JOHN J NEWCAVER

HEAVENLY FATHER
SET MY
SPIRIT
ABLAZE

TELLING THE GOSPELS WITH AN INSIDER'S EYE

Heavenly Father Set My Spirit Ablaze

Copyright ©John Newcater

Published By:

GROVEHILL PUBLICATIONS,

150 St Agnells Lane,
Hemel Hempstead,
Hertfordshire, HP2 6EG
ENGLAND

grovehill.publications@googlemail.com

All rights reserved.

ISBN 9788190634984

3000/0111/SR

All rights reserved. No part of this publication may be reproduced, stored in a retrieval system, or transmitted in any form or by any means – for example, electronic, photocopy, recording – without the prior written permission of the publisher. The only exception is brief quotations in printed reviews.

Unless otherwise stated, Scripture quotations are taken from the Authorized King James Version (KJV) of the Bible, published in 1611.

The Scripture quotations marked LB are taken from the Living Bible, copyright © 1971 by Tyndale Publishing House, Wheaton, Illinois 60187. All rights reserved.

The Scripture passage taken form the translation by, J.B. Phillips is from, The New Testament In Modern English For Schools, J.B. Phillips, 1959.

There are also two quotations from the New American Standard Bible, Copyright © 1960, 1962, 1963, 1968, 1971, 1972, 1973, 1975, 1977, by THE LOCKMAN FOUNDATION, La Habra, California, USA. All rights reserved.

Cover and Title Page Rationale :

The front cover showing the eye incorporates the Hebrew word "emeth" which means "true", for all we learn in the gospels is indeed true.

Cover and Title Page Designed by Scott J Wong

DEDICATION

The Scriptures teach that God always has a number of Jews that are loyal to Him. It was from this group that many were chosen to be prophets and to write the Bible. On the other hand, all through Jewish history the people have turned away from their God, but there were always the faithful few, known in the Bible as the remnant, as if they are like a small piece of cloth left over after some clothing has been made by a tailor. All the remnant alive today are believers in the Lord Jesus Christ, and know that He is the promised Jewish Messiah. Today, some of these Messianic Jews have outstanding Christian ministries and include brilliant Bible scholars and teachers. It is to all such men from Israel's remnant, Messianic Jews, used by my Heavenly Father to help me understand His word and bring me closer to Him, that this book is dedicated. To God be the glory.

How This Work Has Been Formatted

The word Church written with a capital "C," when not part of a title, such as in, "the Church of England," refers to the invisible Church, made up only of those people that have the Holy Spirit in them, with Jesus as their Spiritual Head and Leader.

The word church written with a small "c," refers to the visible church of all known denominations, seen by people of the world, but its members are often not recognized by Jesus as having anything to do with Him.

LORD written as shown in capital letters indicates the name of God, in the quoted Bible passages.

Lord written as shown with just the first letter a capital indicates a title of God, such as in, Lord God, in both the text of this book and the quoted Bible passages.

Personal pronouns in this book are capitalized when referring to God in any of His manifestations be it God the Father, God the Son or God the Holy Spirit/Ghost. However, personal pronouns quoted in Scripture passages are the same as written in the particular Bible under reference.

Words in brackets found in Bible quotations are of two kinds. Rounded brackets, (like these), have been copied from the Bible, but square brackets, [like these], contain added clarifications which refer to the proceeding word or words, to explain the present day meaning of the original seventeenth century text of the King James Bible.

Contents

DEDICATION	3
HOW THIS WORK HAS BEEN FORMATTED	5
Table Of Contents	7
FOREWORD by Wiman Chew	31
PURPOSE	34
1. FIRST STEPS	35
2. THE BIBLE IS A JEWISH BOOK	39
THE THEMES OF THE GOSPELS	41
3. THE ARRIVAL OF JESUS AMONG THE JEWS	53
THE ANCESTRY OF JESUS	
Matthew 1:1-16, Jeremiah 22:24-30, Luke 3:23-38	53
AN ANGEL PROCLAIMS THE BIRTH OF JOHN THE BAPTIST	
Luke 1:5-23	58
THE PROCLAMATION OF THE BIRTH OF JESUS TO MARY	
Luke 1:26-38	61
MARY VISITS ELIZABETH	
Luke 1:39-45	64
THE SONG OF MARY	
Luke 1:46-56	65
Advice to the Young - Learn from God and Mary	66
THE BIRTH OF JOHN THE BAPTIST	
Luke 1:57-80	67
THE MESSAGE TO JOSEPH OF THE BIRTH OF JESUS	
Matthew 1:18-25	69

THE BIRTH OF JESUS
　　Matthew 2:1-16, Luke 2:1-7　　　　　　　　70
THE ANNOUNCEMENT OF THE BIRTH OF JESUS TO THE SHEPHERDS
　　Luke 2:8-20　　　　　　　　　　　　　　71
THE CIRCUMCISION
　　Luke 2:21　　　　　　　　　　　　　　　73
FORTY DAYS AFTER HIS BIRTH JESUS WAS PRESENTED TO THE LORD
　　Luke 2:22-38　　　　　　　　　　　　　74
THE INFANT JESUS IN BETHLEHEM
　　Matthew 2:1-12　　　　　　　　　　　　77
HIS EARLY YEARS IN EGYPT
　　Matthew 2:13-18　　　　　　　　　　　80
HIS EARLY LIFE IN NAZARETH - INCLUDING FOUR DIFFERENT WAYS GOD LED THE NEW TESTAMENT WRITERS TO QUOTE THE OLD TESTAMENT
　　Matthew 2:19-23　　　　　　　　　　　81
GROWING UP
　　Luke 2:40　　　　　　　　　　　　　　87
God Still Speaks to His People　　　　　　　88
JESUS A BOY IN THE TEMPLE
　　Luke 2:41-50　　　　　　　　　　　　　90
THE YEARS TO MATURITY
　　Luke 2:51-52　　　　　　　　　　　　　92
THE CALL TO JOHN THE BAPTIST
　　Luke 3:1-2　　　　　　　　　　　　　　92
JOHN'S MESSAGE
　　Matthew 3:1-6, Mark 1:2, Luke 3:3　　　93
JOHN EXPLAINS WHY THE PEOPLE NEED TO REPENT
　　Matthew 3:7-9, Luke 3:7-14　　　　　　95
JOHN MAKES A PROMISE WITH TWO PARTS, GOOD AND BAD
　　Matthew 3:11-12　　　　　　　　　　　97

Contents

    THE BAPTISM
        Matthew 3:13-17, Mark 1:9-11, Luke 3:21-23, John 1:29-34   99
    THE TEMPTATION
        Matthew 4:1-11, Mark 1:12-13, Luke 4:1-13   100
    THE RELIGIOUS LEADERS PROBE AND QUESTION JOHN THE BAPTIST
        John 1:19-28   104
    JOHN TELLS THE CROWD THAT JESUS IS THE SAVIOUR OF THE WORLD THE SON OF GOD
        John 1:29-34   106

4. HOW JESUS WAS ACCEPTED   109
    THE FIRST FIVE DISCIPLES BELIEVED IN HIM
        John 1:35-51   109
    THE FIVE DISCIPLES' FAITH WAS BUILT UP BY THE FIRST MIRACLE
        John 2:1-11   112
    JESUS TAKES POSSESSION OF THE TEMPLE
        John 2:13-22   115
    HIS ACCEPTANCE IN JUDEA
        John 2:23 to 3:21   118
    THE WITNESS OF JOHN THE BAPTIST
        John 3:22-36   123
    JOHN THE BAPTIST IS ARRESTED AND PUT IN PRISON
        Luke 3:19-20, John 4:1-4   124
    HOW JESUS WAS ACCEPTED IN SAMARIA
        John 4:5-42   125
    JESUS WAS ACCEPTED IN GALILEE
        John 4:43-45   132

5. THE AUTHORITY JESUS HAS AS KING   133
    AUTHORITY TO PREACH
        Luke 4:14-15, Mark 1:14-15   133
    HE HAD AUTHORITY TO HEAL THE SICK
        John 4:46-54   134

REJECTED IN NAZARETH
    Luke 4:16-30   136
HIS HEADQUARTERS
    Luke 4:31   138
HIS AUTHORITY OVER DEMONS
    Luke 4:32-37, Mark 1:21-28   138
HE HEALED ALL WHO WERE SICK AND DEMON POSSESSED
    Mark 1:29-34, Matthew 8:14-17, Luke 4:38-41   140
HIS TEACHING THAT HE WAS THE MESSIAH
DREW LARGE CROWDS
    Mark 1:35-39, Matthew 4:23-25   141
AUTHORITY OVER NATURE
    Luke 5:1-11   143
AUTHORITY TO PURIFY UNCLEAN PEOPLE
    Mark 1:40-45, Matthew 8:1-4, Luke 5:12-16   145
JESUS HAS AUTHORITY TO FORGIVE SINS
    Mark 2:1-12, Matthew 9:2-8, Luke 5:17-26   149
AUTHORITY OVER MEN
    Mark 2:13-17, Matthew 9:9-13, Luke 5:27-32   152
THE AUTHORITY OF JESUS IS ABOVE JEWISH TRADITION
    Luke 5:33-39, Matthew 9:14-17, Mark 2:18-22   154
HIS AUTHORITY OVER THE SABBATH
    Matthew 12:1-14, Mark 3:1-6, Luke 6:1-11, John 5:1-47   160
The First Sabbath Dispute – *THE HEALING OF THE PARALYTIC ON THE SABBATH*
    John 5:1-47   161
The Second Sabbath Dispute – *THE ARGUMENT ABOUT THE WHEAT*
    Luke 6:1-5, Matthew 12:1-8   166
The Third Sabbath Dispute – *JESUS HEALED THE MAN WITH A WITHERED HAND*
    Luke 6:6-11, Mark 3:1-6, Matthew 12:9-14   167
HE CONTINUED TO HEAL MANY
    Mark 3:7-12   170

Contents 11

JESUS CHOOSES TWELVE APOSTLES
    Mark 3:13-19, Luke 6:12-16, Matthew 10:2-4   170

JESUS AUTHORITATIVELY EXPLAINS THE LAW OF MOSES – Or, The Sermon On The Mount
    Matthew 5:1 to 7:29, Luke 6:17-49   173

Three things the Sermon on the Mount is not.   175

What is the Sermon on the Mount?   176

The Place And The Historical Background To The Sermon On The Mount
    Matthew 5:1-2, Luke 6:17-19   176

The Quality Of True Righteousness
    Matthew 5:3-16, Luke 6:20-26   177

The Code Of True Righteousness
    Matthew 5:17-48   180

The Behaviour Of True Righteousness
    Matthew 6:1-18   185

The Practice Of True Righteousness
    Matthew 6:19 to 7:12, Luke 6:27-42   192

Words Of Warning About True Righteousness
    Matthew 7:13-27, Luke 6:43-49   195

The Deductions From The Sermon On The Mount
    Matthew 7:28-29   196

JESUS' AUTHORITY IS RECOGNIZED IN CAPERNAUM
    Matthew 8:5-13, Luke 7:1-10   197

JESUS' AUTHORITY IS RECOGNIZED EVERY WHERE IN THE LAND
    Luke 7:11-17   200

6. THE DISPUTE OVER JESUS   201

JOHN THE BAPTIST IS REJECTED
    Matthew 11:7-19, Luke 7:18-30   201

JESUS CURSED THREE CITIES IN GALILEE
    Matthew 11:20-30   205

Doomed For Not Believing In Jesus   205

The Reason People Did Not Believe Jesus ... 207
Jesus Wanted To Teach Them ... 207
A PROSTITUTE SHOWS HER TREMENDOUS FAITH, LOVE AND THANKS
   Luke 7:36-50 ... 208
MESSIAH'S THIRD MAJOR PREACHING TOUR
   Luke 8:1-3 ... 211
THE UNFORGIVABLE SIN (THE UNPARDONABLE SIN)
   Matthew 12:22-37, Mark 3:20-30 ... 212
Rejected Of Men (Isaiah 53:3 – written by Isaiah 700 years before it happened) ... 212
How Jesus Answered His Accusers ... 214
The Judgement ... 216
THE NEW POLICY REGARDING MIRACLES
   Matthew 12:38-45 ... 218
Only One More Sign For That Generation ... 218
How God Was Going To Judge That Generation ... 219
THE REJECTED KING REVEALS A MYSTERY
   Matthew 8:24-34, 9:27-34, 12:46 to 13:52,
     Mark 3:31 to 5:43, Luke 8:4-56 ... 222
A Very Important Turning Point ... 222
Only Believers Can Enter The Spiritual Kingdom ... 225
Five Parts Of God's Kingdom ... 227
The Nine Parables That Jesus Used To Explain The Mystery Kingdom To His Disciples And To Hide It From The Jews ... 231
The Parable Of The Sower
   Matthew 13:3-23, Mark 4:2-20, Luke 8:4-15 ... 231
The Parable Of The Seed That Grows Inexplicably
   Mark 4:26-29 ... 232
The Parable Of The Tares
   Matthew 13:24-30 and 36-43 ... 233

The Parable Of The Mustard Seed
  Matthew 13:31-32   233
The Parable Of The Leaven
  Matthew 13:33, Luke 13:21   234
The Parable Of The Hidden Treasure
  Matthew 13:44   234
The Parable Of The Pearl Of Great Price
  Matthew 13:45-46   235
The Parable Of The Net
  Matthew 13:47-50   235
The Parable Of The Householder
  Matthew 13:52   236
THE KING'S POWER OVER NATURE
  Matthew 8:23-27, Mark 4:35-41, Luke 8:22-25   238
THE KING'S POWER OVER DEMONS
  Matthew 8:28-34, Mark 5:1-20, Luke 8:26-39   240
THE KING'S POWER OVER SICKNESS AND DEATH
  Matthew 9:18-26, Mark 5:21-43, Luke 8:40-56   245
THE KING'S POWER OVER BLINDNESS
  Matthew 9:27-34   250
THE FINAL REJECTION OF THE KING IN NAZARETH
  Matthew 13:54-58, Mark 6:1-6   251
JESUS CHANGES HIS APROACH AFTER THE REJECTION
  Matthew 9:35 to 10:42, Mark 6:7-13, Luke 9:1-6   252
Business As Usual With A Difference   253
How The Disciples Are To Work Now Israel Has
  Rejected Jesus   255
How The Disciples Are To Manage Increasing Persecution   258
How The Disciples Are To Manage Rejection   259
Some Effects Of The National Rejection Of Jesus   261
Rewards For Those That Believe The Disciples
And Support Them   262

The Result Of The Disciples Work	263
THE DEATH OF JOHN THE BAPTIST	
Matthew 14:1-12, Mark 6:12-29	264
7. JESUS TRAINS THE TWELVE	**267**
THE FEEDING OF THE FIVE THOUSAND	
Matthew 14:13-21, Mark 6:30-44, Luke 9:10-17, John 6:1-14	267
THE PEOPLE OF GALILEE TRY TO MAKE JESUS THEIR KING	
John 6:15	272
TRAINING FOR THE STORMS OF LIFE	
Matthew 14:22-33, Mark 6:45-52, John 6:16-21	273
WELCOMED IN GENNESARET	
Matthew 14:34-36, Mark 6:53-56	276
THE BREAD OF LIFE	
John 6:22-71	277
WHAT DEFILES A MAN? WHAT DEGRADES HIM?	
Matthew 15:1-20, Mark 7:1-19	282
A WELCOME IN TYRE AND SIDON	
Matthew 15:21-28, Mark 7:24-30	287
A WARM WELCOME IN DECAPOLIS	
Matthew 15:29-39, Mark 7:31 to 8:10	288
REJECTED IN MAGADAN	
Matthew 15:39 to 16:4	292
WARNING AGAINST FALSE TEACHERS	
Matthew 16:5-12, Mark 8:14-26	295
PETER'S CONFESSION	
Matthew 16:13-20, Mark 8:27-30, Luke 9:18-21	297
The First Thing Jesus Tells Peter	298
The Second Thing Jesus Tells Peter	298
The Third Thing Jesus Tells Peter	299
The Fourth Thing Jesus Tells Peter	300
The Fifth Thing Jesus Tells Peter	303

PREPARING THE DISCIPLES FOR HIS DEATH AND RESURRECTION
Matthew 16:21-28, Mark 9:30-32 — 305

REWARDS IN THE MILLENNIAL KINGDOM
Mark 8:38 — 307

HIS GLORY IN THE MILLENNIAL KINGDOM
Matthew 16:28 to 17:8, Mark 9:1-8, Luke 9:27-36 — 307

The Transfiguration Was Significant In Five Ways — 311

JOHN THE BAPTIST, ELIJAH, AND THE TWO COMINGS OF MESSIAH
Matthew 17:9-13, Mark 9:9-13, Luke 9:36 — 313

FAITH
Matthew 17:14-21, Mark 9:14-29, Luke 9:37-42 — 315

MORE ABOUT HIS COMING DEATH AND RESURRECTION
Matthew 17:22-23, Mark 9:30-32, Luke 9:43-45 — 319

A LESSON FOR SONS
Matthew 17:24-27 — 319

CHILDLIKE HUMILITY
Matthew 18:1-6, Mark 9:33-37, Luke 9:46-48 — 321

ELITISM AND SELF-IMPORTANCE (PRIDE)
Matthew:18:7-14, Mark 9:38-50, Luke 9:49-50 — 325

Salt — 327

FORGIVE AND FORGET
Matthew 18:15-35 — 328

The King That Forgave A Servant — 332

THE HALF-BROTHERS OF JESUS TRY TO PROVOKE HIM
John 7:1-9 — 333

JOURNEY TO JERUSALEM
Luke 9:51-56, John 7:10 — 335

MORE TRAINING ON BEING A GOOD DISCIPLE
Matthew 8:19-22, Luke 9:57-62 — 336

8. THE GATHERING OPPOSITION — 341

DIFFERENCES AT THE FEAST OF TABERNACLES
John 7:10-53 — 342

The Jews Questioned The Authority Of Jesus
    John 7:11-15 343
Jesus' Explanation
    John 7:16-24 344
The Jews Question Who Jesus Really Is
    John 7:25-27 346
Jesus' Answer
    John 7:28-30 346
The Effect On The Crowd And The Leaders
    John 7:31-36 346
The Holy Spirit Is Promised To Believers
    John 7:37-44 347
The Pharisees Become Even More Aroused
    John 7:45-52 349

THE TRAP TO GET JESUS TO DISAGREE WITH THE LAW OF MOSES
    John 8:1-11 351

THE DISPUTE ABOUT THE LIGHT
    John 8:12-20 354

ONLY BELIEVERS IN JESUS WILL HAVE THEIR SINS FORGIVEN
    John 8:21-30 356

JESUS THE RESCUER
    John 8:31-59 357

He Rescues Us From Sin
    John 8:31-40 357
He Rescues Us From Satan
    John 8:41-48 359
He Rescues Us From Death
    John 8:49-59 361

THE HEALING OF THE MAN BORN BLIND
    John 9:1-41 363

The Healing
    John 9:1-12 363

The Man Is Brought In For Questioning
    John 9:13-17   366
The Parents Are Brought In For Questioning
    John 9:18-22   366
The Man Is Again Brought In For Questioning
    John 9:23-34   367
The Spiritual Healing
    John 9:35-41   369
THE DISPUTE ABOUT THE SHEPHERD
    John 10:1-21   370
Jesus Is The True Shepherd
    John 10:1-6   371
Jesus Is The Door
    John 10:7-10   375
Jesus Is The Good Shepherd
    John 10:11-18   375
Once Again The Jews Are Divided
    John 10:19-21   377
THE WORK OF THE SEVENTY DISCIPLES
    Luke 10:1-24   378
The Seventy Are Sent Away In Pairs
    Luke 10:1-16   378
The Seventy Return In Triumph
    Luke 10:17-20   381
Jesus Thanked God The Father In Prayer And Rejoicing
    Luke 10:21-24   383
A HOSTILE QUESTION ABOUT ETERNAL LIFE
    Luke 10:25-37   384
A WOMAN'S SPIRITUAL FELLOWSHIP
    Luke 10:38-42   386
JESUS TEACHES HIS DISCIPLES HOW TO PRAY
    Luke 11:1-13   387
How Our Prayers Should Be Planned   388

**THE DISPUTE ABOUT THE HEALING OF
ANOTHER DUMB MAN**
    Luke 11:14-36   390
The False Accusation Starts To Spread
    Luke 11:14-16   390
Jesus Explains Why The Accusation Is Not True
    Luke 11:17-23   391
Jesus Explains The Spiritual Mess The Nation Is In
    Luke 11:24-28   391
The Sign For That Generation
    Luke 11:29-32   392
An Appeal To The Jewish People
    Luke 11:33-36   393
THE DISPUTE OVER KEEPING RELIGIOUS CUSTOMS
    Luke 11:37-54   393
JESUS HAS NINE LESSONS FOR HIS DISCIPLES
    Luke 12:1 to 13:21   399
The First Lesson: Hypocrisy or Insincerity
    Luke 12:1-12   399
The Second Lesson: Covetousness or Desire
    Luke 12:13-34   400
The Third Lesson: Watchfulness or Keeping On The Alert
    Luke 12:35-40   404
The Fourth Lesson: Faithfulness or Loyalty
    Luke 12: 41-48   405
*The Fifth Lesson: Three Things Will Result From The First
Coming Of Jesus*
    Luke 12:49-53   406
*The Sixth Lesson: The Signs Of This Time
(the time for the Messiah)*
    Luke 12:54-59   407

    The Seventh Lesson: Everyone That Does Not Believe Jesus Is The Messiah Needs To Repent, Because The Judgement Of Unbelievers Is Certain

        Luke 13:1-9   408

    The Eighth Lesson: A Demonstration Of How Israel Needs The Good Shepherd

        Luke 13:10-17   409

    The Ninth Lesson: The Mystery Kingdom, Christendom

        Luke 13:18-21   413

    THE CLASH AT CHANUKA, THE FEAST OF DEDICATION

        John 10:22-39   413

9. JESUS PREPARES HIS DISCIPLES   419

    HE MOVES OUT OF JUDEA

        John 10:40-42   419

    HOW CAN WE ENTER THE KINGDOM OF GOD?

        Luke 13:22-35   420

    JESUS TEACHES FOUR LESSONS IN A PHARISEES' HOUSE

        Luke 14:1-24   423

    Keeping The Sabbath Day Holy

        Luke 14:1-6   423

    Humbleness Or Self-Importance?

        Luke 14:7-11   424

    Respect For Others

        Luke 14:12-14   424

    The Supreme Supper They Snubbed

        Luke 14:15-24   425

    WHAT IT TAKES TO BE A DISCIPLE OF JESUS

        Luke 14:25-35   427

    GOD'S APPROACH TO SINNERS

        Luke 15:1-32   429

    The Parable Of The Lost Sheep

        Luke 15:3-7   430

The Parable Of The Lost Coin
    Luke 15:8-10   430

The Parable Of The Lost Son
    Luke 15:11-32   431

LESSONS ON MAMMON (OR RICHES AND WORDLY PROSPERITY)
    Luke 16:1-31   432

The Parable Of The Unrighteous Steward
    Luke 16:1-13   433

The Pharisees Sneer At Jesus Who Then Rebukes Them Even More
    Luke 16:14-18   436

The True Story Of The Rich Man And Lazarus The Beggar
    Luke 16:19-31   437

JESUS' PEOPLE SHOULD BE FORGIVING PEOPLE
    Luke 17:1-4   441

INCREASE YOUR FAITH
    Luke 17:5-10   442

THE RESURRECTION OF LAZARUS
    John 11:1-54, Luke 17:11-37   443

The Resurrection Of Lazarus – THE SIGN FOR THE NATION
    John 11:1-44   444

The Death Of Lazarus
    John 11:1-16   444

A Conversation Between Martha And Jesus
    John 11:17-27   446

A Conversation Between Mary And Jesus
    John 11:28-32   447

Jesus Gives The Sign Of Jonah By Bringing Lazarus Back To Life
    John 11:33-44   447

Contents 21

The Resurrection Of Lazarus – THE SIGN IS REJECTED BY THE NATION
    John 11:45-54 — 450
The Resurrection Of Lazarus – THREE RESULTS OF THE REJECTION
    Luke 17:11-37 — 452
First: A Special Messianic Sign For Caiaphas
    Luke 17:11-19 — 452
Second: The Kingdom Of God Is Changed In Make-Up
    Luke 17:20-21 — 453
Third: Jesus Will Have To Come Again
    Luke 17:22-37 — 454
TWO POINTS CONCERNING PRAYER
    Luke 18:1-14 — 456
Never Get Tired Of Praying For Jesus To Come Again
    Luke 18:1-8 — 456
Prayers Should Be Humble Identifying Our Personal Needs
    Luke 18:9-14 — 457
DIVORCE
    Matthew 19:1-12, Mark 10:1-12 — 458
WHAT WE NEED TO ENTER THE KINGDOM
    Matthew 19:13-15, Mark 10:13-16 — 462
TEACHING ABOUT EVERLASTING LIFE
    Matthew 19:16 to 20:16, Mark 10:17-31, Luke 18:18-30 — 463
JESUS TALKS ABOUT HIS COMING DEATH AND RESURRECTION AGAIN
    Matthew 20:17-28, Mark 10:32-45, Luke 18:31-34 — 469
JESUS HEALED THE TWO BLIND MEN
    Matthew 20:29-34, Mark 10:46-52, Luke 18:35-43 — 473
INDIVIDUALS WITH FAITH WILL ENTER THE KINGDOM OF GOD
    Luke 19:1-10 — 475

THE DELAYED KINGDOM OF GOD
    Luke 19:11-28 — 477

10   KING JESUS ARRIVES AT HIS CITY — 481

JESUS STOPS IN BETHANY
    John 11:55 to 12:1, 12:9-11 — 481

THE TRIUMPHAL ENTRY OF THE KING INTO JERUSALEM
    Matthew 21:1-17, Mark 11:1-11, Luke 19:29-44, John 12:12-19 — 483

JESUS CURSES A FIG TREE
    Matthew 21:19, Mark 11:12-13 — 490

JESUS COMPLETELY CONTROLS THE TEMPLE
    Mark 11:15-18, Luke 19:45-48 — 491

AN OPEN INVITATION FROM THE KING
    John 12:20-26 — 493

FOR THE GLORY OF GOD'S NAME
    John 12:27-43 — 495

JESUS TELLS IT LIKE IT IS
    John 12:44-50 — 497

THE POWER OF GOD IS RELEASED THROUGH PRAYER
    Matthew 21:19-22, Mark 11:19-26 — 498

THE LAMB OF GOD IS SCRUTINIZED AND TESTED
    Matthew 21:23 to 22:40, Mark 11:27 to 12:34, Luke 20:1-40 — 500

The Priests And Elders Try To Find Fault With The Lamb
    Matthew 21:23 to 22:14, Mark 11:27 to 12:12, Luke 20:1-18 — 500

The Pharisees And Herodians Unite To Attack The Lamb Of God
    Matthew 22:15-22, Mark 12:13-17, Luke 20:20-26 — 508

The Attack From The Sadducees
    Matthew 22:23-33, Mark 12:18-27, Luke 20:27-40   **509**
The Fourth Challenge Came From The Pharisees
    Matthew 22:34-40, Mark 12:28-34   **513**
A QUESTION FROM THE KING
    Matthew 22:41-46, Mark 12:35-37, Luke 20:41-44   **514**
THE JEWISH LEADERS ARE JUDGED
BY THEIR KING
    Matthew 23:1-39, Mark 12:38-40, Luke 20:45-47   **516**
Jesus Talks About The Pharisees
    Matthew 23:1-12, Mark 12:38-40, Luke 20:45-47   **516**
Jesus Talks To The Pharisees Delivering Seven Woes
    Matthew 23:13-36   **520**
The Lament Over The City Of Jerusalem
    Matthew 23:37-39   **524**
THE OUTWARD AND INWARD KEEPING
OF THE LAW
    Mark 12:41-44, Luke 21:1-4   **526**

11. THE PROPHECIES OF JESUS   **527**

THE SETTING FOR THE OCCASION
    Matthew 24:1-2, Mark 13:1-2, Luke 21:5-6   **528**
THREE QUESTIONS FROM FOUR APOSTLES
    Matthew 24:3, Mark 13:3-4, Luke 21:7   **529**
FEATURES OF THIS AGE WHICH INCLUDES
THE TIME OF THE CHURCH
    Matthew 24:4-6, Mark 13:6-7, Luke 21:8-9   **531**
A SIGN THAT THE NEXT AGE (WHEN JESUS
WILL BE KING OVER ALL THE EARTH) IS
DRAWING NEARER
    Matthew 24:7-8, Mark 13:8, Luke 21:10-11   **532**
WHAT WILL HAPPEN TO THE APOSTLES
BEFORE THEY DIE?
    Mark 13:9-13, Luke 21:12-19   **539**

THE SIGN THAT JERUSALEM WILL SOON BE
DESTROYED
    Luke 21:20-24   542
THE GREAT TRIBULATION
    Matthew 24:9-28, Mark 13:14-23   545
THE SIGNS OF THE SECOND COMING
OF MESSIAH JESUS
    Matthew 24:29-30, Mark 13:24-26, Luke 21:25-27   555
THE RESTORATION OF ISRAEL
    Matthew 24:21, Mark 13:27   557
LIFT UP YOUR HEADS
    Luke 21:28   558
THE PARABLE OF THE FIG TREE
    Matthew 24:32-35, Mark 13:28-31, Luke 21:29-33   559
THE RAPTURE
    Matthew 24:36-42, Mark 13:32-37, Luke 21:34-36   560
FIVE PARABLES FOR THE GENTILES
    Matthew 24:43 to 25:30, Mark 13:33-37   564
1st. The Parable Of The Porter Or Doorkeeper
    Mark 13:33-37   564
2nd. The Parable Of The Goodman Of The House
    Matthew 24:43-44   565
3rd. The Parable Of The Wise Servant And
The Evil Servant
    Matthew 24:45-51   565
4th. The Parable Of The Ten Virgins
    Matthew 25:1-13   566
5th. The Parable Of The Talents
    Matthew 25:14-30   569
WHEN, WHERE AND HOW, JESUS WILL
JUDGE THE GENTILES
    Matthew 25:31-46   570

12. SETTING THE STAGE FOR DEATH — 575
JESUS PREDICTS HIS CRUCIFIXION
Matthew 26:1-2, Mark 14:1 — 575
THE RULERS PLOT THE DEATH OF THEIR MESSIAH
Matthew 26:3-5, Mark 14:1-2 — 576
MARY PREPARES THE BODY OF JESUS FOR BURIAL WHILE HE IS ALIVE
Matthew 26:6-13, Mark 14:3-9, John 12:2-8 — 577
THE PRICE IS SET TO BETRAY JESUS TO THOSE WHO WANT HIM DEAD
Matthew 26:14-16, Mark 14:10-11, Luke 22:1-6 — 579
JESUS ARRANGED THE LAST PASSOVER MEAL HIMSELF
Matthew 26:17-19, Mark 14:12-16, Luke 22:7-14 — 582
THE LAST PASSOVER AND THE FIRST LORD'S SUPPER
Matthew 26:20-35, Mark 14:17-31, Luke 22:14-38, John 13:1-38 — 585

The Introduction By Jesus
Luke 22:14-16 — 585

The Cup Of Thanksgiving
Luke 22:17-18 — 586

Jesus Takes The Role Of A Servant And Speaks Of Betrayal
John 13:3-20 — 587

Karpas: Vegetable
Matthew 26:20-25, Mark 14:17-21 — 591

This Is My Body
Matthew 26:26, Mark 14:22, Luke 22:19, 1 Corinthians 11:23-24 — 593

Jesus Gave The Sop To Judas Iscariot
John 13:21-30 — 597

The Cup Of Remembrance
    Matthew 26:27-29, Mark 14:23-25, Luke 22:20-23   **599**
Great Men Of God
    Luke 22:24-30   **604**
Jesus Commands His Disciples To Love Each Other As Much As He Loves Them
    Matthew 26:31-35, Mark 14:27-31, Luke 22:31-38, John 13:31-38   **605**
Jesus And His Disciples Sing Praises To God
    Matthew 26:30, Mark 14:26   **609**
AN EXPLANATION OF WHAT WE ARE GOING TO DO NEXT   **611**
TWENTY-FIVE PROMISES MADE BY JESUS
    John 14:1 to 16:33   **612**
THIRTEEN INSTRUCTIONS FROM JESUS
    John 14:1 to 16:33   **620**
THE ACCUSER HAD NO EVIDENCE TO BRING A CASE AGAINST JESUS
    John 14:30-31   **625**
ANOTHER WARNING ABOUT HIS DEATH AND RESURRECTION
    John 16:20-22   **626**
THE PRAYER OF JESUS IN HIS POSITION OF HIGH PRIEST
    John 17:1-26   **627**
Jesus Prays For Himself
    John 17:1-8   **627**
Jesus Prays For His Disciples
    John 17:9-19   **628**
Jesus Prays For All Believers
    John 17:20-26   **630**

THE AGONY OF JESUS IN THE GARDEN OF GETHSEMANE

Isaiah 49:1-6 *(a prophetic Scripture concerning His agony)*,
Matthew 26:36-46, Mark 14:32-42,
Luke 22:39-46, John 18:1 — 632

Five Facts Concerning His Agony — 633

13. THE ARREST, TRIALS AND DEATH OF JESUS — 641

The Laws Of The Sanhedrin That Were Broken By The Sanhedrin — 641

THE ARREST
Matthew 26:47-53, Mark 14:43-52, Luke 22:47-56,
John 18:2-12 — 644

JESUS IS TRIED BY ANNAS
John 18:12-23 — 650

JESUS IS TRIED BY CAIAPHAS AND THE SANHEDRIN
Matthew 26:57, 26:59-68, Mark 14:53, 14:55-65,
Luke 22:54 — 652

THE APOSTLE PETER'S DENIAL
Matthew 26:58, 26:69-75, Mark 14:54, 14:66-72,
Luke 22:54-62, John 18:15-18, 18:25-27 — 657

JESUS IS MOCKED AND BEATEN
Luke 22:63-64 — 660

THE SANHEDRIN PASSES JUDGEMENT ON THE MESSIAH OF ISRAEL
Matthew 27:1, Mark 15:1, Luke 22:66-71 — 660

THE DEATH OF JUDAS ISCARIOT AFTER HE BETRAYED JESUS
Matthew 27:3-10, Acts 1:18 — 661

THE FIRST TRIAL HEARD BY PONTIUS PILATE
Matthew 27:11-14, Mark 15:1-5, Luke 23:1-7,
John 18:28-38 — 664

THE TRIAL HEARD BY HEROD ANTIPAS
Luke 23:7-12 — 670

THE SECOND TRIAL HEARD BY PONTIUS PILATE
  Matthew 27:15-31, Mark 15:6-20, Luke 23:13-25,
  John 18:38 to 19:16 671
JESUS IS MOCKED BY THE WHOLE ROMAN COHORT
  Matthew 27:27-31, Mark 15:16-19 680
JESUS IS LED AWAY TO CALVARY
  Matthew 27:31-34, Mark 15:20-23, Luke 23:26-33,
  John 19:16-17 681
THE FIRST THREE HOURS OF THE CRUCIFIXION
  Matthew 27:35-44, Mark 15:24-32, Luke 23:33-43,
  John 19:18-27 685
THE SECOND THREE HOURS OF THE CRUCIFIXION
  Matthew 27:45-50, Mark 15:33-37, Luke 23:44-46,
  John 19:28-30 694

Ten Implications Of The Death Of Jesus 698

MIRACLES HAPPENED WHEN JESUS DIED
  Matthew 27:51-54, Mark 15:38-39, Luke 23:47-48 699
THE BURIAL OF JESUS
  Matthew 27:57-61, Mark 15:42-47, Luke 23:50-55,
  John 19:31-42 702
THE TOMB IS SEALED
  Matthew 27:61-66, Luke 23:55-56 708

How Long Was The Body Of Jesus In The Tomb? 709

14. FROM THE GRAVE TO THE EARTH AND THEN THE SKY 713

Nine Implications Of The Resurrection Of Jesus 713

THE BEGINNING OF RESURRECTION DAY
  Matthew 28:1, Mark 16:1 714
AN ANGEL OPENED THE TOMB
  Matthew 28:2-4 715

THE WOMEN VISIT THE TOMB
Matthew 28:5-8, Mark 16:2-8, Luke 24:1-8, John 20:1 — 715

THE APOSTLES RECEIVE THE NEWS THAT JESUS HAS RISEN
Luke 24:9-12, John 20:2-10 — 717

THE FIRST PERSON TO SEE JESUS ALIVE WAS MARY MAGDALENE
Mark 16:9-11, John 20:11-18 — 717

THE SECOND APPEARANCE OF JESUS WAS TO THE WOMEN
Matthew 28:9-10 — 721

THE SECOND SIGN OF JONAH IS REJECTED
Matthew 28:11-15 — 722

THE THIRD APPEARANCE OF JESUS WAS ON THE ROAD TO EMMAUS
Mark 16:12-13, Luke 24:12-31 — 724

THE FOURTH APPEARANCE OF JESUS WAS TO PETER
Luke 24:34 — 726

THE FIFTH APPEARANCE OF JESUS WAS TO THE TEN
Mark 16:14, Luke 24:36-43, John 20:19-25 — 727

THE SIXTH APPEARANCE OF JESUS WAS TO THE ELEVEN
John 20:26-31 — 731

THE SEVENTH APPEARANCE OF JESUS WAS TO THE SEVEN
John 21:1-25 — 732

THE EIGHTH APPEARANCE OF JESUS WAS TO OVER FIVE-HUNDRED BELIEVERS INCLUDING THE APOSTLES
Matthew 28:16-20, Mark 16:15-18, 1 Corinthians 15:6 — 738

THE NINTH APPEARANCE OF JESUS WAS
TO JAMES
 1 Corinthians 15:7   742
THE TENTH APPEARANCE OF JESUS WAS TO
THE ELEVEN
 Luke 24:44-49, Acts 1:1-8, 1 Corinthians 15:7   743
JESUS ROSE INTO THE SKY
 Luke 24:50-53, Acts 1:9-11   745

EPILOGUE IN THREE PARTS   749

Epilogue Part 1 - Advice   749

Epilogue Part 2 - Encouragement For Believers   751

Epilogue Part 3 - Prayer   752

GLOSSARY   755

FOREWORD

I gather that it took the author 20 years to write this book. Not quite as long as the 26 years Edward Gibbon spent to produce *The History of the Decline and Fall of the Roman Empire*. Nevertheless having gone through this book, I believe every minute of John's research has been well spent for the result is a highly informative and eye-opening work that is bound to leave its reader gripped in awe.

John J Newcater was one of those British planters sent to Malaysia to develop rubber and oil palm estates in the former British colony. While the planters of those days were notorious for their hard drinking and cussing habits, John was the exception.

I first knew John in the late 60s as my Senior Assistant Manager. He was never loud and I never heard him engage in vulgarities. Always gentle, I remember most vividly an incident when John and I were working under a local born Malaysian Manager. This was a rare occurrence at a time when the *orang puteh* (white man) was always the *tuan besar* (big boss). One day a local visitor addressed John in the presence of his superior as if he (John) was the *tuan besar*. Immediately John politely corrected him and pointed him to the Manager with a little chuckle – this was typically how John was and always has been, a quiet unassuming and humble man. At the time I knew him, both of us were not believers in Jesus Christ. So it is really an honour and privilege, when John recently asked me to read his book and pen this *Foreword*.

Many of us find it difficult to understand the Bible. The trouble is, as John says, "the Bible is a Jewish book and we need to read the Scriptures, not according to the language of the twenty-first century, but how they were understood in the first century". Not only does John enlighten us on the delicate nuances of the language used in the writing of the Gospels, he also explains the geographical location, customs, traditions, mannerisms, culture and thinking of a unique race, the father of whom was their patriarch Abraham. By reason of the fact that we are non-Jewish, John's book provides for us fresh perspectives and insights of the Gospels.

From the discussion of the genealogy of Jesus Christ to His crucifixion on the cross, John explores, examines, dissects and analyses the words of the four Gospel writers with the skill and precision of a surgeon in an operating theatre. When he discusses the Lord's trials or His encounter with the accusers of the woman caught in adultery, he is comparable to Sir Lionel Luckoo, the born-again lawyer who is listed in the Guinness Book of Records as the most successful lawyer who had won the most number of murder cases consecutively.

The observations of John Newcater concerning the birth of our Lord deserve special mention. I for one, have not really given much thought either to how the shepherds were able to identify Jesus from amongst other babies born at that time or the type of material He was wrapped in until John points out that the cloth the Lord was wrapped in was actually "burial cloth", opening our eyes to its significance in the light of His entombment after His crucifixion.

In his rendering of the calling of the Lord's disciples, John provides a background of how rabbis pick their students and the reader will get to understand a phrase like "Come see where I live".

John then draws our attention to Jesus' claim to be the Messiah of the Jewish people, and how the Jewish leaders and the Pharisees disputed and rejected Him despite all the signs and wonders He performed. This led to the Lord "giving up" on His own people, at least at His first coming, and His decision to speak in parables. What are parables? Personally I always found parables hard to fathom, but John with his research on the Jewish language, culture and background enlightens us on their respective features and explains them clearly in simple language.

One of the things that has puzzled me in my reading of the Gospels was why Jesus on occasions told persons He had healed to tell others but at other times, gave instructions to those He had healed not to do so. I am glad that John has cleared that up for me in his book.

Another area where I always had doubts on the veracity of the Bible was the calculation of the 3-day period from Jesus' death on Friday until His ascension on Sunday. John deftly explains the traditional way Jews reckon time thus eliminating any doubts sceptics may have.

By far the biggest fear in my life has been, that is, until I read this book whether I was liable or capable of committing the unforgivable or unpardonable sin knowingly or unwittingly. Thankfully John tells the reader what this sin actually is.

I was astonished when John described the traditional Passover feast observed by the Jews even to this day and his detailed account from the number of glasses of wine taken during the meal, the various items of food served and their significance. What he said is amazing. You really must read this book for yourself and I will not hinder your enjoyment of this book by telling you more here.

I believe the writing of this book has been inspired by the Holy Spirit who has seen John's diligence, perseverance and desire in helping his grandchildren come to a fuller knowledge of the Word of God. I am reminded of the Lord's promise in Isaiah 44:3 *"For I will pour water on the thirsty land, and streams on the dry ground; I will pour out my Spirit on your offspring, and my blessing on your descendants"*. Truly John, not only your grandchildren are blessed, but we, your readers, are too!

Incidentally John Newcater rose to become one of Guthrie Corporation's top executives moving from Malaysia to Liberia before retiring to manage his own farm. John is married to a very gracious and elegant Chinese lady, Lucy. They have been together now for over 46 years. They have 2 children, Robert and Lisa. To John and Lucy, I thank God my wife and I can count you as our good friends.

I commend you John J Newcater for the excellence of your book. May the Lord the God and Father of our Lord Jesus Christ abundantly bless you and Lucy!

Wiman Chew
Christchurch, New Zealand

PURPOSE

This book is written especially for the grandchildren of John and Lucy Newcater, Charis, Leonidas, Talia, Zachary and Anya, in the hope that they, together with all other readers, will find the everlasting life, Jesus has promised us who believe.

1
FIRST STEPS

To start with you will need a Bible. I shall be using the King James Version first published in 1611, but you might like to get a more modern Bible because they have no old fashioned words and are easier to understand.

The original ancient manuscripts from which the King James Bible, also called the Authorized Version, was translated, called the Greek Textus Receptus, were carefully chosen for their accuracy. The writers of some later versions of the Bible use other manuscripts, which are certainly slightly corrupted, picking and choosing from several different old documents, to try and make the Bible agree with their own particular view points. That is why I use the Authorized Version and recommend it to you. By the time you have finished this book you will be very competent in the English language of the King James Bible, so do not fear to use it. A Bible that has the words of Jesus printed in red will be best because we are especially interested in what Jesus said. The Living Bible, like the more recent New Living Translation, to make things clearer is paraphrased, that is to say the meaning is given but in different words and so it is not word for word accurate.

You will see that your Bible is divided into two sections, the Old Testament and the New Testament. We will be looking at the whole Bible but mostly the first four books of the New Testament, Matthew, Mark, Luke and John, which are known as the gospels. The word "gospel" means "glad tidings" or "news that brings joy," and they all tell the story of Jesus.

The ABC of the Bible are its books, and once we have learned them we can easily find any small portion of Scripture quickly, just like people who know the alphabet can find a word in a dictionary. At school, before we could read we used to chant the alphabet together. After we could read we chanted the books of the Bible and had learnt them all by the age of ten. Our chanting did not include the number of the book if there were two or more with the same name, such as First Kings and Second Kings. All the children repeated the names of the books together like this, "Genesis Exodus Leviticus Numbers Deuteronomy Joshua Judges Ruth." We then took a breath of air and continued, "Samuel Samuel, Kings Kings, Chronicles Chronicles, Ezra," and so on all the way through, ending with, "Peter Peter, John John John, Jude and Revelation," which is the last book. There are 66 books in the Bible, so if you can remember only six a day, you will know the whole lot in eleven days.

It is important to know that everybody who has eternal life believes in Jesus. John, who wrote the fourth gospel had been given eternal life and he was so pleased that he wanted us to have it too, but knowing we would have to believe in Jesus first, he wrote his gospel and then towards the end in chapter 20, verse 31, which is usually written, John 20:31, he said, ... these things are written, that ye might **believe** that Jesus is the Christ, the Son of God; and that **believing** ye might have **life** through His name.

The Bible tells us how we can get the kind of faith in Jesus that will end in God giving us everlasting life in the following quotation.

> Romans 10:17 So then faith cometh by hearing, and hearing by the word of God.

In this book the Scriptures are explained, but it is the word of God itself that leads to conviction, and I encourage all readers to look up and check any Bible verses indicated that they are not sure about, to build their faith.

The word "church" has more than one meaning, but what Jesus means by His Church is that group of people from all over the world that have been given eternal life, because they believe in Him. His Church, the true Church, is not a building and it is not a denomination, such as

Assemblies of God, Baptist, Church of England, Roman Catholic, or any named group, and it is not made by men or women. It is made up of men and women but not by them. It is being made by Jesus, and as the years go by and people are born, live and die, He chooses from them, those of us that He wants in His Church, and to protect us from being tricked into joining a false church, because of the many misleading preachers He told Simon Barjona, better known as the apostle Peter, "I will build My church."[1] Jesus is building His Church.

The first true Church started in Jerusalem with about 120 Jews.[2] Jesus had told them to wait there in the city until they had been given the Holy Spirit.[3] He, the Spirit, came into each of them at Pentecost.[4] At the first Pentecost, about 1,500 years before the Holy Spirit was given to the Church in Jerusalem, God had given the Law to the Jewish people through Moses. If they kept that Law, God considered them righteous. At this Pentecost, God sent the Holy Spirit to the Church for two reasons, first to give them power to preach in a way that made people believe them and to perform miracles, secondly as a sign to each one of them that God considered them righteous.

> Ephesians 1:13-14 13 Ye [Christian believers] were sealed with that Holy Spirit of promise,
>
> 14 Which is the earnest [guarantee] of our inheritance [eternal life].

God had appeared to Moses from a burning bush that was not burnt by the fire.[5] At the start of the true Church everyone present had fire on their heads and they also were unharmed, they spoke in languages they had not learned and the loud sound of rushing wind filled the room.[4] These first Jewish Christians knew that the fire that did not consume the bush represented God, and would realise that the fire that did not harm them meant that the Holy Spirit had come upon them in the form of fire. Jesus sent the Holy Spirit to help them in their work[6] and show them the previous way of becoming righteous through keeping the Law was no longer in operation. He was declaring that everyone there at the meeting was righteous by giving them the Holy Spirit,[7] and to emphasize the point it was done at the Feast of Pentecost, so that they would know that from now on the righteousness of God would be received, not by keeping the Law, which was given to Israel at the first Pentecost, but would be given free, as an act of grace or blessing from God.[8]

So the Church started in a very mystical kind of way and the true Church is still supernatural to this day. Jesus is building us into His Church and using the Holy Spirit to do so.

[1] Matthew 16:17-18

[2] Acts 1:15

[3] Acts 1:4-5

[4] Acts 2:1-4

[5] Exodus 3:2

[6] John 15:26

[7] Ephesians 1:13-14

[8] Romans 6:23

2

THE BIBLE IS A JEWISH BOOK

The Old Testament was written for Jews by Jews, but we non-Jews or Gentiles also benefit from these Jewish Scriptures. The New Testament was written for both Jews and Gentiles, I believe it was written entirely by Jews. However there are others who disagree saying that Luke who wrote the third gospel was a Gentile. All the gospels tell the Jewish story of the life and death of Jesus. It is set in first century Israel, that had a very Jewish civilization, and so the gospels are written in the background of their culture. To get a better grasp of the gospels we need to know more about the traditions and customs of the Jews living in Israel 2,000 years ago. We need to understand the reason things were written the way they were and why things happened the way they did. In other words we need to learn how the Jews lived in those days.

From about the fourth century the church started to ignore the cultural side of the gospels, and as the years rolled by forgot most of it, and for that reason, churches split and wars were fought. Then they began to misunderstand certain phrases like, "to be born of water," and not thinking to ask a Jew what it meant, a new denomination was established based on that one phrase. The writers of the gospels did not bother to explain what a certain phrase meant as it was common knowledge at the time, but now it may be misunderstood. To understand what is happening when we read the gospels we need some knowledge of the culture of the Hebrews in those days.

Usually when people study the life of Jesus they see where He was and then list what He said and did in that place. It is an easy way to do it but they often miss out the connections with what had happened already and what would happen later. **In this book we are going to follow the theme, God's promised Deliverer of the Jews is Jesus their King.** The use of a theme or idea in telling the story will help us see how one event or teaching leads to another event or teaching, and give us a better knowledge of the Jewish Messiah or Deliverer, and the people associated with Him. Matthew, Mark, Luke and John each had their own themes from their own special understanding of the gospel, because of the slightly different effects or impressions it made on each of their minds, and since it was not possible for them to tell us everything about Jesus[1] they carefully selected what was important to each of them.

To help get the idea, let's imagine a large circle, and let's suppose that everything about Jesus is in that circle, everything He said and everything He did, His whole life. Each of the gospel writers knows what is in the circle and each chooses something that will demonstrate his theme. Suppose Matthew looks in the circle and decides that (A) explains his theme clearly, so he takes it out and writes it down for us. He looks again but (B) does not help him and he leaves it there. He likes the way (C) helps prove his theme and includes it in his book.

Next, Mark has a look in the circle. His theme is not helped by (A) so he leaves it there but his attention is caught by (B) which although it did not help Matthew, is very useful to Mark, so he quotes it for us along with (C), but Mark has a different theme to Matthew and so he uses (C) in a different way. However, although the gospels sometimes tell us of different things that happened at the same event, none of the four gospels ever contradict each other.

The Themes of the Gospels

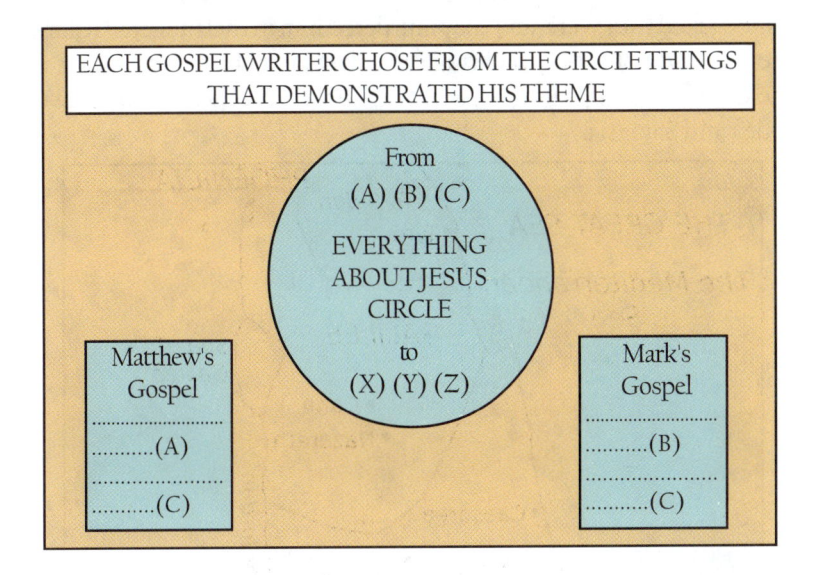

```
EACH GOSPEL WRITER CHOSE FROM THE CIRCLE THINGS
         THAT DEMONSTRATED HIS THEME
```

From
(A) (B) (C)

EVERYTHING
ABOUT JESUS
CIRCLE

to
(X) (Y) (Z)

Matthew's Gospel
..........(A)
..........(C)

Mark's Gospel
..........(B)
..........(C)

1. Matthew

Matthew's theme is, "Jesus the Messiah the King of the Jews." "Messiah" is a Hebrew word meaning "anointed" and is used to identify the coming deliverer of the Jews. The same word in Greek is "Christ" from where we get the word Christian. Matthew's gospel is most likely the first one written, but of course there are many who would not agree. Some people think Mark's was first because it is the shortest but more and more it has been shown that Mark's was not the first. Some think that Luke's gospel was first, but it seems to me that Matthew wrote first.

Writing for the early Church which was Jewish, we find Matthew writing for the needs of Jewish believers. To start with the whole Church was in Jerusalem, and if anyone wanted to know anything about Jesus they could ask His disciples, His mother Mary, or other relatives and people who had known Him. The Church grew and grew and became very large and the unbelieving Jews, could not argue against the truth being preached by the believers. They secretly persuaded men to lie about one of the Christians called Stephen, and then took him to be tried in court.[2] They were unable to disprove anything that Stephen said in his defence,[3] and more than that Stephen showed them just how wicked they were, and they murdered him in their anger.[4] Killing Stephen did not satisfy their rage and they next started attacking all the Christians in Jerusalem, and the Church was scattered all over Judea and Samaria.

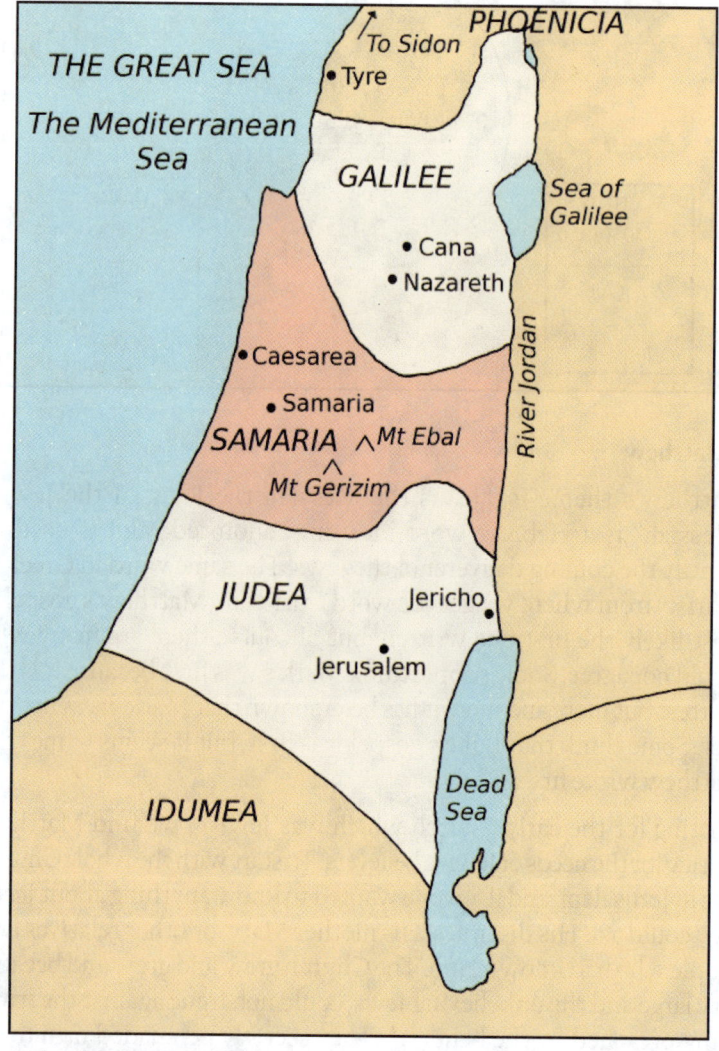

The Church Scattered From Jerusalem Throughout All Judea And Samaria

Scattered all over the place they started to preach the gospel (glad tidings) and the Church grew even more, but they were not able to answer all the questions the new believers were asking, so Matthew wrote his gospel for the Jews to give them the information needed. The Old Testament has many prophecies about the Messiah, and Matthew shows how Jesus fulfils these prophecies in the hope that more Jewish people will believe Jesus is their Messiah or promised Deliverer and King. To an unbelieving Jew this made them ask, "If Jesus is the Messiah, where is the kingdom and where is the world peace He is going to establish?" And Christians preaching to Jews still get asked the same questions.

Matthew took care to explain why Jesus did not set up the Messianic Kingdom when He was here the first time, and he says much more about God's Kingdom than the other gospel writers do because a key question in Jewish minds is, "Where is the Kingdom?" He gives the reasons why the kingdom is not yet set up in chapters 12 and 13 of his gospel, and shows that Jesus is still their future King.

Another thing about Matthew was his concern about the judgement that was soon to come upon Israel, and which God accomplished by means of the Roman army. He records the prophecies of Jesus warning the Jews that because they rejected their King and committed the unpardonable sin, Jerusalem and the Temple would be destroyed.

2. Mark

Mark's theme is, "Jesus the Messiah the Servant of God." Mark wrote his gospel for the Romans, the world superpower of those days. Roman power came from its well managed, disciplined and highly efficient army. The Romans were more interested in successful exploits than in learning, and so Mark's gospel records, the accomplishments and deeds of Jesus rather than what He taught, showing Him as a man with an urgent mission to carry out. Romans liked men who could receive a command, carry it out quickly, and report back that the job had been done. Mark tells them about Jesus in the same way. Jesus had a job to do, and was keen to get it done quickly and well.

In the gospel of Mark there is rapid action, a sense of urgency. More than 40 times he uses the Greek word, *"euthus."* It is translated as "immediately" or "straightway" or "forthwith." In that way Mark reaches out to his Roman readers, but he wants them to get the Jewish content of the message and does this by referring to the Servant of God prophecies made at least 700 years before by Isaiah the prophet to describe the coming Jewish Messiah. Mark shows Jesus as a servant of God, a man of action with a job to do, immediately, straightway or forthwith.

3. Luke

Luke's theme is, **"Jesus the Messiah the Son of Man,"** and he emphasizes the humanity of Jesus. Matthew's gospel was written for the Jews, Mark's for the Romans and Luke's for the Greeks. The Greeks had two special interests. The first was a perfect body and mind. Greek philosophers or thinkers, are famous for their love of study and knowledge, and their athletes are remembered by the Olympic games. The ideal Greek was physically strong and mentally self disciplined, and Luke shows that Jesus is just such a man.

The second special interest of the Greeks was history, and they were most particular about its accuracy, and it is this concern for historical accuracy that prompted Luke to write.

Matthew, Mark and John all saw Jesus at work for themselves, but Luke was not an eyewitness, and tells us so at the beginning of his gospel.[5] When Luke wrote his gospel, Matthew and Mark had written theirs and there were a good number of eyewitness writings, not in the Bible, already circulating in the early Church, so why did Luke, who was not a witness, feel the need for another account? He gives the answer in Luke 1:3.

> "It seemed good to me also, having had perfect understanding of all things from the very first, to write unto thee in order."

Luke wants his readers to have the gospel in the order the events happened, in chronological sequence. He tells the life of Jesus in the way the Greeks would understand, and for them accurate history was necessary to prove the message. Matthew, Mark and John were more concerned with their themes, and when they place events in a different sequence to Luke, we follow Luke because he was the only one who claimed to write in consecutive order.

Although not an observer himself, Luke does use eyewitness reports. He obviously had a talk with Mary the mother of Jesus, because he tells us what she had been thinking.[6] He would have had plenty of opportunity to talk to witnesses while living in the Jerusalem area for two years, waiting for Paul to be released from the prison in Caesarea.[7]

Another thing about Luke, he had three special concerns, that were important to him, Jerusalem, Gentiles and women. He tells us things that Jesus taught, said and did in Jerusalem that the other three gospel writers left out, making a special study of the actions and teachings of the Messiah in the City of Jerusalem.

Luke also tells us things about the Gentiles that the others gospels do not. The reason is probably his close friendship with Paul, the apostle to the Gentiles,[8] and their regular travels together.[9] It was Paul who led Luke to the Lord and so Luke shares Paul's concern for the Gentiles.

His third concern is women, and from Luke we learn that the ministry of Jesus was financed by several wealthy women,[10] and we would not know that if he had not told us. We learn more about Mary and Martha from Luke, and about other women in the life of Jesus, their serving Him and His looking after them, His teachings to them and about them, than from the other gospels.

4. John

John's theme is, **"Jesus the Messiah the Son of God."** John emphasizes that Jesus is God. In Luke we read how Jesus was hungry, thirsty and tired like normal men and women. God doesn't get tired or thirsty. Psalm 121:4 shows He is always looking after His people.

> "He that keepeth Israel shall neither slumber nor sleep."

People get hungry and sleepy and so did Jesus because He was human, but He was also God and that's what matters to John.

Although widely circulated, the gospels of Matthew, Mark and Luke were written mainly for the Jews, Romans and Greeks. John's gospel, written after the other three, was intended for the Church everywhere.

He was anxious to record those things that the others left out, and there is a lot in John's book about Jesus that you won't find in Matthew, Mark or Luke.

Mark was interested in what Jesus did, but in the Book of John the emphasis is on the teachings of the Messiah and so there are more teachings and sermons. In addition to his main theme, **"Jesus the Messiah the Son of God,"** John has two other themes. His secondary themes are, **"the conflict of light and darkness,"** and **"the Son came to reveal the Father to men."**

He uses the terms light and darkness to point to good and evil, or he may say night and day. He sometimes tells us things that seem to be irrelevant, until we remember his sub-themes. For example during the last Passover meal with His disciples, after Jesus identifies Judas as the one who is going to betray Him, John tells us that Judas went out and then adds, "and it was night."[11] The Passover meal is always eaten between sunset and midnight, so it had to be night when Judas went out. There would be no point in John telling us it was night except for his sub-theme of, "the conflict between light and darkness." Judas himself is of the darkness, and what he was doing was wrong and so he did it secretly at night, not in the light of day.

The second sub-theme, "the Son came to reveal the Father to men," is the reason why John spends much more time on what Jesus said and taught than on what He did, because although the nature of the Father was revealed by what Jesus did, what He said was very informative. John records seven signs that Jesus performed to show the Jews He was their Messiah, seven of the talks or discourses Jesus preached and seven "I am," statements He made, so three times John works with the number seven, seven signs, seven talks and seven "I am," statements.

In John 1:1 we read,

> "In the beginning was the Word, and the Word was with God, and the Word was God."

Nearly all Bible scholars, because they can read the original Greek, give great emphasis to the Greek when explaining this verse and the following verses. They forget that John was a Jewish fisherman, not a Greek scholar. He used Greek to reach out to the Church of the first century because Greek was used in many nations. However, his message was influenced by his Jewish upbringing and education, and we are going to look at the Hebrew religious culture of those days to get a deeper understanding of the Book of John.

The rabbis after studying the Old Testament thoroughly, discovered six truths about the Word, and John brings all six out in his first eighteen verses.

1. The Word was sometimes distinct from God and sometimes the same as God.

The rabbis never explained how the Word was distinct from God and yet at the same time it was God, but they taught it and left it at that. John did the same thing in his first verse. He says, "the Word was with God," making Him distinct from God, but then he says, "the Word was God," making Him the same as God. Later he explains that the Person he is writing about is distinct from God because He is not God the Father and He is not God the Holy Spirit, but He is the same as God because He is the second member of the Trinity, of Father, Son and Spirit as constituting one God, He is God the Son. The explanation of this first truth can only be explained in terms of the Trinity, something the rabbis themselves did not understand. Even today Jewish rabbis do not understand the explanation of their own discovery and teaching, unless and until they believe that Jesus is their Messiah, in which case they are Christians. Christian Jews recognise Jesus is their Messiah and are called Messianic Jews.

2. The second thing the rabbis taught was that the Word was the agent of creation.

Everything God created He did by His Word, and so without His Word nothing at all would exist. Look at the first chapter of Genesis at the beginning of your Bible and those passages which read, "And God said, Let there be ..." and you will discover that after God said, "Let there be, ..." whatever He called for immediately came into existence. In John 1:3, it says,

> "All things were made by Him; and without Him was not any thing made that was made."

John agrees with the rabbis and says the same is true about the Word he is talking about, without Him nothing that exists would exist and so the Word is the agent of creation.

3. The rabbis also realised from the Old Testament that the Word was the agent of salvation.

In the Old Testament whenever God saved it was always by His Word. People were saved by God physically, spiritually or both physically and spiritually, but always by means of His Word. In John 1:12, it says,

> "But as many as received Him, to them gave He power to become the sons of God, even to them that believe on His name."

John is saying that Jesus is the Word the agent of salvation because God saved through His Word, and those who believe in the name of Jesus are empowered to become sons of God.

4. The fourth truth is that the Word is the means by which God becomes visible.

Many times in the Old Testament, God visibly showed Himself to the Jewish people. The rabbinic term for the clearly seen presence of God was the Shekinah. It was frequently coupled with God's glory and the two words are often joined together, the Shekinah glory of God. The Shekinah glory came mostly as light, fire or cloud or a combination of them, but whenever it came it came by God's Word. John 1:14, begins with,

> "And the Word was made flesh."

The invisible Word which in verse one was with God and was God now became visible, not as light, fire or cloud but as a person. John continues in verse 14,

> "And dwelt among us."

After the Israelites had left Egypt, they built a portable tent temple, called a tabernacle where God spoke to Moses and the Shekinah glory of God came and stayed in the holy of holies,[12] for about six centuries, first in the tabernacle and later in the Jerusalem temple. Then, when the nation became more and more wicked, the Shekinah glory departed from Israel in four reluctant stages.[13] But after hundreds of years the Shekinah glory returned to Israel, not as light, fire or cloud but as flesh, as a man demonstrating once again the presence of God was in Israel, and John immediately makes the connection because verse 14 continues,

> "(and we beheld His glory, the glory as of the only begotten of the Father,) full of grace and truth."

Often the Shekinah glory has a brightness of fire and tends to give off light, but the human body of Jesus veiled the brightness of His glory, and so He looked just like any other Jewish man of the period, except for the time when the Shekinah glory burst through His flesh. His face shone like the sun, His clothes became extremely white, and three apostles saw His glory,[14] so John could write in verse 14 as an eye witness, "we beheld His glory," and just as the rabbis taught the Jewish people the Shekinah glory came by God's Word, so this is true of John's Word. Jesus was the visible manifestation of God's presence.

5. The rabbis also taught that the Word was the agent of revelation, or discovery.

The rabbis figured this out from the Old Testament because so many times we read, the word of the Lord came to this prophet or that prophet, followed by a message from God.[15] God used His Word as the agent of revelation. In John 1:18, we read,

> "No man hath seen God at any time; the only begotten Son, which is the bosom of the Father, He hath declared [revealed] Him."

We said earlier that one of John's sub-themes is, "Jesus came to reveal the Father to men." It is only John that tells us the disciples asked Jesus to show them the Father, and His reply was, "He that has seen Me has seen the Father."[16] The nature of God the Father, is the same as the Son, and if we know the Son, we also know the Father. In the Old Testament, God revealed Himself in many ways but in the New Testament, He revealed Himself through His Son,[17] and so the Son, the Word, is the agent of revelation.

6. Lastly the Word, is the way by which God signed His promises or covenants.

God made eight covenants in the Old Testament, three with the people of the world and five with the Jewish people, and all were signed, sealed and authenticated by His Word. The last point does not come out so clearly as the first five, but in John 1:17 he says,

"For the Law was given by Moses, but grace and truth came by Jesus Christ."

The Law of the Old Testament was based on the covenant God made with the Jewish people through Moses, which was signed and authenticated by the Shekinah glory.[18] No Jew was ever able to keep the Law of Moses perfectly until Jesus came on the scene. He kept the Law flawlessly and by so doing showed His holiness, and proved His righteousness according to the Law. Up until His crucifixion Israel was under the Law but from then on until the end of the Church Age,[19] the whole world, Jewish and Gentile, has been given a period of grace in a New Covenant (Testament) signed by Jesus by the shedding of His blood.[20] In that way the Son, the Word, is a covenant signer.

What is the message of John, in the first eighteen verses of his book, that we have briefly looked at? It is that the six things the rabbis had been teaching about the Word is true of Jesus of Nazareth. In other words He is their long awaited Saviour sent by God, their Messiah.

Another thing that comes out here is John's sub-theme of light and darkness in John 1:4-9. Jesus is the light, and people who do not have the light are in the dark and cannot see.

In verse 18, John calls Jesus, "the only begotten Son." Certain cults or religious groups that refuse to believe that Jesus is God, like the Jehovah's Witnesses, use this kind of verse to show that Jesus was a begotten Son, who has not eternally existed, and therefore cannot be God. They forget that the Bible is a Jewish book and are trying to understand Jewish literature with a Gentile mind set.

In Jewish writings, "only begotten" or "only" does not emphasize a starting point or origin, but uniqueness or individuality, (i.e. of which there is only one). An example from the Bible is in Genesis 22, where God tells Abraham to sacrifice Isaac, and He speaks to Abraham in verse 2, "Take now thy son, thine only son Isaac." God knew Abraham's first son Ishmael was still alive when He recognized Isaac as, Abraham's only son, so the word "only" cannot mean origin because Ishmael and Isaac both had the same father. But Isaac was Abraham's only son in the sense of uniqueness, and God's covenant with Abraham would be continued not through Ishmael but **only** through Isaac. Later Abraham had six more sons but uniquely Isaac was the only covenant son. Isaac remember was the father of Jacob, later called Israel by God,[21] and the father of the Jewish people, so again, the Bible is a Jewish Book.

Jesus is not the only person called the Son of God. Angels are called sons of God,[22] Israel is called the son of God,[23] and we believers are called sons of God.[24] Jesus is the only Son of God, exclusively because He always existed. He was "in the beginning with God," (John 1:2), and God existed from eternity past.

To sum up this is what we learn from John in chapter one verses 1-18 of his gospel.

1. The Word came in a visible form.
2. (Sadly). The world in general failed to recognize Him.
3. (Even more tragic). His own Jewish people failed to recognize Him.
4. Some individual Jews and Gentiles did recognize Him and they are the children of the Shekinah light and received eternal life from the Agent of Salvation.
5. To understand the Bible we need to remember it is Jewish, and we require some knowledge of their culture in the first century, when Jesus walked around the Galilee and Jerusalem, to help us understand why things were written the way they are.

[1] John 21:25
[2] Acts 6:9-14
[3] Acts 7:2-53

[4] Acts 7:54-60
[5] Luke 1:2
[6] Luke 2:19
[7] Acts 23:33 & 24:27
[8] Romans 11:13
[9] Colossians 4:14, 2Timothy 4:11, Philemon 1:24
[10] Luke 8:3
[11] John 13:30
[12] Exodus 40:34-38
[13] Ezekiel 7:23 – 11:23
[14] Matthew 17:1-2
[15] Three examples are, Jeremiah 1:2, Ezekiel 1:3 & Hosea 1:1
[16] John 14:9
[17] Hebrews 1:1-3
[18] Exodus 24:10-11
[19] Matthew 13:49 & 28:20
[20] Mark 14:24, 1 Corinthians 11:25
[21] Genesis 32:28
[22] Genesis 6:4, Job 1:6
[23] Exodus 4:22
[24] Galatians 3:26

3

THE ARRIVAL OF JESUS AMONG THE JEWS

THE ANCESTRY OF JESUS
Matthew 1:1-16, Jeremiah 22:24-30, Luke 3:23-38

In the Bible there are two different records of the birth of Jesus. Matthew tells the story from Joseph's angle, as if Joseph had told him what happened. In Matthew's gospel the angels speak to Joseph, not to Mary, and he tells us what Joseph was thinking, but not what Mary was thinking. He records the ancestry of Jesus from Abraham through King David down to Joseph, the stepfather of Jesus.

Luke tells us about the birth of Jesus from Mary's point of view, the thoughts that went through her mind, but not Joseph's thoughts, and the angel appearing to Mary, but nothing about angels appearing to Joseph. He gives the line of descent from Adam, through King David down to Mary, the mother of Jesus, using Mary's husband's name Joseph as a proxy, in substitution for Mary's name. The reason for using the proxy and why we know it to be true will be explained in detail towards the end of this section.

Joseph was only the step father of Jesus, and not blood related, so why do you think God has given us two different family trees for Jesus in His Word? To understand this we need to investigate the requirements He had laid down for kings of the Jewish people. There were two sets of rules, one for the southern kingdom, of the two tribes of Judah and Benjamin with their king in Jerusalem, and another for the ten tribes in the northern kingdom ruled from Samaria. At the time Jesus was born there were no Jewish kings on their thrones because both kingdoms were ruled by the Romans, but God's rules for kingship were still there.

The first rule was that the king of the Jews had to be a descendent of King David and applied to the southern kingdom with its throne in Jerusalem.[1] The second rule for the northern kingdom was that the king had to be chosen by God or authorized by a prophet. Anyone who tried to become king in Samaria without approval always ended up being murdered. For example God told Jehu that his family would rule in Samaria for four generations,[2] and God kept His Word, but when Zacharias, the fifth generation took over he was assassinated after only six months as king.[3] The reason we have different family trees in Matthew and Luke is because of the two different requirements for being king.

Matthew 1:1-16 tells the family history of Joseph the step father of Jesus beginning with Abraham. Remember Matthew's theme is, Jesus the Christ the King of the Jews, and because Jewish history begins with Abraham he does not need to go back any further. In verses 11 and 12 we read that someone called Jechoniah was an ancestor of Joseph,

> "And Josias begat Jechoniah and his brethren, about the time they were carried away to Babylon: and after that they were brought to Babylon, Jechoniah begat Salathiel."

Finally the family tree ends in verse 16 with Jacob, the father of Joseph, the husband of Mary. So Joseph was not only a descendent of David through Solomon but also through Jechoniah, a bad king God had cursed saying that none of his descendants would ever be allowed to sit on David's throne, as we will learn from the Book of Jeremiah.

In the Old Testament God used the prophet Jeremiah to spell out judgement on Jechoniah. Jeremiah calls him Coniah a shortened form for Jeconiah, and his father Jehoiakim, but they are same father and son found in Matthew.

3 The Arrival of Jesus Among the Jews

Jeremiah 22:24-30 [24] As I live, saith the LORD, though Coniah the son of Johoiakim king of Judah were the signet upon My right hand, yet would I pluck thee thence;

[25] And I will give thee into the hand of them that seek thy life, and into the hand of them whose face thou fearest, even into the hand of Nebuchadrezzar king of Babylon, and into the hand of the Chaldeans.

[26] And I will cast thee out, and thy mother that bare thee, into another country, where ye were not born; and there ye shall die.

[27] But to the land whereunto they desire to return, thither [there] they shall not return.

[28] Is this man Coniah a despised broke idol? Is he a vessel wherein is no pleasure? Wherefore are they cast out, he and his seed, and are cast into a land which they know not?

[29] O earth, earth, earth, hear the Word of the LORD.

[30] Thus saith the LORD, Write thee this man childless, a man that shall not prosper in his days; for no man of his seed [descendants] shall prosper, sitting upon the throne of David, and ruling any more in Judah.

God cursed Jeconiah because of the kind of person he was, and the curse gets worse and worse until just before the climax is reached in verse 29 God calls on the earth three times to listen to the high point which is that no descendent of Jeconiah will ever have the right to rule in Jerusalem.

The rule for kingship has been changed slightly because now only descendents of David that are not from the line of Jeconiah are allowed to sit on the throne of David. Matthew presented the Jeconiah problem which meant that Joseph or his son could not be heir to the throne, but then he solved it with the story of the virgin birth,[4] pointing out that Jesus was not the real son of Joseph.

Matthew's family tree breaks Jewish tradition by skipping names and including the names of women. The women he mentions are, Tamar in verse three, Rechab and Ruth in verse five, and in verse six, "her" refers to Bathsheba. Tamar was guilty of incest, Rechab of prostitution and Bathsheba of adultery. Ruth was not directly guilty of sexual sin but she was a Moabite and the Moabites were descended from Lot through an incestuous relationship with one of his daughters, and what Matthew is hinting at is that Jesus came to save sinners. Secondly none of these four women were Jews, and Matthew is again hinting that although Jesus only came to the Jewish people, the Gentiles would also benefit.

Luke keeps to Jewish tradition, skipping no names and not mentioning any women, but this procedure presented Jewish writers with a problem, how to trace a women's family tree without using her name? It was done by using her husband's name as a replacement, but if someone was reading the family line how would they know if the author was referring to the husband or the wife? Our problem is with English grammar because in English we do not use the definite article before a proper name. We do not say, "the Mary, the John," and so on, but in the original languages it was allowed. In the Greek text every single name in the family history has the definite article in front of the proper name except one, the name Joseph. In that way the reader knows that this is not really Joseph's line but Mary's. Other examples in the Old Testament where a man's name replaces his wife's are Ezra 2:61 and Nehemiah 7:63. So Luke's account gives Mary's family tree, not Joseph's.

Luke records his family tree differently from Matthew, instead of starting at the beginning of the Jewish race and ending with Jesus, he starts with Jesus and goes back through history all the way to Adam, Luke 3:23-38. Why Adam? Luke's theme is the humanity of Jesus and the history of humanity starts with Adam. He begins in verse 23 with Jesus the son of Joseph, which means the son of Mary, and in verse 31 it says, "Nathan, the son of David." Mary, like Joseph is of David's line, not through Solomon but Nathan, which means Jeconiah is not her ancestor. Mary is the real biological mother of Jesus and Jesus is therefore a member of the house of David apart from Jeconiah. He was not the only one because there were many others who were also of the house of David apart from Jeconiah around at the time. We will see why Jesus was the only one able to claim the throne and not the others under our heading, "The Proclamation Of The Birth Of Jesus To Mary."

In the Bible Jesus has many titles and two are found in Matthew's family tree and two in Luke's. In Matthew 1:1 they are, "the Son of David," and the, "Son of Abraham," and in Luke 3:38 they are, "the Son of Adam," and, "the Son of God."

Son of David means Jesus is a king.

Son of Abraham means Jesus is a Jew.

Son of Adam means Jesus is a man.

Son of God means Jesus is God.

God made four everlasting covenants (promises) with Israel, and calling Jesus, the Son of David, connects Him with the Davidic covenant, the promise God gave to David, and calling Him the Son of Abraham, connects Him with the covenant made with Abraham, but more of that later.

[1] 2 Chronicles 13:5, Psalm 89:35-36, Jeremiah 33:17

[2] 2 Kings 10:30

[3] 2 Kings 15:8-10

[4] Matthew 1:20-25

AN ANGEL PROCLAIMS THE BIRTH OF JOHN THE BAPTIST
Luke 1:5-23

The parents of John the Baptist were a priest called Zacharias, his name means, "God remembers," and Elizabeth, her name means, "the promise of God."

> Luke 1:5 There was in the days of Herod, the king of Judea, a certain priest named Zacharias, of the course of Abia: and his wife was of the daughters of Aaron, and her name was Elizabeth.

The tribe of Levi had been divided into 24 courses by King David. The order of the priesthood was, one high priest in charge of 24 chief priests one for each course, and then the common priests. Zacharias was a common priest and Luke tells us he was of the course of Abia.[1] A course would serve in the temple for one week twice a year and by casting lots a priest would be given a job to do, and that would be the only thing he did in the temple during his life time. Zacharias' lot was to burn incense.[2]

Zacharias and Elizabeth both trusted God, and at that time there were not many Jews like them. They were part of God's very small believing remnant, [3] the last few that believed God.

> Luke 1:6 And they were both righteous before God, walking in all the commandments and ordinances of the Lord blameless.

They were not without sin, no one is, but whenever they realised they had done something wrong they followed the Law of Moses, making the necessary offerings and sacrifices for forgiveness, and were therefore blameless. They were God's saved people, living in a way that everyone could see was according to God's instruction bringing honour to His name, they were "righteous before God."

Zacharias' work in the temple for the week was to take a hot ember from the altar of sacrifice outside the building into the first room, the holy place and put it on the altar of incense. Next to the holy place was the holy of holies and the two rooms were separated by a thick curtain. Zacharias would put incense on the hot ember and a beautiful perfume would fill the air, passing through the curtain as a sweet smelling offering to God in the holy of holies.

Two sons of Aaron had died when they were not careful to burn the incense as Moses had instructed,[4] and because of this there was a strongly held conviction at the time of Zacharias, that if the priest did the slightest thing wrong, he would die in the holy place. To this there had been added the belief that if a priest had done something wrong and was about to die, the Angel of Death would appear on the right side of the altar of incense. Zacharias went in to burn the incense and a large crowd of people were praying outside.

Luke 1:11 And there appeared unto him [Zacharias] an angel of the Lord standing on the right side of the altar of incense.

He would conclude from what he had been taught that he was going to die because an angel was standing on the right side of the altar.

Luke 1:12 And when Zacharias saw him, he was troubled, and fear fell upon him.

To Zacharias' relief, the message was not about death and judgement but blessing and everlasting life, and the angel was about to make some wonderful announcements.

Although he was an old man he was told by the angel he would soon have a son and he must call him John.[5] In Hebrew that would be Yohannan and it means "grace". The name shows that God is introducing a new age, a new way of salvation, not by keeping the Law, but a free gift of everlasting life by grace.[6] The angel then says six things about Zacharias' promised son, John the Baptist, in Luke 1:15-17.

1. "For he shall be great in the sight of the Lord." Jesus said, "Among them that are born of women there hath not risen a greater than John the Baptist."[7]

2. "[He] shall drink neither wine nor strong drink." This means he would be a Nazirite, his hair would not be cut and he would not take grapes, fresh, dried, as wine or in any form. It was a mark of separation and was usually something undertaken voluntarily. Two previous prophets had been Nazirites from birth,

Samson, who did not keep the Nazirite vows and Samuel who did. John was the third and last.

3. "He shall be filled with the Holy Ghost, even from his mother's womb." The angel was telling Zacharias here that John would be controlled by the Holy Spirit, and we will see later how the Spirit of God had influence on the child long before he was born.

4. "And many of the children of Israel shall turn to the Lord their God." He would turn many back from not believing in God, and make them ready to accept their Messiah, when they found out the promised deliverer was Jesus.

5. "And he shall go before him in the power and spirit of Elijah." Notice the angel does not say John is Elijah, but that he comes with Elijah's power and spirit. Like Elijah he will encourage the relatively small believing remnant[3] during a time of national wickedness.

6. "To make a people ready for the Lord." He would prepare groups in various places to be ready to accept the person he later identified as the Messiah. People baptised by John made a commitment, which was that when John eventually told them who the Messiah was, they would believe. We will see this in Scripture, when John tells them Jesus is the Messiah they believe. Some people refused John's baptism, and they ended up rejecting Jesus. John's special task was to go before Jesus, and to be the herald of the King.

Eventually, after the angel stopped talking Zacharias asked him a question showing he had doubts about the message. "Whereby shall I know this? For I am an old man, and my wife well stricken in years."[8] The angel detected the doubt and unbelief in the question and told John he would not be able to speak again until the prophecy was fulfilled, and from then on Zacharias became dumb. The conversation with the angel in the holy place slowed up Zacharias' work, and the people outside began wondering why he was taking so long. Finally he came out and they could see something supernatural had happened but when he tried to tell them about it he could not speak.[9]

[1] 1 Chronicles 24:10
[2] Luke 1:9
[3] Isaiah 46:3, Romans 9:27
[4] Leviticus 10:1-2
[5] Luke 1:13
[6] John 1:17
[7] Matthew 11:11
[8] Luke 1:18
[9] Luke 1:21-22

THE PROCLAMATION OF THE BIRTH OF JESUS TO MARY
Luke 1:26-38

Still in the first chapter of Luke, Gabriel, the angel that stands in the presence of God,[1] the one who spoke to Zacharias, is sent to Mary in the sixth month of Elizabeth's pregnancy.

> Luke 1:26-28 26 And in the sixth month the angel Gabriel was sent from God unto a city of Galilee, named Nazareth,
>
> 27 to a virgin espoused to a man whose name was Joseph, of the house of David; and the virgin's name was Mary.
>
> 28 And the angel came in unto her and said, "Hail, highly favoured, the Lord is with thee:"

Mary is highly favoured because God has chosen her to be the mother of the Messiah, but she doesn't know this and gets very frightened, and the angel then calms her down and tells her what is going to happen.

> Luke 1:31 And behold, thou shalt conceive in they womb, and bring forth a Son, and shalt call his name JESUS.

Actually, Jesus is English, His name in Hebrew was Yeshua, a common name at the time from the word "yeshuah" meaning salvation, and when the angel tells Joseph to name his step son Jesus (Yeshua), he is told, "for He shall save His people from their sins."[2]

Luke 1:32 He shall be great, and shall be called the Son of the Highest; and the Lord God shall give unto Him the throne of his father David.

Here is the fulfilment of the second rule for kingship, being chosen by God or authorized by a prophet. Many Jewish men could have been king on the basis of being a descendant of King David, but only Jesus met the second condition of being appointed by God, "the Lord God shall give unto Him [and no one else] the throne of His father David." No one else ever claimed the throne, because no one else met the second condition, and because of His resurrection He now lives forever and there will be no need for any successor.

Gabriel's announcement to Mary had five points.

1. The incarnation (the embodiment or clothing the Spirit with a body of flesh) will be in a man.
2. The man's name will be Jesus, (Yeshua = salvation).
3. He shall be great.
4. He will be the Son of God.
5. He will fulfil God's promise to David, the Davidic covenant, made more than 1,000 years before.

God had promised four things in the Davidic covenant which are repeated several times in Scripture but all can be found in one verse, 1 Chronicles 17:14, and they are:

1. An eternal house or dynasty.
2. An eternal throne.
3. An eternal kingdom.
4. An eternal descendant.

The first three are guaranteed because Jesus, the Seed of David will live forever. There are three key words in the Davidic covenant, house, throne and kingdom. All these words are used in Gabriel's proclamation, in verses 31 and 32, and the fourth, the eternal descendant is Jesus, the Son of the Highest,[3] the Son of God.[4]

Mary, like Zacharias has a question for the angel Gabriel because she is a virgin and is not married. "How shall this be, seeing I know not a man?"[5] Mary's question is not because she doubts the angel like Zacharias did, and so Gabriel answers her, "The Holy Ghost shall come upon thee, and the power of the Highest shall overshadow thee: therefore that holy thing that shall be born of thee shall be called the Son of God."[4] The Spirit of God will stimulate one of her eggs so that there will be a family connection from Jesus through Mary back to King David, Abraham and Adam, and her Child will not have a human father because the Holy Spirit will overshadow her and trigger one of her eggs. Notice that Jesus will be holy because of the power of God that will overshadow His mother, "the power of the Highest shall overshadow thee: therefore that holy thing that shall be born of thee,..."

Some people wrongly teach that for Jesus to be holy His mother must have been holy. She was not, that is why she went to the temple after the birth of Jesus to give her sin offering.[6] Also if Jesus was holy because His Mother was holy, then her mother and father would have had to be holy for her to be holy, and their mothers and fathers before them, and the further back you go the more holy people there would have to have been and the idea is clearly unbelievably stupid. Jesus was holy because His Father was God, and 700 years before, the prophet Isaiah had told the Jews to watch for a special sign.

> Isaiah 7:14 Therefore the Lord himself shall give you a sign; Behold, a virgin shall conceive, and bear a son, and shall call his name Immanuel.

Immanuel means, God with us.

Mary made her mind up.

> Luke 1:38 And Mary said, Behold the handmaid of the Lord; be it unto me according to thy word. And the angel departed from her.

She trusted God to look after her and she had three good reasons to do so.

1. The penalty for a woman engaged to be married who became pregnant was to be stoned to death, and she needed security.
2. If she was not stoned to death she would still be out of favour with the Jewish community, and she needed God to protect her from being hated.

3. She had to trust God to look after her relationship with Joseph, and this was serious because when Joseph found out she was pregnant he decided not to marry her, until the angel explained her situation to him.[7]

[1] Luke 1:19
[2] Matthew 1:21
[3] Luke 1:32
[4] Luke 1:35
[5] Luke 1:34
[6] Leviticus 12:6-8, Luke 2:22-24
[7] Matthew 1:19-25

MARY VISITS ELIZABETH
Luke 1:39-45

The angel had told Mary that her cousin Elizabeth who was known by the name Barren, meaning infertile, was six months pregnant and that nothing is impossible for God.[1] Elizabeth was old and long past the age when women have children and if God could cause her to have a child, then He for whom nothing is impossible could arrange for a virgin to give birth. Knowing that Elizabeth was pregnant, Mary went to see her.

The angel had told Zacharias that his wife Elizabeth's baby, John the Baptist would be controlled by the Holy Spirit in her womb and this is seen in action when Mary enters Elizabeth's house because the baby jumps in her womb. More than that, Elizabeth is filled with the Holy Spirit, and so she speaks out knowledge obtained from God, not from her own cleverness.

> Luke 1:41 And it came to pass, that, when Elizabeth heard the salutation of Mary, the babe leaped in her womb; and Elizabeth was filled with the Holy Ghost:

Next come the words of Elizabeth given to her by the Holy Ghost.

Luke 1:42-43 ⁴² and she spake [spoke] out with a loud voice, and said, Blessed art thou among women, and blessed is the fruit of thy womb.

⁴³ And whence is this to me, that the mother of my Lord should come to me?

How could Elizabeth possibly have known that Mary was the mother of her Lord?

Luke 1:44 ⁴⁴ For, lo, as soon as the voice of thy salutation surrounded mine ears, the babe leaped in my womb for joy.

She knew clearly but it was not through human understanding. She understood by being filled with the Spirit of God.

[1] Luke 1:36-37

THE SONG OF MARY
Luke 1:46-56

Mary's song is similar to Hannah's song in 1 Samuel 2:1-10, and shows that this young Jewish girl knew the Scriptures, and that she really and deeply loved God. In verse 47 she says, "And my spirit hath rejoiced in God my Saviour." What kind of people need a Saviour? Sinners need a Saviour! This verse shows that the Catholics have got it wrong by claiming that Mary was sinless. Mary needed a Saviour and knew it because she was a sinner.

The song is in two parts; first she talks about what God has already done for her and then she prophesies what God is going to do for Israel. The most important point of the first part of the song is that God is her Saviour. In the second part the key point is her clear understanding that the Son of God in her womb will fulfil God's covenant with Abraham.

Luke 1:54 ⁵⁴ He hath holpen [helped] his servant Israel, in remembrance of his mercy,

⁵⁵ As he spake [spoke] to our fathers, to Abraham, and to his seed [offspring] for ever.

At the end of the song we are told she stayed with Elizabeth for three months, and left for her own home just before John was born.

Advice to the Young - Learn from God and Mary

As I write this page, our granddaughter Charis is seven years old, Leo and Talia are five and Zack is four. Leo and Zack will be getting a brother or sister in about six month's time. You are all attractive and intelligent young people and when you grow up you will probably get married and have children of your own. You can learn from the Bible what kind of person you should marry.

God chose a virgin to have His Son. We will see later that Joseph was going to break off his intended marriage to Mary because he thought she was not a virgin, so it is best not to have sex before marriage, and this rule is the same for boys as it is for girls. I know that schools in England, unlike years ago, now teach children that they can decide for themselves what they do regarding sex, and because you are all good looking you will very probably be asked to have sex and you may be made fun of by your friends if you don't. However, be strong and brave and stay a virgin until you are married.

Mary's song teaches us that she was clever for two reasons. First she could remember Hannah's song almost by heart and secondly in the original language her song was very good poetry, so she was intelligent. The next rule is, don't marry a dumb twit, look for someone who has a good brain as well as looks.

We learned from looking at Mary's song that she loved God very much, and so God chose a young lady to have His Son who loved Him. Marry someone who loves you, because life is not always easy and people sometimes suffer hard times. It is then that you need a husband or wife that loves you and sticks by you through thick and thin. Lucy has gone through a lot for me. She has left her town life, her country, her family, the people who speak her language and come to live on a farm, which she knew nothing about, because she loves me.

THE BIRTH OF JOHN THE BAPTIST
Luke 1:57-80

The Jews name their boys after a dead relative when they are eight days old during the circumcision ritual. The custom at the time of Jesus was different because then they could also use the name of a living relative, and when John was about to be circumcised they decided to call him Zacharias after his father. Elizabeth had already been told by the angel to call him John and said, "Not so, but he shall be called John."[1] Her neighbours refused to accept this because no one in the family was called John, and they decided to find out what the baby's father wanted to call him, and they made signs to him. If they made signs to Zacharias it shows he was not only dumb but deaf as well. Zacharias, because he could not speak signalled for a writing tablet and wrote on it, "His name is John," the name given by the angel, and because He had been obedient to the angel of God, the curse was broken and he could hear and speak again.

The breaking of the curse made the neighbours of Zacharias afraid because they knew that something supernatural and eerie had happened and for many miles around they all wondered, what kind of man John would grow up to be.[2] Now Zacharias could talk he was filled with the Holy Ghost and prophesied, in Luke 1:68-79. So under the guidance of the God's Spirit, Zacharias speaks, and the prophecy he makes relates to three of God's covenants with Israel.

1. The Davidic covenant. "(Blessed be the Lord God of Israel; for he hath) raised up a horn of salvation for us in the house of his servant David."[3]
2. The covenant with Abraham. "To remember his holy covenant; the oath which he sware [made] with our father Abraham."[4]
3. The New Covenant (The New Testament). "To give knowledge of salvation unto his people by the remission [forgiveness] of their sins."[5]

The prophecy focuses on two people, the Messiah Jesus and John the Baptist. John will be a prophet, "And thou, child, shalt be called the prophet of the Highest."[6] He will be the greatest of all the Old

Testament style prophets, as we will see. John will have the job of preparing the way for Jesus, "for thou shalt go before the face of the Lord to prepare his ways."[6] In Malachi 4:2, Jesus is called the Sun of righteousness, and like the morning star that comes before daybreak, so John's ministry will be to announce the coming of Jesus, "through the tender mercy of our God; whereby the dayspring from on high hath visited us."[7]

The prophecy also says that when the Messiah comes the Jews and the Gentiles will both benefit. Up until the time of Jesus the Gentiles did not have the Scriptures and so were in darkness, but as the prophet Isaiah had said 700 years beforehand, Jesus would change all that.

> Isaiah 9:2 The people that walked in darkness have seen a great light: they that dwell in the land of the shadow of death, upon them hath the light shined.

The work of the Messiah will be, "to give light to them [the Gentiles] that sit in darkness and in the shadow of death, to guide our [the Jews] feet into the way of peace."[8] Jesus has not yet brought peace to Israel but He will bring them peace at His second coming.[9] There will be many attempts to bring peace to the Middle East but true peace will not come until Jesus returns.

In Luke's gospel notice how he talks more about Mary and Elizabeth than the other gospel writers, showing the important part women have in God's work, and how he tells us more about the role of Gentiles, two of his major concerns.

The early life of John the Baptist was not in a city or town.

> Luke 1:80 And the child grew, and waxed [changed by growing] strong in spirit, and was in the desert till the day of his shewing [showing] unto Israel.

Growing up in the desert away from the religious leaders meant that John was not contaminated by false teaching but was able to learn from the Scriptures for himself. Later when he gave his message it was very different from the Judaism of that time.

[1] Luke 1:60
[2] Luke 1:65-66
[3] Luke 1:68 & 69
[4] Luke 1:72 & 73
[5] Luke 1:77
[6] Luke 1:76
[7] Luke 1:78
[8] Luke 1:79
[9] Romans 11:26

THE MESSAGE TO JOSEPH OF THE BIRTH OF JESUS
Matthew 1:18-25

In Matthew's telling of the nativity of Jesus we get the story as Joseph saw it, and three times he reminds us of the virgin birth, beginning in verse 18.

> When his mother Mary was espoused to Joseph, before they came together, she was found with child of the Holy Ghost.

In verse 23 he quotes Isaiah 7:14, and this shows how Jews in the first century understood the prophecy of Isaiah to be talking about a virgin, not a young woman, because remember Matthew was writing for Jews. The virgin birth also overcomes the Jeconiah problem. Mary's virginity is mentioned a third time in verse 25.

> Matthew 1:25 And knew her not [kept her a virgin] till she had brought forth her firstborn son: and called his name JESUS.

So after the wedding there was no sexual union between husband and wife until after Jesus was born, but afterwards there was plenty of love making between them because Jesus had at least four half brothers and two half sisters.[1]

The proclamation of the birth of Jesus to Joseph was by an angel, like the announcements to Zacharias and Mary but this time the communication came in a dream. In his dream the angel gave him three messages.

1. He must keep his promise to marry Mary.
2. He must believe her story because she has not been unfaithful to him.
3. The birth of Jesus is according to God's plan, told by the prophet Isaiah more than 700 hundred years before.

[1] Matthew 13:55-56

THE BIRTH OF JESUS
Matthew 2:1-16, Luke 2:1-7

Looking at Matthew, Luke and historians of the time, especially Josephus, we know roughly the year Jesus was born. Herod died in 4 BC and the gospels tell us that Herod was alive when Jesus was born, so Jesus must have been born before 4 BC. The decree from Caesar Augustus that was issued in the days of Cyrenius[1] was issued in 8 BC, and was before the birth of Jesus, so He was born between 8 BC and 4 BC.

Josephus says that Herod left Jerusalem in 5 BC and went to live in Jericho and stayed there until he died. Matthew says that when Herod met the wise men, he was still in Jerusalem,[2] and Jesus was already two years old or less,[3] so when the wise men met Herod it was a long time after the birth of Jesus, not while He laid in the manger. (I have heard of one historical report that talks about Jesus standing beside His mother when the wise men saw Him). Put all that together and Jesus was born between 7 BC and 6 BC. How can Christ be born seven or six years before Christ? The answer is that calculations made when the Christian calendar was first set up years after the birth were not accurate.

The Virgin Mary became pregnant by the Holy Spirit six months after her cousin Elizabeth had conceived John the Baptist,[4] and because a woman's pregnancy is nine months, Jesus would have been born 15 months after the angel told Zacharias that Elizabeth his wife was going to have a son.[5] Zacharias was a priest of the course of Abia,[6] and it is known from the Tulmud and Qumran sources that one of the two weeks in the year the priests of the course of Abia served in the Temple was the end of June. If Zacharias did serve that week, then Jesus would have been born 15 months later, at the end of September of the following year, at the Feast of Tabernacles. The apostle John hints at this by saying that Jesus tabernacled among us, although the KJV Bible translates it, "dwelt."

> John 1:14 And the Word was made flesh and dwelt [tabernacled] amongst us.

The feast begins on the 15th of the month of Tishray, which the Jews call, - the Month of the Mighty Ones, - because Abraham, Isaac and Jacob were all born during Tishray. Sadly they do not yet realise that the Mightiest One of all, Jesus Christ, was also born in Tishray.

[1] Luke 2:1-2

[2] Matthew 2:1

[3] Matthew 2:16

[4] Luke 1:24-27

[5] Luke 1:13

[6] Luke 1:5

THE ANNOUNCEMENT OF THE BIRTH OF JESUS TO THE SHEPHERDS
Luke 2:8-20

Some shepherds were looking after their sheep in the pastures near Bethlehem when two things happened. The Shekinah glory appeared as light in the sky and lit up the ground all around. The Shekinah glory had not appeared in this way for 600 years since the time of Ezekiel. Also, the angel of the Lord suddenly materialized among the shepherds, and they were very frightened. The message from the angel covered three points.

1. Do not be afraid of what you are seeing.

2. A Saviour has been born. (Israel had had saviours before such as

the judges in the Book of Judges in the Old Testament, so what is special about this One?)

3. This One is Christ the Lord. (The Messianic Saviour).

The shepherds were told to go and find this child but we know from Matthew that there were many babies born in Bethlehem at the time,[1] so the angel gave them a sign to look for.

> Luke 2:12 And this shall be a sign unto you; Ye shall find the babe wrapped in swaddling clothes, lying in a manger.

The word "sign" shows that they were to look for something a bit unusual, and there were two uncommon things about the sign, the baby would be wrapped in swaddling cloths and would be lying in a manger. We will start with the place because that will help explain the cloths.

The thought of a manger would tell the shepherds not to look in a house or hotel but somewhere where animals were kept. The farmers around Bethlehem used caves in the area to shelter their animals when the weather was wet and cold, but when the weather was fine then the animals stayed out. Mangers would be found in the stable caves, and because they were shepherds they would know where these stables around Bethlehem were, but why a manger in a stable? Joseph and Mary tried to find good accommodation when they got to Bethlehem, but the town was filled with people, and the only place they could find was a stable cave. The second sign was the baby wrapped in swaddling cloths. The word for "cloths" in the original text comes from the Greek word "*sparganoo*," and it means strips of cloth like bandages that were used to wind around the bodies of dead people. The shepherds were to look for a baby wrapped in strips of burial cloth, and there is a reason for that.

Scattered among the stable caves were caves used for burying people, and these caves had and still have niches in the walls where burial cloth was stored. When someone died in Bethlehem the funeral procession would go to one of the caves where the cloth was kept and the body would be wrapped and taken to a burial cave. Joseph and Mary made use of the burial cloth that was available in the cave where Jesus was born. Interestingly Jesus was wrapped in the same cloth on the first day of his life that He would be wrapped in on the last day of His life, showing the reason for His birth. We are born to live but Jesus was born to die.

While the angel was talking, suddenly a large number of angels were standing with him, praising God and said two things.
1. "Glory to God in the highest, and
2. "on earth peace, and good will toward men."[2]

The shepherds quickly found the right stable with the help of the two clues and worshipped Jesus. Notice that the first recorded Jewish worship of the Messiah was brought about by the Shekinah Glory.

[1] Matthew 2:16-18
[2] Luke 2:14

THE CIRCUMCISION
Luke 2:21

The angel, as was the case with John, revealed the name of Jesus before He was born, but again the actual naming took place on the eighth day, the day of circumcision.[1] The circumcision was in obedience to two Jewish covenants, the Abrahamic covenant and the Mosaic covenant. The Abrahamic covenant required all Jews and people living in a Jewish household to be circumcised as a sign of being Jewish. Circumcision under the Mosaic covenant was slightly different because it was a sign of submission to the Law.

Paul warned us Gentiles not to get circumcised because we would then have to keep the whole Law of Moses, not just that one commandment.[2] Jesus has made the Law of Moses and the Mosaic covenant inoperative by His death, and there is no basis anymore to circumcise Jews or Gentiles under the Mosaic Law, which is Paul's point,[2] because circumcision does not make a man righteous.

The covenant with Abraham is an everlasting covenant[3] and all Jews, whether believers in Jesus or otherwise, must still circumcise their sons when they are eight days old. Paul has been criticized because in Acts 15 he refused to allow Gentiles to be circumcised but in Acts 16, the next chapter, he instigates the circumcision of Timothy, but Timothy's mother was Jewish.

Circumcision shows the obedience of the child's parents, the child has no part in the decision. One reason why baptism is not a type of or symbol for circumcision is because baptism shows the obedience or faith of the person being baptised.

[1] Luke 2:21
[2] Galatians 2:14 – 3:14
[3] Genesis 17:9-14

FORTY DAYS AFTER HIS BIRTH JESUS WAS PRESENTED TO THE LORD
Luke 2:22-38

The Law of Moses says that a woman is unclean for 80 days after she has given birth to a daughter and 40 days for a son.[1] In verse 22 it says that the days of Mary's purification were complete, meaning that Jesus was 40 days old, when they took Him to the temple to be presented to the Lord. The presentation had two purposes.

1. The purification of the mother through immersion (baptism) and a blood sacrifice (for the forgiveness of sins).
2. Jesus being her first born son, it was for the redemption of the first born.[2]

Mary took to the temple in verse 24, a pair of turtle doves or two young pigeons for the burnt offering and blood sacrifice, and this offering was only accepted by the priests if the person could not afford anything better, so Joseph and Mary were a poor couple.

Old Testament passages such as Isaiah 11:1, talking about the then future Messiah showed He would come from a poor background, when the powerful family of King David had been reduced to a stump of a tree with the root of Jesse. David's much poorer father's name was Jesse.

Joseph and Mary met with a very old man called Simeon, who had been guided by the Holy Spirit to be in the temple at the same time. Simeon was righteous and devout, so he was a member of the believing remnant, of whom there were very few left, waiting for the consolation (Greek *paraklesis*) of Israel,[3] meaning waiting for the One who was coming to the aid and comfort of Israel. God had revealed to Simeon that he would not die until he had seen the Messiah, and when he saw this 40 day old Boy he knew immediately who He was.

> Luke 2:29-32 [29] [Simeon said] Lord, now lettest [allow] thy servant depart in peace, according to thy word:
>
> [30] for mine eyes have seen thy salvation,
>
> [31] Which thou hast prepared before the face of all people;
>
> [32] A light to lighten the Gentiles, and the glory of thy people Israel.

Keep in mind Luke is writing and because his gospel is for the Gentiles, he makes sure he tells them Simeon's prophecy that Jesus will be a light for the Gentiles. Earlier in Luke we noticed Isaiah said the Gentiles sat in darkness,[4] and now to those who sit in darkness, the light, the glory of Israel, is given. For Mary herself he has two pieces of depressing news.

> Luke 2:34 Behold, this child is set for the fall and rising again of many in Israel; and for a sign which shall be spoken against.

Simeon is saying that Jesus will cause division among the Jews, for some He will be a falling and for others a rising. The remnant will believe and they will rise, but the others will not believe and they will fall, He will be a sign which they speak against.

> Luke 2:35 (Yea, and a sword shall pierce through thy own soul also,) that the thoughts of many hearts may be revealed.

Mary is warned she is going to agonise and suffer over her Son, a sword will pierce her soul. We will see how she was there when the nation and leaders of Israel rejected His clear claims of being their Messiah, saying He was possessed by Beelzebub, meaning His power came from Satan not God. Worse than that she was there when He was tortured and died on the cross, but her agonising is necessary, "that the thoughts of many hearts may be revealed," that the sinfulness of His enemies, of mankind as a whole be shown for all to see, for whom He suffered and died.

Next, Joseph and Mary met Anna, a prophetess who was also old and part of the believing remnant. She was of the tribe of Asher, one of the wrongly called ten lost tribes, that some say did not return from the captivity in Babylon,[5] but Anna's forefathers did and she was not lost. Several cults claim to be descended from the ten lost tribes but there are no lost tribes. The people in the cults may be lost but amazingly after thousands of years without a country of their own, the tribes of Israel are not. An example of Bible prophecy coming true today is that God said He would scatter Israel in all the nations of the world and then bring them back to their own land again.[6] The Jews had their own country again after nearly 2,000 years when the United Nations decided to re-establish Israel as a nation from 14 May 1948, and God's promised gathering of the Jews from around the world has been in progress since then.

As soon as she saw the baby, Anna knew He was the Messiah, just as Simeon did, and thanked God for Him.

> Luke 2:38 And she coming in that instant gave thanks likewise unto the Lord, and spake [spoke] of him to all them that looked for the redemption in Jerusalem.

She told members of the believing remnant, those that were looking for the redemption in Jerusalem, that Jesus was the Messiah they were looking for.

[1] Leviticus 12:1-8
[2] Exodus 13:2, Numbers 18:15-16
[3] Luke 2:25
[4] Luke 1:79
[5] Ezra 2:1
[6] Ezekiel 36:22-24

THE INFANT JESUS IN BETHLEHEM
Matthew 2:1-12

Every Christmas in Camelford, Cornwall, a shop and two pubs erect the same nativity scenes. They are well made antiques, and add old fashioned quality to the cheap and garish decorations in the rest of the town. The scenes are set in an old English barn, that Jews living in Israel would not recognize. In the barn are Joseph and Mary with the baby Jesus, either in Mary's arms or in a manger. Also there are some shepherds that look like Muslims not Jews, and three kings wearing golden crowns. Nativity scenes like these are traditional but definitely not biblical. The result of ignorance, they are nevertheless still warmly approved by most Christians and churches.

To begin with the shepherds and the kings never met each other, because the two events were more than a year apart. Starting with the kings, the Bible does not say they were kings or that there were three of them. There were at least two men because the word is plural but there may have been two, twenty, two hundred or many more, but when they arrived they caused a great deal of excitement throughout the whole city of Jerusalem,[1] and this probably means there was a large number of them. The Bible does not call them kings but wise men, from the Greek word, "*magos*" meaning astrologers, and if you have read the Scripture, Matthew 2:1-12, which has been pointed out for you to read you will know they came from the east.

In the Bible east is not China, because being a Jewish book it is centred in Jerusalem, and east of Jerusalem are Mesopotamia and Babylonia. The astrologers arrived in Jerusalem asking people, "Where is he that is born King of the Jews?" It is interesting that Gentile astrologers from Babylon knew about the Messiah, the King of the Jews, and wanted to come and worship Him? In the Old Testament there are stories, in the Book of Daniel for instance, about Babylonian astrologers and Jewish kings, and the kings were not worshipped, so why now? By the way, in the Bible the practice of astrology is forbidden,[2] so do not have your fortune told or your palm read even in fun, it leads people away from the light of God's Word to the darkness of Satan, but back to the questions.

How did they know? They knew because they had seen a "Star" in the east. To understand the Bible correctly we always interpret the words literally unless it is very clear that we should not do so. Here is an example where we cannot believe that it was an ordinary star.

1. The "Star" appeared and disappeared at least twice.
2. It was His "Star," the "Star" belonging to the King of the Jews.
3. The "Star" moved from east to west.
4. It also moved from north to south.
5. It came down low and hovered over one house in Bethlehem.

It was not a normal star.

The sun is a star, and the reason other stars look smaller than our sun is because they are far away. If a star like the sun came and stood over a house, the planet earth would be destroyed, so the "Star" we read about in Matthew 2, is something else. The Greek word for star has a root meaning of, "radiance or brilliance," and what the Babylonian astrologers saw was the same as the shepherds, the Shekinah glory, informing them of the birth of Jesus. Somehow these foreigners knew there was going to be a Jewish messianic King whose coming would be proclaimed by a "Star."

At the time of Jesus astronomy, the study of the stars, and astrology, fortune telling by the stars, (which we have just said is forbidden by God), were joined together. Astronomers were astrologers and vice versa, and this had been the case for thousands of years. In Numbers 22-24, is the story of one of these astrologers who came from Babylon called Balaam, and people believed he could bless and curse whoever he liked, but whenever he tried to curse the Jews, God took control of his tongue and he blessed them instead. Once in Numbers 24, God had taken control again when Balaam prophesied.

> Numbers 24:15-17 [15] Balaam the son of Beor hath said, and the man whose eyes are open hath said:
>
> [16] he hath said, which heard the words of God, and knew the knowledge of the Most High, which saw the vision of the Almighty, falling into a trance, but having his eyes open:

¹⁷ "I shall see him, but not now: I shall behold him, but not nigh: there shall come a Star out of Jacob, and a Sceptre shall rise out of Israel.

A sceptre is a symbol of royal authority and Balaam connected the coming of the Messiah with a King and a "Star." The Babylonians stored stacks and stacks of information on clay tablets in huge libraries and the astronomers would have known of any recorded prophecies about their favourite subject, the stars, so here they were in Jerusalem.

Jerusalem was not where Jesus was born, he was born in Bethlehem and the Jews had known their Messiah would be born in Bethlehem for 700 years because that is what the prophet Micah had told them.

Micah 5:2 But thou, Bethlehem Ephratah, though thou be little among the thousands of Judah, yet out of thee shall he come forth unto me that is to be ruler of Israel; whose goings forth have been from of old, from everlasting.

The astrologers from Babylon did not have the Jewish Scriptures so where would they expect a royal baby to be born? The capital city would be a good place to look for a king, but He wasn't there.

The question, "Where is he that is born King of the Jews?", caused tremendous interest throughout the city especially from Herod the Great. He asked to see the wise men and called in the chief priests, who told the Babylonians to look for Jesus in Bethlehem, the place He was born. Later, Herod called the wise men back secretly, because he wanted to know how long it had been since they first saw the "Star,"[3] and later we learn it had been about two years. He sent them away to look for Jesus asking them to come back and tell him when they had found Him, pretending that he also wanted to worship Him, but that was not his intention.

Away to Bethlehem they all went but how could they find the right house and the right baby, because there were lots and lots of babies in the town? The "Star" that had disappeared came back and moving from north to south, from Jerusalem to Bethlehem led them all the way and stopped over the house where the little Boy was. The Bible does not talk about the baby Jesus, but "the young child."[4] They did not have to search, the "Star" pointed out the exact house, something an ordinary heavenly star could not do. They worshipped Jesus in a house, not in the stable where the shepherds found Him.[5]

The first Jews to worship him were the shepherds, the first Gentiles were these wise men, and both groups were led to worship Him by the appearance of the Shekinah glory. The gifts they gave Him, gold, frankincense and myrrh, all had Old Testament symbolic meaning.

Gold, was the symbol for His being a king.

Frankincense, was the symbol for deity. He was God.

Myrrh, was associated with death and sacrifice.

Finally, because God warned them in a dream not to go to Herod, the wise men returned to Babylon by another way.[6]

[1] Matthew 2:3

[2] Isaiah 8:19-22

[3] Matthew 2:7

[4] Matthew 2:9

[5] Matthew 2:11

[6] Matthew 2:12

HIS EARLY YEARS IN EGYPT
Matthew 2:13-18

We learn about Jesus' time in Egypt from Matthew, and his theme is Jesus the Messiah the King of the Jews. Herod the Great was fearful about his security as king and jealously guarded his throne. He was always suspicious that someone was trying to take his throne away. He murdered his favourite wife because he thought she might be plotting against him, and also four of his own sons at different times of his reign for the same reason. After Herod had killed one of his sons Caesar Augustus quipped, "It is safer to be Herod's pig than Herod's son," because being a convert to Judaism, Herod did not eat pork, so if you were Herod's pig you would be safe, but if you were Herod's son you could be murdered at any time.

Herod was afraid that a young Boy in Bethlehem was going to take his throne away from him, and after some time he realised that the wise men would not come back. He did not know which Child the Babylonians had come to worship or the house where He lived, so he sent for some Roman soldiers. Matthew tells the story as it happened to Joseph, who had another dream and the angel of the Lord spoke to him again.

> Matthew 2:13 Arise, and take the young child and his mother, and flee into Egypt, and be thou there until I bring thee word: for Herod will seek the young child to destroy him.

The wise men had come bringing gifts, and before that, the family had been poor, but now they were rich, with gold, frankincense and myrrh, and could easily afford to travel to Egypt and stay there until it was safe to leave. The army arrived and killed all children two years old and under in Bethlehem and the surrounding area, in what is known as, the slaughter of the innocents, but Joseph, Mary and the young Jesus had already left. The Scriptures tell us why Herod wanted the children that were two years old and below killed.

> Matthew 2:16 [Herod] slew all the children that were in Bethlehem and in all the coasts thereof, from two years old and under, according to the time which he had diligently inquired of the wise men.

The wise men had told Herod when the "Star" had fist appeared, the time Jesus was born.

HIS EARLY LIFE IN NAZARETH - INCLUDING FOUR DIFFERENT WAYS GOD LED THE NEW TESTAMENT WRITERS TO QUOTE THE OLD TESTAMENT
Matthew 2:19-23

Historical records tell us that about two years after the slaughter of the innocents Herod the Great died, making Jesus over three years old.

Matthew 2:19-20 [19] But when Herod was dead, behold, an angel of the Lord appeareth [appeared] in a dream to Joseph in Egypt,

[20] Saying, Arise, and take the young child and his mother: and go into the land of Israel: for they are dead which sort the child's life.

After he died, Herod's kingdom was divided between his sons, and Archelaus was given Judea and Samaria. Herod the Great was bad but Herod Archelaus was worse, for when he became king he sent troops into the Temple during the Feast of Passover and killed 3,000 Jews. Joseph was again warned by God in a dream, this time to stay away from the region ruled by Archelaus, so he took Mary and Jesus and lived in Galilee, in a town called Nazareth,[1] where they had lived before,[2] ruled by another son called Antipas.

The New Testament quotes the Old Testament in four different ways and this is a good place to see how because all four ways are shown in Matthew 2, which we are studying. We will number them 1, 2, 3, and 4.

1. Prophecy and Fulfilment.

In Matthew 2:5-6 there is a quotation from Micah 5:2. Micah is prophesying the Messiah will be born in the town of Bethlehem, pointing out it will be Bethlehem in Judea, not therefore the Bethlehem in Galilee. The prophesy was fulfilled exactly as written, an example of a prophecy and its literal fulfilment.

2. Word and a Type of Fulfilment.

Matthew 2:15 quotes Hosea 11:1 **"Out of Egypt have I called my son."** Actually, Hosea was not prophesying anything. God called the whole nation of Israel, His firstborn son,[3] at the time when He brought them out of Egypt, more than 700 years before Hosea was even born. Hosea was just writing a fact of history, the nation of Israel, God's firstborn son, had been called out of Egypt. Matthew thinks to himself, Jesus is God's firstborn Son that lived for a time in Egypt and God sent His angel and called Him out. Matthew notices that once again God has called His Son out of Egypt, so the verse from Hosea is quoted as a type.

The writer of the Book of Hebrews talks of the Old Testament priest of God called Melchizedek, king of Salem,[4] now known as Jerusalem or Zion. He compares him to Jesus, who is also a Priest[5] destined to rule from Jerusalem after His second coming. Melchizedek did not prophecy about the Messiah but once again there will be a Man of God that will be Priest and King in Zion, so Jesus is a type of Melchizedek.[5] You could also say Melchizedek was a type of Christ, but the writer of Hebrews puts it the other way round and makes Jesus to be a type of Melchizedek. Just before He died Jesus asked us who believe in Him to remember Him by taking bread and wine,[6] and Melchizedek gave bread and wine to another believer called Abraham,[4] so again believers are taking bread and wine and we are reminded that Jesus was a type of Melchizedek. The word of the Old Testament was a type of the New Testament truth, so we have the word followed by a type of fulfilment.

3. Word and Application.

Here, "application" refers to a point that is similar in both Scriptures. Matthew 2:17-18, quotes Jeremiah 31:15, where Jeremiah wrote about something that happened while he was alive, the capture of the Jews and their deportation to Babylon. Although Babylon is east of Jerusalem, there is desert between the two cities. In order to make sure of a good supply of water the way from Jerusalem was north to the River Euphrates and then south-east to Babylon, following the river. Going north from Jerusalem the captives would pass through a town called Ramah, close to where Jacob's wife Rachael is buried. If anyone is reading this who has been on a tour of the holy sites in Israel and remembers being shown Rachael's tomb in Bethlehem, then they have seen one of the many wrong locations of holy sites that are shown to tourists. In the Old Testament, Rachael was a symbol of Jewish motherhood and as the young Jewish men were marched off, the mothers in Ramah came out and wept for the sons they would never see again. Jeremiah saw this and thought of it as Rachael, buried nearby and representing Jewish motherhood, weeping for her children, and refusing to be comforted.

In Matthew 2:17-18 and Jeremiah 31:15 there is one point of similarity, Jewish mothers weeping for the children they will never see again.

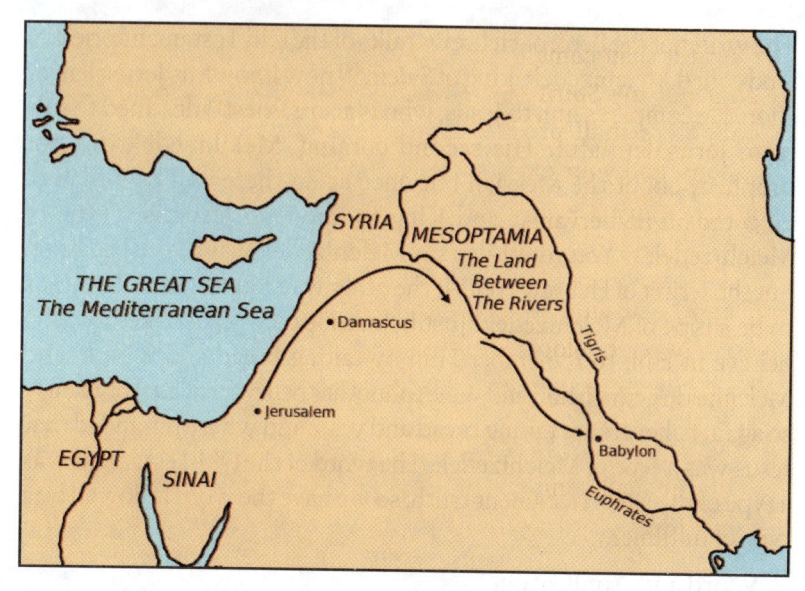

The Captured Jews Were Taken North To Bablylon

Other circumstances are different. In Matthew the town is Bethlehem, south of Jerusalem, in Jeremiah it is Ramah, north of Jerusalem. InMatthew the babies were killed but in Jeremiah the young men were made prisoners. The point of similarity is Jewish mothers weeping for the children they will never see again, and therefore the verse is quoted as an application.

Joel lived between 800 BC and 200 BC, depending on which historian we are reading, but no matter the actual date it was long ago. He talks about a time still in the future today, called the day of the Lord, when armies will be attacking Jerusalem. He saw back in those far off days a kind of war using technology that has not been developed yet. There will be "soldiers" that cannot be wounded,[7] and a new kind of space warfare because the heavens will be shaken.[8] The Jews will have no need to worry because following this they will turn to God,[9] and He will be with them from then on and will pour out His Spirit on all of them. Peter speaks about Joel's prophecy in the Book of Acts.

Acts 2:16-21 ¹⁶ But this is that which was spoken by the prophet Joel;

[17] And it shall come to pass in the last days, saith God, I will pour out my Spirit upon all flesh: and your sons and your daughters shall prophesy, and your young men shall see visions, and your old men shall dream dreams:

[18] and on my servants and on my handmaidens I will pour out in those days of my Spirit; and they shall prophesy:

[19] and I will show wonders in heaven above, and signs in the earth beneath; blood, and fire, and vapours of smoke:

[20] the sun shall be turned into darkness, and the moon into blood, before the great and notable day of the Lord come:

[21] and it shall come to pass, that whosoever shall call on the name of the Lord shall be saved.

Joel was talking about a time when all Israel will be given saving faith, and the Holy Spirit will be received by everyone in the nation resulting in many different kinds of supernatural experiences. Nothing that happens in Joel 2, happens in Acts 2. The one thing that happened in Acts 2, speaking in tongues, was not even mentioned in Joel. The one point of similarity was the outpouring of the God's Spirit resulting in supernatural signs. In Joel the Spirit is poured out on ALL flesh, but in Acts there were twelve people or at the most 120. In Acts the moon did not turn to blood and the sun was not darkened. The prophecy of Joel will come true when the whole nation of Israel is saved. Peter quoted it as an application.

4. A Summing Up.

> Matthew 2:23 And he [Joseph] came and dwelt in a city called Nazareth: that it might be fulfilled which was spoken by the prophets, He shall be called a Nazarene.

The Old Testament can be searched and searched but there is no prophecy saying Jesus will be called a Nazarene. The quotation is a summing up of what the prophets said but not the fulfilment of the words of one prophet. In the first century, a Nazarene was someone who was rejected and despised.

The Jews in Jerusalem and Judea looked down on the people from Galilee where there were no rabbinic schools, and the rabbis used to say, "If you want to get rich you go north, if you want to get wise you go south." If its money you want go to Galilee and be a cheat, but if you want to become wise, come to one of the rabbinic schools in the south. Among the Galileans themselves the people of Nazareth were the lowest of the low. One of the followers of Jesus said, "Can there any good thing come out of Nazareth?"[10] The prophets in the Old Testament did say that Jesus would be rejected and despised,[11] and calling Him a Nazarene in the New Testament, "sums that up."

> Luke 18:31-33 ³¹ [Jesus said] Behold, we go up to Jerusalem, and all things that are written by the prophets concerning the Son of man shall be accomplished.
>
> ³² For he shall be delivered unto the Gentiles, and shall be mocked, and spitefully entreated, and spitted on:
>
> ³³ And they shall scourge him, and put him to death; and the third day he shall rise again.

No prophet had said that but the prophets together did, it is a summing up, but not a direct quotation. So in the New Testament there are four kinds of quotations from the Old Testament:

1. Prophecy and Fulfilment.
2. Word and a Type of Fulfilment.
3. Word and Application
4. A Summing Up.

---

[1] Matthew 2:22-23
[2] Luke 1:26
[3] Exodus 4:22
[4] Genesis 14:18
[5] Hebrews 6:20, Revelation 11:15
[6] 1 Corinthians 11:23-25
[7] Joel 2:7-8
[8] Joel 2:10

[9] Joel 2:12 & 27
[10] John 1:46
[11] Psalm 118:22 (see also, Acts 4:11), Isaiah 53:3

GROWING UP
Luke 2:40

Although Luke emphasized the humanity of Jesus, he covered His development from about four years old to twelve in one verse.

> Luke 2:40 And the child grew and waxed strong in spirit, filled with wisdom; and the grace of God was upon him.

To find out more about Jesus in those eight years while He was growing up, there are two other places we can look. First we know a lot about how Jewish children were brought up at the time. Jesus grew up in a spiritual home with both Joseph and Mary being from the believing remnant of Israel. A child began studying the written Law, the Torah at the age of five, and the oral law, (both of which we will examine later), at the age of ten. He would receive His Bar Mitzva, (from, "mitzvos" – Divine command) when He was 13 years old. Somewhere between the ages of 12 and 16 He would normally get married but this was not so with Jesus. A boy was apprenticed to a profession when he was 12, and if he followed his father's business he would stay at home like Jesus did, but if he was to follow a different occupation he would be sent away to learn. Jesus had some basic education at home and in the synagogue, but that would not have given Him the tremendous knowledge He already had at 12 years of age when He surprised the experts in the temple at Jerusalem.[1]

Our second source of information on Jesus comes from the Old Testament where the prophets often give us details of the life of the Messiah, not recorded in the New Testament.

> Isaiah 50:4-6 4 The Lord GOD hath given me the tongue of the learned, that I should know how to speak a word in season to him that is weary: he wakeneth [wakes] morning by morning, he wakeneth [opens] mine ear to hear as the learned.

⁵ The Lord GOD hath opened mine ear, and I was not rebellious, neither turned back.

⁶ I gave my back to the smiters, and my cheeks to them that plucked off the hair: I hid not my face from shame and spitting.

Verse 4 tells us that every morning while Jesus was growing up, God the Father would wake Him up and teach Him and give Him the training He would need to be the Messiah. Jesus was both man and God, and had two different natures. As a human He had to be taught just like all of us, and as to His Godly mission He had to learn, in verse 5, that he would have to suffer greatly and even die but He was not rebellious. He accepted the plan for His life and death which God the Father was teaching Him. In verse 6, the training for His suffering is given and when the time came, He did not try to shield Himself from the Roman whips, or protect Himself while His beard was pulled out and His wounded face spat upon. Part of His growing up included a private education by God the Father.

God Still Speaks to His People

I was "born again" and received everlasting life in March 1983 in Malaysia, and after about three months, in June that year resigned from managing a group of rubber and oil palm plantations. One day while I was still working out my contract, the company offered me another job, this time in Liberia. I thought about it for several hours and decided to telephone them the next day to say that I did not want the job, and then went upstairs to sleep. Lying in bed on my back, in our lovely old style plantation house, at Ulu Remis, Johore, a masculine Voice spoke to me from inside the room, but no one could be seen. The Voice was above me and came from behind and from the left, the direction of Liberia, and I realised it was Jesus calling me by name, "John." At once I connected this with God speaking to Samuel in, 1 Samuel 3:1-18, of the Old Testament. He wanted me to go to Liberia and I immediately changed my mind and decided to accept the West African job.

Later I learned how very important it was for Lucy and me to spend those three years in Liberia.

Two other people I know have heard God speak to them. An English language teacher from Wolverhampton was asked to go and teach English at a university in China, and found herself telling the story of Jesus Christ to Chinese students who had not heard the gospel before. A Cornish farmer not far from Camelford was spoken to by God also. The farmer, the teacher and me heard God's voice from behind and from above. It is correct therefore for me to quote Isaiah 30:21 as an application.

> "And thine ears shall hear a word behind thee, saying, This is the way, walk ye in it, when ye turn to the right hand, and when ye turn to the left."

The Plantation House at Ulu Remis, where I was "born again," and heard Jesus speak.

Don't think that when God spoke to Jesus every morning, Jesus was hearing something that other people never hear. If God wants to give His people a message He still sometimes speaks to us audibly (we can hear Him with our ears), so that we can have the chance to walk the right way, or do the thing He wants us to do.

[1] Luke 2:47

JESUS A BOY IN THE TEMPLE
Luke 2:41-50

Joseph and Mary went to Jerusalem every year for the feast of Passover, showing they were part of the believing remnant, and when Jesus was twelve they took Him with them. Twelve was also the age He would be apprenticed to a profession, in Jesus' case a carpenter. The word "carpenter" in Greek does not only mean working with wood but also a stone cutter, and in Israel that would make sense because there is not much wood but plenty of stone.

The feast was a two day event and when it was over Joseph and Mary set off with the group they had travelled with back to Nazareth. They travelled for a day before they realised that Jesus was not with them, and then had to travel another day to get back to Jerusalem to look for Him. Three days after that they found Him in the temple sitting in the middle of the doctors, not medical doctors but the nations top experts in the Law of Moses and the spoken religious laws. It says He was hearing them, meaning that at twelve years old He understood their deep theological talks, and they recognized His questions were not the usual kind a boy would ask.

> Luke 2:47 And all that heard him were astonished at his understanding and answers.

Jesus not only understood them but He could answer their difficult questions. The doctors realized that Jesus could not have got His knowledge from the Nazareth schools, which were known to be dreadful. You know from the previous section, "Growing Up," how Jesus had obtained His knowledge that baffled the experts. As in the churches and schools of England today, the educational authorities in Nazareth did not know what they were talking about when teaching about the things of God, and so God the Father gave His Son some home schooling. Home schooling is now necessary again, not for every subject but for a correct understanding of the Bible. My grandfather, was a headmaster and always taught Scripture himself. He took it seriously, telling me that in those days it was the only compulsory subject and the most important one he ever taught.

Joseph and Mary found Jesus in the middle of the doctors. It was five days since His mother had seen Him, she had spent one day walking towards Nazareth, one day walking back, and three days searching in Jerusalem. Not many parents with a twelve year old son would start the three day walk from Jerusalem to Nazareth without making sure the boy was with them, and Jesus was not with them. I suppose it was because Jesus was the only faultless child there has ever been and his parents had got so used to Him never being naughty they had trusted Him. Mary was very cross.

> Luke 2:48 And when they saw him [Jesus], they were amazed: and his mother said unto him, Son, why hast thou thus dealt with us? Behold, thy father and I have sought [looked for] thee sorrowing.

She was trying to make Him feel guilty, like mothers do, but we are still sorry for Mary, and she told Him that He had caused them to sorrow, to be anxious. Jesus replied pointing out that Mary was wrong to call Joseph the carpenter His father

> Luke 2:49 And he said unto them, How is it that ye sought [looked for] me? wist [understand] ye not that I must be about my Father's business?

Jesus reminded them that they should have known to look in His true Father's house or that He would be involved with His true Father's business. Jesus was obeying His true Father. At the age of twelve He was not only apprenticed to Joseph as a carpenter, He was also apprenticed to His Heavenly Father and His business. He clearly knew at twelve years old that while He was human His real Father was God.

THE YEARS TO MATURITY
Luke 2:51-52

Again notice this is Luke who is interested in the humanity of Jesus. In two verses he covers the life of Jesus from twelve to about 30 years old. We learn that Jesus was subject to Joseph and Mary, He obeyed them, and Mary kept all that was said in her heart, she was careful to remember it. Verse 51 shows that being obedient is not a case of superiority or inferiority. It is only an arrangement, a matter of God's order. Here is the sinless God/man putting himself under two sinners, two human beings who were not up to his standard. A wife is in subordination to her husband because it is God's order, not because she is inferior, but a co-equal obeying her partner according to the divine plan. If a man has a clever wife then he is wise to listen to her before making important decisions, just as God told Abraham.[1] Abraham being the husband still had to make the decision but Sarah was right and he was wrong, and God told him so.

In maturing we develop in four areas and verse 52 shows that Jesus developed in these four areas just like everyone else, showing His humanity.

Jesus increased in wisdom, meaning He developed mentally.

Jesus increased in stature, indicating He grew physically.

Jesus increased in favour with God, signifying He grew spiritually.

Jesus increased in favour with man, showing He grew socially.

Everyone of us needs time to undergo development and mature the same way Jesus did.

[1] Genesis 21:12

THE CALL TO JOHN THE BAPTIST
Luke 3:1-2

John had matured in the wilderness of Judea separated from Jewish society and now in a certain year he was asked to start the work for which he was born. Luke wrote his gospel for the historically minded Greeks and so he identified the year.

> Luke 3:1 Now in the fifteenth year of the reign of Tiberius Caesar.

He then mentions other notable people, Pontius Pilate who was procurator from AD 26 to AD 36/37, Herod tetrarch of Galilee, (that was Herod Antipas who was deposed in AD 39), his brother Philip who died in AD 34, and Lysanius who we know nothing about. In verse 2 he names two high priests, Annas who served from AD 7-14, and Caiaphas, high priest from AD 18-36. From all that information we know that John the Baptist began his ministerial work in the year AD 26 .

> Luke 3:2 [In that year], the word of the Lord came to John the son of Zacharias in the wilderness.

The Greek here is *"rhema"* the spoken word, the audible voice of God telling him to start the work he was to carry out.

JOHN'S MESSAGE
Matthew 3:1-6, Mark 1:2, Luke 3:3

Matthew, Mark and Luke are called the synoptic gospels because they are written from a similar point of view. The gospel of John is different in character from the three gospels we are looking at in this section.

> Mark 1:2 As it is written in the prophets, Behold, I send my messenger.

Meaning the person God sent, which was John, was in fulfilment of prophecy. Hundreds of years before, two prophets, Isaiah and Malachi spoke about the forerunner or herald of Jesus.

> Isaiah 40:3 The voice of him that crieth in the wilderness, Prepare ye the way of the LORD.

> Malachi 3:1 Behold, I will send my messenger, and he shall prepare the way before me: and the Lord, whom ye seek, shall suddenly come to his temple, even the messenger of the covenant, whom ye delight in: behold, he shall come, saith the Lord of hosts.

In Malachi 3:1, the title, the Lord of hosts, means the Lord of the heavenly hosts, the Lord of all the heavenly angels. The messenger to be sent is John the Baptist. The Lord whom you seek is Jesus the Messiah. The temple is the Jerusalem temple where Jesus taught. The covenant is the new covenant from Jesus, who gives God's people eternal life as a gift, not by them working hard to be accepted.[1]

In 1985 we were in Liberia, and Lucy was very interested in her new Chinese Bible. She wanted to be one of God's children and wanted to make sure she was one, so she prayed to God to show her in a dream that she belonged to Him. She dreamed that God had given her three verses from her Bible which she still remembered when she woke up, so she quickly opened her Bible to see what the verses said, but they did not mean anything to her. I came in from the rubber fields for brunch, a kind of half breakfast and half lunch, at about half past ten and she told me in a very disappointed way how she had prayed, how God had given her three verses in a dream, but she did not know what they meant. All the verses were important messages from God to Lucy, and one of them was Malachi 3:1, which we have just read.

I was so happy to read the prophesy which God had sent as an application, and explained that when we believe or trust Jesus to save us, he sends the Holy Spirit to live inside us.[2] In the old days where was God? He was in the temple and so now people who have the Spirit of God in them are temples.[3] God was saying that He would send His Spirit, to live in Lucy, that she had been chosen by God to be His temple, and when the Spirit came she would know that she was His child. I have never seen Lucy so happy and in a moment she changed from a state of sad disappointment to high excitement, and started jumping up and down for joy.

John the Baptist's basic message is seen in Matthew 3:2, where he says, "Repent." He was asking the Jews to turn back to God, "for the kingdom of heaven is at hand." We have to repent and turn to God before we can be in His kingdom.

In Luke 3:3, John told the people to be baptised, a baptism of repentance. The people John baptised were committing themselves to believe that whoever John later told them the Messiah was, they would recognize that person as the Messiah. Later we read that those who were baptised by John and met Jesus, believed in Him, because John was preaching for at least six months before he told anyone Jesus was the Messiah. A lot of Jews from other countries were baptised and returned to their homes abroad, and more than 20 years later in Acts 19:1-7, the apostle Paul found a group of Jews in Ephesus that John had baptised, but they still did not know who the Messiah was. Paul told them that Jesus was the Messiah, John had proclaimed and they accepted Him, so John's work reached far and wide.

John dressed something like the prophet Elijah, and ate locusts and wild honey, both commonly found in the wilderness of Judea.[4] The kind of locusts John ate are the only insects Jews are allowed to eat under the Law of Moses. It is amazing that out in the desert, when he first started preaching, John attracted such huge crowds of people, from Jerusalem, all around the River Jordan and the whole of Judea.[5] The people that came to him in those early days were the common people, not the rabbis and priests, and they confessed their sins and were baptised in the Jordan.[6]

[1] Ephesians 2:8-9

[2] Galatians 3:8-9 and 3:14

[3] 1 Corinthians 3:16, 1 Corinthians 6:19

[4] 2 Kings 1:8

[5] Matthew 3:5

[6] Matthew 3:6

JOHN EXPLAINS WHY THE PEOPLE NEED TO REPENT
Matthew 3:7-9, Luke 3:7-14

Lots of men have claimed to be the Messiah, and at the time of Jesus the Jews had a system for checking such groups or persons. The first stage was observation, when religious experts would be sent out to watch what was being done, taught and said, but they were told not to ask questions or say anything. After some time they would go back to Jerusalem, make a report and give their decision or verdict. The verdict would say either that the movement (the person or persons) was important, or it was unimportant. If they decided it was unimportant then they did not go any further, they just ignored the whole thing, but if they decided it was important, then questioning would begin.

The questions could be hostile, casting doubt on the movement and raising objections, that would help them decide whether to accept or reject the claim that a certain person was the Messiah.

John was announcing that a King and a kingdom was coming, and that sounded like it could be the Messiah.

> Matthew 3:7 But when he saw many of the Pharisees and Sadducees come to his baptism, he said to them, O generation of vipers, who hath warned you to flee from the wrath to come?

The Pharisees and Sadducees it says, came to his baptism, to observe, they did not repent. On the other hand Luke spoke about a different group of people.

> Luke 3:7 Then he said to the multitude that came forth to be baptised of him, O generation of vipers, who hath warned you to flee from the wrath to come?

Here it says the multitude, the crowd of common people came to be baptised by John, but the Pharisees and Sadducees only came to his baptism.

John could tell by what the religious authorities, the Pharisees and Sadducees did and did not do, that they needed to repent.[1] They were good at talking but they were not good people. He taught the crowds to do things that they would not normally do, that were very unusual for them. For example men often had two coats, in case one got wet. John said that if they knew someone without even one coat they should give him their own spare one, and if they became aware that another person was hungry, they should give him some of their own food.

> Luke 3:11 [John said] He that hath [has] two coats, let him impart [give] to him that hath [has] none; and let he that hath [has] meat [food], let him do likewise.

We like to save things so that we can use them later, but John said use what you need and give the rest away, and people don't like doing that, its against our nature.

The tax collectors asked him what they should do, and he told them.

> Luke 3:13 Exact no more than that which is appointed you.

Tax collectors were not well paid but they became rich by cheating. The Romans would tell the collector they wanted ten silver shekels from Zechariah the doctor, but the collector would tell Doctor Zechariah he needed to pay 20 shekels. The collector would pay the Romans the ten they had asked for and keep ten for himself. John the Baptist told the collectors not to take more than the correct amount, which was not the normal behaviour of a collector. They did not become tax collectors for the low wages paid by the Romans, they did it to cheat their own people.

Some Jewish soldiers had joined the Roman army and they asked John how they needed to repent. Soldiers at that time used to bully people to get money and accuse them of committing crimes like stealing when it was not true, in order to make them pay a fine.

> Luke 3:14 [John told the soldiers] Do violence to no man, neither accuse any falsely; and be content with your wages.

The Pharisees and Sadducees were able to watch and see that John was telling the people to change their ways and not to follow the selfish behaviour which was normally practised by others. John demanded that his disciples behaved in ways which were far different from the standards of those days. Later we will learn that they went back to Jerusalem and made their report, with the verdict that the movement of John the Baptist was important.

[1] Matthew 3:8

JOHN MAKES A PROMISE WITH TWO PARTS, GOOD AND BAD
Matthew 3:11-12

The father of John the Baptist, prophesied that John would prepare the way for Christ and be the person who would announce to the Jews that

Jesus was their Messiah, he was to be the herald of the King. John baptised people with water but said that the person coming after him, would baptise people with Spirit and fire.

> Matthew 3:11 He shall baptise you with the Holy Ghost, and with fire.

The Greek construction here of one sentence in two parts individually explained is common. It means Jesus will also baptise, not with water but with two things, a baptism of the Holy Spirit, and a baptism of fire, and there is a difference between the two kinds of baptism.

> Matthew 3:12 He will separate the chaff from the grain, burning the chaff with never-ending fire, and storing away the grain. (Living Bible)

The Living Bible translation has been given because it is easy to understand, the same verse in the King James Version reads as follows.

> Matthew 3:12 Whose fan is in his hand, and he will gather his wheat into the garner; but he will burn up the chaff with unquenchable fire.

In this verse the wheat (grain) represents the people who believe in Jesus, and the chaff stands for the unbelievers, those who reject Him.

The wheat, the believers, will be baptised by the Holy Spirit, and gathered into His garner (His granary or barn), which is the Messianic kingdom. They are the ones who will get the good part of John's promise, everlasting life in the kingdom of God. The others, the people who are called chaff, the unbelievers will be baptised by fire, unquenchable (never-ending) fire, found in the lake of fire.[1] John is very clear, it is either one or the other, believers will be baptised by the Holy Spirit, and unbelievers by fire.

It was prophesied by Zacharias that his son John would be a forerunner of Jesus and we will see that the things that happen to John later on also happen to Jesus.

---

[1] Revelation 20:10

THE BAPTISM
Matthew 3:13-17, Mark 1:9-11, Luke 3:21-23, John 1:29-34

Baptism, complete immersion under water, is an old Jewish custom showing that a person who had been unclean or impure had been made clean. The initial root word in Greek of baptism is *"bapto"* – to dip or to dye. If a piece of cloth is dipped into dye, the colour is changed, it is not the same any more, and so another idea of baptism is that there has been a change. It shows that the person now belongs to a new group of people, or agrees with a message or a person.

Jesus went to John to be baptised,[1] but John tried to stop Him because he had been telling people to repent and turn back to God, and Jesus had no need to repent or turn back to God. Jesus would not take no for an answer and His baptism was the last action of His private life and the first step in His public life.

At His baptism all three members of the triune (three in one) God were there. God the Son, God the Holy Spirit or Ghost, and God the Father.

> Matthew 3:16   And Jesus, when he was baptised, went up straightway out of the water.

Coming out of the water meant He had been in it, He had not been sprinkled or had a wet finger pulled across His forehead, He had been baptised and He was soaking wet all over.

The second member of the triune God, the Holy Spirit was also there.

> Matthew 3:16 And he saw the Spirit of God descending like a dove, and lighting upon him.

It was not a real dove, it was the Holy Spirit coming down in the form of a dove, not a ghostly appearance, but structured like a dove.

> Luke 3:22 The Holy Ghost descended in a bodily shape like a dove upon him.

An old rabbinic clarification on Genesis 1:2, says, "The Spirit that brooded over the waters was like a dove." Jesus came to the Jews and because the rabbis had said the Holy Spirit was like a dove, then the significance of the form of a dove would be clear to them. Now the Jewish witnesses at the baptism had seen the Son and the Spirit.

God the Father next appeared at the baptism, not visibly but audibly.

> Matthew 3:17 And lo a voice from heaven, saying, This is my beloved Son, in whom I am well pleased.

At His baptism God the Father told everyone there that Jesus was His Son, and the Holy Spirit anointed Him with power for service.[2] God the Father and the Holy Spirit had shown their approval of the Son. He was about 30 years old.[3]

[1] Matthew 3:14
[2] Luke 4:14
[3] Luke 3:23

THE TEMPTATION
Matthew 4:1-11, Mark 1:12-13, Luke 4:1-13

The full details of Satan tempting Jesus are only in Matthew and Luke, but in Luke the arrangement is different to Matthew, and because Luke claimed to write down the things in the sequence in which they happened we will follow Luke's order. All three gospels tell us Jesus was led by the Spirit into the wilderness to be tempted. God organised it and Satan was pleased to do the testing. God wanted to prove that Jesus had no sin and Satan wanted to make Him sin. At His temptation Jesus represented two groups of people, first the children of Israel, the Jews and secondly all individuals.

> Luke 4:3-13 ³ And the devil said to him, If thou be the Son of God, command this stone that it be made bread.
>
> ⁴ And Jesus answered him, saying, It is written, That man shall not live by bread alone, but by every word of God.
>
> ⁵ And the devil taking him up into a high mountain, showed unto him all the kingdoms of the world in a moment of time.

⁶ And the devil said unto him, All this power will I give thee, and the glory of them: for that is delivered unto me; and to whomsoever I will, I give it.

⁷ If thou therefore wilt worship me, all shall be thine.

⁸ And Jesus answered and said unto him, Get thee behind me, Satan: for it is written, Thou shalt worship the Lord thy God, and him only shalt thou serve.

⁹ And he brought him to Jerusalem, and set him on a pinnacle of the temple, and said unto him, If thou be the Son of God, cast thyself down from hence:

¹⁰ for it is written, He shall give his angels charge over thee:

¹¹ and in their hands they shall bear thee up, lest at any time thou dash thy foot against a stone.

¹² And Jesus answering said unto him, It is said, Thou shalt not tempt the Lord thy God.

¹³ And when the devil had ended all the temptation, he departed from him for a season.

We have already discovered near the end of Chapter 2, the Bible is a Jewish book, that the nation of Israel was called the son of God.[1] Twice during the temptation Satan said to Jesus, "If you are the Son of God," linking Jesus with Israel. Jesus was tested in the wilderness and so was Israel.[2] Israel spent 40 years in the wilderness[3] and Jesus was tempted for 40 days, so there is an association with the number 40. Jesus went in the presence of the Holy Spirit, and so did Israel.[4] In His temptation therefore Jesus represented Israel, the Son of God, and in the wilderness where Israel failed, Jesus triumphed.

As a representative of all people Jesus our High Priest was tempted the same way we are.

> Hebrews 4:15 [He] was in all points tempted like as we are, yet without sin.

The temptations of the world are in three areas.

- The lust of the flesh.
- The lust of the eyes.
- The pride of life.

The Bible has pointed these areas out for us in, 1 John 2:16, and the temptations of Jesus cover all three, but He did not sin. How could I be tempted in these three ways?

- For the lust of the flesh I could be tempted to eat someone else's food who needed it, or I could be tempted to go to bed with a beautiful girl who was not my wife.
- For the lust of the eyes I could be tempted to lie to get an expensive car or even steal one given the chance.
- For the pride of life I could be tempted to become a world famous person like a Lord or a Knight by cheating.

The beautiful girl could say, "Come to bed with me," or she might say, "You can have my brand new Ferrari car if you lie to the police and say we were together all day yesterday." A government minister might say that he likes my house and if I sell it to him he will make sure I am made a Lord, and become famous. Those would be temptations but it is up to me whether I do the wrong thing or not.

The first temptation of Jesus was to turn stone into bread, and it was made after he had not eaten for forty days, and He was very hungry. I could not be tempted to turn stone into bread because it is not possible for me to do that, but for Jesus it was a temptation because He could have done it easily. However, God did not give Him His power so that He could make a fuss of Himself. It was a temptation of the lust of the flesh. Jesus answered Satan by quoting Deuteronomy 8:3, **"It is written, That man shall not live by bread alone, but by every word of God."**

In His second temptation Satan gave Him a vision of all the kingdoms of the world at a certain time. Satan does sometimes give us visions, and he said to Jesus, "All this power I will give thee," because he does have authority over the kingdoms of the world, as he claimed in verse 6, which Jesus did not deny. In verse 7 he added, **"If thou therefore wilt worship me, all shall be thine."** Satan was offering Jesus a short cut to His future kingship of the world which is the plan of God for Him.

God's way was by His crucifixion, not by worshipping Satan. It was a temptation of the lust of the eyes. Jesus answered Satan by quoting Deuteronomy 6:13, **"It is written, Thou shalt worship the Lord thy God, and him only shalt thou serve."**

For His third temptation Satan took Jesus to the pinnacle of the temple, which was in the south east corner of the city wall and in those days was 216 feet high. Psalm 91 says that if the Messiah trips on a stone the angels will catch Him so that He will not fall or be harmed before His time. Knowing the Scriptures, Satan said to Jesus, who was standing above a 216 foot drop, "If thou be the Son of God, cast thyself down." In other words prove it to me, because if You really are the Messiah the angels will rescue You. If Jesus had done that He would have been showing off. The third temptation dealt with the pride of life, and Jesus answered Satan by quoting Deuteronomy 6:16, **"It is written, Thou shalt not tempt the Lord thy God."**

Jesus was tempted in the same three ways that ordinary people are. He resisted Satan by quoting Scripture appropriate to the temptation. We are to do the same when we resist Satan. If Satan used someone to tempt me to lie to get a brand new Ferrari car, I should say, "It is wrong to lie or to desire anything that belongs to someone else,"[5] and leave it at that. Jesus did not shout, or say how wicked the person tempting Him was, He just quoted a Scripture appropriate to the temptation. After that Satan gave up and left Jesus.

Every few years the electric supply company that owns the pylons carrying the power cables over the farm sent men to paint the pylons. One year a painter knocked on our door with three large tins of paint. He said the paint was very thick and it was hard work painting the pylon, would I give him three tins full of tractor diesel oil in exchange for three tins of paint. He wanted to mix some oil into his paint to make it runny and easier to brush on. The trouble with diluted paint is that it washes off in the rain. Now it would have been a good bargain for me because the grey paint the electric company used was the best quality and the colour was suitable for farm buildings and roofs. I looked at the man and told him it would be sinful for me to do that. He froze stiff for a moment, then grabbed his paint and ran back to the pylon as fast as he could, and I saw an example of the Scripture, James 4:7 in action.

> James 4:7 Resist the devil, and he will flee from you.

The man did not show his face again. You may think I am telling you this to boast about how righteous I am and how honest. No, it is not that, none of us are righteous, not one,[6] I know some of the things that go through my mind, and wish they did not. The story is told to demonstrate that when we make a stand against the devil, he will leave, and we get the victory, just as he left Jesus, and I want to encourage all my grandchildren to refuse to submit to their friends or anyone who wants them to do wrong. Just say, "No," and if you can remember a verse from the Bible that supports you, that would be even better, because Jesus used Scripture too.

> James 1:12 Blessed is the man that endureth [does not give in to] temptation: for when he is tried, he shall receive the crown of life, which the Lord hath promised to them that love him.

The last words in Luke 3:13, tell us that although Satan had left Jesus it was only for a while, for a season, temporarily. We must be wary of more spiritual attacks later on, right up until we die. In the Lord's prayer in Luke 13, Jesus taught us to pray, "And lead us not into temptation; but deliver us from evil."

[1] Exodus 4:22

[2] 1 Corinthians 10:1-13

[3] Numbers 13:25ff, Numbers 14:3-34

[4] Isaiah 63:9-14

[5] Exodus 20:16-17

[6] Romans 3:10

THE RELIGIOUS LEADERS PROBE AND QUESTION JOHN THE BAPTIST
John 1:19-28

The second stage of the checking of John the Baptist by the Sanhedrin or religious council is recorded for us by the other John, Jesus' disciple.

Remember they are now going to ask questions and three times we are told that this is the authorized delegation. John tells us that they were priests and Levites, meaning they were sent by the Sanhedrin. Priests and Levites were generally Sadducees.

> John 1:19 And this is the record of John, when the Jews sent priests and Levites from Jerusalem to ask him, Who art thou?

They needed to get answers to their questions to take back to the Sanhedrin in Jerusalem.

> John 1:22 Then said they unto him, Who art thou? That we may give an answer to them that sent us.

For the third time John reminds us they were officially sent.

> [24] And they which were sent were of [from] the Pharisees.

In answer to their questions John denies he is three things, first he says he is not the Messiah.

> John 1:20 I am not the Christ.

He also denied he was Elijah the prophet who had lived over 800 years before.

> John 1:21 Art thou Elijah? And he saith, I am not.

We have already learnt that John came in the spirit and power of Elijah,[1] but he was not Elijah himself. Thirdly he denied being the prophet.[2]

> John 1:21 Art thou the prophet? And he answered, No.

In the end they asked him who he was.

> John 1:23 I am the voice of one crying in the wilderness, Make straight the way of the Lord, as said the prophet Isaiah.

He claimed to be the forerunner of the Messiah, and told them that Jesus was already there but had not yet been identified.

> John 1:26-27 [26] I baptise with water: but there standeth one among you, whom ye know not;
>
> [27] He it is, who coming after me is preferred before me, whose shoe latchet [lace] I am not worthy to unloose.

The questioning of John by the Sanhedrin was now over, but remember what happened to John the Baptist was also going to happen to Jesus.

[1] Luke 1:17

[2] Deuteronomy 18:15

JOHN TELLS THE CROWD THAT JESUS IS THE SAVIOUR OF THE WORLD THE SON OF GOD
John 1:29-34

Many years before Jesus, when the Jews were slaves in Egypt, God told them to kill a lamb for every household, and paint its blood on the outside of the house above the door and on the two door posts. God then sent the angel of death through the land and killed the firstborn sons of every person and animal, but wherever he saw the blood of the lamb, he would pass over the house and no person inside, or their animals would be killed.[1] Every year the Jews celebrate this at the feast of Passover, and they remember when the angel of death passed over their houses because of the blood of the lamb.

In Isaiah 53 there is a prophecy about Jesus which tells of His torture and death 700 or more years later, which happened just as Isaiah had said. The prophecy also says that because of His death many people will have their sins forgiven, and now we know something that Isaiah did not say. The many people who will have their sins forgiven are the ones who believe Jesus died for them.

John the apostle tells us that on the day after the religious leaders questioned John the Baptist, he saw Jesus coming.

> John 1:29 [John the Baptist said], Behold the Lamb of God, which taketh away the sin of the world!

Calling Jesus the Lamb of God identified Him with the Passover lamb of Exodus 12, and the Messianic Lamb of Isaiah 53.

> John 1:30 [John the Baptist then said], This is he of whom I said, After me cometh a man which is preferred before me; [He came before me] for he was before me.

Jesus came after him and before him because as a man he was born after John the Baptist, but as God He was before him.

John was sure that Jesus was the Messiah because John was filled with the Holy Spirit even before he was born, and the Spirit had made known to him, that when he was baptizing he would see the Holy Spirit come down, and the One on whom He descended would be baptised in, with or by the Holy Spirit, and He would be the Messianic King.

John 1:34 And I saw, and bear record that this is the Son of God.

Jesus had been clearly made known as King, Saviour and Son of God first of all by the Old Testament prophets, after that His coming birth was told to Mary and later to Joseph by an angel, then to the shepherds also by an angel, and the Gentiles knew by His Star. He was introduced to the crowds being baptised by John in the River Jordan, by God the Father speaking from heaven, and by John the Baptist, his forerunner and herald. Baptised with power from on high, He was about to begin His work.

[1] Exodus 12

4

HOW JESUS WAS ACCEPTED

THE FIRST FIVE DISCIPLES BELIEVED IN HIM
John 1:35-51

The day after John the Baptist had completed his mission of pointing out to the Jewish public that Jesus was their Messiah, he pointed Him out again in private to two of his own followers, John the son of Zebedee and Andrew, saying, "Behold, the Lamb of God." John and Andrew immediately believed and wanting to be disciples of Jesus, they began a traditional Jewish ritual of the time.

In the Israel of those days they did not have schools like we have. There were some well known rabbis in an assortment of rabbinic schools in and around Jerusalem, and if a man wanted to study under a certain rabbi, he would have to become his disciple. It was not acceptable to go and ask the rabbi, "Can I be your disciple?" The man would show the rabbi he was interested by following him around, not so far away that he would not be seen and not too near to be a nuisance. He would do this for hours, days or weeks, until the rabbi turned to the man and asked, "What are you looking for?" The man would then answer, "Rabbi, where do you live?" If the rabbi did not want the man to be his disciple he would answer, "That's none of your business," and the man would go away, but if the rabbi wanted him to be his disciple he would reply, "Come, and you will see."

The proper way of becoming disciples of Rabbi Yeshua (Jesus), was faithfully followed by John and Andrew, and it was such a life changing important moment for John that he wrote down the time it happened.

> John 1:39 He [Jesus] saith [said] unto them, Come and see. They came and saw where he dwelt, and they abode with him that day: for it was about the tenth hour [The tenth hour would be four o'clock].

Later, Andrew went and told his brother Peter they had found the Messiah, and took him to Jesus.

> John 1:42 And he brought him to Jesus. And when Jesus beheld [saw] him, he said, Thou art Simon [Hebrew name, meaning obedient] the son of Jona [John]: thou shalt be called Cephas [an Aramaic name, meaning stone or rock], which is by interpretation, A stone [In Greek, Peter means, "stone"].

Another day went by and then just before they went to Galilee, Jesus Himself called Philip, and Philip found Nathaniel, the fifth disciple. The conversation between them shows how the people from Nazareth were thought of by Nathaniel, who knew the place well because he himself was from Galilee. Philip told Nathaniel that Jesus of Nazareth was the Messiah, and Nathaniel asked, "Can anything good come out of Nazareth?" Philip replied, "Come and see," and then a strange conversation took place between Jesus and Nathaniel. Remember, Nathaniel had never seen Jesus before.

Jesus saw Nathaniel coming and said, "Behold, an Israelite indeed, in whom is no guile!" Nathaniel heard Jesus and asked how Jesus knew him, and Jesus answered, "Before that Philip called thee, when thou wast under the fig tree, I saw thee."[1] Nathaniel then made a most surprising answer. "Rabbi, thou art the Son of God; thou art the King of Israel."[2] How could being seen under a fig tree make Nathaniel know that Jesus was the King of Israel?

The first Israelite was Jacob, because God gave him the name of Israel at Penuel,[3] and this first Israeli, on one single occasion, was guilty of guile or deceit when he deceived his father Isaac into giving him the blessing intended for Esau.[4] By calling Nathaniel an Israelite without guile, Jesus is pointing out that this descendant of Jacob is different from his ancestor because he is not a deceiver. Jesus then said, "Before that Philip called thee, when thou wast under the fig tree, I saw thee." Nathaniel was doing something under the fig tree that only he and Jesus knew about.

Two thousand years ago it was impossible for everyone to own a copy of the Scriptures, and so the Jews spent hours and hours memorising them by heart. Having learned the words they then meditated on them thoroughly to ensure they got the most they could from the Word of God. The rabbis believed and taught that the best place to meditate on the Word was under a fig tree. An ancient Jewish commentary on part of the Bible, called the Midrash, tells us that some famous rabbis held their classes under a fig tree because it was a better place for meditation, where the Scripture would be better understood.

Nathaniel realized at once when Jesus said, "when thou wast under the fig tree, I saw thee," that Jesus knew exactly which passage of Scripture, he had been meditating on, that Jesus could read his mind, and this becomes clear as the story unfolds. Jesus then said to Nathaniel, "Verily, verily [Truly, truly], I say unto you, Hereafter ye shall see heaven open, and the angels of God ascending and descending upon the son of man."[5] In the Bible there is one other place where we read about angels ascending and descending, when Jacob dreamt of a ladder reaching to heaven,[6] and the dream was on the first night he was running away after deceiving Isaac, his act of guile. Nathaniel for that reason understood that Jesus knew he had been thinking about Jacob's ladder in Genesis 28, and recognized that Jesus was the Son of God, the King of Israel.

[1] John 1:48
[2] John 1:49
[3] Genesis 32:28-30
[4] Genesis 27:1-29
[5] John 1:51
[6] Genesis 28:10-17

THE FIVE DISCIPLES' FAITH WAS BUILT UP BY THE FIRST MIRACLE
John 2:1-11

In his gospel, John often works in sevens. He describes seven signs shown by Jesus, writes down seven of his talks or discourses and seven of His, "I am," claims. He has just told us about six days in the life of Jesus, so this miracle will be on the seventh day, again showing John's use of the number seven. The first day of the story began with the religious leaders questioning John the Baptist,[1] the second day was when John told the crowd that Jesus was the Saviour of the World, the Son of God,[2] the third day began with the words, "Again the next day, ..." when John the son of Zebedee, Andrew and Peter became disciples,[3] and, "The day following, ..." when Philip and Nathaniel became disciples,[4] was the fourth day. The passage we are looking at now begins, "And the third day there was a marriage in Cana of Galilee," because it would take three days to walk from Judea to Galilee, so this is the seventh day.

Jewish weddings then were in two parts, the marriage ceremony to which a few individuals were invited, and then the wedding feast lasting seven days to which many people were invited. Jesus with the five disciples He had collected so far went to the feast and a terrible thing happened, they ran out of wine, something that should never take place at a Jewish wedding. Mary was so disturbed when the wine had run out she told Jesus about it, and He said to His mother, "Woman, what have I to do with thee? Mine hour is not yet come."[5] He often said, "Mine hour is not yet come," when talking about the hour of His crucifixion, but here He means it is not yet time for Him to start performing miracles to show the Jews that He is their Messiah. The best place to begin His miracles would be Jerusalem. However, He performed the miracle there in Cana but rather quietly and most people at the wedding would not have known that a miracle had happened.

At a certain time in our lives we stop being submissive to our parents, and move from obedience to Mum and Dad, to honouring them, and when Jesus said, "Woman, what have I to do with thee?" He is pointing out that what He is about to do is not because He is under her authority, but to give her honour. Mary understands and at once tells the waiters serving the wine, "Whatsoever he saith unto you, do it." Mary's command to the waiters has been preached to Christians for centuries, and I repeat it again, if you hear or understand somehow that Jesus wants you to do something, do it. Whatever He says to you do it! Anyway, there were six large stone water pots able to hold altogether about 150 gallons or 680 litres of water which would be over 900 bottles full, (using the most common modern 75CL wine bottles). Jesus told the waiters to fill the pots with water right to the top, then He told them to take some out and take it to the governor of the feast, the man in charge of the party. The water had changed into wine, not grape juice but alcoholic wine, the Greek word used in the Scripture can only be used for fermented wine. It was good strong stuff. The Bible does not teach us to stay away from strong drink, it teaches self-control and moderation.

The governor when he tasted the wine told the bridegroom that he had made a mistake and left the best wine until last.[6] Wedding feasts lasted a week and they would start by serving the best wine, and after drinking for a few days the guests sense of taste would be less sensitive and they would then bring out the cheaper stuff. The wine that Jesus made from water was high quality, better than the best wine used at the beginning of the wedding. In the Old Testament wine is a symbol of joy and in Psalm 104:15 it talks about wine that makes men's hearts glad. Grape juice has never had that effect on me.

> John 2:11 This beginning of miracles did Jesus in Cana of Galilee, and manifested forth his glory; and his disciple believed on him.

Three points can be noted from this verse.

> 1. This is the first miracle Jesus performed. Changing the water into wine was the first of John's seven signs. Lots of old writings claiming to have knowledge of Jesus while He was a boy, tell of previous miracles which are not true. One story is that when Jesus was playing with other children they all made model birds out of clay, and the children made fun of Jesus because His bird did not look very good. Jesus is then supposed to have said, "Yes, but my bird can fly," and His bird became alive and flew

away. We should only believe what the Bible says when there are differences like that.
2. He manifested (clearly showed) His glory, because His power to create was made obvious.
3. His disciples believed in Him, meaning their original belief had been confirmed before their eyes and strengthened. He was without doubt their Messiah, King of Israel and Son of God.

After the wedding Mary and some of her family, Jesus with His brothers and the five disciples went to Capernaum on the north shore of the Sea of Galilee and stayed a few days.[7] Later Jesus would make the town His headquarters.

[1] John 1:19-28
[2] John 1:29-30
[3] John 1:35
[4] John 1:43
[5] John 2:4
[6] John 2:10
[7] John 2:12

JESUS TAKES POSSESSION OF THE TEMPLE
John 2:13-22

Following the baptism and temptation of Jesus, four Passovers are mentioned. Starting from the first Passover, the second Passover came one year later, the third two years later and the fourth three years later, when He died. The first Passover was four to six months after His baptism and that is how we know Jesus preached to the Jews for about three and a half years. At the first Passover He went to Jerusalem[1] and brought Himself to the attention of the people, by publicly making claims that He was the Messiah. During the Feast of Passover hundreds of thousands of Jews from all over the nation and other countries of the world where Jews lived, went to Jerusalem. Afterwards they would take back to their countries, towns and villages the news that a man named Jesus of Nazareth had claimed to be the Messianic King.

In the Temple he saw thriving businesses with some people selling cattle, sheep and doves, and others changing money. Turning the Temple of God into a business enterprise was a wicked thing to do and some Pharisees of the time, who were very much against the practice, wrote down what was going on. The businesses were all under the control of a man called Annas, who had been the High Priest. The businessmen in the Temple compound were all members of Annas' family, and the Pharisees called it the Bazaar or Market of the Sons of Annas.

Annas was not a Pharisee, he was a Sadducee, and the historian, Flavius Josephus, a Jew and Roman citizen, who was born in Jerusalem in AD 37, described Annus as a collector of money, very rich and a robber of the common priests by using open and violent brutality. Rabbi Shaul of Jerusalem wrote that Annas made his sons the treasurers and his sons-in-laws assistant treasurers.

Like so many men down the centuries, Annas was into religion in a big way to make money. His actions show that he was not interested in God, only himself and his organization. The same attitude is seen in the false churches today, and that includes some people in most of the "Christian" denominations, so be very careful indeed who you give money to for the work of Jesus. It is probably best not to give any money to any church or Christian ministry until after you have been born spiritually and are in close direct unity with Jesus, (not through a priest who might be an Annas in disguise), and even then you should pray first and check them out. Christians are often easily duped by religious crooks that think up all kinds of ways to convince us to give money to them.

In Liberia where Lucy and I lived in the 1980's there was a mixture of good Christian folk and false, and as the people were poor, many "churches" tried to get money from anyone who was easy to fool. One "minister" used to write letters to wealthy Christian organizations, and he wrote to one American group leader telling him that he had an important Christian ministry in Liberia and that God had told him to write and request $100,000 dollars. The American wrote back saying that God had not told him to give anything at all.

Getting back to Annas and the animal sellers, under the Law of Moses, the Jews had the right to take their own animals to the Temple to be sacrificed, but they had to be animals without spot or blemish, and so the priests would inspect them to make sure they were perfect. Under the system Annas and his checking priests were operating, if someone brought their own animal, something was always found to be wrong with it. If they lived close to Jerusalem they could change the animal but if they had come from Galilee they could not go back and get another animal because it was a six days round trip and by then the festival would be over. Conveniently animal stalls had been erected and these were full of animals that had already been approved by the Sadducees for sacrifice. The approved animals had to be bought at very high prices, and the money would go to Annas and his family.

The money changers were there because Passover was the time everybody paid their annual Temple tax of a half shekel, (a shekel was a Jewish weight and also a silver coin). Roman money had an image of Caesar stamped on it and you could not pay the Temple tax with money that had an image on it.[2] Money had to be converted from Roman coins into temple coins and there was a charge for this service which went to the family of Annas. Annas was guilty of making the Temple of God into a business house, just as Jesus said he was,[3] and by calling the Temple, His Father's house, Jesus was claiming to be the Son of God, and He then acted in a very public way. He made a scourge and whipped the people working for Annas, driving them out of the Temple, those selling animals, the money changers together with the sheep and cattle, and asked those selling doves to leave. He poured the money on the ground and turned the tables over,[4] so the news of Jesus of Nazareth, who was claiming to be Messianic King of Israel, would spread everywhere Jews lived when they returned home after the Passover.

His disciples seeing Jesus in action remembered a prophecy from David's Psalm 69:9.

John 2:17 The zeal of thine house hath eaten me up

In Hebrew the language is stronger and says, "The zeal for Your house will be the cause of My destruction." Taking possession of the temple resulted in Annas and the other Sadducees hating Jesus and being hostile towards Him. At His trial Annas was His first judge and Caiaphas, the son-in-law of Annas was His second judge. After He had taken control of the Temple the Jews asked Him for a sign to prove He was the Messiah as He claimed,[5] and He gave them a mysterious answer, one they did not understand.

John 2:19 [Jesus said] Destroy this temple, and in three days I will raise it up.

He was prophesying about the temple of His body which would be destroyed on the cross and then come to life again three days later.[6]

---

[1] John 2:13-16
[2] Exodus 20:4
[3] John 2:16
[4] John 2:15-16
[5] John 2:18
[6] John 2:19-22

HIS ACCEPTANCE IN JUDEA
John 2:23 to 3:21

As well as publicly announcing in the Temple His claim to be the Messiah, Jesus also performed miracles while He was in Jerusalem,[1] and because of the miracles lots of Jews believed in Him. Changing the water into wine, as we said earlier, had been done rather quietly but these miracles were done for many people to see. To begin with the reason for the miracles was to show Israel, Jesus was their Messiah, that they should believe His message. He wanted them to make a decision about Himself, was He the Messiah or not? If they would accept Him, He was offering Israel the kingdom spoken of by the Jewish prophets, and they would see the kingdom set up on earth right then, some 2,000 years ago. But they would first have to believe in Him, and accept Him as the Messianic King, therefore the miracles to start with were to serve as signs to Israel to make that decision. Later on the reason He performed miracles was very different.

The first of the seven talks given by Jesus that John shares with his readers is about the new birth, and involves a man called Nicodemus.

John 3:1 There was a man of the Pharisees, named Nicodemus.

In rabbinic writings he is referred to as, "a rabbi". Pharisees held certain beliefs and we therefore know some of the things Nicodemus believed, in the same way we know what some people believe today. If someone tells you he is a Baptist, you know immediately that he believes that the proper way to be baptised is to be completely immersed in water, and only believers in Jesus are qualified to be baptised. If someone else tells you he is a Presbyterian, you know he believes you can baptise babies who do not believe in Jesus, that do not even know anything about Him, and that a spot of water dabbed on the forehead will do. In the same way we know certain differences between the Jews of those days, Pharisees, Sadducees, the Essenes and others.

The key belief of the Pharisees was, "All Israel has a share in the age to come." The meaning of this was that all people who were born Jews would have automatic rights into the kingdom of God. The Pharisees were quite wrong in this but that is what they believed. You will remember when we were talking about John the Baptist and he was telling the people to repent, to stop sinning, he warned them not to think to themselves that there was no need to repent because they were descendants of Abraham,[2] that is to say because they were Jews.

Another teaching of the Pharisees was that anyone who was circumcised would not end up in Hell, but would go into God's kingdom. Rabbis in the second century were troubled by this because Jewish believers in Jesus were having their sons circumcised, and the rabbis could not accept that Christians would not end up in Hell, but that was what their own theology said, "Anyone circumcised won't end up in Hell." They added to their theology to overcome their problem by claiming when a Jewish believer in Jesus died, an angel from heaven came down and put his foreskin back on, so that he would end up in Hell. Also, in Pharisaic writings, "to be born of water," meant to be born physically, the way everyone in the world is born.

Nicodemus believing what all Pharisees believed came to Jesus secretly, at night. He accepted Jesus was from God because of the miracles.[3] Jesus said to him, "Except a man be born again, he cannot see the kingdom of God."[4] Pharisees believed there were six ways a man could be born again, but only physically because they had no idea or concept of the spiritual birth. The six ways very briefly are the following.

1. When a Gentile converted to Judaism he was said to be born again. This did not apply to Nicodemus because he was born a Jew.
2. Second was when a man was crowned king, again this did not apply, because Nicodemus was not a king.
3. At the age of 13 a Jewish youth goes through the Bar Mitzva ceremony, (nothing to do with circumcision which happens at eight days old), when he becomes responsible to keep the Law and is recognised as an adult. Nicodemus was long past his Bar Mitzva when he came to Jesus and so he had already been born again for the first time when he was 13 years old.
4. A Pharisee was said to be born again when he married a wife. We know Nicodemus was married because he was, "a ruler of the

Jews,"[3] which meant he was a member of the Sanhedrin (Council), and only married men were admitted. Men usually married between the ages of 16 and 20, when Nicodemus would have been born again for the second time.

5. A man was declared born again when he was ordained a rabbi, and Nicodemus being a member of the Sanhedrin had been ordained. In those days this happened at 30 years of age, when Nicodemus had been born again for the third time.

6. The only other way to be born again was to become a Rosh Yesheva, the head of a rabbinic Yesheva (an academe or seminary), which Nicodemus was. We know this because in John 3:10, Jesus called him "the teacher of Israel," and the words, "the teacher," were a title used only for the head of a rabbinic academe. (This is one of the rare occasions when the translation given in the King James Bible is wrong because it has Jesus saying, "a teacher of Israel," other versions such as the New King James Bible, and the New American Standard Bible, are correct). Therefore Nicodemus had the title of, Rosh Yesheva, which means, The Teacher. A man would be around 50 years old when he became the head of a rabbinic Yesheva, and it was then that Nicodemus had been born again for the fourth and last time.

Nicodemus had been born again four times and there was no other way for him to be born again, and so when Jesus told him he would not be able to see the kingdom of God unless he was born again, he answered, "How can a man be born when he is old?"[5] Jesus was using a common Jewish way of teaching, by going from what Nicodemus knew to what he did not know. The term "born again" in the physical sense was known, but the spiritual ramifications or branches were unknown, and Jesus moved from the physical to the spiritual.

> John 3:5 [Jesus said] Verily, verily [Truly, truly], I say unto thee, Except a man be born of water and of the Spirit, he cannot enter into the kingdom of God.

By saying you must be born of water and of the Spirit, Jesus is denying the Jewish belief that all Israel shall have a share in the age to come. Natural birth is not enough, we must also be born spiritually to be able to enter the kingdom. The Spirit means the Holy Spirit, which brings to life our dead human spirits, and makes us alive to God. Nicodemus must experience this new birth before he will be able to see or enter into God's kingdom.

Next Nicodemus starts to wonder, "How can I be born again spiritually?" and Jesus tells him the two necessary steps, the first is the work of God, but he has to take the second step. The work of God is shown in verse 14 that follows, and the response needed by Nicodemus in verse 15.

> John 3:14-15 [14] And as Moses lifted up the serpent in the wilderness,[6] even so must the Son of man be lifted up:
>
> [15] that whosoever believeth in him should not perish, but have eternal life.

Three years later Jesus was nailed to the cross, which was lying down, and then the cross was lifted up and dropped in a hole in the ground to stop it falling over. First God had to send His Son to make eternal life available to everyone, but although salvation is there for everyone, not a single person is saved until they take the necessary human action, "that whosoever believeth in him should not perish, but have eternal life." Probably the most famous verse in the Bible is John 3:16, and it contains the same two steps, God's provision and man's response.

> John 3:16 For God so loved the world, that he gave his only begotten Son, that whosoever believeth in him should not perish, but have everlasting life.

Unless Nicodemus comes to believe that Jesus is the Messianic King, the Son of God, he will not be able to see or enter God's kingdom.

It is uncommon for a Jew to believe the gospel as soon as he hears it, he has to learn to think differently which is a difficult mental and psychological struggle. For Nicodemus the struggle now begins and it will continue for three years. In John 7, although not yet a believer he defends Jesus' right to be heard, and in John 19, he identifies himself as a believer at the time Jesus is buried. Rabbinic writings tell us that Nicodemus was a well-digger and one of the wealthiest men in Jerusalem.

After emphasizing the need to believe in Jesus, John gives another example of his sub-theme spoken by Jesus, on the conflict between light and darkness.

> John 3:19-21 [19] And this is the condemnation, that light is come into the world, and men loved darkness rather than light, because their deeds were evil.
>
> [20] For everyone that doeth evil hateth [hates] the light, neither cometh to the light, lest his deeds should be reproved [punished].
>
> [21] But he that doeth truth cometh to the light, that his deeds may be made manifest, that they are wrought of God [because people can see they are doing what God wants them to do].

An important truth can be learnt from the three verses we have just read. Jesus is the Sun of righteousness,[7] and just as the sun shines in the darkness and gives light to the world, Jesus shines on us who are sinners so that we can gladly and joyfully join our holy and almighty God in heaven, because Jesus will make us just like Himself.[8] We will be given holiness and righteousness as a free gift, we will not have to struggle to be good, righteousness from Jesus is free,[9] and because we will be righteous, we will not feel guilty, for we will be holy and that is why we will enjoy being with our righteous God forever.

We like everyone to think we are virtuous and respectable, and as you grow up you will notice many people and charities doing good humanitarian work. You will also notice that the leaders of some of the hardest working charities, make it very clear to everybody that they are not Christian, and many considerate, generous and helpful people refuse to ask Jesus for the gift of life. Jesus says in the three verses we have just read, that people, which includes those that try to make themselves and others believe they are so kind and honourable, are actually wicked, if they refuse to come to the light, the Sun of righteousness., "men loved darkness rather than light, because their deeds were evil."

In, 1 John 3:2 [8], not the John 3:2, you should have read, "when he [Jesus] shall appear [at his second coming], we shall be like him." If we will be like Him, it means we are not like Him now, we are not holy or righteous yet, and this is true of every living Christian. Sadly you will find that believers in Jesus sometimes behave badly, worse than many non-Christians. If this happens to us we need to pray, telling God what we have done and then our close friendship with Him will be renewed.

> 1 John 1:9 If we confess our sins, he is faithful and just to forgive us our sins, and to cleanse us from all unrighteousness.

Everlasting life comes through Jesus so don't be afraid to come to His light, let the Sun of righteousness shine on you and you will become like Him.

[1] John 2:23
[2] Luke 3:8
[3] John 3:1-2
[4] John 3:3
[5] John 3:4
[6] Numbers 21:9
[7] Malachi 4:2, 2 Samuel 23:4
[8] 1 John 3:2
[9] Romans 5:17 and 6:23

THE WITNESS OF JOHN THE BAPTIST
John 3:22-36

John's gospel tells us that John the Baptist was baptising at Aenon near Salim because there was plenty of water there. John usually baptised further south on the east bank of the River Jordan near where it flowed into the Dead Sea, but at the end of the dry season, before the rain came the river there was shallow, and so he moved north along the river towards the Sea of Galilee, where there was plenty of water to baptise. If a little dab of water on the forehead was enough, he could have stayed in his usual place, but that was not the way Jews were baptised.

The disciples of Jesus were baptising believers[1] and John's disciples were jealous because more and more were being baptised by Jesus and less and less by John, and they told John about it. John explained to them God wanted it to be that way because Jesus was the Christ, and then he spoke of three orders among the people of God, the bride, the bridegroom and the friend of the bridegroom. Later in the New Testament we learn that the bridegroom is Jesus and the bride is the spiritual Church of true believers. John does not put himself in either of these categories because the saints in the Old Testament are not part of the bride, the Church, they are the friends of the bridegroom, and John the Baptist is pleased to be counted among this group.

John explains that God has given Jesus the Spirit without measure.[2] In Isaiah 11:2 we are told He will receive the seven fold Spirit of God which is described as, (1) the Spirit of the LORD, (2) the spirit of wisdom, (3) the spirit of understanding, (4) the spirit of counsel, (5) the spirit of might, (6) the spirit of knowledge, and (7) the spirit of the fear of the LORD, and these seven Spirits represent the fullness of the Holy Spirit. We believers all receive the Holy Spirit in measure, not according to how spiritual we are but upon what God wants us to do, and therefore we all have different spiritual gifts, some have more than others, so that we are equipped to do the work God has planned for each of us in the true Church, the body of Christ. We are given a measure of the Spirit for that reason, but Jesus received the Spirit without measure.

[1] John 4:2
[2] John 3:34

JOHN THE BAPTIST IS ARRESTED AND PUT IN PRISON
Luke 3:19-20, John 4:1-4

Luke says that John was a prisoner of King Herod, actually this was Herod Antipas the son of Herod the Great. John had been preaching against the Herod's marriage to his brother Philip's wife Herodius, because Philip was still alive,[1] and Herod had John arrested to stop his message reaching the people. Remember John was the herald of

King Jesus and what happened to John will later happen to Jesus.

Jesus now decided to leave Judea and go to the district of Galilee. The Bible gives us three reasons why Jesus went to Galilee. We have just discovered that the disciples of Jesus had been baptising more people than John the Baptist and because of this the Pharisees are beginning to take an interest in Jesus, just like they took an interest in John, and as He is starting to attract attention Jesus moves away from Judea.[2] The second reason Jesus left Judea was because John had been put in prison. The third reason was because God wanted Jesus to go through Samaria on His way to Galilee.[3]

> Luke 4:14 And Jesus returned in the power of the Spirit into Galilee.

God had more work for Him in Cana of Galilee and also on the way there was work for Him in Samaria.

[1] Leviticus 18:16

[2] John 4:1-3

[3] John 4:4

HOW JESUS WAS ACCEPTED IN SAMARIA
John 4:5-42

The people who lived in Samaria were called Samaritans, and the Jews and the Samaritans hated each other. By saying that the Jews had no dealings with the Samaritans,[1] John was simplifying the difficult and unfriendly association between the two. He does not mean that Jews were forbidden to have contact with Samaritans. The fact was that Jews could not accept a kindness from a Samaritan for fear of putting themselves in his debt. If they were hungry Jews could buy food from Samaritans but they had to pay for it, because they were not allowed to put themselves in a position where they owed them any favours.

The Jews that returned to Jerusalem after the captivity in Babylon would not allow the Samaritans to help build the Temple[2] because the Samaritans were racially mixed and also their religion was mixed.

The Assyrian empire had captured the tribes of Israel that lived in Samaria, deported them to other countries and repopulated the place with foreigners that brought their phoney gods and idols with them. The God of Israel was worshipped in Samaria but along with a large number of false gods.[3] In response to not being allowed to help build the Temple the Samaritans said Mount Gerizim, one of the two mountains overlooking the towns of Shechem and Sychar, was the holy mountain, not Moriah. Next they went through the five books of Moses, and removed all references that applied to Jerusalem. Genesis 22 tells the story of the sacrifice of Isaac on Mount Moriah, but the Samaritan version of the Torah reads Mount Gerizim.

Samaritans would stop, even murder Jews passing through their country going to Jerusalem, but never coming from Jerusalem to Galilee, the way Jesus was going in His famous meeting with the Samaritan woman, because they enjoyed seeing Jews leave Jerusalem and going past what was for them the holy mountain of Gerizim.

John's sub-theme is to reveal God to men and he does that in five steps when telling us about Jesus and the woman at the well.

1. Jesus tells her about a new kind of life in John 4:10-14.
2. In verses 15-19 He shows that she is a sinner. She had to understand she was a sinner before she realised she needed a Saviour.
3. He shows her the nature of true worship in verses 20-23.
4. God the Father is revealed to her in verse 24.
5. And in verses 25-26 He tells her that He is the Messiah.

It is interesting to listen to the woman during the meeting, showing how her faith grew all the time she was with Jesus. At the start in verse 9, she calls Jesus a Jew, and coming from a Samaritan woman that was an insult. In verse 11, she calls Him, 'Sir', showing some respect, and in verse 19 she says He is a prophet. By verse 29 she finally understands and goes into the city and speaks to the men there.

> John 4:29 Come, and see a man, which told me all things that I ever did: is not this the Christ [the Messiah]?

In demonstrating how John explained his sub-theme of revealing God to men (and women), we have gone ahead of the actual story. We now need to go back to the time when Jesus first arrived at Jacob's well.

> John 4:5-6 Then cometh he to a city of Samaria, which is called Sychar, near to the parcel of ground that Jacob gave to his son Joseph. Now Jacob's well was there.

Sychar was a suburb of the well know Bible city of Shechem, the modern city of Nablus. It is in between Mount Gerizim to the south and the larger Mount Ebal to the north.

> John 4:6 Jesus therefore, being wearied with his journey, sat thus on the well: and it was about the sixth hour.

Jesus sent the disciples to Sychar to buy some food and while they were away, a woman from the town came to get some water, and Jesus asked her for a drink, which really surprised her, because He was asking for a kindness, putting Himself in her debt.

> John 4:9 How is it that thou, being a Jew, askest [ask for a] drink of me, which am a woman of Samaria? For the Jews have no dealings with the Samaritans.

Jesus then begins to tell the woman she needs eternal life.

> John 4:10 If thou knewest the gift of God, and who it is that saith to thee, Give me to drink; thou would have asked him, and he would have given thee living water.

Living water had the meaning of running water as from a fast flowing stream. Some wells reached down to water running in a vein or tunnel underground and Jacob's Well is like that, but Jesus is talking about living spiritual water. The woman does not yet understand but she will soon.

> John 4:11-12 Sir, thou hast nothing to draw with, and the well is deep: from whence then hast thou that living water? Art

thou greater than our father Jacob, which gave us the well, and drank thereof himself, and his children, and his cattle?

She is beginning to wonder if Jesus is greater than Jacob, and He certainly is, so He begins to move from the physical or natural world to the spiritual. He tells her that anyone drinking from the well will get thirsty again, but He has a different kind of water.

> John 4:14 Whosoever drinketh of the water that I shall give him shall never thirst; but the water that I shall give him shall be in him a well of water springing up into everlasting life.

The water Jesus is giving will give everlasting satisfaction, not of physical thirst, we all get thirsty, but of spiritual thirst, because the water from the well inside us is from the Holy Spirit and gives us spiritual life which is forever. She does not yet fully understand and asks Him to give her some of His water so that she will not have to keep coming to the well, but she has now been told the need for eternal life.

Jesus next shows her that she is a sinner because unless we realise that we are sinful we cannot see the need for a saviour, and He begins this by asking her to bring her husband to the well. She has to admit that she is not married and then Jesus shows her that He really is greater than Jacob.

> John 4:17-18 Jesus said unto her, Thou hast well said, I have no husband: for thou hast had five husbands; and he whom thou now hast is not thy husband: in that saidst [spoke] thou truly.

She had been married and divorced five times and the man she was sleeping with now was not her husband, that identifies her sin. Often when unbelievers have their sins pointed out to them, they avoid the problem of sin by asking questions about religion, such as, "Where did the sons of Adam and Eve get their wives?", which has nothing to do with how sinners are forgiven. Her religious issue is about a prophet.

> John 4:19 Sir, I perceive that thou art a prophet.

The question is a very major advance for her because Samaritans are taught the only prophet to come after Moses will be the Messiah. The

Samaritans reject all of the Old Testament and the prophets except the first five books of Moses, and even there they refuse to accept anything about Jerusalem, and when she says, "Sir, I perceive that thou art a prophet," she is already wondering if Jesus is the Messiah. By asking her religious question she was avoiding talking about her own sin and she goes happily on about religion.

> John 4:20 Our fathers worshipped in this mountain; and ye say, that in Jerusalem is the place where men ought to worship.

The mountain she was talking about was Mount Gerizim because the well and the city of Sychar are at the foot of the mountain, which even today is the holy mountain for the Samaritan religion.

Her question has nothing to do with what Jesus had said and He could have ignored it, because she was just trying to change the subject, but He chose to answer her before getting back to the point He was making.

> John 4:21-23 Jesus saith unto her, Woman, believe me, the hour cometh, when ye shall neither in this mountain, nor yet at Jerusalem, worship the Father. Ye worship ye know not what: we know what we worship; for salvation is of the Jews. But the hour cometh, and now is, when the true worshippers shall worship the Father in spirit and in truth: for the Father seeketh such to worship him.

He answered her that the Samaritan worship at Mount Gerizim was wrong, they worshipped what they did not know. Jerusalem was the right place, and the Jews worshipped what they knew according to the Law of Moses. The Jews worshipped wherever the Temple or the Tabernacle was, when the Tabernacle was at Shiloh they had worshipped there and after the Temple was built, Jerusalem was the right place to worship up until the time of Jesus. The Samaritans were wrong and the Jews were right, but that was not her real problem.

She did not yet know that she needed a saviour and eternal life, that she needed to have living water and to recognize true worship. In view of the fact that God is a Spirit, He must be worshipped in spirit and in truth, and because of the work of Jesus, the time is coming when there will be no central place of worship, neither Gerizim or Jerusalem. The way to worship God is going to be in spirit and in truth anywhere in the world. Jesus is prophesying the Church Age in which we now live, the Age of Grace, when He forgives the sins of those who believe in Him.

Under the Law of Moses the place to worship was in the Tabernacle or the Temple,[4] and when Jesus returns to rule the world from Jerusalem, Jerusalem will again be the place for those people left alive on the earth to worship,[5] as many prophets have told us. However, now between the time of the Law of Moses and the coming Kingdom of Jesus on earth, we can worship God anywhere but it must be in spirit and in truth. For that reason Jesus leads the woman back to the proper way to worship and deals with the subject of faith. She must believe that He is the Messiah!

> John 4:25-26 The woman saith unto him, I know that Messiah cometh, which is called Christ: when he is come, he will tell us all things. Jesus saith unto her, I that speak unto thee am he.

The woman had suspected that He was the Messiah earlier when she called Him a prophet, and here Jesus clearly tells her, He is Christ! At this point the disciples returned, and they were absolutely amazed that He was talking to the lady, not only because she was a Samaritan but because she was a woman. It would have been un-Jewish enough to speak to a Samaritan man let alone a Samaritan woman.

She left her water pot beside the well and went back to Sychar telling the people of the town Jesus had told her everything she ever did, He knew all her memories, who she was and what she was like, "Is not this the Christ?" she asked them.[6] The disciples had returned to the well with food they had bought in town, but Jesus again moves from the physical to the spiritual, telling the disciples He has had food already.

> John 4:34 Jesus saith unto them, My meat [food] is to do the will of him that sent me, and to finish his work.

By talking to the Samaritan woman, Jesus had led her to eternal life through faith in Him, and this was His food, the work God gave Him.

The woman then came back from Sychar bringing others with her and Jesus taught the disciples the principle of preaching both the gospel (or evangelism) and salvation, eternal life. It is usually done in two steps, sowing and reaping.

Often a person we lead to Jesus will already have heard about Him, maybe at Sunday school or from other people including friends or even strangers, and we come right at the end of the development of their faith. When this happens then we have reaped where others have sown, and that is the principle of evangelism taught by Jesus, some sow and others reap.

> John 4:36-38 And he that reapeth receiveth wages, and gathereth fruit unto life eternal: that both he that soweth and he that reapeth may rejoice together. And herein is that saying true, One soweth and another reapeth. I sent you to reap that whereupon ye bestowed no labour: other men laboured, and ye are entered into their labours.

Christians who work hard telling others about Jesus sometimes get jealous when another person comes along and does the reaping after all their effort, which is quite the wrong attitude. If someone we have been teaching the gospel to is led to eternal life by another person after we have struggled hard to teach them, we rejoice together,[7] because the fruit of eternal life has been produced.

In John 4:39-42, the disciples saw the principle in action.

> John 4:39 And many of the Samaritans of that city believed on him for the saying of the woman, which testified, He told me all that ever I did.

The woman sowed the gospel, the good news that Jesus is the Messiah, and reaped the harvest because some Samaritans believed her, others believed when they met Jesus after the woman had told them about Him.

> John 4:41-42 And many more believed because of his own word; and said unto the woman, Now we believe, not because of thy saying: for we know that this is indeed the Christ, the Saviour of the world.

The woman had sowed and Jesus had reaped.

[1] John 4:9
[2] Ezra 4:1-3
[3] Exodus 20:3-6
[4] Joshua 18:1, 1 Chronicles 29:19
[5] Zechariah 14:16-21
[6] John 4:29
[7] John 4:36

JESUS WAS ACCEPTED IN GALILEE
John 4:43-45

Eventually after spending two extra days in Samaria Jesus got to Galilee, where many people already believed in Him because they had been to the feast of Passover in Jerusalem, and knew He had claimed to be the Messiah and had performed many miracles.

> John 4:45 Then when he was come into Galilee, the Galileans received him, having seen all the things that he did at Jerusalem at the feast: for they also went unto the feast.

At the start of His effort to get the Jews to believe He had found acceptance in Judea, Samaria and the Galilee of the nations. He had not been accepted in Jerusalem but had taken possession of the Temple. After His second coming He will be worshipped in Jerusalem for a thousand years.[1]

[1] Revelation 20:6

5

THE AUTHORITY JESUS HAS AS KING

AUTHORITY TO PREACH
Luke 4:14-15, Mark 1:14-15

Jesus used to go around the country preaching, and this tour around the Galilee was the first. He had publicly claimed to be the Messiah in Jerusalem and now He began to actively offer the Jews their own kingdom with Himself as King. On these tours He had three roles.

1. The role of Rabbi.
2. The role of Teacher.
3. The role of Prophet.

In Mark 1:15, He said, "The time is fulfilled," because this was the time God had arranged for the Jews to be offered the Messianic kingdom under Jesus, so the message continued, "the kingdom of God is at hand." In addition to a kingdom they were also being offered social change, salvation, as well as deliverance from sin, "repent ye, and believe the gospel." The question we must ask is, "What gospel?" Paul describes the gospel in, 1 Corinthians 15:1-4, making the three points of the gospel of Christ.

1. Messiah died for our sins.
2. He was buried.
3. He rose again on the third day.

But that gospel did not apply while Jesus was alive, it could only be preached after His death on the cross. Obviously that was not the gospel (good news) being preached. The preaching was, "the kingdom of God is at hand, repent ye," He was offering the Jews living at the time a kingdom and salvation in their day.

The gospel was not always the same as it is now, and those who teach that it has never changed are in serious error, because the result is that they do not always correctly understand the words Jesus spoke to the Jewish people. A look at Luke 4:14-15 shows us three things about the preaching of Jesus during this trip to Galilee.

1. It was under the guiding of the Holy Spirit because Scripture says He returned to Galilee in the power of the Spirit. Jesus was being directed where to go and what to say.

2. It spread all over the place and through the surrounding district by word of mouth. It was the talking point of the people there.

3. He taught in their synagogues and was praised by all. See also Matthew 4:23.

HE HAD AUTHORITY TO HEAL THE SICK
John 4:46-54

The healing of the nobleman's son is the second of the seven signs given in the John's gospel.

> John 4:46 So Jesus came again into Cana of Galilee, where he had made the water wine. And there was a certain nobleman, whose son was sick at Capernaum.

The word "again" means this visit to Cana, was after He changed the water into wine. The word "nobleman" means a king's officer, a government official of Herod Antipas, who would have been in charge of the area. The distance from Cana to Capernaum is about twenty miles with a climb of over 2,000 feet, because Capernaum on the north shore of the Sea of Galilee is about 600 feet below sea level, while Cana of Galilee is about 1,600 feet above sea level, and this walk of the nobleman shows he had faith.

> John 4:47 When he heard that Jesus was come out of Judea into Galilee, he went unto him, and besought him that he would come down, and heal his son: for he was at the point of death.

Notice the phrase "come down" because of the difference in height between Cana and Capernaum.

> John 4:48 Then Jesus said unto him, Except ye see signs and wonders, ye will not believe.

Jesus wanted to know from the king's officer if his faith depended on a sign. Did he want to see a sign to build up his faith, or had he got enough faith already?

> John 4:49 The nobleman saith unto him, Sir, come down ere my child die.

He was certain Jesus could heal his son, he did not ask for a sign but only that Jesus would go with him before the child died.

> John 4:50 Jesus saith unto him, Go thy way; thy son liveth. And the man believed the word that Jesus had spoken unto him, and went his way.

The royal official did not doubt Jesus and went away believing that his son was already well.

On his way back to Capernaum the nobleman's servants met him with the news that his son was no longer sick.

> John 4:52 Then he inquired of them the hour when he began to amend [get better]. And they said unto him, Yesterday at the seventh hour the fever left him.

If John was using Roman time the seventh hour would be 7.00 pm, and if he was using Jewish time it would have been 1.00 pm, but note the word "yesterday." The man had apparently stayed the night in Cana showing his faith in Jesus, more especially if John was using Jewish time. Everyone in the man's house believed in Jesus,[1] also this was the second of John's seven signs, or miracles.

> John 4:54 This is again the second miracle that Jesus did, when he was come out of Judea into Galilee.

[1] John 4:53

REJECTED IN NAZARETH Luke 4:16-30

Nazareth is important because what we see happen there will eventually happen in the whole nation. Jesus returned to His home town of Nazareth after becoming popular throughout all the towns and villages of Galilee for His teaching and miracles.

> Luke 4:16 And he came to Nazareth, where he had been brought up: and, as his custom was, he went into the synagogue on the Sabbath day, and stood up to read.

Jews still stand to read the Scroll in their synagogues, whether they are reading the Law (Torah) or the Prophets, but they teach sitting down. In the gospels we are told many times that Jesus sat down to teach as is the custom of all rabbis. Jesus may have read from the Law and from the Prophets but only the prophetic Scriptures are mentioned by Luke. His reading given in verses 18 and 19, is from Isaiah 61, and He read all of verse one and part of verse two, stopping half way through.

> Luke 4:20 And he closed the book [it was actually a scroll], and he gave it again to the minister, and sat down.

He sat down because he was going to explain and talk about the Scriptures He had just read, and rabbis teach while seated. However everything he had done was not according to Jewish custom. The tradition is that whoever reads the scroll of either the Law or the Prophets must read not less than three verses, and by reading only one and a half verses Jesus shocked and greatly surprised the congregation.

> Luke 4:20 And the eyes of all them that were in the synagogue were fastened on him.

He had got their intense interest because He had only read one and a half verses and because He was going to instruct them. Whatever was He going to say?

> Luke 4:21 [He said] This day is this Scripture fulfilled in your ears.

If you look in Isaiah 61, in the last part of verse two and carry on into verse three, those are things He is going to do at His second coming.

Jesus had read that part of the prophecy that told about His first coming only, and that is why He read less than the stipulated three verses. The rabbis knew and taught that Isaiah 61 was a Messianic prophesy, and when He said, "This day is this Scripture fulfilled in your hearing," the people in the synagogue recognized He was saying that He was the Messiah, but they had seen Him grow up in their town.

> Luke 4:22 And all bare him witness, and wondered at the gracious words which proceeded from his mouth. And they said, Is this not Joseph's son?

Jesus had much more to say than Luke has recorded, and the people loved to hear Him, but then came their rejection, "Is this not Joseph's son?"

They knew about His miracles but had not seen any, and following their rejection, Jesus told them about two miracles performed by God, not for Jews but for Gentiles.

> Luke 4:25-27 ²⁵ But I tell you the truth, many widows were in Israel in the days of Elijah, when the heaven was shut up three years and six months, when great famine was throughout the land;
> ²⁶ but unto none of them was Elijah sent, save unto Zarephath, a city of Sidon, unto a woman that was a widow.
> ²⁷ And many lepers were in Israel in the time of Elisha the prophet; and none of them was cleansed, saving Naaman the Syrian.

The purpose of His story was to indicate that what Israel rejects, the Gentiles will accept, and just as Israel was unworthy in the days of Elijah and Elisha, so they still were, and saying that in the town where He grew up and was trained caused ferocious anger.

Nazareth is in a small valley that has a cliff at the top with a sharp drop, and they took Him there.

> Luke 4:28-30 ²⁸ And all they in the synagogue, when they heard these things, were filled with wrath,

²⁹ and rose up, and thrust him out of the city, and led him unto the brow of the hill whereon their city was built, that they might cast him down headlong.

³⁰ But he, passing through the midst of them, went his way.

HIS HEADQUARTERS
Luke 4:31

After being rejected by His own people in Nazareth, Jesus moved on to Capernaum and this became His headquarters. Situated on a major road highway on the north shore of the Sea of Galilee, where there was constant traffic passing between Israel and continental Europe and Asia, Capernaum was strategically placed to send His message far and wide.

HIS AUTHORITY OVER DEMONS
Luke 4:32-37, Mark 1:21-28

First we will talk about demons. Demons are spirit persons without flesh and blood under the authority of Satan.[1] They have nowhere nice to live, and they love to enter someone's body or even an animal's body and make it their home, or as Jesus said, their house.[2] In Mark 5:6-13, you can read how Jesus cast out many demons from one man, and how the demons had a conversation with Him using the voice box of the man, asking if they could go into some pigs after they came out of the man. Spirits speak through a medium at a séance in the same way, using the voice box of the medium. Lucy and I have heard a demon speaking through someone and the voice was not the natural voice of the person, but whether we always recognize them because they speak differently I doubt. We need the help of the Holy Spirit to be sure about these spirit enemies. In the New Testament demons are also called, evil spirits[3] and unclean spirits.[4]

On the first Sabbath after arriving in Capernaum, Jesus went into the synagogue and began to teach.[5]

> Luke 4:32 And they were astonished at his doctrine [religious teaching]: for his word was with power [authority].

Rabbis got their authority from the rabbinic school where they had studied, but Jesus had not been to any such school and yet His teaching was very impressive and remarkable. The question which puzzled them greatly was, where did the authority for His inspiring and exciting interpretation of Scripture come from?

> Mark 1:22 And they were astonished at his doctrine [religious teaching]: for he taught them as one who had authority, and not as the scribes.

How the scribes taught will be dealt with later, but Jesus was teaching something new in the power of the Holy Spirit. The Jews did not immediately understand that He was teaching with the Spirit's authority, but the demons knew clearly where His authority came from. Demons recognized Him at once and even cried out in public as happened in the Capernaum synagogue.

> Luke 4:34 [A demon said to Jesus] I know thee who thou art; the Holy One of God.

Every time a demon or a group of them cried out who Jesus was, He silenced them as He did here.

> Luke 4:35 [Jesus said to the demon] Hold thy peace [keep quiet] and come out of him [come out of the man who's voice the demon was speaking through].

Jesus did not want any acknowledgement from demons, they were not acceptable as character witnesses. His purpose was to get all Israel to recognize and accept Him.

To the astonishment of everyone in the synagogue on that Sabbath morning, the demon left the man when Jesus told it to,[6] and they saw that He not only taught with authority but He cast out demons with authority,[7] causing Him to quickly become well-known and talked about throughout the region.[8] Especially interested were families having relatives that behaved oddly and wickedly, in the same way that the guy with the demon had behaved before Jesus had cast the evil spirit out of him, and who was now a perfectly normal man. Even before this Jesus was already famous for being able to heal all kinds of diseases.

[1] Ephesians 6:12
[2] Matthew 12:43-45
[3] Luke 7:21 and 8:2
[4] Matthew 10:1 and Mark 1:23
[5] Mark 1:21
[6] Luke 4:36
[7] Mark 1:27
[8] Mark 1:28

HE HEALED ALL WHO WERE SICK AND DEMON POSSESSED
Mark 1:29-34, Matthew 8:14-17, Luke 4:38-41

Jews then and now, after the morning synagogue service either go home or they are guests at the traditional Sabbath meal, and after the service Jesus was invited to the home of Peter. Peter's mother-in-law was living with Peter, and was very ill. The Roman Catholics claim that Peter was the first Pope, but the Bible shows he was not. The Pope is forbidden to marry, but Peter was married, so he could not have been Pope. All three gospels tell us Jesus healed Peter's mother-in-law, but each writer tells the story differently according to his theme.

Mark 1:31 And he came and took her by the hand, and lifted her up.

Mark's theme is Jesus the Servant, and here Jesus acted in the way a servant would have done.

Matthew 8:15 And he touched her hand.

Matthew's theme is Jesus the King, and the touch of the King is all that is needed.

Luke 4:39 And he stood over her, and rebuked the fever.

Luke's theme is the humanity of Jesus and this work was a demonstration of what is best or idyllic in men.

Each gospel account is different, depending on the theme of the writer, but nowhere is there any contradiction, all are true. Doctor Luke always gives more details about illnesses and healing, and the Greek tense used by Luke shows that her illness had been with her for a long time. He noticed her lying without strength and ill in bed and how she got physical strength suddenly, because she got up immediately,[1] and started to serve the Sabbath meal.

In the evening, and all three writers agree about this, a large crowd came along for healing.

> Mark 1:32 And at even, when the sun did set.
>
> Matthew 8:16 When the even was come.
>
> Luke 4:40 Now when the sun was setting.

Why had they not come after the morning service in the synagogue? The rabbis taught that you do not go for healing on the Sabbath, and because the Sabbath ends at sunset they had all waited before coming to be made well, and then rushed to Peter's house while the sun was still setting. Notice who they took with them.

> Mark 1:32 They brought unto him all that were diseased, and them that were possessed with devils.

Some Christian teachers say that certain physical illnesses are demonic, and while this is true,[2] the idea that every infirmity is the result of evil spirits is taking things too far. Here Mark makes a distinction between the two, some people were sick and others demon possessed.

[1] Luke 4:39

[2] Luke 13:11-16

HIS TEACHING THAT HE WAS THE MESSIAH DREW LARGE CROWDS
Mark 1:35-39, Matthew 4:23-25

Jesus got up early while it was dark and went to a quiet place where He could pray,[1] to prepare Himself for an important preaching journey throughout all Galilee, teaching in their synagogues and preaching the gospel (good news) of the kingdom.[2] He was not, as we said before, preaching the gospel that He had died for their sins, during this His second teaching tour, because He was still alive, but He was preaching the good news that they could have their own kingdom with Himself as King, and the proof that He could give them such a kingdom was there for them all to see in the way He healed every kind of sickness and disease. Matthew tells us His fame spread far and wide.

> Matthew 4:24-25 24 And his fame went throughout all Syria: and they brought unto him all sick people that were taken with divers [different] diseases and torments [aches and pains], and those which were possessed with devils [evil spirits], and those which were lunatick [lunatics], and those that had palsy [paralysis]; and he healed them.
>
> 25 And there followed him great multitudes of people from Galilee, and from Decapolis, and from Jerusalem, and from Judea, and from beyond Jordan.

Decapolis was a political grouping of ten Greek cities east of the River Jordan, so that Jesus was famous among the Greeks and all of Syria, as well as the Jews, the Samaritans and their Roman masters. To say Jesus was a little known local rabbi as Jews that refuse to accept Him have done, is very far from the truth.

[1] Mark 1:35

[2] Matthew 4:23 and Mark 1:38-39

5 The Authority Jesus Has as King 143

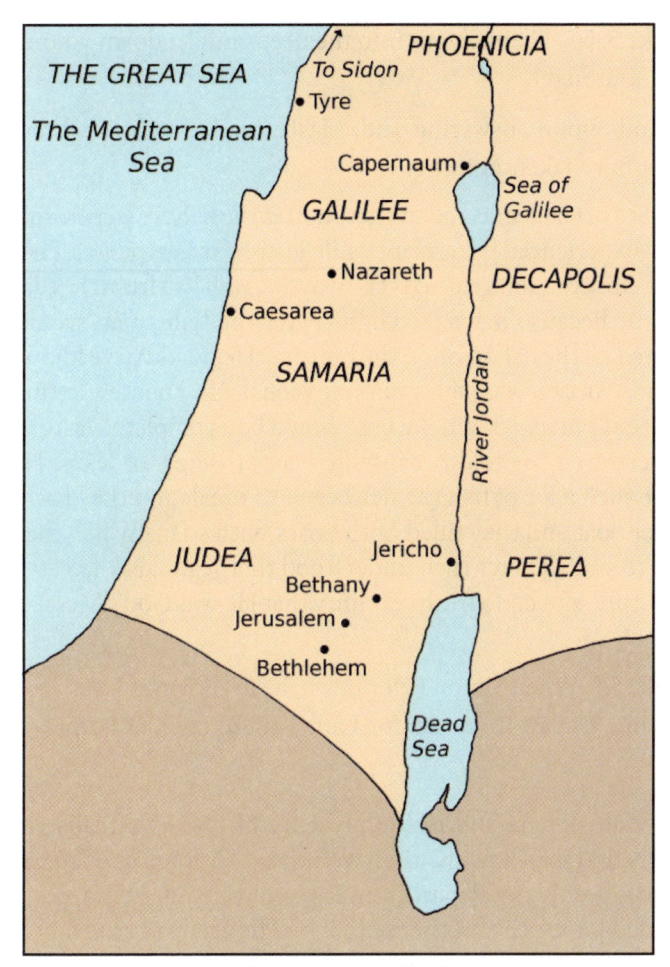

Where Jesus Walked

AUTHORITY OVER NATURE
Luke 5:1-11

The lake of Gennesaret[1] is another name for the Sea of Galilee, and notice that after getting into Simon Peter's boat, Jesus sat down and taught the people who were still on shore. The gospels time after time tell us that Jesus preached from a sitting position, the teaching position of a rabbi. At the end of the lecture Jesus spoke to Simon.

> Luke 5:4-5 ⁴ Launch out into the deep, and let down your nets for a draught.
>
> ⁵ And Simon answering said, Master we have toiled all night, and have taken nothing.

In the Sea of Galilee, as the sun gets hotter the fish go deeper, and Peter was an experienced fisherman, while Jesus was a carpenter. Fishing at night before the sun gets up is the way to catch fish from the top of the lake, but because it was daylight Peter the fisherman would have expected all the fish to be on the bottom. He would have known that Jesus' instruction was highly unprofessional. After politely letting Jesus know that putting down the nets would be a complete waste of time, he agreed to do as told because he was a disciple of Jesus. He then caught such a lot of fish the net began to break and they had to call another boat and they filled both boats with so many fish they both began to sink.[2] Peter then understood that Jesus also had authority over nature, and had a fresh certainty that He was God's Messiah from heaven.

> Luke 5:8 When Simon Peter saw it, he fell down at Jesus' knees, saying, Depart from me; for I am a sinful man, O Lord.

We are all sinners and in the presence of Jesus we realise it most strongly, and then how thankful we are that He forgives us completely, but Jesus would not depart from Peter, or the other disciples, in fact He added James, the brother of John to His group of students.

> Luke 5:9-11 ⁹ For he [Peter] was astonished, and all that were with him, at the draught of the fishes which they had taken.
>
> ¹⁰ and so was also James, and John, the sons of Zebedee, which were partners with Simon. And Jesus said unto Simon, Fear not; from henceforth thou shalt catch men.
>
> ¹¹ And when they had brought their ships to land, they forsook all, and followed him.

They left their business, their source of money to live on, to follow Jesus, trusting Him for everything.

[1] Luke 5:1

[2] Luke 5:7

AUTHORITY TO PURIFY UNCLEAN PEOPLE
Mark 1:40-45, Matthew 8:1-4, Luke 5:12-16

Under the Law of Moses, Jews would become unclean if they touched an unclean animal, a human corpse or the body of a dead animal. Normally they were allowed to touch living people that were sick but if they touched someone with leprosy they became unclean. The Law had so much to say about leprosy that it is too long to repeat but you should read Leviticus 13 and 14, to understand how very detailed God's instructions were, so that you get the most benefit from this section and other sections that will follow.

Only a priest could say a man was a leper, and on that day the leper would tear his garments and forever after walk about in torn clothes, with his face covered from the nose down. He was not accepted by other Jews and could only live with other lepers in a special section of town. Worst of all, he could not enter the tabernacle or Temple compound to worship God. He was untouchable by human hands and if he saw someone in the street he had to shout a warning, "Unclean, unclean."

Jewish rabbis, although they were forbidden to do so, could not resist adding to the Scriptures regarding leprosy, as well as many other matters, much to the harm of their relationship with God and therefore the nation's well being.

> Deuteronomy 4:2 Ye shall not add unto the word which I command you, neither shall ye diminish ought from it, that ye may keep the commandments of the LORD your God which I command you.

In the Midrash rabbis have added to the Law on leprosy, which was complicated enough already. A certain rabbi said, "One is not permitted to pass within four cubits to the east of a leper." A second said, "Within a hundred cubits." The other rabbis were not happy with the apparent contradiction and resolved it like this. "There is no contradiction. The one who said, 'Within four cubits,' meant that there was no wind blowing. The one who said, 'A hundred cubits,' was saying it when there was a wind blowing."

It is important for us to know that from the time the Law of Moses was completed, no Jew was ever healed of leprosy. The healing of Miriam[1] was before the Law had been completed, and Naaman[2] was a Syrian, not Jewish, but Moses wrote two long chapters about what had to be done if a Jewish leper was healed. If a Jew had gone to a priest and said, "I was a leper but now I am healed." Two birds would have been offered to God on the same day, one would have been killed and the other dipped in the blood and freed. The next seven days would have been a busy time for the priests as they had to answer three questions.

1. Had the man been a leper? Only a priest could declare a man a leper and therefore it would have been written down in the records, so a search would have to be made, and if the answer was, "Yes," a second question arose.
2. Had the man been perfectly healed and was all trace of the disease gone? If the answer was, "Yes," then another very important question had to answered.
3. How was the man healed?

If all three questions could be answered by the seventh day, then on the eighth day the priests would have to make four sacrifices, a trespass offering, a sin offering, a burnt offering and a meal offering.

1. The priests would have to take the blood of the trespass offering and put it on the right ear, the right thumb and the right big toe of the man who used to be a leper.
2. They would have to do the same with the blood of the sin offering.
3. They would then have to anoint the same three parts of the healed man's body with oil.

After that the man would have been free to return to Jewish society and worship God in the tabernacle or the Temple. The religious leaders had the Law written down and could find out what they had to do if a Jewish leper had been healed, but they had never had any experience in applying the Law because there was no record of a Jew ever being healed of the disease. The rabbis had written out many cures for many diseases, but not for leprosy. They noticed God had used leprosy as a punishment, as in the case of King Uzziah,[3] and therefore thought they would never be able to cure the disease, but decided that when the Messiah came, He would be able to heal Jewish lepers.

Many years before the time of Jesus, the rabbis separated miracles into two kinds, ordinary miracles that anyone could do if God gave them the power, and Messianic miracles that only the Messiah would be able to perform, of which there were three important ones. As we go through the gospels you will see that the Jews reacted differently when Jesus performed a Messianic miracle, (one of which was the healing of a leper), to when He performed an ordinary miracle. Anyone healing a Jewish leper would be claiming to be the Messiah, so notice the reaction whenever Jesus claims to be the Messiah by performing a miracle that the rabbis themselves had said only the Messiah would be able to perform.

Matthew and Mark both say that the man was a leper but Doctor Luke, who always gives a bit more information about diseases and healings, tells us he was full of leprosy,[4] meaning the sickness had fully developed and the man would soon have died. The Jewish leper, a believer, came to Jesus and all three gospels record the words he said to Jesus, "If thou wilt, thou canst make me clean," meaning, "You are the Messiah, and because of that, You can make me clean." Remember, leprosy meant that the man was forever unclean, and so he did not say, "You can heal me," but, "You can make me clean."

Jesus was very, very sorry for the man,[5] and again all three gospels say that He reached out and touched the leper. Since he had been declared a leper by the priest the man had not been touched by another human being until Jesus in an act of love touched and healed him.

> Luke 5:14 And he [Jesus] charged him to tell no man: But go, and show thyself to the priest, and offer for thy cleansing, according as Moses commanded, for a testimony unto them.

Why did Jesus ask the man to go to the Temple in Jerusalem and show himself to the priest? "For a testimony unto them," and the word "them" means the Jewish religious leaders.

He was asked to go to the Temple where the priest would have to carry out the Law of Moses you read about in Leviticus 13 and 14. The Jewish leaders would then perhaps understand that Jesus was not pretending to be the Messiah, He really was the King of the Jews.

On the day, the man reported to the Temple priest and said, "I was a leper but have been healed," the two birds were offered up, and for the next seven days the three important questions were answered.

1. Had the man been a leper? The record after it had been found would tell them, yes, he had been declared a leper by a certain priest on a certain date.

2. Was he healed? They would not have been able to find the slightest sign of leprosy and so had to answer, "Yes!"

3. **Most important.** How was the man healed? The answer was that the Man, Jesus of Nazareth had healed the leper, and the Jewish leaders would know without doubt that Jesus was claiming to be the Messiah.

The result of healing the leper made Jesus more famous than ever, because before this He had carried out "ordinary" miracles, but now he had performed a Messianic miracle.

> Luke 5:15 But so much the more went there a fame abroad [far and wide] of him.

Large crowds followed Jesus to hear Him and to be healed, and then He went off alone and prayed. Maybe He was asking God's help for what was going to happen next.

---

[1] Numbers 12

[2] 2 Kings 5

[3] 2 Chronicles 26:16-21

[4] Luke 5:12

[5] Mark 1:41

JESUS HAS AUTHORITY TO FORGIVE SINS
Mark 2:1-12, Matthew 9:2-8, Luke 5:17-26

We said at the start that using a theme to tell the story of Jesus is better than the geographic approach because it is then easier to see how one event leads to another. Our theme is, "Jesus the Messiah the King of the Jews," the same as Matthew's. His theme is perfect for us because he wrote for the Jews and we are writing to re-establish in the minds of non-Jews, that the Bible is a Jewish book, because a knowledge of Jewish culture at the time of Jesus opens up the Scriptures to us in ways that have long been forgotten. What is going to happen next came about because Jesus healed the leper, something the rabbis said only the Messiah would be able to do.

After His preaching tour of Galilee, Jesus returned to Capernaum,[1] on the north coast of the Sea of Galilee, and remember Capernaum was a good three days walk from Jerusalem where the rabbis were centred.

> Luke 5:17 And it came to pass on a certain day, as he was teaching, that there were Pharisees and doctors of the law sitting by, which were come out of every town of Galilee, and Judea, and Jerusalem.

Luke is saying that religious leaders were there from all over the country, from every village in Galilee, every village in Judea and every single village in and from around Jerusalem. Why were all these leaders in Capernaum? It was because Jesus had healed the leper and the Temple priests in Jerusalem had confirmed it and were absolutely amazed. The first of the two investigative stages, (we talked about them under, John Explains Why The People Need To Repent, in Chapter 3), had now started, and this was the observation stage. During this stage they had to keep silent, they could not ask any questions, just watch and listen. At the time they investigated John the Baptist, only a small group were sent to observe, but the difference now was that someone was claiming to be the Messiah, and He had performed a Messianic miracle. Jesus decided to take the opportunity now He had the leadership in front of Him to say something only God can say. Jesus was teaching in a house and the power to heal was with Him,[2] but no one could get near because of all these Pharisees and doctors of the law crowding around to watch and listen to Him. Some men with a paralysed man on a stretcher, climbed onto the top of the house, smashed a hole through the roof, which must have really displeased the owner, and lowered the man on the stretcher into the room in front of Jesus.

Up until now Jesus just healed the sick, but not this time, instead He announced, "Man, thy sins are forgiven thee," knowing that anyone who had, had their sins forgiven was acceptable to God. In fact the way Jesus used the Hebrew language at this time would have alerted the leaders present that Jesus was claiming authority that only God has, but although they had some serious objections, this was the observation stage of their investigation and they were not allowed to speak. We are told there were, "scribes sitting there, and reasoning in their hearts,"[3] and, "certain of the scribes said within themselves,"[4] "Why doth this man speak blasphemies? Who can forgive sins but God only?"[5] The scribes, the doctors of the law were correct, because although my wife Lucy can forgive me if I am rough with her, only God can forgive me in the sense that He then sees me as holy and fit to join Him in heaven. God's kind of forgiveness means I am saved for eternal life, and we understand from the Hebrew that was what Jesus had told the paralysed man, and which the scribes had understood correctly. The scribes had only two choices to make, either Jesus was a blasphemer, (an ungodly man speaking dishonestly), or He really was God's promised Messiah.

Jesus had now got the close attention of the crowd, and He answered the question they were thinking, by asking them another question, a very Jewish method of teaching. Rabbis would often answer a question by asking another question, in order to prompt their students to think carefully and perhaps arrive at the right answer without being told, and Jesus often taught the same way.

There is a story that illustrates the Jewish custom of asking a question to answer a question. A rabbi and a priest were great friends and loved to talk about the things of God, but the rabbi always answered the priest's questions by asking another. The priest put up with the rabbi for a long time, but one day he asked, "Why do you always answer my questions with another question?" The rabbi answered, "Why not?" Anyway Jesus used the same technique.

> Mark 2:8-9 Why reason ye these things in your hearts? Whether it is easier to say to the sick of the palsy [paralysis], Thy sins be forgiven thee; or to say, Arise, and take up thy bed, and walk?

His question is, what is easier to say? The answer is, it is easier to say, "Your sins are forgiven," because there is no need for any visible demonstration. Any preacher can tell his congregation that their sins have been forgiven and they are on their way to heaven, and many are fooled by such men. It is an easy thing to say, and they cannot be proved wrong. The harder thing to say to a paralysed man is, "Stand up on your paralysed legs, pick up your bed with your paralysed arms and hands, which are so useless you cannot even feed yourself, and carry your bed all the way home without being helped by anyone." That is a hard thing to say because there are plenty of witnesses to see if the man is so completely healed that he does it easily. Jesus was using the rabbinic teaching method of going from light to heavy, or from easy to difficult. He was going to prove He had authority to say the easy thing, "Your sins are forgiven," by demonstrating his power to say the difficult thing, "Stand up, pick up your bed and walk." After Jesus had said the more difficult thing, notice how quickly the man was healed.

> Mark 2:12 And immediately he arose, took up the bed, and went forth before them all; insomuch that they were all amazed, and glorified God, saying, We never saw it on this fashion.

> Luke 5:25 And immediately he rose up before them, and took up that whereon he lay, and departed to his own house, glorifying God.

The outcome was that Jesus had done the difficult thing to show He could do the easier thing, and the easier thing was to say, "Your sins are forgiven," but the forgiveness of sins is something only God can do. The conclusion to be drawn is that Jesus is the Messiah, the God/Man, with the authority to forgive sins leading to eternal life.

Although it is not stated in the Bible we know from reading between the lines that the leaders went back to Jerusalem and reported that the claims of Jesus of Nazareth were significant, because from now on the investigation moves to the second stage of interrogation or cross-examination. From now, beginning in the next section, one or more Pharisees will always follow Him, making objections and asking questions, in order to help them decide whether to accept or reject His claim that He is the Messiah.

[1] Mark 2:1
[2] Luke 5:17
[3] Mark 2:6
[4] Matthew 9:3
[5] Mark 2:7

AUTHORITY OVER MEN
Mark 2:13-17, Matthew 9:9-13, Luke 5:27-32

Matthew, also known as Levi, was a publican and in the language of the Bible that does not mean he kept a pub, but he collected taxes for the Roman government. For a Jew to be a publican was against Jewish law, but as the Romans were in charge the Jews could not stop someone being a publican if he wanted to be one. Publicans were poorly paid but, as we have already seen, became rich through cheating other Jews, making them pay more tax than Rome wanted and putting the extra money in their own pockets. Publicans were hated because they got rich through cheating and because they worked for Rome. Jewish writings show that of the two kinds of publican, income tax collectors and collectors of customs duties, customs officers were the most hated.

> Matthew 9:9 And as Jesus passed forth from thence, he saw a man, named Matthew, sitting at the receipt of custom.

Matthew then was not only a publican, he was the worst kind of publican. No publicans were accepted in Jewish society, and by Jewish law the only people allowed to be friendly with a publican were other publicans and prostitutes. In the Bible the word "sinner" often means a prostitute, and the Pharisees said that it was almost impossible for publicans and prostitutes to be forgiven. Publicans were considered to be so unreliable they could not be used to give evidence in a court of law. It was this man that Jesus called to be His disciple.[1]

Publicans paid a lot of money to get their jobs, but Matthew left his custom collectors seat, without selling it and without making arrangements for someone else to take over. After being spiritually born again, he understood at once that Jesus had more authority than Rome.

> Luke 5:28 And he left all, rose up, and followed him.

Matthew then decided to give himself an, "I'm born again birthday party", and invited all his friends who of course were publicans and prostitutes. Jesus and the few disciples He had collected so far also went to the party, breaking Pharisaic law and Jewish tradition.

The Pharisees had to go along too because they were investigating Jesus' claim that He was the Messiah, and their investigation was now in stage two where questions were being asked and objections made, and their objection was, Why did He eat and drink with publicans and prostitutes?[2] The Pharisees, who never mixed with people like that, did not expect that kind of behaviour from the Messiah. In Matthew 9:12-13 there are three things Jesus points out when answering their objection.

1. The sick need to be healed not those who are well, and as the Pharisees agreed that publicans were spiritually sick, then He should go to them.
2. The Pharisees had many rules and regulations against publicans which showed their lack of mercy, even though they were strict to pray, to tithe and to give thanks to God, which Jesus called sacrifice. Jesus looks for mercy, more than sacrifice.
3. The Pharisees thought they were righteous and that publicans were sinners, but Jesus said He had come to ask sinners, not righteous people to repent.

From now on we will be looking at more objections made by the scribes and Pharisees to what Jesus either says or does.

[1] Luke 5:27

[2] Mark 2:16

THE AUTHORITY OF JESUS IS ABOVE JEWISH TRADITION
Luke 5:33-39, Matthew 9:14-17, Mark 2:18-22

Jesus had now clearly claimed to be the Messiah, and was being interrogated by the Jewish religious leaders, who would eventually reject Him. By that time the Pharisees had for four hundred years, been making many rules and regulations which they wrongly claimed were equal to Scripture, and the reason they rejected Jesus was because He would not accept their traditions. Jesus kept to the original word of God.

The reason the Jews were conquered and taken as prisoners to Babylon was because they worshipped many false gods and deliberately broke the Laws of Moses.[1] The Jews that returned to Jerusalem from Babylon knew why God had sent them into captivity. Digging on the historic site of Babylon before the second world war, archaeologists discovered a street plan something like New York with wide roads laid out in a criss-cross fashion, and each street named in honour of a demonic "god" with temples for the idols of these false "gods" at the corner of every street. It was the stronghold of Satan and worship involved forced immorality. Women were by law, not allowed to get married until they had, had sex in a temple with a priest, and some of the less attractive women would spend three years in a temple before someone would rape them. Sending the Jews to Babylon was God's way of showing them that if they did not want to obey Him, then they would have to serve other "gods," and after their punishment the Jews were so glad to get out of the place, they enthusiastically returned to Jerusalem worshipping the One True God with thanksgiving and enjoyment and rebuilt the Temple.[2]

One of the religious leaders of the Jews was a scribe called Ezra, of the Book of Ezra, who studied the Bible carefully, teaching the people,[3] because he wanted to make sure Israel did not disobey God again. He began a school called the School of Sofer, which is Hebrew for scribe, getting all the leaders together to go through all the commandments

God gave to Moses and explain to the people how to keep them and how not to break them. It was thought that if everyone knew how to keep the Law they would keep it, and God would never punish them again by sending them out of their land to worship false "gods."

> Hosea 4:6 [God said] My people are destroyed for lack of knowledge: because thou hast rejected knowledge, I will reject thee, that thou shalt be no priest to me: seeing thou hast forgotten the law of thy God, I will also forget thy children.

Ezra's idea to teach the people a working knowledge of the law of God, was a good one, but Ezra died and another generation took over his School of Sofer.

The next generation of scribe leaders said, "It is not enough for us to expound the Law, we must build a fence around it." There were not just ten commandments in the Mosaic Law, the Torah, there were 613, and the fence was a list of new rules and regulations, surrounding each of the 613 commandments, no doubt made with good intentions, but in disobedience to the Word of God.[4] The idea was that the laws of the fence might be broken but they would stop a Jew from breaking through the fence, where he might break one of the 613 Mosaic Laws, and bring the judgement of God on the children of Israel, as happened when they were sent to Babylon.

The scribes grouped together in schools and started work, using the principle, a scribe may disagree with another scribe but he cannot disagree with the Torah. The disagreements between the scribes would be discussed and a decision taken by majority vote. Once the vote had been taken and a decision made on a matter of disagreement, it became absolute law for every Jew in the world to follow it.

Here is an example of how a fence was built around a commandment of Moses given in Exodus.

> Exodus 23:19 Thou shalt not seethe [boil] a kid [baby goat] in its mother's milk.

Moses banned them from boiling a baby goat alive in milk from its mother. The Canaanites in their worship of the god, Baal, boiled the first born kid alive in its mother's milk as an offering to Baal. Jews were not allowed to practice idolatry and therefore were not allowed to boil baby goats in their mother's milk. God gave the command to Moses about 1,400 BC, and about 1,000 years later, the School of Sofer was at work. There were no Canaanites in the land, no one was boiling kids in their mother's milk and the reason for the commandment had been forgotten.

The scribes reasoned with each other, "Suppose we eat some meat and drink some milk, although it is unlikely it could be just possible that the milk was from the mother of the meat we had eaten. If this were true then the two would be together in our stomachs and the kid would be seethed in its mother's milk after we had eaten it." The first rule was therefore, Jews cannot eat meat and dairy products at the same meal, and they must be separated by not less than four hours. Even today Orthodox Jews separate their meat meals from their dairy meals, because of this additional law passed by majority vote, which states all Jews have to eat this way.

The scribes thought out these new rules in an orderly way using a system of rabbinic logic named, "peppery and sharp," which they extended further. "Suppose we sit down to a dairy meal and eat cheese from a plate. Afterwards, no matter how well it is washed a tiny speck of cheese might be left on the plate. Four or more hours later we decide to have a meat meal from the same plate and the meat picks up the tiny crumb of cheese left from the previous meal, and while it is most unlikely, it is possible that the cheese came from the mother of the meat, and when swallowed the meat is seethed in its mother's milk." The second law was, every Jewish kitchen must have two sets of plates, and this became four because separate sets are kept for Passover week. It could happen by accident that a dairy plate was used for meat, and if this happened the plate was no longer to be used for anything, and could either be broken or given to a Gentile. The scribes worked their way through all the 613 commandments, issuing hundred's and sometimes thousands of new rules. They began in 450 BC, and ended in 30 BC.

The work having been completed the rabbis set up a second school, known as the School of Teachers, who also used "peppery and sharp" logic and this is what they said, "There are too many holes in the fence!"

The whole system was revised, beginning in 30 BC and ending in AD 200, another two and a half centuries. Remember, the principle of the School of Sofer was, a scribe could disagree with a scribe but not with the Law of Moses. The principle of the School of Teachers was, a teacher can disagree with a teacher but not with a scribe. The result was that by the time of Jesus, thousands of rules passed by the scribes became revered as having the same value as the Word of God. In order to make the Jews believe that the laws of the scribes were equal to the Laws of Moses, they had to invent something convincing, and it went like this.

On Mount Sinai, Moses was given two laws, the written Law found in the Bible, and the oral law, oral because Moses did not write it down, he memorized it. He passed the oral law down to Joshua, who memorized it and passed it down to the judges, who passed it down to the prophets, who passed it down to the scribes. The people were told that the scribes did not think up these rules, they got them from the prophets, who got them from the judges, who got them from Joshua, who got them from Moses, who got them from God! It is true that from the year 450 BC until AD 220, the rules were not written down, and the rabbis arranged for thousands and thousands of laws to be memorized for more than six and half centuries, when the work of the second school ended.

The rabbis then set up a third school and what did they say? "There are too many holes in the fence!" The third school worked until about AD 500, but again the principle of operation was changed. A third school teacher could disagree with a third school teacher, but not with a second school teacher, and as a result they made the work of the second school also equal in value to Scripture. The work of the first two schools, the School of Sofer and the School of Teachers, is called the Mishnah, and the work of the third school is called the Gemara. The Mishnah and the Gemara together make up the Tulmud.

The unwritten oral law of the second school, beginning in 30 BC, is what the differences between Jesus and the Pharisees were about. The Pharisees thought the Messiah would be a Pharisee and accept the oral law, which we can also call the Mishnaic law, the Pharisaic law, or the rabbinic law but which the Jews now refer to as the Mishnah. The

158   Heavenly Father Set My Spirit Ablaze

Mishnah is available in Jewish book stores today in a set of 30 large hard back books, and it is what is written in the Mishnah that Jesus referred to as, TRADITION.

One of the traditions of the Pharisees was fasting, which John the Baptist and his disciples did but which Jesus and His disciples did not do,[5] and the Pharisees wanted to know why, and Jesus made four observations.

The Mishnah – rejected by Jesus,
but believed by religious Jews to this day.

1. **Luke 5:34-35**   And he said unto them, Can ye make the children of the bridechamber fast while the bridegroom is with them? But the days will come, when the bridegroom shall be taken away from them, and then they shall fast in those days.

No one goes to a wedding feast to fast, and while Jesus, (the Bridegroom) remained on earth it was a time for feasting, not fasting. After Jesus began telling the Jews at that first Feast of Passover, He was the Messiah there is no record of Him ever fasting. He said the bridegroom would be taken away, a tragedy that is rare at a wedding and which would be true if the bridegroom died. It had been prophesied about 700 years before Jesus, "He was cut off out of the land of the living: for the transgression of my people [us believers] was he stricken."[6]

2. **Luke 5:36 And he spake also a parable unto them; No man putteth a piece of a new garment upon an old; if otherwise, then both the new maketh a rent, and the piece that was taken out of the new agreeth not with the old.**

In those days new cloth material shrank when it was washed, but old cloth that had been washed many times did not shrink any more. They did not repair holes in old clothes with new material because if the repaired clothes were washed, the new patch would shrink and damage the clothing even more. Jesus is telling them, He did not come to patch up the Pharisaic Judaism, or to repair holes in that fence they were building. He is introducing something different altogether.

3. **Luke 5:37-38 And no man putteth new wine into old bottles; else the new wine will burst the bottles, and be spilled, and the bottles shall perish. But new wine must be put into new bottles; and both are preserved.**

Wine bottles in those days were made from the empty stomachs of freshly killed sheep, and the used old bottles had stretched as much as they were going to. New wine was not put into an old bottle because it was still fermenting and building up pressure. The extra pressure would break an old bottle spoiling it and the wine. Jesus did not come to pour His teaching into the old skin (or mould) of Pharisaic Judaism. His new wine would ferment and fill the nations of the world, and the old skin was not big enough or flexible enough.

4. **Luke 5:39 No man also having drunk old wine straightway desireth new; for he saith, The old is better.**

He was prophesying they would reject the new wine and keep on swallowing the old.

The Bible has been written to teach us, and God used the actions of the Jews to warn us about human nature. How we can be turned against the instructions of God even by those who claim to be our religious leaders, resulting in our being rejected by Him through wrong teaching, teaching that is from the minds of men and not from the Word of God.[7] You should understand that no denomination of the Christian church is perfect and many are taking their congregations to Hell instead of Heaven, because they feed their people man made rubbish just like the Jewish religious leaders feed their people the Mishnah.

Please remember when you grow up, leave school and look for a church, not to choose one that teaches or does those things which are not in the Bible. Some teach, like the scribes that their denomination's teaching is equal to the teaching of Scripture, and introduce extra rules, or relax Bible rules. In my experience I love the presence of the Holy Spirit who has been sent to me by Jesus,[8] and know He does not like it if I am disobedient to Him. Our effort should not be to conform to the teaching of our preacher or denomination, even if it might lead to our being rewarded with respect or high office in the church during this lifetime. We must keep close to Jesus and make Him our best friend, because His rewards in the next life will be everlasting and so much greater than anything the world can offer.[9]

[1] 1 Chronicles 9:1 and Jeremiah 19:14-20:4

[2] Ezra 3

[3] Ezra 7:10

[4] Deuteronomy 4:2

[5] Luke 5:33

[6] Isaiah 53:8

[7] Hosea 4:6

[8] Luke 24:49, John 16:7-15 and Acts 9:31

[9] Luke 9:25

HIS AUTHORITY OVER THE SABBATH
Matthew 12:1-14, Mark 3:1-6, Luke 6:1-11, John 5:1-47

Moses had given Israel one commandment, "Remember the Sabbath day, to keep it holy,"[1] to which the Pharisees had added 1,500 additional Sabbath rules. They personified the Sabbath as, the Bride of Israel, and Jehovah's Queen, as if the day had become a person, and keeping it became a most important religious ritual for them. On Friday night at the synagogue service the door is opened and the Sabbath is welcomed by the singing of a song, "Welcome My Beloved Queen Sabbath."

There were many debates between Jesus and the Pharisees over the Mishnah, but the proper way of keeping the Sabbath was major, and the issue was what does or does not represent Sabbath rest. We are now going to investigate three of these arguments over the Sabbath.

The First Sabbath Dispute – THE HEALING OF THE PARALYTIC ON THE SABBATH
John 5:1-47

John 5, includes the talk Jesus gave on, The Works Of God, which is the second of His seven discourses recorded for us by John. It also includes the third of John's Seven Signs, or miracles showing that Jesus is the Messiah the Son of God.

> John 5:1 After this there was a feast of the Jews; and Jesus went up to Jerusalem.

Usually when a feast is not named it is the Feast of Passover, and this was the second Passover since Jesus started explaining to Israel, He was their Messiah, which means that His public ministry had already been going for one and a half years.

Jesus was at the Pool of Bethesda, the remains of which can be seen today in the Moslem quarter of the Old City. A paralysed man was lying beside the pool where he had been placed by friends, and Jesus went up to him, and we are told how He healed him.

1. Jesus found the man Himself.
2. He did not ask the man if he had faith, because His miracles at this time are still signs to the Jews that He is their Messiah.
3. To begin with Jesus did not tell the man He was the Messiah, although that does come out later on, consequently when the

man was asked who healed him, he didn't know,[2] and he had to go back and find out. Obviously no faith had been involved, and again the reason was because this was another sign to the Jewish people.

4. Jesus asked the man if he wanted to be healed and the answer in a round about way was, "Yes." Jesus told him to get up, pick up his bed and walk, and after being paralysed for 38 years he was immediately completely cured, but it was the Sabbath.[3] One of the 1,500 Pharisaic rules for keeping the Sabbath day is, "You cannot carry a burden from a public place to a private place, or from a private place to a public place," and the man had carried his bed from a private place to a public place, breaking the rabbinic law for the Sabbath.

The Bible account explains the reaction of the religious leaders.

> John 5:10 The Jews therefore said unto him that was cured, It is the Sabbath day: it is not lawful for thee to carry thy bed.

He was breaking their law, but the man's excuse was that the man who healed him had told him to carry the bed, and when they asked him who had healed him, the man did not know.[4]

> John 5:14 Afterwards Jesus findeth him in the temple, and said unto him, Behold, thou art made whole: sin no more, lest a worse thing come upon thee.

The man now knew who Jesus was and went and told the others, who then accused Jesus of two things.

The first was that He had healed on the Sabbath day and that was forbidden by Pharisaic law except on one special condition, if there was danger to life. If the man was not in danger of losing his life he could not be healed on the Sabbath. The second accusation came from what Jesus said.

> John 5:17 My Father worketh [works] hitherto [until now] and I work.

The Jews understood that when Jesus called God, His Father, He meant He was equal with God. One of the reasons cultic groups use to deny

Jesus is God, is that a son is less than a father, therefore if He is only the Son, He is lower than God. In Gentile understanding that may be true, but it is not true in Jewish reckoning, because a Jewish first born son is equal with his father. We need to read the Scriptures, not according to our language of the twenty-first century, but how they were meant in the first century, and we can see this by noticing the reaction of the Jews to Jesus when He called God, His Father. They plainly knew what He was claiming, and so the use by cultic groups of verse 17, to show Jesus is lower than God, can be used against them.

> John 5:18 Therefore the Jews sought the more to kill him, because he not only had broken the Sabbath, but said also that God was his Father, making himself equal with God.

Jesus defended His claim by saying four things.

1. He is doing the works of the Father in three ways and John explains each of these separately in verses 19, 20 and 21.

(i) He is equal with the Father and what One does the Other does. The Father's work is the Son's work and the Son's work is the Father's work.

(ii) The love between the Father and the Son are equal, so both produce mighty works, which will get even greater.

(iii) They share equal power, and just as Jesus raises anyone He chooses from the dead, so the Father raises who He chooses from the dead.

2. He is going to judge all men, and because in the Old Testament, God is the final Judge,[5] if Jesus does the judging He must also be God and be given equal honour. John 5:22-23 "For the Father judgeth no man, but hath committed all judgement unto the Son: that all men should honour the Son, even as they honour the Father. He that honoureth not the Son honoureth not the Father which hath sent him."

3. He has the authority to give eternal life, but again in the Old Testament it was God who gave eternal life,[6] and if Jesus does it He must also be God. John 5:24 "Verily, verily [Truly, truly], I say unto you, He that heareth my word, and believeth on him

that sent me, hath everlasting life, and shall not come into condemnation; but is passed from death unto life."

4. He is going to cause the dead to live again, but in the Old Testament it was God who raised the dead,[7] and once more if Jesus is going to do it then He must also be God. John 5:25-29 "Verily, verily [Truly, truly], I say unto you, The hour is coming, and now is, when the dead shall hear the voice of the Son of God: and they that hear shall live. For as the Father hath life in himself; so hath he given to the Son to have life in himself; And he hath given him authority to execute judgement also, because he is the Son of man. Marvel not at this: for the hour is coming, in which all that are in the graves shall hear his voice, And shall come forth; they that have done good, unto the resurrection of life; and they that have done evil, unto the resurrection of damnation."

His deity is shown in verse 25, "Son of God," and His humanity in verse 27, "Son of man." In the New Testament whenever the word "voice" is used in association with the resurrection, it means the voice of Jesus. There will be two resurrections and I pray that you will all be in the resurrection of life, because then you will go to heaven and join Lucy and me, if we don't misbehave ourselves before we die. Let's all make sure we are not in the second resurrection, which will be for the wicked.[8]

According to the Law of Moses, two or three witnesses were required in order to confirm something, but Jesus gave them four witnesses that He was the Messiah. The first witness was John the Baptist.

John 5:33 Ye sent unto John, and he bare witness unto the truth.

The second witness was miracles, the signs He performed that showed He was God.

John 5:36 But I have a greater witness than that of John: for the works which the Father hath given me to finish, the same works that I do, bear witness of me, that the Father hath sent me.

The third witness was God when He spoke out of heaven at His baptism.

> John 5:37 And the Father himself, which hath sent me, hath born witness of me.

The fourth witness is Scripture, the prophecies of the Old Testament that told about His first coming.

> John 5:39 Search the Scriptures; for in them ye think ye have eternal life: and they are they which testify of me.

The trouble was not to do with not having enough witnesses, it was because the Mishnah had so changed the authority of the words of Moses that they were believing something that Moses did not say.

> John 5:46-47 For had ye believed Moses, ye would have believed me: for he wrote of me. But if ye believe not his writings, how shall ye believe my words?

The Pharisees then, and the Orthodox Jews today believe in Moses but not his writings. The writings they believe in, are the interpretations given in the Mishnah, the Gemara and the Talmud, and that is why they did not then, and do not now recognize Jesus as their Messiah.

It is of the highest importance not to change a single word written in the Bible. Most so called "Christian" preachers today are crowd pleasers that reject Bible believing fundamentalists like me, and they say so over and over again in the press if not in the pulpit. In the same way the Pharisees rejected Jesus when He stuck closely to the Word of God, the crowd pleasing "Christian" preachers of today who throw out God's Word and snub true believers, will like the Pharisees also be rejected by Jesus, because God will not change His Word. If He did change His Word, it would be of no use to us.

If you look at verse 35, you will see John's first sub-theme of the battle between light and darkness, meaning good and evil, where he quotes Jesus talking about John the Baptist.

John 5:35 He was a burning and shining light: and ye were willing for a season to rejoice in his light.

The Second Sabbath Dispute – THE ARGUMENT ABOUT THE WHEAT
Luke 6:1-5, Matthew 12:1-8

> Luke 6:1 And it came to pass on the second Sabbath after the first, that he went through the corn fields; and his disciples plucked the ears of corn, [actually it was wheat], and did eat, rubbing them in their hands.

The Pharisees were watching and following Jesus everywhere he went and they were alarmed to see the disciples breaking four of those extra 1,500 Sabbath rules.

1. By pulling the heads of wheat from the stalk they were reaping on the Sabbath.
2. By rubbing the wheat heads in their hands to separate out the grain from the chaff they were threshing on the Sabbath.
3. By blowing the chaff away leaving the wheat grains in their hands they were winnowing on the Sabbath.
4. By swallowing the grain they were storing the wheat on the Sabbath.

> Luke 6:2 And certain of the Pharisees said unto them, Why do ye that which is not lawful to do on the Sabbath days?

Jesus answered the Pharisees by making six points. He reminded them that King David broke the Pharisaic law when he ate the showbread.[9] Moses never said that the Levites could not give the consecrated bread to others, outside their tribe, but the Pharisees did. Jesus had put them in an awkward position because they could not say that David ate the bread before the oral law, since they claimed the Mishnah had been given to Moses hundreds of years earlier by God, meaning it would have been known by David. If David had broken Pharisaic law, they should have expressed their disapproval, but as they had not, why were they complaining when David's greater Son did no more than David had done?

Secondly, He pointed out that the Sabbath rest did not apply to all situations, in particular to the priests working in the Temple who had more work to do on the Sabbath than on other days of the week,[10] when there were additional Temple rituals and all sacrifices were doubled. Certain work was therefore always allowed on the Sabbath.

Thirdly, Jesus is greater than the Temple,[11] and if the Temple priests allow Sabbath work, so can He, who is the Lord of the Temple.

Fourthly, by quoting Hosea 6:6, He showed that works of necessity, and mercy, were always allowed on the Sabbath day.[12] Eating is a work of necessity, (the disciples were hungry), and healing is a work of mercy.

His fifth point is that being the Messiah, He is Lord of the Sabbath[13] and He can permit anything they don't allow, and can forbid anything they accept.

His final argument is that they do not understand the reason for the Sabbath.[14] The Pharisees taught that God made Israel to honour the Sabbath, and so Israel was made for the Sabbath, but Jesus said, "The Sabbath was made for man, and not man for the Sabbath,"[14] so the opposite is true, the Sabbath was made for Israel. The idea was not to enslave Israel to the Sabbath but to provide a day for resting and uplifting, but because of the 1,500 Pharisaic Sabbath rules, the day had become a burden, because they had completely misunderstood the reason for it in the first place.

The Third Sabbath Dispute – JESUS HEALED THE MAN WITH A WITHERED HAND
Luke 6:6-11, Mark 3:1-6, Matthew 12:9-14

On a different Sabbath day Jesus was again teaching the real meaning of the Word of God in the synagogue, and one of His listeners was a man with a withered hand, which was not a life threatening condition. Mark and Matthew merely say that the man's hand was withered, but as always Dr Luke tells us more about the health problem saying that it was the man's right hand.

It seems that the man had been put there by the Pharisees who were reporting on Jesus in order that a decision could be made on His claim that He was the Messiah.

> Matthew 12:10 And they asked him, [Jesus] saying, Is it lawful to heal on the Sabbath days? That they might accuse him.

Apparently the poor man was a plant, because they wanted Jesus to heal the man and use that as an excuse to reject Jesus.

> Luke 6:7 And the scribes and Pharisees watched him, whether he would heal on the Sabbath day; that they might find an accusation against him.

Jesus again will not come under the authority of the Mishnah, or their man made traditions. Their oral law said that if there was danger to life then it was lawful to heal on the Sabbath, and so when an animal fell down a hole, its life could be in danger from being buried by falling earth, drowning, or maybe thirst, and for that reason they would rescue their own animal on the Sabbath.

> Matthew 12:11-12 And he said unto them, What man shall there be among you, that shall have one sheep, and if it fall into a pit on the Sabbath day, will he not lay hold on it, and lift it out? How much then is a man better than a sheep? Wherefore it is lawful to do well on the Sabbath days.

He was repeating something He said in the previous section when He quoted Hosea 6:6, that according to the Bible, acts of necessity and mercy by Jews are allowed on the Sabbath day, and healing is an act of mercy. He then healed the man's hand, showing His rejection of their unbiblical rules, and also to demonstrate to them His power to perform miracles, which was to show them He was their Messiah, and for that reason He did not ask the man to have faith, as was His custom later on before healing the sick.

The Pharisees reacted in three ways.

1. They were filled with madness.[15] They let their anger get the better of them.

2. Then the Pharisees went out, and held a council against him, how they might destroy him.[16] They rejected Him despite His powers and discussed ways to annihilate Him.
3. And the Pharisees went forth, and straightway took counsel with the Herodians against him, how they might destroy him.[17]

The Pharisees were in opposition to Roman rule but the Herodians were a political group that supported Roman rule under Herod's family, and for that reason the Pharisees and the Herodians were bitter enemies, yet the anger and hatred of the Pharisees against the Jewish Messiah was so aggressive that they immediately went and negotiated help from their enemies to try find a way to destroy Jesus.

[1] Exodus 20:8
[2] John 5:13
[3] John 5:5-9
[4] John 5:11-13
[5] Deuteronomy 1:17, Psalms 75:7, 94:2, Isaiah 66:6
[6] Psalms 41:12, 61:7, 73:26, Isaiah 51:6
[7] 1 Kings 17:21-22, 2 Kings 4:32-35, Ezekiel 37:12-14
[8] Revelation 20:6, 20:15
[9] Matthew 12:3-4
[10] Matthew 12:5
[11] Matthew 12:6
[12] Matthew 12:7
[13] Matthew 12:8
[14] Mark 2:27
[15] Luke 6:11
[16] Matthew 12:14
[17] Mark 3:6

HE CONTINUED TO HEAL MANY Mark 3:7-12

Jesus left the synagogue and went to the Sea of Galilee, and a huge crowd followed this Man that claimed He was the Messiah. His reputation had obviously spread outside the Jewish community because people from the Gentile areas of Idumea, Tyre and Sidon were among the throng. Mark observed that while the leaders would not recognize the authority of Jesus, the demons in those people unfortunate enough to be possessed, caused them to fall down in front of Jesus and shout out, "Thou art the Son of God," but Jesus would not accept acknowledgement from demons and stopped them speaking.

JESUS CHOOSES TWELVE APOSTLES
Mark 3:13-19, Luke 6:12-16, Matthew 10:2-4

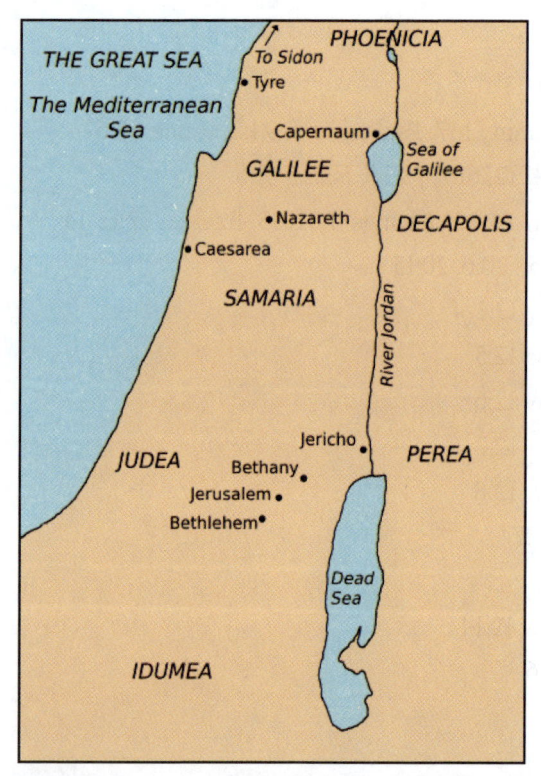

The Huge Crowds Following Jesus Included Many From The Gentile Areas Of Idumea, Tyre And Sidon.

5 The Authority Jesus Has as King

Next Jesus chose the twelve apostles, but before He made His final decision from the huge crowds that were there and from the many, many disciples that He had, He prayed all night to God.[1] The next morning He called the twelve He wanted and Mark gives three reasons why they were selected.

1. They were to be with Him all the time, meaning they were on standby to receive instructions for 24 hours a day.[2] Many disciples would follow him from time to time, like the 70 we will read of later but the 12 were to be with Jesus.
2. They were to be with Him so that He could send them off to preach.[2] The 12 used to spread the news that Jesus was King and were offering the Jews a kingdom ruled by their King.
3. He gave authority to the 12 to cast out demons.[3] A disciple is a follower or learner but an apostle is 'a sent one' and being sent, they went with the authority of the Sender, and were able to cast out demons.

The names of the 12 are given in the gospels of Mark and Luke, and some of them had more than one name, as shown in the following list.

1. SIMON a Hebrew name, he was also known as Caiaphas (which is Simon in Aramaic) and Peter, (Greek).
2. ANDREW.
3. JOHN an English name for the Hebrew, Yohannan, meaning Jehovah is gracious.
4. JAMES an English name for the Hebrew, Jacob. John and James (numbers 3 and 4), were brothers, the sons of Zebedee and his wife Salome.
5. PHILIP a Greek name meaning a lover of horses.
6. NATHANAEL, remember him who Jesus saw under the fig tree and could read his mind? He also went by the Aramaic title (not name) of Bartholomew.
7. THOMAS a Hebrew name meaning "twin", also called Didymus, (Greek meaning "twin").
8. MATTHEW was originally called, Levi the son of Alphaeus,

but he changed his name when he became a follower of Jesus to Matthew, which means, "the gift of God."

9. JAMES the son of Alphaeus, therefore there were two apostles called James, an English name for Jacob. Numbers 8 and 9 are not brothers although their fathers names were Alphaeus. Alphaeus was a common Jewish name then and the fathers were different.

10. JUDAS a Greek name for Judah. He was also known by the Hebrew name of Thaddaeus.

11. SIMON the Zealot, because he was a member of the political party called the Zealots. Zealots were Pharisees that actively resisted Rome, carrying small knives hidden in their clothing used in crowded places to stab Roman soldiers to death, and also Jews that worked for Romans.

12. JUDAS ISCARIOT. Actually Iscariot is not his last name, it is a Hebrew word meaning "town."

Among these 12 apostles there were three groups of brothers, numbers 1 and 2, Simon and Andrew, were sons of John, or Yohannan. Numbers 3 and 4, James and John, were the sons of Zebedee and Salome, and numbers 9 and 10, were brothers as well.

Also among the 12 were two that were extremely opposed to each other, because Simon was a Zealot who would kill Jews that worked for the Romans with his hidden knife, and Matthew was a tax collector working for Rome, but Jesus brought the whole group together and made them an effective team. What do you think Matthew was thinking when Jesus told Simon and him to sit close to each other?

Knowing the significance of the way things were written in those days, both Mark and Luke agree that there were three divisions of disciples, with four men in each division. Both gospel accounts follow the custom of naming the leaders of each group first, followed by the three that were under them. The divisions are also listed in order of seniority, the first being the top group.

1. Simon Peter was the leader of the first division with James, John and Andrew under him.

2. Philip was leader of the second division, with Bartholomew (Nathanael), Thomas and Matthew below him.
3. James the son of Alphaeus, led the third division, with Thaddeus (Judas – not Judas Iscariot), Simon the Zealot and Judas Iscariot. Judas was always last in the list while he was still alive.

[1] Luke 6:12

[2] Mark 3:14

[3] Mark 3:15

JESUS AUTHORITATIVELY EXPLAINS THE LAW OF MOSES – Or, The Sermon On The Mount
Matthew 5:1 to 7:29, Luke 6:17-49

Jesus explains the Law of Moses in the gospels of Matthew and Luke, in what is known as, the Sermon on the Mount, but the problem with a title like that is it does not tells us anything about the teaching in the sermon, only that it was given on a mountain, and when we read the Bible it is usually more important to know what was taught than where it was taught.

Jesus gave this long lecture at a time, as we have already seen, when there was excited and increasing interest in His claim to be the Messiah, from inside and outside the borders of the Land. It was a time when Jewish minds were focused on the coming of their Messiah, and they knew that the prophets in the Old Testament had said that righteousness was necessary to get into the kingdom. It would be a faultless kingdom where total righteousness and perfection reigned at all times. No one would ever do anything wrong, even all their thoughts would be holy. However, for four centuries the Pharisees had been developing a form of righteousness giving a very "wide road" of entry, and as we already know they taught, "All Israel has a share in the age to come." The way in was not through a narrow gate, but through a very wide one that could accommodate everyone.

Jesus had to teach the people that the religious leaders had got it all wrong, they needed to be born again because their old human nature was not suitable for life in the kingdom, and the way to be born again was by accepting Him as the Messiah and King. He would then make them acceptable for the kingdom of heaven miraculously. The people were aware of the Pharisees teaching, but Jesus was saying something quite different, and the question on their minds was, is Pharisaic righteousness good enough and if not what kind of righteousness is needed? Jesus told them the answer to their problem very plainly.

> Matthew 5:20 For I say unto you, That except your righteousness shall exceed the righteousness of the scribes and Pharisees, ye shall in no case enter into the kingdom of heaven.

Jesus' challenge had now been clearly put, first Pharisaic Judaism did not produce enough righteousness for anyone to enter the kingdom, and secondly their interpretation of the true righteousness of the Law of Moses was wrong.

The Jews listening to Jesus giving the Sermon on the Mount were supposed to be keeping the Law of Moses, but most of them were not, they were keeping the Mishnah. Jesus was **not** speaking to Christians, Christianity had not been born yet. The people of God were still under the Old Testament Law, and Jesus was talking about that Law.

Ian is a preacher with much the same understanding of the Bible as myself, and was invited to Canada to address a large Christian gathering. He taught them from the epistles of Paul in the Bible. Paul is a very important teacher of Christianity. Jesus returned from heaven for the special reason to inform Paul that he was to be His apostle to the Gentiles, and so Paul has the authority of Jesus to teach us.[1] Paul in the epistles explains that the righteousness we will need to be able to live with God in heaven, will be given to us as a free gift after we have been born again.[2] Jesus in the Sermon on the Mount was preaching about the Mosaic Law. Now getting back to Ian, and his visit to Canada. During his address Ian was heckled by a man who disagreed with Paul's teaching, and shouted out, "You are wrong. I believe Jesus," and then quoted some words of our Lord from the Sermon on the Mount. The Sermon on the Mount is very important and is there for our benefit[3] but it was given to Jews about their keeping the Law of Moses.

Three things the Sermon on the Mount is not.

The Sermon on the Mount is not a list of principles by which the future kingdom will be governed, although this has been a common teaching, that is not what it is. If it was then we would have to keep all 613 commandments of the Mosaic Law which is not the case because the Law was put out of action when Jesus died.

Secondly, it is not a way to eternal life through keeping its high standards, most especially as some teach through keeping the golden rule of Matthew 7:12.

> "Therefore all things whatsoever ye would that men should do to you, do ye even so to them: for this is the law and the prophets."

Even if anyone could do all the things in the Law without ever once in a lifetime making a mistake, they would still not get to heaven because it would mean that salvation is by works, not by the free gift of God through grace, as Paul taught the Church at Ephesus.[4] It is not the way to everlasting joy and glory in the presence of our holy God.

Thirdly, it is not a list of moral values for the Church to keep, or a catalogue of Christian rules. Some of the principles He gives do become Church ethics, and we know those that do because they are repeated later in the gospels and also by the apostles in the epistles, but taken as a whole, as a complete package, it is not a list of moral principles for the Church. If it was it would again mean that we would have to keep all 613 commandments of the Mosaic Law. Jesus was explaining to them how the Jews should keep the Law.

> Matthew 5:19 Whosoever shall break one of the least commandments.

He was talking about the commandments of the Law of Moses. If the Sermon on the Mount was a list of requirements for the Church then we could not eat pork, we could not wear clothes made from a mixture of cotton and wool, men could not shave, they would have to wear tassels on their clothes, but none of these Old Testament rules apply to Christians.

What is the Sermon on the Mount?

Taken as a whole, as a unit, the Sermon on the Mount is the authoritative interpretation of the true righteousness of the Law compared with the Pharisaic interpretation. The basic difference is that the Pharisees only required external conformity to the Law, but God required external and internal righteousness. Jesus here explained the righteousness of God as required by the Law of Moses, and remember the Law did not end until Jesus died. All the time He was alive all 613 commandments had to be kept.

Our investigation into the Sermon on the Mount is rather a long one and will consist of a number of sub-sections. Scripture references if there are any will be given at the end of each sub-section for ease of reference.

[1] Acts 9:15

[2] Romans 3:22, 4:5, 9:30, 10:10, 2 Corinthians 5:21

[3] 2 Timothy 3:16

[4] Ephesians 2:8-9

The Place And The Historical Background To The Sermon On The Mount
Matthew 5:1-2, Luke 6:17-19

Matthew begins by saying Jesus went up on the mountain, that's why it's called the Sermon on the Mount, and then he says He sat down. Matthew is writing for Jews and because the sermon was about the Jewish Law, Matthew's account is the longest. He tells us Jesus sat down to remind his readers that Jesus was a rabbi, because rabbis always taught while sitting.

Luke says there was a level place on the mountain where a huge crowd had gathered, not just local people but from all Judea, Jerusalem and the coastal plains of Tyre and Sidon.

He gave this message on His way down the mountain after He had chosen all His twelve apostles further up, at a higher level. A great interest in Him from far and wide, inside and outside the Land had been aroused, and there had already been conflict between Him and the Pharisees over the Mishnah.

The Quality Of True Righteousness
Matthew 5:3-16, Luke 6:20-26

In Matthew 5:3-12 Jesus describes people that are righteous as "blessed," actually "happy," from the Greek word, "*makarios.*" He begins with the first of four features of those who have true righteousness in their relationship to God.

> Matthew 5:3 Blessed [happy] are the poor in spirit: for theirs is the kingdom of heaven.

If anyone could achieve righteousness by his own efforts, which would include never, ever, having even one wicked thought, he might be proud of such an achievement, but it is not possible for anyone to obtain righteousness by himself. Righteousness in the kingdom will be holy and pure and it can only be had as a gift from God.[1] The people who are poor in spirit have no pride, but have a right relationship with God and know they are dependent for their righteousness on Him.

> Matthew 5:4 Blessed [happy] are they that mourn: for they shall be comforted.

In this context those that mourn are deeply aware of their sins and ready to confess them.[2]

> Matthew 5:5 Blessed [happy] are the meek: for they shall inherit the earth, [or perhaps the land, which to His Jewish listeners would be the Land of Israel].

Meekness means a quiet confidence in God, recognising and being in submission to His authority.

> Matthew 5:6 Blessed [happy] are they which do hunger and thirst after righteousness: for they shall be filled.

Righteousness here means to live completely according to the standard, the standard being the Law of Moses, and those that kept the Law consistently were happy in their relationship with God.

Jesus then moved on from their relationship with God to their relationship with people, making five observations.

> Matthew 5:7 Blessed [happy] are the merciful: for they shall obtain mercy.

Merciful means to understand the needs of others and to give them what they require.

> Matthew 5:8 Blessed [happy] are the pure in heart: for they shall see God.

People with pure hearts operate from a righteous motive. They do the good things they do, not to get praise from men, but only to please God.

> Matthew 5:9 Blessed [happy] are the peacemakers: for they shall be called the children of God

The peacemaking here is not bringing peace among the nations of the world but bringing peace among the people of God.

> Matthew 5:10 Blessed [happy] are they which are persecuted for righteousness sake: for their is the kingdom of heaven.

The earlier righteousness we mentioned was in relationship to God, here He is talking about righteousness in relationship to men, always doing what is right even when it will mean persecution.

Everything Jesus has said so far in the Sermon on the Mount has been related to the Law of Moses, but He now turns His attention to the coming of the Messiah.

> Matthew 5:11-12 Blessed [happy] are ye, when men shall revile you, and shall say all manner of evil against you falsely, for my sake. Rejoice and be exceeding glad: for great is your reward in heaven: for so persecuted they the prophets which were before you.

One of the things believers in Jesus have to do is to confess Him, to own up that He is the Messiah,[3] and although this may lead to persecution, our reward in heaven will be great.

"Jesus then in Luke 6:24-26, returned to the subject of the religious Jews of the time, showing four ways they did not obtain the righteousness of the Old Testament Law."

1. Their interest was in money and their lives were focused on wealth.
2. They were selfish, only concerned with their own needs and not the needs of other people.
3. They looked for laughter and amusement.
4. They wanted to be famous, and have a high status.

These four points fitted the Pharisees exactly, blind to their spiritual poverty, they saw no need for repentance, and were worried only for their own righteousness. They thought they were better than the authorities and saw no need to obey them, causing conflict between Jews and Jews. In a position of power, concerned only with the external demands of the Mishnah, they refused to help the needy and were in fact persecutors of their own people.

In Matthew 5:13-16, Jesus talks about the relationship of the righteous to the world, and they become two things. First they become the salt of the earth, and salt in those days was used as a preservative and as seasoning. The few Jews who achieved the righteousness of the Law accomplished both those things.

> Isaiah 1:9 Except the LORD of hosts, had left unto us a very small remnant, we should have been as Sodom, and we should have been as like unto Gomorrah. [Sodom and Gomorrah were completely destroyed[4]].

The reason God preserved Israel then was because of a small number of believers, a remnant that kept the Law of Moses, and today Israel is being kept alive by a small remnant of Jews that believe in Jesus. The other characteristic of salt is its use to season food, and believers are the ones who make life in the world worthwhile. We may be in a work place each day with empty unbelievers who are tiresome and unpleasant. After work when we meet friends who are fellow believers of Jesus, we find they have just the opposite effect on us, they are like salt. Then our lives are refreshed, and very satisfying, and we become strengthened.

Secondly believers become the light of the world, because they have the Truth, (the Truth is a person[5]), that can shine spiritual light on those in spiritual darkness. Jesus then warns or advises us who have the Truth.

> Matthew 5:16 Let your light so shine before men, that they may see your good works, and glorify your Father which is in heaven.

[1] Genesis 15:6, 2 Corinthians 5:21, Philippians 3:9, 2 Timothy 4:8, James 2:23

[2] 1 John 1:9

[3] Matthew 10:32-33, Luke 12:8-9, Romans 10:9, 1 John 4:1-6

[4] Genesis 19:24-25

[5] John 14:6, 14:17

The Code Of True Righteousness
Matthew 5:17-48

The epistles demonstrate to us over and over again that the Mosaic Law ended with the death of Jesus on the cross. It is clearly shown in Romans 7:1-4, and the translation of this passage by J.B. Phillips explains the teaching clearly.

> "You know very well, my brothers (for I am speaking to those well acquainted with the subject), that the Law can only exercise authority over a man so long as he is alive. A married woman, for example, is bound by the Law to her husband so long as he is alive. But if he dies, then his legal claim over her disappears. This means that, if she should give herself to another man while her husband is alive, she incurs the stigma of adultery. But if, after her husband's death, she does exactly the same thing, no one could call her an adulteress, for the Law over her has been dissolved by her husband's death.

There is, I think, a fair analogy here. The death of Christ on the Cross has made you 'dead' to the claims of the Law."

Therefore in Romans 7:6, Paul tells us we have been released from the Law, and I would like to quote from his letter to the Colossians to emphasize his point.

> Colossians 2:16 Let no man therefore judge you in meat, or in drink, or in respect of a holyday, or of the new moon, or of the Sabbath days.

The writer of Hebrews shows that with the death of Jesus the whole reason for the Temple in Jerusalem was done away with, because the Law then ended and there was no longer any need for any other priest except Jesus Himself.[1]

> Hebrews 9:28 So Christ was once offered to bear the sins of many.

Many Christians, especially Jewish, use Matthew 5:17 to falsely teach that the Law of Moses is still in effect because they miss the point of the words of Jesus in that verse.

> Matthew 5:17 Think not that I am come to destroy the law, or the prophets: I am not come to destroy, but to fulfil.

Remember, Jesus was speaking while the Law was still active because it only ended when He died, and in His arguments with the Pharisees over the Law, (which is why He preached the Sermon on the Mount), His purpose is to show that while they destroyed the Law of Moses through introducing the oral law, He came to fulfil it as it was written[2] in the Bible, not as the Pharisees said in the Mishnah. Jesus was and will continue to remain the only Jew to perfectly keep the Mosaic Law in all the 613 commandments that applied to Him. We said earlier that the parents of John the Baptist were righteous under the Law because they confessed their sins and made the necessary sacrifices according to the Law, but with Jesus there were no sins to confess and therefore no requirement for sacrifice, He came to fulfil the Law. However, once He had fulfilled the Law, then it could end.

> Matthew 5:18 For verily I say unto you, Till heaven and earth pass, one jot or one tittle shall in no wise pass from the law, till all be fulfilled.

A jot is the smallest letter in the Hebrew alphabet, about a quarter the size of all the other letters, and a tittle is a tiny addition to a Hebrew letter that sticks out, so that readers know to change the sound. Unlike the Pharisees therefore, Jesus is going to fulfil the Mosaic Law exactly, down to the smallest letter in the Hebrew alphabet and even down to the smallest stroke or part of a letter. Jesus was driving home the message that the Mosaic Law was made to be kept perfectly.

> Matthew 5:19 Whosoever therefore shall break one of these least commandments, ...

The commandments He is talking about here in His Sermon on the Mount, are those in the Law of Moses, and the Jews needed to keep them "as they were written," because the Law was still in operation when Jesus was speaking.

> Matthew 5:20 For I say unto you, That except your righteousness shall exceed the righteousness of the scribes and Pharisees, ye shall in no case enter into the kingdom of heaven.

Jesus next gave some examples of the code of true righteousness in Matthew 5:21-48, and notice how some of the verses begin.

> [21] Ye have heard that it was said by them of old time.

> [27] Ye have heard that it was said by them of old time.

> [31] It hath been said.

> [33] Again, ye have heard that it hath been said by them of old time,

> [38] Ye have heard that it hath been said.

> [43] Ye have heard that it hath been said.

Jesus, when talking about the Law of Moses, would say, "as it is written," because He was talking about the written Law, but when He was talking about the oral law, He would say as in these verses something like, "you have heard that it was said," because although they had heard it from their Pharisaic religious leaders, it was not from the Bible. He would choose a commandment of Moses from the written Law and compare their kind righteousness with the kind of righteousness God required.

> Matthew 5:21 Ye have heard that it was said by them of old time, Thou shalt not kill.

Although, "Thou shalt not kill," was from the Mosaic Law, Jesus was talking about what the Pharisees said about that Law in the Mishnah, how they had interpreted the Law written by Moses. The word "kill" here means premeditated murder, and the Pharisees said, "you are not guilty of unrighteousness until you actually murder someone." Jesus said they were wrong, because while the letter of the law was not broken until the murder had been carried out, and there would be no punishment under the Law unless murder had been committed, the righteousness of the command against premeditated murder is always broken before the murder takes place. Anyone who actually performs a premeditated murder, first of all has in his mind hostility towards his victim (which lawyers call *mens rea*), and at that moment he has broken the righteousness of the Law.

> Matthew 5:22 [Jesus said] whosoever shall say to his brother, Raca.

"Raca" is, "you empty head" in Aramaic, and if we call someone an empty head with a feeling of hostility when we say it, we have behaved unjustly, since it is our internal hostility that is not righteous, and it can result in premeditated murder.

The same principle applies when we consider adultery and Jesus explains this in Matthew 5:27-28. The way the Pharisees understood it was that so long as they did not commit adultery they had not broken the righteousness of the Law. True, no one was stoned to death until the adultery had taken place, but the question is, "What is the righteousness of the Law?" The answer is, "The righteousness of this particular rule in the Law is broken before the adultery occurs." A man must develop a sexual desire for a woman who is not his wife before he commits adultery with her, and as soon as he does this, even if he does not actually commit adultery, he has broken the righteousness of the Law.

We will deal with divorce (Matthew 5:31-32) later, and go on to Matthew 5:33-37 where Jesus criticises the Pharisaic practice of taking oaths. The Law of Moses emphasized that your word should be enough, trustworthy, but if you made an oath it was absolutely essential that you kept it. However, in the Mishnah there are many rules allowing a Jew to break an oath, and so they would swear by God in heaven, or by the Temple, or by something else and then find a way to break their promise, breaking the righteousness of the command. Jesus told them they needed to be completely honest and there was no need to use an oath, their "Yes," should mean yes and their "No," should mean no.

> **Matthew 5:37** But let you communication be, Yea, yea; Nay, nay: for whatsoever is more than these cometh of evil.

Matthew 5:38-42 deals with the Law's rule of retaliation, an eye for an eye and a tooth for a tooth,[3] which was an instruction on legal justice about the punishment to be handed out by a court of law, and nothing to do with people taking the law into their own hand for the sake of revenge. The Pharisees used the instruction as an excuse to settle scores and satisfy their anger, ignoring the Bible teaching of, "Vengeance is Mine," says the Lord,[4] and of course breaking the righteousness of the command.

The teaching on loving your neighbour and hating your enemy in Matthew 5:43-48, is remarkable because the main line Pharisees did not teach hatred for an enemy, but a branch of Pharisees known as the Essenes did and this message was probably for them.

> **Matthew 5:43-44** Ye have heard that it hath been said, Thou shalt love thy neighbour, and hate thine enemy. But I say to you, Love your enemies, bless them that curse you, do good to

them that hate you, and pray for them which despitefully use you, and persecute you.

The way the Essenes identified a neighbour was, any fellow Jew, but that was wrong, a neighbour in the biblical language of the time was anyone in need that you are able to help,[5] and for that reason the Essenes were guilty of breaking the righteousness of the Law.[6]

[1] Hebrews 5:1-10

[2] Luke 2:23, 4:4, 4:8 etc.

[3] Deuteronomy 19:15-21

[4] Deuteronomy 32:35, Psalm 94:1

[5] Luke 10:29-37

[6] Leviticus 19:18

The Behaviour Of True Righteousness
Matthew 6:1-18

Jesus begins with an introduction and then gives some examples to explain true righteousness.

> Matthew 6:1 Take heed that you do not your alms before men, to be seen of them: otherwise ye have no reward of your Father which is in heaven.

The righteousness required is a righteousness that pleases God and has nothing to do with pleasing men. Many people in this world do good works in order to get the approval of men, but that is all they get, because they are not concerned about God, whereas those who do the will of God to get His approval, while maybe not pleasing men and perhaps even annoying them, will receive everlasting approval from heaven.

The first example of this principle is in Matthew 6:2-4, and is about giving money or alms, which should be done secretly for the attention of God, not of men.

> Matthew 6:2 Therefore when thou doest [give] thine alms [money to charity], do not sound a trumpet before thee, as the hypocrites [pretenders] do in the synagogues and in the streets, that they may have glory of men. Verily [Truly] I say unto you, They have their reward.

Rich Pharisees would often have a trumpet blown before they gave a large amount of money for a charitable need, in order to gather a huge crowd of people to see how big the gift was. Giving in that way is not the behaviour that God approves, but it does get men's approval especially from those that support the same cause. Recently I put a few small coins in the tin can of a man collecting for charity, and he stuck a sticker on my jacket to show I had paid. I thought to myself, "People will think I am good because of this sticker, but it is what God thinks that matters."

The second example of the same principle in Matthew 6:5-15, is about prayer. Our prayers are to God, and they should never be made to be heard by other people for the sole reason of making them believe we are good Christians. It is not men we need to impress, but our Heavenly Father.

> Matthew 6:5 And when thou [you] prayest [pray], thou shalt [shall] not be as the hypocrites [pretenders] are: for they love to pray standing in the synagogues and in the corners of the streets, that they may be seen by men. Verily [Truly] I say to you, They have their reward.

Prayers to our Heavenly Father should be extemporaneous, which means they should be spoken without preparation in the same way that we speak to a close friend. There are no extemporaneous prayers in any Gentile religion, they are all recited from memory or read from prayer books, whether the religion is Buddhism, Islam or whatever, and over the years the same became true of Judaism. Although in the Bible we read extemporaneous prayers to God made by the prophets, kings and others, today there are no extemporaneous prayers in Judaism. They have Sabbath prayer books, Atonement prayer books, Rosh Hashana prayer books, prayer books for different occasions, so that Judaism has become like a Gentile religion.

At Trewint, Cornwall, there is a Methodist chapel, which is also a museum. In 1743 it was the home of Digory Isbell, whose wife Elizabeth was amazed when two of John Wesley's advance agents, John Nelson and John Downes, stayed there and prayed without a prayer book, just as Jesus taught at the Sermon on the Mount.

TREWINT

In Cornwall, the busy A30 road carries visitors from Launceston to Bodmin and beyond. Near Five Lanes is the hamlet of Trewint with a place all its own in the Wesley Saga.

One summer day in 1743, two of John Wesley's advance agents, John Nelson and John Downes, tired and hungry, asked for refreshment at a house with a stone porch the home of Digory Isbell a journeyman Stonemason. In his absence his wife, Elizabeth, entertained the two strangers who on leaving insisted on paying and then knelt and prayed— "Without a book!"

The story of these such unusual ways, was return. A year later wet and weary, was Stonemason's house ing behind. One evening in his Bible of the built a "Prophet's God." I will do that Trewint became a

A Welcome awaits you at TREWINT

Unusual visitors, with told to Digory on his John Wesley himself, entertained in the and left a rich blessing Digory Isbell read Shunamite woman who Chamber" for a man of said Digory and he did. flourishing Methodist Society but when other chapels were opened the Trewint rooms fell into disuse and eventually became a roofless ruin.

In 1950 the Isbell house and the Wesley rooms were suitably restored. Services are now regularly held in the latter, believed to be the smallest Methodist preaching place in the world.

The A30 road symbolises the stress and strain of modern life. Digory Isbells house at Trewint calls the soul to prayer and peace. For those who will linger and listen there, voices will speak of the riches of yesterday providing a thrill for to-day and a challenge for tomorrow.

The house with the stone Porch

The Prophets Chamber

The Prayer Room, used and loved by John Wesley.

Antique Collecting Box

We are still looking at the teaching of Jesus about prayer in Matthew 6:5-15, and the third point He made was that our prayers should be well thought-out, and to show this He gave us a model, which is known by Christians all over the world as the Lord's Prayer. The Lord's Prayer is an example with six parts for us to follow.

1. We should always speak to God the Father, "After this manner therefore pray ye: Our Father which art in heaven."[1] There are no prayers in the Bible either in the Old Testament or in the New Testament, spoken to the Son of God or to the Holy Spirit, all our prayers are to be made to God the Father.

2. Next we should show our respect and awe of God because He is so holy and almighty. "Hallowed be thy name."[1] We are nothing in comparison to Him and so we think about how wonderful He is and how He is helping us to come to Him.

3. The kingdom of God is very, very important indeed, and He wants us to be part of it and to pray for it. "Thy kingdom come. Thy will be done in earth, as it is in heaven."[2] The kingdom will come but many of us will have the honour of helping bring it in. It is the time we can pray for evangelists, (those people who preach the good news of Jesus), for our church, the preacher, the Sunday School teachers, missionaries and Christian organizations we support with gifts of money, for all our relatives, especially those who do not yet have eternal life. All these things will help bring in the kingdom of God.

4. We are to pray for our needs, "Give us this day our daily bread."[3] Perhaps we are going through a difficult time and if we are, our Heavenly Father is waiting to hear our cry for help. He answers our secret prayers openly for everyone to see,[4] and also the prayers we make together to him when we are in what seems to us to be an impossible situation, but we must agree when we pray as a group, that is why husband and wife prayers are so powerful because they are in agreement together.

In Acts 4:24-30 the believers in Jerusalem prayed in unity, "with one accord" telling God how the government, including Herod the king, Pontius Pilate the Roman governor, the leaders of Israel and of the Gentiles, had united together against God, His Son Jesus, and how they were threatening them. They prayed, "that signs and wonders may be done by the name of thy holy child Jesus." The result was that there was an earthquake, they were all filled with the Holy Spirit and spoke with great power. May be that kind of praying will be necessary again soon because of threats plotted against believers by the false churches, false religions and worldly politicians. True believers are always a minority even in countries that are supposed to be Christian,[5] and therefore cannot control politicians directly, in the way people of the world do. The influence of the people of God is supernatural and is the result of having Jesus in them and being in Him,[6] and it is assisted by secret humble prayer,[7] not prayer for your own worldly fame and pleasure.

In my experience God has been so good in answering prayers of need, both the secret kind which He answers openly and the corporate prayers made by Lucy and me together. In the early nineties a group of hippies set up camp at Davidstow on Bodmin Moor, about three miles from our farm, for what they called the White Witch Festival. The music they played was very loud and heard up to eight miles away and like so many popular gatherings and comic shows it was anti-Christian, and one of the songs they were singing I am told was, "Worship the Devil, worship the Devil, worship the Devil in the house of God." At that time Lucy and I had not yet started praying together on a daily basis, and the trouble with the loud sounds from the camp was that they disturbed my daily prayer times, and so in secret with my door shut, while the music was being played I explained the situation to my Heavenly Father, who is Almighty. The next day the music stopped and it was so good to have my quiet time again. The closure of the festival was mentioned in Parliament and in the media, the Royal Marines moved to Davidstow on exercises and kept people away, the police patrolled all the approaching roads and turned back everyone making their way to the festival, for which the Government announced it would give them extra funds amounting to £200,000, and despite attempts to revive the event in subsequent years, God has continued to reward me openly up to now, May 2007. That is an example of how God, true to His Word, answered a secret, private prayer openly for all the world to see.[4]

Later after Lucy and I had started praying together every day, and were converting a barn on the farm into a cottage, we were down to our last £2,000 in the bank, when the architect informed us that we needed another £7,000 for a new roof. The farming operations were losing money and we needed the rent from letting out the barn, (after converting it into a cottage), to stop us going into debt. In agreement, "with one accord" we told our Father in heaven the situation and asked Him to help. Three days later there was a cheque for £5,000 on the floor beside our letter box, from a solicitor who had decided to issue partial payments to beneficiaries of my mother's estate. He did this without the prompting of anyone named in her will, and because we had the money three days after praying together, it seems the idea probably came into his mind about the time we were praying. This is an example of God answering a prayer of agreement made by two people, whom He continues to bless. If you belong to the LORD and have a need, pray!

We are still looking at the six parts of the model prayer Jesus outlined for us, we have dealt with the first four, and there are two more.

> 5. We must pray for forgiveness. "And forgive us our debts [sins] as we forgive our debtors [people that have behaved wrongly to us]"[8] Forgiveness of sin is important. "For if ye forgive men their trespasses, your heavenly Father will also forgive you: but if ye forgive not men their trespasses, neither will your Father forgive your trespasses."[9] Some people think that God will not listen to their prayers unless they have owned up to their sin, perhaps to the person concerned or to a priest, but Jesus did not say that. It is acceptable to admit our sins in prayer to our heavenly Father, and forgiving someone is a decision we make, not a feeling we get. However it has been my experience that eventually after a certain amount of prayer a feeling of forgiveness comes over me. I put this down to the Spirit of God dwelling in me and not to my own effort because I am still the same person, and so it must be God that is changing me. Since it is God that is working in me and making the change,[10] then how thankful I feel for His gift.

6. We also need to pray for the help of Almighty God in the spiritual warfare we face during our battles with our flesh, that is to say our own sinful natures, and the devil. "And lead us not into temptation, but deliver us from evil."[11]

Jesus gave us this model for prayer, known as the Lord's Prayer, as an outline or strategy, it was not meant to be repeated time after time. He began by saying, "After this manner therefore pray ye,"[1] meaning, in this way, not by repeating the same words but by using them as an outline. Remember at the beginning, before the Lord's Prayer, Jesus told them, "But when ye pray, use not vain [useless] repetitions, as the heathen do; for they think that they shall be heard for their much speaking."[12]

The third example Jesus teaches about the behaviour of true righteousness is in Matthew 6:16-18, and concerns fasting. In the New Testament we are not told to fast, the decision is up to us, but if we fast we should not make a big thing out of it to let people know we are fasting for God, that would not be true righteousness. If we fast we should do it secretly so that only God knows, "and thy Father, which seeth in secret, shall reward thee openly."[13]

[1] Matthew 6:9

[2] Matthew 6:10

[3] Matthew 6:11

[4] Matthew 6:6

[5] Matthew 7:14

[6] John 15:4-5

[7] James 4:3-4

[8] Matthew 6:12

[9] Matthew 6:14-15

[10] Philippians 1:6

[11] Matthew 6:13

[12] Matthew 6:7

[13] Matthew 6:18

The Practice Of True Righteousness
Matthew 6:19 to 7:12, Luke 6:27-42

The Sermon on the Mount, we should remind ourselves, has been given that name because that is where Jesus taught it, on the mount, but that does not tell us what it is about. It is all about the authority of Jesus to interpret the righteousness of the Jewish Law, as distinct from the interpretation and actions of the Pharisees, so what did Jesus teach about the way truly righteous people behave in dealing with money, worry, judging other people, praying (being persistent) and finally in practising the golden rule?

Matthew 6:19-24, is about money, "Lay not up for yourselves treasures upon earth." Heaven, where God is, is the place we should be building up our heaps of riches. The problem is not the money but who we are serving, God above or wealth below.

> Matthew 6:24 "No man can serve two masters: for either he will hate the one, and love the other; or else he will hold to the one, and despise the other. Ye cannot serve God and mammon." ["Mammon" is the Aramaic word for "riches"].

Money is essential, and fathers need a lot of it if they are to provide for their families, especially if they are blessed with many children that are able to make good use of money spent on their education. The question is, "What are we most concerned about?" If our minds are centred on the Lord then we will be well balanced individuals and not materialistic big-spenders or misers.

In Matthew 6:25-34, Jesus talks of worrying, "Take no thought for your life, what ye shall eat, or what ye shall drink; nor yet for your body, what ye shall put on." He reminds us of the birds and the flowers and how God supplies the animal and plant kingdoms with all they require. If this is so then we can be sure He will provide greater care of believers who are searching for righteousness so that they can always be in the presence of God. We can expect God, in normal times, to make available our food, clothing and housing, our basic needs, not everything we want but all the essentials. However, there are and will be times when believers are persecuted,[1] so much that they die, but that is not the end for them, only a more wonderful beginning.[2] If that is so, what should be the focus of our attention?

> Matthew 6:33 "Seek ye first the kingdom of God, and his righteousness; and all these things shall be added unto you."

Jesus, after showing that our most important objective is to enter into eternal life, ends as He began by telling us not to worry about our basic daily needs.[3] We are still responsible to get a job and earn some money because the Bible says that people who refuse to work should not be allowed to eat,[4] and followers of Jesus should not be allowed to live off other believers.[5] Jesus promises that if we direct our lives mainly to finding true righteousness and entry into the kingdom of God for ourselves, God will look after us.

How the righteous are to judge others is explained in Matthew 7:1-6 and Luke 6:37-42, verses that are often wrongly applied.

> Matthew 7:1-2 Judge not, that ye be not judged. For with what judgement ye judge, ye shall be judged: and with what measure ye mete [measure], it shall be measured to you again.

Looking at these three warnings concerning money, worry and judging, they are all made into negatives. Regarding money, "Lay **not** up for yourselves treasures upon earth," and worry, "Take **no** thought for your life," and finally judging, "Judge **not**." Jesus is telling us things we should not do, but some teachers have decided it means we must never judge others at all, but that contradicts other Scriptures where we are told to make judgements. Matthew himself talks about Church discipline,[6] and before discipline is decided a judgement must be made. Jesus is not saying we must never judge, but look at verse two, "with what measure ye mete [measure], it shall be measured to you." The Pharisees were judging by the Mishnah, not by the word of God, and we are not to use standards thought up and approved by men.

Today some churches make the same mistake as the Pharisees by judging a person's spirituality according to their own rules and regulations. We must only judge by God's standards, using men's standards is like trying to move a piece of sawdust from someone's eye while we have a huge beam in our own eye. The sawdust and the beam are both wood but the one with the beam in his eye is completely blind, and the one using men's standards is also completely blind, and needs to get back to the Word of God so that he can see. Jesus warned the Jewish believers that the Pharisees would not accept these truths, and so also we cannot expect many of the religious leaders of today to accept them either.

> Matthew 7:6 Give not that which is holy unto the dogs, neither cast ye your pearls before swine, lest they trample them under their feet, and turn again and rend you.

The fourth teaching is on righteous prayer and is in addition to the three lessons He gave previously, in Matthew 6:5-15, when we looked at the behaviour of true righteousness, and His main point is persistence. In Matthew 7:7 the key words are, "ask," "seek" and "knock," and they are all in Greek present tenses meaning continuous action, "keep on asking," "keep on seeking" and "keep on knocking." We are to persist in prayer until we get an answer or until we no longer have a burden for it. Notice He does **not** say we are to pray in His name, because He is talking about the righteousness of the Law, but later when teaching about the Age of Grace, He added, "And whatsoever ye shall ask in my name, that will I do, that the Father may be glorified in the Son. If ye shall ask anything in my name, I will do it."[7]

Matthew 7:12 is where we find the golden rule, the foundation of true righteousness under the Law. "Therefore all things whatsoever ye would that men should do to you, do ye even so to them: for this is the law and the prophets." In our dealings with others we are to treat them the way we would like to be treated, and regarding our personal relationships, that sums up the Law and the Prophets, but it is not a way to obtain salvation. It is the way a person with everlasting life behaves but it is not a way to earn it.

[1] Hebrews 11:37-40

[2] 2 Corinthians 5:1-8

[3] Matthew 6:34

[4] 2 Thessalonians 3:10-12

[5] 2 Thessalonians 3:7-8

[6] Matthew 18:15-17

[7] John 14:13-14

Words Of Warning About True Righteousness
Matthew 7:13-27, Luke 6:43-49

The Pharisees believed that all Israel had a share in the age to come, and in Matthew 7:13-14 Jesus shatters that by calling their doctrine the broad way to destruction. Churches that teach we will go to heaven if we belong to their denomination and follow their traditions and rules are making the same mistake as the Pharisees. The way to obtain righteousness that will enable us to live in the presence of God is very narrow and only comes by accepting Jesus as the Messianic King, there is no other way apart from Him.[1]

Following the warning of the two ways Jesus then talks of the two trees, the true and false prophets, in Matthew 7:15-20 and Luke 6:43-45. We can tell false prophets from true prophets by their fruit. A true prophet teaches and lives his life in agreement with God's written word, and his prophecies come true. A false prophet is just the opposite, his prophecies do not come true, and he does not live and teach according to Scripture, and in the case of the Pharisees they had their own rules and regulations they followed. The true prophet produces the fruit of righteousness but the false prophet does not.

The next comparisons Jesus warns us of is about two groups of people that both say the same thing, and this is found in Matthew 7:21-23. He warns us that just because we call Him Lord does not mean we belong to Him. "Not everyone that saith unto me, Lord, Lord, shall enter the kingdom of heaven." Observant Pharisees would never use the name of Jesus. However, some of His hearers and readers of the gospels might use His name but will still be false teachers even though they do the works of verse 22, making prophecies that come true, casting out demons and other miracles, because according to Matthew 7:23 He is going to say to them on judgement day, "I never knew you: depart from me, ye that work iniquity." The test of true righteousness is never outward signs, like miracles or speaking in tongues, but keeping to the written word of God, that what is being said, taught and done agrees with Scripture. Satan can perform the outward signs, and in the "church" today there are additional signs that are not in the Bible, but even the signs found in Matthew 7:22, can not be taken as evidence of righteousness. We need to see what they are saying and teaching.

The last warning is a comparison between two builders in Matthew 7:24-27, where Jesus asks the Jews to make a choice between building on the Pharisees interpretation of the righteousness of the Law, a foundation of sand, or on His interpretation of the righteousness of the Law. If they build on His interpretation they will be building on a Rock and what they build will last forever. There is only One Foundation of true righteousness.

[1] John 14:6

The Deductions From The Sermon On The Mount
Matthew 7:28-29

> Matthew 7:28-29 [28] And it came to pass, when Jesus had ended these sayings, the people were astonished at his doctrine [teaching]:
>
> [29] For he taught them as one having authority, and not as the scribes.

Rabbinic writings show us how the scribes used to teach. The method was always the same, Rabbi So-and-so said, of Rabbi Such-and-such this. Rabbi Such-and-such said, of Rabbi So-and-so that. Rabbis always taught from a previous rabbinic teaching. Jesus never quoted a rabbi, a Pharisee or scribe, but taught "as one having authority" to interpret the righteousness of the Law, which was right because He is the Messiah who gave it. The contrast between the teaching of the scribes, those Pharisees who were experts of the Law, and the teaching of Jesus was obvious and the people understood Jesus plainly and knew, as these verses show, how His teaching differed from theirs.

The Sermon on the Mount is two things, first as we have already stated, it is the authoritative interpretation of the true righteousness of the Law compared with the Pharisaic interpretation. Secondly, taken as a whole, it is the public rejection by Jesus to all Israel of Pharisaic Judaism as explained in the Mishnah. We will now see how His rejection of their Mishnaic Judaism results in their rejecting His claim of being the Messiah.

JESUS' AUTHORITY IS RECOGNIZED IN CAPERNAUM
Matthew 8:5-13, Luke 7:1-10

The authority of Jesus here was recognized by a Gentile, a Roman army officer in charge of a hundred men, known as a centurion, and we read in Matthew, "there came unto him a centurion, beseeching him."[1] However, in Luke 7:3 it says, "he [the centurion] sent unto him [Jesus] the elders of the Jews, beseeching him that he would come and heal his servant." Now here is a contradiction people love to point out, Matthew says it was a centurion and Luke says it was the elders of the Jews. As we said, the Bible is a Jewish book, and we will have a better understanding about what it says if we know Jewish ways.

If someone is sent he is sent with the authority of the person who sends him and is looked upon as the sender himself. An example is seen in the Talmud in Berahot 34:2 where it says, "The apostle or emissary of anyone is as he himself." In Luke 7:3 it simply means the Jews did not make the decision to go, the centurion sent them and that is seen as the centurion going himself. Interestingly the Jews are not just message carriers, they try to convince Jesus to do exactly as the centurion asks even though he is a Gentile.

> Luke 7:4 And when they came to Jesus, they besought [asked earnestly] him instantly, saying, That he was worthy.

Why did the leaders of the synagogue say that the centurion was worthy and that a miracle should be done for him? Two reasons are given in Luke 7:5, first, "he loveth our nation," a Gentile that loves the

Jews will receive a blessing from God under His covenant with Abraham, "I will bless them that bless thee."[2] The other reason they gave was, "and he hath built us a synagogue." It was the centurion who had provided the synagogue where Jesus had preached and so he certainly was worthy, and Jesus began His journey towards the centurion's home. Word reached the centurion that Jesus was on His way and he sent Jesus another message.

> Matthew 8:8 Lord, I am not worthy that you should come under my roof.

The Jewish elders think he is worthy but he, not proud in his opinion of himself, thinks he is not worthy or not deserving but what faith he has. Next there is a clear recognition of the authority of Jesus from a Gentile who also uses power he has been given.

> Matthew 8:8-9 8 speak the word only, and my servant shall be healed.
>
> 9 For I am a man under authority, having soldiers under me: and I say to this man, Go, and he goeth; and to another, Come, and he cometh; and to my servant, Do this, and he doeth it.

If a word from me will get the job done, then certainly a word from You will be enough.

Jesus was very impressed with the faith of this Roman soldier.

> Matthew 8:10 When Jesus heard it, he marvelled, and said to them that followed, Verily [Truly] I say unto you, I have not found so great faith, no, not in Israel.

This event was symbolic of the future when the Gentiles understand exactly what the Jewish leaders do not, and so Jesus adds an important prophecy.

> Matthew 8:11 And I say unto you, That many shall come from the east and west, and shall sit down with Abraham, and Isaac, and Jacob, in the kingdom of heaven.

He says that when the messianic kingdom is set up, Gentiles will come from all around the world, from east and west and will "sit down," a better translation would be "recline," in the same way people of those days in Israel reclined on the floor propped up by one elbow, when they feasted round a low table. Gentiles are going to get-together and celebrate with Abraham, Isaac and Jacob, the ancestors of the Jewish nation. Do you think there will be any people who hate the Jews there? Anyway many Gentiles will be at the party, people like the centurion who recognize the authority of the Messiah and who love the Jewish people. Jesus next gives another important prophecy.

> Matthew 8:12 But the children of the kingdom shall be cast out into outer darkness: there shall be weeping and gnashing of teeth.

The Pharisees called themselves the sons of the kingdom, and Jesus is saying that those Jews relying on the righteousness of the Mishnah will go the place of weeping and gnashing of teeth, a description of the fire of Hell.[3]

> Matthew 8:13 And Jesus said unto the centurion, Go thy way; and as thou hast believed, so be it done unto thee. And his servant was healed in the selfsame hour.

The centurion was unusual because he cared so much for his servant, going to great lengths to have him healed, yet in those days servants and slaves were easy to replace.

[1] Matthew 8:5

[2] Genesis 12:3, 27:29, (where Abraham passed the blessing to Isaac).

[3] Matthew 13:42, 13:50

JESUS' AUTHORITY IS RECOGNIZED EVERYWHERE IN THE LAND
Luke 7:11-17

The day after healing the centurion's servant Jesus was still in the Galilee but had travelled more than twenty miles south, to the city of Nain.

> Luke 7:12 Now when he came nigh to the gate of the city, behold, there was a dead man carried out, the only son of his mother, and she was a widow.

Her husband was dead and the Law of Moses was that her sons would be responsible for her, to provide a home, food, clothing and all her needs. In her case she is faced with being a common beggar because her only son is also dead. Jesus was sorry for her and touched the coffin, which would normally make Him unclean, but He did not stay unclean because Jesus said, "Young man, I say unto thee, Arise," and the dead man spoke. The Bible does not tell us what he said, but the incident produced three results.

First the people were gripped by an awful fear. Jesus had shown them His miraculous authority which put them at His mercy, but it was a Godly fear and they glorified God. Secondly they realised that a great prophet was with them, "That God had visited his people." However, their realisation was not enough, Jesus was more than a great prophet, He was their Messianic King. The third result was that the news that the dead man had been raised to life, the fear of the people and the realisation that this was the power of God, spread from the Galilee in the North to Judea in the south and all the surrounding districts.

Finally, Luke was the writer of this account and we are again reminded of his interest in the relationships between women and Jesus. Here by bringing the widow's son back to life He rescued her from beggarly poverty.

6

THE DISPUTE OVER JESUS

This chapter begins with the Jewish leaders rejecting God's prophet, John the Baptist, and ends with his death. We have already seen that Zacharias the priest prophesied that his son, John the Baptist, would be a forerunner of Jesus,[1] and therefore John knew he was the herald of the King.

JOHN THE BAPTIST IS REJECTED
Matthew 11:7-19, Luke 7:18-30

John had been in prison for quite a while but his disciples often visited him and gave him news about Jesus. He learned that Jesus was not being accepted by the Jewish leaders as King, which puzzled him because like the apostles he did not understand about God's programme of Jesus coming twice. Locked up in jail and not sure about what was going on, John, like other believers sometimes, began to doubt, wondering if he had pointed out the wrong Messiah, and sent his disciples to Jesus with a question.

> Matthew 11:3 "Art thou he that should come, or do we look for another?"

John's disciples arrived in Luke 7:21 when Jesus was healing many people, delivering them from evil spirits, curing diseases and blindness, and His answer was not, "Yes," or "No."

Luke 7:22 Go your way and tell John what things ye have seen and heard.

They would have heard what He said, His teaching and His claim to be the Messiah, and they would have seen the miracles He was performing to prove that He was the Messiah. The disciples left to report to John and than Jesus gave us His assessment of His herald, and He had five things to say.

1. He was not a reed shaken by the wind.[2] He was not a coward, he had a strong character, and spoke boldly leaving people in no doubt as to what he meant. He called the Pharisees and Sadducees, a "generation of vipers."[3]

2. He was not a man clothed in soft raiment.[4] He was not a dandy who paid too much attention to being dressed smartly, but was used to roughing it out in the desert, not living a life of ease.

3. He was a prophet.[5] He was given knowledge by God which ordinary people did not know until John told them.

4. He was more than a prophet[5] because he was the person who would come before the Messiah,[6] as spoken of more than 400 years earlier in Malachi 3:1.

5. In Matthew 11:11 Jesus says something about John that is astounding, He says, "Among them that are born of women there has not risen a greater than John the Baptist." He was as great or greater than any saint in the Old Testament, men like Noah, Abraham, Moses and David. Quite rightly the writers of the four Gospels concentrate their stories on Jesus, and therefore we do not know all about the work John did for God, but we know it was very great. In Acts 19:1-7 many, many years afterwards, Paul met some men in Ephesus who were disciples of John but who still knew nothing about Jesus at all, and there are villages in Syria to this day where they still speak Aramaic and still regard John as their prophet. John's influence was much greater than the Gospels alone tell us.

Jesus has left us in no doubt as to how great a man John the Baptist was, but then still talking about John he adds in Luke 7:28, "but he that is least in the kingdom of God is greater than he." The kingdom of God Jesus is speaking about concerns a new kingdom plan which He will tell us more about in Matthew 16:18, His Church, the body.[7] So, those of us who are part of the true Church, who are in the Messiah, are greater than John and the saints of the Old Testament.

John spoke of the coming King and the kingdom but his preaching was received with violent opposition.

> Matthew 11:12 And from the days of John the Baptist until now the kingdom of heaven suffereth violence, and the violent take it by force.

The main opposition had come from the Pharisees and by their strong disputes they were effectively stopping the Jews of that generation from entering the kingdom with Jesus as King, that John was talking about.

> Matthew 11:13 For all the prophets and the law prophesied until John.

So again we are shown that John will be the last of the Old Testament style of prophet. Still talking about the preaching of John, about the coming King and kingdom, Jesus in the next verse made one of those Bible statements that link John the Baptist and Elijah.

> Matthew 11:14 And if ye will receive it, this is Elias, which was for to come.

Previous passages that connect John and Elijah (Elias) are Luke 1:17, where the angel speaking to John's father Zacharias said that John came in the spirit and power of Elijah, and John 1:21, where John said, "No," when he was asked whether he was Elijah the prophet. However, Jesus said to His Jewish audience, "And if ye will receive it, this is Elias, who was to come." Jesus is explaining that if they accept Him as Messiah, He will be their King in a new kingdom, and John will carry out the role of Elijah, which was to restore all things (Mark 9:11-13). Jesus was offering them the kingdom and told them, "If ye will receive it, this is Elias." The last two verses of the Old Testament tell us that before the judgement of the people on the earth, the preaching of Elijah will, "turn the heart of the fathers to the children, and the heart of the children to their fathers," so that the judgement of God will be less severe.[8] John the Baptist did not carry out the task that God has assigned to Elijah because the Jews rejected the kingdom and so one day before the judgement, Elijah will return and do it himself.

Although John did not complete the function of Elijah, his work was outstandingly successful in other ways. His mission was to prepare people to be ready and waiting to recognize the Messiah once He was known, and anyone baptised by John was promising they would accept whoever John told them was the Messiah, which we can see from various verses.

> Luke 7:29 And all the people that heard him [Jesus], and the publicans, justified God, being baptised with the baptism of John.

We see here that the common people who had believed John later believed Jesus, and the Pharisees who rejected John, rejected Jesus.

> Luke 7:30 But the Pharisees and lawyers rejected the counsel of God against themselves, being not baptised of him.

In rejecting John the Pharisees were just like spoilt children who insisted that everybody should do things their way.

> Luke 7:31-32 And the Lord said, Whereunto then shall I liken the men of this generation? And to what are they like? They are like unto children sitting in the marketplace, and calling one to another, and saying, We have piped unto you, and ye have not danced; we have mourned to you, and ye have not wept.

John refused to dance to their tune, he rejected the oral law of the Pharisees and they rejected him because he would not do things their way. However, that was not the reason they gave for rejecting him.

> Matthew 11:18-19 For John came neither eating nor drinking, and they say, He hath a devil. The Son of man came eating and

drinking, and they say, Behold a man gluttonous, and winebibber [drunkard], a friend of publicans and sinners.

John was known for fasting and refusing to drink alcohol because he was a Nazirite from the time he was born,[9] and they used that as a starting point to reject him. Jesus, on the other hand did not fast and He drank alcohol, and that was their basis for rejecting Him, so whatever anyone did the Pharisees would not let them win unless they were Pharisees. But the actual reason they gave for rejecting John was, "He hath a devil," that he was demon possessed.

To repeat briefly what we have learned, John was rejected because he would not do things the way the Pharisees said they should be done, that was the real reason for his rejection, but the reason they gave was that John was possessed by a demon, and remember what happens to John will later happen to Jesus.

[1] Luke 1:76

[2] Matthew 11:7

[3] Matthew 3:7

[4] Matthew 11:8

[5] Matthew 11:9

[6] Matthew 11:9-10

[7] Colossians 1:18

[8] Malachi 4:5-6

[9] Luke 1:15

JESUS CURSED THREE CITIES IN GALILEE
Matthew 11:20-30

Doomed For Not Believing In Jesus

> Matthew 11:20 Then he [Jesus] began to upbraid [reprimand] the cities wherein most of his mighty works were done, because they repented not.

He cursed Chorazin, Bethsaida[1] and Capernaum,[2] three important Galilean cities where most of His miracles were performed because they refused to believe in Him. The Bible records some miracles in Bethsaida and Capernaum, but there is nothing about Jesus even being in Chorazin except that He said He had performed many miracles there. This is because the four Gospel writers only wrote down a brief and selective account of what happened and even though Chorazin was one of the three towns where most of His miracles took place not even one is recorded.

The people of these three towns will be punished in Hell more harshly than people of some other towns where Jesus did not go and perform miracles. Everyone who does not believe in Jesus will end up in the lake of fire[3] but those of us who have been brought up in Christian countries or in Christian families and have been told what Jesus has done for us, and perhaps have even seen His miracles, and still refuse to believe, will suffer more in Hell, than those that were not given the chance to know about Him, as Jesus explains.

> Matthew 11:21-22 Woe unto thee, Chorazin! Woe unto thee, Bethsaida! For if the mighty works, which were done in you, had been done in Tyre and Sidon, they would have repented long ago in sackcloth and ashes. But I say unto you, It shall be more tolerable for Tyre and Sidon at the day of judgement than for you.

Jesus had even stronger words for Capernaum because that was where He had made His headquarters in the Galilee, and so He says Capernaum had been exalted to heaven, and yet they refused to believe.

> Matthew 11:23-24 And thou, Capernaum, which art exalted unto heaven, shalt be brought down to hell: for if the mighty works, which have been done in thee, had been done in Sodom, it would have remained until this day. But I say unto you, That it shall be more tolerable for the land of Sodom in the day of judgement, than for thee.

Remember, Jesus was performing miracles at this time as a sign to Israel to get them to decide whether He was the Messiah or not, and in the Jewish towns of Chorazin, Bethsaida, and Capernaum particularly, they seem to be making the wrong decision. The three towns that would have accepted Jesus, Tyre, Sidon and Sodom, were all Gentile towns and this shows that if the Jews reject Jesus, the Gentiles will accept Him. The Jews considered themselves wise regarding the things of God, but were rejected, which leads us into the next point.

The Reason People Did Not Believe Jesus

As Jesus prays it becomes clear why the Jews did not believe in Him.

> Matthew 11:25-26 I thank thee, O Father, Lord of heaven and earth, because thou hast hid these things from the wise and prudent, and hast revealed them unto babes. Even so, Father: for so it seemed good in thy sight.

Jesus shows here the foresight and carefulness of God, so that no one can come to Him unless God draws them,[4] so until God acts they cannot believe. God decides to call simple people first and therefore they believe but the wise do not. The wise who were so proud of their own cleverness could not see the truth, and the very people they thought were simple were given spiritual light.

Jesus Wanted To Teach Them

> Matthew 11:28 Come unto me, all ye that are heavy laden, and I will give you rest.

The heavy-laden were those Jews who were trying to keep all the laws the Pharisees had made up, which are found in the Mishnah.

> Matthew 11:29 Take my yoke upon you, and learn from me.

Jesus is using a Jewish saying of the time which meant to go to school, and he tells them to take His yoke, go to His school not the Pharisees school, and learn from Him, where they will find it easy to enter eternal life, and also enjoy a more restful time on earth.

> Matthew 11:29-30 ... for I am meek and lowly in heart: and ye shall find rest unto your souls. For my yoke is easy, and my burden is light.

[1] Matthew 11:21

[2] Matthew 11:23

[3] Revelation 20:10, 20:15, 21:8

[4] John 6:44

A PROSTITUTE SHOWS HER TREMENDOUS FAITH, LOVE AND THANKS
Luke 7:36-50

Several times we read of Jesus being invited to the home of one Pharisee or another to join them for a meal, but if we examine what happens we discover the Pharisees always had a hidden agenda, a secret plan which was to try and find a reason to reject Jesus. Pretending to be friends they were in fact enemies. One day a Pharisee invited Jesus to join him at his table.

> Luke 7:37-38 And behold, a woman in the city, which was a sinner, when she knew that Jesus sat at meat [food] in the Pharisee's house, brought an alabaster box of ointment, And stood at his feet behind him weeping, and began to wash his feet with tears, and did wipe them with the hairs of her head, and kissed his feet, and anointed them with the ointment.

The gospel writers following Jewish culture did not like to call a woman a whore, or prostitute, which would have been harsh, and often used the word sinner because it was not so disgusting, but we should consider the woman to be a prostitute. If this was not a trap to try to discover a reason to accuse Jesus, how was it so easy for this prostitute to get into the Pharisee's house? The Roman Catholics believe that the woman was Mary Magdalene, but there is nothing to suggest this or even that Mary Magdalene was a prostitute. She did have seven demons cast out of her by Jesus,[1] but there is not the slightest suggestion in the Bible that she was ever a prostitute, although the Latin tradition is that this is who the woman was.

We are sure that the woman believed in Jesus because of the way she worshipped Him. My heart is stirred by her crying, so many tears that they wet His feet, tears of thankfulness and uncontrollable joy. She took a whole box of expensive perfume and lavishly poured it on His feet, kissing them and wiping them with her hair and crying, but the Pharisee's cold heart was not moved by her tremendous love.

> Luke 7:39 Now when the Pharisee which had bidden [invited] him saw it, he spake [spoke] within himself, saying, This man, if he were a prophet, would have known who and what manner of woman this is that toucheth him: for she is a sinner.

The Pharisee reasoned to himself that Jesus could not possibly be the Messiah because He was associating so closely with a woman from the bottom class of society, and that even if He was a prophet, something less than Messiah, He would not allow the woman to touch even his feet in the way she was doing. We must certainly wonder, in the light of the Pharisee's thoughts, how the woman got into his house in the first place, unless it was all part of a plan to test the behaviour of Jesus, and try to find fault with Him, to find some reason to reject Him.

The Pharisee, named Simon, kept his thoughts to himself, but Jesus had read his mind and told Simon what he had been thinking, which proved to Simon that Jesus was indeed a prophet, something Simon had just decided He was not. Jesus then told Simon a story to show why the woman showed so much love. In the story two men borrowed money from the same lender, one a small sum and the other a very large amount but when they could not pay him back he forgave them both. Jesus asked Simon which of the two men would love the lender the most.

> Luke 7:43 Simon answered and said, I suppose that he, to whom he forgave the most. And he said unto him, Thou hast rightly judged.

The more we are forgiven the more we love the person that forgives us and Jesus having got Simon to agree to this then brought his attention back to the woman, by saying, "Seest thou this woman?" He then compared the way the woman had been treating Him with the way Simon had treated Him.

> Luke 7:44-46 [44] I entered into thine house, thou gavest me no water for my feet: but she hath washed my feet with tears, and wiped them with the hairs of her head.
>
> [45] Thou gavest me no kiss: but this woman since the time I came in hath not ceased to kiss my feet.
>
> [46] My head with oil thou didst not anoint: but this woman hath anointed my feet with ointment.

It was the custom of those days, as a matter of common courtesy, to provide guests with water to wash the dust of the streets from their feet, to give the Middle East kiss of greeting and to provide anointing oil for their head. Simon the Pharisee did none of these things showing that his invitation to Jesus had not been genuine but that he had an underhand reason for asking Jesus to come.

The conclusion Jesus gives in Luke 7:47-50 is so precious to us who have faith and believe.

> Luke 7:47 Wherefore I say unto thee, Her sins, which are many, are forgiven; for she loved much: but to whom little is forgiven, the same loveth little.

The reason Simon treated Jesus so poorly was because he had not been forgiven, since Pharisees thought they were righteous and did not see any need to be pardoned for anything. On the other hand the woman knew she had sinned and that she had been forgiven, and was generous and genuine in showing her love.

> Luke 7:48 And he said unto her, Thy sins are forgiven.

Did you know that **only** God can forgive sins? The friends of the Pharisee certainly knew it.

> Luke 7:49 And they that sat at meat with him began to say within themselves, Who is this that forgiveth [forgives] sins also?

There are two possible answers to their question, either Jesus was speaking wickedly, He was blaspheming, or He is God, He is the Messiah, just as He kept telling them and showing by the many signs and wonders that He performed. Next Jesus made it clear **exactly** why her sins were forgiven.

> Luke 7:50 And he said to the woman, Thy faith hath saved thee; go in peace.

Her belief that He was the Messiah with the power to forgive sins, and her faith that He had forgiven her, had saved her. Washing His feet with her tears, the expensive perfume, and the kisses were only outward signs of the love she had for Him because of what she already knew, but they were not what saved her.

[1] Mark 16:9

MESSIAH'S THIRD MAJOR PREACHING TOUR
Luke 8:1-3

On this tour Jesus took all the recently chosen twelve apostles, many rich women who were supporting Him with their own money, plus a large crowd of followers. Again it is Luke who gives us the most information about the women in the life and ministry of Jesus.

THE UNFORGIVABLE SIN (THE UNPARDONABLE SIN)
Matthew 12:22-37, Mark 3:20-30

Matthew has the most to say about the unforgivable sin and we will be looking mainly in his gospel, but there are two things mentioned by Mark that Matthew left out.

> Mark 3:21 And when his friends heard of it, they went out to lay hold on him: for they said, He is beside himself.

A very important time in the teaching of Jesus had arrived, He was not behaving the same as before, but His friends did not understand that He was about to reach a turning point in His dealing with the Jewish leaders. His enthusiasm was high, they knew something different was happening and thought He needed their protection because He was acting strangely, and they said, "He is beside himself."

> Mark 3:22 And the scribes who came down from Jerusalem.

If you or I had written this verse we would have said, "And the scribes who came up (not down) from Jerusalem," because when we look at the map, the Galilee is north of Jerusalem, but Jerusalem is on a hill and no matter which direction they approached the city, the Jews always went up to Jerusalem, or they came down from it, and Mark uses here a very Jewish way of writing. The point is that the scribes had finished the interrogation stage in examining the claims of Jesus to be the Messiah, they had made up their minds and had come from Jerusalem to announce the decision of the Jewish religious leaders.

Rejected Of Men (Isaiah 53:3 – written by Isaiah 700 years before it happened)

In Matthew 12:22 Jesus cast a demon out of a blind man who was also dumb, healing the man completely so that he could see and speak. It was not unusual for demons to be cast out of people in Israel at that time, the Pharisees, rabbis and their students did it. Later in verse 27 Jesus confronted them with His question, "by whom do your children cast them out?" You will know the Jews had already noticed that the way the Pharisees and Jesus cast out demons was different. The rabbis cast out demons in three stages. First the exorcist would engage the demon in conversation, the demon spoke using the voice box of the person he was controlling. Secondly he would find out the demon's name, and finally using the demon's name he would order him to leave. We will see Jesus using the same method later, but He usually ignored the rabbis ritual and just ordered the demon's out.

The Pharisees could not cast out a demon from a person who could not speak because there was no way to have a conversation with it, and they could not find out its name. Long before Jesus arrived among them, the Pharisees had taught that although they could not cast out a demon from a mute person, when the Messiah arrived, He would cast out dumb demons, and here we have the second of the Messianic miracles. The first was healing a Jewish leper, and the second is the exorcism of a dumb demon. It was understood by those people watching Jesus cast out the dumb demon, that only the Messiah could work such a miracle, and that is the reason events unfolded the way Matthew tells us, beginning in the following verse.

> Matthew 12:23 And all the people were amazed, and said, Is not this the son of David?

The son of David, is a title of the Messiah, and what the people were saying was, "Is He the Messiah?" Previously when Jesus cast out demons they had asked by what "authority" He had cast them out, but when it was a dumb demon the question changed to, "Is He the Messiah?" It was the right question, and the Pharisees they trusted to answer it had to advise them one way or the other, either, "Yes, He is the Messiah," or, "No, He is not." If they said Jesus was not the Messiah, they would have to explain how He could perform miracles that they themselves had been teaching only the Messiah would be able to do. The answer they gave was a deliberate falsehood intended to make the people reject Jesus and trust them, the lying religious leaders. The scribes said that Jesus Himself was possessed by a demon, not a normal demon but Beelzebub the prince of demons, and that is how He could perform all the Messianic signs.

The name Beelzebub came from Beelzebul, a god of the Ekronites, meaning the god of the royal palace. God had finally put a stop to the Jews worshipping other gods by exiling them to Babylon, a huge city built to honour false gods. Babylon was dedicated to idol worship and after being in captivity there for seventy years the Jews that returned to Jerusalem did not worship idols again. They started making fun of all those so called gods which included changing the sound at the end of Beelzebul from 'bul' to 'bub.' In Hebrew the meaning then was not, god of the royal palace, but god of the flies, god of the smelly dung heap, where all the disease carrying flies were, the demon in charge of diseases.

The question again was, "Is not this the son of David?"

> Matthew 12:24 But when the Pharisees heard it they said, This fellow doth not cast out devils, but by Beelzebub the prince of devils.

It was an atrocious lie but that was how the Pharisees explained that Jesus was not the Messiah, even though He could perform miracles they said only the Messiah was supposed to do. Nowhere in the Bible or in the writings of the Jewish rabbis does it suggest that Jesus did not perform His miracles, there were so many witnesses who saw the miracles that they did not try to deny them as actual facts, but in the Bible and other Jewish writings they say that the miracles were done by the power of demons. The official reason given for rejecting Jesus as the Messiah by the Jewish religious leaders was, and still is, that He was demon possessed. The real reason they rejected Him is because He insisted on keeping to the word of God from the Old Testament, and refused to do things their way.

How Jesus Answered His Accusers

Jesus replied to the wicked lie of the religious leaders with four truthful points, the first of which was also a prophecy about how the destruction of Jerusalem would take place forty years later when it was destroyed by the Roman army under the command of Titus Flavius Vespasianus in AD 70. The reason for the fall of city was that the Jewish soldiers inside were in three groups under three leaders, and these

Zealots fought amongst themselves, not having one person in charge of their campaign like the Romans had for their attack under Titus. The Romans when they had got into the city killed and killed until there was no one left alive to kill, not a soldier, child, woman or any civilian, after that they were still angry and destroyed the buildings including the Temple. As we read the New Testament we will see from His prophecies that Jesus knew exactly what was going to happen to Jerusalem, the Jews and their beloved Temple. Anyway back to the story.

> Matthew 12:25-26 And Jesus knew their thoughts, and said unto them, Every kingdom divided against itself is brought to desolation; and every city or house divided against itself shall not stand. And if Satan cast out Satan, he is divided against himself; how shall then his kingdom stand?

Firstly then their accusation that Jesus cast out demons by the prince of demons is nonsense because that would mean there was division in Satan's kingdom, and utter chaos in his house.

Secondly the Pharisees had been teaching for years that to be able to cast out demons was a gift from God, and to accuse Jesus of casting them out by Satan means that their own house is divided against itself, some saying exorcism is a gift of God and others a gift from Satan.

> Matthew 12:27 And if I by Beelzebub cast out devils, by whom do your children cast them out? Therefore they shall be your judges.

Third, the miracle proves to them without doubt that Jesus is the Messiah.

> Matthew 12:28 But if I cast out devils by the Spirit of God, then the kingdom of God is come unto you.

Finally casting out the blind and dumb demon shows that Jesus can tie Satan up in knots and is stronger than Satan.

> Matthew 12:29 Or else how can one enter into a strong man's house, and spoil his goods, except he first bind the strong man? And then he will spoil his house.

The Judgement

Jesus then announced God's judgement on that generation of Israel because of their special sin, the unpardonable sin of blasphemy or insulting the Holy Spirit. Jesus says that their sin is unforgivable and because that is so, no matter what happens from now on judgement is certain.

> Matthew 12:31 All manner of sin and blasphemy shall be forgiven unto men: but the blasphemy against the Holy Ghost shall not be forgiven unto men.

The judgement came 40 years later with the destruction of Jerusalem and the Temple by the Romans, and that was the end of the matter. Some Christians are still concerned that they might commit the unpardonable sin, but they are not seeing the context in which it was made, so what was it?

THE UNFORGIVABLE SIN WAS THE REJECTION BY ISRAEL AS A NATION, OF JESUS AS THE MESSIAH WHILE HE WAS STILL WITH THEM, FOR THE UNTRUTHFUL REASON THAT HE WAS DEMON POSSESSED. Remember that definition while we look into some other aspects of what the unforgivable sin is, and is not.

First and foremost the unforgivable sin is a national sin only, it is not a personal sin. Many, many Jews of the time escaped the judgement that came upon Jerusalem as you will see later. Also, people could not commit the sin today, because it was not an individual sin anyway. The Bible teaches very clearly that every sin is forgivable to any person who is willing to come to God through the blood of Jesus, every sin, no matter what it is. Jesus died on the cross, not just for some kinds of sin, but so that every kind of sin can be forgiven every person. However, for Israel as a nation it was unpardonable.

It was a special sin that could only be made by that generation of Jews that were alive at the time of Jesus, and later generations of Jews cannot be blamed for it in the way certain denominations have preached. Jesus came physically and visibly to only one Jewish generation, claiming to be their Messiah and King, and offered to establish His kingdom then, and it was this generation that rejected Him. As we continue the story you will see two words repeated many times, "this generation." It is only "this generation" that is guilty of this particular sin.

Thirdly, another country today could not commit this sin because Jesus is not visibly and physically present in any other country, claiming to be that county's Messiah. God has made a covenant with only one nation, Israel, and Jesus is their own Jewish Messiah and King, even if they reject Him, which they do.

Now we will look at two penalties "this generation" of Israel were faced with because of the unforgivable sin. To start with the offer of the Messianic kingdom was immediately withdrawn, and they were without hope of seeing the promise of God established during their life times, but the kingdom will be accepted by a future Jewish generation that will believe in Jesus, at His second coming. Details of the Jews, again living in the land of Israel after the people had been spread all over the world for almost 2,000 years (plus I don't know how many more years), that will turn to Jesus at His second coming is given in Matthew 24 and 25.

The other penalty awaiting "this generation" was the divine judgement of destruction, and it was unavoidable. It came, as you already know, forty years later in AD 70, with dreadful slaughter at the fall of Jerusalem, a terrible national punishment. Nothing they did from now on would reduce the price they would have to pay. Later at the triumphal entry of Jesus into Jerusalem before He was crucified, thousands and thousands of people applauded Him as their Messiah, but the response of Jesus was the promise of judgement to come (Luke 19:41-44). Jerusalem would be destroyed and all those within her walls, because her sin had been unforgivable.

THE NEW POLICY REGARDING MIRACLES
Matthew 12:38-45

Only One More Sign For That Generation

After being given such a powerful talking-to by Jesus the Pharisees tried to get some control of their sorry situation, saying, "Master, we would see a sign from thee."[1] The decision had already been made by the religious leaders in Jerusalem to reject Him, and these Pharisees were their willing errand boys in agreement with those higher authorities, but they pretended that His signs had not been enough to convince them that He was the promised Messiah. Their pretence was a sham because ever since Chapter 4, of this book, "How Jesus was Accepted," where He took possession of the Temple in John 2:13-22, at the first Passover, He had performed many more miracles than we have been told about, including miracles that they themselves taught no one except the Messiah could do, and they still rejected Him. Remember also when we studied the first Passover it was the Jews in the Temple that had asked Him to perform these signs,[2] so that they could make a decision. Now they have stated their conclusion, claiming wrongly that He is not the Messiah, but a servant of Satan, and that decision cannot be changed. For that reason Jesus says there will only be one more sign for the nation, the sign of resurrection from the dead, the sign of Jonah.

> Matthew 12:39-40 ³⁹ But he answered and said unto them, An evil and adulterous generation seeketh [looks] after [for] a sign; and there shall no sign be given to it, but the sign of the prophet Jonas:
>
> ⁴⁰ For as Jonas was three days and three nights in the whale's belly; so shall the son of man be three days and three nights in the heart of the earth.

As we read more of the life of Jesus in the gospels after the Jews had rejected Him, we see He performed many, many more miracles, that were nothing to do with the sign of resurrection, and therefore were not signs for the unbelieving Pharisees. What were all these miracles for and why did Jesus perform them? Now that the Jewish leaders had rejected their Messiah, He postponed offering them the kingdom on earth, promised them by God through the prophets in the Old Testament, at this time. If they did not believe in Jesus there were ordinary people among the Jews who would believe in Him together with some Gentiles, including about 2,000 years later Lucy and I, and these believers would receive eternal life. However, Jesus had come to preach only to the Jews, not to the Gentiles.[3] The job of preaching to the Gentiles would be done by His disciples and the early Jewish Church that started in Jerusalem. We Gentiles learned the way to eternal life through the Jewish people. Jesus therefore trained the disciples for their work of preaching the good news after He had been taken back to God, and examples of some of what the disciples did then, are found in the Book of Acts, so His miracles from now on are to train the disciples. For the Jewish nation, from now on there would be no more signs except the sign of Jonah, the sign of resurrection from the dead, and this sign will be given to them three times.

1. The resurrection of Lazarus.[4]
2. The resurrection of Jesus.[5]
3. This will be at the resurrection of the two witnesses after they have prophesied for 1,260 days as we are told in Revelation 11:3-11.

The only sign to be given to Israel will be the sign of resurrection, which they have rejected twice, when Lazarus and Jesus were resurrected, so they had better believe their Messiah the next time they are given their own special sign.

How God Was Going To Judge That Generation

The new reason for miracles has now come into place and Jesus continues His announcement which the Jews interrupted when they asked for more signs. The best thing is to read from the Bible what Jesus said and then consider it carefully.

Matthew 12: 41-45 ⁴¹ The men of Nineveh shall rise up in judgement with this generation, and shall condemn it: because they repented at the preaching of Jonas [Jonah]; and, behold, a greater than Jonas [Jonah] is here.

⁴² The queen of the south shall rise up in the judgement with this generation, and shall condemn it: for she came from the uttermost parts of the earth to hear the wisdom of Solomon; and, behold, a greater than Solomon is here.

⁴³ When the unclean spirit is gone out of a man, he walketh through dry places, seeking rest, and findeth none.

⁴⁴ Then he saith, I will return into my house from whence I came out; and when he is come, he findeth it empty, swept, and garnished [well arranged].

⁴⁵ Then goeth he, and taketh with himself seven other spirits more wicked than himself, and they enter in and dwell there: and the last state of that man is worse than the first. Even so shall it be also with this wicked generation.

Jesus is stressing, this generation; the men of Nineveh will condemn this generation, the Queen of the south will condemn this generation, He is highlighting what is going to happen to this generation, the one that committed the unforgivable sin.

He reminded the Jews that in the Old Testament there were two groups of Gentiles, that had been shown a little spiritual light, the men of Nineveh and the Queen of the south, but when they saw it they responded correctly, they believed. At the great white throne judgement[6] these Gentiles will condemn the Jews of this generation, because they did not believe when they were shown much more spiritual light. Jesus ended His judgement with the story about another kind of demon.

The demon was living in a man and decided to move out and look for a better place to live, but unable to find another place he decided to go back to his old home. After he left no other spirit went into the man, neither a demonic spirit nor the Holy Spirit, and so he found his old home swept clean and empty. He decided not to live there alone, but took seven other spirits with him, more wicked than himself, so that he would not be lonely, and as a result Jesus says, "the last state of that man is worse than the first." To start with the man had only one demon but because he stayed empty he ended up with eight. In this story Jesus stresses something which people often do not notice, "Even so shall it also be with this wicked generation." His illustration was meant for that generation of Jews.

The generation had started when John the Baptist was out in the wilderness, preaching and preparing his followers to accept Jesus as the Messiah, and by way of John's preaching that generation was swept clean, or made ready to receive Jesus. But because they rejected the Son of God, they stayed empty and because they were empty their last condition would become much worse than their first.

At the time John began preparing his followers in the desert, the nation was under Roman control and had to pay taxes to Rome. The Romans were not out to destroy the Jews, but spent money on improving roads, water supplies, shipping ports and other buildings, and their army provided protection. Jerusalem, so precious to Israel was standing, and their splendid Temple built by Herod was operating magnificently in all its glory, while under the Sanhedrin, Israel had a measure of self government, but it was not to last. Forty years after Jesus had spoken the Roman legions invaded and laid siege to the city. After two years they destroyed Jerusalem and the Temple not leaving one stone upon another, and the Jews that were not killed were scattered all over the world, so that the last condition of that generation was worse than at first. Today the lesson is that people who receive the light of the gospel of Jesus Christ and reject it will suffer serious consequences, but it is up to each one of us.

[1] Matthew 12:38

[2] John 2:18

[3] Matthew 15:24

[4] John 11:1-53

[5] Matthew 28:1-10, Mark 16:1-9, Luke 24:1-9, John 20:1-18

[6] Revelation 20:11-15

THE REJECTED KING REVEALS A MYSTERY
Matthew 8:24-34, 9:27-34, 12:46 to 13:52, Mark 3:31 to 5:43, Luke 8:4-56

A Very Important Turning Point

Mark 3:21 spoke about the friends of Jesus going out to take custody of Him, because they said, "He is beside Himself." The word translated into friends here can also be translated as, people, relatives or kinsmen, and in verse 31 His mother and brothers arrived to take charge of Him, but we will continue the story from Matthew.

> Matthew 12:47-50 [47] Then one said unto him, Behold, thy mother and thy brethren stand without, desiring to speak with thee.
>
> [48] But he answered and said unto him that told him, Who is my mother? And who are my brethren?
>
> [49] And he stretched forth his hand towards his disciples, and said, Behold my mother and my brethren!
>
> [50] For whosoever shall do the will of my Father which is in heaven, the same is my brother, and sister, and mother.

Jesus now refused to accept any earthly blood relationships, and only recognized spiritual relationships such as those He had with His disciples. The Pharisees claimed to be fit for heaven because of their blood relationship going back to Abraham, but only the spiritual seed of Abraham, those who like Abraham believe God, will get in.

Next Jesus made some important changes in His teaching programme in the areas of, the miracles, the message and the way He taught. We have already learnt that the miracles are no longer for Israel to make a decision, they have done that, but they are to train the disciples. When Jesus performed signs before, He did not call for faith first. At the Pool of Bethesda the man that was restored to health did not even know who Jesus was and did not ask to be healed.[1] Now faith will be necessary before a miracle is performed plus a personal need.

Previously after performing healing, He always told the person to go and tell what God had done. After He had cured the leper, He sent him to the priests to make the sacrifice Moses commanded, "For a testimony unto them."[2] Now He tells the Jews he heals, not to tell anyone what God has done for them. In the case of Gentiles it will be different, and they are even asked to go and tell people what God has done for them, but for the signs performed among the Jews the change is from, spread the news, to, keep it secret.

Jesus and the disciples had gone all over Israel from city to city and from synagogue to synagogue publicly announcing that He was the Messiah, but after the Jewish leaders committed the unforgivable sin there was a change in the message being preached, the disciples being forbidden to tell anyone that He was the Messiah. After Matthew 16:16, where Peter says to Jesus, "Thou art the Christ, the Son of the living God," the disciples were told in verse 20, not to tell anyone, and until the Great Commission in Matthew 28:18-20, they had to keep His identity secret.

The change in the way Jesus taught after the unforgivable sin is enormously significant, because He had been teaching in ways the people clearly understood, as we learned in the Sermon on the Mount, where it was explained how they recognized His teaching was different from the scribes and Pharisees. From now on He would only teach in parables, and notice the timing.

> Matthew 13:1 The same day ...

On the day the unforgivable sin was committed, the same day the nation rejected Him.

> Matthew 13:3 And he spake [spoke] many things unto them in parables, ...

Why do you think He spoke to the crowds in parables?

> Matthew 13:10 And the disciples came, and said unto him, Why speakest thou unto them in parables?

Jesus gave three reasons why He spoke in parables. The first reason was for the disciples, to teach them about the mystery kingdom, because later on after the crucifixion, they would establish the Church.

> Matthew 13:11 And he answered and said unto them, Because it is given unto you to know the mysteries of the kingdom of heaven.

The second reason is to keep the people at large from learning the mysteries of the kingdom. They could hear the message but were not meant to understand, because the truth had been preached to them and they had, had enough time to accept it but their response had been the unforgivable sin, and they simply could never be forgiven, "but whosoever speaketh against the Holy Ghost, it shall not be forgiven him."[3]

> Matthew 13:11-13 ... but to them it is not given.
>
> [12] For whosoever hath, to him shall be given, and he shall have more abundance: but whosoever hath not, from him shall be taken away even that he hath.
>
> [13] Therefore speak I to them in parables: because they seeing see not; and hearing they hear not, neither do they understand.

At least 700 years before Jesus, Isaiah, (Esaias, in the KJV version of the New Testament), had prophesied in Isaiah 6:9-10, exactly what was going to happen now, that the people would see and hear but not understand and their hearts would not be healed, so the third reason Jesus spoke to the people in parables was because Isaiah's prophecy had to be fulfilled.

> Matthew 13:14-17 [14]And in them is fulfilled the prophecy of Esaias, which saith, By hearing ye shall hear, and shall not understand; and seeing ye shall see, and shall not perceive:
>
> [15] For this people's heart is waxed gross, and their ears are dull of hearing, and their eyes they have closed; lest at any time

they should see with their eyes, and hear with their ears, and should understand with their heart, and should be converted, and I should heal them.

¹⁶ But blessed are your eyes, for they see: and your ears, for they hear.

¹⁷ For verily [truly] I say unto you, That many prophets and righteous men have desired to see those things which ye see, and have not seen them; and to hear those things which ye hear, and have not heard them.

Only Believers Can Enter The Spiritual Kingdom

Matthew 13:34 All these things spake Jesus unto the multitude in parables; and without a parable spake [spoke] he not unto them.

This scripture would not have been true before the unforgivable sin but from now on it will be true. From this time forward whenever Jesus teaches in public He will always speak in parables that they cannot understand, but Mark adds an aspect of Christ's teaching which Matthew omitted.

Mark 4:33-34   ³³ And with many such parables spake he the word unto them, as they were able to hear it.

³⁴ But without a parable spake he not unto them: and when they were alone, he expounded all things to his disciples.

The teaching of Jesus from this day forward will be in parables that the people will not understand, but later when He is alone with His disciples He will explain the meaning of the parables carefully, because they are the ones He is training in the truth. It is a very crucial turning point, in preparation for the second half of His campaign, for the events yet to take place in the Book of Acts, for the Church, the body of Christ to get started, and for the history of the Jews over the next 2,000 years.

A parable is a way of teaching or illustrating a spiritual or moral truth, based on reality from everyday life. For example, in the parable of the Good Samaritan the truth was pointed out through something that had actually happened. The reason Jesus preached the nine parables that we are going to examine next, and later explained them to His disciples, was to instruct them about God's kingdom plan, but before we study the parables concerned, we must find out what the kingdom of God is.

Two terms used in the Bible are, "the kingdom of God," and, "the kingdom of heaven," and some teachers have tried to tell us the difference between the two, but actually they are the same thing. Matthew only spoke about the kingdom of heaven, but he meant the kingdom of God. We can see this by comparing parallel scriptures from the gospels of Matthew, Mark and Luke.

> Matthew 13:11 Because it is given unto you to know the mysteries of the kingdom of heaven.
>
> Mark 4:11 Unto you it is given to know the mystery of the kingdom of God.
>
> Luke 8:10 Unto you it is given to know the mysteries of the kingdom of God.

Mark and Luke talk about the kingdom of God, while Matthew talks about the kingdom of heaven, but it is absolutely clear that they are all talking about the same kingdom.

The reason Matthew uses "heaven" is because he is writing to Jews, and back then and even now the Jews never use God's name anymore, although it was used by the Jewish writers of the Old Testament. At the time of Jesus and still today they will call God, "Adonai" meaning Lord, and some of them won't even use that, using "Hashamayim" – the heaven. Matthew writing to his Jewish audience would have been aware of their ways and not wanting to cause offence, spoke of the kingdom of heaven, but he meant the kingdom of God.

Five Parts Of God's Kingdom

Although the terms, "kingdom of heaven" and "kingdom of God" mean the same, and there is no variation between them, there are five segments of God's kingdom, and when people talk about the kingdom of God, we need to understand which aspect they are talking about, because there are differences. God's kingdom is something He rules over or will rule over, so let's look at the five areas of His rule.

God rules over all of His creation, and Bible scholars call this the Universal Kingdom or the Eternal Kingdom. Universal because God controls the entire universe, and eternal because He is always in control. Nothing occurs in the entire universe ever, unless it is the will of God, either He has ordered it, or allowed it, and whatever takes place anywhere is the will of God. He is in complete control of His creation.[4]

God also rules the hearts of people that believe in Jesus, and scholars call this the Spiritual Kingdom, which includes all Christians that have been born again through the work of the Holy Spirit. There have always been men and women ruled by God that because of faith in Him were careful to be obedient. Between Acts 2, when the Holy Spirit was poured out on the believers and the Church was established, and the snatching away of the Church from the earth to heaven, which will happen in a moment of time,[5] the Spiritual Kingdom and the Church are the same thing, because all believers are part of the Church and they are in the Spiritual Kingdom. However, there is much, much more to the Spiritual Kingdom than the Church, because the Spiritual Kingdom was there long before the Church started, and it will last forever, but the Church will not.[6]

The Jews are special because they were chosen by God to be ruled by Him. The government of Israel by God began with Moses, a man God used as His first go-between or judge. The last judge was Samuel, and God used him to introduce a new form of go-between, the kings of Israel. Samuel the last judge anointed Saul as the first king of Israel but he was disobedient to God, so Samuel then anointed David as king, a man after God's own heart.[7] The descendants of David ruled in Jerusalem until the time of Zedekiah, when Jerusalem was destroyed by the Babylonians and Israel was taken captive in 586 BC. A kingdom ruled by God is called a theocracy, and His rule over Israel is called the Theocratic Kingdom. It lasted from Moses to Zedekiah and you can read about it in the Bible beginning in Exodus 20, and ending with, 2 Chronicles 36.

The rule of Jesus on earth from Jerusalem, which will take place after His second coming, is called the Messianic Kingdom, because that is when the Jewish people will be ruled by their Messiah. It is also called the Millennial Kingdom because it will last for 1,000 years.[8] Most Jews call it the Messianic Kingdom since their Messiah will be on the throne, and most Christians call it the Millennial Kingdom as it will last for a millennium. There are many Bible prophecies about the Messianic Kingdom, such as, 2 Samuel 7:8-17, 1 Chronicles 17:10-15 and Luke 1:32, but by far the most are in the Old Testament promising the Jews that their Messiah will rule from David's throne.[9] It was this kingdom that John the Baptist and Jesus proclaimed was at hand in Matthew 3:2, 4:17 and 10:5-7. If the Jews had not rejected Jesus this is the kingdom that would have been established for them then, about 2,000 years ago, but because they rejected their Messiah, the establishment of the Millennial Kingdom was postponed until their Messiah comes back a second time.

Some people believe that if Israel had accepted Jesus at His first coming He would not have died, but that is quite wrong. The Messiah had to die because He is the Lamb of God, that had to be sacrificed, in order that our sins could be covered over with His blood,[10] and it made no difference whether Israel accepted Him or not, He would still have had to die. Sinners cannot come into the presence of God the Father, because He is holy, but believers will live with Him forever in the holy place because although we have sinned, we will be given holiness as a gift. On the cross Jesus was made sin that we might be made righteous, with the righteousness of God.[11]

Suppose Israel had made Jesus King, then the reaction of Rome would have been to crucify Him, as they would have seen it as a political challenge to their rule. The difference would have come at His resurrection three days later when the Roman empire would have been brought to nothing and the Messianic Kingdom would have begun. Now the kingdom has been delayed but it will come as Jesus told His disciples it would.

> Matthew 24:14 And this gospel of the kingdom shall be preached in all the world for a witness unto all nations; and then shall the end come.

The fifth part of the kingdom of God came into existence because the Jews rejected Jesus as King. Known as the Mystery Kingdom, it does not appear in the Old Testament and so its establishment was not foreseen. Mystery, in the New Testament does not denote something strange or inexplicable in the way the word is used today in the English language, but it means something not found in the Old Testament that is revealed for the first time in the New. Look at the way the apostle Paul used the word, "mystery."

> Ephesians 3:3-5 ³ How that by revelation he [God] made known unto me the mystery; (as I wrote afore in few words,
>
> ⁴ Whereby, when ye read, ye may understand my knowledge in the mystery of Christ)
>
> ⁵ Which in other ages was not made known unto the sons of men, as it is now revealed unto his holy apostles and prophets by the Spirit.

Paul is telling us about something that is being exposed for the first time which he calls a mystery and the following passage emphasises that the revelation is being made for the first time.

> Ephesians 3:9-10 ⁹ And to make all men see what is the fellowship of the mystery, which from the beginning of the world hath been hid in God, who created all things by Jesus Christ:
>
> ¹⁰ To the intent that now unto the principalities and powers in the heavenly places might be made known by the church the manifold wisdom of God.

It was something hidden in God for ages, now being revealed by God through the apostles and prophets. The name, Mystery Kingdom, comes from these verses in Ephesians, and from the words of Jesus, Himself.

> Mark 4:11 And he said unto them [His disciples], Unto you it is given to know the mystery of the kingdom of God: but to them that are without, all these things are done in parables.

The Mystery Kingdom was born when the Messiah was rejected and it will last until He comes again to set up the promised Millennial Kingdom. It is the rule of Jesus on the earth while He is in heaven seated at God's right hand,[12] and to some extent it includes everyone that lives as a Christian whether they are born again or not. It is not pure honest to goodness Christianity, but it is Christendom as a whole, including so-called Christian people, so-called Christian churches where ever they may be, and so-called Christian countries. It has several distinctive features when compared with other aspects of the Kingdom of God.

1. The Mystery Kingdom is not the same as the Universal Kingdom because it will not last forever, it is not eternal. Having begun with Israel's rejection of their Messiah, it will end when they accept Him.
2. It is not the same as the Spiritual Kingdom because it includes believers and unbelievers. Jesus speaking in a parable called the believers wheat, and the unbelievers tares.[13]
3. It differs from the Theocratic Kingdom because it is not just God's rule over Israel, but includes Gentiles as well as Jews.
4. This Mystery Kingdom is not the same as the Church, although the Church is in it, in fact it is not Christianity, but everyone beneath the umbrella of Christianity.[14]
5. It cannot be mistaken for the Messianic Kingdom because Jesus is not ruling it from David's throne and also the Messianic Kingdom, with so many prophecies about it in the Old Testament, is not a mystery.

The Nine Parables That Jesus Used To Explain The Mystery Kingdom To His Disciples And To Hide It From The Jews

The parables were not meant to be interpreted from every single detail in the story, but from some central points which we will now examine regarding the Mystery Kingdom. You should take your Bible and read at least one of the gospel accounts for each of the following nine parables.

The Parable Of The Sower, Matthew 13:3-23, Mark 4:2-20, Luke 8:4-15

Jesus explained this parable very carefully to His disciples, because being the first one it had some dominant ideas or motifs that would apply to the other parables He was going to preach later, and they would be able to understand all of them if they clearly knew the meaning of this one. Obviously the parable speaks of a sower, and Matthew 13:37, identifies the sower of the good seed as the Son of Man, Jesus. The seed that Jesus sowed was the Word of God and this seed would be sown in all the world (Matthew 24:14). The Word is preached or sown among people. Individuals respond to the Word in different ways as Jesus prophesied they would in the parable.

Mark 4:13 And he said unto them, Know ye not this parable? And how then will ye know all parables?

Consequently, Jesus explained this parable in order that they would understand all the others. The parable of the sower tells us several facts about the Mystery Kingdom.

- ❖ During the time of the kingdom the gospel seed will be sown.
- ❖ The soil in which the seed is planted will be prepared in different ways.
- ❖ There will be opposition to the kingdom from the devil, the flesh and the world.
- ❖ There will be four different responses to the gospel.

1. Some seed will fall by the wayside and the birds will eat it, showing us that certain people that hear the gospel will not believe it.
2. Other seed will fall among rocks where there is little soil so it will not grow well. Here Jesus is talking about people that believe the gospel but their roots do not go down deeply into the Word of God, and they never mature or produce as they should.
3. Then there will be seeds that fall among thorns in thorny ground. The thorny ground stands for people who also believe and take root, meaning they may have a good knowledge of Scripture, unlike those corresponding to the rocky places, but they do not live their lives as they know they should. The cares of the world have too much of a pull on them and their Christian life becomes choked, and therefore they also do not produce as they should. A good knowledge of Scripture is of no use if we do not apply it in our daily living.
4. Finally there will be the seed sown in good ground, representing people that believe, become deeply rooted in the Word of God and live according to the Word and produce a good crop. Not all these produce at the same rate, some yield 30 times as much seed, some 60 times and some 100 times, but they all reproduce a worthwhile harvest.

The Parable Of The Seed That Grows Inexplicably, Mark 4:26-29

The meaning of the parable is that the seed that is sown grows by itself, bursting mysteriously into life. The gospel message is three simple truths, Jesus died for our sins, He was buried and He rose again.[15] How can we explain the way such a simple message, when believed gives us eternal life? The seed strangely comes to life and we cannot explain it. Notice that after sowing the seed the sower did nothing else, having preached the word the rest was out of his control.

The Parable Of The Tares, Matthew 13:24-30 and 36-43

The tares in this parable are a tall strong grass, now rare in England, called Darnel, that used to grow in wheat fields, in those days when cereal crops were heavily contaminated with many weeds. Darnel was a grass very much like wheat and was often not noticed until just before harvest time because it developed a different seed head to wheat.

Matthew 7:16 Ye shall know them by their fruits.

Until the ears or seed heads develop, Darnel looks very much like wheat. The lessons from the parable are strikingly accurate of Christendom today and at the coming judgement.

- There will be true sowing and false sowing.
- The true and the false will both grow together, side by side.
- There will be a judgement when the Mystery Kingdom comes to an end, and the wheat will go into the Messianic Kingdom, but not the tares. The Messianic Kingdom is pictured as the barn where the wheat is stored, and Hell is pictured as fire where the tares will be burned. (John the Baptist also preached about the Messianic Kingdom, the one that was postponed when the Jews rejected their King, and he also described it as the place where the wheat would be stored, and Hell as the fire where the chaff would be burned.[16])
- Each sowing will be made known by its fruitfulness or unfruitfulness.

The Parable Of The Mustard Seed, Matthew 13:31-32

In the parable Jesus says that the mustard seed, "is the least of all the seeds." He did not mean that there were no seeds smaller than a mustard seed, because there were and there are. He was using a common comparative saying of the time about seeds, it was said to be less than all the seeds. In the parable, the mustard seed, which would normally grow as big as a small bush, grew into something astonishing, a monstrous tree where the birds came to rest, but what did it mean?

- The Mystery Kingdom will grow and grow until it reaches a monstrous size.
- The monstrosity will become attractive to birds that will rest in its branches. Going back to the first parable, the birds were working for Satan, so these birds are unclean. In Christendom's massive tree there is so much that is false, like cultic groups that claim to be Christian, such as Jehovah's Witness, Christian Science, Mormonism and many more, which are all the birds in the tree.

The Parable Of The Leaven, Matthew 13:33, Luke 13:21

The parable of the leaven is about a woman who puts leaven in three different mixtures of flour, and each mixture had a different amount of leaven to the other two. A woman is often used symbolically in the Bible, but she does not always represent the same thing. One thing she commonly represents is false religion, and examples are, Jezebel in Revelation 2:20, and the Great Harlot in Revelation 17:1-8. Leaven when used in the Bible is always used symbolically and it always signifies sin. In the four gospels of the New Testament it stands for just one sin, false doctrine, meaning that what is taught is not true. Jesus used this parable to warn us of two dangers.

- Lying teachers will gain access to the Mystery Kingdom and false religions will be thought to be good by many. People who do not read and learn from the Bible are the ones that will be easily tricked.
- The three measures of flour coincide with the three major Christian groups, Catholicism, Eastern Orthodoxy and Protestantism, all of which teach false doctrine, some more some less.

The Parable Of The Hidden Treasure, Matthew 13:44

Exodus 19:5, Deuteronomy 14:2 and Psalm 135:4 in the Old Testament teach us that treasure is sometimes a symbol for Israel, the

Jews are God's special treasure. The parable means that there will be believing Jews in the Mystery Kingdom.

The Parable Of The Pearl Of Great Price, Matthew 13:45-46

The Old Testament does not teach us what a pearl represents but it is probably a symbol for the Gentiles that are in the Mystery Kingdom. Jesus had just spoken about the Jews in the parable of the hidden treasure, and it would be appropriate for Him to say something about the Gentiles as well. Another clue is that pearls come form the sea, and the salt sea is symbolic of the Gentile world as we can see from Daniel 7:1-2, Revelation 17:1 and 17:15. In order that the Gentiles could become members of the Mystery Kingdom the Jews paid a great price, their Messianic Kingdom was postponed for two thousand years or more, Jerusalem and the temple were destroyed, and they were scattered all over the world without a country of their own, persecuted, tortured and killed. More than that, many of them were spiritually hardened or blinded by their God, and this blindness will continue until the full number of the Gentiles have come into the true Church.[17] The parable of the pearl of great price certainly fits with the Gentile entry into the Church.

The Parable Of The Net, Matthew 13:47-50

In this parable Jesus is telling us that when the Mystery Kingdom ends the Gentiles will be judged. We have just learned that the sea symbolizes the Gentile world and now the net is cast into the sea, to catch the Gentiles and hold them for judgement. The King James Bible is a most trustworthy translation of the Word of God, taken from reliable ancient manuscripts, but I want to compare its version of Matthew 13:49 with other translations because the King James in this case is a little misleading.

"So shall it be at the end of the world." KJV.

"So it will be at the end of the age." More than one modern translation uses this wording.

The parable is not talking about the destruction of our planet or the universe but the end of the age we are living in, after which things will be very different in this world of ours. The judgement pictured here is identical with the judgement of the Gentiles in Matthew 25:31-46, where Jesus talks about separating the sheep from the goats. Following the judgement, the righteous Gentiles will go into the Messianic Kingdom and the unrighteous will be thrown into the furnace of fire.

The Parable Of The Householder, Matthew 13:52

The ninth and last parable about the Mystery Kingdom, tells us that there will be some things about it, depicted as old, that are found in other segments of the Kingdom of God. One of these is that some believers will be found there. On the other hand there will be other things about it that are entirely new, but then after all, it is called the Mystery Kingdom isn't it?

The parables are ended but what do they teach us? We can get a picture of the things Jesus prophesied for His people and others in this age of the Mystery Kingdom, by briefly looking at each parable in turn.

1. The Sower. The gospel seed will be sown during the entire age.
2. The Seed Growing By Itself. The seed can grow by itself after planting.
3. The Tares. After the true seed has been sown, others will come along and plant weeds.
4. The Mustard Seed. The Mystery Kingdom will grow into something monstrously large.
5. The Leaven. There will be a great deal of corruption in the kingdom.
6. The Hidden Treasure. God will bring in believing Jews.

7. The Pearl Of Great Price. God will also bring in believing Gentiles.
8. The Net. The consummation of the age will come with the judgement, when the righteous Gentiles will go into the Millennial Kingdom, and the unrighteous will be burned.
9. The Householder. The Mystery Kingdom will have in it a mixture of old and new features.

Living in this age of the Mystery Kingdom, I am often concerned at the way the Bible is trashed, true Christians are ridiculed and the gospel seed they sow is thrown out by the world, particularly when it comes to believing children and their Hell bent educators. Jesus taught us exactly what to do in such a situation, because when the Jews rejected Him, He stopped teaching them, allowing them to follow the path they had chosen for themselves, which led all the way to the everlasting fire. Our job is to sow the gospel seed, and if the person that hears it has been chosen by God, the seed will grow by itself, there will be no need to argue for the truth. The more Jesus proved to the Jews that He was their Messiah the angrier they became, because knowing the truth they did not want to believe it, so I advise my grandchildren not to argue with unbelievers, Jesus didn't.

[1] John 5:1-9
[2] Matthew 8:4
[3] Matthew 12:32
[4] 1 Chronicles 29:11-12, Psalm 10:16, Lamentations 5:19, Daniel 4:17, Acts 17:24
[5] 1 Corinthians 15:48-54, 2 Corinthians 5:1-5
[6] 1 Thessalonians 4:15-18
[7] 1 Samuel 13:14, Acts 13:22
[8] Revelation 20:4-6
[9] Psalms 2, Isaiah 11, Jeremiah 23:5-6, Ezekiel 34:23-31 and 37:24-28, Hosea 3:4-5, Micah 4:6-8, and 5:2, Malachi 3:1-4, etc.
[10] John 1:29, Romans 5:9, Ephesians 1:7, etc.

[11] 2 Corinthians 5:21
[12] Colossians 3:1
[13] Matthew 13:24-30
[14] Matthew 7:22-23
[15] 1 Corinthians 15:1-4
[16] Matthew 3:11-12
[17] Romans 11:25

THE KING'S POWER OVER NATURE
Matthew 8:23-27, Mark 4:35-41, Luke 8:22-25

After postponing the Messianic Kingdom of God, and teaching the disciples about the previously unheard of Mystery Kingdom, through the nine parables we have just studied, Jesus now begins a new set of miracles, and the reason for them is to train His disciples.

Mark 4:35 And the same day, when the even was come, ...

Look what Mark says, "And the same day, when the even was come," the day Jesus was officially rejected, a long and busy day when the unforgivable sin was committed, the day He had announced the Mystery Kingdom, a most important day in world history yet overlooked by historians, towards the end of that day Jesus got into a boat and asked the disciples to take them all across the Sea of Galilee.

Mark 4:35... he saith unto them, Let us pass over unto the other side.

It had been a tiring day and while the boat sailed across the sea, Jesus fell fast asleep,[1] when suddenly they were hit by a fierce life threatening storm. The Sea of Galilee behaves just the same way today, out of the blue very strong winds blow down the mountains on both sides of the lake and the water is abruptly in an absolute turmoil. While Jesus slept, the boat was filling up faster than the disciples could bail the water out.

Mark 4:37 ... and the waves beat into the ship so that it was now full.

It was an unusually violent storm and these experienced fishermen had completely lost control of the situation. Doctor Luke, being a medical man says their lives were in danger.

> Luke 8:23 ... and they were filled with water, and were in jeopardy.

The disciples had done everything that was humanly possible, the boat was full of water and just about to sink, so what did they do?

> Matthew 8:25 Lord, save us: we perish.

> Luke 8:24 Master, master, we perish.

Mark says that they tried to make Him feel guilty because He was not helping.

> Mark 4:38 Master, carest thou not that we perish?

They were all shouting different things at once, but they were all calling to Jesus, and this was the reason for the lesson, to make them depend solidly on Jesus. What do you think Jesus did after they had asked Him to save their lives?

> Mark 4:39 And he arose, and rebuked the wind, and said unto the sea, Peace be still. And the wind ceased, and there was a great calm.

Two miracles happened at once, the wind completely stopped and the sea was absolutely calm. It was not a case of the waves dying down slowly and the wind easing off.

> Mark 4:40-41 [40] And he said unto them, Why are ye so fearful [cowardly]? How is it that ye have no faith?
>
> [41] And they feared [awe, reverence, God fearing] exceedingly.

The miracles remember are to train the disciples, so what did they learn from them.

> Matthew 8:27 But the men marvelled, saying, What manner of man is this, that even the winds and the sea obey him!

The disciples learned on the Sea of Galilee that the wind and the water obey Him.

Luke 8:25 ... He **commandeth** even the winds and water, and they obey him.

The lesson is that Jesus is more than a man, He is the God/man Messiah of Israel, and He proves here that the Pharisees were wrong in saying He was under the authority of Beelzebub (Satan), because angels, authorities and other spiritual powers are under His control.[2] He can instantly control Satan and his wind.

[1] Luke 8:23
[2] 1 Peter 3:22

THE KING'S POWER OVER DEMONS
Matthew 8:28-34, Mark 5:1-20, Luke 8:26-39

Jesus' next lesson is about demons, and He gives it just after He has been accused by the Pharisees of working with the prince of these evil spirits. Mark 5:1-5 gives us a detailed report on demon-possession and the dramatic effect the demon had on the poor man's behaviour. The man was suffering from the most severe degree of demonic control recorded in the entire Bible, and Jesus who had been accused by the Jews of being demonised by Satan himself, confronted this unfortunate human being, and proved that He was stronger than Satan.

According to Mark 5:1 and Luke 8:26, this confrontation took place in Gadarenes, but Matthew 8:28 says it was Gergesenes, and so opponents of the Bible say that the discrepancy shows the story is unreliable. However, they are only showing their ignorance of these places which were not Jewish by the way but were in a Gentile region. Jesus and the disciples had crossed the lake to the Gentile side which was divided up into districts, one of which was Gadara, and there was also a town called Gadara in the district of Gadara, just like New York in America is a city in the state of New York. Just as there are two places called New York, the city and the state, so Gadara was both a district and a city, but the district of Gadara had other cities in it as well as Gadara, and one of these was called Gergesa. Gergesa was in the district of Gadara and so when Matthew emphasises Gergesa he is talking about the city, but all three gospel writers are talking about the district of Gadara. After being rejected by Israel, Jesus went to the city of Gergesa in the district of Gadara and turned his attention to the Gentiles living there.

The demons were speaking to Jesus using the voice of the man they possessed and from Matthew 8:29 we can see they understood two things, first they knew who Jesus was, "What have we to do with thee, Jesus, thou Son of God?" They also knew they were going to everlasting torment after God's judgement, "art thou come hither to torment us before the time?"

Jesus began His exorcism in the traditional Jewish way.

> Mark 5:9 And he [Jesus] asked him, What is thy name? And he answered, saying, My name is Legion: for we are many.

There were between three thousand and six thousand soldiers in a Roman legion, which means there were between 3,000 and 6,000 demons in the two men, (Matthew says two men, but Mark refers to only one of them, the more significant of the two, as will become clear later on), and this is going to show how much stronger Jesus is than Satan and his kingdom. The demons knew they had no chance, that they would be cast out, and were afraid of where Jesus might send them.

> Luke 8:31 And they [the demons] besought him [Jesus] that he would not command them to go out into the deep, [the abyss].

In the middle of the world there is a place called Sheol, in Hebrew, or Hades, in Greek. It is a place that used to have two main sections. The Old Testament tells us that when people died they went to Sheol, it made no difference whether they were good or bad, everyone when he died went to Sheol but not to the same section, because the good went to one side and the bad to the other. The good side of Hades had two names, Paradise and Abraham's bosom, but they both meant the same place, on the good side. The bad side had three subsections of which we will discuss only two, Hell and, the abyss.

The bodies of unbelievers when they died were buried in the ground but their soul went into Hell. The abyss is a prison holding fallen angels and demons temporarily. Revelation 9, tells us that some of them will be freed during the great tribulation to torment unbelieving men and women, that have accepted the mark of the beast. Satan will spend 1,000 years in the abyss, but after that he will be released for a short while,[1] so the abyss is a temporary demonic prison, before their short-term release or their final judgement. The demons are asking Jesus in Luke 8:31, not to command them to go to the abyss.

Jesus teaches us about the situation in Hades as it was before He was crucified, when all the souls of the dead went there, in Luke 16:19-31, and if you haven't read these verses you should read them now. When they died the believer's bodies were buried and their souls went into Abraham's bosom, because although these believers had performed the sacrifices for their sins God required, the blood of animals while it could cover their sins, it could not remove their sins. They were not pure and holy, just like God, and able to enjoy being in close company with Him without feeling guilty or ashamed, only the blood of Jesus could work that miracle.

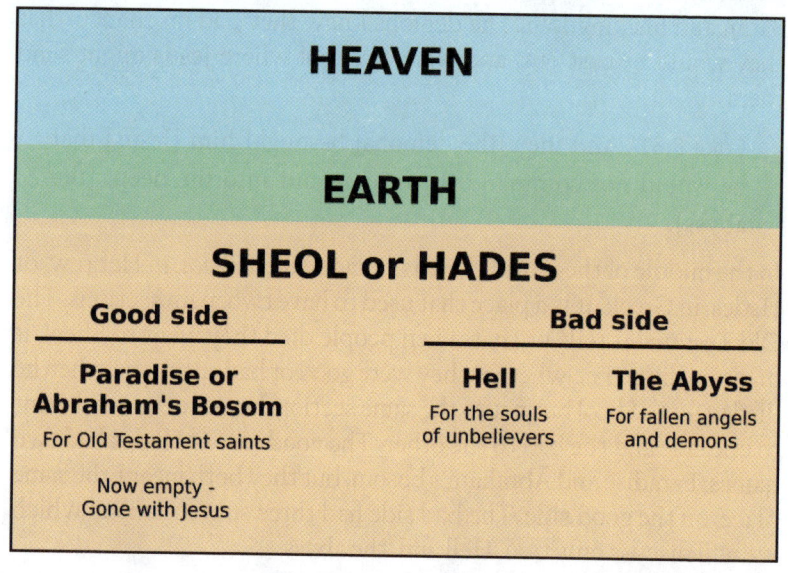

HEAVEN

EARTH

SHEOL or HADES

Good side	Bad side	
Paradise or Abraham's Bosom For Old Testament saints Now empty - Gone with Jesus	**Hell** For the souls of unbelievers	**The Abyss** For fallen angels and demons

Heaven, Earth And Hell

In Luke 16:24-26, Abraham was in Paradise and explained that in between him and those poor souls in Hell there was a great chasm or gulf that could not be crossed, although the souls in Paradise and the souls in Hell could talk to each other across the chasm.

After the crucifixion the body of Jesus was buried in Joseph of Arimathea's tomb,[2] and His soul went to Abraham's bosom or Paradise,[3] but He did not go to Hell as some teach, the chasm between Hell and Paradise could not be crossed and Jesus was never in Hell for a moment, He was in the good side of Hades. Hanging on the cross before he died, Jesus said to one of the men crucified with Him, "To day shalt thou be with me in paradise."[3]

In Paradise Jesus spoke across the chasm to the souls in Hell,[4] so that they understood that His death not only secured the perfection of the Old Testament saints and their release from Paradise into the presence of God in heaven, it also guaranteed the final judgement of those condemned and waiting in Hell. At His ascension Jesus took with Him the souls from Paradise,[5] leaving it empty. Ever since then when a believer dies his soul goes straight into the presence of God in heaven.[6] For the bad side of Hades, nothing has changed. Unbelievers die, their bodies are buried or cremated and their souls go to Hell, where they will stay until the end of the Millennial Kingdom. They will then be removed at the time of God's construction of a new heaven and a new earth,[7] to stand trial at the great white throne judgement before going into the lake of fire forever.[8] Getting back to the demons, living in the two men on the Gentile side of the Sea of Galilee, they all asked Jesus not to send them into the abyss, but to allow them to enter a herd of pigs that were rummaging for food on the mountain side nearby, grunting and sometimes squealing as they ate like pigs do.

Jesus agreed to the request of the demons, with the result that they left the bodies of the two men and entered into the bodies of the pigs, upon which the entire herd of about 2,000 hogs charged down a steep slope and were drowned in the lake.[9] I used to ask myself, "Why did Jesus allow the demons to go into the pigs?" and thought it was because Jews were not allowed to eat pork, and were breaking the Law of Moses by keeping pigs, but now I see that the pigs were not in Israel and they did not belong to Jews. Gentiles are quite entitled to keep pigs and so I still don't know why Jesus allowed the demons to enter the pigs, and another question I don't know is, "Where are the demons now?"

The two men, free from the demons were now normal sound minded people. Mark only tells us about one of the men but Matthew says there were two.[10] How pleased they must have been to have been changed from raving mad lunatics into intelligent men, but the owners of the pigs were not at all pleased, because their porkers once worth perhaps £150,000 in today's money, were corpses in the Sea of Galilee, a grisly sight as they floated silently in the water. The lost money along with the sight of the dead pigs was too much for their owners who filled with fear and terror, asked Jesus to leave their country.[11] One of the men, most likely the one that had been the worst of the two, was so pleased to be sane, he wanted to be one of Jesus' disciples. The problem was he was a Gentile and only Jews could be His disciples at this time, but Jesus did give him a job to do.

> Mark 5:19 Howbeit Jesus suffered him not, but saith unto him, Go home to thy friends, and tell them how great things the Lord hath done for thee, and had compassion on thee.

Although Jesus was now asking the Jews not to tell anyone when He had worked a miracle, this was not the case with Gentiles, and so He asked the man to spread the news about the miracle and give the glory to God, which he did going to all the ten Greek cities in the Decapolis.

> Mark 5:20 And he departed, and began to publish in Decapolis how great things Jesus had done for him: and all men did marvel.

Later we will come to the feeding of the four thousand and see how this man's work prepared the population to receive Jesus, because the next time Jesus came to this place where they had asked Him to leave, He was warmly welcomed.

[1] Revelation 20:1-3

[2] Matthew 27:57-60

[3] Luke 23:43

[4] 1 Peter 3:18-20

[5] Ephesians 4:8-10

[6] Philippians 1:23, 2 Corinthians 5:8

[7] Revelation 21:1-5

[8] Revelation 20:11-15

[9] Mark 5:11-13

[10] Matthew 8:28-32

[11] Luke 8:37

THE KING'S POWER OVER SICKNESS AND DEATH
Matthew 9:18-26, Mark 5:21-43, Luke 8: 40-56

After being asked to leave by the Gardarenes, Jesus and His disciples got into the boat and sailed across the Sea of Galilee, back to the Jewish side. As soon as Jesus came ashore while He was still beside the sea an official of the synagogue, a ruler, called Jairus came and fell down at the feet of Jesus, pleading strongly for Jesus to go and see his dying daughter who was only twelve years old.[1] Notice that this synagogue ruler had faith, believing that if Jesus touched the little girl she would not die, even though she was already almost dead, and she actually did die before Jesus got to her.[2] Jesus went with Jairus to visit his daughter, but Mark and Luke tell us that the people thronged Him, this word "thronged" in Greek means their bodies were touching and pressing tightly in on Him from every direction. As the crowd was moving along with Jesus squashed up in the middle a woman interrupted their journey.

> Matthew 9:20 And, behold, a woman which was diseased with an issue of blood twelve years, came behind him, and touched the hem of his garment.

The woman had had her disease for as long as Jairus' daughter had been alive. She was like a young woman having a monthly period that never ever stopped, and because of this, according to the Law of Moses she was legally unclean[3] and separated from other people. Like lepers and other separated people she had never felt the loving touch of another person for twelve years, nor had she ever touched another person for all that time. Doctor Luke tells us about the poor woman in one way, while Mark who was not a doctor tells us in a different way.

> Luke 8:43 And a woman having an issue of blood twelve years, which had spent all her living upon physicians, neither could be healed of any.

Luke has just told us that doctors had taken all her money but had not healed her.

> Mark 5:25-26 ²⁵ And a certain woman, which had an issue of blood twelve years,
>
> ²⁶ And suffered many things of many physicians, and had spent all she had, and was nothing bettered, but rather grew worse.

Mark, not being a doctor himself felt free to give us more information, and tells us that many doctors had made her suffer a lot, none of them had done anything that helped, but they only made her worse. Luke carefully missed those details out and we can see that even two thousand years ago there was a certain amount of professional loyalty between doctors. We can get an idea of the things she could have suffered at the hands of the doctors from instructions given in an old Jewish manuscript on how to cure a woman of an issue of blood.

Old Jewish Remedy For A Woman With An Issue Of Blood.

> Take the gum of Alexandria, alum and crocuses, let them be bruised together and given in wine to the woman with the issue of blood. If this does not work, take Persian onions and larks, boil them in wine and make her drink it and say, "Arise from your flowing." If this does not work make her squat down at some cross roads, give her a cup of wine to hold and send someone to creep up behind and scare her, and say, "Arise from your flowing." If that does not work, take a handful of cumin and

a handful of crocuses, boil them in wine and give them to her to drink and say, "Arise from your flowing." If this does not help get some labourers to dig seven ditches, and burn some vine cuttings less than three years old. Put a cup of wine in her hand and ask her to sit down over the first ditch and say, "Arise from your flowing." Then go on to the next ditch, and so on from ditch to ditch and at every departure you must say, "Arise from your flowing." (Here the instructions stop).

After spending all her money and suffering many things at the hands of doctors she found Jesus, crept up behind Him and touched the hem of His clothing (the tassel). She did not touch Jesus, just His tassel, because if she had touched Jesus she would have made Him unclean according to the Law of Moses, and she was careful not to do that.

> Mark 5:28-29 [28] For she said, If I may touch but his clothes, I shall be whole.
>
> [29] And straightway the fountain of her blood was dried up; and she felt in her body that she was healed of that plague.

She had been totally healed at once.

Jesus stopped the crowd, which must have made Jairus very frustrated because he knew his daughter was almost dead, and said, "Who touched my clothes?"[4] Remember the miracles now are for personal need and to train the disciples, and although He asked them who touched His clothes, He knew who it was because He turned and looked straight at the woman, and the lady knew she could not hide. He asked the question to get their attention because this miracle was mainly for them. The disciples had been asked a difficult question because the crowd was pressed tightly around Him.

> Mark 5:31 And his disciples said unto him, Thou seest the multitude thronging thee, and sayest thou, Who touched me?

Jesus wanted to teach them and Jairus something important.

> Luke 8:46-47 [46] And Jesus said, Somebody hath touched me: for I perceive that virtue [miracle power] is gone out of me.
>
> [47] And when the woman saw that she was not hid, she came

trembling, and falling down before him, she declared unto him before all the people for what cause she had touched him, and how she was healed immediately.

All this was preparation for the lesson, for the woman, Jairus and the disciples. The woman instinctively knew that if she touched His clothes she would be healed, that was faith, she touched in faith, and if she did not have faith she could have touched as much as she liked but she would not have been healed.

Matthew 9:22 But Jesus turned him about, and when he saw her, he said, Daughter, be of good comfort; thy faith hath made thee whole.

The woman thought she had been healed because she had touched his clothes but Jesus taught them all that, that was not true, it was her invisible faith that had healed her. Her touching his garment was only the outward visible sign of her inner faith. During the stop for this lesson, Jairus' daughter died.

Mark 5:35 While he yet spake, there came from the ruler of the synagogue's house certain which said, Thy daughter is dead: why troublest thou the Master any further?

Remember Jairus had originally asked Jesus to go and touch his daughter, because like the woman he thought touching was important but touching was not the main issue, having faith was.

Touching and the laying on of hands have become common in some churches and on Christian television shows, because it looks impressive. Once in a Pentecostal church we used to attend, one of the elders was suffering from cancer of the liver and had been given less than a month to live. He sat in the front row of chairs, thin and with deep dark yellow skin. My father had died of liver cancer and I recognised the symptoms, the man had not got long to live. The pastor called me by name along with some others to go out to the front, lay hands on our friend, and pray for his healing. I had no faith whatsoever that he would be healed, and I knew this before I got up from my seat, but I had been asked in front of the congregation and thought to myself, "Well I can't refuse in front of all his friends, and I can't do any harm," so I went out to the front, knowing that God had not given me the gift this time,[5] touched the man on the shoulder, and prayed as best as I could under the circumstances, but within two weeks the man died. We all obeyed our pastor, laying hands on our jaundiced elder and praying, but touching is not the issue, faith is the issue, and I doubt if any of us had faith for healing, or the man himself.

After Jairus learned about faith from the miracle of the healing of the woman with the issue of blood, Jesus used the lesson in the very next verse.

> Mark 5:36 As soon as Jesus heard the word that was spoke, he saith unto the ruler of the synagogue, Be not afraid, only believe.

After the unforgivable sin you will remember, miracles are no longer signs for the Jewish public, and therefore Jesus only allowed three of His disciples, Peter, James and John into the room where the dead girl was lying, plus her mother and father.[6] Her parents are there because of their personal need and faith, and the disciples to learn the lesson.

It was well known by now that the girl was dead, and when Jesus said she was sleeping they laughed at Him scornfully, with contempt. In the New Testament, when the word sleep is used for someone who is physically dead, it always means the person is a believer, that they are not spiritually dead, because God has given them everlasting life. Everyone was then bundled out of the house except for the disciples, Jairus and his wife, then Jesus went with them into the room where the girl's body was lying.

> Mark 5:41-43 [41] And he took the damsel by the hand, and saith unto her, Talitha cumi; which is, being interpreted, Damsel, I say unto thee, arise.
>
> [42] And straightway the damsel arose, and walked; for she was of the age of twelve years. And they were astonished with a great astonishment.
>
> [43] And he charged them straitly that no man should know it; and commanded that something should be given her to eat.

Luke wrote, "her parents were astonished: but he charged them that they should tell no man what was done."[7] From now on this will be the rule, tell no one. Jairus and his wife were left with faith in Jesus, and the disciples were taught that where there was a personal need combined with faith, they would be able to raise the dead to life, something Paul later did in Acts 20:9-12.

[1] Luke 8:42

[2] Mark 5:22-23

[3] Leviticus 15:19-30

[4] Mark 5:30

[5] Matthew 17:14-20, 1 Corinthians 12:4-11, James 5:15

[6] Mark 5:37-40

[7] Luke 8:56

THE KING'S POWER OVER BLINDNESS
Matthew 9:27-34

These verses begin with two blind men following Jesus and shouting out, "Son of David, have mercy on us." By calling Jesus, Son of David, they are basing their request on the fact that He is the Son of David, the Messiah, but the Jews have already rejected Jesus as Messiah and He does not respond to the two men. They do have a personal need though, and make it known by crying out, "have mercy on us." In the next verse Jesus and the men are inside a house and because they have need, He is prepared to heal them secretly on condition that they have faith, but away from the Jews and asked them, "Believe ye that I am able to do this?" They did believe, they had faith and said so, then Jesus touched their eyes and said, "According to your faith be it unto you." The men could see perfectly well after that, but Jesus following His new policy told them, "See that no man know it." The men did not do as they were told although Jesus had given them the command to tell no one.

> Matthew 9:31 But they, when they were departed, spread abroad his fame in all that country.

After being rejected by Israel, Jesus is asking for faith in Him from individuals, and from now on He will only heal on that condition, but before they had rejected Him, He had healed and performed signs for unbelieving Jews who did not have faith in Him. In Matthew 9:33, Jesus cast out another dumb demon, as He had done before and which we noted was the second of His three messianic miracles. No one before Jesus had ever cast out a dumb demon, He was the first person in the history of Israel to do so.

> Matthew 9:33 . . . and the multitudes marvelled, saying, It was never so seen in Israel.

The Pharisees knew the multitudes were right, that the miracle was one they themselves taught only the Messiah would be able to do, but they again showed their made-up reason for rejecting their King.

> Matthew 9:34 But the Pharisees said, He casteth [casts] out devils through the prince of devils.

THE FINAL REJECTION OF THE KING IN NAZARETH
Matthew 13:54-58, Mark 6:1-6

Early in Chapter 5, when talking about the rejection of Jesus in Nazareth, we said that what happens in Nazareth eventually happens in the whole nation, then we were talking about His first rejection, and now His final rejection in Nazareth will be a small scale representation of His final rejection by the nation. Nazareth remember is the town He grew up in and on the Sabbath day He was teaching there in the synagogue.

> Mark 6:2 And many hearing him were astonished, saying, From whence has this man these things? And what wisdom is this which is given unto him?

The people had known Jesus from a boy and they knew that He could not have learned His wisdom in the schools of Nazareth. In verse 4, Jesus had quoted a proverbial saying of the time, "A prophet is not without honour, but in his own country, and among his own kin, and in his own house," and the citizens of Nazareth prove the truth of the saying by their reaction. They knew He had great wisdom and were jealous because being from Nazareth He was supposed to be like them, not well educated. They just would not accept it and their unbelief in Him, blocked the supernatural from taking place because now, having faith in Him was necessary.

> Mark 6:5 And he could do no mighty work, save that he laid his hands upon a few sick folk, and healed them.

No doubt these few sick people He healed were people with faith.

These two passages from Matthew and Mark are enlightening in other ways, because Mark 6:3 tells us that Jesus was a carpenter, and Matthew 13:55 that He was the carpenter's son, meaning Jesus was apprenticed to the profession of His step father. They also give the names of four of His half brothers, James or Jacob, Joses or Yossi, Judas or Judah, and Simon or Simeon. He also had at least two half sisters because the word sisters is plural, meaning that Mary had at least six children after Jesus, so she definitely had seven children and maybe more. The Catholic Church claims that after giving birth to Jesus, Mary stayed a virgin, and that the word "brothers" here means cousins, but clearly Matthew and Mark are talking about Mum, Dad and their children, the close family, not cousins from different marriages all together.

JESUS CHANGES HIS APROACH AFTER THE REJECTION
Matthew 9:35 to 10:42, Mark 6:7-13, Luke 9:1-6

We are going to see the new approach mainly through Matthew's gospel because he has much more to say about it. Notice that although Jesus sends out His disciples throughout the whole land to teach and preach, they focus their attention on the believers only, God's faithful remnant[1] of that time, because both the disciples and their message are going to be rejected by the nation as a whole, and the time is over for reaching out to people that have rejected Jesus. They have made their choice and will suffer the consequences.

Business As Usual With A Difference

Jesus continued going to the synagogues, preaching the gospel of the kingdom, and validating the truth of His message by healing all kinds of sickness.

> Matthew 9:35 And Jesus went about all the cities and villages, teaching in their synagogues, and preaching the gospel of the kingdom, and healing every sickness and every disease among the people.

He appeared to be doing just what He had been doing earlier, but something different is beginning to be seen.

> Matthew 9:36 But when he saw the multitudes, he was moved with compassion on them, because they fainted, and were scattered abroad, as sheep having no shepherd.

When we moved to Cornwall, the first animals I bought to eat the grass were sheep, and in a sense I was similar to Jesus to them because I was their shepherd, and they were my flock, just as Jesus is the Good Shepherd[2] and believers are His flock. One day I was driving out of the farm and passed a gate where a ewe was standing by herself. She had left the flock which were out of sight and come to the gate where I used to go in and out to see my sheep, and was looking for help from her shepherd. I thought, "You look alright to me, I will see you when I come back in a short while," but when I returned a little later she was lying by the gate dead, so she must have felt very ill. Perhaps she died because I did not stop on the way out and she felt abandoned, but what impressed me is the way she went to the gate for help from her shepherd. Another incident happened with the sheep which was confirmed by a veterinary surgeon. One morning I found a big fat lamb that had come to the gate next to the back door of our house when he felt ill and died there during the night while I was in bed. The next day there was another fat lamb dead at the same gate and another, one or two days later. I called the vet to do a post mortem to find out why the sheep were dying. It was an infection that sometimes takes hold of lambs when they are moved on to better pasture. I told the vet that they came to the gate to die, as if they were looking for me. "Yes," she said, "they often do that."

In Matthew 9:36, we saw the people were like sheep without a shepherd, and they fainted. The verse stirs emotions in me because the people were fainting and were like sheep without a shepherd, and my sheep died looking for their shepherd. The scribes and Pharisees had rejected Jesus, but to begin with the people did not follow their leaders, and were discussing among each other whether they should follow the old shepherds or, the New One, and because they were still undecided they were like sheep without a shepherd.

Getting back to Jesus and His Jewish flock, most of them decided to follow the old shepherds, but there were a few among them that followed Jesus or would follow Him, and it is for the benefit of those few, that Jesus prepared His disciples for the work ahead.

> Matthew 9:37-38 ³⁷ Then saith he unto his disciples, The harvest truly is plenteous, but the labourers are few;
>
> ³⁸ Pray ye therefore the Lord of the harvest, that he will send forth labourers into his harvest.

It is difficult to ask God for labourers to help with the harvest and then to refuse to labour yourself, and the lesson is that they need to work as well as pray, and to pray as well as work. Here Jesus is calling the disciples together before telling them how they are to go out into the harvest field and preach to those that believe and will believe, three points should be noted.

> First in Mark 6:7, He sent them out in pairs so that they could encourage and help one another.
>
> Second in Luke 9:2, they were to preach the kingdom of God, which would include the Mystery Kingdom, but we will see later that the disciples were not yet absolutely clear about the difference between it and the Messianic Kingdom.
>
> Thirdly in Matthew 10:1, they were given authority to cast out evil spirits and to heal every kind of disease, which would con-

firm the truth of their message and encourage the believers. Notice that evil spirits and disease are considered separately, which shows that not all disease is the result of demon possession, as has been taught in some churches. I have arthritis in my foot, and one well known preacher would have said that I need to cast out the demon of arthritis to be healed.

The twelve apostles are listed in Matthew 10:2-4, which we dealt with in Chapter 5, under the heading, Jesus Chooses The Twelve, and you can refer there if you need to. Jesus then begins to give the disciples some very sensible advice for the work He is sending them out to do.

How The Disciples Are To Work Now Israel Has Rejected Jesus

First Jesus said they were to work with Jews only, and He forbade them to go into Gentile or Samaritan areas.

> Matthew 10:5-6 ⁵ Go not into the way of the Gentiles, and into any city of the Samaritans enter ye not;
>
> ⁶ But rather go to the lost sheep of the house of Israel.

Not everything Jesus said in the Bible was meant to be obeyed by everybody forever. The instruction here, not to preach to the Gentiles, was only meant for the apostles for the short time they were preaching to the Jewish believers before He died and rose to life again. Later in the same gospel, we will see the need for another change to their work after His death, so in Matthew 28:19 they are told to teach all nations, but before the resurrection they were to go only to the Jews.

Secondly their work would be to preach the message of the kingdom, although their understanding of the Mystery Kingdom remained something of a mystery to them also, as we will see by the questions they ask Jesus later, but as time went by their knowledge about it increased. They were well informed about the Messianic Kingdom from prophecies in the Old Testament, but it would no longer begin with that generation, something the disciples were not yet clear about themselves, but the essential facts about the Messianic Kingdom had not, and would not change, and they could reassure the believing remnant of Jews that it was still in God's programme.

> Matthew 10:7 And as ye go, preach, saying, The kingdom of heaven is at hand.

The preaching of the disciples would be authenticated by miracles.

> Matthew 10:8 Heal the sick, cleanse the lepers, raise the dead, cast out devils: freely ye have received, freely give.

They were told to share whatever they had been given with all the other Jewish believers.

Thirdly everything they needed would be provided and they were not to worry about the daily necessities of life, but to just trust God.

> Matthew 10:9-10 ⁹ Provide neither gold, nor silver, nor brass in your purses,
>
> ¹⁰ Nor scrip [bag] for your journey, neither two coats, neither shoes, nor yet staves: for the workman is worthy of his meat [support].

Once again this is definitely not an instruction for believers in future times, because after His resurrection Jesus will tell them to take those same things with them. You should be aware of what seems like a discrepancy in the three gospel accounts regarding the staves, staffs or walking sticks of verse 10, because not all are the same.

> Matthew 10:10, says they are not to take staves,
>
> Luke 9:3, also says they are not to take staves, but
>
> Mark 6:8, says, they should take nothing for their journey, except a staff only.

There are many speculations we can make to account for this apparent difference when translated into English, but there are different words used in the Greek texts for the verbs, "to take," and, "to provide," found in the King James translations. Matthew used, "*ktieseisthei*," Luke used, "*airete*," and Mark used, "*arosin*," which also means to lift up, all this should be considered.

Fourthly the disciples were to stay with worthy people, and the worthy ones were those that believed in Jesus. The disciples were to teach those worthy individuals only, because the days of making broad appeals to the masses had ended with the unforgivable sin.

> Matthew 10:11 And into whatsoever city or town ye shall enter, inquire who in it is worthy; and there abide till ye go thence.

When they had been invited into a home of a worthy family the disciples were to salute them and give them their blessing. If the people there were true believers, (not individuals who had listened to Jesus but had fallen away for some reason), then the disciples were to bless them with peace, but if the householders weren't worthy, they were not to give them their peace.[3] If they had given their peace to the householders and later on discovered they were not worthy, then they should take their blessing of peace back.

> Matthew 10:12-13 ¹² And when ye come into an house salute it.
>
> ¹³ And if the house be worthy, let your peace come upon it: but if it be not worthy, let your peace return to you.

The important change to notice is that the disciples were to teach and heal only worthy individuals, not the general public.

Fifthly the disciples were given strict instructions how they must treat unworthy people. The truth was, and still is, that unbelieving Jews were going to face judgement, and they should be told so. The sign of the coming judgement was made by the disciples shaking the dust from their feet.

> Matthew 10:14 And whosoever shall not receive you, nor hear your words, when ye depart out of that house or city, shake the dust of your feet.

The subject of judgement causes Jesus to emphasize cities and nations more than individuals.

> Matthew 10:15 Verily I say unto you, It shall be more tolerable for the land of Sodom and Gomorrha in the day of judgement, than for that city.

Whole cities will be judged with various degrees of punishment depending on their particular sins.

How The Disciples Are To Manage Increasing Persecution

Jesus realised that sending out the disciples was like putting two sheep, (they were sent out in pairs), into a pack of attacking wolves, and yet they were instructed to be harmless but also wise.

> Matthew 10:16 Behold, I send you forth as sheep in the midst of wolves: be ye therefore wise as serpents, and harmless as doves.

They needed wisdom because of the rejection, with skills like a snake but without its poison. He told them plainly that they would be rejected and that they should persevere in spite of it all.

> Matthew 10:17-18 [17] But beware of men: for they will deliver you up to the councils, and they will scourge you in their synagogues;
>
> [18] And ye shall be brought before governors and kings for my sake, for a testimony against them and the Gentiles.

At this moment the disciples are to go only to the lost sheep of Israel, and this talk of the Gentiles means He is teaching them here to continue to expect persecution when they preach to the Gentiles after the resurrection, which is what they are being trained for. The intimidations will be opportunities for them to show their faith in practice.

A most remarkable instruction was, not to prepare what they would say to their tormenters before being asked to give an account of themselves.

> Matthew 10:19-20 [19] But when they deliver you up, take no thought how or what ye shall speak: for it shall be given you in that same hour what ye shall speak.
>
> [20] For it is not ye that speak, but the Spirit of your Father which speaketh in you.

They are not to worry because Jesus promises them the Holy Spirit will give them the absolutely perfect answers to all the tricky questions.

Another warning is that the persecutions will get worse and worse, and going through the next three verses of Matthew 10, we see in verse 21, they will be persecuted by their own families, in verse 22, they will be hated by the general population, but not of course by other believers, and in verse 23, they will be persecuted by cities, and they were told that when they were persecuted in a city to move to another one.

> Matthew 10:23 But when they persecute you in this city, flee ye into another: for verily I say unto you, Ye shall not have gone over the cities of Israel, till the Son of man be come.

This verse probably refers to the first coming of Jesus to Jerusalem, when He rode in on a donkey,[4] because the rejecting cities are all Jewish and it seems to be these cities that are rejecting the apostles He sent out. It could also be prophetic of His second coming when He will descend from the sky,[5] but there are many Gentile cities around the world that have and will reject Him, whereas verse 23 is talking about the cities of Israel.

How The Disciples Are To Manage Rejection

Jesus emphasizes four points to the disciples as to how they are to deal with rejection.

First of all He reminded them that He had been rejected on the basis of the absolute lie that He was demon possessed. Logically it follows therefore, that if that were the case, then all His disciples would be the same as their leader, and it would be easy to claim that the whole movement was demonic.

> Matthew 10:25 If they have called the master of the house Beelzebub, how much more shall they call them of his household?

They must expect to be rejected on the false basis that they are demon possessed.

Secondly, in spite of this wicked lie that they will be taunted with, they must keep on preaching the message of the kingdom, even climbing onto the roofs of houses and shouting it out.

> Matthew 10:26-27 ²⁶ Fear them not ...
>
> ²⁷ preach ye upon the housetops.

They must get the message out despite opposition.

Thirdly, they are not to fear men, but they must fear God. Everything they suffer is for a reason because nothing can happen to them unless God makes it happen or else lets it happen. God is always in complete control, although we may be tempted to think the opposite sometimes. In such difficult times we should wonder for a while, "What is God trying to teach me."

> Matthew 10:28 And fear not them which kill the body, but are not able to kill the soul: but rather fear him which is able to destroy both soul and body in hell.

They are in God's loving care, and need to fear Him only.

Fourthly, He reminds them that the issue now rests with individuals, not the masses, and anyone that rejects Jesus publicly will be judged accordingly on judgement day, and everyone that accepts Jesus publicly, will be rewarded.

> Matthew 10:32-33 ³² Whosoever therefore shall confess me before men, him will I confess also before my Father which is in heaven.
>
> ³³ But whosoever shall deny me before men, him will I also deny before my Father which is in heaven.

Looking at the Scriptures as a whole we can see that Jesus here is not threatening believers with losing eternal life, but is offering incentives of good rewards in the Messianic Kingdom for those that confess Him, and disincentives for those that deny Him.

Some Effects Of The National Rejection Of Jesus

Jesus told the disciples that He had now become the cause of division among the Jewish public.

> Matthew 10:34 Think not that I am come to send peace on earth: I came not to send peace, but a sword.

He is the reason for the division between Jews, between those that reject Him and those that believe Him. If He had been made King then the Messianic Kingdom would have come into being during that generation, and there would have been peace, but there was to be no kingdom unless He was made King, so instead of peace, it would be the sword. The division among the Jews over Jesus would be especially painful within families.

> Matthew 10:35-36 35 For I am come to set a man at variance against his father, and the daughter against her mother, and the daughter in law against her mother in law.
>
> 36 And a man's foes shall be they of his own household.

The Jewish family is well known for being a tight knit mutually supporting group so long as none of them become Christian, once that happens the division is immediate and firm. The prophet Isaiah had warned that when the Messiah came He would bring division between the remnant and the majority, to the remnant He would be a sanctuary (holy place), but to the majority a stumbling stone and an offence.

> Isaiah 8:14-15 14 And he shall be for a sanctuary; but for a stone of stumbling and for a rock of offence to both the houses of Israel, for a gin [a trap that catches the foot] and for a snare [a noose that strangles] to the inhabitants of Jerusalem.
>
> 15 And many among them shall stumble, and fall, and be broken, and be snared, and be taken.

The division as we already know would not only be within families, but would result in the destruction of Jerusalem and the Temple, along with the Jews living in the city that were not believers, as the prophet Isaiah had predicted hundreds of years before.

Jesus next spoke in Matthew 10:37-38, about those that were not worthy of Him, and if we compare these verses with Luke 14:26-27, we realise that He is talking about discipleship. Being a disciple will affect family relationships and we will have to identify ourselves totally with His rejection.

> Matthew 10:37-38 [37] He that loveth father and mother more than me is not worthy of me: and he that loveth son or daughter more than me is not worthy of me.
>
> [38] And he that taketh not his cross, and followeth after me, is not worthy of me.

Disciples that are worthy will love Jesus more than members of their families and they will be prepared to be rejected by the people of the world, just as Jesus was, because they are His followers. Eternal life is given to those that have faith and trust in the death of Jesus for their sins, but discipleship requires a greater dedication that should be carefully considered beforehand, as Jesus is about to explain.

The third effect of the rejection is the need to lose our old life because of our focus on the Messiah.

> Matthew 10:39 He that findeth his life shall lose it: and he that loseth his life for my sake shall find it.

When we lose our lives because the centre of our attention is on Jesus, we will be rewarded.

Rewards For Those That Believe The Disciples And Support Them

The rewards in the Messianic Kingdom will also apply to those that focus their attention on the disciples, because the principle we learned when the Roman centurion was talking about authority was, that when we receive an ambassador it is the same as receiving the one who sent the ambassador, and the disciples were ambassadors of Christ, as Jesus explained.

> Matthew 10:40 He that receiveth you receiveth me, and he that receiveth me receiveth him that sent me.

If we receive a prophet, we will receive a prophet's reward, and if we receive a righteous man, we will receive a righteous man's reward.

> Matthew 10:41-42 [41] He that receiveth a prophet in the name of a prophet shall receive a prophet's reward; and he that receiveth a righteous man in the name of a righteous man shall receive a righteous man's reward.
>
> [42] And whosoever shall give to drink unto one of these little one's a cup of cold water only in the name of a disciple, verily I say unto you, he shall no wise lose his reward.

Giving water to a believer in Jesus, because he is a believer in Jesus will result in a reward. The smallest thing will be rewarded if it is done because we are doing it to help believers in Jesus. Seeing the children of a school for believers safely across the road, or cleaning their toilets, will get a reward.

The Result Of The Disciples Work

In Matthew 11:1, Jesus finishes His instructions to the disciples and sends them out to preach, and their message includes the need for repentance.

> Mark 6:12 And they went out and preached that men should repent.

In telling the people to repent they were in effect saying, "Change your minds," and what they had to change their minds about was Jesus. He was not demon possessed, He was the Messiah of Israel, the King, and those that did change their mind about Him, those that believed He was the Messiah, became part of the remnant, and would receive eternal life.

[1] Micah 7:18-20, Romans 9:27, Romans 11:5

[2] John 10:14

[3] John 14:27, Philippians 4:7

[4] Zechariah 9:9

[5] Acts 1:9-11

THE DEATH OF JOHN THE BAPTIST
Matthew 14:1-12, Mark 6:12-29

We are told about the death of John the Baptist in a round about way, because both Matthew and Mark talk about the beheaded John first, and then return to the beginning, to tell us how it all came about. The conscience stricken Herod Antipas, after having John the Baptist beheaded, heard of the miracles being performed by Jesus, and feared He was John the Baptist who had returned from the dead.

> Mark 6:14 And king Herod heard of him; (for his name was spread abroad:) and he said, That John the Baptist was risen from the dead, and therefore mighty works do show forth themselves in him.

Only then do the gospels turn back and give us their accounts of how John had died.

The characters involved all descended from Herod the Great, the one who tried to kill Jesus in Bethlehem when He was less than two years old. They are his granddaughter Herodias, his son Philip and another son Herod Antipas. Herodias had a number of liaisons with different men, in and out of marriage. She married her uncle Philip which was incest, and while he was still alive she married another uncle, Herod Antipas, which was adultery and incest, and it was not the first time she had committed adultery either. By marrying Herodias, Herod had broken the Law of Moses by marrying his brother's wife.[1]

> Matthew 14:3-4 ³ For Herod had laid hold on John, and bound him, and put him in prison for Herodias' sake, his brother Philip's wife.
>
> ⁴ For John said unto him, It is not lawful for thee to have her.

Herodias was furious with John for pointing out that her marriage was sinful, and wanted him killed, but after arresting John, Herod at first refused to kill him because he knew John was a man of God.

> Mark 6:19-20 [19] Therefore Herodias had a quarrel against him, and would have killed him; but she could not:
>
> [20] For Herod feared John, knowing that he was a just man and an holy, and observed him;

Herod watched over John, observed him, and kept him safe, until Salome, (his wife Herodias' daughter from another man), danced for Herod and his high ranking guests, at an extravagant party on Herod's birthday. Herod was so infatuated with his wife's daughter, that he made a fool of himself by promising her anything she asked for, up to half his kingdom. Salome did not know what to ask for so she went to ask her mother Herodias, and returned to ask Herod for the head of John the Baptist, presented to her there in a charger, a large flat dish.[2] Salome was very enthusiastic about having John's head presented to her there at the party on a plate, as the words emphasized in the following Scripture show.

> Mark 6:25 And she came in **straightway** with **haste** unto the king, and asked, saying, I will that thou give me by and by in a charger the head of John the Baptist.

Herod was extremely upset at finding himself in the position of being responsible for harming John, the man he had been protecting, knowing he was righteous, holy and innocent of any crime. However, because he had sworn an oath to Salome he sent and had John killed.

> Matthew 14:11 And his head was brought in a charger, and given to the damsel: and she brought it to her mother.

Later Pontius Pilate would also kill an innocent Jesus, because remember what happens to John the Baptist will also happen to the King. The Jewish historian Josephus wrote that Herod deliberately killed John to quell a possible uprising, that is to say for a political reason, and this is not inconsistent with the gospel story. Certainly

Herodias moved among the very highest political circles, and may well have used politics, as well as Salome, in order to achieve the assassination of John, she so unwaveringly pursued. To the political historian then, the charge against John was political, John was planning an uprising, but the actual reason from the gospels was a personal one coming from Herodias. Later the charge against Jesus that brought about His death was political, He claimed to be king, but the actual reason was personal, coming from the Jewish religious leaders. Right to the very end we see that what happens to John, later on happens to Jesus.

[1] Leviticus 18:16, 20:21

[2] Matthew 14:8

7

JESUS TRAINS THE TWELVE

The training of the disciples we are going to learn about covers a period of roughly fifteen days in AD 29. It took place sometime between the third Passover after Jesus began to claim Himself to be the Messiah, and the Feast of Tabernacles of the same year. During this training session He withdrew from Galilee four times, usually into places controlled by Gentiles, which were not under the rule of the man that had killed John the Baptist, Herod Antipas. He also went into the region governed by Herod Philip, and when the gospels here speak of Bethsaida, it would be Bethsaida Julius which was under Herod Philip's jurisdiction. It seems from the gospel accounts that He used to withdraw into mountainous regions. The training of the twelve was necessary because of Israel's unforgivable sin and rejection. It prepared the disciples for the wonderful work they would do in the name of Jesus, in the Book of Acts after He had gone into heaven.

THE FEEDING OF THE FIVE THOUSAND
Matthew 14:13-21, Mark 6:30-44, Luke 9:10-17, John 6:1-14

The miracle happened in Bethsaida Julius, during Jesus' first withdrawal to the region, and it is the fourth of the seven signs recorded in the Gospel of John. Notice also the time the miracle took place.

> John 6:4 And the Passover, a feast of the Jews, was nigh.

Jesus taught in Israel for about three and a half years, during which time there were four Passover festivals. John is talking here about the third Passover, so at the next one Jesus will die. The feeding of the five thousand therefore occurred at the beginning of His last year.

> AD 26 Jesus began His ministry about the autumn of the year.
>
> AD 27 In the spring, was the first Passover of His ministry.
>
> AD 28 In the spring, was the second Passover of His ministry.
>
> AD 29 In the spring, was the third Passover of His ministry.
>
> AD 30 In the spring, was the last Passover of His ministry, the fourth in less than four years.

Only two miracles are reported in all four gospels, the resurrection of Jesus from the grave which was performed by God the Father, and this miracle of Jesus the Son of God, the feeding of the five thousand. Many more than five thousand were fed by Jesus because there were women and children in addition to the five thousand men that were also in need, and Jesus' new policy you will remember, is to perform miracles for people in need, but it did not occur until the disciples had returned. Again the reason is that the miracle was to train the disciples, and in this case to teach them that He was able to give them everything they needed for the work He would ask them to do. Actually Jesus set the whole thing up by moving to a desert area where there was not enough food for all the people that were following Him.

> Mark 6:30-31 [30] And the apostles gathered themselves together unto Jesus, and they told him all things, both what they had done, and what they had taught.
>
> [31] And he said unto them, Come ye yourselves apart into a desert place, and rest a while: for there were many coming and going, and they had no leisure so much as to eat.

From now on Jesus begins to pay more attention to his disciples and less to the crowds as the emphasis I have made in a couple of the following Scriptures shows.

> Luke 9:10 And the apostles, when they were returned, told him all that they had done. **And he took them, and went aside privately** into a desert place belonging to the city called Bethsaida.

Again, this was Bethsaida Julius, under Herod Philip, not the solidly Jewish Bethsaida under the control of Herod Antipas. After their rest they went four or five miles by boat to the other side of the Sea of Galilee,[1] (also called the Sea of Tiberius), a distance of four or five miles. Huge crowds followed them by foot[2] showing that in spite of his rejection by the leaders, many were still intensely interested. The crowds travelled the long way round by land which was a walk of about ten miles. The reason for the crowds was that Jesus was healing the sick, so they were after physical benefits, and were not interested in the spiritual significance of what was taking place by the power of God, through His Son.

> John 6:2 And a great multitude followed him, because they saw his miracles which he did on them that were diseased.

The crowds by now knew that Jesus claimed to be the Messiah, and that the scribes and Pharisees were saying He performed messianic miracles by the power of Satan. They were undecided about Him, but they followed Him because, out of pity, He was healing them.

> Mark 6:34 And Jesus, when he came out, saw much people, and was moved with compassion toward them, because they were like sheep without a shepherd.

> Matthew 14:14 And Jesus went forth, and saw a great multitude, and was moved with compassion toward them, and he healed their sick.

> Luke 9:11 (He) spake unto them of the kingdom of God, and healed them that had need of healing.

Notice something from each of the three verses above. First He shows it is not the sheep who should look for food, it is the responsibility of their shepherd to feed them. The crowds did not know whether to follow the old shepherds or the new One, and that is why they were like sheep without a shepherd. Secondly from Matthew 14:14, He healed them because He was very concerned for their needs, and thirdly as their pastor and teacher he did three things.

1. He taught them the truth.
2. He cared for the flock by healing them.
3. He also cared for the flock by feeding them.

All this was intended to teach the disciples, and sometimes he picked out certain apostles for special attention.

> John 6:5 And when Jesus lifted up his eyes, and saw a great company come unto him, **he saith unto Philip, Whence shall we buy bread, that these may eat?**

The area they were in was where Philip came from,[3] and if anyone knew where to get bread there, it would be Philip. He would know that the crowd was so big that there was not enough food in the whole district to feed them, and that even if there was, the disciples could not find anywhere near the money to pay for it even if they collected from everyone they could.

> Mark 6:37 Shall we go and buy two hundred pennyworth of bread, and give them to eat?

The two hundred pennies in Mark's account, (actually two hundred denarii) represents two hundred days wages, and even that would not be enough to buy enough bread.

> John 6:7 Two hundred pennyworth of bread is not sufficient for them, that every one of them may take a little.

They are in an absolutely impossible situation, they do not have enough money and if they did, there is not enough food in the district of Bethsaida Julius to feed them anyway.

Paying attention to John's gospel for a moment, the problem is to provide physical food, but later it will be spiritual nourishment. Andrew the brother of Peter, also got caught up in the problem.

> John 6:8-9 [8] One of his disciples, Andrew, Simon Peter's brother, saith unto him,

⁹ There is a lad here, which hath five barley loaves, and two small fishes: but what are they among so many?

In other words Andrew was saying, "We have got five bread buns and two tiny fish, to feed five thousand[4] men plus all the women and children with them, and it is just not possible." It is then, when we are in an impossible situation while working for the Lord, that He supplies all we need for His work. Nothing is impossible for God and so Jesus asked the disciples to get everyone to sit down in groups of 100 and of 50. Knowing that Jesus was claiming to be Israel's Messiah, promised to them by God about 1,500 years before, that He had performed many miracles that had never been seen on earth before that time, and had healed everyone that needed healing, the crowd would be getting more and more excited. When the disciples told them to sit down in groups they did so, because they wanted very much to know what ever was going to happen next.

Mark 6:39-40 ³⁹ And he commanded them to make all sit down by companies upon the green grass.

⁴⁰ And they sat down in ranks, by hundreds, and by fifties.

Jesus then looked up to heaven and gave a blessing over the bread,[5] and started to break the small buns and the tiny fish, giving the pieces to His disciples to distribute among all the groups. They must have worked for hours and hours while the bread and fish kept coming and coming because everyone had enough to eat.

Luke 9:17 And they did eat, and were all filled: and there was taken up of fragments that remained to them twelve baskets.

After the crowds had finished their meal, twelve baskets full of uneaten bread and fish were collected, so there was much more food given out than was needed.

The apostles were meant to learn three things from this miracle to guide them in their future work.

1. It is their responsibility to feed the people. This is clear from Luke 9:13, where Jesus says, "Give ye them to eat." That will be their job, but now the food is physical, later it will be spiritual, the Word of God.

2. They are not to rely on their own ability because it will not be possible for them to feed the flock of God by themselves.[6]
3. They must only share out what Jesus provides them with, just as happened in Matthew 14:19, "... and he gave the loaves to his disciples, and the disciples to the multitude."

The Holy Spirit reminded all the four gospel writers of this miracle and teaching of Jesus,[7] which emphasizes the importance of it. Too many Christian leaders today ignore this message and rely on their own ability, giving out information that does not come from Jesus or His Word, with the result that in the spiritual sense, Christians are getting a lot of junk food, even poisoned food.

[1] John 6:1

[2] Matthew 14:13, Luke 9:11, John 6:2

[3] John 1:43-44

[4] Luke 9:13-14

[5] Matthew 14:19

[6] John 6:5-9

[7] John 14:26

THE PEOPLE OF GALILEE TRY TO MAKE JESUS THEIR KING
John 6:15

The five thousand that Jesus fed were Galileans, and when they had eaten that miracle food, they decided that they would like Jesus to be King of Galilee, but Jesus, seeing they were trying to force Him to be king moved away to a mountain.

> John 6:15 When Jesus therefore perceived that they would come and take him by force, to make him a king, he departed again into a mountain himself alone.

He went to the mountain to pray.[1] Devoted at all times to close friendship with His Father, and committed to carrying out God's plan perfectly, there were three reasons Jesus refused to accept the offer of the Galileans to make Him their king.

1. The leaders had committed the unforgivable sin, and being unforgivable it was no longer possible for Him to become king over the people of that generation.
2. According to prophecy Jesus will be made King on Mount Zion, ruling over the whole world, with His throne in Jerusalem.[2] Galilee is not where He will rule from.
3. The reason they want Jesus to be king is completely wrong, because they were only concerned about a life of ease, and not having to work for their food, as Jesus expands on later when talking about the Bread of Life.

[1] Mark 6:46

[2] Psalm 2

TRAINING FOR THE STORMS OF LIFE
Matthew 14:22-33, Mark 6:45-52, John 6:16-21

This is the fifth of John's seven signs, and the lesson is, put your trust in Jesus. The three gospels combined give us a fairly clear description of the circumstances. To begin with it was sunset time and the disciples were in a boat by themselves in the middle of the Sea of Galilee.[1] After it became dark, the time when storms on the Sea of Galilee often occur, a particularly strong tempest with violent winds hit the boat.[2] They fought the sea and the waves for about nine hours, because Mark 6:48 and Matthew 14:25 both say it was about the fourth watch of the night, which would be between 3:00 a.m. and 6:00 a.m., or about nine hours after sunset.

As the nine hours passed, their situation became more and more desperate until they believed they were all going to die. The work of rowing in the very rough weather was strenuous because they were heading into the wind,[3] no doubt to keep the waves coming towards the bow of the boat. The bow of the vessel was designed to float over the waves coming towards it, lifting the boat over them. That is why they had to face the waves head on because waves hitting the ship from any other direction would fill it and sink it. In nine hours of hard rowing against the wind and the waves they only travelled twenty-five or thirty furlongs,[4] which would be less than 740 yards an hour. At this point they saw Jesus walking past them on the water.

> Mark 6:48 … and about the fourth watch of the night he cometh unto them, walking upon the sea, and would have passed by them.

If you were in the dark, in the middle of the sea and thought you could see someone walking on top of the waves, would you think it was a real person or a ghost? Lots and lots of people have seen ghosts doing funny things, but not many have ever seen a real person walking on the sea. The disciples thought Jesus was a ghost, and because in their culture an angel was often supposed to visit people just before they died, they would naturally think He was the angel of death.

> Matthew 14:26 And when the disciples saw him walking on the sea, they were troubled, saying, It is a spirit; and they cried out for fear.

The lesson Jesus wanted them to learn by seeming to walk passed them was that they should call on Him in times of danger.

> Matthew 14:27 But straightway Jesus spake unto them, saying, Be of good cheer; it is I; be not afraid.

The discovery that this really was Jesus put them at ease. Every day when we had the farm I used to visit my cows, and as soon as they saw me coming they would stop grazing the grass and watch me, getting ready to run away in case of danger, but after I spoke and they recognized my voice they would all relax and start peacefully eating again. Some would come up and lick me, the way they licked their calves. Sheep are the same with their shepherd, apart from the licking that is, and so were the disciples.

The famous story of Peter walking on the water comes from the Gospel of Matthew.[5] Peter asked Jesus to let him walk on the sea, and when Jesus asked Peter to join Him, Peter got out of the boat and walked on the water towards Jesus. He walked along nicely while he was looking at Jesus, but for some reason he looked away to see the waves, and then he started to sink. Fortunately for Peter he shouted out to Jesus for help.

> Matthew 14:31 And immediately Jesus stretched forth his hand, and caught him, and said unto him, O thou of little faith, wherefore didst thou doubt?

The point of the lesson is faith in God, we should never start anything without faith, but having begun in faith, whatever happens we must continue to have faith right to the end, then we really praise God because He works through us when we have faith. Notice also that Peter only got out of the boat to walk on the water after Jesus had called him, and because Peter obeyed Jesus it did not mean that Peter was going to have an easy time. The wind did not stop blowing and the sea was just as rough as before, therefore when we obey Jesus it does not mean there will not be any problems or that He is going to make things easy for us. Difficulties that are more than we can cope with may occur that only God can remove, and Jesus will remove them when we apply the faith we have in Him.[6] The disciples should have learned to have faith in Jesus to handle impossible situations from the feeding of the five thousand, as Mark tells us.

> Mark 6:51-52 51 And he went up to them into the ship; and the wind ceased: and they were sore amazed in themselves beyond measure, and wondered.
>
> 52 For they considered not the miracle of the loaves: for their heart was hardened.

They were only frightened because they had not learned the lesson to depend on Jesus from the feeding of the five thousand.

As we face the storms of life we need to understand the Bible correctly, we must grasp its teaching, then we have to do what the Bible tells us, or to put it another way, we must apply the message in our lives.

> Matthew 14:33 Then they that were in the ship came and worshipped him, saying, Of a truth thou art the Son of God.

To be successful in our spiritual life we need a good knowledge of the Bible, but many people that know the Bible well do not have victory spiritually, God's promises seem to pass them by. The reason is that these know-it-alls, don't apply their knowledge, they don't put it into practice from day to day, it's very sad.

[1] Mark 6:47

[2] John 6:17-18

[3] Mark 6:48

[4] John 6:19

[5] Matthew 14:28-31

[6] John 14:12-14

WELCOMED IN GENNESARET
Matthew 14:34-36, Mark 6:53-56

After the storm they sailed back across the lake to Jewish territory, to a region called Gennesaret, where Jesus was warmly welcomed, not because they recognized Him as Messiah but because He healed the sick. The reason for their acceptance was wrong but still it is better to be appreciated than to be made unwelcome. He healed them because of their personal need.

> Mark 6:56 And whithersoever he entered, into villages, or cities, or country, they laid the sick in the streets, and besought him that they might touch if it were but the border of his garment: and as many as touched him were made whole.

> Matthew 14:36 And besought him that they might only touch the hem of his garment: and as many as touched were made perfectly whole.

In both gospels we learn that they besought Him, they pleaded with Him, meaning they had personal needs, and everyone that touched the border of His garment was completely healed. The garment that Jesus wore was bordered or hemmed with tassels, according to the Law of Moses,[1] which Law Jesus kept perfectly down to the last jot and tittle,[2] and His keeping the Law made the Pharisees so angry because they could not find a single fault with Him. The tassels are still worn by observant Jews and it was these that the sick people were touching to get healed, so these people that were cured had faith, but as we are soon to find out most of the people did not.

[1] Deuteronomy 22:12
[2] Matthew 5:17-18, John 8:46

THE BREAD OF LIFE
John 6:22-71

The discourse by Jesus on the Bread of Life, is the third of His seven talks given to us by John. In His talk Jesus is presenting another kind of life to the Jews, but because they have rejected Him as the Messiah, He explains it to them parabolically, in a way they do not understand, as their questions and conversations among each other show. He tells them four things about this other life.

1. This new life is everlasting, it will never ever end.

John 6:27 Labour not for the meat which perisheth, but for the meat which endureth unto everlasting life, which the Son of man shall give unto you.

The word 'meat' here is used in the same way it was used in the seventeenth century, when the Authorized Version of the Bible was written, and it means food, including of course, bread.

2. The new life will be heavenly life, because it comes from heaven.

John 6:32-33 [32] Moses gave you not that bread from heaven; but my father giveth you the true bread from heaven.

[33] For the bread of God is he which cometh down from heaven, and giveth life unto the world.

3. A lovely thing about this new life is that it gives satisfaction, and for that reason it brings spiritual happiness and contentment.

John 6:35 ... he that cometh to me shall never hunger; and he that believeth on me shall never thirst.

4. The life Jesus is offering is resurrection life, and just as Jesus was resurrected so will everyone with the new life.

John 6: 39-40 And this is the Father's will which hath sent me, that of all which he hath given me I should lose nothing, but should raise it up again at the last day.

[40] And this is the will of him that sent me, that every one which seeth the Son, and believeth on him, may have everlasting life: and I will raise him up at the last day.

Such a wonderful new life was being offered but it was portrayed in a way that the majority would never understand, and we see their disbelief and utter blankness in several verses.

John 6:41-42 [41] And the Jews murmured at him, because he said, I am the bread which came down from heaven.

[42] And they said, Is not this Jesus, the son of Joseph, whose father and mother we know? How is then that he saith [says], I came down from heaven?

John 6:52 The Jews therefore began to strove [argue] among themselves, saying, How can this man give us his flesh to eat?

Obviously the Jews did not understand the offer being made to them, but that of course was intentional following their rejection of Jesus. Physical things they understood well, but the spiritual meaning had been hidden from them.

Jesus had already given the signs that showed He was the Messiah and these were rejected on the false grounds that His power came from Beelzebub, and the reason the Galileans had wanted to make Him king was not because they saw the signs, as Jesus knew very well.

> John 6:26 Ye seek me, not because ye saw the miracles, but because ye did eat of the loaves, and were filled.

The situation was still the same, they liked the bread, the physical food but were not even aware of the spiritual message it represented.

> John 6:28-29 ²⁸ Then said they unto him, What shall we do, that we might work the works of God?
>
> ²⁹ Jesus answered and said unto them, This is the work of God, that ye believe on him whom he hath sent.

What do we have to do to get eternal life, what work does God require from us? The work that will save us is to believe in the One Person, God sent. Their question was something to say to make an opening for what was really on their minds, that physical, tasty, miraculous bread.

> John 6:31 Our fathers did eat manna in the desert; as it is written, He gave them bread from heaven to eat.

In other words, Moses gave our forefathers manna,[1] what are you going to give us? Jesus then went on to explain that God provided the manna. Moses had only taught them about the manna and how to use it.

In John 6:35 is the first of John's seven, "I am," statements, "I am the bread of life." Following that, in spite of their disbelief, Jesus states emphatically in verses 36-39, that He will be completely successful, and all who believe will be resurrected after their death. We have quoted John 6:41 already, but notice it tells us they murmured against Him. John probably chose the word, "murmured" because after the Hebrews left Egypt, God had provided water and manna in the dessert, but they were a bunch of moaners and murmured against both Moses and God,[2], and now their descendants are murmuring against Jesus, the Bread of Life, also provided by God.

Believers in Jesus should never, ever, murmur or grumble because God is watching us all the time and He does not like it, since all our lives are under His control, and He allows difficulties to come into our lives to help us mature spiritually. Any problem that is impossible for us, remember, is not impossible for God, so who should we turn to in times of trouble? After leaving Egypt the Jews murmured in their tents, and although they thought no one knew about what they said in their tents, God heard them.[3] My grandmother would stop people moaning by saying, "We mustn't grumble, all these things are sent to try us." It was a common expression of the time and reflects the Bible based Christian heritage of England following the Reformation, and the people's understanding that God did not like moaners. After the Jews murmured against God in the wilderness, He cursed them and refused to allow any of them to enter the promised land, except for Joshua and Caleb, the two that did not murmur.[4]

Jesus explained to the crowd the reason why they did not believe.

> John 6:44-45 [44] No man can come to me, except the Father which hath sent me draw him: and I will raise him up on the last day.
>
> [45] ... Every man therefore that hath heard, and hath learned of the Father, cometh unto me.

Jesus told the multitude that to have eternal life they must eat His flesh,[5] but He was speaking parabolically so that they would not understand, therefore we must find out what He actually meant. He had already clearly said that to have eternal life we must believe in Him, so when He told the crowds they had to eat his flesh, He was saying in effect they must believe in Him, but they were thinking of physical food and did not understand.

> John 6:47 ... He that believeth on me hath everlasting life.

Eating His flesh and drinking His blood, in the context of John 6:22-71, has nothing to do with taking communion,[6] which we do to remember the Lord's death. The Jews could not understand how they would be able to eat the flesh of Jesus, who answered their question in John 6:53-57, again in a way they would not understand.

> John 6:53-54 [53] ... Except ye eat the flesh of the Son of man, and drink his blood, ye have no life in you.
>
> [54] Whoso eateth my flesh, and drinketh my blood, hath eternal life; and I will raise him up at the last day.

Once again, to eat His flesh and drink His blood, is not to take the bread and the cup at communion, it is His parabolic way of saying it is necessary to believe in Him, as He had said earlier.

> John 6:29 ... This is the work of God, that ye believe on him whom he hath sent.

The food that we eat makes us grow and becomes part of us, so when we have believed or we could say, swallowed, the fact that Jesus is the Son of God, He will live in us, we become united with each other. Faith in Jesus results in eternal life, but eating manna did not do that,[7] it only kept people alive physically.

> John 6:63 It is the spirit that quickeneth; the flesh profiteth nothing: the words that I speak unto you, they are spirit, and they are life.

Although many do not grasp and accept the words Jesus is saying here, yet His words bring eternal life to the believer. He then explains again the reason for their unbelief.

> John 6:65 ... Therefore said I unto you, that no man can come unto me, except it were given unto him of my Father.

The talk about the Bread of Life led to three important results.

1. Many of His disciples, but not any of the twelve apostles, left Him.

> John 6:66 From that time many of his disciples went back, and walked no more with him.

2. Peter, speaking for the twelve apostles declared once more their belief in Jesus, although Peter had misjudged one of the twelve.

> John 6:69 ... we believe and are sure that thou art the Christ, the Son of the living God.

Jesus could not allow Peter and the others to be misled, and so we come to the third result from His talk.

3. Judas Iscariot is identified here as the one who would betray Jesus, and therefore Judas did not have the eternal life Peter thought he had.

John 6:70-71 ⁷⁰ Jesus answered them, Have I not chosen you twelve, and one of you is a devil?

⁷¹ He spake of Judas Iscariot the son of Simon: for he it was that should betray him, being one of the twelve.

[1] Exodus 16:31-32
[2] Numbers 16:41, 17:5
[3] Deuteronomy 1:27
[4] Numbers 14:26-32
[5] John 6:51
[6] 1 Corinthians 11:23-26
[7] John 6:58

WHAT DEFILES A MAN? WHAT DEGRADES HIM?
Matthew 15:1-20, Mark 7:1-19

The man made rules of the Pharisees, the oral law, now written down in the Mishnah, were often proved to be false by Jesus. We have dealt with fasting, in addition to keeping the Sabbath, and now we come to a third matter, washing your hands before eating. By the time of Jesus, you may remember, the Mishnah had equal authority with, or sometimes more authority than Scripture. Just look at four quotations from the Mishnah about itself.

1. He that says something against his rabbi causes the Shekinah to depart from Israel.
2. He that contradicts his rabbi is a he that would contradict the Shekinah. He that would speak against his rabbi is a he that would speak against God.
3. My son, give more heed to the word of the rabbis than to the words of the Mosaic Law.

4. Our rabbis taught, to engage in the study of Scripture is neither good nor bad, but to engage in the study of the Mishnah is a good habit and brings reward.

The Pharisees were so proud of themselves they put their oral law above the word of God, and one of their key topics was hand washing. Mark, who was writing to the Romans, carefully explained in his gospel the Jewish hand washing ritual,[1] before coming to the question the Pharisees asked Jesus.

Mark 7:5 … Why walk not thy disciples according to the tradition of the elders, but eat bread with unwashed hands?

The New Testament name for the Mishnah is shown in this verse, 'the tradition of the elders.' They would not even eat one seed unless they had washed their hands. We will now look at four more quotations from the Mishnah, this time about washing hands.

1. It is better to have to walk four miles to water, than to incur the guilt of neglecting hand washing. (You are out in the countryside and think to yourself, "Those blackberries look scrumptious, I'll walk four miles back to the stream I saw, wash my hands and come back and try one.")
2. One that neglects hand washing is as bad as a murderer.
3. One who neglects hand washing is like one who went unto a prostitute.
4. Three sins bring poverty after them, one of which is neglecting hand washing. (If you don't want to be poor, wash your hands before you eat.)

They were told to wash their hands from the elbow to the tips of their fingers.

The question, as to why the disciples ate bread with unwashed hands, was an attempt to find something wrong with Jesus, so that they could accuse Him of being a sinner. Jesus never bothered with their oral law, in fact sometimes He would break the rules on purpose, but He kept the Law of Moses perfectly, and try as many times they did, they were never able to accuse Him of breaking the Law as written in the Bible, never, ever. Jesus responded to their question, by explaining the sins they were committing by keeping the Mishnaic law.

1. They are hypocrites and therefore their religious traditions are fake.

Mark 7:7 Howbeit in vain do they worship me, teaching for doctrines [rules] the commandments of men.

People who carefully follow religious rituals sometimes do it believing God will be pleased with them, sometimes to impress other people, and sometimes for personal gain, but Jesus says, keeping man made rules is vain, absolutely useless. The word of God is in the Bible, and we must follow Scripture.

2. They are so keen to keep their traditions they break the commands of God to do so.

Matthew 15:3 Why do ye also transgress the commandment of God by your tradition?

They break the Law of Moses, given by God, to keep the laws they made up themselves. Jesus gave just one of many examples He could have given, choosing to point out the wickedness of the Corban.

Corban, mentioned in Mark 7:11, means "dedicated" in Hebrew, and it was used by the Pharisees to identify something that had been dedicated to God. At any moment of the night or day, a Pharisee could wave a hand and say, "Corban!" From that moment all his material possessions were set aside or dedicated, and he could only do two things with them. He could give some of it or all of it to the Temple, or, he could keep it for his own use, but he could not, from then on, give any of it to someone else for them to use. He could not even give it for a good cause or for charity, if he did not give it to the Temple he had to keep it.

In the Ten Commandments, God said, "Honour thy father and thy mother,"[2] and Moses expanded on this in the Law, saying that children are responsible to make sure their parents are looked after when they are unable look after themselves. That was the Law of Moses.

The Pharisees had new converts in their ranks, with old and infirm parents who were physically or mentally disabled, but were not Pharisees, and the Pharisees were unwilling to share their wealth with non-Pharisees. A Pharisee would see his father coming to visit him, and knowing his deep need of help, he would say, "Corban" (Dedicated). The father when he arrived would explain his difficulty, and the son would say, "I have just made all my possessions Corban, I am sorry but I cannot help you. Nothing I own can be given for anyone else's personal use, what a pity you did not arrive earlier." The money did not have to be given to the Temple, he could still keep all of it for his own use, and so they broke the Law of Moses to keep their traditions, as Jesus knew very well.

> Mark 7:9-13 [9]And he said unto them, Full well ye reject the commandment of God, that ye may keep your own tradition.
>
> [10] For Moses said, Honour thy father and thy mother; and, Whoso curseth father or mother, let him die the death.
>
> [11] But ye say, If a man shall say to his father or mother, It is Corban, that is to say a gift, by whatsoever thou mightest be profited by me; he shall be free.
>
> [12] And ye suffer him no more to do ought for his father or his mother;
>
> [13] Making the word of God of none effect through your tradition, which ye have delivered: and many such like things do ye.

Chapter 7, of Mark shows Jesus' new method of preaching. In verse 14, He called all the people and told them to listen and understand, then in verse 15, He spoke parabolically so that none of them would understand, then in verse 17, he went indoors with His disciples and explained the meaning to them privately. Since Israel rejected Him, His intention is to hide the truth from the multitude and to explain it to His disciples, so that later on they can teach the Gentiles.

The disciples came to Jesus in Matthew 15:12-14, saying that He had offended the Pharisees by what He said, but that is necessary

sometimes and Jesus made three comments about the Pharisees.
1. They are plants that God did not plant and must be pulled up.
2. They are leaders but are blind and walking towards a pit. They were heading for annihilation at the siege of Jerusalem in AD 70, and they were leading their followers to destruction along with themselves.
3. They were defiled internally and that resulted in sinful behaviour. This comes out in Matthew 15:15-20 which we will look at more closely.

Interestingly, it was Peter who asked Jesus to explain the parable,[3] because it was Peter who did not learn the lesson at this time. The real issue is, what defiles a man?, where does sin start? For the Pharisees it was external, but the true righteousness of the Law is internal. Moses said they could not eat pork, and as far as the Pharisees were concerned they had not sinned until they ate the pork. Now suppose a Jew saw some Gentiles tucking into some roast pig, and smelt the appetizing aroma, and thought to himself, "That smells good, I am going to try some of that," he had already sinned internally, and it is the internal sin that leads to the external. In the same way, watching pornography on television can lead to internal sin, resulting in the actual sinful act. Listen to Jesus.

> Matthew 15:19-20 [19] For out of the heart proceed evil thoughts, murders, adulteries, fornications, thefts, false witness, blasphemies:
>
> [20] These are the things which defile a man: but to eat with unwashen hands defileth not a man.

Coming back to Peter, the man that asked the question, two times God had to teach him the lesson, that eating certain foods does not defile a man. In Mark 7:18-19, Jesus said that anything that goes into a man from the outside cannot defile him because it does not go into his heart, only his stomach from where it is flushed out. Peter had to learn the lesson again in Acts 10:1-16, when God gave him a vision in which Peter was told to eat all kinds of unclean animals and birds. When Peter complained, God told him again, that He had declared them all clean. It is what is in our hearts that is important to God.

[1] Mark 7:1-4
[2] Exodus 20:12
[3] Matthew 15:15

A WELCOME IN TYRE AND SIDON
Matthew 15:21-28, Mark 7:24-30

For the second time in this chapter about Jesus training the twelve, He goes away to a Gentile area, to what is now Lebanon, because He wanted to spend some time privately with the disciples.

> Mark 7:24 … (He) entered into a house, and would have no man know it: but he could not be hid.

He was famous in the area and a Gentile woman came looking for Him, note she was not Jewish, but still she cried out to Him.

> Matthew 15:22 … saying, Have mercy on me, O Lord, thou Son of David; my daughter is grievously vexed with a devil.

She makes her appeal to Him as the Messiah of Israel, but the Jews have rejected their Messiah, and even if they had not, she is not Jewish, so Jesus ignores her.

> Matthew 15:23 But he answered her not a word.

She keeps on asking and eventually Jesus tells her why He has not helped her.

> Matthew 15: 24 But he answered and said, I am not sent but unto the lost sheep of the house of Israel.

The woman then understood that He had been sent to Israel, and because she was a Gentile, it was no good her asking help on the basis that He was the Jewish Messiah, so she changed the way she made her request.

> Matthew 15:25 Then came she and worshipped him, saying, Lord, help me.

Her appeal was now on the basis of personal need, but Jesus wanted to make sure she had learned this correctly and that faith was also required, so he continued.

> Matthew 15:26 But he answered and said, It is not meet [right] to take the children's bread, and cast it to dogs.

We Gentiles sometimes don't like the fact that Jesus called us dogs, but the Greek root word means young dogs or puppies, which are very lovable as they scamper around the table and beg for food. The message to the woman was that just as good food meant for children, should not be taken away from the children and fed to puppies, so that which God promised the Jews, should not be taken away from them and given to Gentiles. The Jews may have rejected Him, but He hadn't rejected them. Her answer shows she understood the lesson very well indeed.

> Matthew 15:27 And she said, Truth, Lord: yet the dogs [puppies] eat of the crumbs which fall from the master's table.

She says she is not asking for the children's food, but only for that which is meant for the Gentiles, and the Old Testament does promise that the Jewish Messiah will also be the Saviour of the Gentiles.[1] Jesus then helped the woman because of her personal need and her faith.

> Matthew 15:28 Then Jesus answered and said unto her, O woman, great is thy faith: be it unto thee even as thou wilt. And her daughter was made whole from that very hour.

[1] Isaiah 49:6

A WARM WELCOME IN DECAPOLIS
Matthew 15:29-39, Mark 7:31 to 8:10

For the third time during this training session Jesus moves into Gentile territory, to the region of Decapolis, which we have already learnt is a Greek speaking area with ten towns. One town, Scythopolis, (called Bethshean in the Old Testament), was west of the River Jordan and all the others were east of the Jordan. The last time Jesus was here, you will remember, He cast a legion of demons out of two men and let them go into some pigs, and the pigs committed suicide by drowning themselves. One of the men wanted to be a disciple of Jesus but Jesus was not looking for Gentile disciples at that time, and refused to take him, but He asked the man to go and tell everyone what God had done for him.

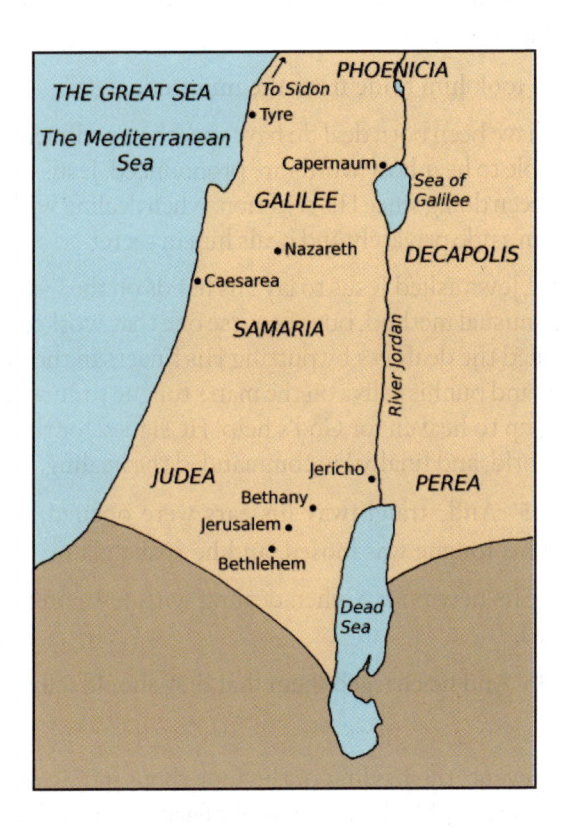

Where Jesus Walked

The man had worked hard spreading the news because now crowds of people from the ten towns welcomed Jesus, while before He had been asked to leave. We are going to notice two things from this passage of Scripture, one Jewish and the other Gentile.

The ten towns of the Decapolis had small Jewish communities, living among the Gentiles, and we can tell by the details in Mark 7:32-37, that a man that came to Jesus to be healed was a Jew living in a Greek city, and that those that brought him were also Jewish.

> Mark 7:32-33 [32] And they bring unto him one that was deaf, and had an impediment in his speech; and they beseech him to put his hand upon him.
>
> [33] And he took him aside from the multitude.

People that have been born deaf do have speech impediments because they are unable to hear how words are pronounced. Jesus behaves the way He has been doing since His rejection, when dealing with Jews. He takes the man aside privately and heals him in secret.

Although the Jews asked Jesus to lay His hands on the man, this time He uses an unusual method, but of course one that worked perfectly. First He healed the deafness by putting His fingers in the man's ears, then He spit and put his saliva on the man's tongue to cure his speech, and looking up to heaven for God's help, He sighed for the results of sin in this world, and finally He commanded the healing.

> Mark 7:35 And straightway his ears were opened, and the string of his tongue was loosed, and he spake plain.

Now notice His new policy when dealing with Jews on the basis of personal need.

> Mark 7:36 And he charged them that they should tell no man.

The Gentile event, the feeding of the four thousand, is recorded by Matthew as well as Mark. This has similarities to, and differences from the feeding of the five thousand. Here the 4,000 men plus women and children are mainly Gentiles, there he had a Jewish crowd of 5,000 men plus women and children. The Gentiles came to Jesus because of the preaching work of the healed demoniac, and the way Jesus had been dealing with Jewish crowds did not apply to them. He would tell the Gentiles, just as he had told the demoniac, to go and spread the news of what He had done, to proclaim it, but He told the Jews not to tell anyone. In Matthew 15:30-31, crowds of Gentiles came bringing the lame, blind, dumb and maimed for healing, because of the man that had told them about Jesus casting out the demons, and the result was that the Gentiles, "glorified the God of Israel." They were turning to the Jewish Messiah in large numbers, the man had done the sowing, and Jesus was reaping the harvest. The people were so enthusiastic they had stayed there without food, and the feeding of the four thousand was soon to take place, but once again the main reason for the miracle was to train the twelve.

> Matthew 15:32 Then Jesus called his disciples unto him.

Jesus wanted the disciples to understand the problem that needed to be dealt with, and so he said to them.

> Mark 8:2-3 ² I have compassion on the multitude, because they have now been with me three days, and have nothing to eat:
> ³ And if I send them away fasting to their own houses, they will faint by the way: for divers [some] of them came from far.

What follows shows that the disciples had not learnt the lesson given at the feeding of the five thousand.

> Mark 8:4 And his disciples answered him, From whence can a man satisfy these men with bread here in the wilderness?

They have not yet learned that Jesus can provide bread or anything else that may be needed, and Jesus, concentrating on His disciples, asks them a question.

> Matthew 15: 34 ... How many loaves have ye? And they said, Seven, and a few little fishes.

These are different numbers from the feeding of the five thousand, and there is probably some significance in the differences. As before Jesus took the loaves and the fish, blessed them and gave them out for the disciples to pass on to the people, who ate, and ate until they were all full up. This time the left over food filled seven baskets, but when the Jews ate there were twelve baskets. It is interesting that twelve is a number we frequently come across in the Bible concerning Israel. There are twelve tribes,[1] twelve springs at Elim,[2] twelve stones in Joshua's memorial,[3] twelve bronze oxen in the Jerusalem Temple,[4] twelve apostles,[5] etc. On the other hand the number seven is often seen in relation with the Gentiles, particularly in God's dealings with Noah when He saved a few Gentiles from the flood. Noah was told to take seven pairs of all clean animals and seven pairs of the different kinds of birds,[6] into the ark.

> Genesis 7:4 For yet seven days, and I will cause it to rain upon the earth.

When the flood was over God sent the rainbow, with seven colours, as a sign to remind Him, not to destroy the earth again by flooding.[7]

The two lessons for the disciples from feeding the four thousand are first, Jesus can provide what is needed in every situation, and secondly, the Gentiles can profit from His care. Although until the resurrection, His attention was first and foremost to Israel, the Gentiles would also benefit greatly from Israel's King. However, don't think He is finished with Israel forever. God never fails in anything, and He will not change his mind to put Jesus on the throne in Jerusalem, where as King of the Jews, He will rule the world. Many Old Testament prophecies speak of this future event, Psalm 2, being a good example, and from the New Testament, Romans 11:25-26.

[1] Genesis 49:28
[2] Numbers 33:9
[3] Joshua 4:9
[4] 2 Chronicles 4:4
[5] Matthew 10:2
[6] Genesis 7:2-3
[7] Genesis 9:12-17

REJECTED IN MAGADAN
Matthew 15:39 to 16:4

Jesus returned to Jewish territory again, and in Magadan, the Pharisees and the Sadducees though separated by many different interpretations of Scripture and religious beliefs, and not friendly with each other, actually united together to try and find fault with Jesus.

> Matthew 16:1 The Pharisees also with the Sadducees came, tempting desired him that he would shew [show] them a sign from heaven.

Jesus had shown them many, many signs but they would not accept them, and here they asked for a sign from heaven. The reason they asked for a sign from heaven is that whenever He gave them a sign they said it was from Hell, through Beelzebub, even when He cast out demons, so what was the point of Jesus giving them any more signs? They were very childish weren't they?

> Matthew 16:2-4 ² He answered and said unto them, When it is evening, ye say, It will be fair weather: for the sky is red.
>
> ³ And in the morning, It will be foul [bad] weather to day: for the sky is red and lowering [threatening]. O ye hypocrites [pretenders], ye can discern the face of the sky; but can ye not discern the signs of the times?
>
> ⁴ A wicked and adulterous generation seeketh [looks for] after a sign; and there shall no sign be given unto it, but the sign of the prophet Jonas. And he left them and departed.

The sign of Jonah (Jonas) is resurrection, bringing the dead back to life, and it will be given to Israel three times, the first two times have passed, the resurrection of Lazarus,[1] and the resurrection of Jesus.[2] There will be one more, the resurrection of God's two witnesses towards the end of the reign of the anti-Christ,[3] then the Jews will believe the sign and accept Jesus as Messiah, after that He will reign over the earth.

The Bible says that Jonah was swallowed by a fish and was in the belly of the fish for three days and three nights.[4] While he was in the fish he died because the story goes on to say he went to Sheol. You will remember in Chapter 6, in the section, The King's Power Over Demons, Sheol at that time had a good side, Paradise or Abraham's Bosom, and a bad side, and everyone that died went there, to one side or the other. After he had died the spirit of Jonah prayed to God from Sheol, but his dead body was in the stomach of the fish.

> Jonah 2:1-2 ¹ Then Jonah prayed unto the LORD his God out of the fish's belly,
>
> ² And said, I cried by reason of mine affliction unto the LORD, and he heard me; out of the belly of hell [Sheol], cried I, and thou heardest my voice.

The fact that Jonah was dead while in the fish was confirmed by Jesus when He prophesied His own death.

> Matthew 12:40 (Jesus said) For as [in the same way] Jonas [Jonah] was three days and three nights in the whale's belly; so shall the Son of man be three days and three nights in the heart of the earth.

Jesus was dead when they buried Him, as we will find out later, and because that was so, Jonah was dead in the fish, in the same way that Jesus was dead in the grave while He was buried. The conclusion is that God brought Jonah back to life after he had died. Jonah was resurrected.

Another interesting point about Jonah was that although Jewish, he was a prophet to the Gentiles, and it was after his resurrection that the people of Ninevah repented and turned to Israel's God,[5] just as Gentiles around the world are doing today after the resurrection of Jesus.

---

[1] John 11:43-46, 12:9-11

[2] Mark 16:14, Luke 24:33-34, 2 Timothy 2:2-9

[3] Revelation 11:3-12

[4] Jonah 1:17

[5] Jonah 1:1 to 4:11

WARNING AGAINST FALSE TEACHERS
Matthew 16:5-12, Mark 8:14-26

It seems that after telling the Pharisees and Sadducees that no more signs would be given except the sign of Jonah, Jesus and the disciples went back across the lake to the Gentile area for the fourth time.

> Matthew 16:4-5 ⁴ ... And he left them, and departed.
>
> ⁵ And when his disciples were come to the other side, ...

Jesus warned the disciples against three kinds of leaven, the leaven of the Pharisees and Sadducees are in Matthew 16:6, but Mark 8:15 also brings in the leaven of Herod or the Herodians. Leaven is anything that is put into bread dough before it is cooked to inflate it with gas or air bubbles. It can be yeast or in ancient times old sour fermenting dough that was going bad was used. The fresh dough was quickly infected by the bad effervescing dough causing the whole lot to puff up. Pride is a sin that puffs us up, because it makes us feel we are better than other people, and leaven puffing up the dough is a symbol of this. Leaven therefore represents sin, something rotten that infects us and makes us proud, stopping us from being humble before God. In the gospels it is the sin of false teaching, and all three groups, the Pharisees, Sadducees and Herodians were spreading their own special lies about Jesus.

1. The leaven of the Pharisees was their teaching that Jesus was possessed by a demon.
2. The Sadducees didn't believe in demons, so they invented another leaven, saying that Jesus was against the system of worship in the Temple.
3. The Herodians taught that Jesus was against the rule of Rome by Herod's family.

The disciples after being warned about the three kinds of leaven, thought they were being told off for not bringing enough bread to eat on the journey.

> Mark 8:16-18 ¹⁶ And they reasoned among themselves, saying, It is because we have no bread.

> ¹⁷ And when Jesus knew it, he saith unto them, Why reason ye, because ye have no bread? Perceive ye not yet, neither understand? Have ye your heart yet hardened?
>
> ¹⁸ Having eyes see ye not? And having ears, hear ye not? And do ye not remember?

He went on to remind them of the feeding of the five thousand, and of the four thousand, because they should have known by now that He could provide for all their physical needs in all circumstances. If they got hungry He would give them all they wanted. The important thing they must get into their heads was to beware of the false teachings about Him and His word, by those who rejected Him. It is the same today. We must beware of the false teachings about Him by religions that reject Him, journalists that reject Him, politicians that reject Him, scientists that reject Him, school teachers that reject Him, parents that reject Him, and probably worst of all ministers of the church that reject His word.

Finally the disciples understood what He had been teaching them.

> Matthew 16:12 Then understood they how that he bade them not beware of the leaven of bread, but of the doctrine of the Pharisees and of the Sadducees.

He is warning them against false teaching coming from people that don't believe in Him.

Jesus next led His disciples back into Jewish territory, and we see the method He had used since His rejection in operation once more.

> Mark 8:22-23 ²² And he cometh to Bethsaida; and they bring a blind man unto him.
>
> ²³ And he took the blind man by the hand, and led him out of the town.

He led the man away from the crowds to heal him privately. The healing was given in two separate steps, the only time in the gospels He ever healed in two stages. The method He used to heal the blindness was first to spit on the blind man's eyes, and then to lay hands on him. Very strangely for Jesus the man's sight was not properly restored, because although he could see, his vision was blurred, people looked like trees walking about. Jesus was teaching His disciples something because He could have healed the man in one go. After Jesus touched the man a second time he saw clearly. Let's record these two steps, so that we remember them.

1. The man (representing the disciples), that had been blind could see but not clearly.
2. After the blindness is completely cured, he could see perfectly.

As we bring this section to a close, notice that after the healing, the request for silence was still being made.

> Mark 8:26 And he sent him away to his house, saying, Neither go into the town, nor tell it to any in the town.

PETER'S CONFESSION
Matthew 16:13-20, Mark 8:27-30, Luke 9:18-21

This section will show that the disciples do not yet have perfect vision regarding spiritual things.

Jesus and the disciples, still just inside Gentile territory, now came to the town of Caesarea Philippi, at the foot of Mount Hermon, which soaring over 9,000 feet above sea level is the highest mountain in the Holy Land. The town has been built out from the base of a towering stone cliff that dwarfs it. At the bottom of this massive overshadowing rock is a cave from where one of the four sources of the River Jordan, the River Banyas, used to shoot out until about a hundred years ago when an earthquake interrupted the flow, and since then the Banyas has flowed from the right of the cave. Today the cave is dry, but at the time of Jesus, the force of the water running from the cave, broke fragments from the rock, and the small pebbles and stones can still be seen a little way down river. It helps to know this bit of geography because Jesus refers to it when speaking to the disciples, Peter in particular.

Imagine Jesus and the disciples together at the foot of the massive rock face, with the River Banyas quickly flowing from the mouth of the cave. The disciples have just been given a lesson on the false teaching of the

Pharisees, Sadducees and Herodians, three kinds of leaven (sin), and Jesus wants to know if they have understood, so He asks them two test questions.

Matthew 16:13 Whom do men say that I the Son of man am?

From the answers we know that there were different opinions among the people, as to who Jesus was. Some thought He was John the Baptist raised from the dead, some remembered the prophecy that Elijah would come before the Messiah,[1] and thought He was Elijah come back again, or Jeremiah or various other prophets from the Old Testament that had returned. The people realized therefore that there was something supernatural about Jesus, but what they did not recognize is that He was the Messiah (the Christ), their future King, so Jesus asked His second question.

Matthew 16:15 But whom say ye that I am?

Peter, speaking for the disciples as a group had no doubt.

Matthew 16:16 Thou art the Christ, the Son of the living God.

Peter's answer shows that they did understand, and had learned the lesson. The disciples were now ready for some more teaching, and speaking to Peter, Jesus has five more things to tell them.

The First Thing Jesus Tells Peter

Matthew 16:17 Blessed art thou, Simon Barjonah: for flesh and blood hath not revealed it to thee, but my Father which is in heaven.

In other words Peter had not learned that Jesus was the Christ, even from Jesus Himself, but God the Father had made him understand supernaturally.

The Second Thing Jesus Tells Peter

Matthew 16:18 And I say also unto thee, That thou art Peter, and upon this rock I will build my church.

The early Roman Catholics saw this verse, and believing it taught that Peter would build the Church, decided to claim that Peter had been the first Pope, and then went on to say that the authority of God is passed down from Pope to Pope all the way back to Peter, and for that reason the Roman Catholic Church is the only true Church. They still believe this story of theirs, but it is based on a completely wrong understanding of the very simple Greek grammar used by Matthew in his gospel.

Matthew tells us that Jesus said, "You are Peter," and the word Peter in Greek is a masculine word *"Petros,"* meaning a small pebble or stone, just like those in the River Banyas, that was flowing from the cave. Jesus went on to say, "Upon this rock I will build my church," and the Greek word used for rock was a feminine word *"petra,"* and it means a massive cliff of solid rock, just like the one overshadowing Caesarea Philippi, where they were at the time. In Greek grammar a feminine cannot modify a masculine, and for that reason Matthew cannot and does not mean that the Church will be built upon Peter.

Peter had confessed, "You are the Christ, the Son of the living God," and Jesus is telling them what Peter is, a small stone, a pebble, but Jesus is going to build His Church on the gigantic rock cliff from which the pebbles have been broken off. In the Old Testament the word 'rock' used symbolically was always as a symbol of the Messiah,[2] and so the meaning is that the cliff represents the Messiah, the Christ, and Jesus is going to build His Church upon Himself. Peter was right, Jesus is the Christ.

The Third Thing Jesus Tells Peter

> Matthew 16:18 ... and the gates of hell shall not prevail against it.

The word "hell" in this Scripture should have been "Hades" if translated correctly, meaning the resting place of departed spirits. In the Old Testament, "the gates of hell" (Hades), meant physical death.[3] See Chapter 6, The King's Power Over Demons. Jesus is going to build His Church upon Himself, "the Rock," and physical death will not prevail against it. If Jesus is killed, the Church will still prevail and triumph, if the disciples die or anyone else that has been born again into the new life dies, the Church will still win through. The physical death of those that belong to the true Church makes no difference; Jesus will continue to build until His Church is complete.

At the time Jesus spoke these words the Church did not exist. He said, "I will build My church." This is the first time the word "church" is used in the Bible and Peter and the other disciples, were being trained for the work of helping to build it.

The Fourth Thing Jesus Tells Peter

> Matthew 16:19 I will give unto thee the keys of the kingdom of heaven.

In the Old Testament, keys are a symbol of authority,[4] and of the right to open and close doors. In Chapter 6, The Dispute Over Jesus, we looked at five parts of the kingdom of heaven, including the Church which is a sub-part of the spiritual kingdom, and Peter is going to be responsible to open the doors to the Church. The Bible tells us later how Peter opened those doors.

The Old Testament divides people into two groups, Jews and Gentiles, but when we come to the New Testament there are three groups, Jews, Samaritans and Gentiles.

> Matthew 10:5-6 ⁵ These twelve Jesus sent forth, and commanded them, saying, Go not into the way of the Gentiles, and into any city of the Samaritans enter ye not:
>
> ⁶ But go rather to the lost sheep of the house of Israel.

These are the three groups of folks we find, and Peter will open the doors of the kingdom of heaven for each group, and after he has opened a door it stays open.

Peter opened the door of the kingdom of heaven for the Jews.

> Acts 2:36-41 ³⁶ Therefore let all the house of Israel know assuredly, that God hath made that same Jesus, whom ye have crucified, both Lord and Christ.

⁳⁷ Now when they heard this, they were pricked in their heart, and said unto Peter and the rest of the apostles, Men and brethren, what shall we do?

³⁸ Then Peter said unto them, Repent and be baptised every one of you in the name of Jesus Christ for the remission of sins, and ye shall receive the gift of the Holy Ghost.

³⁹ For the promise is unto you, and to your children, and to all that are afar off, even as many as the Lord our God shall call.

⁴⁰ And with many other words did he testify and exhort, saying, Save yourselves from this untoward generation.

⁴¹ Then they that gladly received his word were baptised: and the same day there were added unto them about three thousand souls.

The door to the Jews was open, and from then on every Jew that believed was and still is, baptised by the Spirit into the Church.

Peter opened the door to the kingdom of heaven for the Samaritans in Acts 8. Philip the evangelist[5] had preached the gospel to them but Peter had the keys, and so Peter had to go to Samaria after Philip had preached to unlock the door.

Acts 8:14-17 ¹⁴ Now when the apostles which were at Jerusalem heard that Samaria had received the word of God, they sent unto them Peter and John:

¹⁵ Who, when they were come down, prayed for them, that they might receive the Holy Ghost:

¹⁶ (For as yet he was fallen upon none of them: only they were baptised in the name of the Lord Jesus.)

¹⁷ Then laid they their hands on them, and they received the Holy Ghost.

The door was now open for the Samaritans, and ever since then whenever a Samaritan believer is baptised by the Holy Spirit he becomes a member of the body of Christ.

Paul, (previously Saul) was chosen by Jesus to be the apostle to the Gentiles,[6] but again he did not have the key. He preached to Jews in Acts 9:20-22, but before he preached to Gentiles, Peter went to the home of Cornelius. The Gentiles believed Peter and were baptised by the Spirit, and the door to the kingdom of heaven had now been opened for the Gentiles. In the Scripture that follows, "circumcision" means Jews, to distinguish them from the Gentiles who were not circumcised.

> Acts 10:44-48 44 While Peter yet spake these words, the Holy Ghost fell on all them which heard the word.
>
> 45 And they of the circumcision which believed were astonished, as many as came with Peter, because that on the Gentiles also was poured out the gift of the Holy Ghost.
>
> 46 For they heard them speak with tongues, and magnify God. Then answered Peter.
>
> 47 Can any man forbid water, that these should not be baptised, which have received the Holy Ghost as well as we?
>
> 48 And he commanded them to be baptised in the name of the Lord. Then prayed they him to tarry certain days.

Ever since that day everyone that believes is baptised by the Holy Spirit and becomes a member of the true Church, the body of Christ.

> 1 Corinthians 12:13 For by one Spirit are we all baptised into one body, whether we be Jews or Gentiles, whether we be bond or free; and have all been made to drink into one Spirit.

Peter has opened the doors to the kingdom of heaven, and no one can shut them. The way into the Church is by being baptised in the Spirit, and a congregation meeting in a building without the Holy Spirit is not part of the Church, even though it may call itself a church, and believe that it is one.[7]

The Fifth Thing Jesus Tells Peter

Peter is now given authority to make rules and regulations for the Church, which will be the body of Christ on earth, after Jesus has gone into heaven. The Church is the body of Christ because after Jesus went to heaven He sent His Spirit to live in us who belong to Him. His Spirit was in His own body while He was on earth, but now He (the Spirit of Jesus) is in those people who belong to His true spiritual Church.[8] Remember, Jesus at this time was training Peter and the other apostles for the work of setting up the Church, and someone would have to make the rules.

> Matthew 16:19 ... whatsoever thou shall bind on earth shall be bound in heaven: and whatsoever thou shalt loose on earth shall be loosed in heaven.

Many English speaking Christians have misunderstood this verse for hundreds of years, because they did not know the Jewish culture in which Jesus and His disciples lived. Contrary to current church wisdom, Matthew 16:19, has nothing at all to do with binding up Satan or demons so that they can no longer operate. As we shall show, in authorizing Peter to bind and loose, according to the language of the Jews, Jesus was giving Peter authority to allow or not to allow, that is to say, to make rules.

Binding and loosing were well know words in first century Israel, when Jesus was training His apostles, and giving them instructions for establishing His Church in a way and language they would understand. As rabbinic writings of the time show, the Pharisees claimed the right to bind and loose, although God never gave it to them. For example the Pharisees wrote, "If a person made a vow to abstain from milk, he was loosed **(allowed)** to drink the whey." Another example is, "If a person made a vow to abstain from wine, he is loosed **(allowed)** to eat that which is cooked in wine." The authority to bind (meaning: **disallow**) and loose (meaning: **to allow**), just like the keys, was given only to Peter at this time. Later, the other apostles were also given authority to bind and loose,[9] but Jesus never gave anyone else, apart from the apostles named in the New Testament authority to bind or loose.

The apostles did not pass the authority on to anyone else, but they did use the authority themselves, permitting things that used to be forbidden and banning things that had been allowed.[10] The apostles used the authority to make rules for the early Church.[11] In Acts 5:1-11, where Ananias and Sapphira were bound (not allowed) by Peter, to lie to the Holy Spirit, they dropped dead on the spot because they had done so. Notice that neither Peter nor any other apostles used their authority to bind up demons or Satan, because in the Jewish way of things, that was not what binding and loosing were about. I want to make this clear because there is a lot of binding and loosing going on in charismatic churches and meetings by Christians that mean well but do not have the necessary authority. You will see it on Christian television, especially American programmes. You will hear them praying out loud and binding Satan. We were not told to bind Satan, neither were the apostles, we were told to resist him,[12] but people go about binding him out of houses and out of certain streets. If we had authority to bind him we could have bound him out of the planet years ago. The problem is that many Christians do not understand the Bible because they fail to find out what this Jewish Book means from a Jewish perspective.

Notice the new policy of Jesus was still in force and even His disciples were not allowed to tell anyone that He was the Messiah.

> Matthew 16:20 Then he charged his disciples that they should tell no man that he was Jesus the Christ.

[1] Malachi 4:5

[2] Psalm 18:2, 62:6-7

[3] Job 38:17, Psalm 9:13, 107:18, Isaiah 38:10

[4] Isaiah 22:22

[5] Acts 21:8

[6] Acts 9:10-15. Romans 11:13

[7] Acts 1:4-5, 2:4, Romans 8:9, 8:14, 1 Corinthians 2:12, 3:16

[8] John 7:39, Romans 5:5, Romans 12:5, 1 Corinthians 6:19

[9] Matthew 18:18
[10] Acts 15:1-29
[11] John 20:23
[12] James 4:7, 1 Peter 5:8-9

PREPARING THE DISCIPLES FOR HIS DEATH AND RESURRECTION
Matthew 16:21-28, Mark 9:30-32

In this section we notice the disciples are still not able to see clearly. After Peter's confession, Jesus begins to give them details about His coming death and resurrection, and as the last year of His life goes by He will give them more and more information, but no matter how often He tells them, they never understand. Eventually when His crucifixion actually took place, just as He had told them it would, they were all completely surprised. In this first lesson on his approaching death He mentions four stages, in Matthew 16:21.

1. He must go to Jerusalem.
2. He must suffer many things from the elders, chief priests and scribes.
3. He must be killed.
4. He must be raised up on the third day.

In this lesson Peter failed the test, after passing the previous one so well.

Matthew 16:22 Then Peter took him, and began to rebuke him.

Peter had just declared correctly that Jesus was the Christ, the Son of the living God, and here he is rebuking that same Christ, and what did he say?

Matthew 16:22 ... Be it far from thee, Lord, this shall not be unto thee.

Jesus reaction to Peter was;

Matthew 16:23 But he turned and said unto Peter, Get thee behind me, Satan.

Jesus knew He was talking to Peter, but Peter was trying to help Satan's cause by stopping Jesus going through the suffering and the crucifixion. Of course Satan would be pleased to see Jesus killed but not on the cross, not at the Feast of Passover, in Jerusalem, as the Lamb of God, to pay the price for the sins of believers, and exchange them for the righteousness of God,[1] as the prophets had said He would. Peter was trying to do Satan's work.

We get eternal life when we believe that, Jesus died to take the punishment of death that should be given to us for our sins,[2] and that He rose to life again on the third day of His burial. Salvation therefore comes to those that have faith, but discipleship requires more than just believing. Jesus went on to teach them three things about being His disciples.

1. Disciples must be ready to accept rejection in same way Jesus was rejected, that's what the following verse means.

Matthew 16:24 If any man will come after me, let him deny himself, and take up his cross, and follow me.

2. If disciples, try and save their lives, by not facing up to rejection for the sake of Jesus, they will lose their lives anyway, but if they are ready to face rejection they will find life. We must stand firmly on the fact that the only way to eternal life is through Jesus Christ the Son of the living God.[3]

Matthew 16:25 For whosoever will save his life shall lose it: and whosoever will lose his life for my sake shall find it.

3. Every believer should become His disciple because it results in spiritual safety and everlasting treasures.

Matthew 16:26-27 26 For what is a man profited, if he shall gain the whole world, and lose his own soul? Or what shall a man give in exchange for his soul?

27 For the Son of man shall come in the glory of his Father with his angels; and then he shall reward every man according to his works.

The disciples in those days needed to be ready to be rejected by the Pharisees, and disciples today must be prepared to be rejected by the established churches, that do not accept or put into practice some parts of the Bible message.

[1] 2 Corinthians 5:21

[2] Isaiah 53:5-10, Romans 6:23

[3] Acts 4:12, Romans 10:8-11, 10:13

REWARDS IN THE MILLENNIAL KINGDOM
Mark 8:38

Jesus will reward people according to how they respond to Him and the Bible in this life. If we accept Him whole heartedly and with a show of approval to others, praising Him highly, He will welcome us in the same way, but if we are ashamed now of telling others that we are His followers and that we absolutely trust the Bible, He will be ashamed of us in the Messianic Kingdom. You will notice that Jesus was very much concerned with that specific generation.

> Mark 8:38 Whosoever therefore shall be ashamed of me and of my words in this adulterous and sinful generation; of him also shall the Son of man be ashamed, when he cometh in the glory of his Father with the holy angels

He is not talking about believers losing their eternal life, but about their rewards and status in the future kingdom of God. The verse ends with an introduction to His future glory.

HIS GLORY IN THE MILLENNIUM KINGDOM
Matthew 16:28 to 17:8, Mark 9:1-8, Luke 9:27-36

Each of the three gospel accounts shown above begin with Jesus telling His disciples that some of the them will see the glory He will have in the kingdom before they die, and He stresses the fact that they will actually see the glory of the kingdom. There were three, Peter,

James and John, who would see his glory at the transfiguration,[1] (the transfiguration was the change in the appearance of Jesus on the mountain). Matthew and Mark say it was six days later, while Luke says it was eight days later.

> Luke 9:28 And it came to pass about eight days after these sayings.

Luke is counting the day Peter made his confession, right through to and including the day Jesus was transfigured, while Matthew and Mark counted the days in between, which was the time it took for them to climb the mountain. The mountain is not named in Scripture, but we understand from the text that it was a secluded place and very high.

> Mark 9:2 … (Jesus) leadeth them up into an high mountain apart by themselves.

Knowing the region they were in at the time, the mountain of the transfiguration was Mount Hermon. The tourist guides in Israel will take you to Mount Tabor, where the Roman Catholics have built the Church of the Transfiguration, about forty-five miles away. It was much easier for them to build a church on Mount Tabor with its peak of 588 metres above sea level, and a much nicer place for their clergy to live than Mount Hermon with its normally snow clad peak of 2814 meters. Also, Mount Tabor was not secluded being heavily fortified to guard the route from the Sea of Galilee to the Jezreel Valley. The Bible description of the mountain is only true in respect of Mount Hermon.

At the transfiguration three disciples saw the promise of the previous section, Jesus in the glory of His Father, as He will be in the Millennial Kingdom.

> Matthew 17:2 And was transfigured before them: and his face did shine as the sun, and his raiment was white as light.
>
> Mark 9:2-3 [2] … and he was transfigured before them.
>
> [3] And his raiment became shining, exceeding white as snow; so as no fuller on earth can white them.

> Luke 9:29 And as he prayed, the fashion of his countenance was altered, and his raiment was white and glistening.

Jesus, as we discussed in Chapter 2, is the Shekinah Glory, and He exudes light, but His physical body was a veil that blocked the light, it veiled the brightness of His glory, so He looked no different from any other Jewish man of the time. As He prayed the Shekinah light shone and affected His clothes, so that they became white. His face had the brightness of the sun and His clothes according to Luke were dazzling because they were reflecting His light, and the three disciples saw the brightness of His glory.[2]

Moses saw an appearance of the Shekinah glory, which made his face shine,[3] but the shine was a reflected glory, from being in the presence of God, just like moonlight is a reflection of the sun. The glory of Jesus was not reflected because He is the Shekinah Glory, light exudes from Him and His light is very much stronger, when unveiled.

Two men from the Old Testament, Moses and Elijah, also in glory, are suddenly there talking with Jesus on the mountain, and it is Luke that gives us some details of their discussion.

> Luke 9:31 [Moses and Elijah] appeared in glory, and spake [spoke] of his [Jesus'] decease [death] which he should accomplish at Jerusalem.

They spoke about His coming decease, which is interesting because the Greek word for decease used here is *"exodus"* which also means departure. The Jewish exodus from Egypt resulted in their being liberated from slavery, and the departure of Jesus by means of the crucifixion will lead to a double liberation.

First, Jesus will be freed from all the restrictions placed on Him while He was human. Secondly, it will liberate us from being natural sinners, (slaves of sin), because we will be like Him.[4]

At the time Jesus, Moses and Elijah, all in glory, were having their conversation the disciples were asleep, and only heard a little of what was discussed.

> Luke 9:32 But Peter and they that were with him were heavy with sleep: and when they were awake, they saw his glory.

Peter woke up and came up with a suggestion that to us Gentiles seems strange.

> Matthew 17:4 Then answered Peter, and said unto Jesus, Lord, it is good for us to be here: if thou wilt [agree], let us make here three tabernacles; one for thee, and one for Moses, and one for Elias.

Do you think Peter, by building three tabernacles was trying to put Jesus, Moses and Elijah, on the same level? Some Gentiles may think so, but remember we should look at things from a Jewish point of view, and we must not forget that the disciples only knew part of God's future programme, not yet having perfect spiritual sight. Let's try and look into Peter's Jewish mind at the time. He knew Jesus was the Messiah, and had said so. He did not know yet the need for death and resurrection, or that Jesus would come again, that there were to be two comings. In that state of mind he now sees Jesus with the glory He will have in the Messianic Kingdom. Not knowing about the two comings and seeing Jesus in the glory He will have in the kingdom, would have prompted him to conclude that the kingdom had been born, because Jesus had said that some of the disciples would see the glory of the kingdom before they died.

Peter would have known from Zechariah 14:16-21, that after the Messianic Kingdom is established, God will severely punish all the nations that refuse to celebrate the Feast of Tabernacles, and although it was not the correct time for the feast, Peter wanted to make sure that all would be well in what he thought was the establishment of the Messianic Kingdom. It was a lovely response based on what he knew and understood at the time. What he did not understand, was that Jesus had to fulfil the Feast of Passover, by becoming the Lamb of God, at His first coming, before He could fulfil the Feast of Tabernacles, and tabernacle among men, that is to say, dwell together with men, at His second coming.[5]

The Shekinah Glory, as a bright cloud overshadowed the disciples and stopped Peter from going further. God spoke to them from out of heaven, just as he had at the baptism of Jesus. At the baptism God the Father had said,

Matthew 3:17 ... This is my beloved Son, in whom I am well pleased.

At the transfiguration God the Father said the same thing, and then added three words.

Matthew 17:5 ... This is my beloved Son, in whom I am well pleased; hear ye him.

Listen to Him. They knew the Law and the prophets, they had listened to them both, but now God was telling them to listen to Jesus.

Hebrews 1:1-2 ¹ God, who at sundry times and in divers manners spake in time past unto the fathers by the prophets,

² Hath in these last days spoken unto us by his Son.

To hear God speaking directly to them was an unforgettable event for the three disciples, and they would have been obedient, but the command of God was emphasized further, in that when the cloud lifted, Moses and Elijah had gone, and they were left with Jesus only. The Law and the prophets had done what God had intended them to do, from now on they were to listen to Jesus.

Mark 9:8 And suddenly, when they looked round about, they saw no man any more, save Jesus only with themselves.

The Transfiguration Was Significant In Five Ways

1. God the Father reaffirmed that Jesus was the Messiah, after He had been rejected by the nation of Israel.
2. It was an expectation of the Messianic Kingdom on earth as foretold by the prophets, because the purpose of the Messiah, especially from a Jewish viewpoint, is to rule that Kingdom.
3. It reaffirmed the fulfilment of the Old Testament, a conclusion that Peter came to in, 2 Peter 1:16-21. Moses had represented the Law and Elijah had represented the prophets, and together on the mountain they had spoken about the death of Jesus, the

only person to keep the Law perfectly and therefore fulfil it, while prophecy in Scripture is about Jesus.[6]

4. It signifies that there is everlasting life with Moses and Elijah being two examples. Moses died,[7] and is symbolic of those of us that will rise from the dead, but Elijah was translated alive,[8] and he represents those that will be snatched up while they are still living.[9] It is a promise of the future life ahead.

5. Having been glorified by His Father, He had to veil His glory a second time as he came down the mountain, a demonstration of His love for us. The first time He veiled His glory was at his birth. At the ascension, His glory was unveiled forever, so that in Revelation 1:12-16, John saw Him with His glory uncovered. At the second coming He will come with clouds, that will represent the Shekinah glory, and His personal glory will be powerfully bright.

Matthew 24:27 For as the lightning cometh out of the east, and shineth even unto the west; so shall also the coming of the Son of man be.

Matthew 24:30 … and they shall see the son of man coming in the clouds of heaven with power and great glory.

---

[1] Matthew 17:1-2, Mark 9:2-3, Luke 9:29

[2] John 1:14

[3] Exodus 34:29-35

[4] 1 John 3:2

[5] Revelation 21:3

[6] Revelation 19:10

[7] Deuteronomy 34:5

[8] 2 Kings 2:11

[9] 1 Thessalonians 4:17

JOHN THE BAPTIST, ELIJAH, AND THE TWO COMINGS OF MESSIAH
Matthew 17:9-13, Mark 9:9-13, Luke 9:36

We already know three things about John the Baptist.

1. When he was asked by those sent to question him from the Sanhedrin whether he was Elijah, John said, "I am not."[1]
2. Although he was not Elijah, John the Baptist came in the spirit and power of Elijah.[2]
3. If the Jews had accepted Jesus as the Messiah, John would have taken the place of Elijah,[3] as we discussed at the beginning of Chapter 6.

On their way down the mountain the policy of silence, was maintained.

> Luke 9:36 And when the voice was past, Jesus was found alone. And they kept it close, and told no man in those days any of those things which they had seen.

Also, while coming down the mountain, Jesus was careful to remind them not to tell anyone what they had seen and heard.

> Matthew 17:9 And as they came down from the mountain, Jesus charged them, saying, Tell the vision to no man, until the Son of man be risen from the dead.

They were clear in their minds about not telling anybody what had happened, but they were confused about Jesus rising from the dead, first, because they were used to people staying dead, and secondly because they did not realise that Jesus would die, rise from the dead, and then come from heaven again a second time.

> Mark 9:10 And they kept that saying with themselves, [they kept thinking about it], questioning one another what the rising from the dead should mean.

Their questions to each other raised another question, because they did not understand there would be two comings.

> Mark 9:11 And they asked him, saying, Why say the scribes that Elias must come first?

The scribes and Pharisees knew from the Old Testament that Elijah would come first, and that is what they taught the people.

> Malachi 4:5-6 ⁵ Behold, I will send you Elijah the prophet before the coming of the great and terrible day of the LORD:
>
> ⁶ And he shall turn the heart of the fathers to the children, and the heart of the children to their fathers, lest I come and smite the earth with a curse.

The prophecy from Malachi 4, is talking about the second coming of Jesus, and Elijah will come before the second coming, but the prophecy about the first coming of Jesus does not say, Elijah will come first.

> Malachi 3:1 Behold, I will send my messenger, and he shall prepare the way before me.

If the disciples had understood there would be two comings then they would have know the messenger, in Malachi 3:1 was John the Baptist, and that Malachi 4:5-6, was talking about the second coming. In the first part of verse 12, of Mark 9, Jesus confirms the truth of Scripture, talking about His second coming.

> Mark 9:12 Elias verily [truly] cometh first, and restoreth all things.

Jesus then asked how could the Scriptures prophesying His suffering and death be true, if Elijah came now?

> Mark 9:12 and how it is written of the Son of man, that he must suffer many things, and be set at nought.

If Elijah came before the first coming and restored all things, then the prophecies about the suffering of Jesus would not have taken place, so in order that Scripture was fulfilled, Jesus had to suffer many things and be set at nought. Do you realise that Jesus was set at nought on the cross, He had nothing, no clothes, no possessions at all. He was even drained of blood, and of course there was no life left in Him. Elijah will come and restore all things before the second coming, when Jesus will set up the Messianic Kingdom. For the time being however, at the first coming, the messenger heralding Jesus was John the Baptist.

> Mark 9:13 But I say unto you, That Elias has come, and they have done unto him whatsoever they listed [wished], as it is written of him.

Matthew puts it to us in a clearer way.

> Matthew 17:12-13 [12] But I say unto you, That Elias is come already, and they knew him not, but have done unto him whatsoever they listed [wished]. Likewise shall also the Son of man suffer of them.
>
> [13] Then the disciples understood that he spake unto them of John the Baptist.

John was a forerunner of Messiah, but he came at the first coming, while Elijah will come before the second coming. Consequently John was a type of Elijah, who came in the spirit and power of Elijah, although he denied he actually was Elijah.

[1] John 1:21
[2] Luke 1:17
[3] Matthew 11:14

FAITH
Matthew 17:14-21, Mark 9:14-29, Luke 9:37-42

The nine disciples that had been left behind got into difficulty while Jesus was away, and when they all met up again a discussion which had drawn a large crowd was going on.

> Mark 9:14 And when he came to his disciples, he saw a great multitude about them, and the scribes were questioning with them.

The scribes were asking questions and so for some reason they had started the quarrel. The large crowd had gathered because the row between the scribes and the disciples interested them. From reading the Scriptures we know that the disciples had tried to cast out a demon without success, leaving the scribes the opportunity to argue that if the followers of Jesus could not cast out the demon, it meant that Jesus could not be the Messiah. The demon was a very nasty one according to the possessed boy's father.

> Matthew 17:15 ... he is a lunatick [lunatic], and sore vexed [very ill]: for ofttimes [often] he falleth into the fire, and oft into the water.

> Luke 9:39 And, lo, a spirit taketh him, and he suddenly crieth out; and it teareth him that he foameth again, and bruising him hardly departeth from him.

It was a severe case of demon possession with symptoms of epilepsy and suicide, and because the disciples could not cast it out, it caused the scribes to question the claim made by Jesus before the rejection, that He was the Messiah. Jesus replies and again emphasises that generation.

> Mark 9:19-20 [19] He answereth him, and saith, O faithless generation, how long shall I be with you? How long shall I suffer you? Bring him unto me.
>
> [20] And they brought him unto him, [they brought him away from the multitude]: and when he saw him, straightway the spirit tare [convulsed] him; and he fell on the ground, and wallowed foaming [from the mouth].

The demon knew he would have to go and made a supreme effort to destroy him. Don't forget Jesus, after the rejection, was performing miracles on two conditions, personal need, which this certainly was, and personal faith, and both are shown in Scripture.

> Mark 9:21-22 ²¹ And he asked his father, How long is it ago since this came unto him? And he said, Of a child.
>
> ²² And ofttimes he has cast him into the fire, and into the waters, to destroy him. [Next the father tells Jesus of his personal need]: but if thou canst do any thing, have compassion on us, and help us.

By asking Jesus, if He could do anything, the father was showing a lack of faith, and that had to be dealt with before the miracle was performed, and so Jesus dealt with the lack of faith.

> Mark 9:23 If thou canst believe, all things are possible to him that believeth.

The boy's father answered Jesus in the next verse.

> Mark 9:24 And straightway the father of the child cried out, and said with tears, Lord, I believe; help thou mine unbelief.

The father has now shown he has a little faith for the miracle, and a strong faith in Jesus to give him more faith for the miracle. Remember that the boy had been taken away from the crowd, but someone had discovered where he was.

> Mark 9:25 When Jesus saw that the people came running together, he rebuked the foul spirit, saying unto him, Thou dumb and deaf spirit, I charge thee, come out of him, and enter no more into him.

The demon was cast out before the people got there, because Jesus was not performing miracles for the crowds to see anymore, but only for personal need on the basis of faith.

The boy had been miraculously healed but the nine disciples still had a problem.

> Mark 9:28 And when he had come into the house, his disciples asked him privately, Why could not we cast him out?

Jesus gave them two reasons why they could not cast out the demon, and we will learn the first from Mark's gospel.

> Mark 9:29 And he said unto them, This kind can come forth by nothing, but by prayer and fasting.

The disciples had not gone about the job the right way, and many people assume from this verse that in order to cast out demons we need more prayer, but if you look again, Jesus emphasised the type of demon, **"This kind,"** and so what kind of demon was it? We just now saw in Mark 9:25, that Jesus rebuked the demon, "Thou deaf and dumb spirit," and according to the rabbis casting out a deaf and dumb spirit was a miracle that only the Messiah could do. Jesus actually agreed with the Pharisees that deaf and dumb spirits are difficult to force out. The Pharisees could not cast them out although they could order out other kinds of demons, and the nine disciples had had the same difficulty, and commanding them to go in the name of Jesus does not work with deaf and dumb demons. A dumb demon is not cast out or ordered out, it is prayed out. "This kind can come forth by nothing, but prayer and fasting." The first reason then why the disciples could not drive the demon out was because they were using the wrong technique.

The second reason why the disciples could not exorcise the demon is found in Matthew's gospel.

> Matthew 17:20 And Jesus said unto them, Because of your unbelief: [they did not have enough faith].

Deaf and dumb demons according to the oral law, could only be expelled by the Messiah, and the scribes had seen that the disciples of Jesus could not cast out the demon, so they were able to question their belief, resulting in some doubt creeping in.

> Matthew 17:20 And Jesus said unto them, Because of your unbelief: for verily [truly] I say unto you, If ye have faith as a grain of mustard seed, ye shall say unto this mountain, Remove hence to yonder place; and it shall remove; and nothing shall be impossible unto you.

Jesus spoke about moving, "this mountain," and the mountain that they were standing on, although well down on the lower level, was Mount Hermon. There is also another context, because in Scripture, "mountain," is a symbol for a kingdom, king or throne, and the kingdom that had just been defeated was Satan's kingdom, when the deaf and dumb demon had to go. The way the story is told, the most likely meaning for the disciples at that moment was that using the correct method, and with sufficient faith, they would be successful in everything they did. "Nothing shall be impossible unto you."

MORE ABOUT HIS COMING DEATH AND RESERRECTION
Matthew 17:22-23, Mark 9:30-32, Luke 9:43-45

This was the second time Jesus told the disciples that He would be killed and then rise from the dead, and it was done while He was teaching them secretly.

> Mark 9:30-31 ³⁰ And they departed thence, and passed through Galilee; **and he would not that any man should know it.**
>
> ³¹ For he taught his disciples, and said unto them, The Son of man is delivered into the hands of men, and they shall kill him; and after that he is killed, he shall rise the third day.

It was a special time of training for the disciples, but although He told them plainly that He would be killed and rise again, they did not understand, were afraid to ask,[1] and were extremely sorry,[2] therefore when He was killed they were dreadfully surprised.

[1] Mark 9:32
[2] Matthew 17:23

A LESSON FOR SONS
Matthew 17:24-27

All of us, men and women, boys and girls, that have been given eternal life through faith in Jesus is a son of God.

> Romans 8:14 For as many as are led by the Spirit of God, they are the sons of God.

Galatians 3:26 For ye are all the children of God by faith in Christ Jesus.

The following lesson given to Peter is therefore for us as sons of God, as well as for the disciples.

Jesus and his disciples were now back in Jewish territory at his headquarters in Capernaum, which meant they were under Jewish Law, which will become clear from the Scripture.

Matthew 17:24 And when they had come to Capernaum, they that received tribute money came to Peter, and said, Doth not your master pay tribute?

The tribute was the half shekel Temple tax,[1] and was paid by every man in Israel in the early spring, about March. The time now was early autumn, close to the Feast of Tabernacles, meaning that Jesus' payment was about six months late, and that is why the tax collectors asked Peter, "Doth not your master pay tribute?" Peter, without asking Jesus, replied, "Yes," and Jesus who knew what had happened, had something to say to him about it.

Matthew 17:25-26[25] He [Peter] saith, Yes. And when he was come into the house, Jesus prevented him, [stopped him], saying, What thinkest thou, Simon? Of whom do the kings of the earth take customs or tribute? Of their own children, or of strangers?

[26] Peter saith unto him, Of strangers. Jesus saith unto him, Then the children are free.

The point was that Roman citizens did not pay taxes, the empire was financed by taxing the people of nations they had conquered. For that reason the citizens or sons or Rome paid nothing. Additionally at that time, outside of the Roman empire, kings controlled their subjects and the cost of governing was paid for by taxing the citizens, but a king would not tax his own sons, the sons of the king were free.

Regarding the Temple tax, the Messiah is Lord of the Temple, believers are His sons, and as a result are exempt from the tax. Jesus had not paid the tax six months earlier because He was Lord of the

Temple, and no doubt because He knew it would lead to this teaching opportunity. His apostles were sons of the King, (by adoption spiritually speaking), and that is why Jesus had not asked them to pay the tax. However, the Jews had rejected their Messiah, and although Jesus was right, He did not want to offend them. Under the Law of Moses, the Messiah would have been exempt from the Temple tax, but in order not to appear to break the Written Law, (the Temple tax was not collected according to any rule in the Mishnah), Jesus arranged for a miracle payment, for Himself and Peter by sending the fisherman back to his old job.

> Matthew 17:27 Not withstanding, lest we should offend them, go thou to the sea, and cast an hook, and take up the fish that first cometh up; and when thou hast opened his mouth, thou shalt find a piece of money: take that, and give unto them for me and thee.

Peter went fishing, caught a fish with a one shekel coin in its mouth and gave it to the collectors of Temple tribute money, half a shekel for Jesus and half a shekel for Peter.

In the restaurants around the Sea of Galilee, the menus on the tables often list, St Peter's Fish, because that kind of fish is traditionally the one that Peter caught, certainly it is one of the few fish in the lake with a mouth big enough to hold a one shekel coin.

The lesson for the disciples is that Jesus is Lord of the Temple, they are the sons of the King, and have nothing to pay.

[1] Exodus 30:11-16

CHILDLIKE HUMILITY
Matthew 18:1-6, Mark 9:33-37, Luke 9:46-48

Humble people do not think of themselves as important, and show their humility by giving way to other persons who have authority over them, such as parents, school teachers and those they work for. John Bunyan was a famous English preacher who was imprisoned in Bedford

Jail for teaching from the Bible. He wrote some famous Christian books which were very popular at the time, but are not read very much now, and also this poem about Christian humility.

> He that is down, need fear no fall,
>
> He that is low, no pride.
>
> He that is humble ever shall
>
> Have God to be his guide.

Jesus and His disciples were in Capernaum. Jesus had returned there after taking Peter, James and John, just the three of them, up the mountain to see His glory, and maybe those three felt a little too pleased since Jesus had chosen them alone for that special honour. After that there had been the miracle of the coin in the fish's mouth to pay Peter's Temple tax, and perhaps Peter felt a bit self-important as he was the only one whose tax had been paid for by Jesus. Anyway, it is possible some of them were getting a little too proud, because they started talking to each other about which of them would be the most important.

> **Luke 9:46** Then there arose a reasoning [argument] among them, which of them should be the greatest.

Still not understanding the two comings of Christ, Matthew 18:1 tells us they were wondering which of them would hold the highest positions in the kingdom of heaven, by which is meant the Messianic Kingdom. Jesus asked them a question, not because he didn't know the answer, but He wanted them to learn something.

> **Mark 9:33-34** ³³ What was it that ye disputed among yourselves by the way?
>
> ³⁴ But they held their peace, [they kept quiet]: for by the way they had disputed among themselves, who should be the greatest.

They were concerned about their positions in the coming kingdom, not only that they, the apostles should be above everyone else, but also who would be the highest in rank among themselves. Jesus then gave the lesson of their need for childlike humility.

Matthew 18:2-3 ² And Jesus called a little child unto him, and set him in the midst [middle] of them.

³ And said, Verily [truly] I say unto you, Except ye be converted [changed], and become as little children, ye shall not enter into the kingdom of heaven.

They have been arguing who will be the greatest in the kingdom, and Jesus is saying, unless they change their attitude and become like children, they won't even get into the kingdom at all. What does it mean to become like children?

A child is not to blame for being born, his father is; and a child is not responsible for looking after himself, his father is. A child depends for his life and his upbringing on his father. Some modern thinkers may object and say I am wrong, and that the mother is in charge, but in God's order of things it is the husband's duty to provide his wife with everything she needs, and he is as a result responsible for his whole family. Therefore as a child should trust his earthly father in this life, so we must trust our heavenly Father to bring us into His family and give us eternal life.

Matthew 18:4 Whosoever therefore shall humble himself as this little child, the same is greatest in the kingdom of heaven.

To enter the kingdom of heaven then, we must have faith in Jesus and trust Him, but our status in the kingdom will depend on becoming like a child. A small child knows he has no authority in the family and that he has to obey his father until he gets older, and then if he has proved himself, he is put in charge of everything his father owns.

Mark 9:35 If any man desire to be first, the same shall be last of all, and servant of all.

People that want great authority in the kingdom of heaven, must be servants in their earthly lives, not looking for high status but keeping a look out for low positions, from which to serve others.

Luke 9:48 ... for he that is least among you all, the same shall be great.

As a visual aid to this lesson, Jesus sat a child down among the disciples, and the point was, childlike humility is necessary before anyone can become great. Let's go over the things we can learn from this training session from Jesus.

1. Children do not quarrel with their parents about who should be in charge. They accept without question that they are under the control of their parents.
2. He taught that we need to believe, trust and correct our ways like a child, and that is the way into the kingdom.
3. After that we should not be proud, but humble.
4. We also have to be ready to help people that from a worldly view are not important, such as the poor or children, as Jesus explained in Matthew 18:5.

Matthew 18:5 "And whoso shall receive one such little child in my name receiveth me."

5. Just like a very small child depends on his father, so we must put all our trust in God, our heavenly Father.
6. If we are servants on earth, and take up a low position, we will be great in the kingdom.

This lesson was given to the disciples after Peter, James and John had seen the transfiguration and after Jesus had paid Peter's Temple tax with the miracle of the coin in the mouth of the fish. It began because the apostles were arguing about which of them was going to be the greatest in the kingdom of heaven, and we know that Peter learned the lesson because this is what he wrote in his first letter in the Bible.

1 Peter 5:5-6 [5] God resisteth the proud, and giveth grace to the humble.

[6] Humble yourselves therefore under the mighty hand of God, that he may exalt you in due time.

ELITISM AND SELF-IMPORTANCE (PRIDE)
Matthew:18:7-14, Mark 9:38-50, Luke 9:49-50

In the last section Jesus taught the apostles to be childlike, in this section He will teach them to welcome childlike people into the kingdom.

The telling off of the apostles by Jesus, for not being humble like a child, and for wanting to be great, caused John to start talking about something else, to change the subject, but what he said still dealt with status, this time the standing of the twelve in relation to persons outside their small group.

> Luke 9:49 And John answered and said, Master, we saw one casting out devils in thy name; and we forbad him, because he followeth not with us.

John's saying, "he followeth not with us," does not mean the man was not a follower of Jesus, because clearly he was a believer and he was using the name of Jesus to cast out demons. John meant that the man was not one of the exclusive twelve apostles, and therefore should be forbidden to work using Jesus' name, because only they should have that honour. Only the twelve should have the authority to cast out demons, but Jesus would have none of it and the disciples got a second rebuke.

> Luke 9:50 And Jesus said unto him, Forbid him not: for he that is not against us is for us.

> Mark 9:39-40 ³⁹ But Jesus said, Forbid him not: for there is no man which shall do a miracle in my name, that can lightly speak evil of me.

> ⁴⁰ For he that is not against us is on our part.

The lesson is that we don't have to be one of the twelve apostles before we can do wonderful things for Jesus.

The lesson on elitism was now over and Jesus went on to the matter of self-importance.

> Mark 9:41 For whosoever shall give you a cup of water to drink in my name, because ye belong to Christ, verily I say to you, he shall not lose his reward.

In other words, Jesus does not require everyone to do mighty miracles in His name, because even the smallest work in His name will be rewarded, such as giving a follower of Christ a cup of water, but there was more to the lesson.

> Mark 9:42 And whosoever shall offend one of these little ones that believe in me, it is better for him that a millstone were hanged about his neck, and he were cast into the sea.

John and the other disciples had offended the man that had been casting out demons, by asking him to stop, a man that had been using the name of Jesus effectively, doing the work of Christ. We can learn a little more from Matthew's narrative because he adds something.

> Matthew 18:6-7 6 But whoso shall offend one of these little ones which believeth in me, it were better for him that a millstone were hanged about his neck, and that he were drowned in the depth of the sea.
>
> 7 Woe unto the world because of offences! For it must needs be that offences come; but woe to that man by whom the offence cometh!

Giving offence to believers in Jesus, such as the man that had been casting out demons, is very much against the command of Jesus, especially if the believers are children, and the punishment in the after life will be severe. It would be better to be drowned if that would stop the punishment but it won't, because everyone drowned in the sea will be raised for judgement.[1]

Feelings of self-importance and pride are common among people of the world, but they are not typical of believers in Jesus. There will always be proud folk that cause believing children to trip up, but in the end they will be punished, and the disciples were taught not to cause stumbling, a good lesson for us also, because a constant attitude of pride would show that we do not belong to the Lord.

> Matthew 18:8 Wherefore if thy hand or thy foot offend thee, cut them off, and cast them from thee.

The meaning is that anything that causes stumbling should be stopped, even parts of the body doing the Lord's work may have to be cut out, if they are causing offence to young believers. Jesus does not mean that we should cut off our hands or feet or mutilate ourselves, He is talking about the cause of our problem, and if something is causing others to stumble, or even ourselves, it must be dealt with decisively to avoid judgement. Jesus again warned the disciples to be very careful when dealing with children.

> Matthew 18:10 Take heed [be careful] that ye despise not [think you are better than] one of these little ones; for I say unto you, That in heaven their angels do always behold the face of my Father which is in heaven.

It is clear from this verse that children have guardian angels, whose job it is to report to God everything people do that makes believing children stumble.

> Matthew 18:14 Even so it is not the will of your Father which is in heaven, that one of these little ones should perish.

Salt

> Mark 9:49-50 ⁴⁹ For every one shall be salted with fire, and every sacrifice shall be salted with salt.
> ⁵⁰ Salt is good: but if the salt have lost his saltness, wherewith will ye season it? Have salt in yourselves, and have peace one with another.

Let us look at some aspects of the use of salt by the Jews in the Temple and the nation at the time of Jesus.

- ❖ Every sacrifice in the Temple was salted.
- ❖ Salt was symbolic of the morally upright and superior person.
- ❖ Scriptures that were extremely well put were said to be salty by the Jews.

- ❖ A high intelligence, was associated with salt, someone that was clever.
- ❖ Salt was used to preserve food, to stop it going bad.
- ❖ The savoury taste of salt made food tasty and enjoyable to eat.

Jesus was teaching the disciples to stop being offensive and proud, and to make themselves attractive and useful to believers. "Have salt in yourselves," don't fight for high status, "Have peace one with another." If they love one another their saltiness will attract others, and this will help preserve the world and make life really worthwhile for others.

[1] Revelation 20:13

FORGIVE AND FORGET
Matthew 18:15-35

We discovered earlier that only one gospel talks about the Church, and the first time was when Jesus spoke following Peter's confession in Matthew 16:18. Then Jesus was talking about the world wide Church, He being the Rock on which it would be built, and Peter a pebble or small stone that would help get it started. Here Jesus mentions the Church again but He is talking about Church discipline, which points to the local Church congregation. We are going to look at a few verses that are often misunderstood, causing serious mistakes and problems in Church life. In Matthew 18:15-17, Jesus gave us a procedure for Church discipline involving four separate stages.

1. If someone in the Church sins against me, and Jesus is talking about Christians only, brothers in Christ, then it is the command of Jesus that I go to the person that has wronged me in secret and tell him about it privately. If I tell any other person before approaching my Christian brother, then I am guilty of wronging him.

   Matthew 18:15 … if he shall hear thee, thou hast gained thy brother.

The meaning of, "if he shall hear thee," is, if he agrees with you, and so if he concurs and confesses, that is the end of the matter, and I should forgive and forget. If he does not see eye to eye with me, then I am told to move to the next stage.

2. It is now time to involve one or two other Church members, making a total of two or three, because two or three witnesses are necessary before action can be taken.[1]

> Matthew 18:16 But if he will not hear thee, then take with thee one or two more, that in the mouth of two or three witnesses every word may be established.

If he still disagrees then I move on to the next step.

3. I am now told to take my one or two witnesses and tell the Church, and if they agree that the member has sinned against me, and if he still refuses to apologize, then we come to the final action that must be taken.

4. Matthew 18:17 If he neglect to hear the church, let him be unto thee as an heathen man and a publican.

"Let him be unto thee as an heathen man and a publican," would mean to the Jewish apostles Jesus was training, untouchable, excommunicated, thrown out of the Church and banned from attending Church services. Church members would be strictly forbidden from inviting the man into their homes, and would not be allowed to condone his sin or console him in any way.

The succeeding verses continue the teaching on Church discipline and this is where the misinterpretation often occurs.

> Matthew 18:18 Whatsoever ye shall bind on earth shall be bound in heaven: and whatsoever ye shall loose on earth shall be loosed in heaven.

We have already gone over the question of binding and loosing, something Jesus gave Peter the authority to do after he had confessed, "You are the Christ, the Son of the living God." It was not a question of binding and loosing demons or Satan, but you will remember, regarding the law, to bind meant to forbid, and to loose meant to allow, and only the apostles were allowed to bind and loose in the sense of establishing Church rules. The phrases were also used in deciding on the punishment for not keeping the law, in which case, to bind meant to punish, and to loose meant to condone, and as we saw when we discussed the issue earlier, the disciples had authority to punish even to death.[2]

In Matthew 18:18, just quoted, binding and loosing refers to the authority given to the apostles, and to a much lesser extent the Church to punish, but no Church can sentence to death. However, the Church can and should excommunicate or forbid members that sin against their Christian brothers or sisters in the Church, and refuse to be corrected. Binding and loosing here then means the authority to punish or not, and has nothing to do with Satan or demons.

Another verse that is misunderstood, because one miscomprehension will often lead to another, is the one that follows.

> Matthew 18:19 Again I say unto you, That if two of you shall agree on earth as touching any thing that they shall ask, it shall be done for them of my Father which is in heaven.

Christians often use this verse to claim that God is duty bound to answer and agree to anything they ask Him for in prayer, after they have decided on a request. Of course God promises no such thing, He would never hand over His sovereign authority to two imperfect sinful people,[3] and when their prayer is not answered one will accuse the other of not having enough faith. Jesus is not talking here about how to pray, He is still talking about discipline in the local Church, and the two people are the two or three witnesses of verse sixteen. The sinner declines to change his ways and the Church acting on the evidence of the witnesses, stops him from worshipping with them, and God in heaven agrees. Let's look in more detail at the fourth stage, the excommunication of the sinning brother, his being kicked-out of the Church.

The sinner, when he is expelled from the Church is given to Satan, and Satan in turn is given authority to kill him, "deliver such an one unto Satan for the destruction of the flesh."[4] However, Satan cannot send him to hell, and when he dies his spirit will go to heaven.

> 1 Corinthians 5:5 To deliver such an one unto Satan for the destruction of the flesh, that the spirit may be saved in the day of the Lord Jesus.

He is still a believer and he remains a saved person with eternal life.

Usually Satan is not involved in the death of believers, because Jesus is the One who comes and takes His own people.

> 1 Thessalonians 4:14 For if we believe that Jesus died and rose again, even so them also which sleep in Jesus will God bring with him.

In the original Greek the phrase, "them also which sleep in Jesus," actually says, them also that sleep **through** Jesus, meaning that Jesus is responsible for their death, and Satan is not involved. The exception is the excommunicated Church member, in which case Satan puts the believer to death. He can choose the time he dies and the way he dies, but he has no authority over his spiritual life.

Going back to Matthew 18:19, again it has nothing to do with prayer, but with the authority of two or three witness, with agreement from heaven to allow Satan to end a sinful believer's life, and then Jesus continued;

> Matthew 18:20 For where two or three are gathered together in my name, there I am in the midst of them.

Again, for the same reason as before, this verse is usually misunderstood because it is talking about a situation, where two or three believers from a particular local Church, under the authority of Church elders, are gathered together, on Church business. Outside of a Church situation, two or three believers are merely two or three believers, but this verse is dealing with the two or three witnesses that are reporting to the Church on the sinner that has not repented, and if they are being truthful, Jesus is there with them, and therefore God removes his protection from the sinner and allows Satan to take his life.

Peter had been listening carefully to all this and having correctly understood the teaching of Jesus about disciplining a sinning brother, he had a question to ask.

> Matthew 18:21 Then came Peter to him, and said, Lord, how oft shall my brother sin against me, and I forgive him? Till seven times?

According to the oral law of the Pharisees, you only needed to forgive three times, as recorded in the Talmud, tractate, Yoma 82:2. "For they pardon a man once, that sins against another. Secondly they pardon him. Thirdly they pardon him. Fourthly they do not pardon him." By suggesting he forgive his brother seven times, Peter was being generous compared to the rules under which he had been brought up, because he had doubled the existing standard and then added an extra pardon on top of that, but Jesus was more generous.

> Matthew 18:22 Jesus saith unto him, I say not unto thee, Until seven times: but, Until seventy times seven.

Taken literally that would be 490 times, but Jesus is speaking figuratively and He means keep on, keeping on, and never stop forgiving him. Every time your brother comes and asks to be forgiven, then forgive, because if you count the times it shows you are not forgiving him from your heart, you are remembering instead of forgetting, consequently, when it came to the 490th time you would be thinking, "Next time I will be able to condemn you," and that would be wrong.

The King That Forgave A Servant

In Matthew 18:23-35 Jesus told a parable to show the principle of forgiveness among Christian brothers. A servant owed his king 10,000 talents, an extraordinary large sum of money because one talent of silver was the price of a man,[5] and anyone with enough cash to buy 10,000 men would be holding tremendous wealth. The king forgave his servant the debt but later the servant refused to forgive another man that owed him just one talent, and sent the poor man to jail until the debt was paid. Eventually the news reached the king, who was furious and punished the unforgiving servant in a very harsh way indeed. There are three lessons to be learned from the parable.

1. We who have been forgiven by God for everything after we repented, should be ready to forgive our brothers in the Church for everything if they repent. Clearly they must repent and ask for our pardon before we can do that, but we must always be ready to excuse them.
2. As children of God we should copy our heavenly Father.
3. If we do not forgive our Church brothers and sisters we cannot expect forgiveness ourselves.

Matthew 18:35 So likewise shall my heavenly Father do also unto you, if ye from your hearts forgive not every one his brother their trespasses.

[1] 2 Corinthians 13:1

[2] Acts 5:1-10

[3] Romans 3:23, 1 John 1:10

[4] 1 Corinthians 5:1-7

[5] 1 Kings 20:39

THE HALF-BROTHERS OF JESUS TRY TO PROVOKE HIM
John 7:1-9

John 7:2 Now the Jews' feast of tabernacles was at hand.

The setting for this story was the feast, and they were well aware from Zechariah 14:16-21, that the Feast of Tabernacles was a pointer to the Messianic Kingdom, where the feast will have world wide significance. If Jesus was the Messiah, then He would be King in the Messianic Kingdom, and so His half-brothers, sons of Mary, confronted Him.

John 7:3-4 ³ His brethren therefore said unto him, Depart hence [from here], and go unto Judea, that thy disciples also may see the works that thou doest.

> [4] For there is no man that doeth anything in secret, and he himself seeketh [seeks] to be known openly. If thou do these things, shew [show] thyself to the world.

In other words His brothers were telling Him to go to Jerusalem and take over as King and carry out the prophecy of Zechariah. They were provoking Him because they did not believe His claim to be the Messiah, they were making a challenge.

> John 7:5 For neither did his brethren believe in him.

His brothers were disputing His claim because they did not believe Him, and what they meant was, "If you are the Messiah, go to Jerusalem, take over as King at the Feast of Tabernacles, fulfil the prophecy, then we will believe in you."

> John 7:6 Then Jesus said unto them, My time is not yet come: but your time is alway ready.

It was not yet time for the prophecy concerning the celebrating of the Feast of Tabernacles in the Messianic Kingdom to take place, that will be after the Church Age. The time of their own deaths was something they did not know and for that reason they should be careful to behave themselves because they could die at any moment, and should always be ready.

> John 7:7 The world cannot hate you; but me it hateth, because I testify of it, that the works thereof are evil.

Jesus had been speaking of the sin in the world, including the Jewish religious world, and that is why the world hated Him. The situation was that the activities of His brothers were evil, and they were attempting to bring about His death.

> John 7:8 Go up unto the feast: I go not up yet unto this feast; for my time is not yet full come.

By telling His brothers to go to the feast, and that He is not going to this feast, it does not mean He will not attend. It means that He is not going to take instructions from them, and this is not one of the many Feasts of Tabernacles at which He will be worshipped as King, according to the prophecy of Zechariah 14:16, because that time has not yet come.

> John 7:9 And when he had said these words unto them, he abode still in Galilee.

In the next section He and the disciples will make their way to Jerusalem to keep the Feast.

JOURNEY TO JERUSALEM
Luke 9:51-56, John 7:10

John covers the trip in just one verse, and notice Jesus waited until his brothers had gone before going Himself.

> John 7:10 But when his brethren had gone up, then went he also up unto the feast, not openly, but as it were in secret.

Jesus' attendance at the feast was not the result of being provoked to go by His brothers. He chose His own time and manner, going up secretly so as not to attract attention, not openly like a coming king, because after His rejection on the false grounds that His power was from Satan, Israel would now have to wait thousands of years for their Messiah to establish His throne.

Luke tells us that He tried to go to Jerusalem through Samaria, but in Chapter 4, where we looked at how Jesus was accepted in Samaria, we learned that although the Samaritans allowed Jews to travel through their territory from Jerusalem, they resolutely refused to let them go to Jerusalem. Their fanatical objection being based on the claim that the place to worship was on Mount Gerizim.

> Luke 9:51 And it came to pass, when the time was come that he should be received up, he steadfastly set his face to go to Jerusalem.

Jesus knew this would be the last time He would go to the Feast of Tabernacles before His death, resurrection and ascension, and that this particular feast marked the beginning of the last half year of His life.

> Luke 9:52-53 ⁵² And he sent messengers before his face [ahead of Him]: and they went, and entered into a village of the Samaritans, to make ready for him.
>
> ⁵³ And they did not receive him, because his face was as though he would go to Jerusalem.

The refusal to allow Him to pass through Samaria was because He was on the way to Jerusalem, a clear case of what is now a world wide phenomenon, anti-Semitism. In, The Antiquities of the Jews, Book One, verse one, Josephus says that Samaritans would kill Jews going through Samaria on their way to Jerusalem. The mental reaction of the disciples to the Samaritans refusal to let them through was also extreme.

> Luke 9:54 And when his disciples James and John saw this, they said, Lord, wilt thou that we command fire to come down from heaven, and consume them, even as Elias did?

John is the disciple who was later known as the Apostle of Love, because he emphasized love in his gospel and letters. The change in character would only come after the death and resurrection of Jesus, now they feel offended and are set on revenge, but Jesus corrects them.

> Luke 9:55 But he turned and rebuked them, and said, Ye know not what manner of spirit ye are of.

Prevented from going through Samaria, they had to cross the River Jordan and take the long route to Jerusalem through Perea.

MORE TRAINING ON BEING A GOOD DISCIPLE
Matthew 8:19-22, Luke 9:57-62

We have to keep in mind that this teaching is about being a disciple and not about eternal salvation, the gift of life. For eternal life we trust in the death of Jesus who died in our place, it is a matter of having faith in His promises. Discipleship is more than that and we have already learned three lessons about being a disciple of Jesus.

1. A disciple must be ready to be rejected, or in other words deny himself.
2. He must not try to save his life by refusing to face rejection because of Jesus, and must stand firmly on the fact that the only way of salvation is through Him, or in other words take up his cross.
3. He must be a follower of Jesus and no one else.

According to Luke it was while they were on their way to Jerusalem to attend the feast, that Jesus, while they were going along, added to and topped up the lessons He had already taught.

> Luke 9:57 And it came to pass, that as they went in the way, a certain man said unto him, Lord, I will follow thee whithersoever [anywhere] thou goest.

We will continue the story by looking at Matthews version of this man's meeting with Jesus.

> Matthew 8:19-20 [19] And a certain scribe came, and said unto him, Master, I will follow thee whithersoever thou goest.
>
> [20] And Jesus saith unto him, The foxes have holes, and the birds of the air have nests; but the Son of man hath not where to lay his head.

Jesus did not have a home of His own, and was not living a life of luxury, but the scribes were well provided for, and the lesson is, if you want to be a disciple you must count the cost. The scribe had not considered himself living the frugal lifestyle of Jesus and the disciples, breaking the first lesson, being ready to deny himself.

The second lesson is that as soon as you have decided to become a disciple, get started at once, don't wait, and for this we will return to Luke's version.

> Luke 9:59-60 [59] And he said to another, Follow me. But he said, Lord, suffer me first to go and bury my father.
>
> [60] Jesus said unto him, Let the dead bury their dead: but go thou and preach the kingdom of God.

In Jewish society at the time, the term "bury my father," did not mean that the man's father was dead. It meant, in the fist place to wait until his father had died, which could take many years. Secondly it meant waiting for one year after the father had died to say the special Kaddish prayer for him according to the oral law. The situation was that Jesus had called the man to be His disciple, and the man had said, "OK, after my father dies and I have stayed one year after that to say the Kaddish, I will follow you." Some Gentiles, not knowing the Jewish customs of the day, have said that Jesus showed a lack of consideration and kindness, by not letting the man bury his father, but that was not true. The man was putting off following Jesus for a very long time, until it suited him, in other words he was not ready to take up his cross. Jesus was pointing out that His disciples need to live and work for Him, leaving those who are spiritually dead, to bury their spiritually dead relatives, if it is going to take years.

The third lesson is about divided loyalty.

> Luke 9:61-62 [61] And also another said, Lord, I will follow thee; but let me first go bid them farewell, which are at home at my house.
>
> [62] And Jesus said unto him, No man, having put his hand to the plough, and looking back, is fit for the kingdom of God.

As a teenager, I ploughed with a team of horses, two large animals working side by side. A field was ploughed in parallel strips, and in order that the strips met together exactly it was important that the first furrow of each strip was absolutely straight and parallel to the land already ploughed. Then as the new strip was ploughed it got wider and wider until it joined perfectly with the previously ploughed land. In order to be sure my first furrow was straight, I used to keep the team heading directly towards a marker in the field I had placed there before putting my hand to the plough. If I had looked back while ploughing, the horses would have immediately gone slightly off course, the furrow would be crooked, and I would have been heading in the wrong direction. Disciples must not allow themselves to get side tracked.

> Philippians 3:13 ... forgetting those things which are behind, and reaching forth unto those things which are before.

In this example it is not so much that the man wanted to say farewell, but that the family were so important to him that he was not giving his fullest loyalty to Jesus. The lesson is that a disciple cannot have divided loyalties. Such a person would be too undecided, he would not be able to keep a straight furrow, and comply with the command of Jesus to His disciples, "Follow Me."

8
THE GATHERING OPPOSITION

In earlier chapters we saw how publicly, so that everyone would know, Jesus performed some of the miracles the Jewish leaders claimed through their oral law, no one but the Messiah of Israel would ever be able to do. Once these Messianic miracles had become common knowledge throughout the land, the Pharisees plotted to attack the credibility of Jesus by a smear campaign declaring that the miracles were carried out through the power of Beelzebub or Satan, dishonestly arguing Jesus was not their Messiah sent from God, but was from the devil himself.

In this chapter the people begin to believe the lie of the Pharisees that Jesus is possessed by a demon. Up until now they had not been able to make up their minds whether to follow Jesus or the false shepherds, and so they had been like sheep without a shepherd.

The proceedings in this chapter took place in the three months from the Feast of Tabernacles in October, to Feast of Dedication or Hanuka, in December. The details are only found in the gospels of Luke and John, and where the same incident is recorded in both gospels they each highlight different aspects, Luke being concerned with the activities of Jesus in the whole of Judea, and John emphasizing His ministry in the City of Jerusalem. Notice as we study the gathering opposition to Jesus, how the Bible often reminds us of the divisions among the Jews.

DIFFERENCES AT THE FEAST OF TABERNACLES
John 7:10-53

In this section Jesus uses the two most important ceremonies at the Feast of Tabernacles as backdrops and settings for what He says and does. The first was the Outpouring of the Water, and the second was, the Kindling of the Lamp Stands.

For the Outpouring of the Water, the priests would march from the Temple, which was on top of Mount Zion, down a steep hill to the lowest part of Jerusalem to the Pool of Siloam, fill their jugs and pitchers, and then in an orderly procession they would march back up the hill to the Outer Court. There were fifteen very wide and long steps up from the Outer Court to the Inner Court, and on the first of these they would stop and sing, Psalm 120, on the next step they would sing Psalm 121, and so they would sing Psalms 120 to 134, one on each step, all the way to the Inner Court. Usually our Bibles mark these Psalms in some way, such as, A Song of Ascents, A Song of degrees, or A Psalm of Ascents. Inside the Inner Court, they poured the water down beside the altar and then there was wonderful rejoicing. In the Mishnah it says, "Whoever has not seen the rejoicing at the Outpouring of the Water, has not seen rejoicing in all of his life." The Outpouring of the Water represented the outpouring of the Holy Spirit upon all Israel in the last days as promised by God through His prophet Joel,[1] and we need to keep in mind this interpretation was something the Pharisees and rabbis agreed about.

For the Kindling of the Lamp Stands, they erected throughout the whole Temple, including the Outer Court, colossal lamp stands each one having four lights. The brilliance from the lights was so great that according to the Mishnah every courtyard in the City was lit up. The light represented the visible presence of God, the Shekinah glory, and again remember that the rabbis were agreed on that interpretation. In the following sections Jesus will cover both these ceremonies.

In this section, in John 7:37-44, is the discourse on the Water of Life, the fourth of the seven talks given by Jesus found in John's gospel. Also notice how John uses the word Jews in three ways.

1. In John 4:22, where Jesus says, "salvation is of the Jews," John is using the word generally to include all the descendants of Jacob.
2. In John 7:11 where Jesus has arrived from Galilee to attend the Feast of Tabernacles, John wrote, "Then the Jews sought him at the feast," and here he means those Jews that live in Judea, not Galileans.
3. He also uses the word Jews to describe the leaders, for example when they made inquiries into John the Baptist in John 1:19, where it says, "the Jews sent priests and Levites from Jerusalem to ask him, Who art thou?"

We are now ready to examine the differences between Jesus and the Jews at the Feast of Tabernacles under seven separate headings.

The Jews Questioned The Authority Of Jesus
John 7:11-15

The Jews knew from Zechariah 14:16-21 that the Feast of Tabernacles would be fulfilled in the Messianic Kingdom, and because Jesus claimed to be the Messiah they expected Him to be at the feast.

> John 7:11 Then the Jews sought him at the feast, and said, Where is he?

Before the kingdom is established every Jew in Jerusalem will know without doubt that Jesus is King, and they will all mourn because of the part their ancestors had in His crucifixion.[2] On this occasion there was division among them and they held opinions that were poles apart.

> John 7:12 And there was much murmuring among the people concerning him: for some said, He is a good man: others said, Nay; but he deceiveth the people.

The division among the crowds clearly shows they were not of one mind about Him, because some were beginning to believe the teaching of the Pharisees.

> John 7:13 Howbeit no man spake openly of him for fear of the Jews.

Of course everyone there was Jewish, so John is talking about the Jewish leaders.

> John 7:14-15 ¹⁴Now about the midst of the feast Jesus went up into the temple, and taught.
>
> ¹⁵ And the Jews marvelled, saying, How knoweth this man letters, having never learned?

His teaching was recognized to be of a high standard and yet His authority to teach was being questioned because they knew He had never been to any rabbinic school, and that the leaders had rejected Him.

Jesus' Explanation
John 7:16-24

The reason they questioned His authority was because they did not believe He was the Messiah, and the reason they did not believe he was the Messiah was because they were not keeping the Law of Moses, which as Jews they were required to keep, and so Jesus is going to point out three things. He starts by making two claims.

> John 7:16 Jesus answered them, and said, My doctrine is not mine, but his that sent me.

First God had taught Him the doctrine and God had sent Him to teach it.

Secondly, because they were not doing the will of God by keeping the Law they were not able to recognize Him.

> John 7:17 If any man will do his will, he shall know of the doctrine, whether it be of God, or whether I speak of myself.

Also, by saying the things God had told Him to say, He was trying to bring glory to God only, which showed He was completely righteous. Naturally this would be impossible for natural men to believe because no one on earth had ever been perfect before, and to the natural man there is the belief that everyone is wicked. "Every man has his price," is a saying that demonstrates the wickedness of the world.

> John 7:18 He that speaketh of himself seeketh his own glory: but he that seeketh his glory that sent him, the same is true, and no unrighteousness is in him.

The desire of the Jews to have Jesus killed was evidence of their problem which was not keeping the Law.

> John 7:19 Did not Moses give you the law, and yet none of you keepeth the law? Why go ye about to kill me?

The crowd would have known that Jesus was right about them not keeping the Law and their consciences would have made them feel guilty, but look at their reply.

> John 7:20 The people answered and said, Thou hast a devil: who goeth about to kill thee?

Until now the accusation that Jesus had a demon had only come from the leaders, but now the people are beginning to say the same thing.

Jesus next challenged them with another fault, the way they had got the wrong idea about the Law, and He gave the example of the Sabbath, something they had accused Him of breaking.

> John 7:23 If a man on the Sabbath day receive circumcision, that the law of Moses should not be broken; are ye angry at me, because I made a man every whit whole (completely well) on the Sabbath day?

The rabbis knew very well that the Law of Circumcision took precedence over the Law of the Sabbath, that was why they circumcised their children on the Sabbath when that happened to be the eighth day after the birth of a child. Circumcision was something that disfigured a boy for the rest of his life, and if it was correct to disfigure a person on the Sabbath, then it was even better to make someone completely well on the Sabbath. Clearly then they had interpreted the Law incorrectly, because it was definitely right to heal people on the Sabbath.

The Jews Question Who Jesus Really Is
John 7:25-27

> John 7:25-27 ²⁵ Then said some of them of Jerusalem, [these were not visitors to Jerusalem, they lived there], Is not this he, whom they seek to kill?
>
> ²⁶ But, lo, he speaketh boldly, and they say nothing unto him. Do the rulers know indeed that this is the very Christ?
>
> ²⁷ Howbeit we know this man whence he is, [where He is from]: but when Christ cometh, no man knoweth whence he is.

They wonder who Jesus is because they know where he is from and when the Messiah comes no one will know where He is from.

Jesus' Answer
John 7:28-30

Jesus told them that they knew where He was from, humanly speaking but not spiritually speaking, because He was divine. Of course He spoke to them in a parabolic way so that they could not understand, as was His practice following the rejection.

> John 28-29 ²⁸ Then cried Jesus in the temple as he taught, saying, Ye both know me, and ye know whence I am: and I am not come of myself, but he that sent me is true, whom ye know not.
>
> ²⁹ But I know him: for I am from him, and he hath sent me.

In the verse after that they tried to arrest Him but they could not hold Him because it was not yet the time for His death.

The Effect On The Crowd And The Leaders
John 7:31-36

The result was division, there were those that rejected Him and those that believed Him, and so some did have faith.

John 7:31 And many of the people believed on him, and said, When Christ cometh, will he do more miracles than these which this man hath done?

The Pharisees and Sadducees however, were definitely hostile.

John 7:32 The Pharisees heard that the people murmured such things concerning him; and the Pharisees and the chief priests [who were Sadducees] sent officers to take him.

Jesus then told them about His going away, but again He spoke in such a way that they would not understand.

John 7:33-34 [33] Then said Jesus unto them, Yet a little while am I with you, and then I go unto him that sent me.

[34] Ye shall seek me, and shall not find me: and where I am, thither ye cannot come.

It is obvious they did not understand what He had been talking about.

John 7:35 Then said the Jews among themselves, Whither will he go, that we shall not find him? Will he go unto the dispersed among the Gentiles, and teach the Gentiles?

Perhaps, they thought, He would visit the Jews living in the Greek speaking countries to teach them, or even the Gentiles, and this shows that Jesus had obtained the desired result because they had not understood.

John 7:36 What manner of saying is this [what is He talking about] that he said, Ye shall seek me, and shall not find me: and where I am, thither ye cannot come?

The Holy Spirit Is Promised To Believers
John 7:37-44

The seventh and last day of the Feast of Tabernacles was the most important of all, and was known as the great day. For six days they circled the altar once, but on the seventh day they walked around seven times reciting Psalm 118. Also on the last day the pouring of the water held greater emphasis than on the previous six days, furthermore remember, the rabbis linked the outpouring of the water with the outpouring of the Holy Spirit, and Jesus also had something to say in connection with the same ceremony.

> John 7:37-39 [37] In the last day, the great day of the feast, Jesus stood and cried, saying, If any man thirst, let him come unto me, and drink.
>
> [38] He that believeth on me, as the scripture hath said, out of his belly shall flow rivers of living water.
>
> [39] (But this he spake of the Spirit, which they that believe on him should receive: for the Holy Ghost was not yet given; because that Jesus was not yet glorified.)

Jesus agreed with the rabbis that the outpouring of the water was a symbol of the gift of the Holy Spirit, but the rabbis believed that this was promised to all the sons of Jacob, to every Jew. Jesus said here that the Holy Spirit would not be given on a national basis, but on an individual one. The Spirit would be given to every single person that believes in Him, regardless of race or nationality, every one that believes He is the Messiah. "**He** that believeth, ... out of **his** belly," the application was to individuals, but the Spirit would be given after His ascension into heaven, where He now sits in glory,[3] and ever since then all believers have the Holy Spirit in them.

In the crowd at the Temple there were believers and unbelievers, and this promise of Jesus once again caused division among the people, on this occasion a three way split.

> John 7:40 Many of the people therefore, when they heard this saying, said, Of a truth this is the Prophet.

Many of the folks thought He was a prophet.

> John 7:41 Others said, This is the Christ.

Some were believers saying He was the Messiah, but there was third opinion.

> John 7:41 But some said, Shall Christ come out of Galilee?

Obviously they know nothing of His birth in Bethlehem and assume He was born in Nazareth, which was not where the Scriptures said Messiah would be born.[4]

> John 7:42 Hath not the scripture said, That Christ cometh of the seed of David, and out of the town of Bethlehem, where David was?

Next comes further confirmation of the divisions among the people.

> John 7:43 So there was a division among the people because of him.

In John 7:43, some wanted to capture Jesus there and then, but no one laid a hand on Him, because as we know full well by now, the time for His death had not yet come.[5]

The Pharisees Become Even More Aroused
John 7:45-52

The officers that had been sent to capture Jesus[5] of course came back to the chief priests and Pharisees without Him.

> John 7:45 Then came the officers to the chief priests and Pharisees; and they said unto them, Why have ye not brought him?

Although the officers had not understood what Jesus had said, something about His teaching had really moved them.

> John 7:46 The officers answered, Never man spake like this man.

The reply of the officers really got the Pharisees worked up, and they did not mince their words.

> John 7:47-49 47 Then answered them the Pharisees, Are ye also deceived?
>
> 48 Have any of the rulers or of the Pharisees believed on him?
>
> 49 But this people who knoweth not the law are cursed.

Scathing and derisive in their attack, the Pharisees took the position that because the rulers and themselves were well educated in the Scriptures, any one who did not agree with them was ignorant, and deceived, including the officers they had sent to arrest Jesus.

The people that did not know the law, they had scoffed at were called in the Mishnah, the people of the Land, meaning the uneducated, the peasants. However, there was division among them also because one member of the Sanhedrin standing with them had started moving towards Jesus, Nicodemus, of whom we spoke about in Chapter 4, and he made a slight effort to defend Him.

> John 7:50-51 [50] Nicodemus saith unto them, (he that came to Jesus by night, being one of them,)
>
> [51] Doth our law judge any man, before it hear him, and know what he doeth?

Nicodemus reminded the Pharisees to keep to their own law, by having a completely open and fair hearing before condemning Jesus. The Pharisees then turned their contemptuous tongues on their fellow member, and by calling this man from Judea a Galilean they were implying that he was really stupid.

> John 7:52 They answered and said unto him, Art thou also of Galilee? Search and look: for out of Galilee ariseth no prophet.

Interestingly if the Pharisees had known the Bible as well as they knew the oral law, they would have known that they themselves were the ignorant ones because, 2 Kings 14:25, tells us that the prophet Jonah came from, Gath-hepher, a Galilean town near Nazareth. Perhaps they assumed all Galileans were uneducated "people of the Land," because there were no rabbinic schools there.

[1] Joel 2:28-32

[2] Zechariah 12:10-14

[3] Hebrews 1:1-3, 10:10-12

[4] Micah 5:2

[5] John 7:30

THE TRAP TO GET JESUS TO DISAGREE
WITH THE LAW OF MOSES
John 8:1-11

Jesus kept the Law of Moses perfectly in every minute detail down to the last jot and tittle, and as we have already seen, the Pharisees never had a chance to charge Him with breaking the Mosaic Law, therefore they tried to manufacture a situation that would result in Him saying something that contradicted that Law, in order to be able to accuse Him. They were able to charge Him with breaking the oral law, but that did not bother Jesus one tiny bit, because it was not the Law of God, and later we will see Jesus purposely break that Mishnaic law.

This trap set by the Pharisees was the one and only time they tried to get Jesus to say something in contradiction to the Law of Moses. He had claimed to keep the Law,[1] so they very much wanted to be able to accuse Him of not keeping it, or at least saying something that did not agree with it. A time was chosen when Jesus was teaching before a crowd of people, because they wanted to humiliate Him publicly, and the issue they decided upon was one for which the punishment was specific, adultery.

> John 8:3-4 ³ And the scribes and Pharisees brought unto him a woman taken in adultery; and when they had set her in the midst,
>
> ⁴ They say unto him, Master, this woman was taken in adultery, in the very act.

The penalty for adultery was death,[2] and to make sure that Jesus knew she was guilty, they said she was caught in the act, meaning that there were eye witness involved. Remember the Law required the evidence of two or three witnesses.[3]

> John 8:6 This they said, tempting him, that they might have [reason] to accuse him.

So they were tempting Him to try and get some grounds on which to base an accusation. The trap, the tempting, as John called it was obvious. They gave themselves away when they said she was caught in the act, because it takes two people to commit adultery, and both parties are guilty under the Law, and both should get the same punishment, not just the woman. Of course one person alone can be charged with adultery, but when there are witnesses, then why not charge both the man and the woman? Anyway they think they have Jesus in a trap.

> John 8:5 Now Moses in the law commanded us, that such should be stoned: but what sayest thou?

The issue was the Law, "Moses commanded us," the Law of Moses, and the question is, "What sayest thou?" We know what Moses said but what do you say? They wanted Him to say something opposed to Moses.

> John 8:6 But Jesus stooped down and with his finger wrote on the ground, as though he had heard them not.

They kept on and on asking Him to answer, and eventually He did answer them but then He started writing on the ground again with His finger, and in the original text the Greek grammar lays emphasis on His finger. In the Bible we are not told the words that Jesus wrote because that was not what interested John, the apostle was excited because Jesus used His finger.

The Mosaic Law comprises 613 commandments, 603 were written by men on parchment using pens, but ten were written on tablets of stone, not by men using chisels but, and the Bible tells us twice, in Exodus 31:18 and Deuteronomy 9:10, that the stone tablets were written by the finger of God Himself. John, by emphasizing the finger here, is bringing our attention to the fact that Jesus is the author of this and all the commandments given to Moses, the rules and the punishments, the whole Law, all of it. In that light we will look at the answer Jesus gave to the Pharisees.

> John 8:7 He that is without sin among you, let him first cast a stone at her.

Jesus does not mean by this that we should not go round judging others, because that would not be in agreement with other Scriptures.

We are required to judge on certain matters according to what has been written down for us in the Bible, not on rules made by men, as we saw when we learned how to deal with a brother that sins against us, and his excommunication from the Church. Neither was Jesus saying they had to be perfect before casting the first stone, because the Mosaic Law did not say that. If punishment could only be given by people without sin then no one would ever have been punished under the Law. However, death was the punishment for adultery. If He had said the people that carry out punishment have to be perfect, that would have been against the Law, and the Pharisees would have been able to accuse Him.

The words of Jesus need to be considered in regard to the whole Law of Moses. Moses did say that the punishment for adultery was to be stoned to death, but he also said that before anyone could be stoned to death there had to be two or three witness to the crime and of course, they had to give evidence,[3] but none of the witnesses wanted to identify themselves. Furthermore it was those same two or three witnesses that gave evidence that had to cast the first stone, [4] and none of them did, because the woman had been set up, and they were guilty of setting the trap, they were implicated, and one of them may have been the man that committed adultery with her. One by one all her accusers left and the woman was left alone with Jesus.

> John 8:10-11 [10] When Jesus had lifted up himself, and saw none but the woman, he said unto her, Woman, where are those thine accusers? Hath no man condemned thee?
>
> [11] She said, No man, Lord. And Jesus said unto her, Neither do I condemn thee: go, and sin no more.

He did not excuse her, but told her to stop sinning, and true to the Law, he did not punish her either, because the witnesses refused to cast the first stone. That was the only time the Pharisees tried to get Jesus to contradict the Mosaic Law, afterwards they only used the unscriptural, oral, Pharisaic law of their own making, for under the Law of Moses, they themselves had been shown to be guilty.

[1] Matthew 5:17

[2] Leviticus 20:10

[3] Deuteronomy 17:6

[4] Deuteronomy 17:7

THE DISPUTE ABOUT THE LIGHT
John 8:12-20

In this section we find the second of John's, "I am," statements, "I am the light of the world."[1] It came at the time of the second major ceremony at the feast, the Kindling of the Lamp Stands, which the Jews connected with the Shekinah glory, and so Jesus is claiming that He is the Shekinah glory.

> John 8:12 He that followeth me shall not walk in darkness, but shall have the light of life.

The rabbinic remarks in Rabbati 58:4 saying, "Light is the name of the Messiah," would have been well known to the Pharisees and other Jews around Jesus when He said, "I am the Light of the world," meaning, "I am the Messiah."

The beginning of the fifth, of the seven talks given by Jesus, that John recorded for us, is also recorded here, although the whole of the discourse, goes right the way through to verse 59 at the end of the eighth chapter of John.

The dispute began as soon as Jesus had claimed to be the Messiah, the Light.

> John 8:13 The Pharisees therefore said unto him, Thou bearest record of thyself; thy record is not true.

The Pharisees claimed that two or three witness were necessary to ascertain a truth,[2] and if only Jesus was making the claim, then His claim had not been established. In His rebuttal Jesus gave three reasons why the Pharisees were wrong.

> John 8:14 Jesus answered and said unto them, Though I bear record of myself, yet my record is true: for I know whence I

came, and whither I go; but ye cannot tell whence I come, and whither I go.

First, they did not believe the truth of His testimony because they did not know about His divinity.

> John 8:15-16 ¹⁵ Ye judge after the flesh; I judge no man.
> ¹⁶ And yet if I judge, my judgement is true: for I am not alone [in it], but I and the Father that sent me.

Second, they are not judging Him correctly because they do not know His Father, they are not spiritual.

> John 8:17-18 ¹⁷ It is also written in your law, that the testimony of two witnesses is true.
> ¹⁸ I am one that bear witness of myself, and the Father that sent me beareth witness of me.

Third, there were in fact two witnesses to His being Messiah, Jesus Himself who told them He was the Messiah, and validated the claim with the appropriate miracles, signs and wonders. The second witness was God the Father, speaking from heaven for many to hear, "This is My beloved Son," at His baptism by John the Baptist.[3] Therefore everyone that knows who Jesus is, knows who His Father is, and to know Jesus is to know His Father.

> John 8:19 Then said they unto him, Where is thy Father? Jesus answered, Ye neither know me, nor my Father: if ye had known me, ye should have known my Father also.

Once again Jesus was protected from being killed before God's appointed time.

> John 8:20 These word spoke Jesus in the treasury, as he taught in the temple: and no man laid hands on him; for his hour was not yet come.

[1] John 8:12
[2] Deuteronomy 19:15, 2 Corinthians 13:1, Revelation 11:3
[3] Matthew 3:17

ONLY BELIEVERS IN JESUS WILL HAVE THEIR SINS FORGIVEN
John 8:21-30

Jesus here was not teaching the disciples in private, but was teaching the crowd, and therefore He spoke parabolically to make sure they did not understand. This had been His policy since He had been rejected on the false grounds that He had a demon. We can see they did not understand Him by what they were saying.

> John 8:22 Then said the Jews, Will he kill himself? Because he saith, Whither I go, ye cannot come.

> John 8:25 Then said they unto him, Who art thou?

Jesus was teaching them about the One they must believe, about Himself, and some differences between them and Him, and made seven points.

1. He is going somewhere where they cannot go. (John 8:21)
2. They were going to die as sinners. (John 8:21)
3. He was heavenly, but they were worldly. (John 8:23)
4. They must believe He is the Messiah, and must have faith in Him. "If you believe not that I am he, ye shall die in your sins." (John 8:24)
5. He will be their judge, and as the ambassador of the Father, He only says what the Father wants Him to say. (John 8:26)
6. The Father sent Him to them, the Jewish people, to speak to the whole world. (John 8:26)
7. They are going to crucify Him, but of course He tells them in a way they do not understand. (John 8:28)

Many of them were completely baffled by what Jesus had said.

John 8:27 They understood not that he spake to them about the Father.

However there were also many others that did believe Him.

John 8:30 As he spake these words, many believed on him.

JESUS THE RESCUER
John 8:31-59

He Rescues Us From Sin
John 8:31-40

All the Jews in the crowd that Jesus was talking to clearly understood that He was claiming to be their Messiah. Some, the believers, wanted to accept Him. On the other hand the religious leaders thought they would loose their authority and privileges if they acknowledged Jesus to be their Messiah. They became alarmed when they realised that a number of those listening to Jesus believed Him, and felt threatened by this Man who could perform all the miracles the prophets had said the Messiah would perform when He came. They would argue against Him as strongly as they could, and try and convince the undecided individuals not to believe in Him, but thought the best way to save their own positions was to kill Him, however they had kept their desire to murder a secret.

The crowd listening to Jesus therefore, consisted of believers, unbelievers and those that had not yet made up their minds, and so were also unbelievers. We need to understand which group Jesus is talking to in this section, believers or unbelievers, because He sometimes switches His attention from one group to the other. The Pharisees teaching was that all Jews were free from sin because they were descendants of Abraham, (all Israel has a share in the age to come), so remember this as Jesus begins by speaking to the Jewish believers in the crowd. Remember also that these believers had been taught by the Pharisees and therefore needed to be re-educated.

John 8:31-32 ³¹ Then said Jesus to those Jews that believed on him, If ye continue in my word, then are ye my disciples indeed;

> [32] And ye shall know the truth, and the truth shall make you free.

They were saved because of their belief in Jesus, and He told them if they continued in His word, the Bible,[1] they would become His disciples, knowing the truth and being set free. The believers in the crowd then replied to Jesus.

> John 8:33 They answered him, We [Jews] be Abraham's seed, and were never in bondage to any man: how sayest thou [what do you mean], Ye shall be made free?

They were still trusting in the fact that they were blood descendants of Abraham. Jesus will explain in the next few verses that everyone that sins is a slave to sin, and therefore they need to be made free from their slavery to sin by having faith in Him, (by having faith in God, God the Son). Still speaking to the Jews who believed He was their Messiah, but who had grown up being brain-washed by the Pharisees, Jesus continued.

> John 8:39 If ye were Abraham's children [spiritually speaking], ye would do the works of Abraham.

Abraham was not given righteousness by God because of the family he was born into. He was given righteousness because he believed God. "And he [Abraham] believed in the LORD; and he [the LORD] counted it to him [Abraham] for righteousness (Genesis 15:6)." In the same way the believing Jews would be made righteous **only** by believing Jesus was their Messiah. They must stop putting their faith in the false teaching of the Pharisees, that they were without sin because they were blood descendants of Abraham. The blood descendants of Abraham are no better than anyone else until and unless they are declared righteous by God. However, Abraham's spiritual descendants are declared righteous by God **only** through faith in Jesus, not by being born into a certain family, by keeping religious traditions, or doing charitable work.

Jesus next began speaking to the unbelieving Jews in the crowd that wanted Him killed. Again they were blood descendants of Abraham but were definitely not righteous as Abraham had been, and the evidence for this was that, although they had not told anyone, they wanted to murder Jesus.

> John 8:40 (Jesus said) But now ye seek to kill me, a man that hath told you the truth, which I have heard of God [God had told Jesus their plan]: this did not Abraham [Abraham did not behave like that].

The important verse is John 8:36, "If the Son therefore shall make you free, ye shall be free indeed." We are only freed from sin by faith in Jesus.

He Rescues Us From Satan
John 8:41-48

In John 8:44 we will learn that Satan is the spiritual father of unbelievers, but at the beginning of this passage, the unbelieving Jews do not yet know that.

> John 8:41 ⁴¹ Ye do the deeds of your father. Then said they to him, We be not born of fornication; we have one Father, even God.

The Jews opinion of themselves was that they were not illegitimate bastards, they were the sons of God, which is based on Exodus 4:22-23, where it says God is the Father of Israel. If they had been the sons of God spiritually speaking, they would have welcomed Jesus as the Son of God. The fact they rejected Jesus, identified them as sons of Satan because they were doing his work, not God's.

The problem is they have been intellectually blinded, and that is why they cannot understand.

> John 8:43 Why do you not understand my speech? Even because ye cannot hear my word.

The blindness of unbelieving Jews and Gentiles comes from Satan, the god of this world.[2] However the Jews have a second source of blindness which came from the judgement of God.[3] Deliberately making the false accusation that Jesus was demon possessed, deepened the darkness they were in and did not help them to see things any clearer.

Lies and murder were invented by Satan, and it is because of him that people die.

> John 8:44 Ye are of your father the devil, and the lusts of your father ye will do. He was a murderer from the beginning, and abode not of the truth, because there is no truth in him. When he speaketh a lie, he speaketh of his own: for he is a liar, and the father of it.

The Jews were also liars because they said Jesus was demon possessed as shown by the following passages.

> John 8:48 Then answered the Jews, and said unto him, Say we not well that thou art a Samaritan, and hast a devil?

> John 8:52 Now we know that thou hast a devil.

Although the Jews as a nation were the sons of God (Exodus 4:22-23), and were also the physical descendants of Abraham, they were actually doing the works of Satan, which is lying and killing. For that reason they could not possibly be the spiritual sons of Abraham and even more definitely, they were not the spiritual sons of God.

During this time Jesus gave the Jews the perfect chance to give details of anything He had done that was sinful.

> John 8:46 Which of you convinceth [convicts] me of sin?

The answer was nobody, they could not come up with a single sin, because He kept the Law of Moses perfectly.

He Rescues Us From Death
John 8:49-59

Jesus is still speaking in a parabolic way so that the Jews that rejected Him will not understand.

> John 8:51 Verily, verily [Truly, truly], I say unto you, if a man keepeth my saying, he shall never see death.

Jesus is talking about spiritual death but they think He means physical death, and because they do not understand, they once more accuse Him of having a demon.

> John 8:52-53 ⁵² Then said the Jews unto him, Now we know that thou hast a devil. Abraham is dead, and the prophets; and thou sayest, If a man keep my saying, he shall never taste death.
>
> ⁵³ Art thou greater than our father Abraham, which is dead? Whom makest thou thyself? [Who do You think You are?].

After rejecting Him they will never have any chance of understanding Him, and because they believe He is talking about physical death, they say, "Who do You think You are?" He is the Messiah, and Jesus tells them this again in three more ways.

1. He is the One the Father honours. John 8:54
2. He is the One the Father knows. John 8:55
3. He is the One, Abraham was looking for.

> John 8:56 Your father Abraham rejoiced to see my day: and he saw it, and was glad.

Jesus was speaking of a vision given to Abraham by God, He was still speaking in a way they could not understand.

> John 8:57 Then said the Jews unto him, Thou art not yet fifty years old, and hast thou seen Abraham?

At this, Jesus replies by making a statement that is only true of the Divine.

> John 8:58 Jesus said unto them, Verily, verily [Truly, truly], I say unto you, Before Abraham was, I am.

In this verse He told them of His life before the time of Abraham, and His deity, meaning in fact that He had always existed. The words, "I am," are in the present tense, because He always was present and forever will be. He is not just past and future, and He is teaching the Jews that He is the One that showed Himself to Moses as the "I am Jehovah," of the Old Testament.

> Exodus 3:14 And God said unto Moses, I AM THAT I AM: and he said, Thus shalt thou say unto the children of Israel, I AM hath sent me unto you.

Many people in cultic groups and denominations that deny the deity of Jesus are spiritually blind to what this verse means. Who do you think blinded them? Anyway after Jesus had said, "Before Abraham was, I am," the Jews knew that He was claiming to be God, and they would not accept it.

> John 8:59 Then they took up stones to cast at him: but Jesus hid himself, and went out of the temple, going through the midst of them, and so passed by.

Jesus walked right through the middle of the crowd, but they could not see Him, and He survived yet another attempt on His physical life, because His time had not yet come. The Jews were angry because they knew He had again taught that He was their Messiah, both God and man, and that point they always understood from Him.

Looking back over this section we can see that Jesus is our Rescuer from sin, from Satan and from spiritual death.

[1] John 1:1-14

[2] 2 Corinthians 4:4

[3] Isaiah 6:8-10, John 12:40

THE HEALING OF THE MAN BORN BLIND
John 9:1-41

The ninth chapter of John contains the sixth of John's seven signs, the healing of a man that had been born blind. Once again it is convenient to split the study up into subdivisions.

The Healing
John 9:1-12

> John 9:1-2 [1] And as Jesus passed by, he saw a man which was blind from his birth.
>
> [2] And his disciples asked him, saying, Master, who did sin, this man, or his parents, that he was born blind?

If you saw a man that had been blind ever since he was born, would you ask the doctor, "Is he blind because his mum or his dad was wicked?" This was the first part of the question. Actually it was a sensible question for Jews to ask because in the Law Of Moses, God said He would punish the children, grandchildren, great-grandchildren and great-great-grandchildren of men and women who had disobeyed Him.[1] It could be that God had punished the baby before he had been born, while he was still inside his mother's womb because his parents had sinned. The second part of the question the disciples asked Jesus, and like them, would you ask the doctor, "Is he blind from birth because he himself was naughty?" Is it sensible to ask if a baby behaved badly before it had even been born, and because of that had been born blind?

The second part of the question is not based on the Bible, but on the oral law, the Mishnah. The Pharisees said that children were born blind because of sin carried out either by the parents, or by the baby itself, but how could the child sin before it was born? The belief was that from the moment the egg in the womb of the mother was fertilized it had two partialities, one good and the other bad, and these two were always fighting each other, but the good usually won. Rarely, when the bad inclination won and the baby while inside the mother kicked its mother because of hatred, then the Pharisees said that God would punish the baby with blindness before it was born. In all cases they said that children were born blind because of punishment from God, and because God was responsible, only the Messiah would ever be able to heal someone that had been born blind.

Here then is the third kind of the three miracles listed below and performed by Jesus that the Pharisees taught, only the Messiah would ever be able to do.

1. Healing a Jewish leper.
2. Casting out a dumb demon.
3. Healing someone that had been born blind.

It was not considered a miracle of the Messiah to heal someone that had gone blind, only someone born blind, and the teaching was well know, especially by the man in this story who had been born blind and would soon be able to see. He had listened to the rabbis teaching and knew that his only chance of ever being able to see was for the Messiah to come and heal him.

In John 9:3, Jesus told His disciples that the man had not been born blind because of anyone's sin, but to demonstrate the power of God. John then introduces his sub-theme, the conflict between light and darkness, in the words Jesus speaks.

> John 9:4-5 [4] I must work the works of him that sent me, while it is day: the night cometh, when no man can work.
>
> [5] As long as I am in the world, I am the light of the world.

The Father has sent the Light of the World, to give His light to those that are blind. Jesus then healed the blind man, and it was the Sabbath day, the day the Pharisees say it is forbidden to heal anyone. The healing was done in a rather odd kind of way, making use of the fact that it was the Sabbath.

At other times when He had healed the blind it was simple and immediate, but this time it was more complicated. He spat on the ground and made some mud, then He spread the mud over the man's eyes, but he still could not see, so there was this blind man with mud all over both his eyes.

John 9:7 And he said unto him, Go, wash in the pool of Siloam, (which is by interpretation, **Sent**.) He went his way therefore, and washed, and came seeing.

There is a play on words here, Siloam, in English means, **Sent**, and in John 9:4, God **sent**, the Light of the World (Jesus), into a world of darkness, and He **sent** the man who was in darkness to the pool called **Sent**, and when he washed himself his darkness changed to light and he could see. The man showed his faith by obeying Jesus, but when the man's eyes were healed Jesus was not there, so the miracle was not done to please the crowds. Why do you think Jesus made such an elaborate ritual of healing the man, spitting, mixing the mud and pasting it over the man's eyes, and after all that sending him to the pool of Siloam?

We have shown already that, the Talmud bans healing on the Sabbath, but it also especially forbids healing a blind man by spitting, making mud and putting it on the eyes, on the Sabbath day. Jesus knowing the law of the Pharisees, which is not the Law of God, purposely broke it. He went out of His way to heal on the Sabbath day in exactly the way the Pharisees said it must not be done. In Jerusalem there are plenty of pools the man could have washed in which were easy to get to, Bethesda being one, but Jesus sent the man to the Pool of Siloam down a steep hill to the bottom of the City, bad enough for a man that could see and even more difficult for a blind man, but remember it was the Feast of Tabernacles.

The claim of Jesus, "I am the Light of the World," had been a reaction to the Kindling of the Lamp Stands. Now He will act in response to the Outpouring of the Water, because the priests came to the Pool of Siloam and for that reason it was the most crowded of all the pools. The news of another Messianic miracle would quickly become well known and the rabbis would not be able to hide it from the crowds, and yet when it happened Jesus would be nowhere near. Sure enough when the miracle occurred there was a great commotion because they could not understand how it had happened. It was a good thing that a man born blind had been healed, something only the Messiah could do, but three questions needed to be answered.

1. Why was it done on the Sabbath day?
2. Why was it done in the way it was against their law to do on the Sabbath?
3. Would the Messiah break the oral law of the Pharisees? Yes, absolutely.

The Man Is Brought In For Questioning
John 9:13-17

The people had seen a miracle only the Messiah could do, but they were scared to say so openly, so they took the man that had been born blind, who could now see probably better than anyone else in Jerusalem, to the Pharisees for them to decide. They questioned the man closely but nothing he said served their purpose, and this resulted in another division.

> John 9:16 Therefore said some of the Pharisees, This man [Jesus] is not of God, because he keepeth not the Sabbath day. Others said, How can a man that is a sinner do such miracles? And there was a division among them.

Arguing this way and that it dawned on them that if the man had not been born blind then this was not a Messianic miracle. Who would know whether the man had been born blind or not?

The Parents Are Brought In For Questioning
John 9:18-22

The parents of the man that was born blind were asked if he was their son, and they agreed that he was, they had known him ever since the moment of his birth and, "Yes," he had been born blind, he had not gone blind. The next question was, "Then how does he now see?" The Jewish leaders had already made it absolutely clear that if anyone said Jesus was the Messiah, that person would be excommunicated, thrown out of the synagogue, and for that reason the parents answered the question with caution.

John 9:23 Therefore said his parents, He is of age; ask him.

Frightened of being shunned by other Jews, they point out that their son is a mature and intelligent man, and is in a better position than them to answer the question.

The Man Is Again Brought In For Questioning
John 9:23-34

The Pharisees famous for their logic and common sense, are by this time beginning to go a bit crazy.

> John 9:24 Then again called they the man that was blind, and said unto him, Give God the praise: we know that this man [Jesus] is a sinner.

Have you ever heard anyone say, "Praise God, this man is a sinner?" It's an absolutely foolish thing to say or do, "Praise the Lord, this woman has murdered her lovely baby daughter," or, "Praise God, a gang of thieves has stolen everything we own and set fire to our house." I thank God and praise Him almost every day, for His blessings, or when He gives someone the gift of life, but never because someone has sinned, but that is what the Pharisees tell the man to do, "Give God the praise: we know this man is a sinner."

Despite the fact that the Pharisees are becoming irrational, the man still answers them with tact and discretion.

> John 9:25 He answered and said, Whether he be a sinner or no, I know not: one thing I know, that whereas I was blind, now I see.

These were the same Pharisees that had taught him, only the Messiah would be able to make him see, and so he had put them on the spot. What were they going to say about this man called Jesus from Nazareth? As usual they were looking for a loop-hole, a way to deny what was obvious, and so they come back again with more questions.

> John 9:26 Then said they to him again, What did he to thee? How opened he thine eyes?

They want him to go through the entire story all over again, perhaps they had missed something. The man now begins to be less tactful and less diplomatic.

> John 9:27 He answered them, I have told you already, and ye did not hear, [you cannot understand]: wherefore would you hear it again? Will ye also be his disciples? [Are you all trying to become His disciples?].

It was not a wise thing to say to Pharisees, and they replied to him in a rage.

> John 9:28-29 ²⁸ Then they reviled him, and said, Thou art his disciple; but we are Moses disciples.
>
> ²⁹ We know that God spake unto Moses: as far as this fellow, we know not from whence he is.

In other words, if he wants to follow Jesus he can but they will not, they will follow Moses because God spoke to him, as for Jesus they do not know where He is from. Throwing caution to the wind, and forgetting any tact he may have shown earlier the man spoke boldly from the heart.

> John 9:30 The man answered and said unto them, Why herein is a marvellous thing, that ye know not from whence he is, and yet he hath opened my eyes.

Put another way, he expected a much more convincing explanation from the spiritual rulers and they did not impress him.

> John 9:32 Since the world began was it not heard [it has never been known] that any man opened the eyes of one that was born blind.

They had accounts of blind people regaining their sight, but not of people seeing after being born blind, that was why the Pharisees said only the Messiah could do it. The Pharisees did not want to discuss the subject any more and ended the matter by doing their worst in John 9:34.

1. According to their belief you will remember a person was born blind because of sin, and so they say, "Thou wast altogether [entirely] born in sins, and thou doest [how can you] teach us?"
2. "And they cast him out." They excommunicated him from the synagogue.

The Spiritual Healing
John 9:35-41

The man had been told to go and wash in the pool of Siloam, while he was still blind and so he had never seen Jesus, and did not know what He looked like, but after he had been cast out of the synagogue, Jesus went to look for him.

> John 9: 35-38 [35] Jesus heard that he had been cast out; and when he had found him, he said unto him, Does thou believe on the son of God?
>
> [36] He answered and said, Who is he, Lord, that I might believe on him?
>
> [37] And Jesus said unto to him, Thou hast both seen him, and it is he that talketh with thee.
>
> [38] And he said, Lord, I believe. And worshipped him.

A Jew worshipping another Jew is a sign that the first one believes the second one is the Messiah, and as Jesus had prophesied in John 9:3, the power of God had indeed been shown. The chapter finishes on John's sub-theme of the conflict between light and darkness.

> John 9:39-41 [39] And Jesus said, For judgement I am come into this world, that they which see not might see; and that they which see might be made blind.
>
> [40] And some of the Pharisees which were with him heard these words, and said unto him, Are we blind also?
>
> [41] Jesus said unto them, If ye were blind, ye should [would] have no sin: but now ye say, We see; therefore your sin remaineth.

The difference between the man and the Pharisees was that while the man had progressed first from darkness to light, and then from spiritual darkness to spiritual light, the Pharisees remained in spiritual darkness because they did not believe their Messiah. In these three verses Jesus explained that He came into the world so that the blind could see, but since the Pharisees refused to believe, they remained in spiritual darkness. They could have had their sins forgiven but supposing they could see when they could not, and for that reason believing they had no sin, that they were perfect and did not need to be forgiven, their sin and spiritual blindness would remain.

[1] Exodus 34:7

If you would like to be born-again spiritually and receive everlasting life, and **if you believe** Jesus is who He says He is, pray to our Heavenly Father, using your own words would be best. Tell Him you believe Jesus is His Son, the Son of God, the Messiah of Israel, and thank Him for sending Jesus, the Light of the World, and for opening the eyes of your understanding. Ask Him to make you His child, a child of God. He will do as you ask and be so very happy to make you part of His everlasting family, because you believe in His Son. Jesus was born as a baby, just like you, He died and was buried, just like we will be, but He rose from the grave on the third day with eternal life, the Bible says, the first-born of that huge everlasting family of God (Romans 8:29).

THE DISPUTE ABOUT THE SHEPHERD
John 10:1-21

Jesus' talk on the Good Shepherd, the sixth of John's seven discourses is found in this section, together with the third and fourth of His seven, "I am," statements, "I am the Door of the sheep," in John 10:7, and "I am the Good Shepherd," In John 10:11 and 14.

Jesus Is The True Shepherd
John 10:1-6

A sheepfold is a fenced off enclosure where sheep are put to keep them safe during the night, or sometimes the daytime as well. After we bought the farm, we purchased some sheep, an animal I had not had much experience with before, and after one lambing season there were 54 lambs with their mothers that we turned out to eat the grass in Homer Field, behind the house. The western boundary of Homer is the wooded valley that runs down to the river, the home of many animals including foxes and badgers. One day I counted my lambs three or four times because there were only 53, another day there were only 52 and when there were only 50 left, I telephoned a sheep farmer, who told me to fold them. "Make a fold by fencing off about a quarter of an acre with sheep netting, three feet high. Keep the fold well away from any field boundary, and put them in there before dusk, and let them out in the morning," he said. I didn't think a badger would jump three feet, but a fox could. I said, "What about the foxes, surely they can jump a three foot fence?" "They won't jump into a sheepfold," came his reply. Do you know, from that time on none of our lambs ever went missing, because every night they were safe in the fold with their mothers.

> John 10:1-2 [1] I say unto you, He that entereth not by the door into the sheepfold, but climbeth [climbs] up some other way, the same is a thief and a robber.
>
> [2] But he that entereth by the door is the shepherd of the sheep.

In this parable of Jesus, the sheep are the Jewish people living in the land. The thieves and robbers are the Pharisees who have taken control of the sheep through the false teaching found in the Mishnah, which is not the word God, it was the wrong way. Jesus is the true shepherd because He came fulfilling all the appropriate prophecies for His first coming found in the Old Testament, the word of God, and so He came the right way, through the door.

You may have wondered how I used to get the sheep and lambs into the fold every night. Lambs always follow their mothers when they call, so all I had to do was call the mothers, they called their own lambs, and the job was done very quickly. In this story, the shepherd Jesus was talking about worked the other way round, he wanted to get the sheep out of the enclosure, because in those days many flocks of sheep were corralled together, and in the morning the problem was that all the flocks were mixed up. The older sheep knew their shepherd's voice and would leave the fold when they heard him, and the lambs would follow their mothers who never fail to call them. Jesus goes on to say that sheep recognize the voice of their shepherd.

> John 10:3 … the sheep hear his voice: and he calleth his own sheep by name, and leadeth them out.

Zechariah 11:4-14, is prophetic, of Jesus the Good Shepherd, coming to feed all the sheep, but He ends up looking after only the poor of the flock, the few that believe Him, and these are the sheep that hear His voice, and follow Him out, in the parable.

> John 10:4 And when he putteth forth his own sheep, he goeth before them, and the sheep follow him: for they know his voice.

Charlie Biscombe, was a successful farmer, and a good shepherd, and when he visited me one day I wanted to show him my sheep, to hear anything he had to say. We walked in amongst the flock while I told Charlie about my sheep, then when I had finished briefing him I asked a question. Immediately Charlie spoke, the flock panicked and took off at full speed to the farthest corner of the field. I said, "Why was that? They have never done that before." Charlie replied, "Strangers voice."

> John 10:5 And a stranger they will not follow, but will flee from him: for they know not the voice of strangers.

Again, John reminds us Jesus spoke in parables, because He did not want the people that rejected Him to understand.

> John 10:6 This parable spake Jesus unto them: but they understood not what things they were which he spake unto them.

ME AND MY SHEEP

My sheep know my voice

When I call them they follow me

Old and young sheep follow me

They come behind

And wherever I go, they go

Because they have absolute faith in their shepherd

I have opened a gate to a fresh field of grass

It is as if heaven's door is open to the sheep

Jesus Is The Door
John 10:7-10

The third of John's seven "I am," statements of Jesus is found here, "I am the Door."

> John 10:7-8 ⁷ Then said Jesus unto them again, "Verily, verily (Truly, truly), I say unto you, I am the door of the sheep.
>
> ⁸ All that ever came before me are thieves and robbers: but the sheep did not hear them.

The thieves and robbers are the Pharisees, basing their confidence on the Mishnah. The sheep did not take any notice of them but followed the written word of Moses. These included the families Jesus and John the Baptist had been born into, and others of the believing remnant. They are the ones that find pasture to graze, all the food they need for daily living and salvation, and the only way is through the Door.

> John 10:9 I am the door: by me if any man enter in, he shall be saved, and shall go in and out, and find pasture.

Jesus not only gives them all they need in this life but all they need for eternal life as well.

> John 10:10 The thief cometh not, but for to steal, and to kill and to destroy: I am come that they might have life, and that they might have it more abundantly.

Jesus Is The Good Shepherd
John 10:11-18

"I am the Good Shepherd," the fourth "I am," statement of Jesus recorded by John, comes from here, and then Jesus says He is going to die for His sheep.

> John 10:11 I am the good shepherd: the good shepherd giveth his life for the sheep.

Marie Coleman had two sheep that started breaking out of her poorly fenced paddock into a public park, where the locals exercised their dogs. She came to me and said, "I'm having trouble keeping my sheep out of the park, would you be kind enough to let me put them in with yours?" I was pleased to help and Marie brought her two sheep along and put them in with mine, and if they had not been marked, no one would have been able to tell which were which, because they blended in so well.

Soon the grass in the field was eaten up by the hungry sheep, so I opened a gate to another field, called the sheep and shut the gate behind them. I had not gone many steps through the meadow when, surprise, surprise, far away on the other side by the hedge were two sheep grazing by themselves. Marie's sheep had not taken any notice of my call, and when perhaps 60 or so sheep all left the field at a run, her sheep stayed behind not even looking up to see what was happening, they were a separate flock even though they were living together with mine. The same thing happened again and again, every time I moved the sheep to another field. About three months afterwards, it was again time to move the sheep to new pasture, and as usual all my sheep ran out to fresh grass at once, much quicker than if I had used a sheep dog, and Marie's sheep stayed behind all alone, but this time after all the others had left the field, the pair looked up at me still chewing mouthfuls of grass. I called them and they came towards me, so I turned and led them in with the others. The two flocks had become one, with one shepherd.

In the New Testament we learn that Jesus has Jewish sheep and Gentile sheep,[1] unlike the Old Testament where the flock of God was only Jewish. I have told you the story of Marie Coleman's sheep because Jesus now goes on to say that His Jewish sheep and His Gentile sheep will become one flock.

> John 10:16 And other sheep I have which are not of this fold: them also I must bring, and they shall hear my voice; and there shall be one fold, and one shepherd.

The Church of Jesus, was going to be one body, one flock, made up Jews and Gentiles that believed and followed Him.

A hired shepherd when faced by a ferocious attack by thieves and robbers that wanted to kill him, would flee for his life, leaving his sheep to be captured and stolen.

> John 10:13 The hireling fleeth, because he is an hireling, and careth not for the sheep.

Jesus is the Good Shepherd and would rather die for His sheep, and he told the crowd who it was that would be answerable for His death. The Jews are usually held responsible for killing Him, although the Jews gave Him over to the Romans and the Romans did the killing, but in actual fact neither the Jews nor the Gentiles were to blame for His death.

> John 10:17-18 [17] Therefore doth my father love me, because I lay down my life, that I might take it up again.
>
> [18] No man taketh it from me, but I lay it down of myself. I have power to lay it down, and I have power to take it again. This commandment have I received of my Father.

Jesus is clearly saying His death is in His own hands, He will decide the time and the place, and He takes full responsibility.

Once Again The Jews Are Divided
John 10:19-21

The division is over the same old thing, the false reason the Pharisees used to justify their rejection of Him, whether He has a demon or not, and notice how now, "many of them" were agreeing with the Pharisees. The crowds are beginning to turn from Jesus to following the Pharisees.

> John 10:19-21 [19] There was a division therefore again among the Jews for these sayings.
>
> [20] And many of them said, He hath a devil, and is mad; why hear ye him?
>
> [21] Others said, These are not the words of him that hath a devil. Can a devil open the eyes of the blind?

[1] John 10:1-21, 21:15-17, Acts 20:28-29, 1 Peter 5:1-4

THE WORK OF THE SEVENTY DISCIPLES
Luke 10:1-24

Jesus had many, many more disciples than the twelve apostles. The apostles were the specially chosen group that had been close to Him from the beginning, but a lot more kept on joining Him as He went about teaching and healing the sick, and it was from these other disciples that He now chose seventy.

The Seventy Are Sent Away In Pairs
Luke 10:1-16

The special job given to the seventy was to visit all the towns and villages Jesus was going to stay in and prepare lodgings for Him in each place, as He made His way to Jerusalem, for his crucifixion.

> Luke 10:1 After these things the Lord appointed other seventy also, and sent them two and two before his face [ahead of Him] into every city and place, whither he himself would come.

The idea was to find homes for Jesus to stay in where He would be welcomed, and to prepare the local people for the visit of their King. There are eight points of interest in the assignment Jesus gave to the seventy.

1. They were sent out two by two, meaning there were 35 pairs of disciples. If each pair only prepared for Jesus in one town or village, that would mean at least 35 stopping places where He could teach and rest, there could have been more than that but there would have been at least 35.

2. He told them to pray while they were on their mission, to ask God for a good harvest of people to be saved for eternal life, while they sowed the word and prepared the people to be reaped or converted by others or by Jesus when He came later.

> Luke 10:2 Therefore said he unto them, The harvest truly is great, but the labourers are few: pray ye therefore the Lord of

the harvest, that he would send forth labourers into his harvest.

3. He warned them that they would have to be ready for wide-ranging hostility.

   Luke 10:3 Go your ways: behold, I send you forth as lambs among wolves.

4. He gave them the sense that their assignment was so very urgent they should not bother about providing for their trip, God would take care of all their needs, and they should not waste their time chatting to people on the way. Get the job done and have all those places ready for Jesus on His final journey to Jerusalem.

   Luke 10:4 Carry neither purse, nor scrip, [beggar's bag], nor shoes, [spare shoes]: and salute no man by the way.

5. Once they reach their destination and have found a home willing to take them in, they are to stay in that house and not move to another one that is more comfortable.

   Luke 10:5-6 ⁵ And into whatsoever house ye enter, first say, Peace be to this house.

   ⁶ And if the son of peace be there, your peace shall rest upon it: if not, it shall turn to you again.

   Jesus is repeating the instructions He gave to the twelve apostles when He sent them out earlier in Matthew 10, and if the house is worthy, if it is a household of believers they are to bless them with peace, but if the house is unworthy, a family of unbelievers, they are to cancel the blessing.

   Luke 10:7 And in the same house remain, eating and drinking such things as they give: for the labourer is worthy of his hire. Go not from house to house.

   The urgent mission they are on is to find places for Jesus to stay on the principle of the first available house is the most acceptable. They are not to go from one house to another house looking for the best place in town. He also tells them not to worry about food or drink, and promises they will be fed.

6. They are to help the individual people they stay with and other believers in the towns and villages where they lodge, including healing the sick.

Luke 10:8-9 [8] And into whatsoever city ye enter, and they receive you, eat such things as are set before you:

[9] And heal the sick that are therein, and say unto them, The kingdom of God has come nigh [near] unto you.

While the King is physically present there is healing for everyone that comes to Him, something that is not true while He is not physically on earth, but the individuals that accepted the seventy disciples had a foretaste of the kingdom of God, because their sick were healed, and so, "The kingdom of God has come nigh unto you."

7. They are to tell the people of the cities that reject them, that judgement will fall on them, and there is the promise of different levels of punishment, so that towns that reject any of the seventy will be punished more harshly than the people of Sodom, the town God destroyed by fire as an example of His disapproval.[1]

Luke 10:10-12 [10] But into whatsoever city ye enter, and they receive you not, go your ways out into the streets of the same, and say,

[11] Even the very dust of your city, which cleaveth on us, we do wipe off against you: notwithstanding be ye sure of this, that the kingdom of God is come nigh unto you.

[12] But I say unto you, that it shall be more tolerable in that day for Sodom, than for that city.

He then cursed the three cities He had cursed before[2] once again, Chorazin and Bethsaida in Luke 10:13, and Capernaum in Luke 10:15, because most of His miracles had been carried out in them and yet they rejected Him, furthermore any city that rejects any of the seventy will experience the same curse as these three cities.

8. Rejecting or accepting any of the seventy disciples, will be the same as rejecting or accepting the Messiah.

Luke 10:16 He that heareth you heareth me; and he that despiseth you dispiseth me; and he that despiseth me despiseth him that sent me.

Rejecting the disciples is the same as rejecting Jesus, and rejecting Jesus is the same as rejecting God.

The Seventy Return In Triumph
Luke 10:17-20

The seventy did everything Jesus asked them to do perfectly, and for that reason they were very happy to tell Him that their mission had been accomplished, and so we know, not less than 35 homes were ready and waiting to look after Jesus on His way to Jerusalem. Satan had tried to block their work but even the demons had not been able to stop them, and they excitedly told Jesus all about it, and He had even more to tell them.

Luke 10:18 And he said unto them, I beheld Satan as lightning fall from heaven.

Clearly Satan's days are numbered and his doom is very near.

Luke 10:19 Behold, I give unto you power to tread on serpents and scorpions, and over all the power of the enemy: and nothing shall by any means hurt you.

About the time Jesus called me by name back in Chapter 3, I was reading Luke 10:19-20, and these two verses made a very strong impression, and I knew God was saying those very words to me personally. After that three things happened involving snakes. I was running on a paper chase and was just about to tread on a large black cobra lying across the narrow path in the grass, but saw it just in time and managed to miss treading on it, and I remembered the two verses of Scripture and thought, "Satan wants to kill me But God won't let him." Not many days later after work, Soo Fah, the house maid came in to inform me that there was a snake in the garden pond, eating the tropical fish. I went to investigate and found Wong, the gardener and my driver, Kumaran, probing the pond with sticks, on the opposite bank. I was wearing Bermuda shorts and standing close to the pond. Suddenly a fully grown black cobra shot its head out of the water with its hood fully open ready to strike. I did not move, and this snake's head about ten inches from my knee stayed still for a few moments before disappearing into the pond, and I again remembered the two verses of Scripture. The next incidence was in Liberia, where again wearing shorts, I was out in the rubber fields with the manager of an estate and about half a dozen of his field supervisors checking the quality of the rubber harvester's work. Looking at the trees and their tapped panels, and paying no attention to my path, there was suddenly a unanimous cry from the Liberians behind me, not of any words, but loud, "Ooh, urghhh," and "Wahhrr," noises, however, I was dashing ahead and slow to react. They told me I had trodden on a cobra and it had writhed quickly and drastically under my foot, rising well up my unprotected leg, but it did not strike, and I thought God is really protecting me and these Africans have seen it.

The promises in Luke 10:19 were given to the seventy disciples Jesus sent out, and applied to me because of the way God impressed the verse on me while I read it and then confirmed it by experience later on through practical examples. When Jesus spoke to the seventy, the point was that they would be protected while they were on their mission. The protection was a demonstration that they had been chosen by God, by Jesus, and this meant they had been also chosen for heaven, and that is what they should have been rejoicing about, rather than the fact that the demons were under their authority.

> Luke 10:20 Not withstanding in this rejoice not, that the spirits are subject to you; but rather rejoice, because your names are written in heaven.

Jesus Thanked God The Father In Prayer And Rejoicing
Luke 10:21-24

The work of the seventy had been totally successful, with demonstrations of the power of God, and Jesus was absolutely delighted, praying to the Father and pointing out three things.

> Luke 10:21 Jesus rejoiced in the spirit, and said, I thank thee, O Father, Lord of heaven and earth, that thou hast hid these things from the wise and prudent, and hast revealed them to babes: even so, Father; for so it seemed good in thy sight.

First we learn that the reason for unbelief is because these things have been hidden from the wise, and belief is given to babes. The seventy disciples were not just out of their nappies, if they had ever had any, and so the babes, the seventy are new believers. Second, we learn that everything we know about God the Father as believers, is through Jesus only.

> Luke 10:22 All things are delivered to me of my Father: and no man knoweth who the Son is, but the Father; and who the Father is, but the Son, and he to whom the Son will reveal him.

The third thing we learn is that His disciples were blessed because they were witnessing the fulfilment of prophecies that many Old Testament prophets and kings had longed to see, but they had died long before the time of Jesus.

> Luke 10:23-24 ²³ And he turned him unto his disciples, and said privately, Blessed are the eyes which see these things that ye see:
>
> ²⁴ For I tell you, that many prophets and kings have desired to see those things which ye see, and have not seen them; and hear those things which ye hear, and have not heard them.

---

[1] Genesis 19:1-25

[2] Matthew 11:20-24

A HOSTILE QUESTION ABOUT ETERNAL LIFE
Luke 10:25-37

Just a brief reminder about the two ways of obtaining eternal life. It could be given for keeping the Law of Moses or having faith in God, just as it was given to Abraham and the other Old Testament saints. Now in the time of grace in which we are living, our faith has to be faith in Jesus, because since the crucifixion God the Father has made Jesus the only way of salvation.[1]

> Luke 10:25 And behold a certain lawyer stood up, and tempted him, saying, Master, what shall I do to inherit eternal life.

In the Bible a Jewish lawyer was someone who was an authority on the Law of Moses, and this expert tempted Jesus, meaning he was setting a trap, and by calling Jesus, Master, (Teacher), he was recognising that He also was an authority on the Law. The question was, "What shall I do," (the emphasis was on doing something, on works), "What shall I do to inherit eternal life." Jesus answered in the Jewish style by asking another question.

> Luke 10:26 He [Jesus] said unto him, What is written in the law? How readest thou?

The man did not ask about inheriting eternal life by grace, by the free gift of God, he asked what work he had to do, and that way was by the Law of Moses, and for that reason Jesus directed him to the Law. The man answered by quoting in a slightly different way the most important of the commandments from Deuteronomy 6:5, "Thou shalt love the Lord thy God with all thy heart, and with all thy soul, and with all thy strength, and with all thy mind," and the second most important commandment from Leviticus 19:18, "but thou shalt love thy neighbour as thyself."

His first quotation covered man's relationship with God, that is the most important commandment, and his second covered man's relationship with other people, and that is the second most important.

> Luke 10:28 And he [Jesus] said unto him, Thou hast answered right: this do, and thou shalt live.

Notice Jesus said, "this do," and if the man could have kept those two commandments perfectly, he would have been able to inherit eternal life, but he knew he could not keep them without ever failing. He had not trapped Jesus and he had lost the argument, but he thought it would be a good idea to start another argument over the meaning of a point of the Law.

> Luke 10:29 But he, willing to justify himself, said unto Jesus, And who is my neighbour?

In other words, "How are we to decide who this neighbour is, that we are to love as much as we love ourselves?" Jesus replied by telling a story about a Jewish priest, a Levite and a Samaritan.

The Jews had three classes of people, first and foremost the priests, directly descended from Aaron the brother of Moses, secondly the Levites the other descendents of Levi apart from the priests, and lastly the whole house of Israel. In His story Jesus includes a Samaritan, a man of that mixed race so hated by the Jews.

The story Jesus told was about a Jewish man going down from Jerusalem to Jericho, the Jews always went down from Jerusalem, not north, south, east or west, and this phrase supports those of us that think Luke was Jew. Robbers attacked the man on his way down, beat him and left him for dead beside the road. A priest came along but did nothing, walking by on the other side of the road, then a Levite came along and he also did nothing to help. Finally it was a Samaritan who stopped to help the wounded and robbed Jew, took him to an inn, asked the inn keeper to take care of him until he got well and paid the bill.

We have just discovered that the Law of Moses was that a Jew should love his neighbour as much as he loved himself, so had the priest or the Levite been neighbourly to their fellow Jew? The answer is no, they had not, because they both left him beside the road to die. The Samaritan however had been very neighbourly indeed by taking him to the inn, and guaranteeing to pay the inn keeper the full cost of his stay there until he was strong again. After telling His story to the lawyer Jesus asked him a question.

> Luke 10:36 (Jesus said to the lawyer) Which now of these three, thinkest thou, was neighbour unto him that fell among thieves?

The lawyer could not bring himself even to say the word, Samaritan, because Jews hated the Samaritans, but answered in a roundabout way, although you will remember they had called Jesus a Samaritan.[2]

> Luke 10:37 And he said, He that shewed [showed] mercy on him. Then said Jesus unto him, Go, and do thou likewise.

[1] John 6:40, Acts 4:12

[2] John 8:48

A WOMAN'S SPIRITUAL FELLOWSHIP
Luke 10:38-42

We will discover later that one of the 35 or more places prepared by the seventy was in the village of Bethany, at the home of two sisters, Martha and Mary, and their brother Lazarus. Eventually on their way to Jerusalem, Jesus and His followers reached the family's dwelling. It seems from the following verses that Martha was the manager of the house hold, and it was Martha, probably the older of the two women, that welcomed Jesus into the home.

> Luke 10:38-39 38 Now it came to pass, as they went, that he entered into a certain village: and a certain woman named Martha received him into her house.
>
> 39 And she had a sister called Mary, which also sat at Jesus' feet, and heard his word.

Martha was very interested in serving a good meal for Jesus, and wanted to be completely sure that He had the best of everything she was able to provide for His physical comfort. On the other hand, Mary was not concerned with the physical, her interest was spiritual, and she sat at the feet of the Lord in the manner of a disciple listening carefully to His teaching. In doing this she satisfied her own need and importantly, gave spiritual fellowship to Jesus as well, and Jesus gratefully appreciated the spiritual fellowship Mary provided. Mary was an intelligent student and sitting at the feet of the Lord she learned things that even His disciples did not understand. She knew that Jesus was going to die, but although the disciples were told the same thing many times, they had not understood it, and so because of her understanding, Jesus will praise her highly later on. Mary's listening to Jesus eventually brought Martha to the point where she could bear it no longer.

> Luke 10:40-42 ⁴⁰ But Martha was cumbered [distracted] about much serving, and came to him, and said, Lord, dost thou not care that my sister hath left me to serve alone? Bid [Ask] her therefore that she help me.
>
> ⁴¹ And Jesus answered and said unto her, Martha, Martha, thou art careful [worried] and troubled about many things:
>
> ⁴² But one thing is needful: and Mary hath chosen that good part, which shall not be taken away from her.

More often than not it would have been right for members of the household to share the workload of attending to their guests, but in this case Mary was providing Jesus with His spiritual need for fellowship, and was learning about spiritual things herself which was more important than enjoying a good meal. From this we learn two lessons.

1. It is more important to be with Jesus than it is to be busy for Him.
2. It is better to be taught by Jesus than it is to be full of activity in His service.

JESUS TEACHES HIS DISCIPLES HOW TO PRAY
Luke 11:1-13

In Judaism, prayers were and are from prayer books, like the prayers of the Church of England and like so many other denominations and religions, but Jesus did not pray the set prayers of prayer books, He prayed spontaneously, off the cuff, avoiding all forms of religious formality. He did not go round with a prayer book to guide Him, and the disciples brought up in Judaism realised that His prayers were genuine and successful.

> Luke 11:1 And it came to pass, that, as he was praying in a certain place, when he ceased, one of his disciples said unto him, Lord, teach us to pray, as John [the Baptist] also taught his disciples.

The prayers of someone with a strong Bible based faith are always spontaneous and straight from the heart.

Going back for a moment to Chapter 5, the Sermon on the Mount was the explanation by Jesus of the righteousness of the Law of Moses, in which He discredited the Pharisaic interpretation as recorded in the Mishnah. The Sermon on the Mount then was about the Law, but there were a few things in it that need to be taken up by the church, and we know these things because they are repeated later in the gospels and the letters. One example of this is the Lord's Prayer, which was never meant to be used as a set prayer,[1] but as an outline, as previously explained and as again summarized below.

How Our Prayers Should Be Planned

1. We should speak to God the Father. Luke 11:2, "When ye pray, say, Our Father."
2. We should greet our heavenly Father, as holy. Luke 11:2, "Hallowed be thy name."
3. We should pray for the promised kingdom of God. Luke 11:2 "Thy kingdom come."
4. We should pray for the needs of each day. Luke 11:3 "Give us by day our daily bread."
5. We should pray for the forgiveness of our sins. Luke 11:4 "And forgive us our sins; for we also forgive everyone that is indebted to us."

6. We should pray for protection in spiritual warfare. Luke 11:4 "And lead us not into temptation; but deliver us from evil."

The first lesson here comes out in Luke 11:5-8, the parable of the pushy friend, who at midnight wakes up his neighbour to ask for bread, and keeps on disturbing him until he gets what he wants. The point is that the unwilling neighbour gave his friend what he asked for because of his persistence, but we have a God who is eager and ready to answer our prayers, and if we keep praying continually, He will be even more willing to answer us.

> Luke 11:9-10 [9] And I say unto you, Ask, and it shall be given you; seek, and ye shall find; knock, and it shall be opened unto you.
>
> [10] For every one that asketh receiveth; and he that seeketh findeth; and to him that knocketh it shall be opened.

If a reluctant neighbour will give his friend what he wants because of his dogged and repeated asking, how much more will our dedicated heavenly Father answer our unrelenting prayers that we make for our friends, and of course for ourselves as well.

The second lesson comes in Luke 11:13, and it is based on the truth that a wicked man will give good gifts to his children, so how much more will God the Father, who is good, give good gifts to His children!

> Luke 11:13 If ye then being evil, know how to give good gifts unto your children: how much more shall your heavenly Father give the Holy Spirit to them that ask him.

It is said, and I am not suggesting otherwise, that asking God for the Holy Spirit was a good prayer before the crucifixion, (i.e. at the time Jesus was teaching this to His disciples), but is no longer necessary because after Acts 2:4, believers now receive the Holy Spirit the moment they first put their faith in Jesus.

> Acts 2:38 Then Peter said unto them, Repent, and be baptised every one of you in the name of Jesus Christ for the remission of sins, and ye shall receive the gift of the Holy Ghost.

That is how it was with me, I believed, prayed for Jesus to come into my life, and knew the presence of God within me the next morning, but for my mother, Luke 11:13 was her way of getting born again. She prayed to God for the Holy Spirit, received Him and was born again in that way. With God we do not always have to be too finicky about the way we approach Him, it is what is in our hearts that gets His attention.[2]

[1] Matthew 6:7

[2] 1 Samuel 16:7

THE DISPUTE ABOUT THE HEALING OF ANOTHER DUMB MAN
Luke 11:14-36

Casting out a dumb demon was the second of the Messianic signs, and this was the third time Jesus performed the miracle. The first was in the Galilee, Matthew 9:33, the second was in the Decapolis, Mark 7:35, and now He gives the same sign again, this time in Judea while on His way to Jerusalem. We will look at this event under five headings.

The False Accusation Starts To Spread
Luke 11:14-16

> Luke 11:14 And he was casting out a devil, and it was dumb. And it came to pass, when the devil was gone out, the dumb spake; and **the people wondered**, [could He be the Messiah?].

Now notice how some of the crowd respond.

> Luke 11:15-16 [15] But some of them said, He casteth out devils through Beelzebub the chief of the devils.
>
> [16] And others, tempting him, sought of him a sign from heaven.

Increasingly the crowds are beginning to believe the Pharisees, and mimicking them ask for a sign from heaven, but whenever Jesus gives them a sign they immediately say it is from Hell, from Satan.

Jesus Explains Why The Accusation Is Not True
Luke 11:17-23

The same accusations were made by the Jews in Galilee, and the answers Jesus gives here are the same as He gave before, because if the accusations are the same, the answers will be the same, although they are given to other people in different places.

1. It cannot be true that Jesus cast out demons by the power of Beelzebub, because that would mean that Satan's kingdom was divided and fighting among itself (Luke 11:17-18).
2. The rabbis themselves taught that exorcism was something that could only be done through the power of the Spirit of God, and to say Jesus was doing it through the power of Satan, meant they were denying their own faith (Luke 11:19).
3. The miracle was in fact a sign that Jesus is the Messiah (Luke 11:20).
4. It was proof that He was stronger that Satan (Luke 11:21-22).
5. Each person must make up his or her own mind whether they are going to follow Jesus or not.

Luke 11:23 He that is not with me is against me: and he that gathereth not with me scattereth.

I am following Jesus, what about you?

Jesus Explains The Spiritual Mess The Nation Is In
Luke 11:24-28

First in Luke 11:24-26, Jesus repeats what He said in Galilee, in Matthew 12:43-45, when he was rejected by the spiritual leaders. The unclean spirit that left will come back, bringing others with it. The hidden message again is that the final state of the generation He was talking to was going to get much worse, except of course for those that believed in Him. In Galilee, Jesus' disapproval had been directed at the leaders but here in Judea, He also included the increasing number among the crowd that were now following the leaders in rejecting Him.

Secondly Jesus, as before, tells them to give more attention to spiritual things and stop being so concerned about worldly relationships. In the Galilee, Jesus' mother and brothers had come to Him, and there He taught that only those that obey Him are His true spiritual family. The situation this time is different.

> Luke 11:27-28 [27] And it came to pass, as he spake these things, a certain woman of the company lifted up her voice, and said unto him, Blessed is the womb that bare thee, and the paps [nipples] which thou hast sucked.
>
> [28] But he said, Yea rather, blessed are they that hear the word of God, and keep it.

Although the situation this time is different the message is the same, He stresses the importance of spiritual intimacy above worldly contacts.

The Sign For That Generation
Luke 11:29-32

Although in Galilee Jesus spoke to the leaders, in Judea He spoke to the crowds, and notice also He is speaking to that generation.

> Luke 11:29 And when the people were gathered thick together, he began to say, This is an evil generation: they seek a sign; and there shall no sign be given it, but the sign of Jonas the prophet.

The sign of Jonas is the sign of the resurrection of the dead.

> Luke 11:30 For as Jonas was a sign unto the Ninevites, so shall also the son of man be to this generation.

In the following verses, He says the Gentiles will be raised from the dead on judgement day, and will condemn the Jewish generation that rejected Him.

An Appeal To The Jewish People
Luke 11:33-36

His appeal is made in terms of light and darkness, those accepting Him will walk in the light but those rejecting Him will be lost in darkness. Seven points will help us to understand these four verses.
1. The words of Jesus are light.
2. The light Jesus brought was the knowledge of the Father.
3. The knowledge of the Father was given clearly to the whole nation.
4. The Jews rejected the light because they were spiritually blind.
5. The reason for their spiritual blindness was not the fault of the light, but of the blind individuals themselves.
6. Israel remained in the darkness because it rejected the knowledge of the Father, it was not the fault of Jesus who revealed Him.
7. If they had accepted the knowledge of the Father given by Jesus they would have had light.

THE DISPUTE OVER KEEPING RELIGIOUS CUSTOMS
Luke 11:37-54

In the Bible, God has given us certain rules to keep and work to do, but religious people often make up other rules. We need to do what God says but not what men say. It is amazing how, like the Pharisees, the church has started its own customs. People are given a church job because they have passed a difficult examination, as if holiness is given to those that can do clever tests, which it is not, and they are then given great sounding titles, like Reverend or Doctor giving them the right to wear clerical collars, cassocks, official highly decorated robes and mitres. Such people are sometimes insecure and I have noticed when meeting them socially, they often like to talk about politics, the weather, and the repairs needed for the church roof, but not about Jesus. If we start talking about our Lord, they go quiet, and make excuses to talk to someone else. Perhaps the reason is they do not know Him, and are out of their comfort zone.

Righteousness is the gift of God,[1] and is only given to us after we believe in Jesus.[2] Jesus was given the opportunity to teach the Jews about the uselessness of their religious customs, when he was invited into a Pharisee's home where they thought they were being righteous when they washed their hands before eating.

> Luke 11:37-38 [37] And as he spake [spoke], a certain Pharisee besought [asked] him to dine with him: and he went in, and sat down to meat [a meal].
>
> [38] And when the Pharisee saw it, he marvelled [was amazed] that he had not first washed before dinner.

The Pharisee, pretending to be generous, asked Jesus home for a meal, but here again he was actually trying to find a way to accuse Him of sin. Watching carefully he saw at the very start of the meeting that Jesus did not wash His hands before eating, which the Mishnah has much to say about as we learned in Chapter 7, when we asked ourselves, "What defiles a man? What degrades him?" The Pharisee did not say anything but the people there could see from his demeanour that he was shocked, and that he thought Jesus was acting very badly, and so Jesus told them their mistake in the next three verses.

> Luke 11:39-41 [39] And the Lord said unto him, Now do ye Pharisees make clean the outside of the cup and the platter; but your inward part is full of ravening [greed] and wickedness.
>
> [40] Ye fools, did not he that made that which is without make that which is within also?
>
> [41] But rather give alms of such things as ye have; and, behold, all things are clean unto you.

He tells them off for being careful to keep rules that other people can see, the external issues of the oral law, and for not giving the same attention or more to the internal issues of the Law of Moses. It is because they do not worry about the internal issues that they are fools and will have to suffer the terrible woes, He is about to prophesy against them. Later, shortly before He dies, Jesus will tell the unbelieving Jews of a more detailed number of woes that will happen to them, and some of those woes will be similar to these He speaks of here, but the two announcements were quite separate events.

The word, "woe," is not used much in every day conversation today, so what does it mean? Wherever "woe" is used in the New Testament, it always comes from the Greek Word, *"ouai,"* which was a spoken expression of bitter grief and distress or of denunciation. *"Ouai,"* can also be translated, "Alas!" Jesus in listing His woes was hinting, (parabolically in a way they would not understand), at the tremendous judgements that were coming on the Jewish people because they had rejected their Messiah. Our Lord was most concerned about the suffering that would take place, particularly in Jerusalem, as Luke has told us.

> Luke 19: 41-44 [41] And when he [Jesus] was come near, he beheld [looked at] the city [Jerusalem], and wept over it,
>
> [42] Saying, If thou [you] hadst [had] known, even thou, at least in this thy day [your day – because their King was there but they did not know Him], the things which belong unto thy peace! But now they are hid from thine eyes.
>
> [43] For the days shall come upon thee, that thine enemies shall cast [dig] a trench [ditch] about [all the way around] thee, and compass [surround] thee round, and keep thee in [no one will escape] on every side.
>
> [44] And thy shall lay thee [pull you down] even [level] with the ground, and thy children within thee; and they shall not leave in thee one stone upon another; because thou knewest not [did not know] the time of thy visitation [God's visit].

This prophecy of the destruction of Jerusalem will be dealt with more fully in Chapter 11, The Prophecies Of Jesus, but it happened in AD 70, just as the Jewish King said it would. I have included it here just to show how extremely tragic the woes that Jesus was talking about, that the Jews would have to suffer were going to be.

The first three woes found in Luke 11:42-44, were for the Pharisees as a whole group, but the second three woes applied only to the lawyers, those Pharisees who decided on the oral law and kept adding to it.

> The first woe, in verse 42, was because they were so careful to tithe the tiniest things, even giving one tenth of the small amounts of garden herbs they grew to God, to feed the priests, but they were not bothered about justice and the love of God. They were keeping the least important part of the Law but completely forgetting the most important. They should not have picked and chosen the parts of the Law to keep; they were supposed to keep all of it.

> The second woe, in verse 43, was because they were proud of the respect they got from the people, expecting to be given seats of honour in the synagogues.

> The third woe for the Pharisees, in verse 44, was because they were hypocrites, and Jesus was not saying the same here as He said later in the more detailed list of woes already mentioned, where He speaks of the Pharisees being like whitened sepulchres. In this separate and earlier event He was not calling them, whitened tombs, which can easily be seen, but burial places that were difficult to see because they were not whitewashed, so that the hypocrisy of the Pharisees contaminated and polluted people without warning.

After announcing these three woes on the Pharisees as a whole, Jesus was interrupted by one of their lawyers.

> Luke 11:45 Then answered one of the lawyers, and said unto him, Master, thus saying thou reproachest us also.

Remember, these were not civil lawyers but religious lawyers, that were experts, not only on the Law of Moses but also on the laws in the Mishnah which they helped to invent. The Pharisees were following the laws the lawyers had made up and so the lawyer pointed out that by showing His disapproval of the Pharisees, Jesus was in fact condemning them. He probably thought Jesus would apologise for condemning the big-headed law makers, but not one bit, in fact they would suffer three extra woes of their own.

The first woe was because they made up new traditions and rituals forcing the people to keep them as if they were instructions from God. Luke 11:46, "And he said, Woe unto you also, ye lawyers! For ye laid men with burdens grievous to be borne, and ye yourselves touch not the burdens with one of your fingers."

The second woe for the lawyers was because by not recognizing Jesus as the Messiah they were denying the words of every single prophet in the Old Testament that had prophesied about His first coming, and that was why the destruction of AD 70 would happen to Israel. The Jews of that generation by following the teaching of the lawyers, abandoned the truth of God's prophetic Word, and therefore Jesus made sure they were told that their generation was responsible for the punishment that would soon come upon them.

> Luke 11:50-51 50 The blood of all the prophets, which was shed from the foundation of the world, may be required of this generation.
>
> 51 From the blood of Abel unto the blood of Zacharias, which perished between the altar and the temple; verily [truly] I say unto you. It shall be required of this generation.

Abel, a son of Adam and Eve, had sacrificed the first lambs from his flock,[3] and God accepted Abel's sacrifice which pointed thousands of years into the future to Jesus the Lamb of God, sacrificed for us.[4] The Zacharias which perished between the altar and the temple, was the prophet Zechariah the son of Berechiah, the writer of the second from last book of the Old Testament.[5] He made very many prophecies about the coming of Jesus as the Messiah, including the fact that He was humble and would ride on a donkey,[6] that He would be sold for thirty pieces of silver,[7] and also importantly, (because of the punishment, the woe, that would come on the Jews of that generation), how the Messiah would be rejected by the false shepherds of Israel, and as a result the nation would be attacked and the people scattered.[8]

Everything all the prophets were going to say about the first coming of the Messiah had been said, and Jesus had performed the signs of the Messiah just as the prophets had foretold. There was no way out for the lawyers, if the Bible prophets of the Old Testament were genuine, then without doubt Jesus was the Messiah of Israel. If they rejected Jesus, they were rejecting the prophets.

The third woe is in Luke 11:52, Woe unto you lawyers! For ye have taken away the key of knowledge: ye entered not in yourselves, and them that were entering in ye hindered.

Through all their traditions, the lawyers had hidden the truth from the masses, and by saying that the Law of Moses could not be understood without the oral law they had taken away the key of knowledge, so that many Jews were unable to recognize their Messiah.

After the first three woes had been pronounced against the Pharisees and the following three against the lawyers, they were furious and angrily questioned Jesus to try to get Him to say something that they could use against Him, but the Messiah was always perfect in what He did and what He said.

> Luke 11:53-54 [53] And as he said these things unto them, the scribes and the Pharisees began to urge him vehemently [strongly and passionately], and to provoke him to speak of many things:
>
> [54] Laying wait for him, and seeking to catch something out of his mouth, that they might accuse him.

---

[1] Romans 5:17-18, Ephesians 2:4-9

[2] John 14:6, Romans 3:22-24

[3] Genesis 4:4

[4] Hebrews 10:1-18

[5] Matthew 23:35

[6] Zechariah 9:9

[7] Zechariah 11:12

[8] Zechariah 11:3-9

JESUS HAS NINE LESSONS FOR HIS DISCIPLES
Luke 12:1 to 13:21

The First Lesson: Hypocrisy or Insincerity
Luke 12:1-12

The lesson was "first of all," for the disciples, even though there was a huge and tightly packed crowd there so that people were treading on each other. Remember after the rejection He taught the public in ways they did not understand. His instructions to the apostles here were clear and easily understood.

> Luke 12:1 In the meantime, when there were gathered together an innumerable multitude of people, insomuch that they trod one upon another, he began to say unto his disciple first of all, Beware ye of the leaven of the Pharisees, which is hypocrisy.

The question of insincerity comes up here because of the dispute about keeping religious rituals, like the washing of hands we have just been talking about, and that is why Jesus told His disciples, "Beware ye of the leaven of the Pharisees, which is hypocrisy." Apart from Luke 12:1, verses 4 and 8, also show that Jesus was not teaching the huge crowd where the people were treading on each other, but only His disciples.

> Luke 12:4 And I say unto you my friends, …

> Luke 12:8 Also I say unto you, …

Jesus had six things to say about hypocrisy to the apostles.
1. They will never have to hide anything they do from anyone if they are always completely honest.[1]
2. Liars often lie because they are afraid to tell someone the truth, but people that fear God do not lie because they are more frightened of what God might do to them than what men might do, so the disciples must fear God, but not men.[2]

3. God is focusing His attention on them, and they must trust Him only and have faith in nothing and no one else.[3]

4. If they fear God and not men, and if they trust God and not men, then they must tell other people that Jesus is the Messiah.[4]

5. They must not join the Pharisees and the crowds of that generation in denying that Jesus is the Messiah, saying that His miracles were not done by the Holy Spirit, but by the power of demons. As we have already seen, that would have been an unforgivable sin against the Holy Spirit.[5]

6. If they were taken to a law court by the police because they had told people that Jesus was the Messiah, they were not to worry about what they were going to say, since God would teach them.[6]

Luke 12:12 For the Holy Ghost shall teach you in the same hour what ye ought to say.

[1] Luke 12:1-3
[2] Luke 12:4-5
[3] Luke 12:6-7
[4] Luke 12:8-9
[5] Luke 12:10
[6] Luke 12:11

The Second Lesson: Covetousness or Desire
Luke 12:13-34

The second lesson will be divided into three separate sections, A, B and C.

(A) How The Lesson Came About (Luke 12:13-15)

Luke 12:13-15 13 And one of the company said unto him, Master, speak to my brother, that he divide the inheritance with me.

¹⁴ And he said unto him, Man, who made me a judge or a deliverer over you?

¹⁵ And he said unto them, Take heed, and beware of covetousness: for a man's life consisteth not in the abundance of things which he possesseth.

Verse 15, means that real life is not about how rich we are, and leaves us to wonder what real life is. As we study the teaching of Jesus in section (A) remember that He came to bring this real life, but because the Jews rejected Him, He will have to come again before the nation as a whole is given that kind of life.

The cause of the lesson on covetousness was a family argument over an inheritance which a man refused to share with his brother, then the one that had got nothing challenged Jesus to settle the argument, but why did he bring this dispute to Jesus? Psalm 72 is a messianic psalm, a prophecy of what will happen when Jesus actually becomes King of the Jews, reigning in Jerusalem. One of His responsibilities will be to settle disputes between the people, and therefore the man confronted Jesus with the problem to find out if He judged with righteousness, as Scripture said the Messiah would.

Psalm 72:2 He shall judge thy people with righteousness, and thy poor with judgement.

It was another attempt to get a sign from Jesus that He was the Messiah, but Jesus had said that the only other sign in addition to the many signs they had already refused to accept would be the sign of Jonah, the sign of the resurrection of the dead.[7]

If we go back 3,500 years, that is to about 1,500 BC, Moses killed an Egyptian because he was beating a Jewish slave. The very next day He saw a Jew beating another Jew, and when he asked why, the Jew that was in the wrong said to Moses, "Who made thee a prince and a judge over us?"[8] Moses had been trying to assist his fellow Jews, but their answer to Moses from the man that was in the wrong shows how, the first time he came to them, his own people rejected him and his offer of help, so he left them for forty years. What Jesus is saying is that just as Moses was rejected by Israel, now Jesus has also been rejected by those Jews that are in the wrong, and because he has been rejected, He cannot be the One to judge Israel as King, and to settle disputes as Messiah. Moses had to come again to rescue the Jews from Egypt, and it will be the same with the nation of Israel, Jesus will have to come again, a second time, before they are finally rescued for eternal life.

[7] Luke 11:29-32

[8] Exodus 2:14

(B) The Parable (Luke 12:16-21)

The man that had asked Jesus about having a share of the inheritance his brother had seized was from the crowd of unbelieving followers, and so Jesus replied by telling them a parable that they could not and would not understand, according to His guiding principle ever since Matthew 13:13.

In the parable of the rich fool, a wealthy farmer has huge harvests and decides to build new barns to store all his goods in and live a life of ease for the rest of his life. The idea does not seem foolish at all until we check the meaning of the word "fool" when used in the Bible.

Psalm 14:1 The fool hath said in his heart, There is no God.

A wise man will always make his plans remembering God and His ways, but fools never do. The parable shows the madness and sinfulness of storing up much more than we need. God was going to end the man's life that night and his plans for a life of ease would never come to pass.

It is not wrong to prepare for the future as Jesus teaches us later on but it is sinful to leave God out of our thinking, that was why he was called, "You fool." He did not bother with the first and greatest of the commandments.[9] He was selfish and did not concern himself with the poor and needy even though he was a rich man with a big surplus of goods far beyond his needs, meaning that he did not bother with the second most important commandment.[10] Jesus in His final words of the parable to the unbelieving crowd then summed up the rich man's condition.

> Luke 12:20-21 [20] But God said unto him, Thou fool, this night thy soul shall be required of thee: then whose shall those things be, which thou hast provided?
>
> [21] So is he that layeth up treasure for himself, and is not rich toward God.

Laying up treasure on earth for themselves was something the Pharisees did.

[9] Deuteronomy 6:4-5, Matthew 22:35-38
[10] Leviticus 19:18, Matthew 22:39

(C) Jesus Explains The Parable To His Disciples (Luke 12:22-34)

Notice to whom Jesus is talking as He begins to explain the meaning of the parable.

> Luke 12:22 And he said unto his disciples.

The basic teaching is in two verses, and the message to believers is we need not worry so long as we remember to live and work according to the leading of our Heavenly Father, something the rich fool in the parable did not do.

> Luke 12:22-23 [22] And he said unto his disciples, Therefore I say unto you, Take no thought for your life, what ye shall eat; neither for the body, what ye shall put on.
>
> [23] The life is more than meat [food], and the body is more than raiment [clothes].

Jesus gave four examples of how God looks after those of us that are careful to live according to His will, that follow the way He wants us to go, and that do the things He wants us to do, that do not leave God out of the equation.

1. God will make sure we get our food.[11]
2. God will make sure we have the clothes we need.[12]

3. If we make it our business to understand and be part of His kingdom, He will provide us with all the food and clothes we need.[13]

4. God promises us a future with Him in heaven.

Luke 12:32 Fear not, little flock; for it is your Father's good pleasure to give you the kingdom.

As we are heirs to the kingdom of God, we are advised to store up treasures in heaven, not in the world.[14]

Luke 12:34 For where your treasure is, there will your heart be also.

[11] Luke 12:24-26
[12] Luke 12: 26-28
[13] Luke 12:29-31
[14] Luke 12:33

The Third Lesson: Watchfulness or Keeping On The Alert Luke 12:35-40

Jesus sees the disciples as His servants, looking after His interests while He is away, and He makes the point that He wants them to stay alert.

Luke 12:37 Blessed are those servants, whom the lord when he cometh shall find watching.

If I had a number of servants and left them to look after the house and gardens while I went away on business, I would not expect them to stay near the gate and watch and see when I was coming back and do nothing else. I would expect them to work hard so that when I returned the lawns were cut, the flower beds were in bloom, the house swept and clean, and food ready to prepare if needed. Definitely if the house had been perfectly kept while I was away and the servants greeted me with friendly smiles on my return, that would make me happy, so there is work involved for servants who have been asked to be alert.

Jesus promises His servants rewards when He returns if they are alert and welcome Him immediately.
1. Faithful servants will be served.
2. Faithfulness will be taken into account in deciding on the rewards.

The Fourth Lesson: Faithfulness or Loyalty
Luke 12:41-48

The teaching about faithfulness was given because Peter wanted to know if the parable was only for the disciples or for everyone that was there.

Luke 12:41 Then Peter said unto him, Lord, speakest thou this parable unto us, or even to all?

The answer was that it was for everyone who knows the truth, and that is why a servant must carefully look after everything his master has trusted him with. Any servant who behaves responsibly while the master is away will be rewarded by being given more responsibility.

Luke 12:48 For unto whomsoever much is given, of him shall be much required: and to whom men have committed much, of him they will ask the more.

Jesus asks for constant and persistent loyalty from His servants at all times.

Luke 12:47-48 [47] And that servant, which knew his lord's will, and prepared not himself, neither did according to his will, shall be beaten with many stripes.

[48] But he that knew not, and did commit things worthy of stripes, shall be beaten with few stripes.

Even believers will get different amounts of prizes, while for unbelievers there will be punishments of different severity depending upon what they knew. If someone does something he knows is wrong, his punishment will be greater, but if someone else does the same thing but does not know it is wrong, his punishment will be less, although he will still be punished for his sin. The people who sin and do not know they are doing wrong will still be punished, no excuses will be accepted.

The terrible truth is that people who sin without knowing it, that is those that have not called on Jesus to forgive them, will go to Hell, but in Hell some will be chastised more harshly. The severity of the punishment will depend on knowledge. If they have been told the message of the gospel and refused to accept it, their punishment will cause more intense suffering, but those who did not know will also be punished.

The Fifth Lesson: Three Things Will Result From The First Coming Of Jesus
Luke 12:49-53

1. He came to judge. Luke 12:49, "I am come to send fire on the earth; and what will I, if it be already kindled?" If the Jews had accepted Jesus as their King and Messiah, He would have sent peace, but because they rejected Him, He sent judgement instead.

2. He came to die. Luke 12:50, "But I have a baptism to be baptised with; and how I am straightened [distressed] till it be accomplished!" His baptism was the suffering and cruel torture that only ended when He died.

3. He came to split Jewish families. Luke 12: 51, "Suppose ye that I come to give peace on earth? I tell you, Nay; but rather division."

Jewish families are well known for their strength as a unit, something that has helped keep the Jews a separate people. For almost 2,000 years they have been living among the nations of the world, with no country of their own. However, as soon as a Jew believes in Jesus the family is divided, and the believer is no longer accepted, just as Isaiah the prophet said. To the remnant, those Jews that believe in Messiah Jesus, He is a sanctuary, a place of safety, but to the others, the majority, He is an offence, an insult.

Isaiah 8:14 And he shall be for a sanctuary; but for a stone of stumbling and for a rock of offence to both the houses of Israel, for a gin [a trap that catches the foot] and for a snare [a noose that catches the neck] to the inhabitants of Jerusalem.

The Sixth Lesson: The Signs Of This Time (the time for the Messiah) Luke 12:54-59

Jesus is speaking here to the people,[15] words of judgement,[16] because they do not recognize from the signs that this is the time for their Messiah, the time above all others they should have been ready for.

> Luke 12:56 Ye hypocrites, ye can discern the face of the sky and of the earth; but how is it that you do not discern this time?

"Hypocrites" in this verse has the idea of an actor, so that the Pharisees were pretending to be religious but they were fakes acting the part, and that is why they were unable to discern that the time for the Messiah had come.

Today, many people read about the signs of the times spoken of by Jesus and think they can predict His second coming, but in the gospels the term, "signs of the times" always concerns His first coming, never ever his second coming. However, Jesus did give signs for the end of the age in the gospels. The multitudes and Pharisees should have known the signs of His coming from prophecies in the Old Testament. Now judgement is coming and they are strongly advised to reconcile themselves to God while there is still time, that is before the judgement falls. Individual people could do this by leaving the multitudes and accepting Jesus as the Messiah, in which case they would not suffer the judgement. The judgement of AD 70 was now certain for the nation, but there was still time for anyone to accept Jesus before it came, and escape with the other believers that followed the instructions He gave, which were to leave Jerusalem just before the final siege by the Roman army was enforced. When Jesus spoke to the multitude they were separated from God and the only way to be united with Him was to change their thinking, repent and believe that He was the Messiah.

[15] Luke 12:54
[16] Luke 12:58-59

The Seventh Lesson: Everyone That Does Not Believe Jesus Is The Messiah Needs To Repent, Because The Judgement Of Unbelievers Is Certain
Luke 13:1-9

The chapter begins with two sad stories, the first told by people in the crowd and the second told by Jesus. The first was about some Galileans that had gone to the Temple to offer sacrifices, and Pontius Pilate the governor of Judea took them to be rebels. Pilate ordered the army to kill them and their blood was mixed with the blood of their sacrifices. The second tragedy was at the Pool of Siloam where a tower had collapsed killing eighteen people. The Pharisees taught that brutal and unusual deaths such as these showed that those who died had been guilty of secret sin, something far worse than normal, but Jesus rejected that idea completely.

> Luke 13:2-5 ²And Jesus answering said unto them, Suppose ye that these Galileans were sinners above all Galileans, because they suffered such things?
>
> ³ I tell you, Nay: ...
>
> ⁴ Or those eighteen, upon whom the tower in Siloam fell, and slew them, think ye that they were sinners above all men that dwell in Jerusalem?
>
> ⁵ I tell you, Nay: ...

These awful deaths were not because the unfortunate victims had been greater sinners than anyone else, but they were to do with those sins that we are all guilty of.[17] However, Jesus tells them there is a way to have sins cancelled.

> Luke 13:3 "except ye repent, ye shall all likewise [in the same way] perish."

Luke 13:5 "except ye repent, ye shall all likewise [in the same way] perish.

Repent means to change your mind, and they need to change their mind about Jesus. He is not possessed by the devil, He is the Messiah, and that is the change in thinking, the repentance, that is needed. If they refuse to change their minds they will die like the people killed by the Roman soldiers and those killed by the falling tower. In AD 70 the Romans attacking Jerusalem dug under the towers in the wall so that they collapsed and people died in the same way as those killed by the tower of Siloam. Once inside the city at the time the sacrifice was being offered the Roman soldiers fought their way into the Temple and so the blood of the Jews killed by Roman soldiers, was again mixed with the sacrifice, as had happened to the Galileans killed by Pontius Pilate.

The parable of the fig tree that did not produce fruit, in Luke 13:6-9, was for the multitude, and although they could not and did not understand, the hidden message was that judgement would be delayed from AD 30 to AD 70, to give a new generation of Jews the chance to think things over. The fig tree represented Israel and because there was no fruit of repentance by the nation as a whole, after forty years Jerusalem was destroyed and Jews were killed or sold as slaves, and so the fig tree was felled.

[17] Romans 6:23

The Eighth Lesson: A Demonstration Of How Israel Needs The Good Shepherd
Luke 13:10-17

In this, the last Bible record of Jesus in a synagogue, He was teaching on the Sabbath day.

Luke 13:11 And, behold, there was a woman which had a spirit of infirmity eighteen years, and was bowed [bent] together, and could no wise lift up herself.

The poor lady had extreme curvature of the spine, but she had managed somehow to get to the synagogue where Jesus healed her, meaning of course that she believed in Him. The president of the synagogue was furious with anger and publicly condemned Jesus.

> Luke 13:14 And the ruler of the synagogue answered with indignation, because Jesus had healed on the Sabbath day, and said unto the people, There are six days in which men ought to work: in them come and be healed, and not on the Sabbath day.

Jesus would have none of it and answered the president plainly.

> Luke 13:15 Thou hypocrite, does not each one of you on the Sabbath loose his ox or his ass from the stall, and lead him away to watering?

It was the teaching of the Pharisees that works of mercy and genuine need were allowed on the Sabbath, and they made sure their animals were well looked after on the weekly day of rest, consequently it was much more important to look after sick people on that day, and as a result Jesus explained further.

> Luke 13:16 And ought not this woman, being a daughter of Abraham, whom Satan hath bound, lo, these eighteen years, be loosed from this bond on the Sabbath day?

Jesus stressed the lady was Jewish by calling her a daughter of Abraham, and then made it public knowledge that her condition was caused by Satan.

Again, following His rejection by Israel on the wickedly untrue grounds that His messianic miracles were performed by the power of Satan, Jesus would no longer help the nation but He would help individuals in it. There is no doubt that this poor Jewess had a personal need, and as the Jews are His possession, He can take care of the welfare of His individual sheep. It is perhaps appropriate to recall a prophecy from the Old Testament at this point.

> Zechariah 11:11 And it [the covenant] was broken in that day: and so the poor of the flock that waited upon me knew that it was the word of the LORD.

The poor (afflicted) of the flock in this prophecy is associated with individual believers, and this woman was certainly of the flock and also afflicted.

Jesus again teaches here about binding and loosing but notice Satan was not bound or loosed. The woman had been bound by Satan and was loosed by Jesus. An angel of God will bind Satan when the right time comes and the angel will not need our help,[18] and notice that because he is bound Satan will not be allowed to deceive the nations.[19] The act of binding means a person is prevented from doing something, and loosing means a person is freed to do something.

My own experience with so called, "binding and loosing," happened about ten years after being born again. My Heavenly Father for five years put me in training as secretary of the Full Gospel Business Men's Fellowship International, Launceston, Cornwall. We used to host banquets in a large hotel and invite guests, including men women and children to an evening meal. During coffee afterwards there would be a talk from a successful business man about his faith. Many gave their lives to Jesus on those occasions, and some confirmed miracles of healing took place. Apart from the dinners the men of the chapter met once or twice a week for worship, prayer, and to organise the coming banquet.

In those days, "binding and loosing," was popular, and in the evenings after work we used to walk the streets of certain towns desperately in need of Jesus, or so we thought, binding Satan and his demons so that Jesus was loosed to come in. It now seems crazy to me but that is what we did. At the time a revived teaching in church circles was about territorial spirits, that is to say spirit servants of Satan that influence people, living in certain areas of the earth, (people who are not filled with the Holy Spirit and are not being protected by Jesus).

We noticed that the sightings of famous ghosts were reported by many different observers, over many years but always in the same place, which we assumed was their special territory. Also we remembered from the

Bible how the messenger to Daniel from heaven had been held up by the territorial spirit of Satan stationed over Persia, until God's angel Michael came and helped him break through to Daniel.[20] Other references to territorial spirits occur throughout the Old Testament because it often tells us the people used to worship them under trees and on the tops of hills. They were worshipped there because that was their territory, that was where they were.[21] Putting all this together we decided that the territorial spirits over my local town of Camelford were on Roughtor, the second highest peak on Bodmin Moor. Earlier in this chapter there was a photograph with Roughtor in the background of a picture showing my sheep approaching the open gate to a field of fresh grass, following after the heading, Jesus Is The True Shepherd.

The men of the Launceston Chapter of The Full Gospel Business Men's Fellowship International, (FGBMFI), decided to wage war on the spirits over Camelford. One evening a dozen or so of us set off to climb Roughtor. As we approached the top a strong wind started to blow, darkness fell and it began to snow, and we prayed and bound the spirits. Afterwards we had to come down through the dark, the wind and snow, losing our way several times.

Finally arriving back at the farmhouse, where Lucy was sitting by a blazing log fire in the sitting room, I greeted her, but she was in an awfully bad mood. She continued to be upset for three days, then gradually returned to her normal self. At the next prayer meeting of FGBMFI, I told the men about Lucy, and discovered that all the married men that had climbed Roughtor with me, which was all those on the trip except for two, had had similar reactions from their wives.

We decided not to go binding territorial spirits any more, and justified our decision by examining Scripture and finding it was something that Jesus Himself did not do. He stilled the storms on the Sea of Galilee, but if Satan's spirits on earth did not bother Him, He left them alone. He cast demons out of people many times, that is from their human dwelling places but there is no record of Him removing them from their earthly geographical territory. Jesus just left them where they were, and we decided to do the same.

[18] Revelation 20:1-2

[19] Revelation 20:3

[20] Daniel 10:10-21

[21] Deuteronomy 12:2, 2 Chronicles 28:1-4,
 Jeremiah 17:1-2, Ezekiel 6:13

The Ninth Lesson: The Mystery Kingdom, Christendom
Luke 13:18-21

Jesus here once more told two parables about the then unknown kingdom, mentioned in Chapter 6, in the section, The Rejected King Reveals A Mystery. The mystery was the coming founding of Christendom on earth, which would soon be established because the Jews had rejected their Messiah. The new nature of the coming kingdom following the Jewish rejection was told again in two parables.

1. The parable of the mustard seed was to show that Christendom would grow into an exceedingly large organization.
2. The parable of the leaven was to show that some in Christendom would preach lies and false teaching and Jesus emphasized that this would result from external defilement and internal defilement.

The eighth and ninth lessons to the disciples confirm that as a result of being rejected by Israel, Jesus will only deal with people individually, for the time being.

THE CLASH AT CHANUKA, THE FEAST OF DEDICATION
John 10:22-39

"Chanuka" means, dedication, and because candles are lit at this time, the Feast of Dedication is also called the Feast of Lights. One candle is lit on the first day, two the second and so on up until the eighth day when eight candles are lit, but remember Chanuka does nor mean lights, it means dedication. On the 25th day of the Jewish month of Kislev 165 BC, which in that particular year would have been equivalent to the 25th December, a group of Jews known as the Maccabees recaptured the Temple and rededicated it, giving rise to the Feast of Dedication.

After the seven feasts authorized by Moses, two more were added, first the Feast of Purim, or the Feast of Lots, from the Book of Esther in the Old Testament,[1] but the second, the Feast of Chanuka is not biblical although it was validated when Jesus went to the Temple and kept it. John reminds us it was winter and as the feast usually comes in December that would be right, and that Jesus was walking in the Temple through what was called, Solomon's porch, when He was surrounded by Jews accusing Him of being vague and unclear.

> John 10:24 Then came the Jews round about him, and said unto him, How long dost thou make us to doubt? If thou be the Christ, tell us plainly.

It was a lie to accuse Jesus of not speaking plainly, but that was the accusation they brought against Him. Jesus answered by reminding them first that He had told them but they had not believed Him, and secondly that the miracles He had performed confirmed Him as Messiah, "the works that I do in my Father's name, they bear witness of me." The Jews were wrong, Jesus had not been vague at all but had clearly told them He was the Christ, and demonstrated it by His deeds, but despite all this clear teaching there was a reason they did not believe.

> John 10:26 But ye believe not, because ye are not of my sheep.

Jesus then went on to tell them about those of us who are His sheep.

1. His sheep know who He is.
2. They have eternal life.
3. No one can pluck them from the hand of Jesus or from the hand of God the Father. He teaches here eternal security and double eternal security, the sheep are in the hand of Jesus and the hand of His Father, and can be taken from neither, a wonderful and powerful promise.

Getting back to the accusation of His being vague, He goes on to make an absolutely clear statement.

> John 10:30 I and my Father are one.

His claim to be one with God means that He is God Himself, nothing vague about that, and we will see from the reaction of the Jews that they understood clearly what He meant.

> John 10:31 Then the Jews took up stones again to stone him.

As they were about to throw the stones, Jesus asked them a question.

> John 10:32 Many good works have I shewed [shown] you from my Father: for which of these works do you stone me?

Jesus respectfully asked them for which of the miracles He had performed under the power of God, they were going to stone Him.

> John 10:33 The Jews answered him, saying, For good work we stone thee not; but for blasphemy; and because that thou, being a man, makest thyself God.

They knew very well that Jesus was claiming to be God Himself, far from being vague as they accused Him of being, Jesus was absolutely clear, and that is why His audience had drawn the right conclusion as to what He had said.

> John 10:34-38 [34] Jesus answered them, Is it not written in your law, I said, Ye are gods?
>
> [35] If he called them gods, unto whom the word of God came, and the scripture cannot be broken;
>
> [36] Say ye of him, whom the Father hath sanctified [made holy], and sent unto the world, Thou blasphemest; because I said, I am the Son of God?
>
> [37] If I do not the works of my Father, believe me not.
>
> [38] But if I do, though ye believe not me, believe the works, that ye may know, and believe, that the Father is in me, and I in him.

Some evangelical preachers take these verses and teach that we can be little gods, performing miracles by just speaking, but that is not at all what Jesus means. His statement, "Is it not written in your law, I said, Ye are gods?", comes from Psalm 82:6, so with reference to that Psalm and the words of Jesus in John 10, above, let us make some observations about what He meant.

1. The judges of Israel, such as Joshua and Samuel, represented God and were able to prophecy and perform miracles by His power.
2. The works they did were the works of God Himself and were directed by Him.
3. Being God's representatives, doing His works and making announcements on His behalf, they were called in Hebrew, "elohim" or gods.
4. If those agents of God that had been given limited authority were known as "elohim" or gods, it could not be blasphemous for Jesus to call Himself the Son of God, because He had been ordered to carry out His Father's work directly, and the works that He did were far greater, being, the works only the Messiah could do.
5. God used Moses to send messages to Aaron and to Pharaoh, and that is why Moses became, "as God to Aaron,"[2] and, "as God to Pharaoh."[3]
6. If Moses, a man, was as God Himself to Aaron and Pharaoh, what was wrong with Jesus being the Son of God?
7. Moses was the messenger of God, and so was Jesus.
8. The Israelites had listened to Moses.
9. Why would they not listen to Jesus?
10. He also as a man was God's representative and more, much more, because He was and is One with God, and His miracles proved Him to be the God/Man, the Messiah.

[1] Esther 9:24, 9:28
[2] Exodus 4:16
[3] Exodus 7:1

9
JESUS PREPARES HIS DISCIPLES

In this chapter Jesus will repeat two catchphrases several times that express the same idea, "The last shall be first, and the first last," and, "Whosoever shall exalt himself shall be abased; and he that humble himself shall be exalted." In the previous chapter, the Gathering Opposition, the slogan was, "and there was division."

The time of this phase of the preparation of the disciples was from the Feast of Dedication, or Chanuka, in December AD 29, until He began His last journey to Jerusalem for that fateful Passover of AD 30, a period of between three and four months.

HE MOVES OUT OF JUDEA
John 10:40-42

> John 10:40 [Jesus] went away again beyond Jordan into the place where John at first baptised; and there he abode.

Beyond Jordan means east of the River Jordan to the region then called Perea, where the Sanhedrin, (the High Court of religious judges), had no authority. It was there John the Baptist had begun telling the people to accept the Messiah after He became known, and many confirmed they would do so by being baptised by John. The following verses show how the teaching of John had been successful.

> John 10:41 And many resorted unto him [Jesus], and said, John did no miracle: [John did not do a single miracle], but all things that John spoke of this man were true.

The people realized that John's preaching about the Messiah fitted Jesus, and so how did they react?

> John 10:42 And many believed on him there.

John had been successful in the work given to him by God, of preparing the individuals he baptised to pledge to accept the Messiah, once they knew who He was, because now they made good their commitment.

HOW CAN WE ENTER THE KINGDOM OF GOD?
Luke 13:22-35

Eventually the time came for Jesus to move out from the place where John first baptised, and begin His last journey to Jerusalem, then after reaching the city He would have just one week before His crucifixion.

> Luke 13:22 And he went through the cities and villages, teaching, and journeying to Jerusalem.

On this trip Jesus lodged with the people as arranged before hand by the seventy disciples.[1]

> Luke 13:23 Then said one unto him, Lord, are there few that be saved?

The query is based on the rejection of Jesus by the Pharisees, which has now been taken up by the majority of the population. The democratic decision among the Jews was already, as it still is today, (and for Gentiles as well), against obeying Jesus as absolute King, so, will only a few be saved? Now the question was a Jewish one about entering the kingdom of God, which was still perceived as a Jews only kingdom, and so Jesus begins in the following seven verses to teach about eternal life.

> Luke 13:24 Strive to enter in at the strait [narrow] gate: for many, I say unto you, will seek to enter in, and shall not be able.

In Chapter 5, in, Words Of Warning About True Righteousness, concerning the Sermon on the Mount we learned that the Pharisees' road to righteousness was very wide because they taught that all Israel had a share in the age to come. The Roman Catholic Church's road to righteousness is wide like that of the Pharisees because they teach that every baby sprinkled by a priest will go to heaven. Jesus taught something different, that the Way into the kingdom of God was narrow and that individuals must strive to enter in through it, and obviously a baby being sprinkled is not striving is he, he does not even know what is going on. Jesus is the Narrow Way to eternal life and we need to strive to believe that. In the following verses Jesus told those Pharisees, trying to enter by a broad way, a story to illustrate how He would eventually deal with them.

> Luke 13:25-27 ²⁵ Once when the master of the house is risen up, and hath shut the door, and ye begin to stand without, and to knock at the door, saying, Lord, Lord, open unto us; and he shall answer and say unto you, I know you not whence ye are:
>
> ²⁶ Then shall ye begin to say, We have eaten and drunk in thy presence, and thou hast taught in our streets.
>
> ²⁷ But he shall say, I tell you, I know you not whence ye are; depart from me, all ye workers of iniquity [wickedness].

The opportunity to enter eternal life will not last beyond this life. Certainly we must strive to enter before we die because afterwards there will be no opportunity, as those Pharisees and Jews listening to Jesus were clearly warned.

> Luke 13:28 There shall be weeping and gnashing of teeth, when ye shall see Abraham, and Isaac, and Jacob, and all the prophets, in the kingdom of God, and you yourselves thrust out.

The patriarchs, Abraham, Isaac and Jacob, and the prophets will be in the kingdom, but those hoping to get in by the wide road of the Pharisees will not. However we that travel the Narrow Way, that trust in the righteousness given to us that believe in Jesus,[2] will be there in the kingdom, as He told His listeners in the following verse.

Luke 13:29 And they shall come from the east, and from the west, and from the north, and from the south, and shall sit down in the kingdom of God.

A lot of Jews therefore will not be in the kingdom but many Gentiles will be, and because the Jews are God's chosen people, those whose God He was first, this is a good place for the catch phrase often found in this passage of Scripture.

Luke 13:30 And, behold, there are last which shall be first, and there are first that shall be last.

After Jesus had spoken in opposition to the Pharisees some of them went on the offensive against Him in a sneaky and underhanded way.

Luke 13:31 The same day there came certain of the Pharisees, saying unto him, Get thee out, and depart hence: for Herod will kill thee.

We might think it a friendly act of the Pharisees to warn Jesus that Herod Antipas wanted to put Him to death, but as usual they were being very tricky. While Jesus was in Perea, He was under the authority of Herod, but the Pharisees wanted Jesus to cross over to Judea, a Jewish district under the control of the Sanhedrin, where they would have the legal right to arrest Him. Once He was in their power they themselves, not Herod Antipas, wanted to kill Him. Jesus answered them accurately and prophetically, but in a way that would have been hard for them to understand.

Luke 13:32-33 [32] And he said unto them, Go ye, and tell that fox, Behold, I cast out devils, and I do cures to day and to morrow, and the third day I shall be perfected, [I shall reach my destination].

[33] Nevertheless I must walk to day, and to morrow, and the day following: for it cannot be that a prophet perish out of Jerusalem.

Jesus says that He will not die in Herod's territory because He must depart this life in Jerusalem. Finally He grieves over Jerusalem using words that He will repeat later when He ends His message to the Jewish community as a whole, and which we will examine when we come to them then. The point of His grieving, the thing that saddens Him, is that He will not return to Jerusalem until they recognise who He is and ask Him to return.[3]

[1] Luke 10:1
[2] Romans 10:8-11, 2 Corinthians 5:21, Philippians 3:9, 2 Timothy 4:8
[3] Matthew 23:39, Mark 13:35

JESUS TEACHES FOUR LESSONS IN A PHARISEES' HOUSE
Luke 14:1-24

Keeping The Sabbath Day Holy
Luke 14:1-6

Again a Pharisee invited Jesus to his house for a meal, but this time it was a chief Pharisee, the head of a rabbinic school, and the reason was to set another trap so that they could accuse Him of breaking the Law of Moses, because it says, "they watched him." The ruse included inviting a man suffering from dropsy and that is why Jesus asked them a question.

> Luke 14:3-4 ³ Is it lawful to heal on the Sabbath day?
> ⁴ And they held their peace, [they kept silent].

They refused to answer the question. The Pharisees allowed healing on the Sabbath but only if the person's life was at risk. Posing a question He had asked Pharisees before, Jesus showed that resting on the Sabbath and keeping it holy allows healing.

> Luke 14:5 Which of you shall have an ass or an ox fallen into a pit, and will not straightway pull him out on the Sabbath day?

The answer is that they would all pull the poor animal out, and if it is right to help an animal on the Sabbath, then it is even better to be of assistance to a Jewish man. If they had agreed with Jesus their trap would have failed that is why they had refused to answer Him, but Jesus had healed the man, and let him go, so what could they do?

Luke 14:6 And they could not answer him again to these things.

Nothing Jesus had said or done could be used against Him.

Humbleness Or Self-Importance?
Luke 14:7-11

Luke 14:7 And he put forth [spoke] a parable to those that were bidden, [invited].

Other Jews had been invited to the meal along with Jesus because the chief Pharisee wanted them to see how he was going to humiliate Him. These visitors after they arrived tried to find a room or place to eat nearest to the most famous members of society, a place of distinction, and that was why Jesus addressed His parable to them. His lesson was, do not chose the important place for yourself, but wait for those in authority to show their opinion of you by giving you a position of honour, then everyone will know how highly you are admired. If you try to grab the spot yourself, you could be embarrassed and humiliated by being asked to move to a less significant place. This provided another opportunity for Jesus to come out with His catch phrase for this chapter.

Luke 14:11 For whosoever exalteth himself shall be abased; and he that humbleth himself shall be exalted.

Respect For Others
Luke 14:12-14

Jesus, after speaking to the guests, had something to say to the organiser of the meal who had invited Jesus into his house, the chief Pharisee.

Luke 14:12 Then said he also to him that bade [invited] him.

The lesson in this case was about the righteousness of the Law of Moses. The chief Pharisee in inviting people to his house was keeping the letter of the Law, because it was meant to demonstrate love, but if the persons invited were wealthy and ready to invite him back later, that would show his selfish aim of receiving honour from them, which was not the behaviour of a righteous man. The kind of action that would have shown the righteousness of the Law would have been to invite people that could not pay him back, from whom he could expect nothing in return, as Jesus pointed out.

> Luke 14:13-14 ¹³ But when thou makest a feast, call the poor, the maimed [crippled], the lame, the blind:
>
> ¹⁴ And thou shalt be blessed; for they cannot recompense thee: for thou shalt be recompensed at the resurrection of the just.

The Supreme Supper They Snubbed
Luke 14:15-24

> Luke 14:15 And when one of them that sat at meat [the meal] with him heard these things, [they were all enjoying the food at this time] he said unto him, Blessed is he that shall eat bread in the kingdom of God.

The thought of feasting in the kingdom of God gave Jesus the perfect opportunity to tell them the parable of the rejected invitation, showing how they had refused the call to the banquet of God.

> Luke 14:17 [He] sent his servant at supper time to say to them that were bidden, [invited], Come, for all things are now ready.

In the story many had been expecting to be invited to the dinner but when the request was made they all started giving reasons for not going..

> Luke 14:18 And they all with one consent [in the same way] began to make excuse.

The first excuse was from a man who was more interested in his possessions.[1] The second was from a man who was intent on running his business,[2] and the third excuse was from a pleasure seeker,[3] who could not have cared less. All this made the one who had prepared the feast very angry.

> Luke 14:21 Then the master of the house being angry said to his servant, Go out quickly into the streets and lanes of the city, and bring in hither [here] the poor, and the maimed, [crippled], and the halt, [lame], and the blind.

The men that refused the invitation were from the upper class, a land owner, a business man, and a man that did not need to work. After the poor, crippled, lame and blind people had arrived for the grand feast, there was still room for more and so others were urged to join.

> Luke 14:23 And the lord said unto the servant, Go out into the highways and hedges, and compel them to come in, that my house may be filled.

Jesus ended the parable with a comment concerning those men that had refused to go.

> Luke 14:24 For I say unto you, That none of those men which were bidden shall taste of my supper.

The supper was given at the end of the day, and the parable tells in a forceful way how things will turn out at the end of the age. God organized the feast, and told the Jews it was being prepared through the Old Testament prophets. The servant He sent to Israel to tell them that everything was ready, was John the Baptist, and very soon after John started preaching, Jesus the Messiah of Israel came for His people, just as John said He would. The upper class citizens that were invited first were the leading Jews of the time, but they refused to go. The dinner was ready, but the invited guests excused themselves from going, so needy people from the city and the country were searched for, found and brought in to feast with the LORD. Those from the city represent Jews that believe in Jesus, and those from the country represent believing Gentiles. The generation of Jews that rejected the invitation will never see the kingdom of God, because just as Jesus said, none of the men that were invited shall taste His supper.

[1] Luke 14:18

[2] Luke 14:19

[3] Luke 14:20

WHAT IT TAKES TO BE A DISCIPLE OF JESUS
Luke 14:25-35

We learned in the section, More Training On Being A Good Disciple, Chapter 7, there is a big difference in being saved for eternal life and being a disciple. Eternal life is given by God to us that believe, but to be a disciple is much more demanding, as shown by the three things Jesus teaches next.

First, a disciple must be ready to leave his friends and relatives.

> Luke 14:26 If any man come to me, and hate not his father, and mother, and wife, and children, and brethren, and sisters, yea, and his own life, also, he cannot be my disciple.

If anyone gets in the way and holds you back from being a full time disciple, then you must be ready to choose Jesus rather than them. The word "hate" used by Jesus cannot mean emotional hatred, because that would be out of character with our God of love,[1] and with other teachings of Jesus,[2] it is a matter of choice, as in the following passage from the Old Testament.

> Malachi 1:1-3 ¹ The burden of the word of the LORD of Israel by Malachi.
>
> ² I have loved you saith the LORD. Yet ye say, Wherein hast thou loved us? Was not Esau Jacob's brother? Saith the LORD: yet I loved Jacob,
>
> ³ And I hated Esau.

God chose to make His covenant with Jacob, later renamed Israel, and not with Esau, and in that way Jacob was loved and Esau was hated, it was a question of choice. As a manager I often had to decide who to promote and who not to, and emotional love never came into the decision making. Sometimes I made the wrong choice but God never does. We must choose Jesus, love Him and "hate" those that would steer us away from Him, that is choose not to follow them, even the people we love.

Second, a disciple must expect to be hated, just as Jesus was detested, mocked and tortured to death.

> Luke 14:27 And whosoever doth not bear his cross, and come after me, cannot be my disciple.

To bear His cross, is to be aware of the rejection of Jesus that resulted in His crucifixion, to be ready to be treated badly ourselves also, and willing to be unwanted and unloved.

Third, a disciple must count the cost, because Jesus wants all the resources of His disciples totally committed to Him.

> Luke 14:33 So likewise, whosoever he be of you that forsaketh not all that he hath, he cannot be my disciple.

Finally, Jesus reminds his disciples that He likes people that are salty.

> Luke 14:34-35 34 Salt is good: but if the salt have lost his savour, wherewith shall it be seasoned?
>
> 35 It is neither fit for the land, nor yet for the dunghill; but men cast it out. He that hath ears to hear, let him hear.

Disciples are more salty than ordinary believers for the three reasons we have just learned, which are, they choose to follow Christ rather than people, they are prepared to be hated and they commit everything they have to Jesus. Along with the gift of eternal life, God gives other gifts which are meant to be used to help the other members of His Church.[3] People that do not use their gifts will be condemned to outer darkness by Jesus,[4] having lost their saltiness. Nobody is to blame but themselves, because no one can take them out of the hands of the Son of God,[5] but they can leave if they wish or if they do not use their gifts, a stupid thing to do. If we are salty we will bring joy to other true believers, remain close to our Lord and act as a preservative. It is not politicians and other individuals trying to stop global warming that by scientific means will prolong the age we live in, it is the presence in the world of salty disciples of Jesus. He, the creator of all things,[6] who upholds everything by His power,[7] will take notice of them.

[1] 1 John 4:7-11

[2] Matthew 5:44-45, Luke 6:35

[3] Romans 12:6-8, 1 Peter 4:10

[4] Matthew 25:24-30

[5] John 10:28-29

[6] Colossians 1:16

[7] Colossians 1:17

GOD'S APPROACH TO SINNERS
Luke 15:1-32

The three parables here give us three ways God deals with sinners, the first emphasises the attitude of the Son, the second the Spirit and the third the Father. They were spoken to the Pharisees at a time when all the tax collectors [publicans] and prostitutes [sinners] in the region had arrived and were listening to Jesus.

> Luke 15:1-2 ¹ Then drew near unto him all the publicans and sinners for to hear him.
>
> ² And the Pharisees and scribes murmured, saying, This man receiveth sinners, and eateth with them.

The approach of God to sinners is so different to that of the Pharisees, God wants to draw them to Himself and forgive them, while the way of the Pharisees is to reject and condemn them. A few laws and directives of the Pharisees show us their approach.

1. They were not allowed to buy from or sell anything to a tax gatherer or a prostitute.
2. They were not allowed to eat at the table of a tax collector or a prostitute, in case tithes had not been paid from the food.
3. They could not permit a tax collector or a prostitute to sit at their table unless they put on the clothes of a Pharisee, which would mean they had to become a Pharisee.
4. Pharisees taught that there was joy before God in heaven at the death of a tax collector or a prostitute.

You can now see why one reason the Pharisees did not believe that Jesus was the Messiah, was because He spent time with tax collectors and prostitutes. That is the Jewish background to the parables.

The Parable Of The Lost Sheep
Luke 15:3-7

The main point here is being lost. Sheep tend to wander about searching for tasty herbs and plants to eat and may end up lost and alone. The shepherd with only ninety-nine of his one hundred sheep will leave them to look for the lost one, and will be pleased and thankful when he finds it, so this parable shows the attitude of Jesus, the Son of God, towards sinners.

> Luke 15:7 I say unto you, that likewise joy shall be in heaven over one sinner that repenteth, more than over ninety and nine just persons, which need no repentance.

The Parable Of The Lost Coin
Luke 15:8-10

The importance of this parable is the search. The woman knew the coin was in the house but not where in the house, and she rummaged around and hunted for her coin until she found it. This is an example of the work of the Holy Spirit and His delight when success comes, and so the woman rejoices when she finds the coin.

> Luke 15:10 Likewise, I say unto you, there is joy in the presence of the angels of God over one sinner that repenteth.

The Parable Of The Lost Son
Luke 15:11-32

Better known as, the parable of the prodigal, (or wasteful), son, this well known story is about returning and being reinstated, calling our attention to the love of God the Father.

The younger of two sons asked for his inheritance in advance, left home and used the money he had been given on loose living like parties and prostitutes. He spent everything and when he had nothing left all his friends left him, and he got a job feeding pigs, disgusting work for a Jew but he was starving. He then understood how wickedly he had behaved by wasting all his dad's money, and not being thankful to him. Eventually he decided to go home anyway and ask to become an ordinary paid worker, knowing he had behaved too awfully and stupidly to be accepted as a son again, but at least he would not be hungry anymore.

> Luke 15:20 And he arose and came to his father. But when he was yet a great way off, his father saw him, and had compassion, and ran, and fell on his neck, and kissed him.

His dad saw him coming when he was a long way away, because he was looking out hoping he would come back, and although the son would have been pleased to become a paid worker, his dad would not allow him to do such a job, but instead he gave him three things.[1]

1. He was dressed in the best robe, a sign that his original birthright was still his.
2. A ring was put on his finger, a sign that he was reinstated as a son, with the authority of a son.
3. A pair of shoes were put on his feet, a sign that he was his dad's son.

He had now been completely restored and a great feast was prepared because he had returned to his dad. The elder son was jealous of all the attention given to his younger brother, and thought his dad was unfair because the young brother had wasted his dad's money, when the older brother had not, but had worked faithfully all the time his young brother was away and had never been rewarded.[2] The answer his dad gave him shows that no rewards will be given for good work done.

Luke 15:31-32 [31] And he said unto him, Son, thou art ever with me, and all that I have is thine.

[32] It was meet [necessary] that we should make merry, and be glad: for this thy brother was dead, and he is alive again; and was lost, and is found.

Rewards will be based on forgiveness, the younger son returned in need of pardon, and his dad was so very pleased to show mercy. The older son wanted to be rewarded because of all he had done, but got nothing, and he represents the Pharisees. Pharisees believe God will reward them because they deserve it, but God will only accept us if we come to Him, knowing we deserve nothing and that we need His forgiveness.

The father told his elder son, "All that I have is thine," meaning that the privileges given to his younger brother could also be given to him, but he refused to humble himself and ask for them on the grounds of forgiveness, therefore like the Pharisees he did not receive what was there waiting for him.

[1] Luke 15:22
[2] Luke 15:29-30

LESSONS ON MAMMON
(OR RICHES AND WORDLY PROSPERITY)
Luke 16:1-31

The Pharisees thought that being wealthy proved they were righteous, being a blessing from the Almighty, and in order to show everyone that they were loved and accepted by Him they did all they could to get rich, then believing that poor people were unrighteous they looked down their noses at them. How proud they were of themselves, because they were rich in this world believing that they would spend eternity with God. Sadly some churches teach the same message today, stay away from them. Knowing this false belief of the Pharisees about prosperity helps us understand the messages, which come in three parts.

The Parable Of The Unrighteous Steward
Luke 16:1-13

The parable tells of a dishonest and crooked steward who misused his authority by frittering away his employer's possessions, as well as squandering and wasting what he was supposed to be taking care of, in short he was unrighteous. The point Jesus is making is that the Pharisees had been unrighteous in the way they had belittled and demeaned what they were given to look after, which was the Word of God.

Once he was found out, this shady character was given a short time to explain how he had lost so much money and produce, which he could not do because he had not been faithful. True to his nature he decided to use the time he had before he was kicked out to give away even more of his employer's goods, so that those he helped would be friendly to him and be of assistance after he had been dismissed.

> Luke 16:8 And the lord commended the unrighteous steward, because he had done wisely:

The steward was not commended for being unrighteous and wicked, but for using the short time he had left to prepare for the days ahead when he would be out of work, and Jesus then makes an observation.

> Luke 16:8 for the children of this world are in their generation wiser than the children of light.

The comment continues to be true because unbelieving people of the world put God out of their mind and concentrate on their careers and other interests and are wiser when it comes to riches and prosperity, and in planning for the future. Believers tend not to worry, thinking that God will take care of them, and this is unwise because there is a difference between trusting the Lord and tempting Him.[1] It is right that we prepare for our retirement, look after our health, take out insurance to protect the value of our possessions, none of these safety measures go against anything in the Bible.

At the time of Jesus, the word "mammon" was used often by the Jews in their writings, and it meant any good stuff found in the world that had value, so with this in mind listen to Jesus again.

> Luke 16:9 And I say unto you, Make to yourselves friends of the mammon of unrighteousness; that, when ye fail, they may receive you into everlasting habitations.

The instruction above is that we are to use our mammon now to make sure of our welcome in the future spiritual kingdom of God. Take note that Jesus does not say we are to give everything away and become a burden to other people, including the welfare state, we still have to provide for our families and for our old age. Jesus is asking us to make friends for Him so that there will be more of us in the kingdom, all friends together, forever. We can use our mammon in this way by supporting the printing and distribution of tracts which we have approved and Bibles, missionaries, evangelists and teachers of sound Christian guidelines. Look at Luke 16:9 quoted above, again, piece by piece.

> **"And I say unto you,"** Jesus is telling us.

> **"Make to yourselves friends"** It becomes clear later that these friends are believers in Jesus.

> **"of the mammon of unrighteousness;"** By using our worldly wealth.

> **"that, when ye fail,"** When we leave this life, and our wealth is no more use to us.

> **"they"** The people we have helped bring to Jesus, our spiritual friends.

"may receive you into everlasting habitations." Some of the people we help bring to Christ will die before us, and will be there in the places prepared for them by Jesus,[2] to greet us as we enter our new homes in heaven.

The resources we have during our earthly lives are to be used for our needs and responsibilities now, as well as to win more friends and enjoyment for us, when we pass over into everlasting life.

Remember, that Jesus was teaching His disciples by talking to the Pharisees, those great lovers of money, and in the following verse their earthly wealth is "least" compared to the "much" which is spiritual wealth.

> Luke 16:10 He that is faithful in that which is least is faithful also in much: and he that is unjust in the least is unjust also in much.

In the next verse, "unrighteous mammon" is worldly wealth, while "true riches" are everlasting spiritual wealth.

> Luke 16:11 If therefore ye [the Pharisees] have not been faithful in the unrighteous mammon, who will commit to your trust the true riches?

The true riches cannot be obtained until the gospel of Jesus the Son of God is believed and acted upon, and this spiritual wealth then becomes our own.

> Luke 16:12 And if ye have not been faithful in that which is another man's, who shall give you that which is your own?

We need to go all-out for what is spiritual and holy, not for physical financial wealth.

> Luke 16:13 No servant can serve two masters: for either he will hate the one, and love the other; or else he will hold to the

one, and despise the other. Ye cannot serve God and mammon.

The Pharisees were unable to serve God because they were serving mammon, and we must not make the same mistake.

The Pharisees Sneer At Jesus Who Then Rebukes Them Even More
Luke 16:14-18

The Pharisees had not liked hearing Jesus speaking on the use of money and wealth, because He had correctly identified serious errors in their teaching about mammon and their use of it.

> Luke 16:14 And the Pharisees also, who were covetous [eager for money], heard all these things: and derided [mocked, ridiculed, and laughed scornfully at] him.

If they thought that laughing and sneering would put Jesus off or frighten Him, then they were absolutely wrong, because he had four more things to tell them.

He first criticized their habit of telling others how good they were,[3] and one of the catchphrases for this chapter is, you may remember, "Whosoever shall exalt himself shall be abased."

Secondly He told them that the time of the Law and the prophets ended with the last of the Old Testament style prophets, John the Baptist. Beginning with John, the gospel of the kingdom was preached, but because the Pharisees refused to believe the new message, the kingdom was only offered to those individual Jews that believed Jesus was the Messiah.

> Luke 16:16 The law and the prophets were until John: since that time the kingdom of God is preached, and every man presseth into it.

Thirdly, although the Pharisees broke the Law by keeping their traditions instead, Jesus kept the Law, so that when He died and the time for keeping the Law ended, there was not any part of the Law, right down to the last tittle, that had not been kept perfectly by Him.

Luke 16:17 And it is easier for heaven and earth to pass, than for one tittle of the law to fail.

Fourthly, by way of example Jesus accused the many Pharisees that had divorced their wives, and the many that had married divorced women, of committing adultery and therefore of breaking the Law.[4]

The True Story Of The Rich Man And Lazarus The Beggar
Luke 16:19-31

Often called the parable of the rich man and Lazarus, this story from the lips of Jesus is not a parable, but is a true account of an unnamed rich man and a poor beggar called Lazarus. Parables do not have names of people in them, they are stories from daily life with a moral or spiritual lesson.

The rich man, according to the Pharisees, would have been rich because God was so pleased with his righteousness, that He blessed him with great prosperity. According to them all wealthy Jews were highly favoured by God. On the other hand they would have been uncertain about Lazarus, probably a beggar they knew from visiting the rich man's house, because Lazarus lay outside his gate always needing food and medical treatment.[5] Lazarus was sick, hungry and covered with many sores, but the rich man did not attend to the beggar's hunger or disease, neither did his servant or his visitors, but the stray dogs from the streets came and licked his wounds. Every time he went in and out of his stately home the rich man could see the suffering Lazarus beside the gate, and could have easily kept the second most important Law of Moses, to love his neighbour as himself.[6]

In due course both men died and in their after-lives it was Lazarus that received the blessing of God, not the rich man, in fact the exact opposite of what the Pharisees believed happened. The rich man found himself in Hell, and Lazarus had the honour of being in Abraham's bosom. These two sections of Sheol or Hades were covered in Chapter 6 under the heading, The King's Power Over Demons, if you would like to refresh your memory, or you may recall that the rich man and Lazarus could see each other and talk, but because of a great chasm or gulf they could not change places. The rich man in the bad side of

Hades, that is to say, Hell, spoke to Abraham in the good side and reminded him that they were all Jews, by calling Abraham his father.

Luke 16:24 And he cried and said, Father Abraham, have mercy on me, ...

Luke 16:30 And he said, Nay, father Abraham: ...

Abraham agreed that there was a blood relationship between him and the rich man by calling him, son or child.

Luke 16:25 But Abraham said, Son, remember ...

The rich man found out too late that being a blood relative of Abraham, had not protected him from spending eternity in Hell, showing that the teachings of the Pharisees, "All Israel has a share in the age to come," and, "None of the descendents of Abraham will ever be in Hell," were not from God, because they were not in the Bible. Not only was this rich Jew in Hell, but he was suffering from the torture of everlasting fire, to such a severe degree that even if Lazarus wet his finger and touched the sufferer's tongue, it would have given tremendous comfort, but they could only talk about it and think about it, no relief from the agony of Hell being possible.

Luke 16:25-26 [25] But Abraham said, Son, remember that thou in thy lifetime receivedst the good things, and likewise Lazarus evil things: but now he is comforted, and thou art tormented.

[26] And beside all this, between us and you there is a great gulf fixed: so that they which would pass from hence to you cannot; neither can they pass to us, that would come from thence.

The rich man then remembered his five brothers who were still alive, and understood that like him they would all end up in Hell, this place of torment from where there was no escape. He asked Abraham to give Lazarus his life back again, to raise him from the dead, and send him to those five brothers because if something like that happened they would believe, but Abraham's answer is interesting, belief does not come after listening to the dead that have come back to life, it only comes from one source, which is reading and/or listening to the words of the Bible.[7]

> Luke 16:29 Abraham saith unto him, They have Moses and the prophets; let them hear them.

Abraham in other words is saying, they only need the Scripture, (not the teaching of the Pharisees), what they should do is read and believe the word of God to escape from Hell, but even in Hell the rich man did still not believe in the power of the prophetic word.

> Luke 16:30 And he said, Nay, father Abraham: but if one went unto them from the dead, they will repent.

Like many Christians, the rich man thought that the Scriptures alone were not enough, he wanted a miracle as well, just like people today who are attracted by miracles, signs and wonders of preachers today. The Bible for them is hardly read, they want signs, but signs will not lead to everlasting life, as Abraham knew very well.

> Luke 16:31 And he [Abraham] said unto him, If they hear not Moses and the prophets, neither will they be persuaded, though one rose from the dead.

The fact of the matter is that to inherit eternal life we must believe the Scriptures, because signs do not lead to repentance. Jesus performed miracles for three years attracting huge gatherings of people all eager to see the show, but they rejected Him. They agreed they had seen miracles but said they were the work of Beelzebub.[8]

Going back to the time when Jesus was rejected by Israel, and He stopped performing miracles for the nation, you may recall the reason for miracles after that, was for training the twelve. He told the Pharisees there would be no more signs for the nation except one, the sign of Jonah, which is the sign or resurrection.[9] Again the sign of resurrection would come to the nation three times, and the first of these would be when Lazarus was raised from the dead, an event which we will soon come to. Jesus told this story about Lazarus shortly before He would perform the promised sign of resurrection by raising another man, also called Lazarus from the grave. Interestingly, He had already prophesied by telling the Pharisees about Lazarus and the rich man, that when another Lazarus was brought back to life, the first sign of Jonah, they would reject it.

The true story of the rich man and Lazarus show us some important lessons about those that are lost.

1. They will be separated from God forever.
2. They will know without doubt, that they are lost, they will not be unconscious or asleep, but very much aware of their situation.
3. Once lost, always lost, there is nothing that can be done to comfort them.
4. Their suffering is never ending and extremely painful.
5. They never forget the chances they had before they died to go to a much better place and how they always refused.

Those five points from the teaching of Jesus, show that the most important thing in life is to hear the gospel, and to believe it.[10]

---

[1] Psalm 78:17-18, Luke 4:12

[2] John 14:2-3

[3] Luke 16:15

[4] Luke 16:18

[5] Luke 16:20-21

[6] Leviticus 19:18, Matthew 22:39, Mark 12:31

[7] Romans 10:17

[8] Luke 11:15

[9] Luke 11:29-30

[10] Matthew 16:26, Mark 8:36, Luke 9:25

JESUS' PEOPLE SHOULD BE FORGIVING PEOPLE
Luke 17:1-4

Jesus, when he had finished showing how and why the Pharisees were wrong in their teaching about mammon, warned the disciples not to look down on them or hate them.

> Luke 17:1 Then said he unto the disciples, It is impossible but that offences will come: but woe unto him, through whom they come!

In the first four verses of Luke 17, He gave the disciples three important lessons.

1. As far as possible we must try not to offend other people. The emphasis was that a disciple of Christ should not offend the Pharisees just because they did not understand the teaching of the Son of God. In the same way, today, we believers must try not to offend anyone that does not understand the teaching of Jesus.

2. On the other hand we need to make up out own minds not to be offended by other people if possible. Of course there are those that will set out to do everything in their power to offend us, and some of us are offended very easily, but Jesus would prefer it if we do not offend anyone, and we refuse to be offended by others, but there is a condition we must keep. The Pharisees did everything they could to offend Jesus and they themselves were greatly offended by His teaching, because He did not soft peddle the truth, and neither must we. Wishy-washy cowardly Christians that are scared to upset others with the truth will not be wanted in the kingdom of God.[1]

3. He repeated the teaching of always being ready to forgive those that ask for our forgiveness.

---

[1] Revelation 21:7-8

INCREASE YOUR FAITH
Luke 17:5-10

Jesus taught this lesson to the disciples because they asked Him for more faith, and here it should be noted that faith in the Bible is not faith in faith itself or belief in our own ability. Christian faith is knowing that Jesus will organise people and events in our lives so that we will be successful in what He wants us to do for Him. We must never rely on other people to help us, including church officials,[1] but on Jesus only.[2] It is important that our faith is in what Jesus wants us to do, not in what we want to do for Him, because He is the Head of the Church.[3]

> Luke 17:5 And the apostles said unto the Lord, Increase our faith.

It is clear from Jesus' answer that with strong faith we can, through the power of God, do the impossible.

> Luke 17:6 And the Lord said, If ye had faith as a grain of mustard seed, ye might say unto this sycamine tree, Be thou plucked up by the root, and be thou planted in the sea; and it should obey you.

The servants of Jesus then, with faith, can achieve great things for God, and that is why Jesus goes on to remind them that they are servants or slaves.

> Luke 17:7 But which of you, having a servant ...

The relationship between master and servant is then described, and the point is that a servant is not thanked for doing routine work, meaning that people with strong faith in Jesus who achieve wonderful results that prove it, should not consider themselves great.

> Luke 17:10 So likewise ye, when ye shall have done all those things which are commanded you, say, We are unprofitable servants: we have done that which was our duty to do.

If God were to perform mighty miracles through us, it may result in our being noticed, but our joy must be in working for the Lord and seeking His approval only, not in accepting the praise of men, because what we do for the Lord is our duty as servants. There are four ways in which the disciples were taught how to increase their faith.

1. Jesus wants us to be sincere and trusting in Him to give us success in all He wants us to accomplish.
2. We must remember that He is our Master and we merely servants, and that what we do is the work of a servant.
3. Faith increases with results, and therefore to get more faith we need to complete more work. The work of course will be a servant's work, something the Master expects of us. People involved in the Lord's work know that He arranges things in a helpful way, answers prayer, and gives them success beyond their capability, and therefore their faith grows stronger and stronger.
4. Our faith increases when we exercise the small amount of faith we have, and it gets more and more so long as we keep on working for the Lord.

[1] Jeremiah 17:5

[2] Jeremiah 17:7-8, Romans 8:28

[3] Ephesians 1:22, Colossians 1:18, 2:8-10

THE RESURRECTION OF LAZARUS
John 11:1-54, Luke 17:11-37

The resurrection of Lazarus was the last of the seven signs or miracles of Jesus recorded by John in his gospel. Jesus had raised others from the dead before this, but those wonders were all reported in a few words, two or four verses or so, and they were seen by only a few witnesses who were told not to tell anyone, which was the custom of Jesus after He had been rejected. The resurrection of Lazarus on the other hand is told in immense detail and at great length, some forty-four verses, and was witnessed not by a few, but by multitudes of Jews that were in and around Jerusalem to celebrate the feast of

Passover. The reason why Jesus made sure this miracle was seen by so very many Jews, was because this was the sign of Jonah, the sign of resurrection, which Jesus had promised the Jewish leaders, to demonstrate to them that He was and is their Messiah.[1] If we remember this it will be more easily understood why the events here happened the way they did.

The Resurrection Of Lazarus – THE SIGN FOR THE NATION
John 11:1-44

The Death Of Lazarus
John 11:1-16

The story begins with a very sick Lazarus, and Martha and Mary, his sisters, sending a message to Jesus to come and heal him, and as we read further it is clear that they wanted Jesus to come quickly before Lazarus died. At the time Jesus was only a day's walk away from Bethany, the home town of Lazarus and his sisters, so He could have got there long before Lazarus died. You might expect that Jesus would set off to visit Lazarus as soon as He learned of His friend's illness, but He did no such thing.

> John 11:6 When he had heard therefore that he was sick, he abode two days still in the same place where he was.

Preachers often tell us that if you see the word, "therefore" in the Bible you need to find out what it is there for. In the verse we have just read the word "therefore" means, "for that reason," meaning because he was sick Jesus did not go to see him. Jesus waited where He was until Lazarus was dead, because the sickness and death of Lazarus was for an extraordinary reason, as Jesus had told the messengers sent by Martha and Mary.

> John 11:4 This sickness is not unto death, but for the glory of God, that the Son of God might be glorified thereby.

After telling us, through the words of Jesus that the death of Lazarus would bring glory to God and the Son of God, John once again brings in his sub-theme of light and darkness.

> John 11:9-10 ⁹ Jesus answered, Are there not twelve hours in a day? If any man walk in the day, he stumbleth not, because he seeth the light of this world.
>
> ¹⁰ But if a man walk in the night, he stumbleth, because there is no light in him.

The man stumbles because, "there is no light in him," meaning Jesus the Light of the World[2] is not in him. Everyone that does not have Jesus in him stumbles and loses his way because he is in darkness and needs the light. Bringing Lazarus back to life, the sign of Jonah, will show that Jesus really is that Light, the Messiah of Israel.

After two days Jesus knows without anyone coming to tell Him that Lazarus is dead and decides it is time for Him to go to Bethany which was in Judea.

> John 11:14 Then Jesus said unto them plainly, Lazarus is dead.

The disciples were concerned about going back to Judea because it was under the control of the Sanhedrin (the High Court of religious judges) that was looking for Jesus.

> John 11:8 His disciples say unto him, Master, the Jews of late sought to stone thee; and goest thou thither [there] again?

He would not go while Lazarus was alive but now he was dead Jesus told the disciples He was going, which to them made no sense. They could understand taking the risk to heal Lazarus while he was sick, but why do it now he was dead, and Thomas knew that the journey would be very dangerous for Jesus.

> John 11:16 Then said Thomas, which is called Didymus, unto his fellow disciples, Let us go that we may die with him.

[1] Matthew 12:38-41
[2] John 8:12

A Conversation Between Martha And Jesus
John 11:17-27

Eventually Jesus started off for Bethany but He went slowly, and Martha hearing that He was at last on the way went and met Him before He had reached the tomb, and do you know what she did? She told Jesus off for not coming when she told Him to, and suggested that He was to blame for the death of her brother.

> John 11:21 Then said Martha unto Jesus, Lord, if thou hadst been here, my brother had not died.

She then told Jesus that she knew that God would do anything Jesus asked Him to do, and then Jesus spoke to her.

> John 11:23 Thy brother shall rise again.

Martha thought Jesus was talking about the Orthodox Jewish belief of the final resurrection of the dead at the coming of the Messiah.

> John 11:24 Martha saith unto him, I know that he shall rise again in the resurrection at the last day.

Martha's chat with Jesus shows she believed He was the Messiah, and that He had healing power before death, but she did not yet believe He had power over death itself. Next we come to the fifth "I am," claim of Jesus in John's gospel.

> John 11:25-26 25 Jesus said unto her, I am the resurrection, and the life: he that believeth in me, though he were dead, yet shall he live.
>
> 26 And whosoever liveth and believeth in me shall never die. Believest thou this?

Unless we are still alive when Jesus comes for His Church,[3] we who know Jesus is the Messiah will die physically, but not spiritually, and even after our bodies are dead and gone, we will become physically alive once more.[4]

Martha believed Jesus and knew that He was the Messiah, as He claimed.

John 11:27 She saith unto him, Yea, Lord: I believe that thou art the Christ, the Son of God, which should come into the world.

[3] 1 Thessalonians 4:17

[4] Job 19:25-26, Philippians 3:21

A Conversation Between Mary And Jesus
John 11:28-32

The discussion between Mary and Jesus was like the one between Jesus and her sister Martha. She told Jesus off for not hurrying up to get there sooner, she showed she believed Jesus was the Christ, and knew He had power before death, but like Martha she did not realise He had power over death.

Jesus Gives The Sign Of Jonah By Bringing Lazarus Back To Life
John 11:33-44

John 11:33 When Jesus therefore saw her weeping, and the Jews also weeping which came with her, he groaned in the spirit, and was troubled.

The weeping of Mary and the Jews that were with her was in fact the traditional Jewish wailing, they were not quietly weeping as at a British funeral. John tells us Jesus groaned in the spirit, meaning He was angry. They took Jesus to the grave and He quietly wept tears of sorrow, not like the Jews, who because it was their tradition, were wailing at the top of their voices.

John 11:35 Jesus wept.

While Jesus was weeping and some of the Jews were wailing, others were talking.

> John 11:37-38 [37] And some of them said, Could not this man, which opened the eyes of the blind, have caused that even this man should not have died?
>
> [38] Jesus therefore again groaning in himself …

Once again Jesus was angry, of course He could have prevented Lazarus from dying, but not one of these people understood what He was doing not even those He had told. [5] Jesus asked for the stone, that supported an air tight seal to the grave, to be removed, but Martha was opposed to this because Lazarus had been dead for four days and his corpse would stink.

Martha was right when she said the corpse of Lazarus would stink. Years ago on Tanah Merah Estate, Malaysia, after one of my rubber tappers had been missing for four days, her mundor, (a Malay overseer), came into my office to say that her body had been discovered under a rubber tree. He led me to the place which was about a mile away. It had been raining for a few days and the steam from the carpet of fallen leaves could be seen in the slanting shafts of sunlight that came through the few gaps in the new fresh green leaf canopy above us. It was hot and I was perspiring heavily and drenched in sweat as we got near to the place. The first thing to attract my attention was the humming sound of thousands of flies. The lady was lying on her back and although she was scantily dressed, many of her features could not be seen, including her eyes, nose and mouth which were just a mass of fast moving white maggots. What revolted me most was the strong disgusting smell of her four day old corpse. I cannot describe the horribleness of that foul stench, but it haunted me for years.

Jesus did not like Martha objecting to the grave stone being rolled away.

> John 11:40 Jesus saith unto her, Said I not unto thee, that, if thou wouldest believe, thou shouldest see the glory of God?

A four day old corpse was important from a Jewish point of view, and after waiting for him to die, Jesus had to walk very slowly to make sure

Lazarus had been dead that long before arriving at the grave. The rabbis believed that a person's spirit stayed above their dead body for three days after death, and during those three days there was a very slight possibility that the spirit would re-enter the body and the person would begin to breathe and come round again. After three days the spirit moved down to Sheol or Hades and from then on no one could be brought back to life again. The only way for a four days old corpse to be given life was through a miracle performed by the Messiah of Israel, and the Jews believed, as we were told by Martha, this would be in the last days, at the coming of the Messiah.

Jesus therefore made absolutely sure that this sign He had promised to Israel, could not be accounted for by any kind of natural recovery. The Lord then prayed, and notice Lazarus was not resurrected as a kindness to Martha and Mary, but to be witnessed by the crowds that were in Judea for the feast of Passover.

> John 11:41-42 [41] And Jesus lifted up his eyes, and said, Father, I thank thee that thou hast heard me.
>
> [42] And I knew that thou hearest me always: but because of the people which stand by I said it, that they may believe that thou hast sent me.

The miracle was to be witnessed by the Jewish people, because this is the one and only sign He promised them, and when they see the sign they will have to make a decision about who He is, and so we come to the next verse where He shouted loudly to make sure everyone heard Him.

> John 11:43 Lazarus, come forth.

Throughout the gospels and the entire New Testament, when ever a voice is heard calling for the resurrection of the dead it is the voice of Christ.

> 1 Thessalonians 4:16 For the Lord himself shall descend from heaven with a shout, with the voice of the archangel, and with the trump of God: and the dead in Christ shall rise first.

The Lord is going to shout again, and if I am dead by then, which is highly likely, I will hear it, be restored to life, and in my new body will rise up to meet Jesus, but to return to our story.

John 11:44 And he that was dead came forth, ...

[5] John 11:4, 11, 23

The Resurrection Of Lazarus –
THE SIGN IS REJECTED BY THE NATION
John 11:45-54

After the death of Lazarus, a large number of Jews went to visit Mary to comfort her because her brother had died. From, John 11:45, we know that many of these Jewish visitors saw Jesus bring Lazarus back to life, and were from then on convinced that Jesus was the Christ, the Messiah of Israel. The other group, unable to make up their own minds, went and told the Pharisees what had happened, to get their opinion. The Pharisees immediately knew that this was the sign of Jonah, the sign Jesus had publicly promised the nation to confirm that He was their Messiah. The council they called together in verse 47, was the Sanhedrin.

> John 11:47-48 ⁴⁷ Then gathered the chief priests and the Pharisees a council, and said, What do we do? For this man doeth many miracles.
>
> ⁴⁸ If we let him thus alone, all men will believe on him: and the Romans shall come and take away both our place and nation.

They did not try to make people doubt the sign, too many had seen it, but they were afraid that if the Jews believed in Jesus, the Romans would attack and their privileged positions as members of the respected Sanhedrin would end. Caiaphas the High Priest told them what they were going to do.

> John 11:49-50 ⁴⁹ Ye know nothing at all,
>
> ⁵⁰ Nor consider that it is expedient for us, that one man should die for the people, and that the whole nation perish not.

His plan was to murder Jesus, and stop His following getting any bigger so that the Sanhedrin could keep its position, but as John is about to explain, there was truth in what the High Priest had said, but not in the way he had meant it.

> John 11:51-52 [51] And thus spake he not of himself: but being high priest that year, he prophesied that Jesus should die for the nation;
>
> [52] And not for the nation only, but that also he [Jesus] should gather together in one the children of God that were scattered abroad.

Caiaphas' political spin was that by killing Jesus, the nation would be saved from destruction by a Roman invasion. However, John can see the irony in what he said because the death of Jesus will eventually result in the Jewish millennial kingdom being established, comprising the Jewish nation together with non Jewish believers, "the children of God that were scattered abroad." Caiaphas meant one thing, but God will bring about what the High Priest said in a different way altogether. A similar thing happened with Joseph, speaking to his brothers after they had plotted to murder him, in the Book of Genesis.

> Genesis 50:20 But as for you, ye thought evil against me; but God meant it unto good, to bring to pass, as it is this day, to save much people alive.

The Sanhedrin agreed to follow the advice of the High Priest and began plotting the murder of Jesus. Jesus then left Judea and did not go back until just before the Passover, the time God had chosen for Him to suffer and die.

The Resurrection Of Lazarus – THREE RESULTS OF THE REJECTION
Luke 17:11-37

First: A Special Messianic Sign For Caiaphas
Luke 17:11-19

> Luke 17:11 And it came to pass as he went to Jerusalem, that he passed through the midst of [along the boundary between] Samaria and Galilee.

This was the last journey of Jesus to Jerusalem, and on the borders between Samaria and Galilee, ten lepers met Him, nine Jews and one Samaritan. As He was on the borders He could keep out of the clutches of the Sanhedrin. The lepers asked to be healed because of their personal need.

> Luke 17:13 Jesus, Master, have mercy on us.

You will remember that according to the Jewish oral law there were three miracles that only the Messiah would ever be able to do, and one of these was the healing of a Jewish leper. It was when Jesus had healed just one Jewish leper earlier, that the Sanhedrin, had begun to investigate His claim that He was the Messiah. Now Jesus heals ten lepers, including nine Jews, showing us that the Messiah has a sense of humour, and enjoys a joke at His enemy's expense.

Keep in mind that when a Jewish leper was cured, he had to go to the priests, and they would have to go through the long procedure of cleansing required by the Law of Moses, in Leviticus 13 and 14, and when that had happened before with one leper, the investigation into the claims of Jesus began. The High Priest in charge of all this was Caiaphas, the person who led the Sanhedrin to reject the Messianic claim of Jesus, so notice what Jesus does next.

> Luke 17:14 ... he said unto them, Go shew yourselves unto the priests.

They had faith because when they went they were healed, and Caiaphas the man that led the rejection, was unexpectedly challenged by ten witnesses that had all received a Messianic miracle. Caiaphas and the priests had to sacrifice two birds for each of the former lepers, and for seven days they had to carefully examine the facts answering three questions as follows.

> First answer given ten times. "Yes the records show that this man was seen by the priests some time ago and he did indeed have leprosy."
>
> Second answer given ten times. "This man has been thoroughly inspected by us and we are satisfied he is completely healed."
>
> Third answer given ten times. "The name of the man that healed this former leper is Jesus of Nazareth."

Caiaphas is therefore forced to admit and write down in the Temple record that Jesus of Nazareth has performed ten miracles that only the Messiah could do, showing according to his known belief, that his rejection of Jesus as Messiah in the previous section was wrong. We can imagine Jesus laughing to Himself, and Caiaphas fuming in anger.

The Samaritan was the only one of the ten to go back to the Jewish Messiah and thank Him for the miracle, and from Jesus' reply to him we know that he was healed because he had faith in Him.

> Luke 17:19 And he [Jesus] said unto him, Arise, go thy way: thy faith hath made thee whole.

Second: The Kingdom Of God Is Changed In Make-Up Luke 17:20-21

After Israel committed the unforgivable sin of rejecting Jesus as Messiah, on the grounds that He was demon possessed, He stopped preaching clearly to them, and began speaking in parables. From then on He taught in parables about a new style kingdom of God.

> Luke 17:20-21 [20] And when he was demanded of the Pharisees, when the kingdom of God should come, he answered of them and said, The kingdom of God cometh not with observation:
>
> [21] Neither shall they say, Lo, here! Or, lo there! For behold, the kingdom of God is within you.

The Greek word *"entos"* here translated "within" also means "among". The kingdom of God which will last a thousand years on earth with Jesus, the King of the Jews, ruling from Jerusalem has been postponed because Israel rejected his King. In the meantime an invisible, spiritual kingdom,[6] is to be established on earth among the people of Israel and the world. It will not be ruled by world organizations made up of either "churches" or people, it will be invisible, but very real and they, the people of Israel and the world will not be able to say where it is, but it will be among them, it will of course be the true Church.

[6] John 3:6-7

Third: Jesus Will Have To Come Again
Luke 17:22-37

Jesus says six things about His second coming in these verses from the gospel of Luke.

1. When He comes everyone will see Him,[7] unlike His first coming.
2. The second coming will not come about unless He suffers greatly and is rejected by the generation that was living during His first coming.[8] His listeners at the time did not yet realise His programme of coming twice, but we today have a fuller understanding.
3. His second coming will come suddenly without warning.[9]
4. It will be a time of destruction, and everyone will have to make a decision. If they decide to reject Jesus in order to save their physical lives, they will go to Hell, but if they are prepared to be killed rather than reject Jesus, they will be given everlasting life even though they suffer physical death.[10]
5. After people have made their decisions, and those who do not decide for Jesus are against Him,[11] the judgement will come.[12] I have already made my decision.
6. Jesus tells them in a mysterious kind of way, where He will come.

Luke 17:37 "And they answered and said unto him, Where Lord? And he said unto them, Wheresoever the body is, thither will the eagles be gathered together."

The Book of Revelation tells us that when The Word of God,[13] also called the King of Kings and Lord of Lords,[14] that is to say, Jesus, when He fights the armies of the nations, the birds will come to eat their dead bodies.[15] Many believe that this battle will be at Armageddon because that is where the armies will assemble,[16] but I can find no Scripture to support the view that the actual fighting will be at Armageddon. It seems to me, according to the prophet Ezekiel, that although the armies will gather at Armageddon they will be destroyed in the mountains of Bashan, east of the River Jordan,[17] and if that is so, that is where Jesus will be seen when He returns.[18] Isaiah even identifies the actual town of Bozrah as the place of the great slaughter.[19]

[7] Luke 17:22-24

[8] Luke 17:25

[9] Luke 17:26-30

[10] Luke 17:31-33

[11] Matthew 12:30, Luke 11:23

[12] Luke 17:34-36

[13] John 1:1-5

[14] 1 Timothy 6:13-15

[15] Revelation 19:11-18

[16] Revelation 16:16

[17] Ezekiel 39:17-20

[18] Luke 17:30 and 37

[19] Isaiah 34:1-6, 63:1-6

TWO POINTS CONCERNING PRAYER
Luke 18:1-14

Never Get Tired Of Praying For Jesus To Come Again
Luke 18:1-8

> Luke 18:1 And he spake a parable unto them to this end, that men ought always to pray, and not to faint.

Jesus will have to come again to establish the messianic kingdom, and the disciples will still need to pray as He taught them earlier, "Thy kingdom come."[1] To encourage them to keep on praying, He told them about a widow that went to a wicked judge and asked him to provide her with legal protection from an enemy, but the lazy judge did nothing for her. The woman kept going to the judge and eventually he realised that she would keep on coming until she got what she wanted, and to stop her from troubling him anymore, the unrighteous judge said he would give her the protection she needed.

> Luke 18:6-8 6 And the Lord [Jesus] said [to His disciples], Hear what the unjust judge saith.
>
> 7 And shall not God avenge his own elect, which cry day and night unto him, though he bear long with them?
>
> 8 I tell you that he will avenge them speedily. Nevertheless when the Son of man cometh, shall he find faith on the earth?

By saying, "when the Son of man cometh," Jesus shows that the prayers He is talking about are about His second coming.

The line of reasoning is that if an unjust judge will listen to someone because they trouble him with never ending requests, then we can be sure that God, who is not unjust, will listen to our prayers if we keep on praying. It is interesting that the woman wanted protection from her enemy, and that during the messianic kingdom, after His second coming, Jesus will provide protection from Satan, by locking him up.[2] We must never give up praying for the second coming, "Your kingdom come!"

[1] Luke 11:2
[2] Revelation 20:1-3

Prayers Should Be Humble Identifying Our Personal Needs
Luke 18:9-14

Jesus gives us here another parable, this time concerning a Pharisee and a publican, to teach us about humility, and while the first parable was in regard to persistent prayer for the second coming, this second one was for humble prayer, and was to warn the disciples against the proud ways of the Pharisees. In the parable two men went to the temple to pray, a Pharisee and a publican, that is a tax collector.

> Luke 18:11 The Pharisee stood and prayed thus with himself, God, I thank thee, that I am not as other men are, extortioners, unjust, adulterers, or even as this publican.

He begins by telling God how good he is, because he does not take money by force, he is not unjust, and does not commit adultery, but there are many other sins everyone has committed at least once in their lives. After telling God what he does not do, he tells Him all the good things he does. The Pharisees fasted on Mondays and Thursdays, so he says he fasts twice a week, and he pays all his tithes meaning down to the last smallest seed. He just used his prayer time to boast to God about how righteous he was.

On the other hand the publican knew he was not righteous and prayed humbly, knowing his personal need for forgiveness. He stood well away from the holy of holies and the presence of God, he would not lift his eyes to heaven because he knew his sins, and he hit himself on the chest to emphasize the wickedness in his heart, then he prayed the words at the end of the verse below.

> Luke 18:13 And the publican, standing afar off, would not lift up as much as his eyes unto heaven, but smote his breast, saying, God be merciful to me a sinner.

The publican prayed because he knew, he had deep spiritual needs, and was worried and afraid of the judgement to come, and knew he needed to get right with God. Jesus said that God justified the tax collector but not the Pharisee, which teaches three things about prayer.

1. We must remember we are sinners.
2. We must remember we are unworthy.
3. We must remember we need to repent, and be sorry.

The verse ends with the catch phrase for this chapter.

> Luke 18:14 ... for every one that exalteth himself shall be abased; and he that humbleth himself shall be exalted.

DIVORCE
Matthew 19:1-12, Mark 10:1-12

The Pharisees did not agree among themselves over what the Law of Moses said about divorce, because they had different opinions over the meaning of the original Hebrew in the following verse.

> Deuteronomy 24:1 When a man hath taken a wife, and married her, and it come to pass that she find no favour in his eyes, because he hath found some uncleanness in her: then let him write her a bill of divorcement, and give it in her hand, and send her out of his house.

One rabbi said that it showed that a man could divorce his wife for any reason he wanted, and he demonstrated what he meant by this example. "If a wife cooks her husband's soup in a bad way, like putting too much salt in it or over cooking it, she can be divorced." Another rabbi said that the Scripture intended, that a woman could only be divorced if she was guilty of taking part in the sex act separately from her husband.

The Pharisees, who as just explained, did not agree about divorce themselves, brought up the subject with Jesus.

> Matthew 19:3 The Pharisees also came unto him, tempting him, ...

Actually they did not want to know the rights and wrongs of divorce, they were testing, or, tempting Him, but how were they testing Him? The place where this conversation occurred was in Perea, on the east side of the River Jordan, the territory ruled by Herod Antipas, the same Herod Antipas that had beheaded John the Baptist, after John had preached against the unlawful divorce of Herodias and her marriage to Herod afterwards. The Pharisees asked their question to Jesus about divorce in Perea, because if the answer offended Herod, then what he did to John, he could do to Jesus, and they therefore asked their question according to the view of the first rabbi we looked at, which would justify the divorce of Herodias.

> Matthew 19:3 The Pharisees also came unto him, tempting him, and saying unto him, Is it lawful for a man to put away his wife for every cause?

The answer Jesus gave them covered five issues. To begin with, before Adam and Eve sinned, God intended that there would never be divorce at all.

> Malachi 2:15-16 [15] Therefore take heed to your spirit [conscience], and let none of you deal treacherously with the wife of his youth.
>
> [16] For the LORD, the God of Israel, saith that he hateth putting away [divorce].

The first point Jesus made was that God hates divorce and never intended it from the beginning of creation. The Pharisees pressed the issue further quoting the Law of Moses.

> Matthew 19: 7 They say unto him, Why did Moses then command to give a writing of divorcement, and to put her away?

Secondly, Moses never commanded divorce, but he allowed it because the Jews were so hard hearted towards their wives.

> Mark 10:5 And Jesus answered and said unto them, For the hardness of your heart he wrote you this precept.

Thirdly, Jesus was against the injustice of the Jewish laws regarding divorce, and Mark, writing to the Romans included this in his gospel.

> Mark 10:11-12 ¹¹ And he saith unto them, Whosoever shall put away his wife, and marry another, committeth adultery against her.
>
> ¹² And if a woman shall put away her husband, and be married to another, she committeth adultery.

In Jewish law, not the Law of Moses, it is impossible for a woman to divorce her husband. He can divorce her but she cannot divorce him. Look at Mark 10:12 again, "And if a woman shall put away [divorce] her husband, and be married to another, she committeth adultery." Legally the fact was that a woman could not divorce her husband. Jesus was introducing something new here by suggesting that a woman should be allowed to divorce her husband. This was shattering news for the men, and Matthew [1], writing to Jewish readers missed out the information found in Mark 10:12, because he did not want to upset his male Jewish readers. According to Jewish law a husband does not commit adultery against his wife when he goes with another married woman, He commits adultery against the woman's husband. Jesus said that was wrong and that adultery can go either way, but even in Israel today a Jewish divorce can only be taken out by the husband against his wife, because a woman does not have the same right.

Fourthly, Jesus made it plain that fornication is the only acceptable reason for a divorce. Fornication, in the King James Bible of 1611, was a word used the same way as we now use, immorality, and it includes, adultery, homosexuality, lesbianism, incest, bestiality, any of which are acceptable grounds for divorce. However, divorce is not demanded under the Law of Moses, but it is allowed. The Bible teaches forgiveness and unity in both the Old and the New Testaments, because God hates divorce, and clearly He does not approve of the guilty party marrying again.

> Matthew 19:9 [Jesus said], whosoever marrieth her which is put away [divorced] doth commit adultery.

Jesus therefore, only allowed fornication to be used as a reason for divorce, with both men and women having the same right.

> Matthew 19:10 His disciples say unto him, If the case of the man be so with his wife, it is not good to marry.

They were shocked at His teaching, and decided at once that if that were so it would be better not to get married.

Jesus now came to His fifth and last point, which arose because of the way He had just alarmed His disciples

> Matthew 19:11 But he said unto them, All men cannot receive this saying, save they to whom it is given.

The word "given," is used because it means a gift, and one of the spiritual gifts of God is the gift of singleness,[2] and although most people should marry, those with the gift of singleness do not. Many religious people try to live singly, but they are living a lie, which comes out when cases of sexual immorality happen in religious institutions and children's homes. In charismatic churches spiritual gifts are often boasted of, either verbally or by being used often to let everyone else in the congregation know of them. To keep up with these gifted Christians, the ungifted will often fast and pray, asking God for one or more gifts. The gift of tongues was a very popular prayer request when I was born again in the 1980's, but I have never heard of anyone praying for the gift of singleness, they leave that one out, but it is a gift of God, for those servants of His that need to keep very close to Him.

Jesus calls sexually inactive people eunuchs, when teaching His disciples and speaks of three kinds, those with birth defects because they were born deformed, those that were castrated by men, and those that have decided to be eunuchs for the sake of the kingdom of heaven, and Jesus and Paul both agree that singleness is very good for believers that are able to cope with it.[3]

Under the Law of Moses, divorce was allowed because of sexual problems, including having no sexual relationship, that is what the phrase indicates, but adultery was not a reason for divorce. Adultery was so serious that adulterers were stoned to death, and so there was no need for divorce, but divorce because of sexual incompatibility was permitted. There was only one other reason for divorce, and that was when a Jew was married to a foreign wife who worshipped foreign gods.[4] For both these conditions that allowed Jews to divorce, they were allowed to marry again, and we can summarise the situation by saying that remarriage was always allowed if the divorce had been correctly carried out.

In the New Testament there are two new bases for divorce that did not apply in the Old Testament, the first is fornication, which includes adultery in addition to those sexual perversions it included in the Old Testament. The second is where one person in a marriage becomes a believer in Jesus, and the unbelieving partner wants a divorce,[5] in which case the believer should let the unbeliever go. In either of these cases where the divorce is in line with the principles or rules of the New Testament, then remarriage for the believer in Jesus is good, just as remarriage was fine if the divorce had been carried out correctly in the Old Testament.

[1] Matthew 19:9

[2] 1 Corinthians 7:7-9

[3] Matthew 19:12, 1 Corinthians 7:7

[4] Ezra 10:10-11, Nehemiah 13:23-25

[5] 1 Corinthians 7:15

WHAT WE NEED TO ENTER THE KINGDOM
Matthew 19:13-15, Mark 10:13-16

This well known incident happened when some mothers brought their children to Jesus for Him to bless them, and the disciples began telling the women off and sending them away, because they thought children were unimportant, but notice how Jesus reacted.

Mark 10:14 But when Jesus saw it, he was much displeased.

Jesus was upset to discover the mothers were being stopped from coming to Him with their young children, and decided that His disciples needed to be given an important instruction.

Matthew 19:14 But Jesus said, Suffer [Permit] little children, and forbid them not, to come unto me: for of such is the kingdom of heaven.

Mark said it a little differently.

Mark 10:14 Suffer (Permit) the little children to come unto me, and forbid them not: for of such is the kingdom of God.

Everyone that enters into eternal life does so because of believing with faith like a child, and Jesus was quick to make sure the disciples understood the point.

TEACHING ABOUT EVERLASTING LIFE
Matthew 19:15 to 20:16, Mark 10:17-31, Luke 18:18-30

Some of this section repeats what we learned about wealth and prosperity in, Lessons on Mammon.

Mark 10:17-18 [17] And when he was gone forth into the way, [After He had begun His journey], there came one running, and kneeled to him, and asked him, Good Master, what shall I do that I may inherit eternal life?

[18] And Jesus said unto him, Why callest thou me good? There is none good but one, that is, God.

The man came to Jesus running, showing that the question was very urgent, and he could just not let Jesus go without asking it, and by kneeling he showed that he had deep respect. He began by calling Jesus, "Good," a word not used by Jews in those days to address another person. They would speak about someone being good, such as in, "Sarah is a good girl," but would not call her, "Good Sarah," to her face. Moreover the Greeks had two words meaning good, "*kalos*" was used when the goodness was agreeable from the outside, but here the word *"agothos"* indicated the perfect character and genuine internal nature of Jesus was being spoken about. Jesus had told the Jews that He was the Messiah, the Son of God, and believers would therefore know that He was good on the inside. Rabbis sometimes called God, the Good One.

Looking further on in Mark 10, we find that the man was very rich, but he was also a ruler,[1] possibly a member of the Sanhedrin but more probably a synagogue ruler, and he ran to Jesus, kneeled, and asked, "Good Master, what shall I do that I may inherit eternal life?" Don't forget he was rich, and the Pharisees believed and taught that being wealthy was a sign of God's favour. Jesus answered the man in His typically Jewish way by asking another question.

> Mark 10:18 And Jesus said unto him, Why callest thou me good? There is none good but one, that is, God.

Some cults refusing to believe that Jesus is God, use this verse to show, quite wrongly, that Jesus did not claim to be good and did not claim to be God, and because of their unbelief miss the point of Jesus' question which I will rephrase, "Since only God is good, why do you call Me good?" If the ruler had answered Jesus correctly, "I call you good because, - You are God!" he would have answered his question himself. "What you need to do to inherit eternal life is to believe that Jesus is the Messiah and He is God, the Messianic God Man." Jesus had claimed this since He began His teaching to the Jews, meaning He was and is intrinsically good, but the ruler kept silent, and so Jesus brought him back to the Law of Moses, asking several questions, being careful to only ask about those commandments which concerned relationships with other people, and nothing about the commandments concerning relationships with God.

> Mark 10:20 And he answered and said unto him, Master, all these I have observed from my youth.

The ruler could answer that he had kept the Law of Moses as far as personal relationships with other people was concerned, but from Matthew we know that he knew something was still not right.

> Matthew 19:20 What lack I yet? [What else must I do?]

Jesus can now make His point.

> Mark 10:21 Then Jesus beholding [seeing] him loved him, and said unto him, One thing thou lackest: go thy way, sell whatsoever thou hast, and give to the poor, and thou shalt have treasure in heaven: and come, take up the cross, and follow me.

Although the young ruler had kept the commandments regarding his relationships with other people, he had not kept the commandments covering his relationship with God, such as having faith, trusting[2] and loving Him with all his heart, soul and might.[3] His problem was his riches, because wealth was seen as a divine favour, and that is why wealthy Jews believed their riches were a promise of eternal life from God, as a result they loved their money so much, and it was the love of his money that stopped him from loving God with all his heart and strength. His wealth and possessions were actually stopping him from receiving eternal life, but because Jesus loved him, He told him three things he needed to do.

1. Sell everything, because he must learn to trust God.
2. Give the money to the poor, which would show his love for his neighbours.
3. Follow Jesus, which would mean he would be showing everyone that Jesus was the Messiah, and the Way[4] to eternal life.

The ruler had not answered Jesus, and when Jesus told him the answer, he could not carry it through because he was so very rich.

> Mark 10:22 And he was sad at that saying, and went away grieved: [feeling miserable] for he had great possessions.

Jesus turned to His apostles and began to teach them, from what had just happened.

> Mark 10:23 How hardly shall they [How hard it will be for those] that have riches [to] enter into the kingdom of God!

Having said that, Jesus went on to explain that the real obstacle is not the wealth but the lack of **trust in God**, which riches often result in, as seen in Mark 10:24 of the King James Bible and other versions, but not all versions have included the word "trust."

> Mark 10:24 Children, how hard it is for them that **trust** in riches to enter the kingdom of God!

Again, Jesus was showing His disciples that the teachings of the Pharisees were wrong and this was one example. They trusted in their wealth to get them into heaven, because they thought riches were a sign of God's favour, and the barrier this trust in money caused was impossible to cross without a miracle from heaven.

> Mark 10:24 It is easier for a camel to go through the eye of a needle, than for a rich man to enter into the kingdom of God.

Such sayings were common at the time of Jesus, one rabbi wrote, "Open for me a door as big as the eye of a needle and I'll open for you a door which can bring in ten camels." My mother believed there was a special gate in the city wall around Jerusalem which was very small, and a camel could only get through it if the load it was carrying was removed first. This story about a small gate is told to many tourists that visit the Holy Land, but it is not true, there is no Needle Gate in the walls of Jerusalem. Jesus was talking about the eye of a needle, and if you go back to the Greek versions of the gospels, Matthew 19:24 and Mark 10:25 both talk about a sewing needle but doctor Luke, in Luke 18:35, speaks about a surgeons needle. Jesus means it is easier for a camel to go through the eye of a sewing needle or a surgeons needle, than for a wealthy man to stop trusting in his riches and put all his faith in God only. The Jews believed the teaching of the Pharisees about mammon so much that even the disciples could not at first accept what Jesus had told them.

> Matthew 19:25 When his disciples heard it, they were exceedingly amazed, saying, Who then can be saved?

The apostles were absolutely astounded because if the rich could not get to heaven, how could they get there? Jesus had the answer.

> Matthew 19:26 With men this is impossible; but with God all things are possible.

Eternal life is a gift from God,[5] and He can give it to anyone in any condition, including the poor and the rich, and this brings about a question from Peter.

> Matthew 19:27 Behold, we have forsaken all, and followed thee; what shall we have therefore?

Peter told Jesus that the disciples had left everything to follow Him, and he wanted to know how they were going to be compensated, what would they get in return? Jesus made them three promises, the first was for His apostles only.

1. Matthew 19:28 Verily [Truly] I say unto you, That which have followed me, [the twelve apostles], in the regeneration [in the Millennial Kingdom] when the Son of man shall sit in the throne of his glory, ye shall also sit upon twelve thrones, judging the twelve tribes of Israel.

   The first promise is that each of the apostles will be a king over one of the tribes of Israel during the Messianic kingdom, except for Judas Iscariot, because he was the only one that did not believe Jesus was the Messiah, if he had believed he would not have betrayed Him.[6] Obviously this promise was for the apostles only, but the other two are for all believers.

2. Mark 10:29-30 Verily [Truly] I say unto you, There is no man that hath left house, or brethren, or sister, or father, or mother, or wife, or children, or lands, for my sake, and the gospel's,

   But he shall receive an hundred fold now in this time, houses, and brethren, and sisters, and mothers, and children, and lands, with persecutions; ...

This promise of things and people being restored, things or people that believers give up for the sake of Jesus and the gospel, cannot all be physical, because obviously we cannot get new biological natural mothers, so some of these restorations if not all, must be spiritual, which is far better in my experience, but the restorations whether physical or spiritual, will come with persecution as well.

3. But that is not all because **Mark 10:30 continues, "... and in the world to come eternal life."**

The answer then to Peter's question about how Jesus would compensate those believers who give up things, friends and relatives for the sake of Him and the gospel, is that compensation will be a hundred times what is given up, with persecution, plus eternal life.

Jesus next, in the gospels of Matthew and Mark repeats one of the catch phrases common in this chapter.

But many that are first shall be last; and the last shall be first.

Matthew 19:30

Matthew, in the first 16 verses of chapter 20, was the only gospel writer to include the parable of the labourers in the vineyard, which Jesus used to illustrate the secret language of His catch phrase. In the parable Jesus taught us three lessons.

1. We are to work in God's vineyard faithfully, exactly as He asks us, and trust Him to reward us justly.
2. God will treat everyone that works in His vineyard fairly and decently.
3. God retains the right to reward His workers as He chooses.

The parable ends with one of the catch phrases found in this chapter being repeated again.

Matthew 20:16 So the last shall be first, and the first last.

[1] Luke 18:18

[2] Psalms 4:5, 33:20-21, 37:3, Isaiah 50:10
[3] Deuteronomy 6:5
[4] John 14:6
[5] John 17:1-2, Romans 6:23, 1 John 5:11
[6] Mark 3:19

JESUS TALKS ABOUT HIS COMING DEATH AND RESURRECTION AGAIN
Matthew 20:17-28, Mark 10:32-45, Luke 18:31-34

While they were walking along, Jesus, for the third and last time in the gospels, made a prophecy of His death and resurrection, this being the most detailed of all.

> Mark 10:32 And they were on their way going up to Jerusalem.

Going up to Jerusalem for the last time, they were still east of the River Jordan and outside Judea, where the Sanhedrin that wanted to kill Him had authority. However, despite the danger they must go to Jerusalem in Judea, and so verse 32 has more to say.

> Mark 10:32 Jesus went before them: and they were amazed; and as they followed, they were afraid.

The disciples were afraid because when they crossed the river, the Sanhedrin would be looking for Jesus to arrest Him, but Jesus explained about His coming death and resurrection, that it would be a time of fulfilment of Old Testament prophecy.

> Luke 18:31 Then he took unto him the twelve, and said unto them, Behold, we go up to Jerusalem, and all things that are written by the prophets concerning the Son of man shall be accomplished.

For 15 centuries the Jews, the chosen people of God, had faithfully kept the Feast of Passover, remembering how the blood of a lamb, painted on the door posts and lintels of Jewish homes, prevented the death of any eldest son living inside.[1] Now at this Passover, the Son of God, the Lamb of God, the eldest Son of Mary, would surrender His blood so that an even greater, escape from death, could be accomplished. God from now would allow all races to escape death because of the death of His Son at that special Passover. Jesus detailed nine points about the Passover at which he would be sacrificed, and these can all be found in Mark 10:33-34.

1. He must get to Jerusalem.
2. The chief priests and scribes, (the Sanhedrin), will have authority over Him.
3. The Jews will pass the death sentence on Him.
4. The Jews will give Him to the Gentiles.
5. The Gentiles will mock Him.
6. The Gentiles will scourge Him.
7. The Gentiles will spit on Him.
8. The Gentiles will kill Him.
9. He will rise from the dead.

Although this is a clear and detailed account of what was going to happen to Jesus, we know from Luke the disciples did not understand it.

> Luke 18:34 And they understood **none** of these things: and this saying was hid from them, neither knew they the things which were spoken.

The fact that they did not understand is shown by what happened next.

> Matthew 20:20 Then came to him the mother of the sons of Zebedee's children with her sons, worshipping him, and desiring a certain thing of him.

The mother of Zebedee's children was Salome (or Shulamit), the sister of Mary, the mother of Jesus, so that Jesus and the sons of Zebedee, were first cousins. Her request shows that the only thing they understood about the coming events was that Jesus was going up to Jerusalem, but they thought He was going to set up His kingdom there, not die there, and that was why she asked for what she did.

> Matthew 20:21 She saith unto him, Grant that these two my sons may sit, the one on thy right hand, and the other on the left, in thy kingdom.

Obviously the disciples had not understood what Jesus had been telling them.

In the verse above, Matthew stresses the kingdom, but in the verse below, when James and John, the sons of Zebedee and Salome, make their appeal, Mark stresses the glory.

> Mark 10:37 They said unto him, Grant unto us that we may sit, one on thy right hand, and the other on thy left hand, in thy glory.

Mark says James and John did the asking, but the request was actually made on their behalf, or in their names, by their mother Salome, and after hearing her Jesus asked the brothers a question.

> Mark 10:38 Can ye drink of the cup that I drink of? And be baptised with the baptism that I am baptised with?

In fact later on they did suffer as Jesus did, James was the first apostle to be martyred,[2] not the first person to die as a martyr but the first apostle, and John, the only apostle that died of old age, was banished to the island of Patmos.[3] However, those that sit on the right hand and left hand of Jesus, will be chosen by our Heavenly Father.

> Matthew 20:23 And he saith unto them, Ye shall drink indeed of my cup, and be baptised with the baptism that I am baptised with: but to sit on my right hand, and on my left, is not mine to give, but it shall be given to them for whom it is prepared by my Father.

The other disciples were unhappy to learn that James and John had asked for the two highest positions next to Jesus in the millennial kingdom.

Mark 10:41 And when the ten heard it, they began to be much displeased with James and John.

Jesus used this to teach them that in His kingdom, position and importance will be given to those that become servants.

Mark 10:42-44 ⁴⁴ But Jesus called them to him, and saith unto them, Ye know that they which are accounted to rule over the Gentiles exercise lordship over them; and their great ones exercise authority upon them.

⁴³ But so shall it not be among you: but whosoever shall be great among you, shall be your minister:

⁴⁴ And whosoever of you all will be the chiefest, shall be servant of all.

In the kingdom, our own ambitions and requests, will not lead to positions of authority, but they will be given to those that have served faithfully, and the best example of this is Jesus Himself.

Mark 10:45 For even the Son of man came not to be ministered unto, but to minister, and to give his life a ransom for many.

Jesus was the righteous servant of God the Father,[4] and that is why He will be, King of Kings, and Lord of Lords.[5]

[1] Exodus 12:1-13

[2] Acts 12:2

[3] Revelation 1:9

[4] Isaiah 53:11-12

[5] Revelation 17:14, 19:16

JESUS HEALED THE TWO BLIND MEN
Matthew 20:29-34, Mark 10:46-52, Luke 18:35-43

As I have done before I am going to quote the Scriptures, emphasizing certain words, although nowhere in the Bible are words highlighted in this way. The reason for this is to help us see that the gospels here are not in disagreement with each other as some unbelievers say they are.

> Mark 10:46 And they came **to** Jericho: and as he went **out of** Jericho with his disciples and a great number of people, ...

> Matthew 20:29 And as they **departed from** Jericho, a great multitude followed him.

> Luke 18:35 And it came to pass, that as he was **come nigh** unto Jericho, ...

Matthew and Mark say that the event took place while they were leaving Jericho, and Luke says it happened before they got to Jericho, but the Bible attackers are either ignorant of the geography of the land all those years ago, or they purposely forget to mention it.

At the time of Jesus there were two Jerichos, four or five miles apart, the original Jericho of the Old Testament was to the north, with another New Testament Jericho to the south of it. The event took place between the two Jerichos, after coming out of the old Jericho, while on their way to Jerusalem, but before entering the new Jericho. If we know the geography of the area in the first century, the Scriptures give us no reason to doubt their accuracy.

Another difference gospel critics mention is that Matthew says there were two blind men,[1] Luke one,[2] and Mark also one, a man by the name of Bartimaeus, the son of Timaeus.[3] Clearly, Bartimaeus was the main character, the man that stood out most prominently of the pair, and that is why Luke and Mark only speak of the miracle of one of the men, although two blind men were given their sight. Just because Luke and Mark tell us about one man, it does not mean there was not another with him, there is no discrepancy, Jesus healed both of the men. We can see how it all happened by putting the three gospel accounts together.

The blind beggars had found out from people in the crowd that Jesus of Nazareth was passing by, and shouted out to Jesus, asking for mercy. They began calling to Him as He was going into the city, continued their cries as He walked through the city, but Jesus did not reply to them until He was leaving the city. Bartimaeus appears to have been the main speaker for the two because Mark is referring to him in the following passages.

Mark 10:47 Jesus, Thou Son of David, have mercy on me.

Mark 10:48 ... Thou Son of David, have mercy on me.

They based their request to be healed on their personal need.

Matthew 20:30 Have mercy on us, O Lord, thou Son of David.

The Jews knew that when the Messiah came He would heal the blind,[4] and the blind men were asking Him to heal them. Once again the problem was that by calling Jesus, the Son of David, they were claiming He was the Messiah, and He was not healing anyone on that basis anymore because the Jews had rejected Him as their Messiah. However, He was still healing where a request was based on personal need, and in Mark 10:49, Jesus stopped and asked for Bartimaeus to be brought to Him.

Mark 10:50 And he, [Bartimaeus] casting away his garment, [his coat] rose, and came to Jesus.

By throwing his coat away he showed his faith, because without his sight he would never be able find it again in the crowd, but he knew he was going to be healed and he knew that he would be able to see it then. Jesus asked Bartimaeus what he wanted Him to do, which was obvious, but they had to clearly state their personal need.

Matthew 20:33-34 [33] They say unto him, Lord, that our eyes may be opened.

[34] So Jesus had compassion [sympathy] on them and touched their eyes: and immediately their eyes received sight.

Notice the way in which all this was done, Jesus asked for them to be called out and away from the crowd, He asked them their personal need, saw that they had faith, and then healed them. In Mark 10:52, He said, "Go thy way; thy faith hath made thee whole."

[1] Matthew 20:30
[2] Luke 18:35
[3] Mark 10:46
[4] Isaiah 35:5

INDIVIDUALS WITH FAITH WILL ENTER THE KINGDOM OF GOD
Luke 19:1-10

Jesus, on His way to Jerusalem, had crossed over the River Jordan to the Jewish territory on the west side, He had gone through Old Testament Jericho and was passing through New Testament Jericho, when He met Zacchaeus. Zacchaeus was a chief publican, in control of other publicans,[1] including both income-tax collectors and customs officers, a very important official, and a rich man.[1] Publicans were usually rich because they took money from the tax-payers, but Zacchaeus could also have taken money from the publicans that he managed. You will remember that Jesus had strongly taught a little earlier that anyone that trusts in their money to get into heaven, cannot possibly enter.

Zacchaeus was so short he had climbed up a Sycamore tree to see Jesus, who was walking along surrounded by a crowd of people.

> Luke 19:5 And when Jesus came to the place, he looked up, and saw him, and said unto him, Zacchaeus, make haste, and come down; for to day I must abide at thy house.

Publicans were hated by other Jews, their only friends were other publicans and prostitutes, that is why Zacchaeus was delighted to welcome Jesus into his home, because although he was rich, he had few visitors, since most Jews were too self righteous and proud to go inside his house.

> Luke 19:6 And he [Zacchaeus] made haste, and came down, and received him joyfully.

The Jewish crowd was disgusted because Jesus was going to stay in the house of a chief tax collector.

> Luke 19:7 And when they saw it, they all murmured, saying, That he was gone to be the guest with a man that is a sinner.

Zacchaeus had not spent long with Jesus before he understood who Jesus was, and was saved for eternal life, and he proved he had been saved by what he did, that is by his works.[2]

> Luke 19:8 And Zacchaeus stood, and said unto the Lord; Behold, Lord, the half of my goods I give to the poor; and if I have taken any thing from any man by false accusation, I restore him four fold, [four times as much].

Zacchaeus, not like the rich young ruler in Mark 10:17-22, was ready to give up all his money, and Jesus noticed it at once.

> Luke 19:9 And Jesus said unto him, This day is salvation come to this house, forsomuch as he also is a son of Abraham.

Jesus was emphasizing that salvation was now being given to individual believers. Zacchaeus was a son of Abraham in two senses, he was a son of Abraham because he was Jewish and all Jews are descendants of Abraham, but he was also a son because he believed,[3] because he had faith like Abraham had before him. The lesson to the Jews was that although that generation could not enter the kingdom of God as a nation, because the nation had rejected the Messiah, they could still come as individuals. The lesson to Christians is the same, we come as individual believers, not because we belong to this church or that one. However, the main thrust of the message when it was given was for the Jews, the children, the blood relatives, of Abraham. Even though the nation had rejected Jesus, individuals could still accept Him, and so Jesus in the next verse explained what He was doing.

> Luke 19:10 For the Son of man is come to seek and to save that which was lost.

Zacchaeus, a son of Abraham because he was a Jew, had been lost but had now been found, and had received eternal life because of faith in the Jewish Messiah.

[1] Luke 19:2
[2] James 2:20-26
[3] Galatians 3:6-7

THE DELAYED KINGDOM OF GOD
Luke 19:11-28

Jesus was getting nearer and nearer to Jerusalem, and the people, along with the disciples, believed that when Jesus got there He would establish His kingdom. For that reason, immediately after explaining through the conversation with Zacchaeus, that for the time being only individuals could enter the kingdom, he told them a parable. Remember, they did not understand God's plan for His Son was, that He must die in Jerusalem and rise from the dead, although we read in the gospels Jesus had told the disciples three times already, and probably other times as well, but it had been hidden from them.[1] He was not going to set up the messianic kingdom then because of the unforgivable sin of Chapter 6, but He was going to explain the situation in a parable that even the disciples did not understand at the time.

> Luke 19:11 And as they heard these things, he added and spake a parable, because he was nigh to Jerusalem, and because they thought that the kingdom of God should immediately appear.

In the parable, a nobleman called ten servants and gave them ten pounds, one pound each, to trade with while he went away to another country. A correct translation would have been ten minas, and a mina was about 100 days wages, so they were each given about 100 days wages to trade with while the nobleman was away.[2] He was going abroad to be officially made king,[3] but the people hated him and sent messengers after him saying they would not accept him as king.[4] After he had been made king, he went back and asked his servants what they had done with the money he had left with them.

The first servant had traded the pound the nobleman, who was now king, had given him and made another ten.[5]

> Luke 19:17 And he said unto him, Well, thou good servant: because thou hast been faithful in a very little, have thou authority over ten cities.

Another servant had gained five pounds and he was given five cities, then one came along with his one pound which he had done nothing with at all, and the nobleman who was now king was not pleased.

> Luke 19:22 And he said unto him, Out of thine own mouth will I judge thee, thou wicked servant.

The servant, although he knew his master was a strict man, had not followed the instructions he had been given, which was to do business with the money, to occupy his time in trading, and the pound was taken from him and given to the man that had earned ten, because of the following rule.

> Luke 19:26 Unto every one which hath shall be given; and from him that hath not, even that he hath shall be taken away from him.

If what is given to us is not used, it will be taken away and given to someone else who will use it.

The people that had hated the nobleman before he went away and sent messages to say they did not want him to be their king, were not forgotten.

> Luke 19:27 But those mine enemies, which would not that I should reign over them, bring hither, [here] and slay them before me.

The meaning of the parable can be summed up in six points.

1. The Messiah will not be made king now but will leave.
2. His servants that are left behind will carry out the work He has given them.
3. Most of the citizens intended for the kingdom will reject Him as their King.
4. Eventually He will return with authority from heaven as King.

5. His servants will be judged, those that have done well will be given authority in the kingdom, while those that have done nothing will have no authority in the kingdom, and what they were given will be taken away from them.
6. The citizens that did not want Him as King will be killed.

The record was now straight, even if it was not understood, and it was time for Jesus to move on.

Luke 19:28 And when he had thus spoken, he went before, ascending up to Jerusalem.

This would be His last journey to Jerusalem.

---

[1] Luke 18:34

[2] Luke 19:13

[3] Luke 19:12

[4] Luke 19:14

[5] Luke 19:16

10

KING JESUS ARRIVES AT HIS CITY

JESUS STOPS IN BETHANY
John 11:55 to 12:1, 12:9-11

Bethany, on the lower slopes of the Mount of Olives, an easy walking distance from Jerusalem[1], and facing the River Jordan, was the place Jesus chose to stay for the coming week, travelling to and from the city until the last Passover. It was the 8th day of the month of Nissan, or according to our calendar, the 31st March, AD 30, which we know from the following verse.

> John 12:1 Then Jesus six days before the Passover came to Bethany, where Lazarus was which had been dead, whom he raised from the dead.

Jesus began His public ministry to Israel at a Passover feast and ended it at another Passover feast. The first of these feasts had been in AD 27, about four or six months after He had been baptised by John the Baptist, when John had proclaimed that He was the Saviour of the world and the Son of God.[2] His ministry had covered four Passovers or three years, but it had been three and a half years since He had been introduced to the people by John.

After the resurrection of Lazarus, the first of the three signs of Jonah, the Sanhedrin decided to officially reject the sign, and kill Jesus,[3] that is why many people were looking for Him.

> John 11:57 Now both the chief priests and the Pharisees had given a commandment, that, if any man knew where he were, he should shew [show] it, that they might take [capture] him.

The Sanhedrin by this command confirmed that they had rejected the first sign of Jonah, and were making their intentions clear, but the people were curious.

> John 12:9 Much people of the Jews therefore knew that he was there: and they came not for Jesus' sake only, but that they might see Lazarus also, whom he had raised from the dead.

The interest in Lazarus was intensified because he had been dead four days, and the Sanhedrin had not denied it because there had been too many witnesses. It was therefore impossible, according to Jewish oral law, the Mishnah, for the resurrection to be explained away as a natural resuscitation, that is why crowds flocked to see him, and many Jews believed in Jesus because of the miracle. The Sanhedrin, (the High Court of religious judges), was becoming more and more alarmed.

> John 12:10-11 [10]But the chief priests consulted that they might put Lazarus also to death;
>
> [11] Because that by reason of him many of the Jews went away, and believed on Jesus.

Many Jews had believed when Jesus brought the stinking four day old rotting corpse of Lazarus back to life, now others were believing after seeing Lazarus. A living Lazarus was proof to the Jews that Jesus was the Messiah, so the religious leaders strongly felt that they would have to kill him also.

---

[1] Psalms 48:2, Matthew 5:35

[2] John 1:29-34

[3] John 11:47-50

THE TRIUMPHAL ENTRY OF THE KING INTO JERUSALEM
**Matthew 21:1-17, Mark 11:1-11,
Luke 19:29-44, John 12:12-19**

It was the 10th day of the Jewish month of Nissan, which on our present calendar would be the 2nd April AD 30, and significantly every year on the 10th of Nissan the Jews would choose the lamb to be sacrificed for the Passover.[1] The lamb was chosen for sacrifice on the 10th of the month, and separated out from the flock until the 14th, so that it could be tested and scrutinized, to make sure it was perfect before it was killed, therefore there was a spiritual significance for Jesus, the Lamb of God, to ride into the city on that particular day.

Many preachers and teachers will tell you that Jesus rode into Jerusalem to offer the kingdom to the Jews for one more time, but if you check all that He said, you will see that He did no such thing. He did not say, as He used to before the Jews had committed the unpardonable sin, "The kingdom of heaven (or, The kingdom of God) is at hand."[2] His words, concerning the Jewish religious leaders and their followers from now on, were words of utter disapproval and the most severe judgement. No! The spiritual parallel was that this was the day the Lamb of God, was set to one side to be tested and scrutinized, before being sacrificed. John the Baptist, when he introduced Jesus had said, "Behold the Lamb of God, which taketh away the sin of the world."[3]

The journey from Bethany to Jerusalem passes over the Mount of Olives and through Bethphage, a village on the top of the mountain. Bethphage is an Aramaic name meaning, "place of young figs". It was when they got to Bethphage that Jesus sent two of His disciples for a pair of donkeys.

> Matthew 21:2 Ye shall find an ass tied, and a colt with her: loose them, and bring them unto me.

> Mark 11:2 Ye shall find a colt tied, whereon never man sat; loose him, and bring him.

Jesus told his two disciples what to say if anyone asked them why they were taking the donkeys.

Matthew 21:3 Ye shall say, The Lord hath **need of them.**

The word "need" that Jesus told them to say is important because the donkeys were needed to fulfil an Old Testament prophecy, which said that the Messiah would one day ride into Jerusalem on two donkeys, an ass and its colt, and both were necessary to make the prophecy come true. The prophecy had been given to the Jews by Zechariah nearly 500 years earlier.

> Zechariah 9:9 Rejoice greatly, O daughter of Zion; shout, O daughter of Jerusalem: behold, thy King cometh unto thee: he is just, and having salvation; lowly, and riding upon an ass, and upon a colt the foal of an ass.

The crowds knew the meaning of Jesus' riding into Jerusalem on a donkey, because they knew the prophecy of Zechariah, which is even quoted in Matthew 21:4-5, but they wrongly thought that He was going to establish His Messianic Kingdom there and then. We know this for two reasons, by what they say, and by what they do. To begin with they began breaking branches for the donkeys to walk on.

> Mark 11:8 And many spread their garments in the way: and others cut down branches off the trees, and strawed [spread] them in the way.

> Matthew 21:8 And a very great multitude spread their garments in the way; others cut down branches from the trees, and strawed [spread] them in the way.

John was more exact telling us what kind of branches they were.

> John 12:12-13 ¹² On the next day much people that were come to the feast, when they heard that Jesus was coming to Jerusalem,
>
> ¹³ Took branches of palm trees, and went forth to meet him.

Palm branches were used at the Feast of Tabernacles, not the Feast of Passover, and so even the Jews were confused about the Triumphal

Entry of Jesus, because they were behaving as if it was Tabernacles. The Feast of Tabernacles, like other Jewish feasts speaks of two things, what God has done in history and what He is going to do in the future. What God has done in the past will tell us what He is going to do later on, so what did Moses tell us in Leviticus about Tabernacles?

> Leviticus 23:40 And ye shall take you on the first day the boughs of goodly trees, branches of palm trees, and the boughs of thick trees, and willows of the brook; and ye shall rejoice before the LORD your God seven days.

> Leviticus 23:42-43 [42] Ye shall dwell in booths seven days; all that are Israelites born shall dwell in booths [tabernacles]:

> [43] That your generations may know that I made the children of Israel to dwell in booths [tabernacles], when I brought them out of Egypt: I am the LORD your God.

After God had rescued the Jews from slavery in Egypt, Moses built a tabernacle in the desert where he spoke with God.[4] Every family had their tent to live in and there was a special one for God, called the tabernacle, and so God had a tent among the tents of Israel. The historic message of Tabernacles then is that God lived among His people, and this points to two events in the future when God will live with His chosen ones. One event will take place in the Millennial Kingdom, the thousand years of peace, when Jesus will be King in Jerusalem,[5] and the second and final fulfilment will be when God and men live together.[6] "Wonderful," you will say, but notice the order, the sacrifice for sins, the Passover comes first, and Tabernacles after, because sinners cannot live with God until He has made them holy.

Getting back to the story, Jesus had to complete the requirements of Passover, to be the Passover Lamb for the nation, before He could carry out the requirements of Tabernacles, which is to live among them as King in Jerusalem. Also as far as the Church is concerned, He had to be our Passover Lamb before meeting the needs of Tabernacles, which is to build spiritual homes for us to live in, which He has gone to heaven to do.[7]

As Jesus made His triumphal entry riding on a donkey the Jews cut palm branches as they would have done at Tabernacles, thinking that the Messiah was going to establish His kingdom and live among them, because the prophecy of Zechariah 14:16-21 will, when it eventually happens, be a fulfilment of the Feast of Tabernacles. Remember that at the transfiguration,[8] which we studied in Chapter 7, Peter had made the same mistake. It was not realised that Passover had to take place before Tabernacles, and Passover could not be fulfilled without the death of the Lord. Three times Jesus had told His disciples about His coming death and resurrection, but still they did not understand as John pointed out once again.

> John 12:16 These things understood **not** his disciples at first: but when Jesus was glorified, then remembered they that these things were written of him.

It was only after Jesus had risen from the dead,[9] ascended into heaven[10] and sent the Holy Spirit in Acts 2, that they were able to put all the events together and finally realised the enormous significance of what was now beginning to take place.

The resurrection of Lazarus had been very important in making many Jews believe that Jesus was Messiah and King, because it was an established and accepted fact that Lazarus had been dead four days before coming back to life, even by the religious leaders who hated Jesus, everyone knew it was true. That was one reason why such a huge crowd cut down palm branches to welcome Jesus as He was riding into Jerusalem., and again John explains this.[11] Notice also what the people were shouting out.

> John 12:13 Hosanna: Blessed is the King of Israel that cometh in the name of the Lord.

Hosanna, means, "save now," something that is said at the Feast of Tabernacles where a group of prayers are said at the feast, known as the "Hoshana" prayers, meaning, "save us now." We can see then that they are speaking and acting as if it was the Feast of Tabernacles, not Passover, and that their minds are focused on Jesus as King of Israel.

> Mark 11:10 Blessed be the kingdom of our father David, that cometh in the name of the Lord: Hosanna in the highest.

In their minds the everlasting Jewish Kingdom, that will be ruled by a descendent of David who will never die, was about to begin.[12] The most important prayer said at Tabernacles is, in Hebrew, "Hoshana Rabba," meaning, "Hosanna in the highest," or more fully, "Save us in the highest," and that was what they were shouting, the main prayer of the Feast of Tabernacles.

> Matthew 21:9 And the multitudes that went before, and that followed, cried, saying, Hosanna to the Son of David: Blessed is he that cometh in the name of the Lord; Hosanna in the highest.

> Luke 19:38 Blessed be the King that cometh in the name of the Lord: peace in heaven, and glory in the highest.

Clearly they were speaking and acting as if it was the Tabernacles, not Passover, because when the Kingdom is eventually set up, Tabernacles will be fulfilled. Another thing to note is that Matthew, wrote that the crowd was saying, "Blessed is he that cometh in the name of the Lord." The other gospels say something very close to it, and the reason is that the people had been taught that they must welcome the Messiah when He comes with those words, "Blessed is he that cometh in the name of the Lord," something the rabbis had learned from Psalm 118:26.

Multitudes, a huge number of people notice, were loudly proclaiming that Jesus was the Messiah, but the unforgivable sin had been committed and it was too late, their sin was still unforgivable. That is why Jesus, when He spoke did not offer them the kingdom, but told them about the terrible judgement that would come on the people of Jerusalem.

> Luke 19:41-44 [41] And when he was come near, he beheld [saw] the city, and wept over it,

> [42] Saying, If thou hadst known, even thou, at least in this day, the things which belong unto thy peace! But now they are hid from thine [your] eyes.

> [43] For the days shall come upon thee, that thine [your] enemies shall cast [dig] a trench about thee, and compass [encircle] thee round, and keep thee on every side,

[44] And shall lay [level] thee even with the ground, and thy children within thee; and they shall not leave in thee one stone upon another; because thou knewest [knew] not the time of thy visititation [official visit].

Although crowds were enthusiastically shouting "Hosanna!" and laying palms and branches in the road, it was too late, Jerusalem must now be destroyed. However, although the people of Jerusalem would have to be punished, and their city levelled to the ground, nevertheless this was the time, appointed by God for the Messiah's visitation, for His official visit.

Luke 19:39-40 [39] And some of the Pharisees from among the multitude said unto him, Master, rebuke thy disciples.

[40] And he answered and said unto them, I tell you that, if these should hold their peace, the stones would immediately cry out.

It was God's chosen time for the Lamb of God to be set aside to be scrutinized and tested, to make sure He was perfect, and the nation must be told that Jesus had been selected. If the crowds acknowledging Jesus were forbidden to speak, then the message that He was Messiah would have been spoken miraculously by the stones, because it must be made known to everyone that this was the day the Passover Lamb was being set to one side. It was extremely important, that the Jews knew that the result of refusing to accept their Messiah and saying that His miracles were the work of Satan, the unforgivable sin committed by them, would result in the complete destruction of Jerusalem in AD 70, the reason for the destruction given in the Bible was, "Because thou knewest not the time of thy visitation."[13]

The entry of Jesus into Jerusalem was like an earthquake, some Bibles say the city was stirred, our King James Version says the city was moved, the word used in the Greek means shaken in the same way as an earthquake. I was in an earthquake once and my response to it was to fear.

> Matthew 21:10 And when he was come into Jerusalem, all the city was moved, saying, Who is this?

The people did not know who Jesus was but they did know His coming was momentous, but the religious leaders continued to reject Him.

> Matthew 21:15-16 ¹⁵ And when the chief priests and scribes saw the wonderful things that he did, and the children crying in the temple, Hosanna to the son of David; they were sore [annoyed] displeased,
>
> ¹⁶ And said unto him, Hearest thou what these say? And Jesus said unto them, Yea; have ye never read, Out of the mouth of babes and sucklings [un-weaned children] thou hast perfected praise?[14]

The children were telling the truth, Jesus was their Messiah, the Son of David, and He accepted their praise, proving it was true. The trouble was it was too late for Him to set up the kingdom now because of the unforgivable sin. After entering the city and visiting the temple that day He returned to stay the night with His friends in Bethany.

> Mark 11:11 And Jesus entered into Jerusalem, and into the temple: and when he had looked round about upon all things, and now the eventide [evening] was come, he went out unto Bethany with the twelve.

[1] Exodus 12:3-6

[2] Matthew 4:17, 10:7, Mark 1:15

[3] John 1:29

[4] Exodus 33:9

[5] Zechariah 14

[6] Revelation 21:2-3

[7] John 14:2-3

[8] Luke 9:27-36

[9] Luke 24:1-7, 24:33-36, 2 Timothy 2:8
[10] Acts 1:6-9
[11] John 12: 17-18
[12] 1 Chronicles 17:7-12, Isaiah 9:6-7, Luke 1:32-33
[13] Luke 19:44
[14] Psalm 8:2 (Written by King David more than 1,000 years before Christ).

JESUS CURSES A FIG TREE
Matthew 21:19, Mark 11:12-13

Once again we see the authority the King has over nature.

> Mark 11:12 And on the morrow [following day], when they were come from Bethany, he was **hungry:**

Jesus was human, and just like other men he needed to eat.

> Mark 11:13 And seeing a fig tree afar off having leaves, he came, if haply [perhaps] he might find **any thing** thereon: and when he came to it, he found nothing but leaves; for the time of figs was not yet.

The Scripture does not say that Jesus was looking for figs, it was not the season for figs, but Jesus went to the tree because he might perhaps find something on the tree to eat.

Since I began writing this book, we have moved from our farm in Cornwall, to Hemel Hempstead in Hertfordshire, and Mario, our next door neighbour here grows figs, harvesting two crops every year, in the summer and the autumn. When his fig trees produce leaves in the spring, they also produce edible nodules, that will later develop into figs. If you want to see these nodules look for a fig tree with leaves in the spring and if the tree is going to fruit early in the year, you will find the nodules, later towards the summer you will find the nodules have become figs. Lucy, translating directly from her native Chinese language, calls figs, No-Flower-Fruit, because the flower is hidden inside the nodule and never blooms. When Jesus looked at the fig tree He may have been looking for the nodules to eat, because it was not yet time for figs.

Some people may reason that Jesus was unfair to curse the tree because it had no figs when it was not the season for figs, but once we know just a little about this strange fruit, it becomes clear that a fig tree in the spring with leaves will also have nodules, if it is going to fruit in the first fruiting season. When Jesus reached the fig tree He did not find, "any thing thereon," meaning there were no edible nodules and He cursed the tree. Earlier when we saw that Jesus was hungry it showed He was human, now that He can curse a fig tree it shows He is a divine being.

The cursing of the fig tree could be symbolic of the cursing of Pharisaic Judaism, especially of that generation, because after rejecting their Messiah they would not be able to produce any fruit. The leaves of the tree may represent the false religion of the Pharisees, that would cause people to look to them for the fruit, but like the fig tree they had no fruit and nothing that could develop into fruit, they were barren.

> Matthew 21:19 And when he saw a fig tree in the way, he came to it, and found nothing thereon, but leaves only, and said unto it, Let no fruit grow on thee henceforward for ever.

The disciples took note of what Jesus had said to the fig tree, as shown in the following Scripture, and as we will see again later.

> Mark 11:14 And Jesus answered and said unto it, No man eat fruit of thee hereafter for ever. And his disciples heard it.

JESUS COMPLETELY CONTROLS THE TEMPLE
Mark 11:15-18, Luke 19:45-48

The cursing of the fig tree showed the authority of the King over nature, here He shows His authority over the Temple. In Chapter 4, we saw how Jesus took possession of the Temple at the start of His teaching programme to Israel, three years earlier, proclaiming to be their Messiah, now at the completion of His assignment, He again took possession, as the Messiah and Lord of the Temple. Three years before He had cleaned out the Temple but once more the business of money making was going strong.

> Mark 11:15 Jesus went into the temple, and overthrew the tables of the money changers, and the seats of them that sold doves.

You may like to look back to Chapter 4, and remind yourself of the Temple procedures, but on this occasion He was more thorough.

> Mark 11:16 And he would not suffer [allow] that any man should carry any vessel [container] through the temple.

This time He stopped all goods from going through the Temple, and again accused them of turning the place into a den of thieves. In doing this He proved His authority over the Temple in three areas.

1. Authority to clean.
2. Authority to own.
3. Authority to protect.

The religious rulers had lost control, and they were furious.

> Mark 11:18 And the scribes and chief priests heard it, and sought how they might destroy him: for they feared him, because all the people was astonished at his doctrine [teaching].

They did not kill Jesus straight away because the people were on His side, and so they wanted to get rid of Him secretly without the crowds knowing, and this is where Judas would come in.

> Luke 19:47-48 [47] And he taught **daily** in the temple. But the chief priests and the scribes and the chief of the people sought to destroy him,
> [48] And could not find what they might do: for all the people were very attentive to hear him.

Jesus taught in the Temple every day from Monday to Thursday of that last week, but whenever they saw Him He was surrounded by people very keen to hear Him, and arresting Him in front of His fans would make them unpopular.

AN OPEN INVITATION FROM THE KING
John 12:20-26

The invitation from Jesus found in John 12, is to all kinds of people including Gentiles.

> John 12:20-22 [20] And there were certain Greeks among them that came up to worship at the feast:
>
> [21] The same came therefore to Philip, which was of Bethsaida of Galilee, and desired him, saying, we would see Jesus.
>
> [22] Philip cometh and telleth [told] Andrew: and again Andrew and Philip tell Jesus.

Greeks going to the Jewish feast would have converted to the Jewish religion, but would not actually be Jews. Philip and Andrew were not too sure about taking the Greeks to see Jesus because He had come only to the lost sheep of the house of Israel,[1] and that is why they asked Jesus if it was all right for them to come to Him. A quick look at the Scriptures may give us the impression that Jesus did not answer their question or request, but when we study what He said carefully, we find that He did give them the information they needed.

1. Jesus will create much more life after He has died, and this is promised in the following two verses.

> John 12:23-24 [23] And Jesus answered them, saying, The hour [time] is come, that the Son of man should be glorified.
>
> [24] Verily, verily [Truly, truly], I say unto you, Except a corn [seed] of wheat fall into the ground and die, it abideth [stays] alone: but if it die, it bringeth [brings] forth much fruit.

2. Also as a result of His death, the world will be judged.

John 12:31 Now is the judgement of this world:

3. Again, because of His death, Satan will be defeated.

John 12:31 now shall the prince of this world be cast out.

4. It will be after He has been crucified that the Gentiles will be able to come to Him.

John 12:32-33 [32] And I, if I be lifted up from the earth, will draw all men unto me.

[33] This he said, signifying [spelling out] what death he should die.

After His death, everyone, Gentiles and Jews will be able to come to Him, this is the meaning of verse 32, above, "And I, if I be lifted up from the earth, will draw all men unto me." However, before His death He had come only to the lost sheep of the house of Israel,[1] and so we see that Jesus did give Philip and Andrew the answer to their question, which was that the time for the Greeks to meet Jesus would be after He had died, but not before. All this leads to the invitation which you will see is given us on an individual basis, and each of us must make up our own minds about accepting it.

John 12:25-26 [25] He that loveth [loves] his life shall lose it; and he that hateth [hates] his life in this world shall keep it unto life eternal [everlasting].

[26] If any man serve me, let him follow me; and where I am, there shall also my servant be: if any man serve me, him will my Father honour.

---

[1] Matthew 15:24

FOR THE GLORY OF GOD'S NAME
John 12:27-43

Read the following Scriptures carefully to understand what Jesus said and meant. Notice that He did not ask God to save Him from dying, because that is what He came for, to die.

> John 12:27-28 ²⁷ Now is my soul troubled; and what shall I say? Father, save me from this hour: but for this cause came I unto this hour.
>
> ²⁸ Father, glorify thy name.

After Jesus had prayed for God to glorify His name, a voice came from heaven, for the third time in the gospels.[1]

> John 12:28 Then came a voice from heaven, saying, I have glorified it, and will glorify it again.

The huge crowd of people heard God speak but none of them recognized it was from God, some thought it had thundered while others said an angel had spoken to Jesus who decided to explain what had actually happened and why.

> John 12:30 Jesus answered and said, This voice came not because of me, but for your sakes.

God had spoken for the multitude to hear Him for the third time from heaven because they should have known by now that Jesus was the Son of God, and He had come from above. Jesus knew where He was from[2] but most of the people were not catching on.

Jesus was still speaking to the crowds parabolically, and after telling them about His coming death and the reason for it, their reply shows that they did not understand.

> John 12:34 The people answered him, We have heard out of the law that Christ abideth for ever: and how sayest thou, The son of man must be lifted up? Who is this Son of man?

They knew from the Old Testament that the Messiah would live forever, so how could He die? The fact that Jesus was both man, (who can die), and God, (who cannot die), was not understood, and so they were left in the dark. John then leads on to another illustration of the conflict between light and darkness, where of course, Jesus is the Light of the world.[3]

> John 12:35-36 [35] Then Jesus said unto them, Yet a little while is the light with you. Walk while ye have the light, lest darkness come upon you: for he that walketh in darkness knoweth not whither he goeth.
>
> [36] While ye have the light, believe in the light, that ye may be children of the light.

The Jews had already been offered eternal life, not the nation as a whole, that was being reserved for Christ's second coming, but believing Jewish individuals would be given eternal life now, and so Jesus asked them to walk in the light and believe Him before He left them. Time was getting short.

> John 12:37 But though he had done so many miracles before them, yet they believed not on him.

The unbelief of the Jews had been prophesied 700 hundred years before by the prophet Isaiah,[4] after he had seen the glory of God.[5]

> John 12:39-41 [39] Therefore they could not believe, because that Esaias [Isaiah] said again,
>
> [40] He hath blinded their eyes, and hardened their heart; that they should not see with their eyes, nor understand with their heart, and be converted, and I should heal them.
>
> [41] These things said Esaias [Isaiah], when he saw his glory, and spake [spoke] of him.

John then added his own observation which is very sad.

> John 12:42-43 [42] Nevertheless among the chief rulers also many believed on him; but because of the Pharisees they did not confess him, lest they should be put out of the synagogue:

⁴³ For they loved the praise of men more than the praise of God.

Many Jews, even from among the religious leaders, knew in their hearts that Jesus was the Messiah, but they were too cowardly, too afraid to say so in public, because if they did, the Pharisees would stop them from going to the synagogue.[6] Looking for glory for themselves, they preferred to be praised by the unbelieving men from the synagogue, rather than to praise God for His Son and give the glory to Him. The lesson for us is not to be afraid like them to tell others that we are believers in Jesus,[7] and to never try and make ourselves famous among true believers, who are the true Church. If any of us are ever used by Jesus for the benefit of His Church it will be for His glory, not ours.[8]

[1] Luke 3:22, 9:35, John 12:28

[2] John 8:23S

[3] John 8:12

[4] Isaiah 6:9-10

[5] Isaiah 6:1-3

[6] John 9:22, 12:42, 16:2

[7] Revelation 21:7-8

[8] Luke 17:10

JESUS TELLS IT LIKE IT IS
John 12:44-50

1. Everyone who believes in Jesus believes in God, and everyone who has seen Jesus has seen God (John 12:44-45).
2. Jesus was sent by God the Father (John 12:44).
3. Jesus is light, something very important to John who wrote this gospel and these words of Jesus, "I am come a light into the world, that whosoever believeth on me should not abide in darkness" (John 12:46).

4. Everyone that believes in Jesus no longer needs to wander about in the dark, and can find the way out of the darkness into the light of eternal life (John 12:46).
5. Everyone that rejects Jesus and what He said, will be judged according to the words He spoke (John 12:48).

THE POWER OF GOD IS RELEASED THROUGH PRAYER
Matthew 21:19-22, Mark 11:19-26

The date was now the 11th of Nissan in the week of the crucifixion, equivalent on our calendar to, Monday 3rd April AD 30. The daily routine for Jesus was that He would sleep at Bethany each night, and travel to Jerusalem every day to teach.

Mark 11:19 And when even [evening] was come, he [Jesus] went out of the city.

He slept in Bethany that night and on Tuesday morning travelled back to Jerusalem, passing the fig tree He had cursed the day before, which had withered away.[1]

Matthew 21:20 And when the disciples saw it, they marvelled, saying, How soon [quickly] is the fig tree withered away.

Remember by looking for food on the tree when He was hungry Jesus showed He was human, but when the tree withered away so quickly, He showed He was God.

Mark said that it was Peter who spoke to Jesus about the withered fig tree.

Mark 11:21 And Peter calling to remembrance saith unto him, Master, behold [look] the fig tree which thou cursedst [cursed] is withered away.

Mark often wrote his gospel as if he was familiar with the experiences of Peter. One of the early church leaders, Papias, wrote that Mark was Peter's translator, which would account for his great knowledge of the famous apostle's life.

Jesus used the withered fig tree to teach His disciples about two conditions that are needed for prayers to be answered, the first of which is faith.

> Matthew 21:21 If ye have faith and doubt not.

We will look at the message again more deeply as Mark wrote it.

> Mark 11:22-23 ²² And Jesus answering saith unto them. Have faith in God.
>
> ²³ For verily [truly] I say unto you, That whosoever shall say unto this mountain, Be thou removed, and be thou cast into the sea; and shall not doubt in his heart, but shall believe that those things which he saith shall come to pass; he shall have whatsoever he saith.

The first condition for answered prayer then is faith, and we will make the point again, as we began, with Matthew.

> Matthew 21:22 And all things, whatsoever ye shall ask in prayer, believing, ye shall receive.

This saying of Jesus must be put along side the teaching that everything we ask in prayer must be according to the will of God.[2] Clearly God is not our servant and will not fulfil our prayers if we ask Him to do something which is against His will. The Lord's prayer which Jesus gave as a pattern for His disciples to use when praying, includes the words, "Thy will be done."[3] If what we ask for in prayer is the will of God, and if we believe God will answer our prayer, He will, because of our faith.

The second condition needed for answered prayer is that we must forgive others.

> Mark 11:25 And when ye stand praying, forgive, if ye have ought against any: that your Father which is in heaven may forgive you your trespasses.

The lessons we are to learn from the cursing of the fig tree are, that for our prayers to be answered we need to forgive others before we pray, and have faith in God.

[1] Matthew 21:19
[2] 1 John 5:14-15
[3] Matthew 6:10. Luke 11:2

THE LAMB OF GOD IS SCRUTINIZED AND TESTED
Matthew 21:23 to 22:40, Mark 11:27 to 12:34, Luke 20:1-40

Again, at every Passover, the lamb to be sacrificed was chosen on the 10th day of Nissan and separated out for testing until the 14th of Nissan, to make sure it was perfect before it was slaughtered, and what we are going to see next is the testing of Jesus, the Lamb of God, before He was killed. Jesus was tested four times by various groups or combined groups of people. There were two main reasons for the tests, the first of which was to try and make the people turn against Him, because He was so popular that the Jewish leaders were extremely afraid to arrest Him in front of the crowds.

Another reason for scrutinizing Jesus was that He had not broken any Roman Law, and as only the Romans had the legal power to kill anybody, they needed to show the Romans that Jesus was guilty of a crime that carried the death penalty.

The Priests And Elders Try To Find Fault With The Lamb
Matthew 21:23 to 22:14, Mark 11:27 to 12:12, Luke 20:1-18

The priests were Sadducees and the elders were Pharisees, and these two conflicting groups that held the religious authority, came together to examine Jesus, and what they wanted Him to tell them was, where did He get His authority from.

> Mark 11:28 By what authority doest thou these things? And who gave thee this authority to do these things?

We know from Luke that this attack took place in the temple,[1] while Jesus was teaching and preaching the gospel, because they wanted to put Jesus to shame in front of as many people as possible. According to the Sadducees and Pharisees, no one could teach or preach unless a rabbi had given them authority to do so, and a check of all the rabbinic schools would show that Jesus had not been authorized by any of them, and so their trap was, "Who gave thee authority to do these things?"

Jesus answered them in the typical Jewish way, by asking them another question.

> Luke 20:3-4 ³ And he answered and said unto them, I will also ask you one thing; and answer me:
>
> ⁴ The baptism of John, was it from heaven, or from men?

Jesus had asked them a question like their own, about authority, had John the Baptist baptised by the authority of heaven or the authority of men? Where had John's authority come from? This question turned the tables on them completely, and they were trapped. The people were convinced that John was a prophet, (and prophets are men of God), and if the priests and elders said that John's authority was human, the crowds would turn against them, therefore although they did not approve of John's baptism they were not ready to say so publicly. Alternatively, if they said John's authority came from heaven, then Jesus could say, "My authority came from John," because John, speaking about Jesus had said, "Behold the Lamb of God, that taketh away the sin of the world."[2] Realising after a thorough discussion among themselves that they were stuck which ever way they answered, they finally said that they did not know.[3]

> Luke 20:8 And Jesus said unto them, Neither tell I you by what authority I do these things.

Jesus then told them three parables while the crowd in the temple listened as well.

The parable of the two sons is found in Matthew 21:28-32, and the point of it is that the Pharisees will not be allowed into the kingdom, but sinners will. The story was that there were two brothers and their father asked them to go and do something. The first said he would not obey his father but later he did. The second said he would obey his father but he did not, accordingly, it was the first son who actually did the work and obeyed his father. The Pharisees were like the second son who said the right things but did nothing, while on the other hand the prostitutes and tax-collectors where like the first son who at first refused but then went and did the right thing.

Matthew 21:31-32 [31] Jesus saith unto them, Verily [Truly] I say unto you, That the publicans [tax-collectors] and harlots [prostitutes] go into the kingdom of God before you.

[32] For John [John the Baptist] came unto you in the way of righteousness, and ye believed him not: but the publicans and the harlots believed him: and ye, when ye had seen it [seen that the publicans and harlots had believed John the Baptist was a prophet], repented not afterward, that ye might believe him.

The Pharisees had refused to say where John had got his authority, but here Jesus plainly said it came from heaven. However, the tax-collectors and prostitutes, the two groups of people rejected by the Pharisees as sinners, understood that John's authority was from God, and would be allowed into the kingdom, but the Pharisees who thought they were the most spiritual would be kept out.

The second parable, the parable of the vine-growers, is found in Matthew 21:33-46, Mark 12:1-12 and Luke 20:9-18. It is based upon a parable of Isaiah written 700 years earlier, which identifies the vineyard as the 12 tribes of Israel, and the tribe of Judah as the vine.[4] In the same passage Isaiah also prophesied that the people of Judah (the vine), would not pay attention to the miracles of Jesus (the LORD),[5] and as Jesus is about tell them in His parable also, that they would for that reason be judged and condemned.[6] The point of Jesus' parable of the vine-growers is that the Jewish leaders had killed John the Baptist, the prophet and forerunner of Jesus, and they would soon kill the Son of God.

The vineyard belongs to God, and the Jewish leaders in charge of God's vineyard, are supposed to give Him all He is due. God sent three sets of servants to make the collection but each time the servants of God were rejected with force and even killed.[7]

1. The first set of servants were the prophets that kept warning Israel before God finally fulfilled their prophesies by allowing

the nation to be captured and the people taken as prisoners to Babylon.[8]

2. The second group were the prophets of Israel who prophesied after the Jews returned to Jerusalem from Babylon.[9]
3. The third lot were John the Baptist and his disciples.

All these groups of prophets sent by God over many hundreds of years, had been viciously rejected and in many cases like John, killed. We will follow what would happen after John's death by reading the parable as told by Jesus.

> Luke 20:13-15   ¹³ Then said the lord of the vineyard, What shall I do? I will send my beloved son: it may be they will reverence him when they see him.
>
> ¹⁴ But when the husbandmen saw him, they reasoned among themselves, saying, This is the heir: come, let us kill him, that the inheritance may be ours.
>
> ¹⁵ So they cast him out of the vineyard, and killed him. What therefore shall the lord of the vineyard do unto them?

Of course the parable means that the rulers are going to kill Jesus and the question is what will God (the owner of the vineyard) do to the vine-growers or in other words, the husbandmen.

> Luke 20:16   He shall come and destroy these husbandmen, and shall give the vineyard to others.

Forty years later in AD 70 the city of the great King[10] was destroyed along with over a million Jews, as punishment for the unforgivable sin.

Earlier when we were learning how the crowds shouted out, "Blessed is He that comes in the name of the Lord," during the triumphal entry of Jesus into Jerusalem, we found that their words came from Psalm 118:26, a Psalm prophesying the coming of the Messiah. Earlier in the same messianic Psalm it says in verse 22, "The stone which the builders refused is become the head stone of the corner." The Psalm therefore shows that the Messiah would first of all be refused, but later accepted and will become the, Head Stone of the Corner, which will be after the whole nation has cried in unity, "Blessed is He that comes in the name of the Lord."

> Luke 20:17 And he [Jesus] beheld them and said, What is this then that is written, The stone which the builders rejected, the same is become the head of the corner?

The point of Luke 20:17 is that the prophesy in Psalms had only been fulfilled in part. At the time Jesus spoke, He, the stone, had already been rejected, fulfilling the first part of the prophecy. At His second coming He will become the Head of the Corner, the meaning of which will soon be explained, and then the whole prophecy of Psalm 118:22, will have become fact.

Many believe and teach that God has taken the Millennial Kingdom away from the Jews and given it to the Church, because it says in Luke 20:16, "He shall come and destroy these husbandmen, and give the vineyard to others," but such an idea does not tie in with something Matthew tells us of what Jesus said.

> Matthew 21:43 Therefore say I unto you, The kingdom of God shall be taken away from you, and given to a nation bringing forth the fruits thereof.

Here Jesus has ruled out the Church replacing the Nation of Israel because the kingdom is going to be, "given to a nation bringing forth the fruits thereof," and the Church is not a nation. The nation that will be given the kingdom of God will be the one that cries out, "Blessed is He that comes in the name of the Lord," and that will be the Jewish nation with Jesus, the King of the Jews,[11] also being the Head Stone of the Corner. You may ask, "Isn't Jesus the Head of the Church?" and the answer is, "Yes, He is,"[12] and when the Jews have accepted their King, He will also be the Head of the Corner, that joins the Jews and the Church together under One Head.[13] To this day however, the Jews have not changed their position and as far as their nation is concerned, Jesus still remains the Stone that the builders reject.

Another aspect of Jesus as a stone concerns individual people, not the nation as a whole, and this was prophesied by Isaiah.

> Isaiah 8:14-15 14 And he shall be a sanctuary; but for a stone of stumbling and for a rock of offence to both the houses of

Israel, for a gin [trap] and a snare to the inhabitants of Jerusalem.

¹⁵ And many among them shall stumble, and fall, and be broken, and be snared, and taken.

Isaiah meant that Jesus would be a sanctuary, a place of safety, for those Jews that accepted Him, but for unbelievers he would be a stumbling stone, something they would trip up on, causing them to fall down. He would also be a rock of offence, that would take the offensive and attack His enemies. How they tripped on the Stone was by not believing Jesus when He told them He was their Messiah, that was their downfall, and the consequence was that the Stone would later take action against them. He, Jesus, the Rock of Offence did this in AD 70 with the destruction of Jerusalem.

Luke 20:18 Whosoever shall fall upon that stone shall be broken; but on whomsoever it shall fall, it will grind him to powder.

Although Jesus spoke in parables so that the people would not understand, in this case, because He had spoken about Old Testament prophesies, He was understood.

Matthew 21:45 And when the chief priests and Pharisees had heard these parables they perceived that he spake about them.

Mark 12:12 And they sought to lay hold on him, but feared the people: for they knew that he had spoken the parable against them: and went their way.

The religious leaders had attacked Jesus in the Temple in front of the crowds, but it was they that had to leave in defeat.

The third parable, the marriage of the king's son, is only found in Matthew 22:1-14. The parable stresses the fact that the people invited to the marriage, such as the Pharisees, would not actually attend the wedding feast, although many others would. The wedding feast in this parable and later ones is a picture of the Messianic Kingdom, and the first invitation was given by John the Baptist, when he said, "Repent ye: for the kingdom of heaven is at hand."[14] In other words, "Make sure you are ready." Invitations were also given out by servants which included the disciples of John the Baptist and the disciples of Jesus, but the Pharisees and their friends always argued and gave reasons why they would not accept their invitation, making the king in the parable very angry.

The rejection by the Jewish leadership of the invitation to the kingdom, and their decision instead to kill the King, resulted in the destruction and burning of Jerusalem, which happened as we keep saying in AD 70.

> Matthew 22:7-8 ⁷ But when the king heard thereof, he was wroth: and sent forth his armies, and destroyed those murderers, and burned up their city.
>
> ⁸ Then saith he to his servant, The wedding is ready, but they which were bidden [invited] were not worthy.

After the destruction of the invited guests and their city, others would be invited to the wedding feast.

> Matthew 22:9 Go ye therefore into the highways, and as many as ye shall find, bid to the marriage.

The invitation will keep on going out and eventually it will be given to the generation of Jews living during the great tribulation,[15] and after they have accepted, the wedding hall will be filled with guests.

> Matthew 22:10 So those servants went out into the highways, and gathered together as many as they found, both bad and good: and the wedding was furnished [supplied] with guests.

The king then took action against one of his wedding guests, which is often misunderstood as being brutal, because he saw a man who was not wearing the right clothes, or garment for the occasion.

> Matthew 22:13 Then said the king to the servants, Bind him hand and foot, and take him away, and cast him into the outer darkness; there shall be weeping and gnashing of teeth.

All the guests invited to a Jewish wedding at the time of Jesus were provided with the right wedding clothes by the host, everyone, whether rich or poor looked the same for the feast. Returning to the parable, the wedding garment was a symbol of righteousness,[16] and therefore the man without the right clothes had refused to wear the clothes provided. Maybe he thought his own clothes were better than the ones he was offered, but no matter how good we think we are, none of us can get into heaven because of our own righteousness,[17] we must receive our righteousness as gift from God,[18] because only His righteousness is good enough. The "outer darkness" and the "gnashing of teeth" are used elsewhere in the Bible to describe the fire of Hell.[19]

[1] Luke 20:1-2

[2] John 1:29

[3] Luke 20:5-7

[4] Isaiah 5:7

[5] Isaiah 5:12

[6] Isaiah 5:14

[7] Matthew 21:34-36

[8] Psalm 137

[9] Ezra 1

[10] Psalm 48:2, Matthew 5:35

[11] Matthew 2:2, 21:5, 27:37, Mark 15:9, 15:18, 15:26, Luke 23:38, John 12:13, 12:15, 18:39, 19:3, 19:14, 19:15, 19:19, 19:21-22

[12] Colossians 1:18

[13] Ephesians 2:12-20

[14] Matthew 3:2

[15] Matthew 24:21, Mark 13:19

[16] Revelation 19:8

[17] Romans 3:10

[18] Romans 3:21-22, 2 Corinthians 5:21, Philippians 3:9

[19] Matthew 13:42, and 50

The Pharisees And Herodians Unite To Attack The Lamb Of God
Matthew 22:15-22, Mark 12:13-17, Luke 20:20-26

It was unusual for the Pharisees, who were absolutely against any kind of Roman government, to unite with the Herodians, who fully supported Roman rule through the family of Herod. The reason they united was because they both feared and hated Jesus. The priests and elders had failed to find fault with the authority of Jesus, and so this time the question was political. The idea was to make Jesus do or say something against the government that would make the Romans angry so that they could execute Him.

> Mark 12:13-14 ^{13} And they send unto him certain of the Pharisees and of the Herodians, to catch [trap] him in his words.
>
> ^{14} And when they were come they said unto him, Master, ... Is it lawful to give tribute [tax] to Caesar, or not?

If He said, "Yes, you should pay taxes to Caesar," the crowds would get angry and turn against Jesus, but if He said, "No, you should not pay taxes to Caesar," the Romans would be furious. Jesus knew it was a trap and asked to see a coin.

> Mark 12:16 And they brought it. And he saith unto them, Whose is this image [picture] and superscription [name written on the coin]? And they said unto him, Caesar's.

Jesus then answered their question.

> Matthew 22:21 Then saith he unto them, Render [pay back] therefore unto Caesar the things which are Caesar's; and unto God the things that are God's.

The Roman coin they had brought to Jesus, according to Jewish law, could not be used to pay the Temple tax, but it could be used to pay

Roman taxes. The answer Jesus gave could not be used against Him by either the religious Pharisees or the Herodian politicians.

> Luke 20:26 And they could not take hold of his words [trap Him with His own words] before [in front of] the people: and they marvelled [were amazed] at his answer, and held their peace [were silent].

The Attack From The Sadducees
Matthew 22:23-33, Mark 12:18-27, Luke 20:27-40

The challenge here was about religion, and it had to do with the resurrection of the dead. The Pharisees believed in a future resurrection but the Sadducees did not, that is why preachers like to joke that without any hope of the resurrection the Sadducees were, sad-you-see. They liked to ask difficult questions about the resurrection to the Pharisees, to make them look stupid, and then have a good old laugh at them, and so they tried one of these on Jesus, but before they asked their question they told Him the following story.

A woman married a man who died before she had any children, so according to the Law of Moses, she married her dead husband's brother.[1] Her second husband also died before she had any children, so she married another brother, and kept on marrying all the seven brothers in the family without ever having a baby from any one of them. Eventually the last brother died, but let's see how the Sadducees finished their story and asked their question to Jesus.

> Luke 20:32-33 [32] Last of all the woman died also.
>
> [33] Therefore in the resurrection whose wife of them is she? For seven had her to wife.

I am a bit suspicious about this woman, and sorry for the younger bothers that married her in order not to break the Law of Moses. However, Jesus did not talk about that side of the story but kept His answer strictly in line with the question He had been asked.

> Matthew 22:29 Jesus answered and said unto them, Ye do err, not knowing the scriptures, nor the power of God.

The question the Sadducees had asked showed Jesus two things, first they did not understand the Scriptures, and secondly they did not know about the power of God, and because of this, He answered them by explaining three things.

The first thing Jesus told the Sadducees they were wrong about was that they very much underestimated God's power.

> Luke 20:34-36   34 And Jesus answering said unto them, The children of this world marry, and are given in marriage:
>
> 35 But they that shall be accounted worthy to obtain that world, and the resurrection of the dead, neither marry, nor are given in marriage:
>
> 36 Neither can they die any more: for they are equal unto the angels; and are children of God, being the children of the resurrection.

Matthew made it clear that Jesus said that those of us that are resurrected will be like the angels in heaven, which is very good to know because the Devil and his angels will end up in Hell,[2] and some very wicked ones are already imprisoned in the deep, also called the abyss, as we learned in, The Kings Power Over Demons, of Chapter 6, but people that are resurrected by the power of God to eternal life will be like the angels in heaven.

> Matthew 22:30   For in the resurrection they neither marry, nor are given in marriage, but are as the angels of God in heaven.

The resurrection will not be an awakening of the dead back to this kind of life, it will be an absolutely amazing change to something much higher, eternal life, and the Sadducees did not understand the power of God, which will cause us to be completely transformed altogether into an infinitely superior life form.

> 1 Corinthians 15:52-53   52 In a moment, in the twinkling of an eye, at the last trump [blast of the trumpet]: for the trumpet

shall sound, and the dead shall be raised incorruptible, and we shall be changed.

⁵³ For this corruptible must put on incorruption, and this mortal must put on immortality.

In our next life then, there will be no death, with no need for children and no need to marry, and so we will not be married, but we will be like the angels in heaven. In the Bible every time it talks about a heavenly angel, it always, always talks about his appearing as a strong young man, so if any of the members of the feminist movement believe Jesus and trust Him for eternal life, they will then get full equality.

The second thing Jesus told the Sadducees they were wrong about was God's covenant with Abraham, they did not understand Scripture.

Matthew 22:31-32 ³¹ But as touching the resurrection of the dead, have ye not read that which was spoken unto you by God, saying,

³² I am the God of Abraham, and the God of Isaac, and the God of Jacob?

In Bible times the Abrahamic covenant was written as it was spoken by Jesus, "I am the God of Abraham, and the God of Isaac, and the God of Jacob," but today we just say, "The Abrahamic covenant." The Sadducees had many doubts about the Jewish Scriptures, but one thing they firmly believed in was the Abrahamic covenant, and that is why Jesus used it to prove His point to them, but how does the Abahamic covenant promise a resurrection?

The resurrection exists in the Abrahamic covenant because of the rule that if God promises something to a person, and the person dies before it is fulfilled, then God will bring that person back to life to carry out His promise. It was for that reason that Abraham, at God's request, was willing to kill Isaac before the covenant had been completed, because he knew that if Isaac died, God would bring him back to life and complete His pledge.[3] To begin with, God made His covenant with Abraham, then He renewed it with Abraham's son, Isaac, and then renewed it again with Isaac's son, Jacob, and to all three men He said the same thing.

> Genesis 13:15 [God here is speaking to Abraham]. For all the land which thou seest, to thee [you] will I give it, and to thy seed [descendants] for ever.
>
> Genesis 26:3 [God here is speaking to Isaac]. I will be with thee, and will bless thee; for unto thee [you], and unto thy seed [descendants], I will give all these countries, and I will perform the oath which I sware [guaranteed] unto Abraham thy father.
>
> Genesis 28:13 [God here was speaking to Jacob in a dream]. I am the LORD God of Abraham thy father, and the God of Isaac: the land whereon thou liest [are lying down], to thee [you] will I give it, and to thy seed [descendants].

The land then has been promised, not only to the descendants of these three men, but to each of them personally, to you, you and you, but all of them are dead and they have never owned the land promised to them by God. How are the Patriarchs, Abraham, Isaac and Jacob going to own the land? First they will be resurrected from the dead, and then the land will be restored to the Jewish people, which is why Jesus was able to speak as He did earlier in Matthew's gospel.

> Matthew 8:11 And I say unto you, That many shall come from the east and the west (all over the world), and shall sit down (feast) with Abraham, and Isaac, and Jacob.

We will be in the land because of the resurrection.

The third thing Jesus told the Sadducees they were wrong about was that God has a living relationship with the Patriarchs, which is everlasting. In the following Scripture, Jesus is speaking to the Sadducees.

> Matthew 22: 31-32 [31] But as touching the resurrection of the dead, have ye not read that which was spoken unto you by God in heaven,
>
> [32] I am the God of Abraham, and the God of Isaac, and the God of Jacob? God is not the God of the dead, but of the living.

10 King Jesus Arrives at His City

Abraham, Isaac and Jacob are not dead, they are alive in heaven with God.

There were three results from the attack by the Sadducees.

1. Jesus had shone a new light on Exodus 3:6, and from then on the Scripture was seen to have a much wider meaning.
2. Even the scribes, who belonged mainly to the party of the Pharisees, were amazed and pleasantly surprised, because Jesus had given them support for the resurrection.
3. After this the Sadducees never asked Jesus another question.

The Pharisees, on the other hand, were still looking to win an argument with Jesus over the question of religion, or more correctly, theology, and their subject was, what was the most important commandment?

[1] Deuteronomy 25:5-6

[2] Matthew 25:41

[3] Hebrews 11:17-19

The Fourth Challenge Came From The Pharisees
Matthew 22:34-40, Mark 12:28-34

After the Sadducees had decided not to cross-examine Jesus any more, the Pharisees plotted together to find a way to continue questioning Him.

> Matthew 22:35-36 ³⁵ Then one of them which was a lawyer [an expert in the Law of Moses], asked him a question, tempting [testing] him, and saying,
>
> ³⁶ Master, which is the great commandment in the law?

Jesus answered by telling him more than he had asked, beginning with the greatest commandment from Deuteronomy.

> Deuteronomy 6:4-5 ⁴ Hear, O Israel: The LORD our God is one LORD:

⁵ And thou shalt love the LORD thy God with all thine heart, and with all thy soul, and with all thy might.

Out of the 613 commandments in the Mosaic Law, the most important was to love God in every possible way. Jesus did not stop there, because the second one is important like the first.

Mark 12:31 And the second is like, namely [which is] this, Thou shalt love thy neighbour as thyself.

After giving the two main commandments, Jesus highlighted their importance.

Matthew 22:40 On these two commandments hang all the law and the prophets.

These two commandments are central to the Law and the Prophets because every commandment is either about our association with God, or with men. If we loved God our relationship with Him would always be according to the Law, and if we loved our neighbours as ourselves, our relationship with them again, would also be according to the Law. The religious rules of the Pharisees agree with this, and that is why they were unable to accuse Jesus of anything, in fact in Mark 12:32-33, they fully supported everything He had said, and from then on no one at all tried to trick Him with any more questions.

Mark 12:34 And no man after that durst [dared] ask him any question.

The Lamb of God, after being thoroughly scrutinized and tested, had been found to be perfect, without any fault.

A QUESTION FROM THE KING
Matthew 22:41-46, Mark 12:35-37, Luke 20:41-44

Jesus had just been tested with four questions, and now He asked them one, which they quickly answered.

Matthew 22:42 What think ye of Christ? Whose son is he? They say unto him, The Son of David.

The answer, which they got from the Old Testament[1] was correct, the Messiah would be a descendant of David. Jesus would now put them to the test by reminding them of Psalm 110, which was written by David about the coming Messiah, and in verse one, he calls the Messiah, Lord. The question Jesus asked them was, if the Messiah was David's son, why did David call Him Lord? After all, a father is not usually under the authority of his son, treating him as his lord.

Matthew 22:45 If David then call him Lord, how is he his son?

They had studied the Scriptures very much, especially about the coming Messiah, but they could not answer the question, because we do not understand Bible prophecy through our own efforts, no matter how hard we try.

2 Peter 1:20-21 [20] No prophecy of scripture is of any private interpretation.

[21] For the prophecy came not in old time by the will of man: but holy men of God spake [spoke] as they were moved [led] by the Holy Ghost.

The stumbling block was that Jesus was both a man and God, something the rabbis are unable to accept because, not having the Holy Spirit, they try to interpret prophecies by themselves, and that is why they sometimes get them wrong. As a man Jesus was the son, or descendant of David, through His mother Mary, but as God, He was also the Son of God,[2] and God the Father confirmed this.[3] Unlike the Lamb of God, who passed all the tests, the religious leaders of Israel, failed theirs, a very serious mistake for them.

---

[1] 2 Samuel 7:12-13, 1 Chronicles 17:11-12

[2] Luke 1:34-35

[3] Matthew 3:17, Mark 1:11, Luke 3:22

THE JEWISH LEADERS ARE JUDGED BY THEIR KING
Matthew 23:1-39, Mark 12:38-40, Luke 20:45-47

The judgement is given in detail by Matthew, but only briefly in the other two synoptic gospels, and so we will be looking mostly at Matthew. Jesus finished His teaching to the public with this long condemnation at the Feast of Passover, three years after He began at the time of the same feast. After this final talk to the crowds that had gathered for the yearly celebration, He only spoke to His apostles until His arrest, which led on to His trial, death, resurrection and ascension into heaven.

In this judgement Jesus uses strong words against the Jewish leaders, and some preachers make use of it to teach that the New Testament is anti-Semetic, but two points of clarification should be remembered.

1. Jesus was not condemning the Jewish crowds, only their leaders.
2. Remember that in the Old Testament, the teachings of the major and minor prophets, including Isaiah, Ezekiel, Daniel and especially Jeremiah, condemned the Jewish leaders time and time again for leading the people astray and causing the judgement of God to fall on the nation. Jesus was continuing the established method of the Old Testament prophets of holding the leaders responsible for the coming judgement.

Jesus Talks About The Pharisees
Matthew 23:1-12, Mark 12:38-40, Luke 20:45-47

To start with Jesus, as He had done before, condemned the Pharisees as hypocrites, which they most definitely were.

> Matthew 23:3 All therefore whatsoever they bid you observe [abide by], that observe and do; but do not ye after their works [actions]: for they say, and do not.

Verses two and three are often misunderstood, because they have been used to teach that we should obey everything the rabbis say, so here is verse two with the first part of verse three repeated again.

> Matthew 23:2-3 ² The scribes and the Pharisees sit in Moses seat:
>
> ³ All therefore whatsoever they bid you observe [abide by], that observe and do.

We have already seen, time and again that Jesus deliberately broke the laws of the Pharisees, when their law was different from God's Law, which was the Law given by God through Moses. If Jesus meant that we should keep the rabbis laws when He refused to do so, then He would have been a hypocrite. The misunderstanding comes from the term, Moses seat. The synagogue served three purposes, worship, education and government of the civil life of the community.

Moses seat was where a local judge would sit to listen to cases concerning civil law, not religious law, brought by members of the community, just as Moses used to judge the people after the Jews left Egypt.[1] An example of Moses seat can be seen in Israel among the ruins of the town of Chorazin, at the, Black Basalt Synagogue, made of the rock commonly found there. The civil law was case law, based on previous cases brought before the courts, and the Pharisees would sit on the seat of Moses and make judgements based on the established laws and cases. They could not make new laws or cancel old ones but made judgements according to the civil law, as magistrates do in our magistrates' courts today. It was those cases that came before the judges sitting on the seat of Moses, that Jesus said should be obeyed, just like we have to obey the judgements handed down in our magistrates' courts. Jesus did not mean we had to obey the laws of the rabbis, because He refused to do that Himself.

The next thing Jesus said about the Pharisees was that they forced others to keep the rules of the Mishnah, but invented ways not to keep the same rules themselves.

> Matthew 23:4 For they bind heavy burdens and grievous [back breaking] to be borne [carried], and lay them on men's

shoulders; but they themselves will not move them with one of their fingers.

Notice the use of the word, "bind," which is not used in the sense of binding Satan or demons, but it means those things which the Mishnah forbids.

Another thing Jesus had to say about the Pharisees was that they were selfish and self-righteous. He admitted that they did keep some of the requirements of the Law of Moses, but in the wrong way and for the wrong purpose. The main reason they obeyed the Law was to impress men and women, not to please God, as Jesus clearly revealed.

Matthew 23:5 But all their works they do for to be seen by men: they make broad their phylacteries, and enlarge the borders of their garments.

The phylacteries were the little boxes that the orthodox Jews still put on their foreheads and arms in accordance with the Mosaic law.[2] By wearing the boxes they were keeping the Law, but broadening their phylacteries means that they made their boxes much too big, making sure they could be seen. At the borders of their garments the Law required that they were to wear tassels with one blue cord in them,[3] and again they made them much too long so that they would be sure to be noticed.

The idea of obeying the commandments was to show God that they loved Him, the same reason that we obey Jesus, as He said.

John 14:15 If ye love me, keep my commandments.

The Pharisees kept some parts of the Law because they were self-righteous and self-centred, not God-centred.

Jesus had still more to say about the Pharisees, they loved men to call them by exalting titles, such as Rabbi, Father and Master, such titles were religious in character, and so Father referred to a religious father, not to a person's dad. The power of these titles was tremendous and a Rabbi would have more authority over his disciple than the man's dad, so that if the father of a rabbi's disciple was in need, no help could be given unless the Rabbis' need had been met first. The Rabbi decided who his disciple worked for and who he married, he was in fact, the most important person in a disciple's life, and Jesus was against the system.

> Matthew 23:12 And whosoever shall exalt himself shall be abased; and he that shall humble himself shall be exalted.

The fifth and final thing Jesus had to say about the Pharisees is that they perverted and corrupted their religion by hiding their greed. Widows when they lost their husband also lost his income, and often got into debt, and to recover this the Pharisees, cast the poor women out of their homes. However, in order to show other men how righteous they were, before they expelled the poor woman from her home, they prayed long prayers in public for her well-being, happiness and safety.

> Mark 12:40 Which devour [dispose of] widows' houses, and for a pretence make long prayers: these shall receive greater damnation.

The Law of Moses was clear, widows should be well cared for and not taken advantage of,[4] even being provided with money from the tithes due to God.[5] James the half-brother of Jesus, described pure religion as looking after orphans and widows, and not following the ways of the world,[6] but the Pharisees' religion was a pretence and their actions wicked.

[1] Exodus 18:13-16

[2] Deuteronomy 6:8

[3] Numbers 15:38, Deuteronomy 22:12

[4] Exodus 22:22-24, Deuteronomy 14:29, 24:19-21, 27:19

[5] Deuteronomy 26:12-13

[6] James 1:27

Jesus Talks To The Pharisees Delivering Seven Woes
Matthew 23:13-36

Having said five things about the Pharisees, Jesus goes on by speaking directly to them, declaring seven coming judgements because of six sins, the first and last judgements being for the same sin. The judgements are known as the seven woes.

The first woe was coming because they had rejected Jesus as the Messiah.

> Matthew 23:13 But woe unto you scribes and Pharisees, hypocrites! For you shut up the kingdom of heaven against men: for you neither go in yourselves, neither suffer ye them that are entering to go in.

Moreover they were guilty of leading the nation to reject the Messiah also.

The second awaiting woe was for turning their followers into people that thought God would be satisfied if they kept a set of religious rules,[1] through forcing them to learn and keep the oral laws of the Mishnah.

> Matthew 23:15 Woe unto you, scribes and Pharisees, hypocrites! For ye compass [travel] sea and land to make one proselyte [follower], and when he is made, ye make him twofold [twice] more the child of hell than yourselves.

The third woe they had waiting for them was because they gave more religious importance to the ordinary things of the world that had been donated to God, than they did to God Himself, to His altar or to His Temple. Jesus showed this by repeating some of their religious rules and customs.

> Matthew 23:16 Woe unto you, ye blind guides, which say, Whosoever shall swear by the temple, it is nothing; but whosoever shall swear by the gold of the temple, he is a debtor.

They taught that anyone making a promise on the authority of the Temple did not have to keep it, but if their promise was on the authority of the gold in the Temple, then they had to keep it. Gold is gold wherever it is, but what made the gold in the Temple special was that it belonged to God.

> Matthew 23:17 Ye fools and blind: for whether [which] is greater, the gold, or the temple that sanctifieth [sets aside for God, making holy] the gold?

They also taught that you did not have to keep your promise made on the authority of the altar, but you did have to keep a promise made on the authority of the sacrifice being offered on the altar. The dead animal body on the altar was the same as any other dead body, but because it had been sacrificed on the altar it belonged to God, and if it had not been put on the altar, it would not have belonged to God.

> Matthew 23:18-19 [18] [You fools who say], whosoever shall swear by the altar, it is nothing; but whosoever sweareth by the gift that is upon it, he is guilty.
>
> [19] Ye fools and blind: for whether [which] is greater, the gift, or the altar that santifieth [sets aside for God, making holy] the gift?

They were guilty of putting the things given to God, that had been accepted and blessed by Him, before Him, before His altar or His Temple, through which the blessing had been given.

The fourth woe was approaching them because they paid more attention to the trivial or least important parts of the law, while not bothering to keep the most important key points at all. Some of the smallest agricultural seeds known in Israel at the time of Jesus were the herbs of mint, dill and cummin. Although the Mosaic Law required tithing the Talmud states that the tithing of herbs was from the rabbis, meaning it was from the oral law, and Jesus had something to say about the practice.

Matthew 23:23 Woe unto you, scribes and Pharisees, hypocrites! For ye pay the tithe of mint and anise and cummin, and have omitted the weightier [more important] matters of the law, judgement, mercy, and faith:

Nevertheless, they had not been wrong to tithe the herbs because Jesus went on to say, "these [less important matters of the law] ought ye to have done, and not to leave the other undone." They ignored the major points of the law but were very fussy about keeping the minor points.

The fifth woe coming their way, detailed in Matthew 23:25-26, was because they were careful to keep the visible points of law but not the hidden parts. Jesus said they washed the outside of the cup but not the inside, meaning that anything put in their cup would become spoiled. They needed to concentrate on keeping the Law totally, not just the parts other people could see, otherwise all their efforts would be of no use.

Notice that between the third and fifth woe, Jesus said they were blind five times.

1. Verse 16, "blind guides."
2. Verse 17, "Ye fools and blind."
3. Verse 19, "Ye fools and blind."
4. Verse 24, "Ye blind guides."
5. Verse 26, "Thou blind Pharisee."

The sixth woe was because they were hypocrites, (pretending to be good when they were not). In Israel, even today, sepulchres, (burial tombs) are still whitened every year as they were in the time of Jesus. The priests of the tribe of Levi, namely those with the surname Cohen must not come in contact with tombs because it would make them ceremonially unclean, and the tombs are whitewashed to make them clearly visible. The whitened tombs look nice and clean on the outside, but inside are the rotting corpses of the dead.

Matthew 23:27-28 Woe unto you scribes and Pharisees, hypocrites! For ye are like unto whited sepulchres, which indeed appear beautiful outward, but are within full of dead men's bones, and of all uncleanness.

[28] Even so ye outwardly appear righteous unto men, but within ye are full of hypocrisy and iniquity [wickedness].

The fact of the matter is that keeping sets of laws and agreements made by men, (no matter if they are church based or Jewish from the Mishnah), does not change the nature of us on the inside, it only makes us look spiritual and religious from the outside.

The seventh woe, like the first was for rejecting their Messiah, in particular because they had not accepted the predictions about the Messiah made by their own prophets. The words of Jesus are found in Matthew 23:29-36, and we see that He held them answerable for all the blood of all the prophets in the Old Testament. How could that be? The Old Testament writings had been completed more than four and a half centuries before the time of Jesus.

In rejecting Jesus as the Messiah they rejected the words the prophets had written about Him. Many people think that the orthodox Jews believe in the Old Testament prophets, but obviously they do not because they refuse to accept Jesus as the Messiah, and in so doing they are denying the words of the prophets. Jesus proved His claim to be the Messiah by many, many miracles and signs, just as the prophets had said, including also those signs that the Pharisees had openly taught the people, only the Messiah would ever be able to do.

In Matthew 23:35, Jesus named Abel and Zechariah, and we need to remember that although the Jewish Old Testament has the same books in it as our Old Testament, they are in a different order. The first book in the Jewish order is Genesis, where Abel is written about, and the last book is, 2 Chronicles, where we find Zechariah, and so when Jesus says they are responsible for the blood of all the prophets from Abel to Zechariah, He means all the prophets from the start to the finish of the Jewish Old Testament. Jesus summed up the seven woes as coming on, "this generation," those guilty of the unforgivable sin, and of not believing the words of the prophets recorded in the Scriptures, that had been given to them by God.

> Matthew 23:36 Verily [Truly] I say unto you, All these things [seven woes] shall come upon this generation.

[1] Romans 9:30-32

The Lament Over The City Of Jerusalem
Matthew 23:37-39

For over three years Jesus had walked the length and breadth of the land, telling the Jews and the nation to accept Him as their Messiah, so that He could reign as King in the City of Jerusalem, and look after them forever as the prophets have said He will, but for the time being it was not to be, and so Jesus lamented.

> Matthew 23:37 O Jerusalem, Jerusalem, thou that killest the prophets, and stonest them which are sent unto thee, how often would I have gathered thy children together, even as a hen gathereth her chickens under her wings, and ye would not!

By rejecting their Messiah they had decided to do without His protection, thinking they could manage very well on their own. He wanted them to look to Him for safety, but they, "would not."

> Matthew 23:38 Behold, your house [the Jewish Temple] is left unto you desolate.

It would be destroyed 40 years later in AD 70.

> Matthew 23:39 For I say unto you, Ye shall not see me henceforth, till ye shall say, Blessed is he that cometh in the name of the Lord.

Remember when we were talking about His triumphal entry into Jerusalem, at His coming as Messiah they must call out, "Blessed is He that cometh in the name of the Lord!" In verse 39 Jesus told them that before He returns as Messiah, they must cry out those same words from the Temple as the prophet wrote in Psalm 118:26. The point is that as the religious leaders of Israel led the people against their Messiah, only after they turn around and lead the people to accept Jesus, will He return again at the second coming.

I will repeat what I just said because it is important for us to know. The second coming of Jesus will not happen until the Jewish religious leaders teach the Jews that Jesus is the Messiah and make them cry out from the Temple in Jerusalem,[1] "Blessed is He that comes in the name of the Lord!" This of course means that the Jews will rebuild the Temple, and I would expect the Muslims to object strongly because their Mosque, called the Dome of the Rock is standing on the Temple site. Another pointer from the Bible that the Temple will be rebuilt, in addition to Psalm 118:26, is found in Revelation 11:1-2, where John in a vision was asked to measure the Temple. John saw and wrote down the vision on the Isle of Patmos, where he had been imprisoned in his old age,[2] around about AD 95, and he would have known that the Temple had already been destroyed in AD 70. In order to measure the Temple, then obviously another one would have to be built.

It is helpful if we realise that Satan knows Scripture, and therefore if he could stop the Jews calling out, "Blessed is He that comes in the name of the Lord," from the Temple in Jerusalem, then Jesus would not come again, and Satan would remain free forever. It is because of this that Satan hates the Jews and those Christians that have been given eternal life, resulting in persecution of Christians and Jews. Anti-Semitism or hatred of Jews is not logical and yet history is full of it, including the crusades, the Spanish inquisition, the Russian pogroms (the organised massacre of Jews and destruction of their homes) and Hitler's holocaust. The reason for all this is that the destruction of the Jews would prevent the second coming of the Lord Jesus Christ.

In this lament Jesus, in making such a precondition for His homecoming to Jerusalem, showed that before He returns, Israel would be a nation again led by Jewish people. He ended His teaching where He began it, in John 2:13-17, in the Jerusalem Temple.

---

[1] Psalm 118:26

[2] Revelation 1:9-11

THE OUTWARD AND INWARD KEEPING OF THE LAW
Mark 12:41-44, Luke 21:1-4

The way out of the Temple was through the treasury, which contained thirteen large chests where offerings were put. On His way out Jesus stopped to watch people putting their money in the chests, and then gave His disciples a lesson on the outward and inward keeping of the Law. Many rich men and women were putting large amounts of money into the boxes, and this would have made a strong impression on those watching, but then a widow came along and put in two mites, (the minimum amount allowed, you could not put in less than that). Anyone watching may have thought the widow was being stingy, compared to the rich folk, but Jesus knew how much money each person owned.

> Mark 12:43-44 ⁴³ And he called unto him his disciples, and saith [said] unto them, Verily [Truly] I say unto you, That this poor widow hath cast [paid] more in, than all they which have cast [paid] into the treasury:
>
> ⁴⁴ For all they did cast [pay] in of their abundance [large amount]; but she of her want [what she needed] did cast [pay] all that she had.

The widow after paying her two mites into the treasury had nothing left, meaning that she was trusting God to come to her help, and if He did not help her she would go without the things she needed. She kept the Law inwardly, not for everyone to see, and so which of all the offerings do you think was most pleasing to God?

11

THE PROPHECIES OF JESUS

The prophecies we will be finding out about next, are usually together called, The Olivet Discourse, because Jesus made them while leaving the Temple and when He was sitting down on the Mount of Olives, with His disciples, looking towards the Temple.[1] In the previous chapter Jesus made it known to the Jews that He would not return to them again until they cried out, "Blessed is He that comes in the name of the Lord!" In this chapter He shows the pressures that will become more and more intense until Israel is finally convinced that it must make that cry for help. At the end of Chapter 9, there was a section called, The Delayed Kingdom Of God, and in the Olivet Discourse we are told how that delayed kingdom, the Messianic Kingdom is going to begin.

Jesus is often spoken of as, Prophet, Priest and King, although He did/does/will not function as all three at the same time, but one after the other. At His first coming He was a prophet, getting information directly from God, telling the people of His day God's will for them, and predicting future events. After He had been crucified and had ascended into heaven He became our High Priest,[2] proclaiming us to be righteous before God the Father. It might go something like this, Satan says to God, "John Newcater is a sinner, because he has done this, that and the other, and that is why he must join me in Hell." Jesus says, "John believed in Me in 1983."[3] God says to Satan, "Case dismissed. John is righteous."

Jesus was a prophet, He is High Priest, and after His second coming He will be King of the Jews and King of the World, as we are about to find out.

[1] Matthew 24:1&3, Mark 13:1&3

[2] Hebrews 7:21-25

[3] John 1:12, 3:18, 8:24

THE SETTING FOR THE OCCASION
Matthew 24:1-2, Mark 13:1-2, Luke 21:5-6

As Jesus was leaving the Temple complex for the last time, His disciples asked Him to look at the Temple buildings, which were destroyed in AD 70, except for the Wailing Wall, which is still there today.

> Matthew 24:1 And Jesus went out, and departed from the temple: and his disciples came to him for to shew [show] him the buildings of the temple.

The disciples were very impressed with the stones in the walls of the temple buildings.

> Mark 13:1 Master, see what manner of stones and what buildings are here.

> Luke 21:5 And some spoke of the temple, how it was adorned with goodly stones, and gifts.

The Temple had been built about 20 BC, but the whole building complex was not completed until 84 years later in 64 AD, and at the time of Jesus there was a lot of building work still going on in the Temple compound, which King Herod was organizing to please the Jews. The stones that were of interest are known by archaeologists as the Herodian stones, and were some of the largest being used for construction work in Israel at the time, measuring up to ten feet long and weighing as much as ten tons. Visitors to Israel today can see some of these stones, especially along the south wall, and they are still very imposing, so we can imagine how impressed the disciples must have been, at the massive strength and solid construction of the heavily built Temple. It was at this point that Jesus made a detailed prophecy.

> Matthew 24:2 Verily [Truly] I say unto you, There shall not be left here one stone upon another, that shall not be thrown down.

Before he attacked Jerusalem in AD 70, which was God's judgement for the unforgivable sin, General Titus told his soldiers not to damage the Temple, but in the heat of the battle, a soldier threw a burning torch into the building causing the wall coverings to catch fire. The walls inside were covered with gold, which melted in the intensely burning fire and flowed into the crevices between the stones. After the fire had died down the soldiers moved all the stones to get to the gold, which had by then hardened in between them and underneath the bottom row. The prophecy made by Jesus forty years earlier then came true, because no stone was left upon another, all were thrown down. The prophecy that no stone would be left upon another, raised three questions in the minds of four of the disciples.

THREE QUESTIONS FROM FOUR APOSTLES
Matthew 24:3, Mark 13:3-4, Luke 21:7

The questions were all asked in such a way that each was also a request for a sign, but notice Jesus answered the questions sitting down, which was how rabbis taught their disciples, and it emphasises the importance of what He said.

> And as he sat upon the mount of Olives.
>
> Matthew 24:3

The questions came from two pairs of brothers, and they were made privately, apart from the other disciples.

> Mark 13:3 And as he sat upon the mount of Olives over against [opposite] the temple, Peter and James and John and Andrew asked him privately.

Peter and Andrew were brothers and so were James and John. The questions are given in Matthew 24:3.

1. "Tell us, when shall these things be?"
2. "What shall be the sign of thy coming?"
3. "And of the end of the world [age]?"

It is obvious that the last two of these questions are asking for a sign, but so was the first, which we can see by turning to Luke's gospel.

> Luke 21:7 Master, but when shall these things be? And what sign will there be when these things shall come to pass.

I want to put these questions in a way that makes it easier for us to understand, but before I do we need to know that the Jews spoke about two ages, this age – the age we are living in, and the age to come – the messianic age, which will last for a thousand years.[1] The three questions in other words.

1. What will be the sign that Jerusalem and the Temple are about to be destroyed, that is the destruction of AD 70?
2. What will be the sign that the second coming is about to happen?
3. What will be the sign of the end of this age and the beginning of the thousand years of peace?

All these questions will be answered by Jesus in His Olivet discourse, that is to say in this chapter, but not in the order, one, two and three. He answered the last question first, then the first question and finally the second question. Another thing is that we need to look at all three synoptic gospels to get the answers, because Matthew and Mark do not answer the first question at all.

---

[1] Revelation 20:6

FEATURES OF THIS AGE WHICH INCLUDES THE TIME OF THE CHURCH
Matthew 24:4-6, Mark 13:6-7, Luke 21:8-9

Jesus begins by talking about the last question first, giving two features of our time, without telling us what signs will tell us the age is coming to its end. The first feature He gives of the age we are living in is not a sign of the end of the period.

> Matthew 24:5 For many shall come in my name, saying, I am Christ; and shall deceive many.

During the whole time of the Church on earth there will be false-messiahs, they will be a sign of the age, but not of its ending. The first person in history that claimed to be the Jewish Messiah, was Jesus of Nazareth. Since then many Jews have claimed to be the Jewish Messiah, the last and most famous being Jacob Frank of Poland, in the eighteenth century who said he was the reincarnation of King David, and of Sabbati Levi, a false messiah of the seventeenth century.

The number of Gentile false messiahs has been tremendous, and one with many followers at the moment is the Reverend Sun Myuang Moon. Born in North Korea, Moon has said he is the Second Coming of Christ, the Saviour, and the returning Lord, and is founder of the Unification Church. Going back to Chapter 6, and the parable of the mustard seed, Moon can be identified as one of the birds resting in the tree, which represents Christendom, and from the parable of the sower, we know the birds eat up the seed, which represents the Word of God. Moon by lying to his followers is preventing them from hearing the truth, and so the seed never gets planted in their hearts. Like both Sabbati Levy, and Jacob Frank before, Moon will soon fade out of the picture.

The second characteristic of the age in which we live is war.

> Matthew 24:6 And ye shall hear of wars and rumours of wars: see that ye be not troubled: for all these things must come to pass, but the end is not yet.

The wars in this prophecy of Jesus are local wars or battles. Many Christians put great significance on certain wars, especially those in the Middle East involving the USA, but local wars are a feature of the age, not the end of it, and the USA has no revealed position in Biblical prophecies. Jesus put these things, false messiahs, wars and rumours of wars, in their correct position of importance by saying, "For all these things must come to pass, but the end is not yet." We next come to a definite sign that the age we are living in now is approaching its end.

A SIGN THAT THE NEXT AGE (WHEN JESUS WILL BE KING OVER ALL THE EARTH) IS DRAWING NEARER
Matthew 24:7-8, Mark 13:8, Luke 21:10-11

> Matthew 24:7-8 7 For nation shall rise against nation, and kingdom against kingdom: and there shall be famines, and pestilences [diseases], and earthquakes, in divers [different] places.
>
> 8 All these things are the beginning of sorrows [birth pangs].

The Greek word which has been translated, "sorrows" in verse 8, was translated, "travail" - of a woman about to give birth in, 1 Thessalonians 5:3 of the King James Bible, but in modern English it simply means, birth pangs. It means the pains a woman feels when she goes into labour before giving birth to a baby. The pains start and stop slowly to begin with and then get faster and faster and more and more painful, with the greatest pain coming at the time the baby is born. The idea comes from Old Testament prophecies that tell about the rebirth of the Jewish nation, prior to the Messianic Age.

Also in verse 8, notice He is speaking about the beginning of birth pangs, the start of it all, that is, "nation against nation, and kingdom against kingdom," which must be different from, "wars and rumours of wars," because Jesus said that they were not a sign of the last days. The Jewish background of Jesus and the apostles is so helpful in understanding what was said. The rabbis would use the words, "nation against nation, and kingdom against kingdom," for a world war. The prophecy of Jesus is that when you see a world war, that will be the first sign that this age is drawing to a close and that Israel will be reborn as a nation. During the rebirth however, the Jewish people will suffer many sorrows before Jesus eventually appears and saves them. It is amazing that there is so much pressure from world powers and institutions being directed against Israel right now. Clearly God's chosen people are a thorn in the side of the rest of the world, because what has happened to them proves God's Word, the Bible, is true and most people do not like to be reminded of that. Also what is happening and what will happen to them will confirm the truth of Scripture again, and will keep on doing so until the return of Christ. Our Bibles are more up to date than next year's newspapers. In the three synoptic gospels the prophecies given in the Olivet Discourse speak of the world or the earth in ten verses[1], showing that Jesus was talking about the world and world war, not just Israel.

The first sign then was, World War 1, of 1914-1918, followed by World War 2, of 1939-1945, which was basically the same war. The importance of both these wars as signs that they are the beginning of birth pangs, is obvious when we see their impact on the Jews and the re-establishment of the nation of Israel in the land of their ancestors. There are many Bible prophecies which tell that the Jews will be scattered around the world and then brought back by God to Israel.[2] Israel and the Jews are the key to understanding Bible prophecy, because it is about them. In World War 1, the Turks were forced out of Israel and the City of Jerusalem, by British forces led by General Allenby. This paved the way for the Jews negotiating with the British to start working for a land of their own. After World War 2, in which it is widely accepted that 6 million Jews were murdered by the German Nazis and their followers, the Jews were desperate for a safe place to live, a land of their own. The United Nations debated the matter and voted in favour of a national homeland for the Jews in Palestine, as a result of which the state of Israel came into existence on the 14th May 1948. The nation was born in a day, just as had been prophesied 2,700 years before by Isaiah.

> Isaiah 66:8 Who hath heard such a thing? Who hath seen such things? Shall the earth be made to bring forth in one day? For as soon as Zion travailed [started her birth pangs], she brought forth her children.

In Matthew 24:7 the first birth pang included, famines, earthquakes and disease. After the 1st World War, there was a very severe famine in China in 1920 which shocked the world, and in which millions of people died. It made such a strong impression that even my Mum, who was a country girl and did not know much about the outside world, always reminded me of it when I was fussy about the poor quality food we were given to eat during the 2nd World War. "Eat it up," she used to say, "Remember the starving in China!" After the famine in China there was another terrible famine in Russia in 1921, and again millions of people died.

There is no doubt that earthquakes are increasing, and the time before and after the 1st World War, of 1914-1918, shows the changing pattern.

1905   India   20,000 dead.

1908   Italy   75,000 dead.

1915   Italy   30,000 dead.

1920   China   180,000 dead.

1923   Japan   143,000 dead.

Another study gave the following findings.

14th century major earthquakes   157

15th century major earthquakes   174

16th century major earthquakes   253

17th century major earthquakes   278

18th century major earthquakes   640

19th century major earthquakes   2,119

20th century nearly 900,000 earthquakes.

It is much easier to detect earthquakes now than it was in the olden days, but that is not the only reason for the differences. The increasing number of quakes is a sign that go along with the sign of world wars, and they tell us we have entered into the last days.

Moving on to diseases, the plague that went along with World War 1, was pneumonia and it continued long after the war, because after the soldiers from the battle fronts returned home, the people in the towns and villages where they returned to caught it and some died. The disease spread rapidly around the globe, reminding us of the way Jesus spoke about the whole world while giving His prophecy. My Dad was a boy in Norfolk at the time, where my Granddad was the village school master, and what impressed them was that the pneumonia kept on killing many strong young men in their late teens, long after victory was won and the soldiers had returned from the war. The notorious disease of World War 2, was tuberculosis, also known as TB, and it continued to be a world wide problem years later. At school I was tested for it like everyone else but to my surprise I was resistant to the disease. The reason was that we kept a herd of cows with TB that I used to help milk by hand, and close contact with the diseased cows, had given me immunity. I was really pleased that I did not have to be vaccinated against TB like the other kids.

It is clear, putting all these things together, that the first sign that Israel as a nation would soon be reborn was World War 1. After the war the realisation of the huge number of young men and women from the British Isles killed in the conflict caused deep sorrow all over the nation, and to make sure future generations would not forget, war memorials were set up across the land, listing the dead, town by town and village by village. To me in addition to being a tribute to those who died, the memorials signalled something the people that built them never thought about but God did. It is that the count down to the re-establishment of a Jewish nation and the second coming of Jesus their King had begun.

536 Heavenly Father Set My Spirit Ablaze

The War Memorial, Mevagissey, Cornwall

A Sign Seen All Over Our Land Reminding Us That Jesus Will Come Again As King Of The Jews, Because It Commemorates The First World War.

Many of these memorials have the cross of Christ at the top, and have inscriptions beginning with the words, "TO THE GLORY OF GOD," and a reference to the Great War of 1914 – 1918, followed by the names of former local residents that were killed. Another inscription often seen is, "LEST WE FORGET." The people that decided on the words, "TO THE GLORY OF GOD," realised that winning the war would not have been possible without the help of the Almighty, and gave God the glory. They are a strong reminder to me that the prophecy made by Jesus at the beginning of this section in Matthew 24:7-8, is being fulfilled now. The words, "To the Glory of God," have added significance because they describe the second coming of Jesus. "And then shall they see the Son of man coming in a cloud with power and great glory" (Luke 21:27).

Now I am going confess the sin of my English people to our God, the God of Abraham, Isaac and Jacob. In past years we were too self righteous. The words on so many war memorials throughout England, "TO THE GLORY OF GOD" imply that God helped us win the Great War because we had more and better Christians, than our enemies. It suggests God gave the victory to us because we were His favourites, therefore He answered our prayers, and so our triumph was to the glory of God. God hates that kind of thinking.[3] The reason God helped and honoured England and her allies win both world wars was because He wanted to use us in His plan to re-establish Israel as a nation according to Bible prophecy. It was not because we were or are a righteous nation. Surely not many people would disagree with that, especially those of us that live here. "Heavenly Father, draw millions, millions, millions and millions, of the people of England and Britain, of every tribe and language here, to Yourself, I plead with You, in the name of the Lord Jesus Christ, the name which is above every name.[4] Amen."[5]

Another thing that was prophetic was the time the First World War ended. The Germans signed the Armistice Agreement, accepting the Allied Armies' terms of surrender, early on the 11th November 1918. The guns fell silent six hours later at 11:00 a.m., that is at the 11th hour of the 11th day of the 11th month. We sometimes say, "It is the eleventh hour," when we are expecting an important event to take place in a very short while. The 1914-1918 War, was one of the birth pangs warning of the coming birth of the Nation of Israel on the 14th May 1948. On that day the Jews were again governing themselves in their land, something they had not done since the time of King Nebuchadnezzar of Babylon who had conquered them about 2,500 years before. Therefore in terms of history, 11 o'clock on the 11th November 1918, really did signify that the Nation of Israel would soon be born.

If the sorrows are going to be like birth pangs that get worse and worse before a baby is born, and if the First World War was the beginning of them, then we would expect them to intensify in the Second World War, and sure enough things got worse, more terrifying, (with the use of atomic bombs), and more inhumane, especially for the Jews, with anti-Semitism reaching new depths of depravity on the biggest ever scale.

Image: Auschwitz: 'A History In Photographs' compiled by Teresa Sweibocka.

Jews Waiting In The Snow Outside A Nazi Gas Chamber In The Second World War.

[1] Matthew 24:14,21,30,31,35, Mark 13:27,31, Luke 21:26,33,35
[2] Jeremiah 30:9-10, 31:7-10, Ezekiel 11:17, 20:40-42, 36:23-24
[3] Deuteronomy 9:4-6, Isaiah 64:6, Romans 3:9-18
[4] Philippians 2:9
[5] Ephesians 3:20-21

WHAT WILL HAPPEN TO THE APOSTLES BEFORE THEY DIE? Mark 13:9-13, Luke 21:12-19

Looking at Luke's version, after the sign of the beginning of birth pangs,[1] there is something not found in the other gospels, that gives us the time the next prophecy will take place, which will be before the rebirth of the Nation of Israel.

> Luke 21:12 But before all these [signs], they shall lay hands on you [the apostles Jesus was talking to], and persecute you, delivering you up to their synagogues, and into prisons, being brought before kings and rulers for my [Jesus'] name's sake.

Nine things are then listed that will happen to the apostles Jesus was talking to, Peter, James, John and Andrew.[2]

> Luke 21:12 But before all these, they shall lay hands on you.

Peter, James, John and Andrew were in for a hard time as we shall see.

1. Jewish society would throw them out. The councils and synagogues they would be taken to were Jewish, and they would reject them.[3]
2. Gentile society would throw them out. The governors and kings they would stand before were Gentiles,[3] and wherever they went in the world they would be rejected.
3. All the persecutions by Jews and Gentiles will be their chance for the apostles to tell them about Jesus.

> Luke 21:13 And it shall turn [change to an opportunity] for you for a testimony.

4. The hostility to the message will not prevent it being preached to all nations. The Bible does not tell us how this was done, and although the fifth book of the New Testament is called the Acts of the Apostles, it only tells us about the preaching of Peter and Paul, (although John is mentioned as being there), but the other ten apostles were also busy. The titles of the books of the New Testament were not inspired by God, but were made up later on by men. The Book of Acts, might have been better called, the Acts of Two Apostles.

   How the message was preached to all nations, in the face of such world wide hatred,[4] we don't know, but the fact is it was done because it is recorded by Paul, that the gospel had been preached to all creation under heaven.[5]

5. If ever the apostles were taken to a law court to be tried, God would control the words coming out of their mouths, therefore they should not be bothered about what they were going to say.

   Mark 13:11 But when they shall lead you, and deliver you up, take no thought beforehand what ye shall speak, neither do ye premeditate [worry earlier]: but whatsoever shall be given you in that hour, that speak ye: for it is not ye that speak, but the Holy Ghost.

   Luke 21:14-15 [14] Settle it therefore in your hearts, not to meditate [think] before what ye shall answer:

   [15] For I will give you a mouth and wisdom, which all your adversaries [opponents] shall not be able to gainsay [deny] nor resist.

   An example of the wisdom spoken by the apostles appears in the Book of Acts, when Peter and John were arrested and brought before a Jewish court in Jerusalem of the very highest priests, and their wisdom silenced their accusers.

   Acts 4:13 Now when they [the high priests] saw the boldness of Peter and John, and perceived [understood] that they were unlearned [uneducated] and ignorant men, they marvelled [were amazed].

6. They would be rejected by their own families, and in some cases killed.[6] The same kind of thing is still happening in Jewish society today, whenever a Jew believes in Jesus he is often disowned by his own family.
7. They would be hated by all men and some of them would be killed. Ten of the eleven original apostles chosen by Jesus were martyred, they were killed because they would not give up being Christians. The only one to die of old age was John.

Luke 21:16-17 ¹⁶ And ye shall be betrayed both by parents, and brethren [brothers], and kinsfolks [relatives], and friends; and some of you shall they cause to put to death.

¹⁷ And ye shall be hated of all men for my name's sake.

Remember this would all happen before the false messiahs, wars and rumours of wars, etc. They would die before the signs of the last days.

8. Although physical security was not promised to them, their spiritual future was absolutely sure.

Luke 21:18 But there shall not an hair of your head perish.

Some believe that Luke 21:18 is a promise of physical safety, but it cannot be in view of the fact that some will be betrayed and even put to death,[6] however, although their earthly lives were in danger, their eternal lives were not!

9. In the face of strong and determined opposition from the Jews, the Gentiles, friends and families, they would in spite of it all be successful in winning souls to Christ.

Luke 21:19 In your patience [endurance] possess [acquire] ye your souls.

By the time all the apostles had died, churches had been established both in and beyond the Roman Empire, and many souls had been saved.

[1] Luke 21:10-11

[2] Mark 13:3

[3] Mark 13:9, Luke 21:12

[4] Mark 13:10

[5] Colossians 1:5-6, 1:23

[6] Mark 13:12, Luke 21:16

THE SIGN THAT JERUSALEM WILL SOON BE DESTROYED
Luke 21:20-24

Jesus here answers the first of the three questions the four apostles asked Him, giving the sign that would tell them when Jerusalem and the Temple would be destroyed.

> Luke 21:20 And when you see Jerusalem compassed [surrounded] by armies, then know that the desolation [destruction] thereof is nigh [near].

In AD 66 the Jews revolted against Rome, and Cetus Gallus, the Roman general at Caesarea took his legions to Jerusalem and surrounded the city. The Jewish followers of Jesus, the messianic Jews, knew it was the sign that the city would soon be destroyed, and they also knew what Jesus had said they should do, which Luke has told us.

> Luke 21:21 Then let them which are in Judea flee to the mountains; and let them which are in the midst of it depart out; and let them not that are in the countries enter thereinto.

Those in the city had to escape and those outside the city must not go in, but the city was surrounded, and no one could get out. The Jewish revolt was more than Cetus Gallus could handle. His lines of supply to feed and provide for his army were being cut by Jewish guerrillas, and he decided to lift the siege of Jerusalem temporarily and return to Caesarea. On the way back he was killed by Jewish guerrillas. The Jewish Christians in Jerusalem were waiting for such an opportunity, and 20,000 left the city, joining up with 80,000 believers from the surrounding areas, including Judea, Galilee and the Golan Heights.

11 The Prophecies of Jesus

The 100,000 followers of Jesus went and stayed at Pella, one of the ten Greek cities of the Decapolis, east of the river Jordan. There they were perfectly safe until the war ended avoiding the wrath of God that was poured out on Jerusalem, and on those Jews that had refused to believe that Jesus was their Messiah.

> Luke 21:22-23 [22] For these be the days of vengeance, that all things which are written may be fulfilled.
>
> [23] But woe unto them that are with child, and to them that give suck, in those days! For there shall be great distress in the land, and wrath upon this people.

He was talking about the judgement that was coming, "on this generation," and their children because they had committed the unforgivable sin. The siege and destruction of Jerusalem from AD 66 to AD 70 was carried out thoroughly, with the loss of 1,100,000 Jewish lives, but the amazing thing was that not one Jewish believer lost his life, because they had all obeyed Jesus and left the city when Cetus Gallus, withdrew his Roman legions.

> Luke 21:24 [Jesus, still speaking about Jerusalem, continued, saying], And they shall fall by the edge of the sword, and shall be led away captive into all nations: and Jerusalem shall be trodden down by the Gentiles, until the times of the Gentiles be fulfilled.

It is not yet time for the Jews to live in their own land permanently, this will not happen until Jesus sets up the Millennial Kingdom, after the times of the Gentiles have been fulfilled.

In 1967 an Islamic assault was prepared against Israel, led by Egypt and Syria both heavily armed by Russia, and supported by Jordan, who had a defence agreement with Egypt. Egypt amassed 900-950 tanks, 100,000 troops and 1,100 armoured personnel carriers. The Islamic nations of, Iraq, Saudi Arabia, Sudan, Tunisia, Morocco and Algeria, also sent troops to be employed in the attack. The Israeli government, seeing that its military forces were heavily outnumbered, ordered a pre-emptive strike in what is now known as the Six Day War. In six days Jewish forces had captured the Sinai Peninsula and the Gaza Strip from Egypt, the Golan Heights from Syria, and the West Bank, (known in the Bible as the mountains of Israel), and East Jerusalem, from Jordan, so that Israel now controlled the whole city. Jerusalem was now under Jewish control and many Christians believed that the times of the Gentiles, spoken of by Jesus, had come to an end. The error of that conclusion lies in the fact that during the times of the Gentiles, the Jews may have temporary control for certain periods, as has happened already.

From the Book of Daniel, the times of the Gentiles is defined as the period from the destruction of Jerusalem by the Babylonians, until the second coming. In Daniel 2, Nebuchadnezzar the king of Babylon had a dream about the future, and God gave Daniel the meaning of the dream. The king had dreamed of a statue, which represented the Gentile kingdoms that would rule the world, and Daniel said that the golden head of the statue represented Nebuchadnezzar. Nebuchadnezzar had made the Jews slaves, destroyed the Jewish Temple, and Jerusalem, and so the times of the Gentiles began with him. Daniel interpreted the dream going down the body of the statue until he came to the feet which represent the last Gentile world powers. They will be destroyed, Daniel said, to make way for a kingdom that will last forever, which must be the Kingdom of God, the Millennial Kingdom, because after the 1,000 years is up it is not destroyed.

> Daniel 2:44 [Daniel is speaking to Nebuchadnezzar]. And in the days of these kings shall the God of heaven set up a kingdom, which shall never be destroyed: and the kingdom shall not be left to other people, but it shall break in pieces and consume all these kingdoms, and it shall stand forever.

Ever since the Babylonian capture of Jerusalem, we have been in the times of the Gentiles, and during these times the Jews have controlled Jerusalem for periods and then lost control again. The first time was from 165 BC to 63 BC, during the Maccabeen period. The second time was from AD 66 to AD 70, during the first Jewish revolt. The third time was from AD 132 to AD 135, during the second Jewish revolt, and the fourth time was from AD 1967, during the Six Day War until now, but they will lose it again, because Bible prophecy says that Jerusalem will be under the control of the Gentiles when Christ comes.[1] If you come across Christian teachers that tell you the times of the Gentiles ended in 1967 with the Six Day War, then you should not let the idea take root in your minds. Later on in the Olivet Discourse Jesus will speak about the destruction of Jerusalem which is yet to come, but remember we are still in the times of the Gentiles.

After first answering the third question from the four apostles, Jesus had now secondly, answered their first question, the sign that the Temple and Jerusalem were about to be destroyed in AD 70. He now finally starts to deal with the second question, the sign of His second coming, but He first has to talk about the times that will come immediately beforehand, in the Great Tribulation. During that time the people of the world will get so mad with each other, and will have discovered such terrible ways to kill each other, that God will have to intervene to stop the human race from destroying itself completely.

> Matthew 24:22 And except those days should be shortened, there should no flesh [life] be saved: but for the elect's [the people chosen by God] sake those days shall be shortened.

[1] Zechariah 14:1-6

THE GREAT TRIBULATION
Matthew 24:9-28, Mark 13:14-23

- In every country in the world, followers of Jesus will be hated, and many will be arrested, tortured and killed.

    Matthew 24:9 Then they shall deliver you up to be afflicted [tortured], and shall kill you: and ye shall be hated of all nations for my [Jesus'] name's sake.

- The people that are used to mould public opinion, those that control what is taught, in schools, universities, news papers, magazines, on television, and even in churches, will teach lies just as they do today only more so, especially attacking Bible truths, and many will believe them. You can expect their arguments to be very convincing. They will probably include highly honoured and respected scientists, experts, clerics and educationalists as is already the case today.

Matthew 24:11   And many false prophets will arise and deceive many.

- People will get more and more wicked. Jesus said sin will increase, and sin would include, breaking God's laws, such as worshipping other "gods" including the idols and spirits of other religions, murder, adultery, stealing, lying, jealousy, pride and so on.

Matthew 24:12   And because iniquity [sin] shall abound [overrun the world], the love of many shall wax [become] cold.

- Jesus promises all believers, Jews and Gentiles, they will be saved if they are alive at the end of the tribulation.

Matthew 24:13   But he that shall endure unto the end, the same shall be saved.

- Jesus makes it very clear that during this time, before He comes again the gospel, (the good news about the kingdom of God), will be preached throughout the world. In the Scripture below, giving us the words of Jesus, take note of two phrases which are, "in all the world," and, "unto all nations."

Matthew 24:14   And this gospel of the kingdom shall be preached in all the world for a witness unto all nations; and then shall the end come."

Jesus is talking about the Great Tribulation and that the gospel will be preached to all nations during that terrible time.

- A major turning point when pressure will be very severely stepped up during the Great Tribulation will be the abomination of desolation, spoken of by Daniel.

Daniel 9:27 And he shall confirm the covenant with many for one week: and in the midst of the week he shall cause the sacrifice and the oblation to cease, and for the overspreading of abominations he shall make it desolate, even until the consummation, and that determined shall be poured upon the desolate.

The KJV translation of Daniel 9:27 above is difficult to understand, so we will look at how the translators of the Living Bible have paraphrased the same verse.

Daniel 9:27 This king will make a seven-year treaty with the people [Jewish people], but after half that time, he will break his pledge and stop the Jews from all their sacrifices and their offerings; then, as a climax to all his terrible deeds, the Enemy shall utterly defile the sanctuary of God. But in God's time and plan, his judgement will be poured out upon this Evil One. (Living Bible).

The way the Evil One, also known as the anti-Christ, will defile the Jewish Temple, (which will have been rebuilt), is by sitting in the Temple and forcing people to worship him as Almighty God. The Bible calls this, the abomination of desolation. The apostle Paul explained it in his second letter to the Church in Thessalonica.

2 Thessalonians 2:3-4 [3] Let no man deceive you by any means: for that day shall not come, except there come a falling away first, and that man of sin be revealed, the son of perdition [eternal death];

[4] Who opposeth [is against] and exalteth [raises] himself above all that is called God, or that is worshipped; so that he as God sitteth [sits down] in the temple of God, shewing [portraying] himself that he is God.

The seven-year treaty, or covenant, (one week in the KJV of the Bible, and in some other versions), is the Great Tribulation. The Hebrew word used is "shabua" meaning a period of seven, such as days, weeks, or years. Although translators have different opinions as to the time period, the same event described elsewhere in Scripture brings us to the conclusion that the treaty will be for seven years.

This has been a very brief introduction to what is known as the abomination of desolation, in order that we better understand the words of Jesus in the following verse.

Matthew 24:15-16 ¹⁵ When ye therefore shall see the abomination of desolation, spoken of by Daniel the prophet, stand in the holy place, (whoso readeth let him understand:)

¹⁶ Then let them which be in Judea flee into the mountains:

The abomination of desolation, will be the world leader sitting in the Temple and demanding to be worshipped as God. Anyone that refuses to worship him will be hunted down and killed with a technical efficiency never known before in world history. "For then shall be great tribulation, such as was not since the beginning of the world to this time, no, nor ever shall be" (Matthew 24:21). Jesus says it will be time for the Jews to run to the mountains to save their lives.

- Jesus goes on to emphasise the need for everyone to move out as fast as they possibly can to escape from the Evil One. The signal to get out will be the abomination of desolation.

Matthew 24:16-17 ¹⁶ Then let them which be in Judea flee into the mountains.

¹⁷ Let him which is on the housetop not come down to take anything out of his house.

The danger will be so close that someone on the roof of his house should run as soon as he touches the ground, and not go inside his house for anything at all.

Matthew 24:18 Neither let him which is in the field return back to take his clothes.

From the field where they get the news of the abomination of desolation, they must immediately start their journey out of the country, as fast as they can. It will be especially dangerous for pregnant women, and for mothers with suckling babies to move fast enough, and perhaps crying babies will be heard by government agents.

Matthew 24:19 And woe to them that are with child, and to them that give suck in those days!

- Jews are advised to pray that the abomination of desolation does not begin in the winter, and you may wonder why. At the moment there is hardly any snow or frost in Israel during the winter. It may mean that the weather will be different by then with colder winters, but on the other hand winter in Israel can be dangerous for travellers even now. Israel has a dry season with no rain whatsoever, and a wet season, beginning with light rains at the end of October, building stronger through November with heavy rains in December, January and February, lessening in March and ending completely in mid-April. The mountainous regions have many long dry valleys cutting through the higher ground. To get from one high area to another roads have been built down the sides of the valleys and up the opposite sides, without the use of bridges in the bottom of the dry valleys. In the wet winter months heavy rain in the hills can cause torrents of water to pour into the valleys sending tonnes of rocks, stones and debris hurtling down, ripping the roads up and causing havoc and loss of life further down the valleys where it may not even have rained.

The Jews are also advised to pray that the abomination of desolation does not begin on the Sabbath. From sunset on Friday to sunset on Saturday, public transport in Israel stops, and at the time I write this, most people in Israel do not own a car, and have to rely on buses and trains.

Matthew 24:20 But pray ye that your flight be not in the winter, neither on the Sabbath day.

- During the Great Tribulation there will be world wide anti-Semitism. Satan knows that Jesus will only return after the Jews ask Him to by crying out, "Blessed is He that comes in the name of the Lord," as we learned in the previous chapter, when He lamented over Jerusalem. If all the Jews are dead then they will not be able to cry out, and then Jesus will not come back. Satan will use the anti-Christ, who will be in charge of almost all governments, to try and exterminate all the Jews and believers in Jesus, all over the world. Hitler's Germany, when 6,000,000 Jews were killed was just a dry run, and almost nothing in comparison. In Revelation the anti-Christ with power from Satan is shown in action during that terrible time to come.[1]

Matthew 24:21 For then shall be great tribulation, such as was not since the beginning of the world to this time, no, nor ever shall be.

- Despite a determined world wide campaign to kill every follower of Christ and every Jew, using much more sophisticated technology than is available now, the huge wicked majority of mankind will fail, and a significant remnant of Jews will survive.

Matthew 24:22 And except those days should be shortened, there should no flesh be saved: but for the elect's sake those days shall be shortened.

We have already seen this verse at the end of the previous section, in which we dealt with the sign of the coming destruction of Jerusalem. In considering "elect," where it says, "for the elect's sake those days will be shortened," we need to know the three ways the Bible uses the word.

1. Although Satan deceived many of heaven's angels, persuading them to follow him, others were not deceived. They have become God's chosen angels, His elected heavenly host.[2]
2. The saints have been elected for eternal life as individuals.[3]
3. Finally out of all the people throughout the entire history of the world only Israel has been elected by God to be His chosen nation.[4]

In this verse, Matthew 24:22, Jesus uses the word "elect" to mean the Jewish nation. It must be so because in the previous seven verses, Matthew 24:15-21, He spoke about the abomination of desolation in the Temple, and the Jews fleeing for their lives from Jerusalem and Judea. We do not know how many Jews will survive to call out to Jesus, but two thirds of them will die and one third will remain alive.

Zechariah 13:8-9 [8] And it shall come to pass, that in all the land, saith the LORD, two parts therein shall be cut off and die; but the third shall be left therein.

[9] And I will bring the third part through the fire, and refine them as silver is refined, and will try them as gold is tried: they shall call on my name, and I will hear them: I will say, It is my people: and they shall say, the LORD is my God.

It says in this verse, "they shall call on my name," do you know what they will say? They will say, "Blessed is He that comes in the name of the Lord."

- While the Jews are expecting Jesus to come, many false Messiahs will try to fool them into thinking they are the Messiah, but they will be liars, trying to trick Jews, so that they can be captured and killed. The anti-Christ will be one of them.

Matthew 24:23-24 [23] Then if any man shall say unto you, Lo, here is Christ, or there; believe it not.

[24] For there shall arise false Christs.

- Further on in the same verse, Jesus says there will be false prophets. He already warned against false prophets in Matthew 24:10-11, at the beginning of the Great Tribulation, and now they are mentioned again at the end of the tribulation, so they will be used to trick the Jews right through the Great Tribulation. The false prophets at the end of the tribulation with power from Satan, will do mighty miracles, something Jesus did not say about the false prophets He mentioned earlier.[5]

Matthew 24:24 For there shall arise false Christs, and false prophets, and shall shew [show] great signs [miracles] and wonders; insomuch that, if it were possible, they shall deceive the very elect.

- Rumours will circulate that the second coming of the Messiah has already occurred, and Jesus warns His people not to believe any such rumours.[6] They must stay hidden until they see Him come themselves,[7] because unlike the first time He came, His second coming will be so spectacular that everyone will see it.

  Matthew 24:27 For as the lightening cometh out of the east, and shineth [shines] even unto the west; so shall also the coming of the Son of man be.

- Jesus then tells us where He will come, but He does it in the form of a secret code, so that most Christians don't actually know the place.

  Matthew 24:28 For wheresoever [where ever] the carcase [body] is, there will the eagles be gathered together.

  To understand what Jesus means, remember in Chapter 9, the Jewish leaders had rejected Jesus again, after He had raised Lazarus from the dead, the first of three miracles of the sign of Jonah, the only signs they would get from then on. The rejection meant that Jesus could not become King of Israel then, and so He would have to come a second time. Jesus was telling His disciples about the day He would be seen and recognized at the second coming,[8] but they wanted to know where this would be, and He gave the same answer.

  Luke 17:37 And they answered and said unto him, Where, Lord? And he said unto them, Wheresoever the body is thither [there] will the eagles be gathered together.

  Some Bibles say eagles and others vultures, and they will be at the place Jesus comes back to, but what are they and what is the body they will gather around? The eagles are the Gentile armies of the anti-Christ, and the body they are gathered near to is the body of Israel, hiding from its enemies. Remember in the parable of the sower, the birds were the agents of Satan,[9] and Jesus said to His disciples that if they did not know the meaning of that parable, they would not be able to understand the meaning of other parables.[10] The New Testament does not tell us exactly where the body of Israel will hide, only approximately such as the mountains[11] and the wilderness,[12] but the Old Testament tells us the very place they will be, where Jesus their King will meet them and from where He will lead them out.

Micah 2:12-13 I will surely assemble, O Jacob, all of thee; I will put them together as the sheep of Bozrah, as the flock in the midst of their fold: they shall make a great noise by reason of the multitude of men.

The breaker is come up before them: they have broken up, and have passed through the gate, and are gone out by it: and their king shall pass before them, and the LORD on the head of them.

The place the body of Israel will hide is therefore called Bozrah in Hebrew, known today as Petra, its Greek name. It is also the place where the eagles, the Gentile armies will be gathered.

Jeremiah 49:13-14 13 For I have sworn by myself, saith the LORD, that Bozrah shall become a desolation, a reproach, a waste, and a curse; and all the cities thereof shall be perpetual wastes.

14 I have heard a rumour from the LORD, and an ambassador is sent unto the heathen, saying, Gather ye together, and come up against her, and rise up to do battle.

Isaiah 34:1-6 Come near, ye nations, to hear; and hearken [listen], ye people: let the earth hear, and all that is therein; the world, and all things that come forth of it.

2 For the indignation of the LORD is upon all nations, and his fury upon all their armies: he hath utterly destroyed them, he hath delivered them to the slaughter.

3 Their slain also shall be cast out, and their stink shall come up out of their carcasses, and the mountains shall be melted with their blood.

⁴ And all the host of heaven shall be dissolved, and the heavens shall be rolled together as a scroll: and all their host shall fall down, as the leaf falleth from the vine, and as a falling fig from the fig tree.

⁵ For my sword shall be bathed in heaven: behold it shall come down upon Idumea, and upon the people of my curse, to judgement.

⁶ The sword of the LORD is filled with blood, it is made fat with fatness, and with the blood of lambs and goats, with the fat of the kidneys of rams: for the LORD hath a sacrifice in Bozrah, and a great slaughter in the land of Idumea.

The following prophecy is a picture of Jesus after He has destroyed the Gentile armies.

Isaiah 63:1-6 ¹ Who is he that cometh from Edom, with dyed garments from Bozrah? This that is glorious in his apparel, travelling in the greatness of his strength? I that speak in righteousness, mighty to save.

² Wherefore art thou red in thine apparel, and thy garments like him that treadeth [treads] the winefat [wine press]?

³ I have trodden the winepress alone; and of the people there was none with me: for I will tread them in mine anger, and trample them in my fury; and their blood shall be sprinkled upon my garments, and I will stain all my raiment.

⁴ For the day of vengeance is in mine heart, and the year of my redeemed is come.

⁵ And I looked, and there was none to help; and I wondered that there was none to uphold: therefore mine own arm brought salvation unto me; and my fury, it upheld me.

⁶ And I will tread down the people in mine anger, and make them drunk in my fury, and I will bring down their strength to the earth.

[1] Revelation 13:2-10
[2] 1 Timothy 5:21
[3] Romans 8:28-33, 2 Thessalonians 2:13, Titus 1:1-2
[4] Deuteronomy 7:6, 14:2, Isaiah 41:8-9, Romans 11:26
[5] 2 Thessalonians 2:8-12, Revelation 13:11-15
[6] Matthew 24:25-26
[7] Revelation 1:7
[8] Luke 17:30
[9] Mark 4:3-4 and 4:14-15
[10] Mark 4:13
[11] Matthew 24:16
[12] Revelation 12:6 and 12:13-15

THE SIGNS OF THE SECOND COMING OF MESSIAH JESUS
Matthew 24:29-30, Mark 13:24-26, Luke 21:25-27

Jesus having told us what the conditions will be like on earth during the Great Tribulation, just before He comes again, now answers the second question from the four apostles, the sign of His second coming. He brings our attention to four striking events that will happen.

1. There will be a world wide blackout, with no light coming from the sun, moon and stars. By this time people will be getting used to blackouts for this is the fifth one predicted in the Bible for the last days. The first one will be sometime before the tribulation,[1] the second will be in the first quarter of the tribulation,[2] the third will be in the second quarter of the tribulation,[3] the fourth will be in the second half of the tribulation,[4] and this is the fifth which will happen the moment the Great Tribulation ends.

Matthew 24:29 Immediately after the tribulation of those days shall the sun be darkened, and the moon shall not give her light, and the stars shall fall from heaven, and the powers of the heavens shall be shaken.

2. The people of the earth will be bewildered, afraid and panic stricken, by what is happening.

Luke 21:25-26 25 And there shall be signs in the sun, and in the moon, and in the stars; and upon the earth distress of nations, with perplexity; the sea and the waves roaring;

26 Men's hearts failing [stopping] for fear, and for looking after [at] those things which are coming on the earth: for the powers of heaven shall be shaken.

3. The third will be the most impressive so far, the sign in the sky that Jesus is on His way.

Matthew 24:30 And then shall appear the sign of the Son of man in heaven.

This sign will be a tremendously bright light, the Shekinah Glory signalling the coming of the Saviour of the world.[5] It is the sign everyone in the world will see, chasing away the terrible darkness of the blackout that was here before. The sign of the coming of Jesus will be world wide darkness, suddenly shattered by a tremendous light as He gets near.

4. Matthew 24:30 "Then all the tribes of the earth shall mourn, and they shall see the Son of man coming in the clouds of heaven with power and great glory."

Jesus had answered the three questions from the four apostles, but there was more He wanted them to know, more prophecies to make before He died.

[1] Joel 2:31
[2] Revelation 6:12
[3] Revelation 9:2
[4] Revelation 16:10
[5] Isaiah 40:5

THE RESTORATION OF ISRAEL
Matthew 24:21, Mark 13:27

The twelve tribes of Israel are scattered all over the world, just as Moses said they would be if they did not obey the Laws of Moses.[1] However, God loves Israel, and the Old Testament is full of prophecies saying that one day God will gather them all together again to their land. You will find references to a selected few of these prophecies[2] at the end of this section made by three of the major Old Testament prophets. Reading all the Bible prophecies that talk of the restoration of Israel we are given a clear understanding of when the final re-gathering will take place. Obviously the fact that Israel was established as a nation in one day, the 14th May 1948 was a fulfilment of prophecy.[3] Although Israel could be born again in a day when Jesus returns, and destroys the Gentile armies in Jerusalem, which will have been abandoned by the believing Jews, that have fled to Bozrah during the Great Tribulation, the prophecy[3] includes the phrase, "as soon as Zion travailed, she brought forth her children," and that will not be true after all the years of travail during the tribulation. In the two verses from Matthew and Mark, Jesus makes it absolutely clear that the final restoration of Israel will only come after His second coming.

> Matthew 24:31 And he shall send his angels with a great sound of a trumpet, and they shall gather together his elect from the four winds, from one end of heaven to the other.

> Mark 13:27 And then shall he send his angels, and shall gather together his elect from the four winds, from the uttermost part of the earth to the uttermost part of heaven.

Those Jews gathered by angels from the earth will be those that are still alive, and those from heaven will be Old Testament saints. Why are the Old Testament saints and all the Jews alive at the second coming, going to live together in the Promised Land? The answer is because God promised the land to Abraham, Isaac and Jacob, and their descendants forever,[4] and so they will live there together forever.

[1] Deuteronomy 28:15, 28:63-64

[2] Isaiah 11:11 to 12:6, 43:5-7, Jeremiah 23:5-8, 31:7-14, Ezekiel 11:16-21,20:40-42, 36:22-31

[3] Isaiah 66:8

[4] God's promise to Abraham and his descendants, Genesis 13:15, 24:7 God's promise to Isaac and his descendants, Genesis 26:1-4 God's promise to Jacob (Israel) and his descendants, Genesis 28:10-13

LIFT UP YOUR HEADS
Luke 21:28

> Luke 21:28 And when these things begin to come to pass, then look up, and lift up your heads; for your redemption [the word "redemption" here means, release after the payment of a ransom] draweth [is coming] nigh [near].

Jesus tells us when these things start to happen our redemption or rescue will be coming near, but what things? What was the start of all these things happening? They all began when Jerusalem was surrounded by armies[1] in AD 66, and so following the destruction of Jerusalem in AD 70, our rescue has been getting nearer and nearer. How will we be rescued?

Ever since the destruction of Jerusalem as judgement for the unforgivable sin, the time when God will remove the true Church of born again believers physically from earth to heaven,[2] that is the rapture, our transportation from earth to heaven, has been getting nearer and could happen at any time. The destruction of Jerusalem was the first signal from Jesus that the rapture is certain to follow, and the signs that He said would come after that, confirm His promise of the rapture, so lift up your heads, it will happen, to all those that have been born again,[3] spiritually.[4] We will see later in this Olivet Discourse that Jesus taught that the rapture of the saints will happen before the Great Tribulation takes place, so don't worry, if you believe in and follow Jesus, He will rescue you before it all happens.

[1] Luke 21:20
[2] Matthew 24:40-41, Luke 17:34-36, 1 Corinthians 15:49-57
[3] John 3:5
[4] John 3:6

THE PARABLE OF THE FIG TREE
Matthew 24:32-35, Mark 13:28-31, Luke 21:29-33

> Matthew 24:32 Now learn a parable of the fig tree; When his branch is yet tender [succulent], and putteth [grows] forth leaves, ye know that summer is nigh.

The leaves growing from fresh newly formed branches on the fig tree, or any other tree,[1] show that summer is coming.

> Matthew 24:33 So likewise ye, when ye shall see all these things, know that it is near, even at the doors.

Here Matthew is talking about the second coming of Jesus, not the rapture, because Matthew had not mentioned the rapture. It was only Luke who said that Jesus had told us to lift up our heads because our redemption, the taking away to heaven of the true born-again-Church, was near. The words of Jesus in the verse above, "When ye shall see all these things," mean, all the things from Matthew 24:15-31, beginning with the abomination of desolation, and ending with the final restoration of Israel, and He continues, "Know that it is near, even at the doors." He is talking about the second coming, and it is the same in Mark's gospel.

> Mark 13:29 So ye in like manner, when ye shall see these things come to pass, know that it is nigh, even at the doors.

Luke makes it especially clear because only he had spoken of the rapture, and now he was talking about the second coming, when the Messianic Kingdom would be established on earth by Jesus.

> Luke 21:31 So likewise ye, when ye see these things come to pass, know ye that the kingdom of God is nigh at hand.

Luke's emphasis that the Kingdom of God is about to be set up, shows he is talking about the second coming.

From the prophet Daniel we know that from the abomination of desolation until the second coming will be 1,290 days or three and half years.

> Daniel 12:11 And from the time that the daily sacrifice is taken away, and the abomination that maketh desolate set up, there shall be a thousand two hundred and ninety days.

The abomination of desolation will be in the middle of the seven year long, Great Tribulation, because it will be three and a half years before the second coming. Jesus referred us back to Daniel and his prophecy in Matthew 24:15, and by doing so He is stressing that the abomination of desolation will be a sign of His second coming and the defeat of the anti-Christ. The attempt by all the nations of the world to kill every single Jew will not succeed, and Israel will become the greatest nation on earth.

> Matthew 24:35 [Jesus is speaking] Heaven and earth shall pass away, but my words shall not pass away.

The above verse does not mean that every word Jesus spoke while on earth will always be remembered, most of them have been forgotten already, it means that every prophecy of Jesus will come true.

[1] Luke 21:29-30

THE RAPTURE
Matthew 24:36-42, Mark 13:32-37, Luke 21:34-36

> Matthew 24:36 But of that day and hour knoweth no man, no, not the angels of heaven, but my Father only.

The verse begins with the word, "But," and although that may not mean much in the English language, in the original Greek, it is "peri de", and it is used to introduce another topic, so while Jesus was talking about the second coming in the previous verse, he is now going to talk about something else. The Greek, "peri de" is often translated, "now concerning," meaning, concerning something else, or, about another thing. In this case Jesus is no longer talking about the second coming, but about the rapture, when the true Church will be physically taken away from the earth into the presence of Jesus, as we learned when in Luke's gospel, Jesus said, "Lift up your heads; for your redemption draweth nigh."

What about this redemption, this thing we are now talking about? "Of that day and hour knoweth no man," and this confirms Jesus is talking about the rapture of the Church. Once the abomination of desolation takes place, many men will know that the second coming will be in 1290 days time, on the other hand no one will ever know when the Church will be removed until after it happens. It could have happened any time after the destruction of Jerusalem and the Temple, by the Roman army under General Titus. When I first learned about the rapture I used to walk around the plantation wondering if I would be taken up that day.

The rapture will happen in normal times, with people doing what they usually do throughout their lives.

> Matthew 24:37-39 ³⁷ But as the days of No-e [Noah] were, so shall also the coming of the Son of man be.
>
> ³⁸ For as in the days that were before the flood they were eating and drinking, marrying and giving in marriage, until the day that No-e [Noah] entered the ark,
>
> ³⁹ And knew not until the flood came, and took them all away; so shall also the coming of the Son of man be.

Everything will be going on as usual, and there will be no sign at all before the born-again-Christians are taken away to heaven, in less than a second,[1] and no one will be given any sign that something unusual is going to take place. On the other hand, there will be many signs before the second coming of Jesus to set up the Millennial Kingdom, including the abomination of desolation, false Christs and false prophets, the world wide plan to kill the Jews, several blackouts, people dying of fear, because of the terrific wind, rain, and roaring of the huge destructive ocean waves, and the stars falling from the sky.[2] Conversely, the point is there will be nothing unusual to warn us before the rapture, it will happen when it is not expected either by the world or by the true Church.

At the rapture the chosen, while they are doing their normal every day work, will be separated out from the world for everlasting glory.

> Matthew 24:40-41 [40] Then shall two be in the field; the one shall be taken, and the other left.
>
> [41] Two women shall be grinding at the mill; the one shall be taken, and the other left.

All believers will be removed as part of the true Church, and Jesus warns us to watch out, and live our lives waiting in expectation of the most important event that will happen to us as ordinary men and women. The event that will result in us beginning a new kind of holy, righteous, everlasting life, as one of God's elect.

> Matthew 24:42 Watch therefore: for ye know not what hour your Lord doth come.

The thought of not being redeemed at the rapture is too horrible to imagine.

Luke tells us that those alive in the last days can escape the Great Tribulation by the rapture. In other words the rapture will be before the tribulation, which is not surprising because it will be at a time of normal every day activities. In Luke Jesus tells us that the tribulation will come on everyone that is left throughout the world.

> Luke 21:35 For as a snare [trap] shall it come on all them that dwell on the face of the whole earth.

Here the snare or trap is the tribulation, it is not the rapture which is not a trap but redemption, a rescue. Again like Matthew, Luke records Jesus telling us to be watchful, and the way to be watchful is to pray always, asking Jesus to rescue us from the tribulation. Prayer to Jesus keeps us close to Jesus, He is our Way of escape, and He saves those who ask for salvation in faith.[3]

> Luke 21:36 Watch ye therefore, and pray always, that ye may be accounted worthy to escape all these things that shall come to pass, and to stand before the Son of man.

Those that are taken in the rapture will stand before Jesus, and avoid the terrors of the Great Tribulation.

You should know some people believe the Great Tribulation will come before the rapture. They base their view on, 1 Corinthians 15:52, which describes the rapture taking place at "the last trump," and the last trump in the Bible comes in Revelation 11:15, which is after the Great Tribulation. On the other hand there are three named trumpets in Judaism, the First Trump, the Last Trump and the Great Trump. The Last Trump was blown every year at Rosh Hashana, (the Feast of Trumpets), and is therefore not the same as the trumpet of Revelation 11:15, which, by the way is not called, "the last trump." At the rapture Jesus will be seen by the believers that meet Him in the clouds of the air, but He will not be seen by the rest of the world. I find this interesting because one of three alternative names for Rosh Hashana, is Yom Hakeseh: the Day of Concealment.

The second and third alternative names given to Rosh Hashana are, Yom Hadin: the Day of Judgement, and Yom Hazikaron: the Day of Remembrance, both of which remind us of the rapture. Judgement, because it is the day Jesus will make His final choice as to who He will take from the earth to be with him, and who He will leave behind.[4] At the blowing of Last Trump, the Jews traditionally remembered the dead, and Jesus will not forget the dead at the rapture. In fact the dead will rise to meet Jesus first of all, before those of us who are alive.[1]

Clearly the Jewish, Last Trump, reminds us of the rapture, because of the three alternative names given to Rosh Hashana, the Day of Concealment, (Jesus will not be seen by the world on that day), the Day of Judgement, (Jesus will decide who He will take to be with Him), and the Day of Remembrance, (Jesus will resurrect the dead, His chosen ones, at the rapture).

[1] 1 Corinthians 15:52, 1 Thessalonians 4:16-17
[2] Matthew 24:15-24, Mark 13:14-27, Luke 21:25-28
[3] Romans 10:13-17
[4] Mark 13:33-37

FIVE PARABLES FOR THE GENTILES
Matthew 24:43 to 25:30, Mark 13:33-37

Luke has now finished saying all he wants to about the prophecies of Jesus from the Olivet Discourse, but Mark and especially Matthew continue with some important messages from our Lord for His Church. Jesus wants the Church to watch, be ready and work, and the first three of the five parables are about these three things. We have already seen the way Jesus teaches in parables, sometimes He gives just one parable and at other times a few parables, before He gives the meaning, or how to put the lessons into practice. Here He tells five parables one after the other, and then shows how the lessons from the parables should be used by Gentile Christians in the following section called, When, Where And How Jesus Will Judge The Gentiles.

To begin with it will be helpful if we understand two things about these parables.

1. The parables were given to inform the Gentiles how and on what basis they will be judged after the second coming.

2. These parables are all about believers and unbelievers, the saved and the unsaved, the true Church and the false church. They are not about Jews as opposed to Gentiles, or Israel as opposed to the Church. The message is that believers will be saved because they will watch, stay ready and keep working, while the unbelievers will not be saved, because they will not be watchful, not be ready, and will not work while Jesus is away.

1st The Parable Of The Porter Or Doorkeeper
Mark 13:33-37

The main theme of this parable is, watch, which I will show by recording only the relevant parts of the verses concerned.

Mark 13:33-37 [33] Take ye heed, watch ...

[34] For the Son of man is as a man taking a far journey, who left his house, ……., and commanded the porter to watch.

³⁵ Watch ye therefore: ...

³⁷ And what I say unto you I say unto all, Watch.

Mark finishes his report on the prophecies of Jesus from the Olivet Discourse with those verses, and the remaining four parables are all from the Gospel of Matthew.

2nd The Parable Of The Goodman Of The House Matthew 24:43-44

The main theme here is being ready at all times.

> Matthew 24:44 Therefore be ye ready: for in such an hour as ye think not the Son of man cometh.

3rd The Parable Of The Wise Servant And The Evil Servant Matthew 24:45-51

The point of the parable is that a wise servant will be busy about his work while the master is away, he is the believer.

> Matthew 24:46 Blessed is that servant, whom his lord when he cometh shall find so doing.

The last verse of this parable is for the evil servant, who does not watch, is not ready, and refuses to work, because he is not a believer, and he will go to the place of weeping and gnashing of teeth, meaning the lake of fire. Weeping because having lost everything he will be forever without hope of escape, and gnashing of teeth because of the pain he is in.

> Matthew 24:51 ... appoint him his portion with the hypocrites: there shall be weeping and gnashing of teeth.

Following these three parables showing the three things Jesus wants us to do while He is away, there are two longer parables stressing the importance of those three activities.

4th The Parable Of The Ten Virgins
Matthew 25:1-13

The parable focuses on, being ready and on watchfulness.

> Matthew 24:10 ... and they that were ready went in with him to the marriage:

> Matthew 24:13 Watch therefore, for ye know neither the day nor the hour wherein the Son of man cometh.

The parable is about a Jewish wedding, and to understand the parable it is necessary to know the Jewish background. We will begin by looking at the four stages of a Jewish wedding.

The first step is taken by the father of the groom, when He pays the father of the bride for his daughter. Years ago this was often when the future husband and wife were small children or even still babies, and as a result many years often went by before the second step was taken. The time between steps one and two is always at least a year, may be much more, and sometimes the bride and groom never meet each other until their wedding day. Looking at this from the point of view of Jesus marrying His bride the Church,[1] God the Father of Jesus, paid the for the bride with the blood of His Son.[2]

A year or more after the bride's price has been paid, the groom goes to the home of the bride, and brings her to his home. This, the second step is known as fetching the bride. Again from the point of view of Jesus marrying His Church, this will happen at the time of the rapture, when Jesus will come and take the Church home.

The third stage is the wedding ceremony, to which only a very few close friends and relatives of the bride and groom are invited. The wedding ceremony between Jesus and His Church will be in heaven before the second coming.

> Revelation 19:7-8 [7] Let us be glad and rejoice, and give honour to him: for the marriage of the Lamb is come, and his wife hath made herself ready.
>
> [8] And to her was granted that she should be arrayed in fine

linen, clean and white: for the fine linen is the righteousness of the saints.

The fourth event in a Jewish wedding is the wedding feast, usually lasting seven days, with a huge number of guests invited. The Messianic Kingdom is often portrayed as a wedding feast in the parables, and that is one reason we know that after our marriage with Jesus in heaven, the celebrations or feast will take place on earth in the new kingdom of God.

> Matthew 25:10 And while they went to buy, the bridegroom came; and they that were ready went in with him to the marriage: and the door was shut.

In the parable of the ten virgins the five wise ones were ready and went into the wedding feast, in the Millennial Kingdom.

In the days when this parable was told, there was no way of knowing where someone was, if they had left town. Most people walked and only the rich rode on donkeys, mules or horses, and there were no telephones. Suppose then that a man went off to fetch his bride from a town that was fifty miles away, how would they know when he was going to come back? Perhaps the bride had some last minute things to attend to when he got there, or perhaps dogs were attacking their sheep and they needed help. They could never be sure when the groom would return to his home with his bride, and so they worked out a clever plan. Girls are often interested in weddings, so they sent the virgins to the edge of the town to keep a lookout for the bride and groom. They had to take lamps with them because the couple might come at any time of the day or night. Now we can understand why Jesus included ten virgins with lamps in His parable about a normal Jewish wedding in those days.

Again looking at the parable from the point of view of Jesus marrying the Church, the Bride Groom has left home but He has not yet returned with the bride. He will bring His bride with Him at the second coming. The virgins are from every nation on earth that hears the gospel preached during the Great Tribulation.[3] In the Old Testament of the Bible someone that does not believe in God is called a fool,[4] and Jesus said that five of the virgins were wise, believing in God, and five were foolish.

>Matthew 25:3-4 ³ They that were foolish took their lamps, and took no oil with them:
>
>⁴ But the wise took oil in their vessels [containers] with their lamps.

All the girls had lamps, the message had been preached in all nations, and they had all heard it. However, only five had oil, they were the wise ones that had believed, had received the Holy Spirit and were saved. The others had no oil, they were the fools that did not believe in God.

When Jesus returns with His bride at the second coming, the fools will be refused entry into the Messianic Kingdom, because they have no oil, and they do not believe the gospel message. The wise will be believers in the gospel, and as a result they will have been born again spiritually, they will have their oil with them, and will be welcomed into the kingdom. The wise, the children born-again of God, were watching and ready, but the fools that had not believed the message of Jesus, had not watched and were certainly not ready.

>Matthew 25:11-12 ¹¹ Afterward came also other virgins, saying, Lord, Lord, open to us.
>
>¹² But he answered and said, Verily [Truly] I say unto you, I know you not.

Jesus would never tell believers, He did not know them. The Good Shepherd knows His sheep very well, and we know Him.[5] The parable of the ten virgins emphasises once again then, the need for watching and being ready.

5th The Parable Of The Talents
Matthew 25:14-30

The parable of the talents stresses the message of the third parable, the importance for a servant to work while his master is away on a long trip to another country. Jesus of course is the Master and we are His servants waiting for Him to return. The comparison is between two believers, who worked, and an unbeliever who did not, and we know the one that did not work was an unbeliever because Jesus called him wicked.

> Matthew 25:26 His lord answered and said unto him, Thou wicked and slothful [lazy] servant.

We also know that he did not work because Jesus said he was lazy. Another thing about the unbeliever was that when asked why he had not worked, he answered by listing some qualities of his Master, showing he knew a lot about Him, he had heard the gospel message. He had been given a talent, but had decided not to use it, he made his own choice not to believe, and so the master took the talent away from him and ordered his punishment.

> Matthew 25:30 And cast ye the unprofitable servant into outer darkness: there shall be weeping and gnashing of teeth.

In the third parable the evil servant was condemned to weeping and gnashing of teeth with the hypocrites, here in the fifth parable another aspect of the lake of fire is added, which is outer darkness. Outer, means it is a very long way away from the glory of God and that is why it is so very dark. Fire usually gives off light but the lake of fire has no light, it is absolutely pitch black. As a young man many of my rubber planter friends, when drinking their beer and whiskey, in a club or at a hotel bar, made jokes and laughed about being dead. They said that when they died they wanted to go to Hell, and keep warm in the fire with all their friends. The lake of fire is not like that, they will not feel warm they will feel pain, and there will be no friends, just the loneliness and isolation of absolute darkness. It is strange how young men should joke about things like that, it shows again they know they are going the wrong way, but refuse to do the sensible thing and look for eternal life.

> James 4:4 Ye adulterers and adulteresses, know ye not that the friendship of the world is enmity [hatred] with God? Whosoever therefore will be a friend of the world is the enemy of God.

It is a dreadful thing to be an enemy of God, because God punishes His enemies by letting them do all the bad things they want,[6] and then sending them to the lake of fire.

Our next section, about the judgement of the Gentiles, follows on from what we have learned in these five parables, and shows how the lessons are to be applied in everyday life.

[1] Ephesians 5:22-33
[2] Acts 20:28
[3] Matthew 24:14
[4] Psalms 14:1, 53:1
[5] John 10:14
[6] Psalm 81:12, Romans 1:24-32

WHEN, WHERE AND HOW, JESUS WILL JUDGE THE GENTILES Matthew 25:31-46

The judgement of the Gentiles is going to be after Jesus has returned to earth in glory at the second coming with all of His angels, and after He has rescued Israel from Bozrah, and led His people out victoriously following the Great Tribulation.

> Matthew 25:31 When the Son of man shall come in his glory, and all the holy angels with him.

Jesus Himself has told us the time, but not the place, for which we have to go back to one of the Old Testament prophets.

> Joel 3:1-2 ¹ For, behold, in those days, and in that time, when I shall bring again the captivity of Judah and Jerusalem,
>
> ² I will also gather all the nations, and will bring them down

into the valley of Jehoshaphat, and will plead with them there for my people and for my heritage Israel, whom they have scattered among the nations, and parted my land.

Jesus will judge the Gentiles in the Valley of Jehoshaphat, which is the valley between the Old City of Jerusalem and the Mount of Olives to the east of Jerusalem. It is in fact the valley in between the Temple and the place Jesus was sitting on the Mount of Olives, while he was speaking to the four apostles and telling them all these things.

The way Jesus will judge the Gentiles is on how they treated the Jews during the tribulation, something Jesus goes into in great detail, and which Joel briefly mentions.[1]

Matthew 25:31-32 ³¹ ... then shall he sit upon the throne of his glory:

³² And before him shall be gathered all the nations:

The word "nations" in the verse above is from the Greek word, "ethnos", from which we get the word "ethnic". It is mostly translated as Gentiles in the Bible, and if the more common interpretation had been used, the meaning of the original Greek would be clearer, which is, "all the Gentiles will be gathered before Him". The judgement will be made to decide who is going to receive eternal life, and who is going to receive eternal damnation. For that reason it will not be a judgement of nations, but of persons. Judgement of the Gentiles will be on an individual basis, some will be saved and some will not. Jesus will sit on His throne in glory, and all the Gentiles that are left alive after the tribulation will be gathered before Him in the Valley of Jehoshaphat, to be judged. Jesus will separate them into two groups like a Middle Eastern shepherd separates a mixed flock of sheep and goats. He will put the sheep on His right, and the goats on His left, before He passes judgement on each group separately.[2] The judgement of all the sheep Gentiles will come first and it is found in Matthew 25:34-40.

Matthew 25:34 Then shall the King say unto them on his right hand, Come, ye blessed of my Father, inherit the kingdom prepared for you from the foundation of the world:

Jesus next gives the reason this group of Gentiles will go into the Messianic Kingdom.

> Matthew 25:35-36 ³⁵ For I was an hungered [hungry], and ye gave me meat [food]: I was thirsty, and ye gave me drink: I was a stranger, and ye took me in:
>
> ³⁶ Naked, and ye clothed me: I was sick, and ye visited me: I was in prison, and ye came unto me.

The sheep Gentiles are surprised because they do not remember doing any of these things for Jesus, but the Scripture continues, calling the sheep Gentiles something very special indeed.

> Matthew 25:37 Then shall the righteous answer him.

The sheep Gentiles are all righteous, and for that reason are believers in Jesus.

> Matthew 25:40 And the King shall answer and say unto them, Verily (Truly) I say unto you, Inasmuch as ye have done it unto one of the least of these my brethren, ye have done it unto me.

Jesus here is speaking to the sheep Gentiles about, "these My brethren," His brothers, who are there with Him. His brothers are not the righteous Gentiles, because He is speaking to them about how they treated another group of people, called His brothers. In the same way His brothers are not the goats, the unrighteous Gentiles, which is obvious, and to confirm this, He speaks to them later, again about His brothers. There are only three groups of people that come through the Great Tribulation, righteous Gentiles, unrighteous Gentiles, and Jews. It is quite natural for Jesus who was born into the tribe of Judah, from where we get the word "Jew," to call the Jews His brothers. Jesus at the judgement of the Gentiles will confirm His prophecy here, and that of Joel 3, and judge them on the way they treated the Jews during the tribulation. He will tell the whole flock of sheep Gentiles gathered to His right, that because they treated the Jews well during the tribulation, their actions will be reckoned as if they had done the same to Him, and He will reward them with everlasting life with Him in His kingdom.

Now we come to the goat Gentiles.

> Matthew 25:41 Then shall he say unto them on the left hand, Depart from me, ye cursed, into everlasting fire, prepared for the devil and his angels.

The goat Gentiles are all cursed and condemned to the lake of fire forever, to be tormented along with Satan and his wicked friends. The reason is that Jesus was hungry but they did not feed Him, thirsty but they did not give Him a drink, a stranger they refused to help, and so on, but the cursed Gentiles tell Jesus they do not remember any of this.

> Matthew 25:45 Then shall he answer them, saying, Verily [Truly] I say unto you, Inasmuch as ye did it not to one of the least of these, ye did it not to me.

The goat Gentiles are then all killed and sent to everlasting punishment. It will be because of the way they treated the Jews during the tribulation that the goat Gentiles will be cursed and sent off to never ending torment, and the sheep Gentiles will be blessed and sent into the Messianic Kingdom. Those with everlasting life will eventually take up the positions prepared for them by God in the eternal New Jerusalem.[3]

> Matthew 25:46 And these [the cursed Gentiles] shall go away into everlasting punishment: but the righteous into eternal life.

It is very important to understand that the sheep Gentiles were not righteous because of their works, that is not the way to be declared righteous by Jesus.[4] Righteousness is only given to us as a free gift through faith,[4] and that faith is only acceptable when it is faith in Jesus.[5] The point is that because they were believers in Jesus they were righteous, and because they were righteous they did the works of righteousness.[6] Those that did not believe in Jesus were automatically unrighteous, and this is clear from their selfish and wicked behaviour during the tribulation.

At the judgement of the Gentiles, the five parables will be shown to be true. The sheep Gentiles will have been kept alive by watching, working, taking care of the Jews, and being ready. The goat Gentiles will not have watched, not have worked and will not be ready.

Jesus, had given His prophecies for the time stretching from His death until the establishment of His kingdom on earth. These included the present age, what would happen to His apostles, the destruction of Jerusalem, the signs of the second coming, the restoration of Israel as a nation, the rapture, life during the Great Tribulation and finally the judgement of the Gentiles. What follows in the next chapter is how Jesus, His friends and enemies prepared for His coming crucifixion.

[1] Joel 3:2-3, 3:6

[2] Matthew 25:32-33

[3] Revelation 21:10

[4] Ephesians 2:8-9

[5] John 14:6

[6] James 2:14-26

12

SETTING THE STAGE FOR DEATH

JESUS PREDICTS HIS CRUCIFIXION
Matthew 26:1-2, Mark 14:1

> Mark 14:1 After two days was the feast of the passover, and of unleavened bread.

It was Tuesday and the Passover was two days away, meaning that the Passover would begin at sunset on Thursday, that year, the supper would be eaten Thursday night, and the Passover lamb would be sacrificed on Friday before sunset. Sunset Thursday to sunset Friday makes the 24 hours of a Jewish day.

> Matthew 26:1-2 ¹ And it came to pass when Jesus had finished all these sayings, he said unto his disciples,
> ² Ye know that after two days is the feast of passover, and the Son of man is betrayed to be crucified.

Jesus had already told His disciples on three occasions that He was going to be killed, and this was the fourth, but now He tells them when it will happen, in two days time. He will die sometime between sunset on Thursday and sunset on Friday.

THE RULERS PLOT THE DEATH OF THEIR MESSIAH
Matthew 26:3-5, Mark 14:1-2

> Matthew 26:3 Then assembled together the chief priests, and the scribes, and the elders of the people, unto the palace of the high priest, who was called Caiaphas.

The chief priests were Sadducees and the scribes Pharisees, and the leader of the plotters was Caiaphas the High Priest.

> Matthew 26:4 And they consulted that they might take Jesus by subtilty [subtlety or deceitfully] and kill him.

The plot was to arrest Jesus secretly, to make sure the crowds of people in Jerusalem for the feast knew nothing about it. Later Judas Iscariot would come to them with his plan, giving them the very opportunity they were looking for. Although they were eager to arrest Jesus, they agreed that this should not be during Passover.

> Matthew 26:5 But they [the rulers plotting together] said, Not on the feast day, lest there should be an uproar among the people.

It is interesting how Satan was at work influencing the plans of the rulers, because it was necessary that Jesus should die at Passover to pay the penalty for men's sins. He had to die at the right time and in the right way, otherwise He could have died as a child in Bethlehem or at any other time, but the "Lamb of God" had to die at Passover.[1] He could not be killed before this because, His hour had not yet come.[2] The plotters decided to wait until after Passover, then the crowds would have left Jerusalem, and would not have known about the death of the Lord. The difficulty they faced was that they were up against God, who had everything under control, and so they found themselves involved in causing Jesus to be crucified at just the very moment, they and Satan were trying so hard to prevent. As we continue with the story, remember they had decided to wait until after the Passover before carrying out their wicked scheme.

[1] John 7:6
[2] John 7:30, 8:20

MARY PREPARES THE BODY OF JESUS FOR BURIAL WHILE HE IS ALIVE
Matthew 26:6-13, Mark 14:3-9, John 12:2-8

The gospels of Matthew and Mark both tell us that Jesus was a guest at the home of Simon the leper, in the town of Bethany. We discussed leprosy in Chapter 5, and you will remember that lepers were only allowed to live with other lepers in a special part of the town. They were untouchable, no one was allowed to get nearer than four cubits or six feet from a leper, and houses thought to be infectious were destroyed.[1] A check of all the Scriptures above shows that there was quite a party in the leper's house, including Martha, Mary and Lazarus, who also lived in Bethany, Jesus and the disciples, and I would not expect them all to be there unless Simon the leper had been healed, and you know from Chapter 5, that healing a Jewish leper was recognized as a miracle only the Messiah could do.

Matthew and Mark speak about a woman, but John tells us it was Mary, who poured ointment over the head of Jesus, and John adds that it was ointment of spikenard, that she also poured it on His feet and wiped His feet with her hair. Ointment of spikenard was very precious, and used normally only by royalty, but for the common people such as Mary it was saved up to be used once in a life time, on her wedding night. It was worth more than three hundred denarii, which the translators of the KJV Bible have written as three hundred pence.

> Mark 14:5 For it might have been sold for more than three hundred pence.

One denarius was one days pay, meaning the ointment was worth about one years wages, and Mary was pleased to use it all up on Jesus. The disciples thought Mary was wasting her precious treasure, especially Judas.

> John 12:4-5 ⁴ Then said one of his disciples, Judas Iscariot, Simon's son, which should betray him,

> [5] Why was not this ointment sold for three hundred pence, and given to the poor?

The other disciples also thought it would have been better to help the poor,[2] but Judas was more interested in helping himself.

> John 12:6 This he [Judas] said, not that he cared for the poor; but because he was a thief, and had the bag, and bare [took up] what was put therein.

He was the group's treasurer, responsible for looking after money and paying for what they needed, and he used his position to steal, he was not a man to be trusted, but Jesus had chosen him for a special purpose.

Why did Mary take her treasure and use it all on Jesus?

> John 12:7 Then Jesus said, Let her alone: against the day of my burying hath she kept this.

Mary had been saving the ointment to anoint the body of Jesus, a custom of the time at Jewish funerals.

> Matthew 26:12 For in that she poured this ointment on my body, she did it for my burial.

> Mark 14:8 She hath done what she could: she is come aforehand [before the time] to anoint my body to the burying.

Mary knew something that the disciples did not yet know. She knew Jesus would die and that He would be raised to life again, and when we read about His resurrection and the women that went to the tomb, Mary is not there. She seems to be the only one who understood that there would be a resurrection, and that there would not be a chance to anoint His corpse after Jesus died. While Martha had been busy getting the food ready, Mary had been sitting at the feet of Jesus, listening to Him, being with Him, and learning, so that she understood more than anyone else, including His disciples.[3] She had done her best to meet the spiritual need of Jesus by staying with Him, keeping Him company, understanding what He said, and acting accordingly, and for this Jesus gave her high honour.

Mark 14:9 Verily [Truly] I say unto you, Wheresoever this gospel shall be preached throughout the whole world, this also that she hath done shall be spoken of for a memorial to her.

This prophecy, made about 2,000 years ago, was fulfilled just now when you read the Scripture. It was at this point that Judas set off alone to make a bit of extra money for himself, by promising the chief priests to betray Jesus to them in a quiet place, secretly where there would be no crowds of people.

[1] Leviticus 14:43-45
[2] Matthew 26:8-9
[3] Luke 10:38-42

THE PRICE IS SET TO BETRAY JESUS TO THOSE WHO WANT HIM DEAD
Matthew 26:14-16, Mark 14:10-11, Luke 22:1-6

If we lie, cheat or do anything that is wrong, then we open our minds to demons. Jesus often dealt with demons in people and if you want to remind yourself about them, then turn back to Chapter 5, and the fifth section before continuing.

Luke 22:3 Then entered Satan into Judas surnamed Iscariot, being one of the twelve.

Judas became unprotected against demon possession because he stole money, but he was not merely demon possessed, Luke says he was Satan possessed.

Luke 22:4 And he [Judas] went his way, and communed [talked it over] with the chief priests and captains, how he might betray him [Jesus] unto them.

After the discussion Judas knew that he would have to betray Jesus in a secret place away from all the crowds that had gathered in Jerusalem for the Passover. Judas was needed for three reasons.

1. Judas knew the habits of Jesus and would be in a good position to figure out a way to betray Jesus while the crowds were not around. The rulers needed Judas for this and he did lead them to Jesus and hand Him over to them in a quiet place.
2. Judas was also needed to fulfil a point of Roman Law. A Roman cohort, which was one tenth of a Roman legion, could not be sent to arrest Jesus, or anyone, until someone accused Jesus of a crime against Roman law. Judas would have to go to Pontius Pilate and testify that Jesus had broken a Roman law, before a cohort would be sent to arrest Him. Again we will see that Judas did testify against Jesus.
3. He was also needed as a witness for the prosecution, to give evidence that Jesus was guilty of a crime deserving punishment according to Roman law. He was not needed to give evidence for any Jewish trial, but he was most certainly needed for the Roman trial. Later we will see that he did not carry out this last requirement.

The price the chief priests agreed to pay Judas for Jesus is significant.

> Matthew 26:15 And he said unto them, What will ye give me, and I will deliver him unto you? And they covenanted [agreed] with him for thirty pieces of silver.

The price they offered was meant to be an insult, because they hated Jesus so much. Under the Law of Moses, if anyone had a cow that killed another person's slave, then the owner of the cow had to pay the slave owner, thirty pieces of silver, and so they were saying that the King of Israel was not worth any more than a dead slave.

> Exodus 21:32 If the ox shall push [gore with its horns] a manservant or a maidservant; he shall give unto their master thirty shekels of silver.

If the chief priests had wanted to avoid insulting Jesus, they had a custom of paying a little more or a little less, 31 shekels or 29, but the price of 30 shekels shows their hatred and intention to be as rude as they could to their Messiah.

There are many prophecies in the Old Testament that speak of the two comings of Jesus. The Jews understood most of those about the second coming but not those about the first coming. One prophecy of the first coming given about 500 years earlier, even said that the Good Shepherd would be valued at 30 pieces of silver by them. In Zechariah 11:4-14, the prophet played the role of the Messiah as the Good Shepherd, but no price was agreed as to how much he should get for looking after the sheep. When he had finished feeding the flock and it was time for him to be paid for his work, he told them to pay whatever they thought he was worth, and if that was nothing, then to pay him nothing.

> Zechariah 11:12 And I said unto them, If ye think good, give me my price; and if not, forbear [keep it]. So they weighed for my price thirty pieces of silver.

It would not have been so insulting if they had paid the prophet of God nothing, but they deliberately chose to offend him, by saying in effect, "Your work could have been done by a dead slave." Interestingly the prophecy does not stop there because God told the prophet to throw the money for the potter in the Temple area, and later we will find that Judas did the same thing with the money he got for Jesus. God told Zechariah that thirty pieces of silver was the price that He, God Himself, had been valued by them, and the prophecy was that in the future the Jewish leaders would sell their God for thirty pieces of silver.

> Zechariah 11:13 And the LORD said unto me, Cast it unto the potter: a goodly price that I [God] was prised [valued] at of them. And I took the thirty pieces of silver, and cast them to the potter in the house of the LORD.

Again, by making the price for Jesus thirty pieces of silver, not 29 or 31 pieces, they are being as offensive and hostile as they know how. The payment was agreed by the chief priests as a group, meaning the money would come from the Temple treasury, and the money in the Temple treasury was meant to buy sacrifices. It was not in their plan to buy Jesus as a sacrifice, but quite unintentionally that is what they did. It did not cross their minds because they had agreed not to arrest Jesus until after the day of the feast, that is after the twenty-four hours between sunset Thursday and sunset Friday. Days in the Bible are Jewish days, starting at sunset, they begin when it starts to get dark and end at sundown on what to us would be the next day, but to them it is the same day. If we do not remember this it is impossible to understand the Scriptures. Jesus was the last ever sacrifice for sin, that was acceptable to God, ever to be made, and He was bought with money from the Temple treasury, by the chief priests.

Luke 22:5-6 ⁵ And they were glad, and covenanted [promised] to give him the money.

⁶ And he promised, and sought opportunity to betray him unto them in the absence of the multitude [away from the crowds].

"They were glad," they were going to get what they wanted for the price of a dead slave, but they had forgotten to say that the betrayal should only be after the Passover day.

JESUS ARRANGED THE LAST PASSOVER MEAL HIMSELF
Matthew 26:17-19, Mark 14:12-16, Luke 22:7-14

Going briefly over the main points, Passover is held every year to celebrate and remember the time when the Jews were freed from being slaves in Egypt. Moses told them to kill a lamb and paint the blood over the lintels and on the door posts of their houses. The angel of death then went through Egypt during the night killing the firstborn sons of all the people and animals, except for the Jews and their animals, because when the angel saw the blood on their lintels and door posts, it passed-over them.[1] No bread, made with yeast or leaven, is eaten during the feast because leaven represents sin, which reminds us that Jesus who called Himself, the Bread of Life,[2] was without sin.[3]

A great deal of effort was involved preparing for the feast, and as the time got very near the disciples were concerned because they still had no idea where they were going enjoy the feast. How would they ever be able to finish everything in time?

> Matthew 26:17 Now the first day of the feast of unleavened bread the disciples came to Jesus, saying unto him, Where wilt thou that we prepare for thee to eat the Passover?

Jesus would not tell them where they would eat the last Passover, but He sent Peter and John to get it ready, and they went off not knowing where they were going.

> Luke 22:8 And he sent Peter and John, saying, Go and prepare us the Passover, that we may eat.

The preparations that had to be made at that time in Jewish history would take a while to complete. First they would have to take their sacrificial lamb to the Jerusalem Temple to be killed by the priests. The blood was collected in a bowl and poured out at the base of the altar. After that Peter and John had to sing Psalms 113-118, the six Psalms known as the Psalms of Praise, or in Hebrew, the Hellel. Next the lamb was cleaned by taking out its entrails and removing its skin, before parts were burnt on the altar, and then what was left was taken home and roasted. Other things required would be, unleavened bread, wine, bitter herbs and charoseth. Charoseth is made from apples, nuts, honey, cinnamon, lemon juice and wine. All these are chopped and mixed together into a brown sticky stuff, which is needed in the ceremony to represent the clay used by the Jewish slaves in Egypt to make bricks for Pharaoh.[4] There was a lot involved for Peter and John when Jesus told them, "Go and prepare us the Passover, that we may eat."

During the Passover feast there were hundreds of thousands of Jews in Jerusalem, from the land itself and from all the Mediterranean and surrounding nations where Jews lived, traded and worked. The city could not possibly house them all, and so there were massive satellite cities of tents around Jerusalem, where visitors ate the Passover with their own families. However, Jesus had made special arrangements for Him and the disciples to eat the Passover within the city walls.

> Luke 22:10 And he said unto them, Behold, when ye are entered into the city, there shall a man meet you, bearing a pitcher of water; follow him into the house where he entereth [enters] in.

Jesus had arranged for the place and for a distinctive sign to follow, which was a man carrying a pitcher of water. Even today in the villages of Middle East men do not carry pitchers of water, it is women's work, and two thousand years ago it was much more so. A man carrying a pitcher of water would have been very easy to spot, and to follow.

> Luke 22:11 And ye shall say unto the goodman [master] of the house, The Master saith unto thee, Where is the guestchamber [guests room], where I shall eat the Passover with my disciples?

The fact that this was a very special Passover is shown in Matthew's gospel, where the message to the master of the house includes these words from Jesus, "My time is at hand."

> Matthew 26:18 And he said, Go into the city to such a man, and say unto him, The Master saith, My time is at hand; I will keep the Passover in thy house with my disciples.

Jesus and His disciples had kept the Passover feast together in previous years, but this Passover was going to be the time when He would accomplish everything God required of Him as a natural human being.

> Luke 22:12 And he shall shew [show] you a large upper room furnished: there make ready.

Mark tells a bit more information, in that the room was furnished and equipped for the Seder, meaning that the low table and pillows to lean back on as they laid on the floor around the low table while eating, drinking, singing and talking, were there.

> Mark 14:15 And he will shew [show] you a large upper room furnished and prepared: there make ready for us.

The gospels do not mention all the parts of the ceremony that would have taken place at the last Passover, and so I will not go into all that either.

[1] Exodus 12:1-14

[2] John 6:35

[3] Hebrews 4:14-15

[4] Exodus 5:15-19

THE LAST PASSOVER AND THE FIRST LORD'S SUPPER
Matthew 26:20-35, Mark 14:17-31, Luke 22:14-38, John 13:1-38

The Introduction By Jesus
Luke 22:14-16

The Old Testament prophetic messages concerning the first coming of the Messiah and His death would be fulfilled at this Passover. Jesus had never broken the Law of Moses, and therefore He was without fault. As the perfect Lamb of God, He was required by God to allow Himself to be crucified according to the prophetic Scriptures,[1] as a sacrifice that would cancel out the sins of men and women all over the world,[2] that would believe and accept this.[3] God is acting here the same way as a town council that has issued a parking ticket to a driver who has broken their rules by parking in a "No Parking" area. The fine must be paid by someone but it does not have to be the driver. The town council do not mind who pays the fine so long as it is paid. It is the same with God. He is quite happy for Jesus to pay the price we should have paid, so that we can go free. The punishment God demands for sin is death, but Jesus took the punishment for us, and God will accept that our debt to Him has been paid by Jesus,[4] if we believe and ask Him to do so.[3] Jesus was looking forward to this last Passover meal with His disciples.

Luke 22:14-16 [14] And when the hour [time] was come, he sat down, and the twelve apostles with him.

[15] And he said unto them, With desire I have desired to eat this Passover with you before I suffer:

[16] For I say unto you, I will not any more eat thereof, until it be fulfilled in the kingdom of God.

It was indeed a very special Passover which is why Jesus said He was looking forward to eating, "this Passover," because it was going to be so important. He would have to fulfil it by dying, and yet after dying He will eat it again and fulfil it again. "I will not any more eat thereof, until it be fulfilled in the kingdom of God."

Ezekiel prophesied the second coming of Jesus in glory, and the founding of the Messianic Kingdom, beginning with Ezekiel 43:1, and in 45:21 we learn that the Passover feast will be established again. The foundation of the Messianic Kingdom will be the blood of Jesus, because Jewish national righteousness will be a gift from God, just as Gentile individual righteousness is. Jesus was telling His Jewish disciples that this Passover meal would be enjoyed again in the Millennial Kingdom, that He would only have to suffer this once, and later He would eat the Passover again after the kingdom had been set up.

[1] Psalm 22:11-18

[2] Isaiah 53:4-12

[3] Romans 10:12-16, 1 Peter 1:18-21

[4] Romans 6:23

The Cup Of Thanksgiving
Luke 22:17-18

The Cup of Thanksgiving, also known as the Cup of Blessing, is the first of four cups of wine drunk during the Passover meal. The gospels only mention the first cup and the third cup directly, with the fourth cup being indirectly referred to. The meal is taken at night after the lady of the house has lit the candles, and begins with the Cup of Thanksgiving, followed by a long formal prayer of thanksgiving. It was this cup that was drunk at the beginning of the meal by Jesus and His disciples.

> Luke 22:17 And he took the cup, and gave thanks, and said, Take this, and divide it among yourselves.

Jesus then reiterated that He would not drink it again until the Kingdom of God had been established, and notice the phrase in the Scripture below, the fruit of the vine.

> Luke 22:18 For I say unto you, I will not drink of the fruit of the vine, until the kingdom of God shall come.

The wine used by Jews at their Passover today, comes in a normal wine bottle, with a normal looking label, on which in large lettering are the words, "Fruit of the Vine". Fruit of the Vine, is a special kind of strong wine used for the Passover, having been naturally fermented without the addition of yeast or sugar. Some Christians say that because Luke calls it, fruit of the vine, Jesus was drinking ordinary grape juice, and then they observe the Lord's Supper by breaking bread and drinking grape juice. The stuff Jesus and His disciples drank was strong natural wine made from grapes, and certainly alcoholic. The words, fruit of the vine, are still repeated by Jews today in their Passover blessing, which is as follows.

"Blessed be the Lord our God,
Who brought forth the fruit of the vine."

Jesus Takes The Role Of A Servant And Speaks Of Betrayal John 13:3-20

We are following the events in the life of Jesus, in the actual order they took place according to Luke, and for that reason I am missing out, John 13:1-2, not because the verses are wrong, but because Satan did not enter Judas Iscariot at this point. It was of course good for John to include those verses as an introduction to his subject of Jesus, washing the feet of His disciples, one of the many things John wrote about after the other three gospels had been written, which they had failed to mention. John introduces the story, with Jesus realising God had given Him complete authority, and yet He was about to play the role of servant to His disciples.

> John 13:3 Jesus knowing the Father had given all things into his hands, and that he was come from God, and went [was going back] to God.

In a traditional Passover setting some one plays the part of a servant, (often the mother or daughter), and she with others go around with a pitcher of water, a bowl, and a towel tied round the waist. The guests put their hands over the bowl, the servant pours water over them and the guests dry their hands with the towel. Peter and John found the place they were eating in by following a man carrying a pitcher of water, and this may have been why it was needed. Jesus changed the normal procedure in two ways.

1. He took the part of the servant.
2. He did not wash the guests' hands, He washed their feet instead.

What was about to happen would have been a strange experience for the disciples, and we can be sure that it got their wholehearted attention.

> John 13:4-5 ⁴ [Jesus] riseth from supper, and laid aside his garments; and took a towel, and girded [bound it around] himself.
>
> ⁵ After that he poureth water into a basin, and began to wash the disciple's feet, and to wipe them with the towel wherewith he was girded.

The disciples may have wondered what was going on, seeing their Messiah and King doing a servant's job, but no one seems to have dared to say anything until Jesus got to Peter.

> John 13:6 Then cometh he to Simon Peter: and Peter saith unto him, Lord, dost [do] thou [you] wash my feet?

To Peter it was not right for the Messiah to do such a thing.

> John 13:7 Jesus answered and said unto him, What I do thou knowest not now; but thou shalt know hereafter.

Peter does not understand what is being taught here, and Jesus tells him so, but he still protests.

> John 13:8 Peter saith unto him, Thou shalt never wash my feet. Jesus answered him, If I wash thee not, thou hast no part with me.

Peter had just called Jesus, Lord, and here he is telling his Lord what He cannot do. Jesus still did not make His teaching clear, but said to Peter, "If I wash thee not, thou hast no part with me." Peter pricked up his ears at that because at the time he did not understand that Jesus would die and then be resurrected. Peter expected Jesus to set up the Messianic Kingdom there and then and he wanted to play his part in the kingdom with Jesus as King, so he quickly changed his mind.

> John 13:9 Simon Peter saith unto him, Lord, not my feet only, but also my hands and my head.

Washing his head, his hands and his feet would almost amount to a complete bath, but Jesus said that a bath was unnecessary.

> John 13:10 Jesus saith unto him, He that is washed needeth not save [except] to wash his feet, but is clean every whit [bit]: and you are clean, ...

Jesus' talking about the need to wash the feet only, fits in with the practices of the day, because only the extremely rich had baths fitted in their houses. Most people in the city bathed in public baths and then walked home through the dusty streets getting their feet dirty, especially at the time of Passover which is in the dry season. There was always provision at the door of peoples city homes to wash your feet before you went in, either a bowl or a pitcher of water. If you were returning from the baths then after washing your feet, you were completely clean.

An application can be made here between bathing and being born again, and feet washing and being forgiven for the sins we commit after we have been born again. Everyone sins in this life, including every single born again Christian, because we are born with a sinful nature and are naturally wicked,[1] but spiritually speaking we can wash our feet, after we have been saved, by telling God privately in prayer what we have done and asking for forgiveness through the blood of Jesus.[2]

> 1 John 1:9 If we confess our sins, he is faithful and just to forgive us our sins, and to cleanse us from all unrighteousness.

Returning to John 13:10, which we did not quite finish, after telling the disciples that when their feet had been washed they would be clean, Jesus added a few more words.

> John 13:10-11 [10]..., but not all.
> [11] For he knew who should betray him; therefore said he, Ye are not all clean.

Jesus knew who was going to betray Him, but apart from the betrayer, who had agreed to deliver Him up for thirty pieces of silver, none of the other disciples knew anything about it, and here Jesus is just giving them a small clue, "Ye are not all clean."

We have an important lesson to learn from Jesus washing His disciple's feet, which is that Jesus is Lord, and if our Lord takes on the work of a servant to His disciples, then we who are His servants, must follow His example and be servants to one another.

> John 13:13-17 [13] Ye call me Master and Lord: and ye say well; for so I am.
> [14] If I then your Lord and Master, have washed your feet; ye also ought to wash one another's feet.
> [15] For I have given you an example, that ye should do as I have done to you.

¹⁶ Verily, verily [Truly, truly], I say unto you, The servant is not greater than his lord; neither he that is sent is greater than he that sent him.

¹⁷ If ye know these things, happy are ye if ye do them.

The word "apostle" means, "one that is sent," and the apostles are to remember later on, when Jesus their Lord and Master sends them out to preach the gospel, that they are merely His servants and must follow His example, by serving one another.

At the beginning of this chapter when Jesus forecast His crucifixion He told the disciples He was going to be betrayed, now He adds to that by saying that one of them will be the one that does it, but they are still not told who it will be.

> John 13:18 I speak not of you all: I know whom I have chosen: but that the scripture may be fulfilled, He that eateth [eats] bread with me hath lifted up his heal against me.

[1] 1 John 1:8
[2] Ephesians 1:7, Hebrews 9:22, 1 John 1:7

Karpas: Vegetable
Matthew 26:20-25, Mark 14:17-21

I like to call the ceremony of Karpas, the Green Vegetable Ceremony, and it comes after the washing of hands, but for this special Passover it was after the washing of feet. In order to carry out Karpas, bowls of salt water had been placed on the table representing the salt tears of the Hebrew slaves in Egypt, and the salt water of the Red Sea, through which they walked to freedom on dry land,[1] before God drowned Pharaoh and the Egyptian army.[2] Some green vegetable was provided representing the humble beginnings of the Jewish people. Green is symbolic of spring time and youth, and the Passover happened during the spring when the Israelites were a newly emerging nation. The green vegetable is dipped in the salt water and eaten, parsley is usually used because when it is dipped in the salt water and shaken the droplets look like tears. The idea behind keeping the Jewish Passover is to remember how they were slaves in Egypt and how God rescued them with great power.

> Mark 14:18 And as they sat [reclined] and did eat.

At Passover there are several occasions when everyone reclines to the left and eats with their right hand, and Karpas is such a time, and while they were still reclining Jesus made an announcement.

> Matthew 26:21 Verily [Truly] I say unto you, that one of you will betray me.

The disciples were very concerned about this, and then Jesus gave them a clue.

> Matthew 26:23 He that dippeth [dips] his hand with me in the dish, the same shall betray me.

The bowls of salt water would have been placed so that everyone was in reach of a bowl to dip the green vegetable in. As Jesus dipped His vegetable, Judas also dipped his in the same bowl, and in that moment was marked out as the betrayer. Judas as we know already had agreed to inform on Jesus, but he was still playing the deceiver and acting as if he was innocent.

> Matthew 26:25 Then Judas, which betrayed him, answered and said, Master, is it I? He said unto him, Thou hast said.

"Thou hast said," or, "You have said," in the original Greek is a saying which means, "Yes certainly." Proceeding with the story we will see that the other disciples had not noticed this short conversation between Jesus and Judas.

---

[1] Exodus 14:22, Hebrews 11:29

[2] Exodus 14:28, Psalm 136:15

This Is My Body
Matthew 26:26, Mark 14:22, Luke 22:19, 1 Corinthians 11:23-24

The order of the Passover meal has changed since AD 70 with the dispersion of the Jews throughout the nations, for they are no longer able to sacrifice the lamb in the Temple, but we will start by examining the way they deal with the bread during the feast today. Three loaves are placed in the middle of the table, inside a single bag with three compartments, or alternatively are wrapped in a large folded napkin. The napkin is folded twice so that it is a quarter of its original size with three compartments for the three loaves of matza, a Hebrew word for unleavened bread, which means these "loaves" have not risen in the oven and are flat like pancakes.

The Jews use these three loaves that are separated and yet in one container to perform the "Aphikomen" ceremony. The middle matza is the Aphikomen and it is removed and broken in two, half is put back and the other half is wrapped in a linen cloth and hidden away somewhere, before the main course is eaten. After the main course has been finished, the linen cloth is unwrapped, the matza is broken and each person is given a piece. Notice that the "Aphikomen" ceremony has two stages, first half of it is wrapped in linen and hidden before the main course, and the second stage comes after eating the main course when the third cup of wine is drunk, it is taken from the place where it was hidden, unwrapped and given out. The matza used for the Passover ceremony must conform to three requirements by Jewish law.

1. It must be unleavened.
2. It must be pierced, the holes are big enough for you to see through when held up to the light.
3. It must be striped by dark lines on its crust that are the result of being slightly burnt in a hot cooking oven.

Now we can return to the gospels.

Luke 22:19 And he took bread, and gave thanks, and brake it, and gave it unto them, saying, This is my body which is given for you:

Matthew 26:26 Take, eat; this is my body.

Mark 14:22 Take, eat: this is my body.

Jesus was not talking about any old bread when He said, "This is my body," but only about matza, the unleavened bread of the Jewish Passover, and the matza represents His body in ways ordinary bread does not.

1. It is unleavened, symbolizing that Jesus had no sin. He kept the Law of Moses to the last jot and tittle, just as He said He would.[1]

2. Matza is pierced, and Jesus was pierced through His hands and feet when He was nailed to the cross, and when the soldier stuck the spear into His side.[2]

3. Matza is striped, and the Roman whips striped His body when He was scourged.[3]

Matza and wine as used by Lucy and me

The only bread that represents the body of Jesus is matza. When Lucy and I take communion at home together we prefer to use matza. It is horrible for us to use ordinary bread made with yeast because when we see it risen and inflated, we think this bread is not the body of Jesus, it is all puffed-up with sin, and it pricks our consciences to use something that reminds us of a sinful person, when remembering and worshipping our Saviour.

Returning to the Passover feast, the three pieces of matza one above another in one bag or cloth represent the Trinity of the God Head, God the Father on the top, God the Son in the middle and God the Holy Spirit (or Holy Ghost), at the bottom. The middle matza, the "Aphikomen," is removed representing the time Jesus left heaven and came down to earth as a man. If we ask Jews why they call the middle matza, "Aphikomen," they do not know. A word in the Greek lexicon sounds exactly like this "Aphikomen," but it is not written the same, and it means, "I CAME." Who came? The one that was without sin, pierced, scourged, the Lord Jesus, the True Passover, that's who came.

Three matzas separated and yet in one napkin

Bible scholars disagree about the way the "Aphikomen" ceremony was performed at the time of Jesus. Some say it was in two stages as it is done by Jews today. Others say that there was only one stage but it makes no difference to the meaning of what Jesus said about the matza, "This is My body which is given for you."

The broken matza is wrapped in a linen cloth and hidden away, just as the body of Jesus was taken from the cross, wrapped in linen and hidden in a tomb. The matza is later unwrapped, as the body of Jesus was when God resurrected His worldly corpse to eternal heavenly life. When the middle matza is unwrapped the third cup of wine is drunk. Why do unbelieving Jews take out the middle matza and call it, "I Came"? Some Jews keep a piece of "Aphikomen" and hide it in a drawer, then if they become ill, they go and break off a piece of "I Came," hold it towards heaven and pray.

> "God of Abraham, Isaac and Jacob.
> I am taking this, LORD God,
> In the name that it represents,
> And I claim my healing."

They pray to Jesus without knowing it and He heals them. At other times they may be in need of money, and then remember the "Aphikomen," the "I Came," in their draw. Again they break a piece off and hold it towards heaven and pray.

> "God of Abraham, Isaac and Jacob.
> We are getting short of cash.
> I am taking this LORD God,
> In the name that it represents."

Their financial difficulties are then solved by their Messiah, Jesus.

Just as the reason for the Passover Feast was to remember, so it is also the theme of the Lord's Supper. We are to keep it so as not to forget what Jesus has done for us.

> Luke 22:19 This is my body which is given for you: this do in remembrance of me.

1 Corinthians 11:24 And when he had given thanks, he brake it, and said, Take, eat: this is my body, which is broken for you: this do in remembrance of me.

[1] Matthew 5:17-19
[2] John 20:24-28
[3] Matthew 27:26, Mark 15:15, Luke 18:33, John 19:1

Jesus Gave The Sop To Judas Iscariot
John 13:21-30

Here again we have an example of John giving us information not found in the other three gospels. The feast has now reached the point where they remember the time when as slaves they were forced to make clay bricks for Pharaoh, and this is when the sticky brown charoseth, prepared by Peter and John, to resemble the clay, is eaten. A sop is a piece of bread dipped in a liquid. At Passover the sop that is eaten in remembrance of the Jews being forced to make bricks, is made by breaking a piece of bread from the matza and dipping it in charoseth. Since they began this feast in that large upper room Jesus had warned them twice that He would be betrayed, and now He warns them again.

1. The first time was when he was washing their feet.[1]
2. The second time was during the green vegetable ceremony.[2]
3. This third time will be when He gives Judas the sop.[3]

Although they have been warned that one of them will betray Jesus, and shown who it was in the green vegetable ceremony, they have not yet realised who it will be and that is what they still want to know.

John 13:22 Then the disciples looked one on another, doubting [puzzled] of whom he spake [spoke].

At this point the apostle John introduces himself into the story as the disciple Jesus loved. In those days it was not considered polite to name yourself when telling a story about your own life such as John was doing here.

> John 13:23 Now there was leaning on Jesus bosom one of his disciples, whom Jesus loved.

A Passover table is so low that you cannot use chairs, you recline around it on pillows. John was next to Jesus and Peter was somewhere further along. A lot of talking may have been going on and Peter could not hear properly everything Jesus was saying, so he signalled to John to find out which one of them would betray Jesus.

> John 13:24-25 [24] Simon Peter therefore beckoned to him, that he should ask who it should be of whom he spake [spoke].
>
> [25] He then lying on Jesus' breast saith unto him, Lord, who is it?

Jesus did not name Judas Iscariot, but he gave them a clue.

> John 13:26 Jesus answered, He it is, to whom I shall give a sop, when I have dipped it. And when he had dipped the sop, he gave it to Judas Iscariot, the son of Simon.

Jesus would have dipped the sop into the charoseth thirteen times, once for each of the twelve disciples and again for himself. Surprisingly, once again the disciples did not understand what they had been told.

> John 13:27 And after the sop Satan entered into him ….

Satan entered into Judas the first time to negotiate a price to betray Jesus away from the crowds.[4] Now he had entered a second time to do the actual betraying, and so Jesus continues in the same verse, John 13:27, … "Then said Jesus unto him, That thou doest, do quickly." In verse 29, we see that the clue Jesus gave as to who would betray Him had not been understood, because when Judas left the disciples thought that because he had the money bag, he was going to buy something more to eat or to give some money to the poor, which is still the custom of Jews at Passover.

John 13:30 He then having received the sop went immediately out: and it was night.

Why do you think John said it was night? Passover is always celebrated at night, to remember the night the angel of death passed-over the Hebrews in Egypt, because he saw the blood of the lamb on their lintels and door posts. We said back in Chapter 2, that John had a sub-theme of the conflict between light and darkness. Judas was being controlled by Satan, he was going to do something wrong, and he did it secretly at night. Something was going wrong here, the chief priests had decided not to arrest Jesus during the feast,[5] but they had forgotten to tell that to Judas Iscariot,[6] so off he went in the dark to do his dirty deed.

Later when we look at the Jewish trial we will notice the chief priests are very poorly organised and not properly prepared. The false witnesses had not been told what to say and all said different things, because the chief priests had not planned for the trial to be during Passover, but Jesus had forced them into action, because every detail of His coming death was always under His absolute control. The Lamb of God had decided that at this Passover, He would be sacrificed for us.

[1] John 13:18
[2] Matthew 26:21
[3] John 13:26
[4] Luke 22:3
[5] Matthew 26:5
[6] Luke 22:5-6

The Cup Of Remembrance
Matthew 26:27-29, Mark 14:23-25, Luke 22:20-23

The Cup of Remembrance is the third cup to be drunk at Passover. The gospels do not talk about the second cup, which is called the Cup of Plagues, it reminds the Jews of the ten plagues that God inflicted on the Egyptians because they refused to let the Israelites go.[1] No one can drink the second cup until he has spilt ten drops of wine from it, calling out the name of each plague as each drop comes out.

1. The water was turned to blood.
2. The plague of frogs.
3. The plague of gnats.
4. The plague of insects.
5. The death of the Egyptian livestock.
6. The Egyptians plagued with boils and sores.
7. The damage from the hail on the Egyptians and their area only.
8. The plague of locusts in the Egyptian areas only.
9. The darkness for three days which caused the Egyptians physical pain.
10. The death of the Egyptians firstborn sons and animals.

Only after the ten drops of wine have been spilled and the ten plagues named with each drop, can the wine be drunk. The reason for this is that it is against Jewish law to rejoice over the hardship of other people, including their enemies, and so the ten drops are a symbol of sadness. The second cup is drunk before the sop is eaten.

The main course was eaten after the sop, it included the roast lamb, unleavened bread and bitter herbs. Next we have the final part of the "Aphikomen" ceremony, when the hidden half of the broken matza is brought out, unwrapped, broken and shared around, and it is with the "Aphikomen," meaning, "I Came," that the third cup, the Cup of Remembrance is drunk.

To the Jews celebrating Passover, the third cup is a symbol of the blood of the lamb that protected the first born male children and first born male animals from the tenth plague. We know Jesus was talking about the third cup because Luke tells us that it was after supper, after the main course.

Luke 22:20 Likewise also the cup after supper, saying, This cup is the new testament [covenant or promise] in my blood, which is shed [poured out] for you.

The first and second cups are consumed before supper, afterwards comes the third cup, which the Jews also call the Cup of Redemption.

Matthew 26:27-28 [27] And he took the cup, and gave thanks, and gave it to them, saying, Drink ye all of it;

[28] For this is my blood of the new testament [promise], which is shed [poured out] for the remission of sins.

From now on the third cup will symbolise the blood of the Lamb of God, who as John the Baptist said, takes away the sin of the world.[2]

Mark 14:25 Verily [Truly] I say unto you, I will drink no more of the fruit of the vine, until that day that I drink it new in the kingdom of God.

Jesus had already said the same thing about the first cup, and now He says it about the third cup, He will not celebrate Passover again until the Messianic Kingdom is set up after His second coming.

Matthew 26:29 I will not drink henceforth of this fruit of the vine, until that day when I drink it new with you in my Father's kingdom.

Judas had gone, and in the Millennial Kingdom, Jesus is going to celebrate the Passover again with His remaining eleven apostles. In the meantime the Church has been told to remember the Passover feast in the form of the Lord's Supper.

1 Corinthians 11:26 For as often as ye eat this bread, and drink this cup, ye do shew [proclaim] the Lord's death until he come.

The bread Jesus asked us to use in the Lord's supper is the "Aphikomen," the "I Came," and we do it to proclaim His death, His body broken for us. He became a man so that He could die a man's death for us, and in exchange we believers will be given His eternal life,[3] the kind of life God has. However we will only celebrate the Lord's supper, "until He comes," because then the Passover feast will be reinstated in the Messianic Kingdom.[4]

The cup Jesus asked us to drink is the third cup, the Cup of Remembrance. It is drunk after the sop is dipped in the charoseth and eaten, and we know that Judas Iscariot went out immediately after the sop had been eaten,[5] but I want to refer you to Luke 22:20-23. At first glance it appears that Judas was still there when the third cup was consumed, but it does not say they drunk from the cup at once, only that Judas was present when Jesus having spoken about the cup, pointed out that His betrayer was still there. Judas Iscariot had been told by Jesus to quickly go and complete what he was going to do,[6] and Judas left immediately after the sop had been eaten, as John says he did, maybe prompted by the remark made by Jesus in Luke 22:21-22, after He announced, "This cup is the new covenant in My blood."

The vital phrase spoken by Jesus at the last Passover and the first Lord's Supper is, "in remembrance of Me." The bread and the wine **do not** turn into the body and blood of Jesus when we drink them, as the Roman Catholics believe they do, and they **do not** contain His body or blood as the Lutherans teach. If you ever go to a Jewish Passover the word you will keep on hearing is, "remember." Everything in the ceremony is done to remember something, this is eaten to remember that, and that is done to remember this. The thrust of the Passover is remembrance, in order that the Jews never forget what God has done for them, and in the same way the thrust of the Lord's Supper is that we remember what He has done for us. We remember His broken body when we take the "Aphikomen," the "I Came," and we remember His blood, which He poured out as a seal, a signature, of His covenant, His promise, to give believers everlasting life.

> 1 Corinthians 11:24-25 [24] And when he had given thanks, he brake it, and said, Take, eat: this is my body, which is broken for you: this do in remembrance of me.
>
> [25] After the same manner also he took the cup, when he had supped [eaten supper], saying, This cup is the new testament

[covenant] in my blood: this do ye, as oft [often] as ye drink it, in remembrance of me.

The words in the verse we just read, "as often as you drink it," make us wonder how frequently we should do so. The minimum is one year, because the Passover is celebrated annually, but on the other hand the early Christians broke bread together much more frequently and the Scriptures show them doing it, continually,[7] daily[8] and weekly.[9] I do it in reverence and with deep and sincere gratefulness to Jesus. It brings me closer to Him, so that I sense His nearness to me and experience the knowledge that He has a special, reserved place for me in His Kingdom, and that just makes me love Him.

John 14:15 [Jesus said] If you love me, keep my commandments.

I have not gone through all the New Testament, searching for and listing the commandments of Jesus, but one commandment I keep results in a wonderful blessing. It is, "This do in remembrance of Me."

Luke 22:19 And he took bread, and gave thanks, and brake it, and gave unto them, saying, This is my body which is given for you: this do in remembrance of me.

---

[1] Exodus 7:1 to 11:10
[2] John 1:29
[3] Hebrews 2:9
[4] Matthew 26:29, Ezekiel 45:21-25
[5] John 13:30
[6] John 13:27
[7] Acts 2:42
[8] Acts 2:46
[9] Acts 20:7

Great Men Of God
Luke 22:24-30

> Luke 22:24 And there was also a strife [rivalry] among them [the disciples], which of them should be accounted [regarded] the greatest.

Jesus had just been teaching them that they needed to be servants to one another, when He washed their feet, and here they were already arguing about which of them was the greatest. Jesus explained that they must not behave like people of the world. In the world the leaders control the people through using the authority or greatness of their position, but amongst believers in Jesus the greatest people are the ones who serve other believers. The greatest example of this is Jesus Himself, because He was the only man who ever lived who was perfect and yet He became our servant, dying for us to give us eternal life. In the Messianic Kingdom things will change, He will be King of Kings and Lord of Lords.[1] The world's greatest servant will be the leader in the Kingdom of God.

> Luke 22:25-26 25 And he said unto them, The kings of the Gentiles exercise lordship over them; and they that exercise authority over them are called benefactors.
>
> 26 But ye shall not be so: but he that is greatest among you, let him be as the younger; and he that is chief, as he that doth serve.

The disciples now learned the lesson and did as Jesus told them right up until they died. Jesus knew they would, that is why He was able to promise each one of them a kingdom of their own after His second coming.

> Luke 22:29-30 29 And I appoint unto you a kingdom, as my Father hath appointed unto me;
>
> 30 That ye may eat and drink at my table in my kingdom, and sit on thrones judging the twelve tribes of Israel.

[1] 1 Timothy 6:14-15, Revelation 17:14, 19:16

Jesus Commands His Disciples To Love Each Other As Much As He Loves Them
Matthew 26:31-35, Mark 14:27-31, Luke 22:31-38, John 13:31-38

John has told us that Judas left the feast to go and betray Jesus, the result of which will end in the crucifixion. Jesus was very pleased about this because it would be for the glory of God and Himself.

> John 13:31 Therefore when he [Judas] was gone out, Jesus said, Now is the Son of man glorified, and God is glorified in him.

The coming crucifixion means that Jesus will soon leave this old world behind.

> John 13:33 Little children, yet a little while I am with you. Ye shall seek me: and as I said unto the Jews, Whither I go, you cannot come.

Jesus has an important instruction to give to His disciples before He goes, which is about the love of God.

> John 13:33-34 ³³ Now I say unto you.
>
> ³⁴ A new commandment I give unto you, that ye love one another; as I have loved you, that ye also love one another.

The Law of Moses stated, "you shall love your neighbour as yourself,"[1] and yet Jesus says His commandment is new. Jesus' new commandment is greater than Moses' commandment, because under Moses, to love your neighbour as yourself was enough, but Jesus wants believers in Him to love each other as much as He loves each one of us, and His love is perfect. Some people don't like themselves very much at all and can keep the Law of Moses, by loving their neighbour as themselves, which is not all that highly, but that is not good enough for Jesus. He wants everyone to recognise us as His people by the way we love each other.

John 13:35 By this shall all men know that ye are my disciples, if ye have love one to another.

Jesus had already said that one of them would betray Him, and Judas had gone off to do it, now He said that the other disciples would run away and leave Him, so that He would be left on His own.

Matthew 26:31 Then Jesus saith unto them, All ye shall be offended [stumble] because of me this night: for it is written, I will smite the shepherd, and the sheep of the flock shall be scattered abroad.[2]

He then told them that after they had been scattered, they should all go to Galilee and regroup, because He would meet them there after He had obtained eternal life.

Matthew 26:32 But after I am risen again, I will go before you into Galilee.

After the Shepherd has been smitten, meaning after Jesus has been killed, the disciples will be afraid and when this happens they must all go to Galilee. He will command them to go to Galilee three times, this is the first time. The trouble is that they still do not understand that Jesus is going to die and then be raised to life again, and that is why they did not obey Him and go to Galilee after the crucifixion.

The story continues in the gospels of Matthew, Mark and John with a discussion between Jesus and Peter.[3] Peter wanted to know where Jesus was going, and Jesus said that Peter could not follow Him now, but he would follow on later. Peter wanted to know why he could not follow now, and said he could follow Jesus anywhere He went, and if all the other disciples scattered, he never would because he was going to follow Jesus even if he had to die.

Unknown to Simon Peter, there was a spiritual war going on between Satan and Jesus, and Satan had demanded that he be given a chance to test Peter, like he had tested Job.[4] Jesus warned Peter about this, and prayed for Peter's protection during the time of testing. Peter would stumble but he would not lose faith.

Luke 22:31-32 31 And the Lord said, Simon, Simon, behold, Satan hath desired to have you, that he may sift you as wheat:

³² But I have prayed for thee, that thy faith fail not: and when thou art [have] converted [returned], strengthen thy brethren.

Although Peter will be tested by Satan, and will stumble, the end result will be him having stronger faith than the other disciples, and then he is to encourage and strengthen them. We will see later that Peter was the first of all the apostles to see Jesus alive after He had been tortured, mutilated, killed and buried.

Peter was absolutely sure of himself, and told Jesus that even if all the other disciples were to leave Jesus and be scattered, he would not be like them, he would not leave.

> Mark 14:29 But Peter said unto him, Although all shall be offended [fall away], yet will not I.

Peter had no doubt in himself. A lot of us are like that and we have to learn that although God will keep his promises to us, we are often not able to keep our promises to Him. I learned this very early in my walk with God, I had vowed to do something but later found I could not. I do not recall what it was now, but for some reason I could not keep my promise. Later I found out that Jesus does not require us to make vows anyway.[5] Getting back to self confident Peter, Jesus prophesied that Peter would deny that he even knew Jesus, not just once but three times.

> Mark 14:30 And Jesus saith unto him, Verily [Truly] I say unto thee, That this day, even in this night, before the cock crow twice, thou [you] shalt [shall] deny me thrice [three times].

The cock crow was not a male chicken trying to wake everyone up while it was still dark. The cock crow was the name given to the sounding of a horn to tell people in the city what the time was, in those days when there were no clocks. There were four cock crows, the first was at mid-night and the second was at three o'clock in the morning, and before the second cock crow, Peter will deny he knows Jesus three times. Peter told Jesus, that he would never do such a thing, and so did the other disciples.

> Mark 14:31 But he [Peter] spake the more vehemently [strongly], If I should die with thee, I will not deny thee in any wise [way]. Likewise also said they all.

Peter and all the other disciples said they would never, ever betray Jesus, never deny Him, and never scatter from Him and leave Him. Jesus did not argue, He had told them, and we will see what happened.

The death of Jesus will mean changes for the disciples and the way they are to live and provide for themselves. While Jesus was with them they had been told not to carry a purse, not to carry two coats, not to carry new shoes, they were to repair their old ones, and not to carry a walking stick.[6]

> Luke 10:4 Carry neither purse, nor scrip [leather pouch], nor shoes, and salute [greet] no man by the way.

Jesus made sure all these needs were provided for while He was with them, but from now on things would be different, and He gave fresh instructions before He died.

> Luke 22:35-36 ³⁵ And he said unto them, When I sent you without purse, and scrip [leather pouch], and shoes, lacked ye anything? And they said, Nothing.

> ³⁶ Then he said unto them, But now, he that hath a purse, let him take it, and likewise his scrip: and he that hath no sword, let him sell his garment, and buy one.

The sword would be needed to defend themselves, not for the defence of the Christian faith. What Jesus was doing was cancelling the previous orders given to His disciples and issuing new ones, He was not asking them to declare war on unbelievers, just telling the apostles that they would have to take care of themselves from now on. The reason is that when Jesus is physically on earth things are different, for example before Jesus was rejected as the Messiah, everyone that went to Him for healing was healed.[7] After His second coming there will be great changes in this world.

Isaiah 2:4 They shall beat their swords into plowshares, and their spears into pruninghooks: nation shall not lift up sword against nation, neither shall they learn war any more.

[1] Leviticus 19:18
[2] Zechariah 13:7
[3] Matthew 26:33-35, Mark 14:29-31, John 13:36-38
[4] Job 1:8-12, 2:3-6
[5] Matthew 5:34
[6] Matthew 10:10
[7] Matthew 8:16, 12:15

Jesus And His Disciples Sing Praises To God
Matthew 26:30, Mark 14:26

In the two verses above, Matthew and Mark say that after they had sung a hymn they went out from the upper room onto the Mount of Olives. Luke does not mention the hymn but he says they went out in Luke 22:39. Luke remember is the only one that claimed to write the story in the correct order, and he is right again here. Although we have dealt with Matthew 26:31-35, and Mark 14:27-33, in the previous section on the new commandment about love, what those Scriptures record, took place before the events in Matthew 26:30 and Mark 14:26, that we are discussing now, although they come afterwards. You can check this by looking back to the time Jesus warns Peter that he will deny Jesus before the second cock crow. Luke records this before they went out in Luke 22:39, but the other two gospels wrongly place the warning to Peter after they went out and sung a hymn.

The Passover ceremony ends with the Hallel, the singing of Psalms 113-118, and the fourth cup of wine, the Cup of Praise, which is drunk while they sing Psalms 117 and 118. Hallel is a Hebrew word meaning, praise.

Matthew 26:30 And when they had sung an hymn.

The Greek word translated as hymn actually means more than one hymn. The same word in Acts 16:25 is translated, "sung praises," "Paul and Silas prayed, and sung praises unto God," and that is how it should have been translated here, because six Psalms are sung at the Hallel.

Psalm 117 " O praise the LORD, all ye nations: praise him all ye people. For his merciful kindness is great towards us: and the truth of the LORD endureth forever. Praise ye the LORD."

Psalm 118 has several verses which are prophetic of Jesus Himself.

Psalm 118:10 All nations compassed me about: but in the name of the LORD will I destroy them.

Psalm 118:17 I shall not die, but live, and declare the works of the LORD.

Psalm 118:20 This gate of the LORD, into which the righteous shall enter.

Psalm 118:22 The stone which the builders refused is become the head stone of the corner.

Psalm 118:26 Blessed be he that cometh in the name of the LORD: we have blessed you out of the house of the LORD.

Psalm 118:28 Thou art my God. And I will praise thee: thou art my God, I will exalt thee.

Psalm 118:29 O give thanks unto the LORD; for he is good: for his mercy endureth for ever.

All those verses quoted from Psalm 118 speak of Jesus, and every year during Passover the Jews sing them while also drinking the fourth cup, the Cup of Praise, and yet they do not know Him, or understand what they are doing.

AN EXPLANATION OF WHAT WE ARE GOING TO DO NEXT

We are now going to look at the Gospel of John, chapters 14, 15 and 16, and we are going to study them through twice, first looking at His promises and then at His advice and other information. The seventh talk given by Jesus, that John wrote down for us, begins in John 13:31 and ends with John 17:26, and so we will cover most of that talk here. In this talk Jesus made two promises I want you to remember.

1. Jesus will go away to His Fathers house, but later on He will come back and take us to be with Him and His Father.[1]
2. Jesus will go away and will then send a Comforter or Helper to stay with us forever.[2]

There are four other things we need to understand from this talk by Jesus.

1. Jesus here is gradually giving up His work as a prophet, and becoming our Priest.
2. Jesus is moving away from the system under the Law of Moses, to the present one in which we are saved by grace, by believing in Him.
3. Jesus in His talk establishes the new foundations of the New Testament way of salvation, which the apostles expand on in their New Testament letters, known as the epistles.
4. The death and resurrection of Jesus, meant that from then on there has been a new relationship between Him and those of us who are saints, including of course the apostles.

The sixth, "I am," statement from Jesus comes in John 14:6, "I am the way the truth and the life," and the seventh one comes in John 15:1, "I am the true vine." We have now discovered all seven signs, all seven talks and all seven "I am," statements of Jesus from the Gospel of John.

[1] John 14:2-3
[2] John 14:16

TWENTY-FIVE PROMISES MADE BY JESUS
John 14:1 to 16:33

Promise No. 1

He is going to prepare a place for us.

John 14:2 I go to prepare a place for you.

Promise No. 2

He will come back and get us.

John 14:3 And if I go and prepare a place for you, I will come again, and receive you unto myself; that where I am, there ye may be also.

Jesus was going to heaven,[1] and He will come back and take us to the place He was going, so when He returns He will take us to be with Him in heaven. This is important because He is talking about the rapture, which we mentioned in Chapter 11, and after the rapture, or when we die if we die before the rapture, we are going to heaven to be with Jesus.[2]

Promise No. 3

They will do greater works than Jesus.

John 14:12 Verily, verily [Truly, truly], I say unto you, He that believeth on me, the works that I do shall he do also; and greater works than these shall he do; because I go unto the Father.

Christian literature, films, videos and sound tracks, all record men and women believers, performing miracles such as stopping storms, raising the dead, healing the sick, and many evangelists have successfully led their hearers into eternal life, which must be the greatest of all miracles. Jesus did all these things on earth by following the leading of His Father,[3] and therefore these men and women of God have not done anything greater than Jesus did. To my knowledge His raising of Lazarus from the dead was the most dramatic case of being raised from the dead ever, after the resurrection of Jesus, and His control of the weather on the Sea of Galilee, is the greatest example of stilling a storm. The greater works that believers do over and above those of Jesus are probably greater in number rather than greater in quality. Even then the number of miracles performed by Jesus was huge. Of course if God gives us the faith to perform a miracle for His glory, nothing is impossible,[4] and Jesus gives us the reason, "because I go to the Father."

Promise No. 4

Jesus promises to answer prayers.

> John 14:13 And whatsoever ye shall ask in my name, that I will do.

Promise No. 5

God will send His Spirit to stay with and in believers forever.

> John 14:16-18 ¹⁶ And I will pray the Father, and he shall give you another Comforter, that he may abide with you for ever;
>
> ¹⁷ Even the Spirit of truth; whom the world cannot receive, because it seeth [sees] him not, neither knoweth [knows] him: but ye know him: for he dwelleth [lives] with you, and shall be in you.
>
> ¹⁸ I will not leave you comfortless: I will come to you.

In the Old Testament, some believers had the Spirit of God and some did not, and some of them that had the Spirit, did not have Him continually,[5] but now in the age of grace, Jesus has prayed to His Father that the Spirit will remain with us forever. His prayer to His Father is for all believers, "He that believeth on me," John 14:12. In verse 17, Jesus told His disciples that at that time before His death, the Spirit was with them, "for he dwelleth [lives] with you," but later, after Acts 2, the Spirit would be in them, not with them but in them, "and shall be in you." In verse 18, He puts it another way, "I will come to you," He is going to come to us like, or in the form of the Holy Spirit, as a Comforter and Helper, "I will not leave you comfortless."

Promise No. 6

God the Father and God the Son will both love us.

> John 14:21 He that hath [has] my commandments, and keepeth [keeps] them, he it is that loveth [loves] me: and he that loveth [loves] me shall be loved by my Father, and I will love him, and will manifest [show] myself to him.

The prize given to those of us who show our love of Jesus by following His instructions, will be the love of God the Father, and Jesus.

Promise No. 7

I have never seen Jesus, but I have heard Him speak to me with my ears, and I have understood His instructions to me as an individual, through a kind of inner knowledge. I am talking about instructions not given to every believer, and not found in the Bible. In these ways Jesus has manifested Himself to me, because although He was not visible He was discernible. Another way the words of the Scripture already quoted, "I will love him, and will manifest myself to him," were fulfilled was in the case of the disciples He was actually making the promises to, when He physically met and spoke with them after His resurrection.[6]

Promise No. 8

The Holy Spirit would comfort them, supernaturally teach them and make them remember everything Jesus had ever told them.

> John 14:26 But the Comforter, which is the Holy Ghost [Spirit], whom the Father will send in my name, he shall teach you all things, and bring all things to your remembrance, whatsoever I have said unto you.

John wrote his gospel decades after Jesus had died, and many Bible scholars say that after such long a time he would not have been able to remember exactly what Jesus had said. Here we have the reason why John is absolutely accurate, the Holy Spirit was sent by God to John and reminded him of every word Jesus had said. Many university educated professors and church men cannot understand how a group of uneducated fishermen can be trusted. They can be trusted completely, and being uneducated and not wanting to make a mistake they only wrote down what they knew they had correctly remembered. Highly educated men sometimes write down things from their own mind, and their thoughts and opinions can be very different from what we find in the Bible. Remember that some promises of Jesus, like this one, were for the apostles only, and others, such as the promise that the Holy Spirit will be in us, were for all believers. Make sure you understand which are which.

Promise No. 9

Jesus promised them peace in their hearts, because although they would be persecuted for preaching the gospel, they would have an inner peace through understanding that God was with them and in control, something unbelievers never experience.

> John 14:27 Peace I leave with you, my peace I give unto you: not as the world giveth [gives], give I unto you. Let not your heart be troubled, neither let it be afraid.

Promise No. 10

> John 15:5 I am the vine, ye are the branches: He that abideth [stays] in me, and I in him, the same bringeth [brings] forth much fruit: for without me ye can do nothing.

Jesus promises believers a new and much more personal and closer working relationship with Himself, because we are, in Christ.

Promise No. 11

They will be friends of Jesus, as well His servants.

> John 15:14-15 14 Ye are my friends, if ye do whatsoever I command you.
>
> 15 Henceforth I call ye not servants; for the servant knoweth [knows] not what his lord [master] doeth [does]: but I have called you friends; for all things that I have heard of my Father I have made known unto you.

They will have the high honour of being the friends of Jesus.

Promise No. 12

They have all been chosen for special assignments, and Jesus wants them to be successful, so if they ever need a hand in their work, God will answer their prayers for help.

John 15:16 Ye have not chosen me, but I have chosen you, and ordained [appointed] you, that ye should go and bring forth fruit, and that your fruit should remain: that whatsoever ye shall ask of the Father in my name, he may give it you.

God will answer the prayers they make for help in completing the good works Jesus has appointed them to do.

Promise No. 13

They will be hated by the world, by unbelievers, for four reasons.

1. True believers are not part of the world system, because the world does not believe that Jesus is the Son of God.

John 15:18-19 ¹⁸ If the world hate you, ye know that it hated me before it hated you.

¹⁹ If ye were of the world, the world would love his own: but because ye are not of the world, but I have chosen you out of the world, therefore the world hateth [hates] you.

2. People find it difficult to persecute Jesus because He is in heaven, but it is much easier for them to be angry with the followers of Jesus who are in the world.

John 15:20 Remember the word that I said unto you, The servant is not greater than his lord [master]. If they have persecuted me, they will also persecute you; if they have kept [heeded] my saying, they will keep [heed] yours also.

3. The third reason they will be hated is because God the Father is not known by the world.

John 15:21 But all these things will they do unto you for my name's sake, because they know not him that sent me.

4. The people of the world know what sin is, and when they see believers living a different lifestyle, they understand that they are not of the same standard, and so they hate them.

John 15:22 If I had not come and spoken unto them, they had not had sin: but now they have no cloak [excuse] for their sin.

Promise No. 14

The Holy Spirit, living in the believer, will bear witness of the real Jesus.

John 15:26 But when the Comforter is come, whom I will send unto you from the Father, even the Spirit of Truth, which proceedeth [comes] from the Father, he shall testify of me.

Promise No. 15

The disciples will bear witness of Jesus.

John 15:27 And ye also shall bear witness, because ye have been with me from the beginning.

Promise No. 16

The disciples will be banned from worshipping God in the Jewish synagogues.

John 16:2 They shall put you out of the synagogues.

Promise No. 17

Some of them will be killed, martyred.

John 16:2 Yea, the time cometh [will come], that whoever killeth [kills] you will think that he doeth [does] God service.

Certain Christian denominations as well as non-Christian religions fit in here, believing they are serving God when they are actually persecuting the people of God, just as Jesus promised would happen. The reason is that they do not know the God of Israel in the first place, and persecute those who do not do things their way, just as the Pharisees persecuted Jesus.

John 16:3 And these things they will do unto you, because they have not known the Father, nor me.

Promise No. 18

The Holy Spirit will find the world guilty.

> John 16:7-11 ⁷ Nevertheless I tell you the truth: It is expedient [right] for you that I go away: for if I go not away, the Comforter will not come unto you; but if I depart, I will send him unto you.
>
> ⁸ And when he is come, he will reprove [criticise] the world of sin, and of righteousness, and of judgement:
>
> ⁹ Of sin, because they believe not on me;
>
> ¹⁰ Of righteousness, because I go to my Father, and ye see me no more.
>
> ¹¹ Of judgement, because the prince of this world is judged.

The Holy Spirit will criticise the world over three things, sin, righteousness and judgement. Sin because they do not believe in Jesus, that is the sin of unbelief. Righteousness, because Jesus has gone to heaven and He could not have gone if He had not been totally righteous. Judgement, because Satan has been judged and found guilty, and therefore everyone that follows him will also be found guilty at the final judgement.

Promise No. 19

The Holy Spirit will guide the apostles in truth, and will show them future events, for the benefit of themselves and the Church.

> John 16:13 Howbeit [Nevertheless] when he, the Spirit of truth, is come, he will guide you into all truth: for he shall not speak of himself; but whatsoever he shall hear, that shall he speak: and he will shew [show] you things to come.

Promise No. 20

The Holy Spirit will bring glory to Jesus by helping the disciples to understand more about Him.

> John 16:14 He shall glorify me: for he shall receive of mine, and shall shew [show] it unto you.

Promise No. 21

He promises His disciples that in a little while they will not be able to see Him, but after a short interval they will see Him again. They could not see Him after His death and burial, which would be very soon, but after a short time He rose from the dead, and they saw Him again.

> John 16:16 A little while, and ye shall not see me: and again, a little while, and ye shall see me.

Promise No. 22

In John 16:25, He promises to change the way He teaches His disciples. We will look at this verse in two separate parts to get a better understanding of this promise.

> ²⁵ These things I have spoken to you in proverbs [symbolic language];

We have seen that so often they had not understood what He had been telling them, and even now this was still true.

> ²⁵ but the time cometh, when I shall no more speak unto you in proverbs [symbolic language], but I shall shew [show] you plainly of the Father.

Clearly they had not understood all He had been telling them about His coming death and resurrection, and that is why during the 40 days after His resurrection and before He ascends into heaven, He will teach them in a way they understand.

Promise No. 23

His disciples will abandon Him and leave Him all alone.

> John 16:32 Behold the hour cometh, yea, is now come, that ye shall be scattered, every man to his own [himself], and shall leave me alone: and yet I am not alone, because the Father is with me.

Promise No. 24

They will be ill-treated and suffer hardship.

> John 16:33 In the world ye shall have tribulation.

Promise No. 25

They should not worry about being wronged or about the things they will suffer in the world, because they belong to Jesus and will share the final victory.

John 16:33 be of good cheer; I have overcome the world.

[1] Acts 1:9-11

[2] 2 Corinthians 5:8

[3] John 5:19-21

[4] Matthew 17:20, Luke 1:37, John 15:5

[5] 1 Samuel 16:14, Psalm 51:11

[6] Luke 24:33-39

THIRTEEN INSTRUCTIONS FROM JESUS
John 14:1 to 16:33

Instruction No. 1

They are not to worry, they just need to trust Him.

John 14:1 Let not your heart be troubled: ye believe in God, believe also in me.

Instruction No. 2

The way to get to heaven.

John 14:6-7 6 I am the way, the truth, and the life: no man cometh unto the Father, but by me.

7 If ye had known me, ye should have known my Father also: and from henceforth [now on] ye know him, and have seen him.

God the Father is in heaven, and the only way to Him and heaven, is through Jesus His Son.

Instruction No. 3

They must believe Jesus.

> John 14:10-11 [10] Believest [Believe] thou [you] not that I am in the Father, and the Father in me? The words that I speak unto you I speak not of myself: but the Father that dwelleth [lives] in me, he doeth [does] the works.
>
> [11] Believe me that I am in the Father, and the Father in me: or else believe me for the very works' sake.

Jesus and God, His Father are One, and those that know Jesus also know His Father, and so they must believe Jesus. The reasons are first of all, "The words that I speak to you I speak not of myself," and, "The Father that dwelleth in me, he doeth the works." If ever Jesus said to a man, "Be healed," God healed the man, and so Jesus and His Father are One, and we must believe Jesus, because God always confirms everything Jesus says.

Instruction No. 4

Keep His commandments.

> John 14:15 If you love me, keep my commandments.

People that love Jesus show their love for Him by keeping His commandments.

Instruction No. 5

We are told to love the Jewish Messiah, Jesus of Nazareth.

> John 14:23-24 [23] If a man love me, he will keep my words: and my Father will love him, and we will come unto him, and make our abode with him.
>
> [24] He that loveth me not keepeth not my sayings: and the word which ye hear is not mine, but the Father's which sent me.

We are to love Jesus, and those of us that do, show it by obeying His commandments.

Instruction No. 6

We need to rejoice over the fact that Jesus has gone to be with the Father.

John 14:27-28 [27] Let not your heart be troubled, neither let it be afraid.

[28] Ye have heard how I said unto you, I go away, and come again unto you. If ye loved me, ye would rejoice, because I said, I go unto the Father: for my Father is greater than I am.

Jesus was concerned that the disciples would be worried and afraid after He had left them behind on earth and gone to heaven, but all believers should rejoice because Jesus has saved us for eternal life with Him. He is in heaven now but have no fear, He is coming back again for us.

Instruction No. 7

Abide or remain in Jesus.

John 15:4 Abide in me, and I in you. As the branch cannot bear fruit of itself, except it abide in the vine; no more can ye, except ye abide in me.

God will do all that is necessary to make us produce loads and loads of fruit, on the condition that we keep close to Jesus.

John 15:2 Every branch in me that beareth (produces) not fruit he (God)[1] taketh away.

The words, taketh away, in the verse above have been translated from the Greek word, "airo," which means, "to lift up." The same word in Revelation 10:5 is translated, "lifted up." "And the angel which I saw stand upon the sea and upon the earth lifted up his hand to heaven." Grape vines today are grown on supports, they are lifted up, to make them produce fruit. A vine growing along the ground will not produce a crop, it will just grow along the surface. In olden days when land was plentiful, the easy way was to let the vine grow by itself and prop up its branches to make them productive. Every one of us that remains in Jesus, God will prop up to make us fruitful.

John 15:2 And every branch that beareth [produces] fruit, he [God][1] purgeth [prunes] it, that it may bring forth more fruit.

Vines are only one of many kinds of plants that can be made to produce more fruit after being pruned. Such plants are pruned to encourage them to put more effort into growing fruit, and less into growing leaves and branches.

John 15:6 If a man abide not in me, he is cast forth as a branch, and is withered; and men gather them, and cast them into the fire, and they are burned.

The burning of the withered branches is referring to the judgement of believers. The believers go through the fire because their work for God is useless. The only way our work will be acceptable is if we remain in Christ, in the Vine. We will look at a short passage of Scripture which speaks about our works, either being burned up in the judgement fire, or coming through the fire without harm.

1 Corinthians 3:11-15 [11] For other foundation can no man lay than that is laid, which is Jesus Christ.

[12] Now if any man build upon this foundation gold, silver, precious stones, wood, hay, stubble;

[13] Every man's work shall be made manifest: for the day shall declare it, because it shall be revealed by fire; and the fire shall try every man's work of what sort it is.

[14] If any man's work abide which he hath built thereupon, he shall receive a reward.

[15] If any man's work shall be burned, he shall suffer loss: but he himself shall be saved; yet so as by fire.

Getting back to the seventh instruction of Jesus, He is talking about believers, and believers are saved, not burnt in the fire of Hell. The fire in this case is the judgement when our useless works will be burned up and we will not be rewarded for them, and in that way we will lose out, but we will still go into eternal life. Yet there is a way we can be sure of being fruitful and of a reward at the judgement.

John 15:5 I am the vine, ye are the branches: He that abideth [remains] in me, and I in him, the same bringeth [brings] forth much fruit: for without me ye can do nothing.

Instruction No. 8

To be exceedingly fruitful.

John 15:8 Herein is my Father glorified, that ye bear much fruit; so shall ye be my disciples.

Instruction No. 9

To abide in His love.

John 15:10 If ye keep my commandments, ye shall abide in my love; even as I have kept my Father's commandments, and abide in his love.

We show our love for Jesus by keeping His commandments, and if we keep His commandments, we remain in His love.

Instruction No. 10

The disciples of Jesus should love each other.

John 15:12-13 ^{12} This is my commandment, That ye love one another, as I have loved you.

^{13} Greater love has no man than this, that a man lay down his life for his friends.

They should love each other so much, they are willing to die to save the life of their friends, not their life on earth but their eternal life.

Instruction No. 11

They are to tell others about Jesus.

John 15:27 And ye also shall bear witness, because ye have been with me from the beginning.

The disciples are to bear witness of Him.

Instruction No. 12

They are to ask in the name of the Messiah.

John 16:23-24 ²³ And in that day ye shall ask me nothing. Verily, verily [Truly, truly], I say unto you, Whatsoever ye shall ask the Father in my name, he will give it you.

²⁴ Hitherto [So far] have ye asked nothing in my name: ask, and ye shall receive, that your joy may be full.

Under the Law of Moses no one prayed in the name of Jesus, but because of their new friendship with the Son of God, they are to pray in His name, that is to say with His authority. Of course praying in the name of Jesus is a huge responsibility, because they must pray as Jesus would pray, that is according to His will, and then whatever they ask their Father in heaven for in Jesus' name will be given to them.

Instruction No. 13

They are to be of good cheer, to take courage. Being of good cheer does not mean to be always laughing and merry. It is a state of confidence that God is with you always and in complete control, no matter what is going on in the world.

John 16:33 These things I have spoken unto you, that ye might have peace. In the world ye shall have tribulation [hardship and suffering]: but be of good cheer; I have overcome the world.

We have already combed John 14 to 16, twice, once for the promises and then for the instructions, but there are two more things there we should look at before moving on. The first concerns Satan's spiritual attack on Jesus, and the second is about the coming crucifixion and resurrection.

[1] John 15:1

THE ACCUSER HAD NO EVIDENCE TO BRING A CASE AGAINST JESUS
John 14:30-31

One of the names given to Satan, the prince of this world, in the Bible is, the Accuser.[1] He loves to go to God, telling tales about all the wicked things we have done, and of course he can find something wrong with all of us, except for one Man, the Lord Jesus.

> John 14:30-31 [30] I will not talk much more with you: for the prince of this world cometh [is coming], and hath [has] nothing in me.
>
> [31] But that the world may know that I love the Father; and as the Father gave me commandment, even so I do.

A spiritual battle of the greatest universal importance we have ever known was about to take place. Satan needed to find something to accuse Jesus of, otherwise the devil and all his followers both people and wicked angels, would spend forever in the lake of fire.[2] Satan tried to keep himself out of the lake of fire but could find nothing wrong with Jesus, not a thing to accuse Jesus of at all. The reason was that Jesus had shown how much He loved God by keeping all the Laws of Moses perfectly.

[1] Zechariah 3:1, Luke 22:31, Revelation 12:10
[2] Matthew 25:41, Revelation 20:10, 20:15

ANOTHER WARNING ABOUT HIS DEATH AND RESURRECTION
John 16:20-22

> John 16:20 Verily, verily [Truly, truly], I say unto you, that ye shall weep and lament [mourn], but the world shall rejoice: and ye shall be sorrowful, but your sorrow shall be turned into joy.

Later when Jesus died they were very sorrowful, while the enemies of truth, the people of the world rejoiced, but the disciples were still not expecting the resurrection, and after that they were delighted.

> John 16:22 And ye now therefore have sorrow: but I will see you again, and your heart will rejoice, and your joy no man taketh [will take] from you.

Once more Jesus promises them He will die, and be resurrected.

THE PRAYER OF JESUS IN HIS POSITION OF HIGH PRIEST
John 17:1-26

Back in Chapter 8, is a section where Jesus taught His disciples how to pray, where we learned that prayer should be well planned, not darting all over the place from one thing to another. The high priestly prayer of Jesus was organised into three sections, and we will take them one at a time as Jesus prayed them.

Jesus Prays For Himself
John 17:1-8

Jesus asked God to glorify Him, and according to the Greek text, the kind of glory He was requesting was of widespread significance and importance.

> John 17:1 Father, the hour is come; glorify thy Son, that thy Son also may glorify thee.

He will be glorified by His resurrection from the dead, and later by His ascension into heaven. In His prayer He tells God why He wants this glory, and we learn from this that it is good to inform God why we ask for what we do. The first reason is, "that thy Son also may glorify thee," He wants to be able to bring widespread glory to His Father. The way He wants to do this is by giving eternal life.

> John 17:2-3[2] That he may give eternal life to as many as thou hast [has] given him.
>
> [3] And this is life eternal, that they might know thee the only true God, and Jesus Christ, whom thou hast [has] sent.

He wants God the Father to receive widespread glory by giving eternal life. The second reason He wants widespread glory is because He has done everything His Father sent Him to do.

> John 17:4 I have glorified thee on earth: I have finished the work which thou gavest [gave] me to do.

He has finished all God asked Him, the crucifixion has been set in motion according to all the prophecies in the Old Testament with nothing more for Him to do but to let things take their course and suffer the consequences. As He faces death, having completed everything God asked, He prays for glory, and He wants the glory He and God the Father shared before the world was created.

John 17:5 And now, O Father, glorify thou me with thine [your] own self with the glory which I had with thee before the world was.

Right back in Chapter 2, we noticed that one of the sub-themes running through the Gospel of John, is to reveal the Father to men, and now Jesus having done that, wants to return home to His former glory.

John 17:6 I have manifested (shown) thy name unto the men which thou gavest [gave] me out of the world.

Jesus Prays For His Disciples
John 17:9-19

Jesus asked God to protect His disciples, to keep them united in His name, and to sanctify them, which means to set them apart from the world. In His prayer He gives God six reasons why He is praying for them.

    1. They should be preserved because they belong to Jesus and God the Father, and they bring glory to Jesus.

    John 17:9-10 [9] ...for they are thine [yours].

    [10] And all mine are thine [yours], and thine [yours] are mine; and I am glorified in them.

    2. They need to be protected by God because Jesus will soon leave the world and will not be here physically to look after them.

    John 17:11 "And now I am no more in the world, but these are in the world, and I come to thee."

    3. The disciples will need to be united by the power of God the Father, to become one with Him and with each other, just as

Jesus is one with God. Unity with each other and with God will preserve them.

John 17:11 Holy Father, keep through thine [your] own name those whom thou have given me, that they may be one, as we are.

4. John 17:12

John 17:12 While I was with them in the world, I kept them in thy name: those that thou gavest me I have kept, and none of them is lost, but [except for] the son of perdition; that the scripture might be fulfilled.

The son of perdition was Judas Iscariot who betrayed Jesus. Perdition means, ever lasting death, and because an Old Testament prophet said that someone close to Jesus would betray Him,[1] that Scripture had to be fulfilled, it had to happen. Apart from Judas Iscariot, Jesus had kept the other eleven disciples safe in the name of God, that is with the authority of God, and His prayer now is that God should look after them Himself.

John 17:13 And now I come to thee; and these things I speak in the world, that they might have my joy fulfilled in themselves.

5. Jesus asks God to protect His disciples from the evil one, from Satan.

John 17:14 I have given them thy word; and the world hated them, because they are not of the world, even as I am not of the world.

The disciples had now been given a new nature, very different from others in the world, a nature similar to that of Jesus, and because Jesus was hated so would they be.

John 17:15 I pray not that thou shouldest [should] take them out of the world, but that thou shouldest [should] keep them from the evil one.

They had work to do on earth and needed to remain to complete it after Jesus had gone, which would make Satan furious with them.

John 17:16 "They are not of the world, even as I am not of the world."

Since they were not of the world, having characters like Jesus, they needed protection from Satan.

6. Jesus also asked God to sanctify the disciples, or to set them apart to do the same work on earth as Jesus Himself had done.

John 17:17-19 [17] Sanctify them through thy truth: thy word is truth.

[18] As thou [you] hast [have] sent me into the world, even so have I sent them into the world.

[19] And for their sakes I sanctify myself, that they also might be sanctified through the truth.

Jesus Prays For All Believers
John 17:20-26

In the final part of His prayer as High Priest, Jesus prayed for everyone in the world who would believe in Him because of the teaching and writings of the disciples. Jesus did not write a single word of the Bible, all of the New Testament was written after Jesus had gone to heaven, and so there is no born again believer in Jesus, alive on earth today who does not owe his belief to the work of those Jewish disciples.

John 17:20 Neither pray I for these [disciples] alone [only], but for them also which shall believe on me through their word.

He began by asking God to give them perfect unity with each other, with Him and with God. They were certainly happy when they died and went to be with Jesus and God, after a prayer like that. As far as we are concerned that unity is the reason their preaching was so powerful.

John 17:21-23 [21] That they all may be one; as thou [you], Father, art [are] in me, and I in thee [you], that they also may be one in us: that the world may believe that thou hast [have] sent me.

²² And the glory which thou [you] gavest [gave] me I have given them; that they may be one, even as we are one;

²³ I in them, and thou [you] in me, that they may be made perfect in one; and that the world may know that thou [you] hast [have] sent me, and hast [have] loved them, as thou hast [have] loved me.

Just as He prayed for unity among the disciples, Jesus has now prayed for unity among all believers, which is achieved by the Spirit of God the Father and Jesus living in believers.

It is wonderful that Jesus ended His High Priestly prayer by asking God to glorify everyone that believes in Him, the thought of it sends my faith soaring to infinite levels, way beyond anything I can imagine.

John 17:24-26 ²⁴ Father, I will [desire] that they also, whom thou [you] hast [have] given me, be with me where I am; that they may behold [look at] my glory, which thou [you] hast [have] given me: for thou [you] lovedst [loved] me before the foundation of the world.

²⁵ O righteous Father, the world hath [has] not known thee [you], and these have known that thou [you] hast [have] sent me.

²⁶ And I have declared unto them thy [your] name, and will declare it: that the love wherewith thou [you] hast [have] loved me be in them, and I in them.

So we see that our glorification will be the result of the Spirit of Jesus in us.

Jesus had ended His prayer which He organised into three parts, first with reference to Himself, second relating to His disciples and thirdly He prayed for all believers. Also, we will discover later that while Jesus hung on the cross, He cried out, "My God, my God, why hast thou forsaken me?"[2] In the light of that, we should take notice that when He prayed His High Priestly prayer, He called God, "Father," six times.

1.   John 17:1 Father, the hour is come;

2. John 17:5 And now, O Father,
3. John 17:11 Holy Father, keep them in thine own name
4. John 17:21 as thou, Father, art in me,
5. John 17:24 Father, I will that they also,
6. John 17:25 O righteous Father,

We will return to this point afterwards when we come to the crucifixion of Jesus.

[1] Psalm 41:9

[2] Matthew 27:46

THE AGONY OF JESUS IN THE GARDEN OF GETHSEMANE
Isaiah 49:1-6 (a prophetic Scripture concerning His agony), Matthew 26:36-46, Mark 14:32-42, Luke 22:39-46, John 18:1

The word agony means, extreme mental or physical suffering, and Jesus agonised in the Garden of Gethsemane, while waiting to be betrayed by Judas Iscariot.

The Passover Supper with His disciples had ended and Jesus and the eleven had reached the Mount of Olives, crossed over the brook called Cedron or Kidron, and entered the garden. Judas Iscariot was not with them because he had gone to betray Jesus to the chief priests. To get a full understanding of the setting and of what happened we need to look at all four gospels and a prophetic passage from the Old Testament as well.

> John 18:1 When Jesus had spoken these words, he went forth with his disciples over the brook Cedron, where was a garden, into which he entered, and his disciples.

He chose Peter, James and John from the eleven, the same three he had chosen for his transfiguration, and asked the other eight to be the first guard near the entrance to the garden.

> Mark 14:32 Sit ye here, while I shall pray.

He continued on up the mountain with the other three, and they were asked to be the second guard.

> Mark 14:34 tarry [remain] ye here, and watch.

He also told them to pray to overcome temptation.

> Luke 22:40 Pray that ye enter not into temptation.

Jesus left His second guard and went on up the mountain alone, to a place about a stone's throw further on, kneeled down and prayed,[1] before falling on His face and praying.[2]

Five Facts Concerning His Agony

1. Mark 14:33 [Jesus] began to be sore amazed.

The King James Bible makes a good rendering of the meaning, which is that Jesus was stunned with surprise, He was sore amazed.

2. Mark 14:33 [Jesus] began to ... be very heavy.

He was troubled and deeply depressed.

3. Mark 14:34 My soul is exceedingly sorrowful unto death.

What ever it was that had amazed and depressed Him, it was so terrible that His body was almost at the end of its endurance, and liable to collapse.

4. Luke 22:44 And being in agony.

The gospels only tell us one of the things He was agonising about, and for the other we have to turn to the prophet, Isaiah. Earlier in Chapter 3, under the heading, "Growing Up," we learned, from an Old Testament prophecy, how God woke Jesus every morning while He was a child and trained Him. Now again it is from the Old Testament that we learn one of the reasons Jesus was so sorrowful and depressed, and we will deal with that reason here, and after that with the other reason found in the gospels when we come to the fifth point about His agony.

Isaiah 49 is one of those, Servant of the LORD passages, about the Messiah although it was written at least 700 years before our Lord was born, and it tells us that Jesus thought that His work among the Jewish nation had been a failure.

> Isaiah 49:4 Then I said, I have laboured in vain, I have spent my strength for nought, and in vain: yet surely my judgement is with the LORD, and my work with my God.

Jesus had laboured hard and yet it appeared to have been a wasted effort because Israel as nation had rejected Him. He agonised over this but reasoned that God the Father would judge His effort and understand that He had worked perfectly. As He was agonising and deeply troubled, God sent an angel to speak to Jesus.

> Luke 22:43 And there appeared an angel unto him from heaven, strengthening him.

Luke does not tell us the message given by the angel, but Isaiah does.

> Isaiah 49:5-6 ⁵ And now, saith [says] the LORD that formed me [Jesus] from the womb [the womb of the Virgin Mary] to be his servant, to bring Jacob again to him, Though Israel [the Jews] be not gathered, yet shall I [Jesus] be glorious in the eyes of the LORD, and my God shall be my strength.
>
> ⁶ And he said, It is a light thing that thou shouldest be my servant to raise up the tribes of Jacob, and to restore the preserved of Israel: I will also give thee for a light to the Gentiles, that thou mayest be my salvation unto the end of the earth.

It was God's plan all along that the Jews would reject their Messiah, as Isaiah's prophecy proves, saving the Jews only would have been, "a light thing." It is true that Jesus was sent to the lost sheep of the house of Israel,[3] but He was also to be a light to the Gentiles,[4] to reach to the end of the earth. The phrase, "end of the earth," is a Jewish saying for that part of the world where Gentiles live.

Jesus had to be rejected by His own people so that He could be a light to the Gentiles for a while, until the full number of the Gentiles are born again,[5] and after that all Israel will accept Jesus as their Messiah.

> Isaiah 49:8 Thus saith the LORD [God the Father], In an acceptable time I have heard thee [Jesus], and in a day of salvation have I helped thee: and I will preserve thee, and give thee for a covenant of the people, to establish the earth, to cause to inherit the desolate heritages.

After Jesus has spent some time as a light to the nations, Israel will be saved and Jesus will fulfil the covenants God has made with Israel, including returning the Land to the Jews and the Jews to the Land.[6]

5. Luke 22:44 And being in agony he prayed more earnestly: and his sweat was as it were great drops of blood falling down to the ground.

Jesus was in such agony that He began sweating blood, a medical condition still observed today with people in extreme agony. To repeat, the first reason for His agony was because He had been rejected by Israel, but the angel had reassured Him about that. The second reason we learn from the gospels, because He kept on praying about it.

> Mark 14:36 And he said, Abba, Father, all things are possible unto thee; take away this cup from me: nevertheless not what I will [want], but what thou [you] wilt [want].

Jesus was concerned about a cup, but He ended His prayer by saying that whatever God wanted, that was what He wanted. The prayers of Jesus are good examples for us to follow, and we also should pray for things that are according to the will of God.

After praying He got up and went to the three disciples guarding Him.

> Mark 14:37 And he cometh [came] and findeth [found] them sleeping, and saith [said] unto Peter, Simon, sleepest thou [are you asleep]? Couldest not [couldn't] thou [you] watch one hour.

Jesus had been praying and agonising for an hour and that is why we know that none of the gospels tell us everything Jesus prayed.

> Mark 14:38 Watch ye and pray, lest ye enter into temptation.

The temptation that would face them, in spite of them promising they would never leave Jesus, was to scatter and run away, because the flesh is weak, and Jesus had told them, the way to overcome temptation was by prayer.

> Mark 14:38 The spirit truly is ready, but the flesh is weak.

For the second prayer of Jesus we will go to Matthew, where we find He is still praying about the cup.

> Matthew 26:42 He went away again a second time, and prayed, saying, O my Father, if this cup may not pass away from me, except [unless] I drink it, thy will be done.

After the second prayer Jesus returned again to the three disciples on guard nearest to Him, but they were all asleep, as they had been the first time and did not know what to say to Him.[7] Jesus left them awake and on guard again before going away to pray for the third time, and notice what He prayed.

> Matthew 26:44 And he left them, and went away again, and prayed the third time, saying the same words.

The third time Jesus finished praying and went back to see, Peter, James and John, the three disciples He had left to guard Him, He found them all asleep again,[8] but now they had to get up, because Judas Iscariot was leading the chief priests and a huge number of armed Jewish men to arrest Jesus.

> Matthew 26:46 Rise, let us be going: behold, he is at hand that doeth betray me.

It is probably a good time now, before going on with the story, to find out what the cup stood for, because three times Jesus prayed and agonised over it. Bible teachers have looked into the meaning of the cup and have come up with three different ideas.

Some say that the cup is bodily death, that Jesus was worried about having to die, and was asking God not to let Him die physically. It would be strange if this was the case, because it would mean that Jesus was asking God to cancel the plan He had made from the foundation of the world, for saving His chosen ones through the Lamb that was slain.

> Ephesians 1:4 According as he hath chosen us in him before the foundation of the world, that we should be holy and without blame before him in love.

The reason for the incarnation, that is to say, for God becoming a man, was so that He could die. God cannot die, that is why He became a man, so that He could die, and if Jesus prayed that He would not die, then He would have been against the main reason for His incarnation. Also Jesus had already told the disciples that He had come into the world to die, so why would He pray that He should not die?

> John 10:17 Therefore doth my Father love me, because I lay down my life, that I might take it again.

More than that, Jesus had ruled out asking God that He should not die, saying that was the reason He had become a man.

> John 12:27 Now is my soul troubled: and what shall I say? Father, save me from this hour: but for this cause came I unto this hour.

Another group of Bible scholars believe the cup represents the fear Jesus had of not being able to stay alive long enough, that He was afraid he might die before He reached the cross. Again it is a shallow answer, not well thought through, because Jesus and God the Father were always in complete control of the entire course of action. Satan arranged the death of Jesus, but he was never in control, the Jewish leaders plotted the death of Jesus, but again they were never in control either, nor were the Romans, Jesus was in total control of His own death, of the way He would die and when He would die, and that is why there is no chance that He would be afraid of dying too soon. In the next section we will see that a Roman cohort of armed soldiers, a cohort was usually about 600 men, was sent to arrest Jesus, and when they said they were looking for Jesus the Nazarene, Jesus said to them, "I am He," at which all the soldiers and the armed Jews that were with them all fell over backwards.[9] The incident proves that Jesus was able to control that Roman battalion of soldiers, and that they could only arrest Him because Jesus let them. Also when we get to the crucifixion we will see that Jesus actually told God when to take His life.[10] The time of His death on the cross was His decision, and if he had wanted He could have hung there forever. The answer to the question, "Who was responsible for the death of Jesus?", is, "Jesus Himself."

> John 10:17-18   17 ... I lay down my life, that I might take it again.
>
> 18 No man taketh [takes] it from me, but I lay it down of myself. I have power to lay it down, and I have power to take it again.

I believe, along with many others, that the meaning of the cup that Jesus agonised over, was the wrath or fury of God, because a cup is sometimes used to mean that in the Old Testament.[11] God is furious with sinners[12] and His wrath was poured out on Jesus for all the sins of mankind,[13] and so Jesus suffered the wrath of God that was due to us, like no one else before or since, and one of the exchanges that took place at the cross was that Jesus took the wrath due to us, and we were justified.[14] Some people say the word justified, means for the Christian, "just-as-if-I'd" never sinned.

The fury of God is also to be feared because it results in separation from God. Every one of us was born spiritually dead, but after we have believed in Jesus and asked Him to come into our hearts and live there, we become spiritually alive, born again. Our relationship with God, spirit to Spirit,[15] is a wonderful joy, comfort and blessing, and once we have experienced the new birth I cannot imagine anyone wanting to be spiritually separated from God ever again. Jesus was closer to God than us, because He had never known a time when He and God were not together. For Jesus, separation from His Father, even for a short while would have been a new experience and would have caused great agony, because they had always been together including before the creation of the universe.[16] I believe that Jesus agonised over the cup because it was the cup of the wrath of God, and He did not want to suffer the wrath, including the separation from God that would result.

[1] Luke 22:41
[2] Matthew 26:39
[3] Matthew 15:24
[4] Luke 2:32, Acts 13:47
[5] Romans 11:25-26
[6] Zechariah 10:6-12
[7] Mark 14:40
[8] Mark 14:41
[9] John 18:6
[10] Luke 23:46
[11] Jeremiah 25:15
[12] Deuteronomy 9:8, 29:23, 29:24-28, 2 Kings 22:13
[13] Isaiah 53:3-6
[14] Romans 5:9
[15] Romans 8:15-16
[16] Colossians 1:13-20

13

THE ARREST, TRIALS AND DEATH OF JESUS

We know from our study so far, that try as much as they might, the Jewish religious leaders could never find a single example of Jesus breaking the Law of Moses or saying anything against it. The excuse they used to find Him guilty of a crime was that He rejected the law found in the Mishnah, the Pharisaic or oral law they had made up themselves. You will remember that Jesus often purposely broke the Mishnaic law because it did not come from God. Now during the arrest, trials and death of Jesus, the Sanhedrin, the religious High Court, broke their own oral law twenty-two times. The list of 22 rules broken by the Sanhedrin is a real eye-opener to us, showing how right Jesus was when He called the religious leaders hypocrites who made laws for others which they themselves did not keep,[1] bearing in mind the real reason they had rejected Jesus was because He refused to keep their oral law.

The Laws Of The Sanhedrin That Were Broken By The Sanhedrin

1. No religious authority could make an arrest that had been brought about by a bribe.
2. All criminal procedures, including trials, had to stop at sunset, and could only begin again at sunrise, to make sure no conspiracy took place under the cover of darkness.

3. Judges and members of the Sanhedrin could not play a part in the arrest. The idea was that they should not be biased either for or against the accused, if they were involved in the arrest it would mean they had already decided against the person they had arrested.
4. No trials could begin before the morning sacrifice, all the Temple morning rituals had to be over.
5. No trials were allowed on a feast day or on a Sabbath eve.
6. Trials were not to be held in secret, only public trials were allowed to guard against conspiracy.
7. The Hall of Judgement in the Temple area, also known as the Chamber of Hewn Stone, was the only place the Sanhedrin were allowed to conduct a trial. In that way the people knew where to go if they wanted to observe a public trial.
8. The trials always began the other way round to trials in our courts today, with the defence first and the accusation after. Character references, and alibis came before the official could introduce his two or three witnesses.
9. Under Jewish criminal law everyone could make a case for the accused person to go free, but they could not all argue for a guilty verdict, the accused had to have someone speaking in his defence.
10. There had to be two or three witness and everything the two or three said had to be in complete agreement.[2]
11. The accused person was not allowed to give evidence against himself. The reason was that the accused might be trying to protect someone else, or he might be trying to commit suicide.
12. The High Priest was not allowed to tear his clothes,[3] that would have been a sign of strong emotion, and the case had to be decided based on reason, not on emotions.
13. The judges could not charge the accused themselves, they could only judge cases brought to them, because if they brought the charges it would mean they had taken sides already.

14. A person could not be found guilty of blasphemy unless he had spoken out loud the name of God, which in Hebrew corresponds to, or matches in sound, the four English letters YHDH, when the missing vowel sounds are inserted to complete the syllables.
15. No one could be convicted by his own words only, there had to be two or three witnesses.
16. To guard against rash judgements being made, the court's decision could not be declared during the night, even if they knew what it would be, they had to wait until the next day to make the announcement.
17. For cases where the accused would suffer capital punishment, that is death, the guilty verdict could only be declared, twenty-four hours after the end of the trial, to allow more time for any information that would help the accused to be brought in and considered.
18. The death penalty could only be given after all the individual court officials had voted, beginning with the youngest, to protect the youngest one from being influenced by the elders and voting along with them.
19. If everyone voted the guilty verdict, then the accused was declared innocent and set free. Not every member of the Sanhedrin had to attend the trial but the minimum number was twenty-three, and it was thought to be impossible for 23 or more men to agree on a verdict unless they had plotted and schemed together in advance.
20. The sentence could not be pronounced until three days after the guilty verdict, which would be four days after the trial, because the verdict itself could only be given twenty-four hours after the trial, as in number 17 of this list. The reason was the same as before, to allow time for any information that would help the accused to be brought in and considered.
21. The judges were to behave in a kind and considerate manner during the trial.

22. Anyone that was sentenced to death, could not be whipped or beaten before he died.

There are thousands of rules in the oral law but these twenty-two were broken by the Sanhedrin, and as we study the arrest and trials of Jesus we will see where each one was broken.

THE ARREST
Matthew 26:47-53, Mark 14:43-52, Luke 22:47-56, John 18:2-12

The date was the 15th of Nissan, or the 7th of April AD 30.

> John 18:2 And Judas also, which betrayed him, knew the place: for Jesus oft-times [often] resorted [assembled] thither [there] with his disciples.

Here the Sanhedrin broke the first of their rules in our list, because Judas had been bribed with thirty pieces of silver to betray Jesus,[4] and so the religious leaders of the Jews, the High Court itself, broke the religious law it had itself made. The Sanhedrin, as we said earlier, wanted the help of Judas for three reasons. The first was to show them a place where they could arrest Jesus secretly, without the crowds knowing about it. Judas was able to do this because he was a disciple and knew that Jesus often went to the Garden of Gethsemane, a quiet place away from other people to be alone with His disciples.

The second reason Judas was needed was to go to the Roman governor, and accuse Jesus of a crime which was against the law of Rome, so that the governor, Pontius Pilate, could release a cohort, we would say a battalion, normally about 600 soldiers to make the arrest. The Sanhedrin had not planned to do any of this during the feast, but when Judas had found the opportunity to betray Jesus that night they had to act, because he had kept his part of the bargain and it was the only chance they would get.

> John 18:3 Judas then, having received a band [cohort] of men and officers from the chief priests and Pharisees, cometh [came] thither [there] with lanterns and torches and weapons.

Judas, when he had left the Passover supper, would have had to go to the chief priests that had employed him. One or more of the chief priests would have taken him to Pontius Pilate, Judas would have accused Jesus of a crime deserving punishment under Roman law, and then would have been given the Roman cohort. The fact that the cohort arrived with lanterns and torches shows it was dark and therefore that the Sanhedrin broke the second of their rules in the list.

The Roman cohort was only part of a large number that came to arrest Jesus, and this we know from Gospel of Luke. The High Priest could not be there because of Passover ceremonial duties, but he sent his servant to keep an eye on what happened, Luke 22:50. Luke 22:52 mentions three other groups, first "the captains of the temple," these were the Jewish Temple police, responsible for keeping order in the inner court where Gentiles, including Gentile soldiers, were forbidden to enter. Secondly were the, "chief priests," and finally, "the elders," both these last two groups belonged to the Sanhedrin, accordingly they broke the third rule in the list, which stated that judges and members of the Sanhedrin could not take part in the arrest.

It was therefore a large number of men, both Jews and Gentiles, armed with swords and staves, or perhaps clubs, that was sent to make the arrest. The Greek word for the wooden weapons is, *"xulon,"* meaning they were properly fashioned weaponry. It seems extraordinary that such a force was sent to arrest one man, and shows the respect they had for Jesus of Nazareth. On their arrival Jesus immediately took the upper hand.

> John 18:4 [Jesus] went forth [forward], and said to them, Whom seek ye? [Who are you looking for?].
>
> John 18:5 They answered him, Jesus of Nazareth. Jesus saith [said] unto them, I am.

The answer, "I am," can be interpreted in two ways. First it can be taken as the name God called Himself in the Old Testament, in the Book of Exodus.

> Exodus 3:13-14 ¹³And Moses said unto God, Behold, when I come unto the children of Israel, and shall say unto them, The

God of your fathers hath sent me unto you; and they shall say to me, What is his name? What shall I say unto them?

[14] And God said unto Moses, I AM THAT I AM: and he said, Thus shalt thou say unto the children of Israel, I AM hath sent me unto you.

The other way to interpret what Jesus said is, "I am He," meaning He is the person they are looking for.

Jesus used the phrase, "I am," twice, once in each of the ways described. First in the verse already partly quoted, He means He is God, because John pointed out that Judas was with the large heavily armed group of Roman soldiers and Jews that had come to arrest Him, as the verse goes on to explain.

John 18:5 And Judas also, which betrayed him, stood with them.

Now see what happens in the following verse.

John 18:6 As soon as he had said unto them, I am, they went backward, and fell to the ground.

In John 18:5 therefore when Jesus says, "I am," He means He is God, because just by saying those two words, He compels the entire force that has come to arrest Him, down on the ground backwards, on their bottoms if not flat on their backs. It clearly shows His divinity, that He is control, and that they will not be able to arrest Him unless He lets them.

After the cohort from the Roman army, the Jewish Temple police, the chief priests and the elders of the Sanhedrin had all landed un-ceremoniously on their back-sides, Jesus asked them again, "Whom seek ye?" and as before they replied, "Jesus of Nazareth," and Jesus again said, "I am," and this time He meant, "I am the one you are looking for." He said this in order that He only would be arrested.

John 18:8 Jesus answered, I have told you that I am: if therefore ye seek me let these go their way.

The arrest was soon to come but not immediately because Judas had arranged to give them a sign to make sure they apprehended the right person.

> Mark 14:44 And he [Judas] that betrayed him [Jesus] had given them [the cohort] a token [signal], saying, Whomsoever I shall kiss, that same is he; take him, and lead him away safely.

Jesus had identified Himself clearly and there was no need for Judas to give the signal to the Romans, but he was determined to play his part and kiss Jesus. To kiss a rabbi was a sign of submission to that rabbi, a declaration of being his disciple, and a sign of reverence.[5] To the Jewish people, betraying a rabbi by kissing him, was treating someone you should respect with complete disregard, it was absolute profanity, how much worse because Jesus was and is the Jewish Messiah. In Luke 22:48 Jesus warned him not to do it, but he would not be put off.

> Mark 14:45 And as soon as he was come, he goeth [went] straightway [straight] to him [Jesus], and saith [said], Master, master; and kissed him.

During the Passover supper Peter had said He was ready to die for Jesus, and he was now about to put his life in extreme danger, he decided it was time for action.

> John 18:10 Then Simon Peter having a sword drew it, and smote the high priest's servant, and cut off his right ear. The servant's name was Malchus.

Imagine the scene, a battalion of Roman soldiers plus a number of Temple police, all armed with swords and staves, and Peter takes them all on. He may have been a good fisherman but he was certainly not a trained soldier. He had declared war on professional soldiers and police who out numbered him by hundreds.

> Luke 22:51 And he [Jesus] touched his ear and healed him [Malchus].

Maybe Peter was thinking like a miniature Pekinese dog called Gin we had in Malaysia. Gin was running for her life, tail tucked tightly down between her legs, she jumped through a flower bed, ran at full speed straight for our patio, where I was admiring the garden from my rocking chair, and jumped onto my lap. Once safe with her master she turned to face a huge Alsatian dog that was chasing her, and really told him off, barking furiously. Perhaps Peter had come to trust Jesus in the way Gin trusted me, but the mission of Jesus at His first coming was not to take on the powers of the world. He will do that at His second coming when the military forces of the nations will be much more advanced scientifically, and many times more powerful. At His first coming Jesus came to die as the Lamb of God, during the Feast of Passover. He healed His enemy Malchus, the only time in the Bible He healed His enemy, to save Peter's life, and to allow His own death to proceed according to the will of God the Father.

> John 18:11 Then said Jesus unto Peter, Put up thy sword into the sheath: the cup which my Father hath given me, shall I not drink it?

Jesus then taught Peter three important lessons.

1. Matthew 26:52 "... all that take [trust] the sword shall perish by the sword."

In our Christian life we must trust in Jesus, not in swords or military action. Weapons can be used to defend ourselves or our country, but when it comes to following God, we are not to use the sword, instead we should be ready to turn the other cheek,[6] or even to be martyred.[7]

2. Matthew 26:53 "Thinkest thou that I cannot now pray to my Father, and he shall give me more than twelve legions of angels."

In our spiritual lives we need to use spiritual methods, and Jesus had more than twelve legions of angels He could have used. He would not have used Peter's sword.

3. Matthew 26:54 "But how then shall the scriptures be fulfilled, ...?"

Everything had to be done the way Jesus wanted it to be done, not the way Peter wanted it done. Jesus' actions duly fulfilled all those prophecies concerning Him, so that there would be no Biblical reason not to believe that Jesus is the Messiah and King of Israel.

The disciples suddenly realised that Jesus was not going to do anything else to defend Himself against the armed group of professional soldiers and police that had come to arrest Him, so they fled for their lives just as Jesus had said they would.[8]

Matthew 26:56 Then all the disciples forsook him and fled.

Mark adds more detail to his story because he was very nearly caught. In Jesus' day, it was the custom of writers telling stories that happened to them, or about things which they actually saw, to include themselves in the article, without actually saying they were there. The apostle John did it in, John 13:23, describing himself as the disciple Jesus loved, and Mark did the same thing, telling us that when he escaped from the soldiers, he was naked.

Mark 14:50-52 [50] And they all forsook him and fled.

[51] And there followed him a certain young man, having a linen cloth cast about his naked body; and the young men laid hold on him:

[52] And he left the linen cloth and fled from them naked.

Mark's escape cannot be used as Biblical approval of those people that call them selves, naturalists or nudists, nakedness is shameful and God hates what they do.[9]

[1] Matthew 23:1-4, 23:27-28

[2] Deuteronomy 19:15

[3] Leviticus 21:10

[4] Matthew 26:14-16

[5] Psalm 2:12

[6] Matthew 5:39, Luke 6:29

[7] Matthew 16:25

[8] Matthew 26:31

[9] Genesis 9:20-27, Micah 1:11, Revelation 16:15

JESUS IS TRIED BY ANNAS
John 18:12-23

Jesus was tried at two religious trials, the first carried out by Annas and the second by his son-in-law, Caiaphas the High Priest. The subject of both the religious trials was blasphemy, that Jesus was claiming to be divine when He was merely human. Normally Annas and Caiaphas would have been prepared for the trial, with all the false witnesses having rehearsed the lies they were supposed to say, so that they agreed in every detail. Tonight they were not expecting a trial and were caught unprepared.

Annas was a corrupt and powerful character, who had been High Priest himself from AD 7 until AD 14, when he was kicked-out by the Roman governor, Valerius Gratus. It may be that the Jews did not recognise the right of the Romans to depose their high priests, as this was a religious matter, not a political one. In his gospel, John refers to Annas as the High Priest, as well as Caiaphas. Luke also had the two men as high priests, when John the Baptist began to preach in the wilderness.

> Luke 3:2 Annas and Caiaphas being the high priests, the word of God came unto John the son of Zacharias in the wilderness.

Annas certainly retained a strong influence over the priesthood and was eventually followed by his son-in-law Caiaphas. He was also the mastermind and head of what was known as, The Bazaar of the Sons of Annas. The Temple money changing and sacrifice selling businesses were all private concerns belonging to Annas and his family. It was the businesses of Annas and his relatives that Jesus overturned in the Temple, during the first and last Passovers of His ministry, and we can imagine that Annas, the judge at the first religious trial of Jesus, had something of a grudge against Him.

> John 18:12-13 [12] Then the band [the band means the Roman cohort] and the captain [the captain of the Roman cohort] and officers of the Jews [the officers of the Jews were the Temple police responsible for the Temple] took Jesus, and bound him,

¹³ And led him away to Annas first; ...

Taking Jesus to be tried by Annas broke rules 4 and 5 in our list, no trial could begin until after the morning sacrifice had been completed in the Temple, and no trial could take place on the eve of a Sabbath.

Much earlier, way back in John 11:48-52, Caiaphas had already decided to kill Jesus and John reminds us of this again now.

> John 18:14 Now Caiaphas was he, which gave counsel to the Jews, that it was expedient [better] that one man should die for the people.

The whole trial, as John reminds us, was a pretence and deception, because they had previously determined what the verdict was going to be long before the hearing took place. It was after they had rejected the first sign of Jonah, the resurrection of Lazarus, that they decided to kill their Messiah.

Annas, the former high priest had no legal right to try Jesus, that was the responsibility of his son-in-law Caiaphas, thus the trial before Annas was hush-hush. Here rule number 6, was broken, only trials open to the public were allowed. At the secret trial Annas wanted to know about His disciples and His teachings.

> John 18:19 The high priest then asked Jesus of his disciples, and of his doctrine [teaching].

He sought to know the teaching of Jesus because he wanted to try and lay blame on Him, and who His disciples were so that he could lay blame on them. Jesus answered by saying that He only ever spoke openly for many people to hear.

> John 18:20-21 ²⁰ Jesus answered him, I spake [spoke] openly to the world: I ever taught in the synagogue, and in the temple, whither the Jews always have resort; and in secret have I said nothing.
>
> ²¹ Why askest thou me? Ask them that heard me, what I have said unto them: behold, they know what I said.

Jesus was on trial and therefore according to Jewish law was not required to answer their questions, it was their responsibility to provide two or three witness, a very easy thing for them to do because He had never spoken in secret, and many had heard Him. In other words, they had no excuse for not keeping their own rules? A perfectly reasonable point and one which Jesus had every right to make.

> John 18:22 And when he had thus spoken, one of the officers which stood by struck Jesus with the palm of his hand, saying, Answerest [Answer] thou the high priest so?

This was the first ill-treatment of many that Jesus would receive that night.

> John 18:23 Jesus answered him, If I have spoken evil, bear witness of the evil: but if well, why smitest [hit] thou me?

Hitting Jesus was illegal, and He pointed it out because He was entitled to a fair trial.

Again, the religious authorities had not planned to try Jesus during the Passover feast and were unprepared and disorganised, therefore as a result of the trial before Annas not a single religious charge could be made, and so still bound they sent Him off to Caiaphas. The way prisoners were often bound in those days was by tying their hands together.

> John 18:24 Now Annas sent him bound unto Caiaphas the high priest.

JESUS IS TRIED BY CAIAPHAS AND THE SANHEDRIN
Matthew 26:57, 26:59-68, Mark 14:53, 14:55-65, Luke 22:54

Caiaphas, the son-in-law of Annas, was High Priest from AD 25 until AD 36, so that the trial of Jesus, in AD 30 was half way through his time in the job. It was Caiaphas who rejected the first sign of Jonah, which was the resurrection of Lazarus, and now following the events according to the order given by Luke, Jesus is taken to his house. The chief priests, elders and scribes, that is the Sanhedrin, described as the council, in Matthew 26:59, were assembled in Caiaphas' house.

Mark 14:53 And they led Jesus away to the high priest: and with him were assembled all the chief priests and the elders and the scribes.

Holding the gathering in the house broke rule 7, in our list, because trials by the Sanhedrin could only be held in the Hall of Judgement in the Temple complex.

Rule 8 in our list, that the defence should come first, before the accusation, was broken when they began by trying to frame Jesus for something He had not done or said using false witnesses.

Matthew 26:59 Now the chief priests, the elders, and all the council, sought false witness against Jesus, to put him to death.

At the same time they broke rule 9, which was that they could not all argue in favour of Him being guilty, the trial was illegal because no one from the Sanhedrin spoke in favour of Jesus.

Mark 14:55 The chief priests and all the council sought for witness against Jesus.

The witnesses were brought in one after another but none of them said the same thing, again because the council had been forced to act quickly and had not had time to teach the witnesses what to say, word for word. In the end they came to their last witnesses who seemed to be saying the same thing, so the two were brought in, but when they had spoken it was clear that their were differences in what they said also.

Mark 14:59 But neither so did their witnesses agree together.

We can find out what each one said because Matthew and Mark each told us what a different witness testified.

Matthew 26:60-61 [60] At the last came two false witnesses.

[61] And said, this fellow said, I am able to destroy the temple of God, and to build it in three days.

However, we know from Mark 14:59 above that these witnesses did not agree, so what did the other one say?

Mark 14:58 We heard him say, I will destroy this temple that is made with hands, and within three days I will build another made without hands.

The question the Sanhedrin could not decide from these witnesses was, had Jesus claimed He could destroy the Temple, or that He would destroy it. All the witnesses had been called, no charges could be brought against Jesus, and according to Jewish Law, Jesus should have been released and set free at once. By keeping Him a prisoner they broke rule 10 in our list, that there had to be evidence from two or three witness which was in agreement.

The difficulty facing the Sanhedrin was that the Romans were in charge, and had made it law that the Sanhedrin could not condemn to death any one they liked. However the Temple was protected by Roman law, and the Sanhedrin could condemn to death anyone under their authority who tried to destroy it. It is obvious then why the last two witnesses had been brought in. If it could be shown that Jesus had threatened to destroy the Temple, the Jews could condemn Him to death, but the plan failed because the witnesses did not agree, and Caiaphas, the High Priest, was getting more and more irritated.

> Matthew 26:62 And the high priest arose and said unto him, Answerest [Answer] thou nothing? What is it which these witness [say] against thee?

Here rule 11, from our list was broken, because an accused person was not allowed to give evidence against himself. If he was asked to testify against himself it was not lawful for him to answer and he should keep quiet, which is what Jesus did. Caiaphas was getting even more worked up, and he adjured Jesus, that is he put Him under oath.

> Matthew 26:63 But Jesus held [kept] his peace [quiet]. And the high priest answered and said unto him, I adjure thee by the living God, that thou tell us whether thou be the Christ, the Son of God.

This verse shows that Caiaphas knew two things.

1. He knew that Jesus claimed to be the Messiah.
2. He knew that the Messiah would also be the Son of God.

In a Jewish civil law court, if you are put under oath, you must answer, which is just what Jesus did.

> Mark 14:62 And Jesus said, I am: and ye shall see the Son of man sitting on the right hand of power, and coming in the clouds of heaven.

When He said, "I am," in answer to Caiaphas, Jesus meant, "Yes, I am the Christ, the Son of God." He then said that Caiaphas would personally see Jesus sitting beside God the Father, and he would also see the second coming, meaning that the second coming of Jesus will be seen from Hell.

We will now look at Matthew 26:65, a little bit at a time, because four more laws of the Sanhedrin are broken in this verse.

> Matthew 26:65 Then the high priest rent [tore] his clothes. ...

According to rule number 12, the High Priest was not allowed to tear his clothes.

> Matthew 26:65 ... saying, He hath spoken blasphemy; ...

Attention has turned away from the accusation that Jesus was going to destroy the Temple, and they are now charging Him with blasphemy, and notice who it was that first laid the charge, Caiaphas the highest of all the judges present, breaking rule number 13, judges could not make accusations, they could only examine allegations brought to them. Further, the charge of blasphemy could not be made unless the accused person, in this case Jesus, had spoken the name of God, which He had not, and so rule 14 was also broken.

> Matthew 26:65 ... what further need have we of witnesses? ...

All the witnesses had been brought before the court, and none of them had agreed on any single thing against Jesus, so Caiaphas suddenly decides he does not need witnesses, again breaking rule 10. Instead he intends to bring about a conviction based on the words of Jesus, Himself, breaking rule 15, no one could be convicted by his own words alone.

> Matthew 26:66 They answered and said, He is guilty of death.

The court had reached its verdict, deciding that Jesus was guilty of death. It was still night and this broke rule 16, decisions could not be declared during the night, only during daylight. Blasphemy was punishable by death, and they had given their verdict on the same day as the trial, breaking rule 17, in cases of capital punishment the judgment could only be made twenty-four hours after the trial. More than that, they arrived at their judgement by a brief verbal approval, breaking rule 18, the death penalty could only be imposed by an individual vote of all the court officials, beginning with the youngest first, so that the younger officials would not be influenced by the older men.

The decision of the members of the Sanhedrin that were there, (and they were not all there), to kill Jesus, was unanimous, they all voted for His death.

> Mark 14:64 And they all condemned him to be guilty of death.

Under rule 19, if everyone voted guilty then the accused was to be declared innocent and set free. Jesus was not declared innocent and was not set free, and this broke rule 19. Further the punishment or sentence, in this case death, could not be announced the same day as the guilty decision was made, it could only be declared three days later, breaking rule 20, of the laws of the Sanhedrin.

> Mark 14:65 And some began to spit on him, and to cover his face, and to buffet [beat] him, and to say unto him, Prophesy: and the servants did strike him with the palms of their hands.

> Matthew 26:67 Then did they spit in his face, and buffeted [hit] him; and others smote him with the palms of their hands.

The last two rules of the laws of the Sanhedrin in our list were broken here, rule 21, the judges were to behave in a kind and considerate manner, and rule 22, anyone sentenced to death could not be whipped or beaten before he died. This was the second time Jesus was mistreated that night.

Jewish civil law laid down fines for the treatment handed out to Jesus by the Sanhedrin. He had been hit by clenched fist (buffeted) and the fine for that was four denarii, equivalent to four days wages. He had been hit by the palm of the hand, which was considered a much greater insult, and the fine for that was two-hundred denarii, or two-hundred days wages. Most insulting of all they had spat on his face, for which the fine was four-hundred denarii, four-hundred days wages, but of course, no one was fined anything in either of these two completely illegal and totally unjust religious trials.

THE APOSTLE PETER'S DENIAL
Matthew 26:58, 26:69-75, Mark 14:54, 14:66-72, Luke 22:54-62, John 18:15-18, 18:25-27

It was during the trial of Jesus before Caiaphas, that Peter three times denied he knew Jesus or had ever been with Him, and his last denial came at about the time the trial ended. After the arrest of Jesus all the disciples scattered,[1] but later John and Peter teamed up again and followed the procession. The families of John and the High Priest were friends, which was shown when John named the servant of the High Priest as Malchus.[2] We are now going to see an indication of the closeness of the two families again.

> John 18:15 And Simon Peter followed Jesus, and so did another disciple: that disciple was known unto the high priest, and went in with Jesus into the palace of the high priest.

Clearly the servants knew John and they allowed him to enter the grounds of the High Priest's palace, but Peter was left standing outside the door, then John decided to use his influence so that his friend Peter could join him.

> John 18:16 But Peter stood at the door without [outside], Then went out the other disciple, which was known unto the high priest, and spake [spoke] unto her that kept the door, and brought in Peter.

The home of the High Priest[3] was big and luxurious, as only men of great wealth could afford to live in. It had enough room for the Sanhedrin and the trial, while the Roman soldiers, the Temple police and household servants were in the courtyard, where a fire had been lit to provide warmth and light on that cold night. It was nice of John to remember Peter outside and arrange for his friend to join him there by the fire, but he did not know he was setting the stage for Peter to deny Jesus three times.

In the light of the fire Peter could be seen clearly and he was recognised, that is the reason he was accused of being a disciple of Jesus three times, and each time he denied his Lord. The Scriptures show that his second denial was stronger than the first, and his third strongest of all. The first person to identify Peter as a disciple of Jesus was a young unmarried woman, or in KJV Bible language, a damsel.

> Matthew 26:69 Now Peter sat without [in the courtyard] in the palace: and a damsel came unto him, saying, Thou [You] also wast [were] with Jesus of Galilee.

She was not only speaking privately to Peter at the time, but also made her remark to others around the fire.[4]

> Mark 14:68 But he denied, ..., and the cock crew [crowed].

The word denied here, means a simple denial, and this was the first cock crowing, meaning it was exactly mid-night. A short while later another servant recognised Peter.[5]

> Matthew 26:71-72 71 This fellow also was with Jesus of Nazareth.
>
> 72 And again he denied it with an oath, ...

This time Peter did not make a simple denial, he swore by an oath that he was not a disciple or that he even knew Jesus. There were a number of people round the fire and so we get what appears to be an error here. Matthew 26:71, identifies Peter's accuser as a maid, "another maid saw him, and said unto them that were there, This fellow was also with Jesus of Nazareth." On the other hand Peter is shown answering to a man in Luke 22:58, "Man, I am not," obviously more than one person was accusing Peter at the same time. He must have been feeling more and more unsafe. It was about an hour after the second denial that Peter was again spotted and remembered for being with Jesus.

> Luke 22:59 And about the space of an hour another confidently affirmed, saying, Of a truth this fellow also was with him: for he is a Galilaean.

Twice Peter had denied being a disciple of Jesus, and then one guy near the fire began to have his doubts about Peter again because of his

Galilean accent, and supported by others began accusing him of being a follower of Jesus.

> Matthew 26:73 And after a while came unto him they that stood by, and said to Peter, Surely thou also art [are] one of them: for thy speech [accent] betrayeth [identifies] thee [you].

> Mark 14:70 Surely [For sure] thou art one of them: for thou art a Galilaean, and thy speech [accent] agreeth [is the same as] thereto [that place].

Jesus did not speak with the posh cultured accent of Jerusalem, He spoke the working class language of the fishermen and carpenters of Galilee, and so did Peter. One of the men who was branding Peter a disciple this third time was known to John because of the friendship between the two families of Caiaphas and John, who, for that reason tells the story in more detail.

> John 18:26 One of the servants of the high priest, being his kinsman [a relative of the man] whose ear Peter cut off, saith [said to Peter], Did not I see thee [you] in the garden [the Garden of Gethsemane] with him [Jesus]?

Notice how Peter denies Jesus this third time.

> Mark 14:71 And he began to curse and to swear, saying, I know not this man of whom ye speak.

In the original Greek language of this verse, it is put very strongly, and it means Peter swore against Jesus, and cursed Him. It was the strongest by far of all his three denials. It was three o'clock in the morning because the cock crowed for the second time. The trial before Caiaphas was ending, or had ended and the door was open.

> Luke 22:61 And the Lord turned, and looked upon Peter.

> Mark 14:71 And the second time the cock crew [crowed]. And Peter called to mind the word that Jesus said unto him, Before the cock crow twice, thou shalt deny me thrice. And when he thought thereon, he wept.

> Luke 22:62 And Peter went out, and wept bitterly.

[1] Matthew 26:56, Mark 14:50
[2] John 18:10
[3] Mark 14:54
[4] Luke 22:56
[5] Luke 22:58

JESUS IS MOCKED AND BEATEN
Luke 22:63-64

After the trial before the Sanhedrin Jesus was mistreated for the third time that night, again by being beaten, and He was also mocked.

> Luke 22:63 And the men that held Jesus mocked him and smote him.

Jesus would be mocked eight times, and this was the first of them.

THE SANHEDRIN PASSES JUDGEMENT ON THE MESSIAH OF ISRAEL
Matthew 27:1, Mark 15:1, Luke 22:66-71

The trial and the judgement had already been made by the Sanhedrin, and it was plain to everyone that the proceedings and condemnation had been illegal. To try and make their decision seem more lawfully correct, they waited until it began to get light in order that rule 2, of the twenty-two they had broken, would appear to have been kept. All the three gospels make the same point.

> Matthew 27:1 When the morning was come.

> Mark 15:1 And straightway in the morning.

> Luke 22:66 And as soon as it was day.

At first light, to make their proceedings look slightly more permissible, they reassembled for the third stage of the religious trial, without any of the necessary witnesses, and they asked Jesus two questions.

> Luke 22:67 Art thou the Christ? Tell us.

Jesus explained it was a waste of time talking to them because they had already decided not to believe, but later they will eventually realise the truth when they see Him seated by the right hand of God the Father. This leads to their second question.

> Luke 22:70 Then said they all, Art thou then the Son of God? And he said unto them, Ye say that I am.

In the original Greek, "Ye say that I am," is like saying, "Yes, without a doubt, I am the Son of God." Although, "Ye say that I am," does not sound like a strong, "Yes," in the English language, the judges knew exactly what Jesus meant, as the next verse shows.

> Luke 22:71 And they said, What need we any further witnesses? For we ourselves have heard of his own mouth.

THE DEATH OF JUDAS ISCARIOT AFTER HE BETRAYED JESUS
Matthew 27:3-10, Acts 1:18

The plot of Caiaphas to condemn Jesus to death for planning to destroy the Temple, failed when his witnesses could not agree. Also, although the Temple was protected by Roman law under the penalty of death, the death sentence could only be carried out by the Romans themselves, because the Romans had taken away that authority from the Sanhedrin. Caiaphas' next idea was to accuse Jesus of blasphemy, but although blasphemy was punishable by death under Jewish law, it was not under Roman law. In order to get Jesus killed the Sanhedrin would have to have Jesus tried in a Roman law court for a crime punishable by death, something entirely different from planning to destroy the Temple or blasphemy, so another accusation would have to be thought up. The man they needed was Judas, because he had already been before Pontius Pilate and accused Jesus of a crime punishable under Roman law, that is how he obtained the cohort of soldiers for the arrest, but in between the trial before Caiaphas and the Roman trial, Judas committed suicide.

> Matthew 27:3 Then Judas, which betrayed him, when he saw that he was condemned, repented [felt sorry] himself, ...

The word repented (felt sorry), has caused some people to ask, "If he repented, was Judas saved?" The answer is, "No!" Jesus warned Judas beforehand that it would be better if the person betraying Him had never been born.[1] It was while He was praying to God the Father, that Jesus called Judas, the son of perdition,[2] which means the son of eternal death, and so he is in Hell the temporary place of torment for the everlasting dead, along with the souls of all other unbelievers, and he will stay there until the end of the Millennial Kingdom. You can refresh your memory about what will happen to him after that in the section, The King's Power Over Demons, of Chapter 6.

Trying to make amends for his crime, Judas went back to the chief priests and elders to return the blood money, but they would not take it, so he threw the coins into the Temple.

> Matthew 27:5 And he cast down the pieces of silver in the temple, and departed, and went and hanged himself.

Luke writing in the Book of Acts seems to say something different and a question then arises, "How did Judas actually commit suicide?"

> Acts 1:18 Now this man [Judas] purchased a field with the reward [payment] of iniquity [wickedness]; and falling headlong, he burst asunder [open] in the midst [middle], and all his bowls [intestines] gushed out.

A knowledge of Jewish law of the time, shows that both statements are true, Judas hanged himself, and he also fell, and when he fell his stomach burst open. We have to remind ourselves again that a Jewish day begins at sunset, not at midnight as we Gentiles suppose it to be. For that reason the Sabbath law ends at sunset on Saturday, and Jews do not keep the Sabbath until midnight on Saturday, only until sunset. Also, in their system the first night of anything, comes before the first day, and it was on the first night of Passover, that Jesus and His twelve disciples ate the Passover.

On the first day of Passover there was a special sacrifice at, 9 o'clock in the morning, that only the priests could eat, but there was a legal requirement that had to be met. If there was a dead body inside the walls of Jerusalem during the first night or the first day of Passover, the city was considered to be unclean, and while the body remained, they could not carry out the special sacrifice. Of course there was a way out, the Jews always found a way of getting round any law that caused a problem by making another one. The second rule was that if the corpse was taken and thrown out of the city, over the wall that faced the Valley of Hinnom, and not any other wall, that would make Jerusalem clean, and they could go on with the special sacrifice. The grave diggers could go out and bury the body, but they would be working outside the city walls, and so the city would not be unfavourably affected.

The city was defiled by the body of Judas when he committed suicide, and that put a stop to the special sacrifice for the priests. To purify the city they ordered that the corpse be thrown over the city wall facing the Valley of Hinnom, and this caused the stomach to burst and the contents to spurt out. It is only with a knowledge of Jewish law of the time, that we can show both Matthew and Luke wrote truthfully.

Another question that is asked is, "Who bought the field?"

> Matthew 27:6-7 [6] And the chief priests took the silver pieces, and said, It is not lawful for to put them into the treasury, because it is the price of blood.
>
> [7] And they took counsel, and bought with them the potters field, to bury strangers in.

Matthew said the chief priests bought the potters field, but Luke said Judas bought it.

> Acts 1:18 Now this man [Judas] purchased a field with the reward of iniquity.

According to Jewish law, both Scriptures are true. The chief priests and Judas both broke the law when Judas was bribed with thirty pieces of silver, and money wrongly obtained could not be put in the Temple treasury, as the chief priests had said. In such a situation they were supposed to return the money to the giver, but Judas was dead, even then they still could not put the money in the treasury. The only thing they were allowed to do with it was to buy something for the good of the people, and they decided when they met and counselled together, to buy a field to bury strangers in, according to Jewish law. The law was that whatever they purchased had to be bought in the name of the donor, who had provided the money, even if the donor was dead, and all the official documents had to have the name of Judas on them. Matthew told us who actually bought the field, while Luke told us who legally bought the field, and both are correct.

Matthew 27:8-10 [8] Wherefore the field was called, The field of blood, unto this day.

[9] Then was fulfilled that which was spoken by Jeremy [Jeremiah] the prophet, saying, And they took the thirty pieces of silver, the price of him that was valued, whom they of the children of Israel did value;

[10] And gave them for the potter's field, as the Lord appointed me.

A discrepancy in verses 9 and 10, is that the prophecy shown was made by Zechariah,[3] not Jeremiah. I have studied several suggested reasons or explanations for this, and for the purposes of this book have decided not to explain the Scriptures in question. Needless to say, I believe the Bible, and am sure there is a very good reason for Matthew writing as he did.

[1] Matthew 26:24

[2] John 17:12

[3] Zechariah 11:12-13

THE FIRST TRIAL HEARD BY PONTIUS PILATE
Matthew 27:11-14, Mark 15:1-5, Luke 23:1-7, John 18:28-38

The religious trial was over, in which Jesus had been condemned for blasphemy, but under Roman law that did not justify the death sentence. For the Roman trial, in order to get Jesus killed, the Sanhedrin brought in a new charge of sedition or treason against Rome. Sedition would be behaving unlawfully against Roman authority, and treason would be things like, making war against Rome, siding with her enemies or being a threat to her government officials, especially Caesar himself. The plan was then, to show that Jesus was guilty of sedition or treason against Rome.

Pontius Pilate had been born in Spain, but he was a citizen of Rome, and was Procurator of Judea and Samaria, from AD 26 until AD 36. He was well known at the time for his cruelty, and for usually keeping strictly to the rules and customs established by Rome. True to his character then, he was dressed for the trial even though it was very early in the morning, because he had sent out a cohort of troops to follow Judas and make the arrest, and was ready and waiting.

According to Roman law, trials had to be in public, as this one was. Pilate would later give in to public pressure for the death of Jesus, even though he knew Jesus was not guilty. Also, trials could not begin without a prosecuting witness making a charge of a crime against Roman law, but because Judas was dead, there was no prosecuting witness.

> John 18:28 And they led Jesus from Caiaphas unto the hall of judgement: and it was early; and they themselves went not into the judgement hall, lest [for fear that] they should be defiled; but that they might eat the Passover.

Many Gentiles seeing the word Passover here wrongly assume that Jesus ate the Passover a day early, because Caiaphas and his gang had not eaten it yet. Jesus always kept the Law of Moses perfectly to the last jot and tittle, and the Law is very clear about when the feast must be eaten. Jewish families eat the feast on the first night of Passover. Only the priests would eat the special sacrifice, made at nine o'clock in the morning on the first day of Passover, and that is what they were worried about. The special sacrifice was offered straightway after the regular morning sacrifices, roasted and eaten later the same day. The hall of judgement was in the Praetorium, the official residence of the governor, and because they would be defiled if they went into the home of a Gentile, they did not enter the house, only the courtyard outside.

Earlier I explained that a Roman trial could not begin until a witness had given evidence of a crime punishable under Roman law, which explains the first question from Pilate.

John 18:29 Pilate then went out unto them, and said, What accusation bring ye against this man [Jesus]?

Judas was then supposed to make his accusation against Jesus, but Judas was now a lifeless corpse. The Sanhedrin then tried to get Pilate to sentence Jesus to death without a witness.

John 18:30 They answered and said unto him, If he were not a malefactor [worker-of-evil], we would not have delivered him up unto thee.

Pilate, following Roman law correctly, refused to listen to them.

John 18:31 Then said Pilate unto them, Take ye him, and judge him according to your law.

The Jews had no witness, meaning there would be no trial, no guilty verdict, and no sentence, but they would not give up easily.

John 18:31 The Jews therefore said unto him, It is not lawful for us to put any man to death.

The Jews here were pointing out that it was Roman law that prevented them using Jewish law, to sentence any man to death. The problem for the Jews had been caused by the Roman Senate, when it stopped allowing the Sanhedrin to carry out the death sentence, so in their opinion Rome should deal with the matter. The Apostle John follows this with a comment of his own.

John 18:32 That the saying of Jesus might be fulfilled, which he spake [spoke], signifying what death he should die.

Jesus had prophesied His death several times including the fact that it would be by crucifixion,[1] and that was not the Jewish way of execution. The Jews stoned people to death and if Rome had not taken away their right to exercise capital punishment, Jesus would have been stoned, and if that had happened, Jesus would have been a false prophet, because He had prophesied death by crucifixion.

The Jewish Talmud shows the year the Roman Senate took away their right to apply the death sentence, where one quote reads, "Forty years before the Temple was destroyed, judgement in capital cases was taken away from Israel." The Temple was destroyed in AD 70, and forty years before that was AD 30, the same year Jesus was crucified. Jesus and some Old Testament prophets had prophesied that He would die by being crucified, and just before His death, God caused the Roman Senate to take away the right of capital punishment from the Jewish Sanhedrin, making sure that all the Bible prophecies of the death of Christ came true, because execution by Rome meant crucifixion, that was their way.

The leaders of the Jews quickly realised that as the matter stood, Pontius Pilate did not intend to try Jesus at all, and quickly accused Him of sedition or treason against Rome, making three accusations, all found in Luke 23:2.

> 1. "We found this fellow [Jesus] ... perverting the nation." What they meant by, perverting the nation, was trying to cause a revolt against the government, and that is how Pilate understood them.[2]
> 2. "We found this fellow [Jesus] ... forbidding to give tribute [taxes] to Caesar." Forbidding people to pay taxes to Caesar was treason, but they were lying because Jesus had said, "Render to Caesar the things which are Caesar's."[3]
> 3. "We found this fellow [Jesus] ... saying that he himself is Christ a King." His claim to be a king would put him in competition with Caesar, which would then be a case of sedition.

The charges had been made and according to Roman law, therefore Pilate could go ahead and question the accused prisoner, so he left the Jews in the courtyard and returned to Jesus.

> John 18:33 Then Pilate entered into the judgement hall again, and called Jesus, and said unto him, Art [Are] thou [you] the King of the Jews?

Pontius Pilate did not ask Jesus if He was Christ, or Messiah, that did not interest him one little bit, but he did want to know if Jesus was opposed to Caesar, the leader of the Roman empire, so he asked, "Are you the King of the Jews?"

> John 18:34 Jesus answered him, Sayest [Speak] thou [you] this thing of thyself [your own idea], or did others tell thee of me.

In other words, "Are you asking this from your position as a Roman, or from the Jewish angle?"

> John 18:35 Pilate answered, Am I a Jew? Thine own nation and chief priests have delivered thee unto me: what hast thou done?

Pilate is saying, "I am asking because of what your Jewish leaders are accusing you of, and as a Roman I want to know if you are in opposition to Caesar." Pilate had made the issue perfectly plain, and Jesus could now give an accurate answer.

> John 18:36 Jesus answered, My kingdom is not of this world: if my kingdom were of this world, then would my servants fight, that I should not be delivered [handed over] to the Jews: but now is my kingdom not from hence [now on].

Again, in other words, "I do not have any rivalry with Caesar, for two reasons." The first reason is, "My kingdom is not of this world." Some Christians believe that this means there will be no Millennial Kingdom on earth, which is nonsense, so we will look at the Scriptures more closely and show they are wrong. A study of the words of Jesus shows there is a difference in what He meant when He said, "of the world," and "in the world." Let us examine again part of the prayer, He prayed for His disciples and us as our High Priest.

> John 17:14-16 [14] I have given them thy word; and the world hath hated them, because they are not of the world, even as I am not of the world.
>
> [15] I pray not that thou shouldest take them out of the world, but that thou shouldest keep them from evil.
>
> [16] They are not of the world, even as I am not of the world.

While we are alive we are in the world, but if we have experienced the spiritual birth we have a different nature, not perfect, our final perfection will be given to us when we go to be with Jesus, but even now our nature is not the nature of the world. Christ's kingdom has another nature, not like this world's nature. Jesus did not want Caesar's throne, His kingdom will not be of the world, but it will be in the world.

The other reason Jesus was not competing for Caesar's throne is that it was not yet time for His kingdom to be created. He told Pilate, "My kingdom is not from hence," or, "Not for now."

> John 18:37 Pilate therefore said unto him, Art thou a king then?

The meaning of the answer Jesus gave boils down to this, "Yes, I am King of the Truth, and every single person that knows the truth, listens to Me."

> John 18:38 Pilate saith unto him, What is truth?

The strange thing was that as Pilate asked the question, he was looking straight at the Truth, but did not recognise Him. Pilate was only one of so many people that never knew, or do not know the Truth.

Pilate had questioned Jesus and was quite sure that He was not a threat to Caesar, and made the first of several judgements saying that Jesus was not guilty, He was innocent.

> John 18:38 And when he had said this, he went out again unto the Jews, and saith unto them, I find in him no fault at all.

The chief priests became frantic, and because Judas Iscariot their witness was dead, they took on the role of accusing witnesses themselves, and started with a whole new list of crimes they said Jesus had committed, but Jesus refused to answer them.

> Mark 15:3 And the chief priests accused him of many things: but he answered nothing.

Pilate pointed out to Jesus how many things they were accusing Him of, but Jesus did not answer a word.

> Mark 15:5 But Jesus yet answered nothing; so that Pilate marvelled [was astonished].

All kinds of furious accusations were coming from the chief priests, until one of them revealed that Jesus was from Galilee.

> Luke 23:5 And they were the more fierce, saying, He stirreth [stirs] up the people, teaching throughout all Jewry, beginning from Galilee to this place.

On hearing this Pilate asked if Jesus was a Galilean and finding out that He was, thought there was a way out of his difficulty, because Herod Antipas was in charge of Galilee, and Herod was in Jerusalem to help keep order during the feast. Pilate therefore sent Jesus and His accusers off to Herod.

[1] Matthew 20:19, 26:2, Mark 10:33-34, Luke 18:32-33, John 3:14, 8:28, 12:32-33

[2] Luke 23:14-15

[3] Matthew 22:21, Mark 12:17, Luke 20:25

THE TRIAL HEARD BY HEROD ANTIPAS
Luke 23:7-12

Herod the Great, the one who met the wise men in Jerusalem and then tried to kill Jesus when He was a child of less than two years old, was the father of Herod Antipas. It was Antipas that had beheaded John the Baptist, a year or more earlier, and when afterwards, he learned of the miracles of Jesus, he thought that Jesus was John the Baptist returned from the dead, and had been wanting to meet Him for some time.[1] Herod now became judge at the trial of the man he had wanted to see, and he wanted to be amused, he wanted to see some miracles. He loved being entertained, and it was because his stepdaughter Salome had pleased him so much when she danced for him, that John the Baptist had been beheaded.[2] Herod was to be disappointed because Jesus never performed miracles to amuse other people. Frustrated because there were no miracles, Herod made fun of Jesus himself. He ordered his soldiers to mock Him, treat Him with scorn and disrespect, dress Him up like someone very important, and send Him back to Pontius Pilate.[3] This was the second time Jesus was mocked that night.

Although the chief priests and scribes had angrily accused Jesus,[4] Herod could see that Jesus was not a threat to Rome, and returned Him to Pilate. In effect the Roman authorities had now declared Jesus innocent twice.

In AD 39, the Roman emperor Caligula banished Herod and his wife Herodias to Leon, which is now part of France, where they came to their end in miserable, degrading poverty, and died, and so they paid the price for the parts they played in the beheading of John the Baptist, and the mocking of Jesus.

[1] Mark 6:14-29, Luke 9:7-9

[2] Mark 6:14-29

[3] Luke 23:11

[4] Luke 23:10

THE SECOND TRIAL HEARD BY PONTIUS PILATE
Matthew 27:15-31, Mark 15:6-20, Luke 23:13-25, John 18:38 to 19:16

In this section Pilate will try several times to get Jesus freed, because he knows that Jesus is innocent of the charges the Jews have made against Him. He called the chief priests, elders and the people to listen to him[1] and told them that he had tried Jesus and found Him not guilty,[2] and that he had then sent him to Herod and Herod had found Him not guilty, as well,[3] but that would not satisfy the Jews. Like many fanatics, the rights or wrongs of the case were of no interest to them and their followers, they were determined to have their way, and they wanted this man Jesus, dead, because they saw Him as a dangerous threat to them and their life styles.[4]

Pilate then thought of another way to let Jesus go free, and decided to release Jesus according to a custom of the time, which was that the

Romans would let a Jewish prisoner loose at Passover.[5] At that time there was another prisoner waiting to be crucified for breaking Roman law, called Barabbas, and the whole crowd cried out together, for Barabbas to be freed and for Jesus to be killed.

> John 18:40 Then cried they all again, saying, Not this man, but Barabbas. Now Barabbas was a robber.

Robbery was not punishable by death under Roman law, and a better translation would be rebel, not robber. Barabbas had rebelled against the Roman government in a revolt or uprising, which the KJV of the Bible calls an insurrection, and had murdered at least one person.

> Mark 15:7 And there was one named Barabbas, which lay bound with them that had made insurrection with him, who had committed murder in the insurrection.

Barabbas had been judged and found guilty of rebelling against Rome, in other words he was guilty of sedition or treason, the very accusations the Jews had brought against Jesus, and although Jesus was innocent they wanted Him killed, and knowing Barabbas was a murderer, and that he had broken the law they were accusing Jesus of breaking, they wanted him freed.

Something strange was taking place in the Jews choice of Barabbas, because Barabbas is not a name, it is a title that comes from two Aramaic words, Bar, meaning, 'son of,' and then Abba, Barabbas means, Son of Abba. His own name is not given in the Bible, but other sources tell us that his first name was Jesus. The guilty Jesus (Barabbas) was set free, and the innocent Jesus was crucified. Even more strange is the fact that 'abba,' in Aramaic means, 'the father,' and therefore the name, Jesus Barabbas, means, Jesus the son of the father. On the other hand our Saviour is, Jesus the Son of the Father (God). The two men were there and Mark tells us why Pilate was trying to get the True Jesus freed.

> Mark 15:10 For he knew that the chief priests had delivered him for envy.

As it had been with John the Baptist, the reasons they hated Him were personal but the accusations against Him were political, both John and Jesus were killed because of the personal envy of the Jewish religious leaders.

Pilate was still trying to get Jesus released when he was interrupted, by a messenger with news from his wife who wanted him to know about a terrible nightmare she had dreamt.

> Matthew 27:19 When he was set down on the judgement seat, his wife sent unto him, saying, Have thou nothing to do with that just man: for I have suffered many things this day in a dream because of him.

The Roman Governor's conviction of the innocence of Jesus had now been reinforced by a strong warning from his wife, just after he had taken the judgement seat, but before he could continue with the case, members of the Sanhedrin had been prompting the crowds to ask for the release of Barabbas.

> Matthew 27:20 But the chief priests and elders persuaded the multitude that they should ask Barabbas, and destroy Jesus.

The Sanhedrin was very successful in convincing the crowd to ask for the death of their Messiah and for Barabbas the murderer and seditious rebel to be set free.

> Luke 23:18 And they cried out all at once, saying, Away with this man, and release unto us Barabbas.

Once again Pilate failed in an attempt to have Jesus freed, but he then tried a third time, by proposing that instead of being crucified, Jesus should be scourged and then released.

> John 19:1 Then Pilate therefore took Jesus and scourged him.

At the time the Gospels were written, scourging was a common and well known punishment, and so John did not tell us anything about the scourge. The Jewish scourge was known as, forty-less-one, because according to the Law of Moses a man could not be whipped more than forty times,[6] and to be on the safe side and make allowance for not counting properly, they only whipped a man thirty-nine times, and so the Jewish scourge was called, forty-less-one. The scourge used by the Jews had short leather thongs attached to a wooden or leather handle. It was terribly painful but it was not a killer, as was shown by the Apostle Paul who was scourge five times and lived on.[7]

The Roman scourge used to whip Jesus was a much more dreadful piece of equipment, and in addition to that there was no limit to the number of lashes a man could receive. The leather thongs were long and attached to a leather handle, with sharp objects inserted at the end of each thong, such as notched iron balls, sharp lamb bone, pieces of glass or metal. The thongs would wrap tightly round the body of the victim, first tearing the skin, after that the muscles exposing the bones at the back, front and sides of the body. Historical records tell us that even family members of scourged persons could not recognise them. No religious paintings show the terrible condition the scourged body of Jesus was in during His crucifixion. The face of a person after the Roman scourge was a swollen, mushy, bloody mess, just as Isaiah prophesied, the face of Jesus would be.

> Isaiah 52:14 As many were astonished at thee [Jesus]; his visage [face] was so marred [spoiled] more than any man, and his form [shape or appearance] more than the sons of men.

His face and His body did not look human any more after this, the fourth mistreatment that night.

Next, because Jesus said He was a King, which to the Romans implied He was challenging Caesar, they began to mock Him for the third time, dressing Him in a royal purple robe, (a sign of royalty), and putting a crown on His head, made with thorns. The thorns that grow in Israel are long, strong and very sharp, and the crown definitely caused severe pain. It was while He was already suffering from such terrible torture that they began to hit Him.[8]

The crown of thorns, representing sin, was a sign of the curse God put on the earth because of Adam and Eve's sin, before which there were no thorns in the world.

> Genesis 3:17-19 [17] And unto Adam he [God] said, Because thou hast hearkened [listened] unto the voice of thy wife, and hast eaten of the tree, of which I commanded thee, saying, Thou

shalt not eat of it: cursed is the ground for thy sake; in sorrow shalt thou eat of it all the days of they life;

[18] Thorns also and thistles shall it bring forth to thee; and thou shalt eat the herb of the field;

[19] In the sweat of thy face shalt thou eat bread, till thou return unto the ground; for out of it wast thou taken: for dust thou art, and unto dust shalt thou return.

Another thing to notice is that because he had sinned, Adam was cursed to work and sweat, as he harvested grain to make bread to stay alive, but Adam's bread was the bread of death, because no matter how much he ate or for how long, it would not give him eternal life, he was doomed to die, and he would die a sinner. His body would rot and turn back into dust, into the chemicals God had taken from the earth and used to make him. Observe the contrast, Adam gave us the bread of death, Jesus gave us the Bread of Life.

John 6:48 I am the bread of life.

John 6:51 I am the living bread which cometh down from heaven: if any man eat of this bread, he shall live forever: and the bread that I will give is my flesh, which I will give for the life of the world.

Jesus is the Bread of Life, and if we swallow it, that is if we believe Him and ask Him to fill us with that Bread, we are changed from being sinners like Adam, to being righteous, like Christ. Righteousness is given to believers in Jesus.

Romans 5:17 For if by one man's offence [sin] death reigned by one [Adam]; much more they which receive abundance of grace and the gift of righteousness shall reign in life by one, Jesus Christ.

If you are looking forward to the return of Jesus then you will be given a very noticeable kind of head dress, a crown of righteousness, like the one the Apostle Paul will get, not a crown of thorns like our Saviour suffered during His trial.

> 2 Timothy 4:8 Henceforth there is laid up for me [Paul] a crown of righteousness, which the Lord, the righteous judge, shall give me on that day: and not to me only, but unto all them also that love his appearing.

The crown of thorns worn by Jesus represented sin, but He will give us a crown of righteousness.

Returning to the second trial before Pilate, Pilate believed that having scourged Jesus the Jews would accept that as sufficient punishment. Jesus had the crown of thorns on His head and was wearing a royal purple robe, which would have covered up his cruelly torn and tortured body, what a disgusting mockery of God's chosen King. Pilate had Jesus brought out for the Jews to see, and said, "Look at the man," in other words, "He has been punished enough," but the Jews had no pity. For the fourth time Pilate declared Jesus innocent, but the crowd shouted, "Crucify Him." Pilate then made his fourth attempt to set Jesus free by refusing to pass the death sentence,[9] and without a sentence there would be no crucifixion.

The Jews were not getting their way, Pilate was stubborn, but they were more stubborn, so they changed tactics, dropped the charge of sedition or treason against Rome, and came to the point that had troubled them right from the time they rejected Him as the Messiah. His crime was that He claimed to be the Christ, the Son of God.

> John 19:7 The Jews answered him, We have a law, and by our law he ought to die, because he made himself the Son of God.

The new charge meant there must be a new enquiry, and so Pilate left the Jews in the courtyard and went back into the judgement hall, but Jesus refused to testify. He had already told Pilate enough for him to understand the truth and make a correct judgement. Also Pilate was being sarcastic when he said, "What is truth?"[10] so would there be any point for Jesus to give any more evidence?

> John 19:10-11 ¹⁰ Then said Pilate unto him [Jesus], Speakest [Speak] thou [you] not unto me? Knowest [Know] thou [you] not that I have power to crucify thee, and have power to release thee?

¹¹ Jesus answered, Thou couldest [could] have no power over me, except it were given thee from above: therefore he that delivered me unto thee hath the greater sin.

The final authority is from heaven, and because we are all guilty of sin, and the penalty for sin is death, God the Father, intended that His Son should pay our penalty for us, so that we can be freed and united with Him and be given eternal life.[11] God was the final authority, but Pilate was still responsible for his actions and because he did not believe in Jesus, he was also answerable for his sins. On the other hand the accusers are more guilty because their sins are more serious.

Pilate then tried for the fifth time to set Jesus free.

John 19:12 And from thenceforth Pilate tried to release him ....

He was unsuccessful the fifth time because the Jews shouted out that if he released Jesus, he was not Caesar's friend. Pilate was terrified because his very good friend and supporter in Rome, who had recommended Pilate for the job of Governor of Judea and Samaria, a man called Sejanus, had just been executed for plotting to kill the emperor, and the Senate was checking all the friends of Sejanus, to see if they too were a threat. If the Senate found out that Pilate had been called, "Not Caesar's friend," Pilate would probably have lost his life.

John 19:12 ... but the Jews cried out, saying, If you let this man go, thou art not Caesar's friend: whosoever maketh [makes] himself a king speaketh [speaks] against Caesar.

The key word in the following verse is, "therefore," and it refers back to the Jews saying, "thou art not Caesar's friend."

John 19:13 When Pilate therefore heard that saying, he brought Jesus forth, and sat down in the judgement seat.

Once he had sat on the judgement seat he had to make a judgement, and he made a sixth attempt to get Jesus set free, by appealing to the Jews again, showing them the sorry sight of Jesus, the King of the Jews, who clearly had already been so very severely punished, he would be likely to die anyway.

> John 19:14 ... Behold your King!

Again they shouted out for Jesus to be crucified, and Pilate asked again, "Crucify your King?

> John 19:15 ... The chief priests answered, We have no king but Caesar.

The chief priest had rejected Jesus and accepted Caesar, refused the Good Shepherd, and gone after the foolish shepherd, so the prophecy of Zechariah the prophet, made nearly 500 years before, was fulfilled.

> Zechariah 11:15-16 [15] And the LORD said unto me, Take unto thee yet the instrument of a foolish shepherd.
>
> [16] For, lo, I will raise up a shepherd in the land, which shall not visit those that be cut off, neither shall seek the young one, nor heal that that is broken, nor feed that that standeth still: but he shall eat the flesh of the fat, and tear their claws in pieces.

Pilate did not try to get Jesus released again, but ordered that He should be crucified. He was not happy about it as we can see from the Gospel of Matthew.

> Matthew 27:24 When Pilate saw that he could prevail [achieve] nothing, but that rather a tumult [riot] was made, he took water, and washed his hands before the multitude, saying, I am innocent of the blood of this just person: see ye to it.

We know that God was in control of what was going on, and that Bible prophecy going back many hundreds of years, meant that it was absolutely certain that Jesus would be crucified, but humanly speaking, where did the responsibility for condemning Jesus to death by crucifixion lie? The decision could only be made by one man, the Roman Governor, Pontius Pilate, and if he thought he could free himself from the guilt of the sentence he passed on Jesus by washing his hands in water, because he had been too scared to make the right judgement, he was very, very wrong.

In the Book of Acts, when Paul was preaching in a synagogue on the Sabbath day at Antioch in Persidia, he blamed the Jewish religious rulers and people of Jerusalem for the death of Jesus, because they had not understood, "the voices of the prophets which are read every Sabbath day,"[12] in the synagogues.

> Acts 13:28 And though they found no cause of death in him, yet desired they Pilate that he [Jesus] should be slain.

The fact still remains that in order for the crucifixion to be performed, the order had to come from Pilate.

The fifth time Pilate declared Jesus innocent was the most important because it came while he was on the judgement seat, and in their reply the Jews cursed themselves and their children.

> Matthew 27:25 Then answered all the people, and said, His blood be on us, and on our children.

The judgement on that generation of Jews, and their children, came in AD 70 when Jerusalem and the Temple were destroyed because of the unforgivable sin, the sin of saying that the miracles performed by Jesus under the power of the Holy Spirit, were the works of Satan.[13]

The final judgement was that the murderer, guilty of sedition and treason against Rome, was set free, and the innocent man was sentenced to die.

> Luke 23:24-25 24And Pilate gave sentence that it should be as they required.
>
> 25 And he released unto them him that for sedition and murder was cast into prison, whom they had desired; but he delivered Jesus to their will.

In AD 36, which was six years later, the Emperor Caligula, removed Pontius Pilate from power and banished him to exile in Gaul, which was near Vienna, where Pilate committed suicide. Pilate had tried to save himself from the suspicion of the Roman Senate investigating the friends of Sejanus, by agreeing to kill Jesus, so after trying to save his life by condemning an innocent man to death, that life later became so terrible that he killed himself.

[1] Luke 23:13

[2] Luke 23:14

[3] Luke 23:15

[4] John 11:47-50

[5] John 18:39

[6] Deuteronomy 25:3

[7] 2 Corinthians 11:24

[8] John 19:1-3

[9] John 19:5-6

[10] John 18:38

[11] John 8:36

[12] Acts 13:27

[13] Matthew 12:31

JESUS IS MOCKED BY THE WHOLE ROMAN COHORT
Matthew 27:27-31, Mark 15:16-19

Jesus had first been mocked after being tried by the Sanhedrin,[1] again after the trial by Herod[2] and after being scourged,[3] so this was the fourth of the eight mockeries He suffered.

> Matthew 27:27-31 ²⁷ Then the soldiers of the governor took Jesus into the common hall, and gathered unto him the whole band of soldiers.
>
> ²⁸ And they stripped him, and put on him a scarlet robe.
>
> ²⁹ And when they had platted a crown of thorns, they put it upon his head, and a reed in his right hand: and they bowed the knee before him, and mocked him, saying, Hail, King of the Jews.
>
> ³⁰ And they spit upon him, and took the reed, and smote him on the head.

13 The Arrest, Trials and Death of Jesus

How cruel people are to one another, especially when there is a large number against one person or a few. The body of Jesus was so torn and swollen after the Roman scourge, that without His clothes He did not look human, and yet they beat Him on the head which had a crown of thorns on it, and they spat on Him, and so Jesus suffered the fifth mistreatment that night.

> ³¹ And after they had mocked him, they took the robe from him, and put his own raiment [clothes] on him, and led him away to crucify him.

[1] Luke 22:63
[2] Luke 23:11
[3] John 19:1-3

JESUS IS LED AWAY TO CALVARY
Matthew 27:31-34, Mark 15:20-23, Luke 23:26-33, John 19:16-17

Under the next six headings, including this one, we are going to look at thirty-two events in the order they happened, which cover the time Jesus was led away to Calvary, until His body was placed in a tomb and the tomb was sealed. In this section alone, which is about the procession to Calvary, the first five of these thirty-two incidents occur.

1st Event.

> John 19:16-17 ... And they took Jesus and led him away.
> ¹⁷ And he bearing his cross went forth ...

At Roman crucifixions the man that was to die had to carry his cross, which was usually just one bar of wood placed on his shoulders to which his hands were tied with the elbows bent, so that he could lift it. Although this was the traditional way the Romans treated criminals that were to die, they did not usually scourge a man before crucifying him. Pilate had ordered Jesus scourged as a substitute punishment, because he could see that it would be wrong to crucify Him. The scourging had weakened Jesus so much that He could not carry His cross all the way to Calvary.

2nd Event.

> Mark 15:21 And they compel one Simon a Cyrenian, who passed by, coming out of the country, the father of Alexander and Rufus, to bear his cross.

Cyrene was a town in North Africa, so they forced this Jewish man called Simon, who had come to Jerusalem from North Africa for the Feast of Passover, to carry the cross. At Passover there was not enough room in Jerusalem for all the Jews that came for the feast, and so outside the walls of the city a huge number of tents were erected where families lived and ate the Passover on the first night. After the darkness of the first night had cleared, then on the first day they would travel into the city to participate in the special Passover sacrifice, and this is what Simon would be intending to do, before he was compelled to join the procession carrying the cross.

It is only in Mark's gospel that we are told that Simon was the father of Alexander and Rufus, Matthew and Luke do not mention it. Mark wrote his gospel for the Romans, Matthew and Luke did not, and so this information would have been of special interest to Roman Christians. In his letter to the believers in Rome, Paul mentions Rufus and his mother.

> Romans 16:13 Salute Rufus chosen in the Lord, and his mother and mine.

Putting it together, Alexander and Rufus were known to Mark and the Christians he was writing to, while Rufus and his mother were known to the Christians in Rome. It must be that something happened to Simon that caused him to believe and lead his whole family to Jesus. At crucifixions the victims would often scream and curse at their tormentors, and sometimes it got so vile and loud that the soldiers would cut their tongues out to stop them. Jesus did not scream or curse but He prayed for those that crucified Him. Simon would have seen this and understand that Jesus was indeed the Messiah of Israel. The church in Rome was begun by Jewish believers that went to live there like Simon and his family, not by an apostle like Paul, and so we see that this second event was a very important one for the spread of Christianity.

3rd Event.

> Luke 23:27-31 ²⁷ And there followed him a great company of people, and of women, which also bewailed [wrung their hands] and lamented [wept for] him.
>
> ²⁸ But Jesus turning unto them said, Daughters of Jerusalem, weep not for me, but weep for yourselves, and for your children.
>
> ²⁹ For, behold, the days are coming, in which they shall say, Blessed are the barren, and the wombs that never bare, and the paps [nipples] which never gave suck.
>
> ³⁰ Then shall they begin to say to the mountains, Fall on us; and to the hills, Cover us.
>
> ³¹ For if they do these things in a green tree, what shall be done in the dry?

Jesus was grieving for what was going to happen to the Jews living in Jerusalem. The women were not His friends that came with Him from Galilee, they were local women and He calls them, "daughters of Jerusalem." It was the custom in those days when a Jew had been sentenced to die, especially by Gentiles, that professional women mourners would weep and cry out for the victim, and this was what was happening. The same thing still happens at some Jewish funerals. Jesus at a certain moment, stopped, turned to the women and said, "Daughters of Jerusalem, weep not for me, but weep for yourselves, and for your children." He said this because all the Jews at the trial had accepted responsibility for the death of Jesus and cursed themselves and their children, "His blood be on us, and on our children." The judgement for the unforgivable sin in AD 70 was going to be terrible for the whole country, but much more so for Jerusalem.

"For if they do these things in a green tree, what shall be done in the dry?" was an idiomatic saying, and what Jesus means is, "If I suffer like this when I am innocent, how much more will you suffer, you that are guilty."

4th Event.

> Mark 15:22 And they bring him unto the place Golgotha, which is, being interpreted, The place of a skull.

All of the gospels say the same thing, the/a place of a skull, which in Hebrew is Golgotha and in Latin is Calvarius, or, Calvary.[1] The gospels never say it is a place that looks like a skull. In Israel, tourists are sold pictures of an old quarry where a cliff has three holes in it looking like the mouth and two eyes of a massive skull. It is popular as a Protestant tourist site for the place of the crucifixion, but the holes in the cliff date from the 1880's, and were not there in the time of Jesus. Golgotha was not given its name because it looked like a skull, but because it was a place of execution. The Roman Catholic site for the death of Jesus may or may not be correct, but I am informed it is a much more realistic possibility.

5th Event.

> Mark 15:23 And they gave him to drink wine mingled with myrrh: but he received it not.

> Matthew 27:34 They gave him vinegar to drink mingled with gall: and when he had tasted thereof, he would not drink.

He was offered a mixture of sour wine, myrrh and gall, which was given to the victims before the nails were hammered through them, to help deaden the pain. The drink dulled the brain, and because Jesus needed to be mentally alert until the moment of His death, He would not drink it.

---

[1] Matthew 27:33, Mark 15:22, Luke 23:33, John 19:17

THE FIRST THREE HOURS OF THE CRUCIFIXION
Matthew 27:35-44, Mark 15:24-32, Luke 23:33-43, John 19:18-27

In this section Jesus suffers the anger of men, and it covers events numbered 6 to 17 of the 32 we will be looking at ending with the sealing of the tomb.

6th Event.

Mark 15:25 And it was the third hour, and they crucified him.

The time of the crucifixion is most important, because the third hour was at what we now call 9 o'clock in the morning, the morning of the first day of Passover, and it was exactly the moment that the special Passover sacrifice of a lamb, was being offered up in the Temple. It was no mere coincidence when the special sacrifice was being made in the Temple, on the Temple Mount inside the city, that Jesus, the Lamb of God, was being offered up and nailed to the cross as a sacrifice for us on Golgotha, another mount, which was outside the city.

The Romans used four kinds of structures for crucifixion, a rough pole such as a tree trunk standing straight up, two rough poles in the shape of the letter X, two rough poles in the shape of the letter T, and the traditional type, something like the T-type, but with the cross pole a little way down from the top of the standing pole. It is not known which type of cross was used to crucify Jesus on but one is more likely than the other three. The first two, the straight pole and the X-type, were not commonly used away from present day Italy, but there is a church tradition that the Apostle Peter was crucified upside down on an X-type cross. Of the T-type and the traditional type, the T-type was unlikely to have been used because of the way the Romans nailed a notice, written on parchment or wood, to the cross saying why the execution was being made. For T-type crosses the notices were nailed under the feet of the sufferer, and for the traditional crosses the notices were nailed above the head of victim. We will see later on that the gospels say the notice about Jesus was nailed to the cross above His head, and that is why the traditional type of cross was probably used, although we don't actually know for sure.

The condemned person was nailed to the cross on the ground, the wood being laid down first and the victim was nailed to it. In the case of the pole type structure, two nails were used, one through both hands that were crossed over each other above the head, and one through both feet that were also placed one on top of the other. In the case of the other crosses, three nails were used, one for the feet and one for each hand. Paintings of the crucifixion usually show the nails going through the hands but that is not where the nails were driven, because the weight of the body would have torn the hands free. The nails were hammered in through the wrists where the tendons are strong enough to keep the body on the cross. The feet were placed over each other and fastened with one nail, in such a way that it went through the back heel into the post. A wooden ledge was fixed just below the feet.

Afterwards, with the nails strongly in position, the cross with its sufferer was picked up and dropped into a hole in the ground that had already been dug. The dropping of the cross caused extreme pain to the victim, and because the body had been arranged in a special way before being nailed, the bones were pulled out of their joints. We know this happened to Jesus because of the prophecy of His death by crucifixion, and the mocking and agony He experienced as He died, found in Psalm 22.

> Psalm 22:14 ... all my bones are out of joint: ...

The next stage was to watch the victim's suffering get worse and worse, for many hours and even days until they died. Life was extended by giving them as much liquid as they wanted, and so their torture was stretched out longer.

7th Event.

> Luke 23:34 Then said Jesus, Father, forgive them; for they know not what they do.

Jesus spoke seven times from the cross, and on this first occasion He prayed for those who crucified Him, but who did not know what they were doing, such as the soldiers who were just doing their job. His prayer did not cover people who were well aware He was not guilty, people such as, Herod Antipas, Annas, Pontius Pilate, Caiaphas, and many of the chief priests and elders.

8th Event.

John 19:23-24 ²³ Then the soldiers, when they had crucified Jesus, took his garments [clothes], and made four parts [lots], to every soldier a part [lot]; and also his coat: now the coat was without seam, woven from the top throughout.

²⁴ They said therefore among themselves, Let us not rend [split] it, but cast [throw] lots [dice] for it, whose it shall be: that the scripture might be fulfilled, which saith, They parted my raiment among them, and for my vesture [coat] they did cast lots [throw dice]. These things therefore the soldiers did.

Jewish men at the time of Jesus were in the habit of wearing five items of clothing.

1. An upper garment, also known as the outer garment.
2. An under garment, also known as the tunic or inner garment.
3. A covering for the head.
4. A pair of sandals, or perhaps shoes.
5. The robe or coat, which contained much more cloth than any other of the clothes. Remember that cloth was expensive because it was all woven by hand.

The soldiers who were ordered to crucify, were entitled to all the victim's clothes. Many artists have painted the crucifixion with Jesus wearing a loin cloth. That is wrong, Jesus was completely naked, on the cross. Four soldiers were sent to each crucifixion, one would get the upper garment, one the under garment, one the head covering and one the sandals. The robe would be split into four and each man would get a piece of cloth as well. The robe Jesus wore was expensive and well made, normally only used by the very rich, and rather than tear it they gambled for it and one of them got His beautiful coat all for himself.[1]

In a worldly sense, Jesus was a poor man. "The foxes have holes, and the birds of the air have nests; but the Son of man [Jesus] hath not where [nowhere] to lay his head."[2] On the other hand many wealthy women supported Him,[3] and maybe one of them gave Him the expensive coat.

9th Event.

John 19:19-22 ¹⁹ And Pilate wrote a title, and put it on the cross. And the writing was, JESUS OF NAZARETH THE KING OF THE JEWS.

²⁰ This title then read many of the Jews: for the place where Jesus was crucified was nigh [near] to the city: and it was written in Hebrew, and Greek, and Latin.

²¹ Then said the chief priests of the Jews to Pilate, Write not, The King of the Jews; but that he said, I am the King of the Jews.

²² Pilate answered, What I have written I have written.

Earlier I said that the notice was nailed above the head of Jesus, and that is why the traditional type of cross is most likely to be the one used to crucify Jesus, and we know this because of Matthew.

Matthew 27:37 And they set up over his head his accusation …

The accusation was more of a title, and the Jews were not satisfied and complained to Pilate, but he was fed up with being pressured by them into doing something he knew was not right, and refused to change it. Also it was a signal to Rome that He had killed the King of the Jews, and was therefore a friend of Caesar, should the Senate inspectors checking up on friends of the rebel Sejanus, have doubts about the loyalty of Pilate to the emperor.

10th Event.

Matthew 27:38 Then were there two thieves crucified with him, one on the right hand, and another on the left.

Again the KJV of the Bible translation could have been better. As was the case with Barabbas, it would have been more accurate to say the two men were criminals or rebels, because thieves were not condemned to death under the laws of Rome. The crucifixion of Jesus together with two criminals fulfilled the Old Testament prophecy, "He was numbered with the transgressors."[4] It is likely that the two men had been part of the uprising against Rome which had been led by Barabbas, who had been set free by Pilate at the request of the chief priests, elders and the Jewish people.

11th Event.

> Mark 15:29-30 [29] And they that passed by railed [taunted] on him, wagging their heads, and saying, Ah, thou that destroyest [destroys] the temple, and buildest [builds] it in three days,
>
> [30] Save thyself [yourself], and come down from the cross.

This was the fifth time Jesus was mocked, and this time it was while He was suffering on the cross by people just travelling by. Calvary was close to a main route into Jerusalem, and many Jews were camped outside the city for Passover, and were travelling back and forth to and from the Temple. Remembering His claim to be able to destroy the temple, (meaning His body), and rebuild it in three days,[5] which the chief priests had mocked Him about, the people passing by jeered at Him for not respecting the Temple.

12th Event.

> Mark 15:31-32 [31] Likewise the chief priests mocking said among themselves with the scribes, He saved others; himself he cannot save.
>
> [32] Let Christ the King of Israel descend now from the cross, that we may see and believe.

The chief priests were Sadducees, and the scribes were Pharisees, so both the Sadducees and the Pharisees mocked Jesus as He suffered on the cross, this was the sixth time Jesus was mocked.

13th Event.

> Luke 23:36-37 [36] And the soldiers also mocked him, coming to him, and offering him vinegar,
>
> [37] And saying, If thou be the King of the Jews, save thyself.

The seventh mocking came from the Roman soldiers, and therefore both Jews and Gentiles mocked Jesus on the cross.

14th Event.

Matthew 27:44 The thieves [rebels] also, which were crucified with him, cast [hurled] the same [insult] in his teeth [at Him].

The two rebels that were crucified with Jesus, both scoffed at Jesus in the early hours of their torture, this was the eighth time He was mocked. Events, 11, 12, 13, and 14 are all mockeries from different groups of people, but they all ridicule one or more different claims He made about being the Messiah, and they all challenge Him to come down from the cross, to show them that He really is the Messiah. It was Satan's final fling to remove Jesus from the cross, because he knew that if Jesus died in this way, at this time and in this place, prophecy about the Messiah would be fulfilled, Jesus would pay the price for man's sin, and men could again be united with God forever. Satan wanted Jesus dead but not as the Lamb of God, taking away the sins of the world through being sacrificed at Passover. It is for that reason that Satan influenced men to mock Jesus in events 11 to 14, to try and make Him come off the cross, using the two things present in all four mockeries, His claims to be the Messiah and the challenges to come down, which Jesus had the power to do and that would have been easy for Him. If Jesus had used His power to come down He would have been a false Christ, because the true Christ had to die exactly at the place, time and in the way Jesus died. Once again as had happened in the wilderness, Satan tempted Jesus using the pride of life, and again he failed. Jesus was obeying His Father God, by allowing Himself to be crucified, and although He did not answer those people that mocked Him, when He was tempted by Satan using the pride of life in the wilderness, He answered by quoting, Deuteronomy 6:16, "It is written, Thou shalt not tempt the Lord thy God." Even on the cross, Jesus obeyed God, and refused to be tempted not to.

The Apostle Paul called the first man, the first Adam, and he called Jesus, the Second Adam, and I find it interesting that when the first Adam, living in luxury, was tempted by Satan, he disobeyed God, but when the Second Adam, under terrible torture and provocation, was tempted by Satan, He obeyed God.

1 Corinthians 15:45-48 [45] And so it is written, The first man

Adam was made a living soul; the last Adam was made a quickening spirit.

⁴⁶ Howbeit that was not first which is spiritual, but that which is natural; and afterward that which is spiritual.

⁴⁷ The first man is of the earth, earthly: the second man is the Lord from heaven.

⁴⁸ As is the earthly, such are they also that are earthly: and as is the heavenly, such are they also that are heavenly.

15ᵗʰ Event.

Luke 23:39-42 ³⁹ And one of the malefactors [criminals or rebels] which were hanged [crucified] railed [taunted] on him, saying, If thou be Christ, save thyself and us.

⁴⁰ But the other answering rebuked him, saying, Dost thou not fear God, seeing thou art in the same condemnation [judgement]?

⁴¹ And we indeed justly, for we receive the due reward [punishment] of our deeds: but this man [Jesus] hath [has] done nothing amiss [wrong].

⁴² And he said unto Jesus, Lord, remember me when thou [you] comest [come] into the kingdom.

To begin with both the rebels crucified with Jesus mocked Him, but after having time to think and to see how Jesus behaved on the cross, one of them decided that Jesus was exactly who He said he was, the Messiah, the Son of God. From the Scriptures we know that he came to four decisions.

1. He realised that he himself was a sinner, and that is so important because unless we know we are sinners, then we cannot see any need for a Saviour to forgive us our sins.
2. He thought it over and decided that Jesus had no sin, because he said, "this man [Jesus] hath [has] done nothing amiss [wrong]."

3. Although Jesus was naked as He suffered, and so bloodied that He did not look human, the rebel had no doubt that Jesus could save him.

4. He could see that he and Jesus were dying and yet he was sure that Jesus will come again as King of the Messianic Kingdom.

He told Jesus that he would like to be in the Messianic Kingdom when it was launched.

16th Event.

Luke 23:43 And Jesus said unto him, Verily [Truly] I say unto thee [you], To day shalt [shall] thou [you] be with me in paradise.

Except for this rebel, Jesus was being mocked, and in this His second statement from the cross, Jesus tells him, he will not have to wait until the Kingdom of God on earth is set up, because they will both meet in paradise that very same day. The Spirit of Jesus and of the rebel would be sent to that side of Hades or Sheol, called Paradise, proving all the mockers were wrong, except for this rebel who repented, changed his mind, stopped mocking, and told Jesus he wanted to be with Him in His kingdom. The Messiah rescued him as soon as he died.

17th Event.

John 19:25-27 25 Now there stood by the cross of Jesus his mother, and his mother's sister, Mary the wife of Cleophas, and Mary Magdalene.

26 When Jesus therefore saw his mother, and the disciple standing by, whom he loved, he saith [said] unto his mother, Woman, behold thy son!

27 And saith [said] he to the disciple, Behold thy mother! And from that hour the disciple took her into his own home.

During this event Jesus made His third statement from the cross, four Jewish women were there and the Apostle John. If we look at John's narrative together with Matthew 27:56 and Mark 15:40, we get more information about the women.

1. Outstanding among the four is Mary or Miriam, the mother of Jesus.
2. The next Mary or Miriam, a common Jewish name even today, was the mother of James and Joses [Joseph], the wife of Cleophas or Clopas. John would not have put the names of James and Joses into the Scripture if they were not known to the believers, consequently these men were followers of Jesus. Cleophas was one of the two disciples that met Jesus after His resurrection on the Emmaus Road,[6] and this second Mary was his wife.
3. The third lady's name was Salome, she was the sister of Mary the mother of Jesus, the wife of Zebedee, and mother of his children, the two apostles, James and John. She was as a result Jesus' aunt, and her sons James and John were His cousins.
4. The third Mary, was Mary Magdalene, from whom Jesus had expelled seven demons.[7]

Jesus spoke first to His mother, Mary, "Woman, behold thy son!" and then speaking to John, He said, "Behold thy mother!" Jesus was not asking Mary to look at Him while He was dying, He was asking her to look at John, and when He told John to look at his mother, He was not asking John to look at Salome, but at His mother Mary. It was the responsibility of a first born son to look after his widowed mother, and now before He died, Jesus was keeping the Law of Moses, totally to the last jot and tittle.

At that time the four half brothers of Jesus did not believe in Him, and rather than leave her with unbelievers, John was given the responsibility to look after Mary.

> John 19:27 ... And from that hour that disciple took her into his own home.

Jesus' first three hours of the crucifixion, suffering the anger of men, ended with this third statement from the cross when He arranged for His mother to be looked after.

[1] Psalm 22:18

[2] Matthew 8:20, Luke 9:58

[3] Luke 8:3

[4] Isaiah 53:12 ... "he was numbered with the transgressors;"

[5] John 2:19-21, 1 Corinthians 3:16

[6] Luke 24:13 and 18

[7] Mark 16:9, Luke 8:2

THE SECOND THREE HOURS OF THE CRUCIFIXION
Matthew 27:45-50, Mark 15:33-37, Luke 23:44-46, John 19:28-30

In these three hours Jesus suffers the anger of God, and as we study His terrible ordeal, we will be looking at events 18 to 25, of the 32 that end with the sealing of the tomb.

18th Event.

> Luke 23:44-45 44 And it was about the sixth hour, and there was a darkness over all the earth until the ninth hour.
>
> 45 And the sun was darkened, ...

The sixth hour was mid-day, and the ninth hour was three o'clock in the afternoon, those three hours are usually the time of day when the sunlight is the strongest, but it was blocked out. There was something strange and creepy about this blackout because a total eclipse of the sun cannot possible last that long. It cannot be explained scientifically, and it was during these three hours of darkness, that Jesus was humanly speaking spiritually dead, because the spirits of men are inactive, when the Holy Spirit is absent. God cannot die, and one reason why the Spirit of God in Jesus left Him, was so that Jesus could die . The three hours of darkness was when the human part of Jesus was alone, without God, suffering the wrath of God.

19th Event.

> Matthew 27:46 And about the ninth hour Jesus cried with a loud voice, saying, Eli, Eli, la-ma sa-bach-tha-ni? That is to

say, My God, my God, why hast [have] thou [You] forsaken me?

Jesus was quoting from Psalm 22:1, bringing our attention to the fact that Psalm 22, is the prophetic Psalm of King David which gives more detail about the crucifixion than any other. David lived more than 1,000 years before Jesus.

> Psalm 22:1 My God, my God, why hast thou forsaken me? Why art thou so far from helping me, and from the words of my roaring?

The prophecy of the crucifixion in Isaiah 53, details the physical suffering of Jesus in our place, for our sins, so that we can be justified and be given righteousness, making us suitable to live with God in heaven. On the other hand Psalm 22, tells how Jesus died, and the cry of Jesus from the cross was a call for help, coming after three hours of darkness, separated from God and suffering the anger of God.

It was the only time Jesus ever called His Father, "My God." In the gospels Jesus usually called God, "Father", and occasionally, "My Father," and the reason for the change at this time is that He was alone on the cross, He was without His Father. He did not have the usual bond of love He had always had with His Father. His relationship now was with an angry God punishing mankind for sin. The cry of Jesus to God for help was answered, because Jesus died spiritually and came back to life spiritually, before His physical death, as we will soon see.

20th Event.

> Matthew 27:47-49 Some of them that stood there, when they heard that, said, This man calleth [calls] for E-li-as [Elijah the prophet].

In Matthew 27:46, Jesus had called, "Eli, Eli," meaning, My God, my God, but the people thought He was calling for Elijah, because in Hebrew, Eli is also a shortened form of, E-li-as.

> 48 And straight way one of them ran, and took a spunge [sponge], and filled it with vinegar, and put it on a reed, and gave him to drink.

Jesus was crucified high up in the air, and the only way they could offer Him a drink was to use a soaking wet sponge on the end of a long reed.

> [49] The rest [others] said, Let be, let us see whether Elias [Elijah] will come and save him.

21st Event.

> John 19:28 After this, Jesus knowing that all things were now accomplished, that the scripture might be fulfilled, saith, I thirst.[1]

"I thirst," was the fifth statement of Jesus from the cross, and He said it after He had suffered the anger of God. Earlier when we read about Lazarus the beggar in Abraham's bosom, and the rich man being tormented in the flames of Hell, in Luke 16:19-31, the rich man was very thirsty. After Jesus had endured the anger of God, He also was thirsty. Fortunately for believers Jesus has suffered for us, but for those people that do not come to God the Father through His Son, Jesus of Nazareth, they will be very thirsty in the flames.

22nd Event.

> John 19:29 Now there was set a vessel full of vinegar: and they filled a spunge [sponge)] with vinegar, and put it upon hyssop, and put it to his mouth.

The hyssop was not the plant we know by the same name, because that is a native of southern Europe. Bible scholars believe that the hyssop used to offer Jesus his drink was the reed-like, Sorgham vulgare. The vinegar was not drugged like the mixture offered to Jesus earlier and it was alright for Him to drink. After six hours on the cross the vinegar would wet His mouth, lips and tongue in readiness for him to speak clearly when making the last two statements, which were the most important of the seven He made while crucified.

23rd Event.

> John 19:30 When Jesus therefore had received the vinegar, he said, It is finished: and he bowed his head, and gave up the ghost.

The sixth statement made while He was on the cross was, "It is finished," which in the original Greek, is all one word, "Tetelestai." Years ago, archaeologists were digging at a Greek historical site, and discovered a large number of bills, or account statements, and across each one was written, TETELESTAI, to show that the money had been received. Tetelestai does mean, "It is finished," but in the special sense of having been, PAID IN FULL.

Under the Laws of Moses sacrifices had to be made frequently, whenever someone broke a Law that required sacrifice, or once a year, such as at the Feast of Passover, like paying instalments or making part payments, but now there would be no more need for repeated sacrifices. Jesus, the Holy Lamb of God had been sacrificed, and had PAID IN FULL for all our sins.

24th Event.

> Luke 23:46 And when Jesus had cried out with a loud voice, he said, ...

Luke does not tell us what it was that Jesus cried out with a loud voice, but we know from John that it was, "Tetelestai," His sixth statement from the cross.

> Luke 23:46 And when Jesus had cried out with a loud voice, he said, Father, into thy hands I commend [commit] my spirit: and having said thus, he gave up the ghost.

Jesus committed His Spirit to God first, and then died, He chose the moment of His death. Once again in this verse, Jesus calls God, "Father," showing that the Father and Son relationship had been re-established, that God heard the cry of the 19th event, and that Jesus was no longer forsaken. Jesus had died spiritually and had been restored spiritually, before His physical death, and so He was able to say, "Father, into Thy hands I commit My Spirit."

25th Event.

> Matthew 27:50 [Jesus] ... yielded up the ghost.

> Mark 15:37 [Jesus] ... gave up the ghost,

Luke 23:46 ... he gave up the ghost.

John 19:30 ... and he bowed his head, and gave up the ghost.

The 25th event was the physical death of Jesus. Usually we would expect that if a man were nailed up on a cross, his head would fall forward after he died, but Jesus bowed His head Himself and then died. His death was the first of the three points that together are the gospel of Jesus Christ, one, He died for our sins according to the prophetic Scriptures, two, He was buried, and three, He rose again on the third day according to the prophetic Scriptures.[2]

Ten Implications Of The Death Of Jesus

1. His death was a ransom or payment, He paid for our sin.[3]
2. His death redeemed us, (or bought us back), for God.[4]
3. His death reconciled, or made friendly, people all over the world who really believe in Jesus, so that we want to be friends of God.[5]
4. His death was a propitiation, or it took away the anger of God, so God is not annoyed with us any more.[6]
5. He died instead of us, so that when we get to heaven we will be just as righteous as God Himself. Just now in the 25th event, we looked at the three points of the gospel, and this was the main point, He died for our sins.[7] "For he [God] hath [has] made him [Jesus] to be sin for us, who new no sin; that we might be made the righteousness of God in Him" (2 Corinthians 5:21).
6. His death proves God loves us.[8]
7. His death ended the need for believers in Jesus to keep the Law of Moses.[9]
8. His death is not just for the sins we did before we found out about Jesus, it is also for the sins we did after we found out about Jesus and for the sins we have not done yet. The forgiveness does not come automatically without us doing anything, we have to tell our heavenly Father about our sins, that may

seem embarrassing but He knows about them anyway before we tell Him.[10]

9. His death was for the forgiveness of sins of people that had lived hundreds and even thousands of years before the crucifixion, including those that were in Abraham's bosom.[11]

10. His death resulted in the defeat and judgement of Satan,[12] and his demons.[13]

[1] Psalm 69:21

[2] 1 Corinthians 15:1-4

[3] Matthew 20:28, 1 Timothy 2:6

[4] Galatians 3:13, Ephesians 1:7, Hebrews 9:11-12

[5] 2 Corinthians 5:18-19

[6] 1 John 2:2

[7] 1 Peter 3:18

[8] Romans 5:8

[9] Romans 10:4, Colossians 2:14

[10] 1 John 1:7-9

[11] Romans 3:25, Hebrews 9:15

[12] John 12:31

[13] Colossians 2:15

MIRACLES HAPPENED WHEN JESUS DIED
Matthew 27:51-54, Mark 15:38-39, Luke 23:47-48

26th Event.

The miracles that occurred the very moment Jesus died, together make up the 26th event. The Bible tells us about four miracles but it is very likely indeed that there were many more than four. The Jewish religious leaders of the time hated Jesus so much that they refused to connect these miracles with His death. However, they and other

Jewish sources let the cat out of the bag in their writings by detailing a number of miracles they claim happened, 40 years before the Temple was destroyed. The Temple was destroyed in AD 70 and 40 years before that was AD 30, which was the year Jesus died. These reports are not Scripture, and for that reason I will not list them, but in my opinion the writings show that there were more than four miracles given as signs from God when Jesus died. We will now look at the four miracles the Bible tells as about.

1. A massive earthquake struck, the moment Jesus died. Matthew 27:51 "... the earth did quake, and the rocks rent [split]."

2. The tombs where the bodies of dead people had been placed were opened. These were not graves that had been dug and filled back with earth, but tombs such as in the cave Lazarus the brother of Martha and Mary had been buried in. Matthew 27:52 "And the graves [tombs] were opened;"

3. The instant Jesus died, many believers that were dead in their tombs, came back to life, but stayed in their opened tombs, until the resurrection of Jesus, after which they began walking about in Jerusalem, meeting many people. They could breathe after they returned to life because their tombs had been opened, if they had been in graves they would have suffocated. Matthew 27:52-53 "... and many bodies of the saints which slept arose, and came out of the graves [tombs] after his [Jesus'] resurrection, and went into the holy city, and appeared unto many." None of these Old Testament saints were given their everlasting bodies at this time, because Jesus would be the first man to get one,[1] and He had not got His yet. The Jews, their chief priests and elders were being given the sign of the resurrection of the dead such as Jesus had done before in the cases of, Jairus' daughter,[2] the son of the widow of Nain,[3] and Lazarus.[4] In a sense it was like the sign of Jonah, the sign Jesus had promised them, on a massive scale.

4. Mark 15:38 "And the veil [curtain] of the temple was rent [torn] in twain [two] from the top to the bottom."

The veil, or curtain, of the Temple was 16 feet long, 30 feet wide and 4 inches thick, and it separated the Holy of Holies, from the holy place. It would have taken tremendous strength to tear, but if men could have done it, they would have torn it from bottom to top. The veil separated God from the priests, and under the Law of Moses no one, apart from the High Priest, was allowed to go behind the veil into the presence of God, and he was only allowed in on one day a year, the Day of Atonement. The fact that it was torn from top to bottom shows that God did it, and He did it to illustrate that everyone with faith in Jesus, could from then on freely approach God the Father. The Law of Moses had been completed, the old veil of the Temple, which separated God from His people was torn, because it was no longer the way into His presence. The new Way[5] to our heavenly Father, is through faith in the death of His Son, Jesus Christ.[6]

The miracles that happened when Jesus died led to two results. Some Gentiles, the Roman centurion, and the soldiers that were with him were afraid, and so impressed, they believed in Jesus,

> Matthew 27:54 Now when the centurion, and they that were with him, watching Jesus, saw the earthquake, and those things that were done, they feared greatly, saying, Truly this was the Son of God.

The Jewish crowd was also afraid, but their fear did not result in them believing.

> Luke 23:48 And all the people that came together at that sight, beholding [seeing] the things which were done, smote their breasts, and returned.

---

[1] Romans 8:29, Colossians 1:18, Revelation 1:5

[2] Mark 5:22-42, Luke 8:41-55

[3] Luke 7:11-15

[4] John 11:38-44

[5] John 14:6

[6] Hebrews 10:19-20

THE BURIAL OF JESUS
Matthew 27:57-61, Mark 15:42-47, Luke 23:50-55, John 19:31-42

In this section we will look at events 27 to 30, of the 32 that will end with the sealing of the tomb.

27th Event.

> John 19:31-37 ³¹ The Jews therefore, because it was the preparation, that the bodies should not remain upon the cross on the Sabbath day, (for that Sabbath day was a high day,) besought Pilate that their legs might be broken, and that they might be taken away.
>
> ³² Then came the soldiers and break the legs of the first, and of the other which was crucified with him.
>
> ³³ But when they came to Jesus, and saw that he was dead already, they brake not his legs:
>
> ³⁴ But one of the soldiers with a spear pierced his side, and forthwith came there out blood and water.
>
> ³⁵ And he that saw it bare record, and his record is true, that ye might believe.
>
> ³⁶ For these things were done, that the scripture should be fulfilled, A bone of his shall not be broken.
>
> ³⁷ And again another scripture saith, They shall look on him whom they pierced.

The 27th event, was the breaking of the legs of the two criminals crucified with Jesus, and the piercing of Jesus. In verse 31 above, it talks about the Day of Preparation, and in all Jewish writings from the first century onwards, the Day of Preparation is always the sixth day of the week, it is always a Friday, and this Scripture will clearly show the day of the week Jesus died. The Jewish weekly Sabbath always begins at sunset on Friday and ends at sunset on Saturday. In AD 30, the Passover was from sunset on Thursday until sunset on Friday, and from sunset on Friday the Feast of Unleavened Bread began, which lasted seven days, and under the Law Of Moses, those seven days were all holy days.[1] Also in verse 31 above, it says the Sabbath which began at sunset on Friday that year was a high Sabbath. Every time a Sabbath was also on a holy day, then it became a high Sabbath. It is therefore obvious from the mention of the Day of Preparation and the high Sabbath, that Jesus died on a Friday, and you can safely ignore any different teaching.

The Jews would not leave a corpse unburied over the Sabbath, and on a high Sabbath it would have been much worse, so the leaders went to Pilate and asked him to speed up the death of Jesus and the two others. Going back to the four kinds of crosses used for crucifixion, we said the fourth or traditional type had a wooden ledge nailed just below the feet of the victim. The cause of death of a crucified person was by suffocation because of the way they were nailed up. The wooden ledge allowed the person to push his feet against it, raise his body up, take a breath of air, and lower himself down again. He would keep doing this, sometimes for days, until all his strength was gone and then he would die through lack of oxygen. Victims were not allowed food, but they could drink as much as they liked, and when Jesus said He was thirsty, He was quickly given vinegar on a soaked sponge. The liquid and the wooden ledge below the feet prolonged the lives and the torture of the sufferers.

One way to make a crucified man die quickly was to break his legs, because then he would not be able to push himself up and take a breath, and that is why they broke the legs of the two criminals. They also meant to break the legs of Jesus, but He had already bowed His head, dismissed His Spirit and died, and so they did not break His legs. Jesus, the Lamb of God, did not have His legs broken because it was against the Law of Moses to break the bones of the sacrificial Passover lamb.[2] It was also a fulfilment of the prophecy of King David in Psalm 34.

> Psalm 34:19-20 [19] Many are the afflictions of the righteous [Jesus]: but the LORD delivereth [rescues] him out of them all.

[20] He keepeth [preserves] all his bones: not one of them is broken.

If an animal or person is given a strong sharp prick in the ribs it usually reacts by moving or twitching, and to see if Jesus was alive, a soldier stuck a spear deep in His side, but the only reaction was that blood and water came out from His dead body. Another prophecy had predicted this event nearly 500 years earlier.[3] It was evidence that Jesus really had died when He dismissed His Spirit, and so from the body of Jesus at the crucifixion there came out, His Spirit, water and blood, and this was important and taken serious note of by John the apostle. John was the most spiritual of the four gospel writers, and in verse 35 above He makes the point that he saw these things, later in his first letter, he remembered it all and wrote about the significance of the Spirit, water and blood.

> 1 John 5:7-9 For there are three that bear record in heaven, the Father, the Word, and the Holy Ghost: and these three are one.
>
> [8] And there are three that bear witness in earth, the spirit, and the water, and the blood: and these three agree in one.
>
> [9] If we receive the witness of men, the witness of God is greater: for this is the witness of God which he hath testified [given evidence] of his Son.

John then goes on to remind us that it is only through the Son of God that we can receive everlasting life.[4]

28th Event.

The 28th event was the request to Pilate for the body of Jesus.

> Mark 15:42 And now when even [the evening] was come, because it was the preparation, that is, the day before the Sabbath.

Mark was writing for Roman readers, and notice how he clearly tells them the day of Jesus' death, "the preparation," and because Romans would not know about Jewish customs, he explains that the preparation is, "the day before Sabbath." Mark was using typical

Jewish words, and unbelieving Jews reading this verse throughout the centuries and even now, would know that Mark is talking about the sixth day of the week, the Friday before the Sabbath.

Two men, both members of the Sanhedrin, collected the body of Jesus from Calvary to bury Him. The first was Nicodemus, whom we know from our studies of chapters 3 and 7 of John's gospel, and the other was Joseph of Arimathaea, of whom the Scriptures tell us several things.

1. He was a rich man.[5]
2. He was known to be a good man.[6]
3. He was also known as a righteous man, which would be more to do with his internal qualities.[6]
4. He was waiting for the Kingdom of God, of which Jesus will be King, and so God had blessed him with spiritual understanding.[7]
5. He believed in Jesus, and up until this time, he had been a secret disciple.[8]
6. He was a member of the Sanhedrin, because he is described as a counsellor.[9]
7. He had not agreed to the decision of the Sanhedrin to have Jesus killed, meaning he was not at any of the meetings that had agreed to it.[10]

Although Joseph had been a secret disciple of Jesus because he was afraid of the Jews, he now plucked up courage to ask Pilate for the body of Jesus.[11] Pilate did not believe Jesus had died so quickly, and asked the centurion if He was already dead, and then because Jesus had died, he let Joseph have the body,[12] and Nicodemus helped Joseph.[13]

29th Event.

> John 19:40 Then took they the body of Jesus, and wound it in linen clothes with the spices, as the manner of the Jews is to bury.

Notice how the body was wound in linen clothes, it actually means strips of cloth like bandages. In Turin, Italy, there is a shroud like a bed sheet, which the Roman Catholic Church claims to be the cloth that wrapped the body of Jesus. It is strange because it has what appears to be a photographic print of the complete body of a man on it, and it definitely predates the invention of the camera, but whatever it is, it is not a picture of the crucified Christ, because Jesus was not wrapped in a single sheet, He was wound round about with strips of cloth, with about a hundred pounds, or forty-five kilograms, of spices between the layers.

30th Event.

The 30th event is the burial of Jesus in a tomb. The tomb had never been used before, it was brand new, it was in a private garden, not a public graveyard, and the fact that a great stone was rolled to seal the tomb, shows that it belonged to a rich man.[14]

> Luke 23:54 And that day was the day of preparation, and the Sabbath drew on.

Again, Jesus was buried late on, the preparation, Friday afternoon as the sun was about to set, because Scripture says, "the Sabbath drew on."

Remember the first point of the gospel is the death of Jesus, this, His burial, is the second point. Preachers like to say that when Jesus became human, He humbled Himself, changing from God to man, and His becoming like us is called His humiliation. His burial was the end of His humiliation, for two reasons. Although Jesus never ever sinned and did not need to die, He chose to die, and because He was dead that was the end of His humiliation. The other reason His burial was the end of His humiliation is that He was not buried by any of His close friends. He was buried by two Pharisees, who were members of the Sanhedrin, the Jewish religious leaders who were also both believers.

After the humiliation of Jesus, preachers talk about His exaltation, because Jesus has now been raised to a place high in power and rank, the right hand of God in heaven.[15] His exaltation began here at the time of His burial, again for two reasons. The first is the tomb He was buried in. No doubt a grave had been dug ready for Him in the criminals grave yard, but He was not buried there, He was laid in a new tomb especially prepared for a rich man, as prophesied by Isaiah.

Isaiah 53:9 His grave was **assigned** with wicked men, Yet He was with a rich man in His death, ... (New American Standard Bible).

Isaiah 53:9 And he **made** his grave with the wicked, and with the rich in his death; ... (KJV).

Another reason that the burial of Jesus was the beginning of His exaltation, was that He was not buried in an ordinary grave yard, but in a private garden. Thousands of years before in another garden, Adam had sinned, bringing judgement and death. Now in this garden Jesus, the second Adam, will bring blessings and everlasting life.[16]

[1] Exodus 23:15, Leviticus 23:6-8, Deuteronomy 16:3-4

[2] Exodus 12:46

[3] Zechariah 12:10

[4] 1 John 5:10-13

[5] Matthew 27:57

[6] Luke 23:50

[7] Mark 15:43, Luke 23:51

[8] Matthew 27:57, John 19:38

[9] Mark 15:43, Luke 23:50

[10] Luke 23:51

[11] Mark 15:43

[12] Mark 15:44-45, John 19:38

[13] John 19:39

[14] Matthew 27:60, John 19:41

[15] Colossians 3:1, Hebrews 8:1, 10:12, 12:2, 1 Peter 3:22

[16] 1Corinthians 15:44-49

THE TOMB IS SEALED
Matthew 27:61-66, Luke 23:55-56

In this section we come to the last two of the thirty-two events that began with Jesus being led away to Calvary.

31st Event.

The 31st event was the preparations that were made to embalm the body of Christ.

> Luke 23:55-56 ⁵⁵ And the women also, which came with him from Galilee, followed after, and beheld [saw] the sepulchre [tomb], and how his body was laid.
>
> ⁵⁶ And they returned, and prepared spices and ointments; and rested the Sabbath day according to the commandment.

The women from Galilee saw the tomb with the body of Jesus in it before the tomb was sealed, because they saw, "how his body was laid." Knowing where the tomb was and that the body was in it, they went and prepared the spices which they intended to use to embalm the body after the Sabbath. Obviously they were not expecting the resurrection of Jesus.

32nd Event.

The 32nd event is found in Matthew 27:62-66, which tells us why the chief priests and Pharisees wanted the tomb sealed, and how it was done.

> Matthew 27:62 Now the next day, that followed the day of preparation, …

The day after the preparation was Saturday, the Sabbath day, the religious leaders were faced with a new dilemma.

> Matthew 27:62-63 … the chief priests and Pharisees came together unto Pilate,
>
> ⁶³ Saying, Sir, we remember that that deceiver said, while he was yet alive, After three days I will rise again.

Notice that the Pharisees did not call Jesus by name, they hated Him so much that they tried to blot His name out, referring to Him as, "that deceiver." Even so they remembered very well that Jesus had prophesied He would die by crucifixion and would come back to life on the third day, the first part of the prophecy had come true and this was the second day. To stop someone stealing His body and then preaching there had been a resurrection, they wanted the tomb sealed and guarded.[1] Pilate agreed that the tomb should be sealed and allowed them to set Roman soldiers to watch or guard the grave.[2]

To seal the tomb, a hook would be fixed into the stone covering the entrance, and another close to it on the outside wall. A rope would be tied tightly to both hooks and a clay seal with the official Roman insignia impressed in it would be put over the rope. Another clay seal would be put between the stone and the wall of the cave, so that the stone could not be moved without breaking the seals. The punishment for anyone that broke the seal was death. Accordingly the tomb was sealed and a Roman guard was set to watch.

How Long Was The Body Of Jesus In The Tomb?

> Matthew 12:40 For as Jonas was three days and three nights in the whale's belly; so shall the Son of man be three days and three nights in the heart of the earth.

This verse has resulted in many people trying to show that Jesus was in His grave for three full 24 hour days. The discussions began in the twentieth century among unprofessional Bible readers. Genuine Bible scholars were not involved because they have long been knowledgeable of the literature of that time. In order to keep the body in the tomb for three full days they moved the time of the death of Jesus forward to Thursday, Wednesday or even Tuesday, depending when they started counting the first 24 hour period.

The way the Jews reckon time, part of a year counts for a whole year, and part of a day counts for a whole day, in fact the whole day and night. If a king came to the throne in the twelfth month of a year, they would call that the first year of his reign, but the first month of the next year, they would call the second year of his reign, although he had not ruled for more than two months. Jesus spoke about how long He would be in the grave in three different ways, which to us Gentiles seem to contradict each other.

1. He would rise on the third day. Matthew 20:19 "And shall deliver him to the Gentiles to mock, and to scourge, and to crucify him: and the third day he shall rise again."
2. He would rise after three days, which to us Gentiles in the twenty-first century would mean the fourth day. Mark 8:31 "And he began to teach them, that the Son of man must suffer many things, and be rejected by the elders, and of the chief priests, and scribes, and be killed, and after three days rise again."
3. He would be in the earth for three days and three nights. Matthew 12:40 "For as Jonas was three days and three nights in the whale's belly; so shall the Son of man be three days and three nights in the heart of the earth."

All these three ways of prophesying how long He would be in the tomb, mean the same thing, because part of a day is taken to be the whole day.

Jesus was in the tomb part of Friday, that was reckoned to be the first day and night. He remained buried all day Saturday, that was the second day and night, and because He was still in the grave early on Sunday, that became the third day and night.

The Bible has a number of examples of this Jewish way of dealing with time, a good one is from the Book of Esther.

> Esther 4:16 to 5:1 [Queen Esther said], Go, gather together all the Jews that are present in Shushan, and fast ye for me, and neither eat nor drink three days, night or day: I also and my maidens will fast likewise; and so will I go into the king, which is not according to the law: and if I perish, I perish.
>
> [17] So Mordecai went his way, and did according to all that Esther had commanded him.
>
> 5:1 Now it came to pass on the third day, that Esther put on

her royal apparel, and stood in the inner court of the king's house, ...

Esther would fast for three days and three nights and then go and see the king, but she went to see him on the third day. The Bible does not contradict itself here because it was written by Jews, for Jews, and we Gentiles will get a better understanding of the Scriptures if we know the Jewish way of saying things.

Jesus was buried late on the Friday afternoon and, as we will find out in our next chapter, He rose early on the first day of the week, that is Sunday morning.

[1] Matthew 27:64

[2] Matthew 27:65-66

14

FROM THE GRAVE TO THE EARTH AND THEN THE SKY

In Luke 11:29-32, Jesus said only one sign would be given to that generation, the sign of Jonah, and we learned in Chapter 9, that the sign of Jonah is the sign of resurrection, and when Jesus rose from the grave, it was the second time He had performed the sign. His resurrection was also the third point of the gospel, and once again let's look at those three points made by Paul in 1 Corinthians 15:1-4.

1. Jesus died for our sins as the Bible foretold.
2. He was buried as the Bible foretold.
3. He rose again the third day as the Bible foretold.

Nine Implications Of The Resurrection Of Jesus

1. It showed Jesus was the Son of God. Romans 1:4
2. It fulfilled His prophecy that He would rise from the dead. Matthew 28:6
3. It showed that everyone that dies will be resurrected. 1 Corinthians 15:20-22

4. It is a guarantee that everyone will be judged. Acts 17:30-31
5. It is proof that believers will be justified. Romans 4:24-25
6. It shows the power that is available to believers. Ephesians 1:17-20
7. It is an assurance to believers that each one of us will be resurrected. 2 Corinthians 4:14
8. It identified and established Jesus as the Head of the Church. Ephesians 1:20-22
9. It signifies that Jesus has the keys of Hell and Death. Revelation 1:18

THE BEGINNING OF RESURRECTION DAY
Matthew 28:1, Mark 16:1

The Bible is Jewish, and the Gospel of Matthew was written for Jews, so be reminded again that a Jewish day begins at sunset. In our English language as the day dawns it begins to get light, but when a Jewish day dawns, it begins to get dark.

> Matthew 28:1 In the end of the Sabbath, as it began to dawn toward the first day of the week, came Mary Magdalene and the other Mary to see the sepulchre [tomb].

It was late Saturday afternoon, the day was drawing to a close, and the two ladies sat beside the grave of Jesus, waiting for the Sabbath sun to set before going off to do some shopping, just as soon as the spice sellers opened for business again after the Sabbath rest, very early on the first day of the week, before it got too dark.

> Mark 16:1 And when the Sabbath was past, Mary Magdalene, and Mary the mother of James, and Salome, had bought sweet spices, that they might come and anoint him.

Why did they want to anoint the body of Jesus? Because they did not understand that He was going to rise from the dead.

AN ANGEL OPENED THE TOMB
Matthew 28:2-4

The ladies had bought their spices and gone somewhere to stay the night, but not to their own homes, because they came from Galilee. Suddenly another earthquake shook Jerusalem, the first earthquake happened at the exact moment Jesus died, and I believe this one happened when He rose from the dead. It was also that instant that God sent an angel to open the tomb, so that anyone going to the cave could see that it was empty.

> Matthew 28:2 And, behold, there was a great earthquake: for an angel of the Lord descended from heaven, and came and rolled back the stone from the door, and sat upon it.

The Roman guard was there watching, and would have seen the whole thing, so that would be how the news of what happened got out. It was the job of the soldiers, to arrest the angel for breaking those special Roman seals, in order that the government could try him and sentence him to death, but angels cannot be controlled by human armies, and this was a spectacular angel.

> Matthew 28:3 His countenance [appearance] was like lightning, and his raiment [clothes] white as snow:

The soldiers were so afraid they were unable to control their own bodies, and began to shake before turning stiff, scared stiff, unable to breathe, move or blink an eye.

> Matthew 28:4 And for fear of him the keepers did shake, and became as dead men.

THE WOMEN VISIT THE TOMB
Matthew 28:5-8, Mark 16:2-8, Luke 24:1-8, John 20:1

Mark tells us it was sunrise on Sunday morning when the women went to the tomb, but Mary Magdalene had gone earlier, while it was still dark.

> John 20:1 The first day of the week cometh Mary Magdalene early, when it was yet dark, unto the sepulchre, and seeth [saw] the stone taken away from the sepulchre [grave].

Although it was still early, she was able to see that the stone had been rolled away, and that the body of Jesus was not in the grave. There were no angels around and she thought that someone had opened the tomb and removed the body. Later when it was getting light the other women arrived, they also noticed that the stone had been rolled away, and they also saw two angels.[1] An angel told the women two things. First that Jesus had risen from the dead,[2] and they should not be looking in a grave for someone that was alive.[3] Secondly an angel gave the women a message to take to the apostles, telling them to leave Jerusalem and go to Galilee, where Jesus would join them.[4] This was the second time the disciples had been told to go to Galilee, the first time was on the Mount of Olives immediately after the last Passover and the first Lord's Supper.[5] They had not gone to Galilee because they had not understood what Jesus had been talking about, and now Jesus had to send an angel to tell the women to remind them to go to Galilee, because He wanted to meet them there. The angel's message to the women caused three things to happen.

1. They remembered the prophecy Jesus had made. Luke 24:8
2. They did not tell anyone except the apostles. Mark 16:8
3. They ran to the apostles to tell them all they had seen, and what they had been told by the angel. Matthew 28:8

[1] Luke 24:4
[2] Matthew 28:6
[3] Luke 24:5
[4] Mark 16:7
[5] Matthew 26:32

THE APOSTLES RECEIVE THE NEWS THAT JESUS HAS RISEN
Luke 24:9-12, John 20:2-10

Mary Magdalene left the grave before the other women got there, believing that someone had opened the tomb and stolen the body, and went and told the two apostles, Peter and John that the tomb was empty.[1] Later the other women arrived, met the angel and went off to tell the others, but the apostles did not believe them.[2] Peter and John ran to the grave, John got there first but did not go in, but being very interested he looked inside and saw the linen strips of cloth still lying there. Peter soon arrived and went into the cave where he too saw the linen clothes lying there, and a separate piece that had covered the head, folded separately and laying by itself. John then followed Peter into the chamber and when he saw the linen clothes without a body in them, he knew Jesus had risen from the dead. John himself said, "he saw, and believed."[3] John and Peter then went back home, John believing in the resurrection but Peter could not make out what had happened, he left the grave, "wondering in himself at that which was come to pass."[4]

[1] John 20:2
[2] Luke 24:11
[3] John 20:3-8
[4] Luke 24:12

THE FIRST PERSON TO SEE JESUS ALIVE WAS MARY MAGDALENE
Mark 16:9-11, John 20:11-18

Mary returned to the tomb after Peter and John had left it, crying and still believing that someone had opened the tomb and taken the body of Jesus away. Two angels were sitting in the cave, one where the head of Jesus had been and other near to where His feet had been.

> John 20:13 And they say unto her, Woman, why weepest thou [why are you crying]? She saith [said] unto them, Because they have taken away my Lord [Jesus], and I know not where they have laid him.

Jesus then appeared behind her but she did not recognise Him.

> John 20:14 And when she had thus said, she turned herself back, and saw Jesus standing, and knew not that it was Jesus.

Mary thought He was the gardener, just the man who would know what had been going on in the garden, and where the body had been taken.

> John 20:15 Jesus saith unto her, Woman, why weepest thou [why are you crying]? Whom seekest thou [Who are you looking for]? She supposing him to be the gardener, saith unto him, Sir, if thou have borne [taken] him hence [away], tell me where thou hast laid him, and I will take him away.

It was not until Jesus spoke her name, "Mary," that she knew who He was. Jesus appeared several times to different people after rising from the dead, and often He was not recognised to begin with, but later on He was. It seems that the resurrection body of Jesus, was different in some ways but recognisable in other ways, and perhaps our own resurrection bodies will be like that too. Anyway Mary knew the voice of Jesus when He called her name,[1] and it was then she recognised Him entirely.

Some unbelievers say that because the Scriptures show Jesus appearing to a woman first, and not men, the Bible record is false. The reason given is that under the Law of Moses, a woman's evidence was not acceptable, and that in any trial the two or three witnesses had to be men, and because the evidence of the risen Lord came first from a woman, it has no authority, and the disciples made up the story. However, if the narrative had been untrue, it would have been invented by Jews, in which case the story would be, that the first witnesses to see Jesus after His resurrection were men, because that would have made their witness acceptable. Anyway the Bible says the first witness was Mary Magdalene because it is the truth, and it is also a good argument against the suggestion that the story was made-up.

In the following verse Jesus is speaking to Mary, who was probably moving towards her Lord with the intention of clinging hold of Him.

> John 20:17 Jesus saith unto her, Touch me not; for I am not yet ascended to my Father: but go to my brethren and say unto them, I ascend unto my Father, and your Father; and to my God, and your God.

Mary Magdalene, and the disciples she was sent to inform, would have known why Jesus was ascending to heaven and why He could not be touched until He had been there. We Gentiles on the other hand, unless we have a good knowledge of Law of Moses, are not likely to understand the tremendous importance of what Jesus was about to do.

Yom Kippur or the Day of Atonement, is known as a day of forgiveness by the Jews, and the ceremonies they were to observe that day in the Tabernacle and later in the Jerusalem Temple, were given them by Moses, in Leviticus 16. Once a year at Yom Kippur the High Priest would take off his usual costume of many colours, undertake a ceremonial baptism, and dress himself all in white, as a sign of purity. He then went into the Holy of Holies to sprinkle the blood of the lamb on the mercy seat. After coming out of the Holy of Holies, the High Priest removed his white clothes, go through a second immersion in water, and dress in his every-day priestly clothing as before. In between the two baptisms the High Priest was untouchable because that was the time he went into the presence of God, and if anyone touched him he became unclean.

God told Moses the design for the Tabernacle and the Jerusalem Temple,[2] and both were a copy of the Heavenly Temple.[3] Jesus, our heavenly High Priest, played the same role as the earthly High Priest, only Jesus did not offer the blood of an animal in the earthly Temple, He offered His own blood in the Heavenly Temple.

> Hebrews 9:11-12 [11] But Christ being come an high priest of good things to come, by a greater and more perfect

> tabernacle, not made with hands, that is to say, not of this building;
>
> [12] Neither by the blood of goats and calves, but by his own blood he entered in once into the holy place, having obtained eternal redemption for us.

The Law concerning Yom Kippur was given to Moses by God about 1,500 years before the time of Christ, to give the Jews a way of forgiveness, and to show in advance what the work of Jesus as High Priest would be.[4] The High Priest apart from covering the sins of himself and the people with the blood of a lamb, was also prophesying how the Messiah would later on present His own blood for the nation and the world in the Heavenly Temple.

> Hebrews 9:7-8 [7] But into the second [the Holy of Holies] went the high priest alone once every year, not without blood, which he offered for himself, and for the errors of the people:
>
> [8] The Holy Ghost thus signifying [showing], that the way into the holiest of all [the heavenly Holy of Holies] was not yet made manifest [known], while as the first tabernacle was yet standing.

It seems to me that Jesus, our High Priest, appeared to Mary Magdalene before He had ascended into the heavenly Holy of Holies to sprinkle His blood on the mercy seat there, and that is why He was untouchable. "Jesus saith unto her, Touch me not; for I am not yet ascended to my Father." Notice also how Jesus, in John 20:17 previously quoted, when speaking to Mary, the first time He appeared to her, called His disciples His brothers, "brethren." After His death, burial and resurrection, that is the new relationship believers have with the Son of God.

> Hebrews 2:11 For both he [Jesus] that sanctifieth [sanctifies or purifies] and they who are sanctified [purified] are all one: for which cause he [Jesus] is not ashamed to call them brethren [brothers].

Mary went off to the disciples, and gave them the message from Jesus, "I ascend unto my Father, and your Father; and to my God, and your God," but the disciples, now brothers of Christ, did not believe her.[5]

[1] John 20:16
[2] Exodus 25:8-9
[3] Hebrews 8:5, 9:23-24, Revelation 15:5
[4] John 5:46
[5] Mark 16:9-11

THE SECOND APPEARANCE OF JESUS WAS TO THE WOMEN
Matthew 28:9-10

After Mary had left to go and tell the disciples that Jesus had risen from the dead and was going to ascend to heaven, to their Father and His Father, to their God and His God, the other women were later on the way to the disciples, when they met Jesus.

> Matthew 28:9 And as they went to tell his disciples, behold, Jesus met them, saying, All hail. And they came and held him by the feet, and worshipped him.

On this His second appearance, Jesus allowed the women to hold Him, and I assume that this was because He had already been to heaven and returned, and was not untouchable anymore. The reason Jesus wanted to speak to the women was to ask them to give a message to His disciples, because He also wanted to meet them, but in Galilee, not here in Jerusalem. They had been told twice already to go to Galilee, the first time was after the Passover supper while they were on their way to the Mount of Olives,[1] and the second time by the women with their message from the angel,[2] but because the disciples did not believe the women,[3] they were still in Jerusalem. So again Jesus sends them a message to get out of Jerusalem, and go to Galilee to meet Him there.

Matthew 28:10 Then Jesus said unto them, Be not afraid: go tell my brethren that they go to Galilee, and there shall they see me.

[1] Matthew 26:32
[2] Matthew 28:7
[3] Mark 16:9-11

THE SECOND SIGN OF JONAH IS REJECTED
Matthew 28:11-15

The Roman soldiers that had guarded the tomb, saw the situation they were in, deserted the army and fled from the scene. Under Roman law, because they had been unable to protect the grave, the soldiers faced the death penalty, that is why they did not go to Pilate. We cannot imagine Pilate believing their story, "An angel that looked like lightening, came down from heaven and rolled the stone away," and neither could they. Instead they went to the men who had asked for a guard on the tomb in the first place, the chief priests, and told them everything that had happened.[1] The chief priests, who were Sadducees, consulted with the elders, who were Pharisees, meaning this was a meeting of the Sanhedrin, that met together to plot how to deceive the people into believing that Jesus had not risen from the dead, and they promised the soldiers a lot of money.[2]

The Sanhedrin told the guards to go through Jerusalem telling the people that the disciples had come while they were asleep and stolen the body.[3] The soldier's lives were already in great danger, and now they were being asked to identify themselves in public as the guards of the tomb, and so the Sanhedrin promised that if they were caught they would be protected from execution.

Matthew 28:14 And if this come to the governor's ears, we [the Sanhedrin] will persuade [influence] him, and secure [protect] you.

Amazingly the story was believed by many Jews.

> Matthew 28:15 So they took the money, and did as they were taught: and this saying is commonly reported among the Jews until this day.

What was the saying the guards spread around? "His disciples came by night, and stole him away while we were asleep." If they were asleep how would they have known who stole the body?

We know that no one stole the body of Jesus, but if someone had stolen it, who could it have been? Since anyone caught removing the stone would have been killed, only close friends or determined enemies would be likely to risk their lives, because crucifixion was a painful and slow way to die, and apart from friends and enemies, who would risk it?

We know who the enemies of Jesus were, and that in the Book of Acts they tried to stop the apostles preaching that Jesus had risen from the dead, but they could not. If they had taken the body then all they would have needed to do was put the body on public display, and that would have silenced the apostles, but the one thing they did not do was to produce the body of Jesus, which shows they did not have it. On the other hand, we also know the friends of Jesus, the apostles. If they had taken the body, why did they allow themselves to be killed and tortured the way they were, instead of stubbornly preaching that Jesus was alive. Why should they suffer so much just to tell a lie? Peter was crucified, James was decapitated, and church tradition says that some were skinned alive, and others were boiled alive in oil like fish in a deep fat fryer at a fish and chip shop. In most instances they could have gone free if they had said that Jesus was not alive, but they knew differently and kept to the truth. No! The idea that the body of Jesus was stolen, if examined closely, does not make any sense.

[1] Matthew 28:11
[2] Matthew 28:12
[3] Matthew 28:13

THE THIRD APPEARANCE OF JESUS WAS ON THE ROAD TO EMMAUS
Mark 16:12-13, Luke 24:12-31

On His third appearance after rising from the dead, Jesus again did not reveal Himself to any of the apostles, but on the road to Emmaus he joined two other disciples who were walking home from Jerusalem. It was Sunday afternoon and the disciples were walking along, discussing all the things that had happened.[1] While they were talking Jesus joined them, and as on other occasions the people He met with did not at first know who He was. He asked them what they were chatting about, and by the answer they gave in Luke 24:19-21, we know four things they believed at the time.

1. They believed Jesus was a prophet, someone that got messages straight from God.
2. They believed that this was confirmed by His words and works. His words were His claim to be the Messiah, and this was shown to be true by His miracles.
3. He was tried by the chief priests and elders, who handed Him over to be crucified.
4. Up until His death they believed He would rescue Israel, but this could not be so after what had happened.

Luke 24:22-24 shows that they did not believe Jesus was alive, even while they were talking to Him. They knew the women had been to the tomb, found it empty, and met with angels, who told them Jesus was alive, but then certain disciples had gone to the grave, (that would have been Peter and John), and found it empty but they had not seen Jesus, and that is why they did not believe the resurrection had happened. Take note, they told Jesus, but they did not know they were talking to Him, that He had been tried by the Sanhedrin, crucified, buried and His tomb was empty, then they added another fact.

> Luke 24:21 and beside all this, to day is the third day since these things were done.

On a Sunday afternoon, that is the first day of the week,[2] the only explanation for it being the third day was that Jesus died on Friday, not on a Tuesday, Wednesday or Thursday.

The things that had happened to Jesus these last three days, weakened the faith of these two disciples and they now thought He could not have been the promised Messiah. In Luke 24:25-26, because they did not believe in Him, Jesus called the two men fools. I am glad I am not a fool, my gifts of righteousness and eternal life, depend on believing Jesus is the Son of God.[3]

>Psalm 14:1 The fool hath said in his heart, There is no God.

Jesus then, in Luke 24:27, began to teach them so that they would become wise men, and put their foolishness behind them. He explained to them the prophecies in the Old Testament that tell of His first coming, beginning with Moses and then going through all the prophets, the things that were written about Himself. The outcome was that the things which had caused the two men to doubt Jesus, had been prophesied and were firm evidence that He is without doubt the Messiah.

On reaching Emmaus, which was about seven miles from Jerusalem, the two disciples finally came to their home, and Jesus kept walking, but they invited Him in for a meal, still not knowing who He was, and Jesus accepted their invitation. In those days, and still today, the Jews say a blessing before eating.

>"Blessed are You, O Lord, our God,
>
>King of the universe,
>
>That brings forth bread from the earth."

It is the host, the person who has invited the guest to a meal, who is responsible to pray the blessing, except when the guest is a Bible scholar. Jesus had been explaining the Old Testament prophets, and His host recognised that Jesus was indeed a Bible scholar and asked Him to perform the blessing.

>Luke 24:30 And it came to pass, as he [Jesus] sat at meat [food] with them, he took bread, and blessed it, and brake [broke the bread], and gave to them.

He broke the bread, He was not a ghost.

> Luke 24:31 And their eyes were opened, and they knew him; and he vanished out of their sight.

All of a sudden they knew who He was, but then He immediately disappeared. The two disciples walked back to Jerusalem to tell the apostles, but the apostles did not believe them.[4]

[1] Luke 24:14

[2] Luke 24:1

[3] Romans 5:17, Romans 6:23

[4] Mark 16:12-13

THE FOURTH APPEARANCE OF JESUS WAS TO PETER
Luke 24:34

> Luke 24:34 The Lord is risen indeed, and hath appeared to Simon.

Simon was the apostle's original name, but Jesus had renamed him Peter.[1] The report, that Peter had seen the resurrected Jesus was being given by the apostles, which means that Peter was the first of them to see the risen Lord. Paul confirmed this when writing to the church at Corinth.

> 1 Corinthians 15:5 And that he [Jesus] was seen of Cephas.

Again Simon was the apostle's original name but Jesus also called him Cephas, which means a small stone or pebble.[2] Peter was the chief of the apostles in the Book of Acts, and perhaps by appearing to him first, Jesus helped establish Peter's authority over the others.

[1] Mark 3:16

[2] John 1:42

THE FIFTH APPEARANCE OF JESUS WAS TO THE TEN
Mark 16:14, Luke 24:36-43, John 20:19-25

I say Jesus appeared to the ten, because Thomas was not there.

> John 20:24 But Thomas, one of the twelve [one of the original twelve which included the now dead Judas Iscariot], called Didymus, was not with them when Jesus came.

It seems to me that the Scripture from Mark's gospel should come here although Mark says that Jesus appeared to the eleven. It might therefore refer to our next section, the sixth appearance of Jesus to the eleven. Alternatively if Mark's Scripture does fit in here, why does he say eleven? If Thomas was not there and Judas was dead, then two of the twelve were absent, leaving only ten present. If you looked up, 1 Corinthians 15:5, which was partly quoted in the previous section about the fourth appearance, you will know that Paul wrote, that Jesus, "was seen of Cephas, then of the twelve," but Judas was already dead, so how were there twelve?

There were two other disciples that had been with the twelve from the time Jesus was baptised until He ascended into heaven and who had witnessed the resurrection, in other words they had also met the risen Lord just like the apostles.[1] One of these called Matthias, after prayers were made to God and the casting of lots, was chosen to officially replace Judas and become one of the twelve, and if he had been counted by Paul in, 1 Corinthians 15:5, and by Mark in, Mark 16:14, that would explain things, although Matthias was only confirmed an apostle after these events took place.

> Acts 1:26 And they gave forth their lots; and the lot fell on Matthias; and he was numbered with the eleven apostles.

The apostles had been told three times to go to Galilee to meet Jesus there, it was late Sunday afternoon before sunset and they were still in Jerusalem. The problem was they did not believe He had risen, and so Jesus kindly decided to appear to them where they were, frightened and hiding behind locked doors within the walled city of Jerusalem.

John 20:19 Then the same day at evening, being the first day of the week, when the doors were shut where the disciples were assembled for fear of the Jews, came Jesus and stood in the midst [among them], and saith unto them, Peace be unto you.

Jesus was there among them, speaking to them, and still they did not believe He had risen from the grave, they thought He was a ghost and were terrified, as Luke's version shows.

Luke 24:36-37 And as they thus spake [spoke], Jesus himself stood in the midst of them, and saith unto them, Peace be unto you.

37 But they were terrified and affrightened, and supposed they had seen a spirit.

Jesus was not going to put up with this any more and gave them a good telling-off, because they had not believed Mary, the women or the disciples from Emmaus, who had all told them that Jesus was alive,[2] and now they did not believe their own eyes. They had shown their unbelief in three ways.

1. They had not gone to Galilee, although they been instructed to go there three times.
2. They refused to believe the witnesses that had told them that Jesus was alive.
3. They saw Jesus Himself and thought He was a ghost.

To make sure they had no doubt that He was real, and not a ghost, He asked them to feel Him, and when they felt him they would have felt His flesh and bones. His resurrected body is a solid body, and He told them that a spirit does not have flesh and bone.[3] Jesus then showed them His hands and His feet,[4] so that they would see the wounds made by the nails when He was crucified. The disciples were really happy to see and hear Jesus, but probably thought they were watching something like a children's fantasy show because although delighted, the Bible says, "for joy, they wondered," meaning they still did not believe,[4] and so Jesus asked them for food, and He ate some fish and honey comb, right there in front of them.[5] After our own resurrections we will also be able to enjoy nice tasty food, because our bodies will be the same.

> Philippians 3:20-21 [20]For our conversation [citizenship] is in heaven; from whence [where] we look for the Saviour, the Lord Jesus Christ:
>
> [21] Who shall change our vile [wretched] body, that it may be fashioned [created] like unto his glorious body.

I am looking forward to enjoying a really good meal in my new and everlasting body, that will always be new and never grow old, when I sit down to eat with Abraham and the Jewish patriarchs,[6] and much more than that, when I am dressed in white linen at the Wedding Feast of the Lamb.[7]

From now on, as we continue to study the appearance of Jesus to the ten, we will do so from the Gospel of John. Jesus next gave the ten the first of their three jobs to do, three final assignments of which this was the first, and it had two parts. The word "apostle" means, "sent one," and they are called apostles because Jesus sent them out. The first point of their job is that they were sent out with the authority of the Son of God.

> John 20:21 … as my Father hath sent me, even so I send you.

The second point of the job was that what had been given to Peter before, was now given to the others.

> John 20:23 Whose soever [Any person's] sins ye [you] remit [forgive], they are remitted [forgiven] unto them; and whose soever [any person's] sins ye [you] retain [do not forgive], they are retained [not forgiven].

The apostles were not given the power to forgive sins in order that the sinners could receive eternal life, that can only be given by God. Jesus is talking here about the authority to bind and loose that we explained in Chapter 7, when we looked into the fifth thing Jesus told Peter. They were being given authority to punish or not to punish, but except for the apostles, Jesus has never given the same authority to anyone else. Today, no bishop or any clergyman anywhere in the world has been given authority from God to punish any of us. He may have assumed authority himself, or have been given political authority by a king or government, but that is worldly, of this world only, and has no power at all in matters concerning the Kingdom of Heaven. Jesus told Pontius Pilate that His kingdom is not of this world.[8]

Jesus also breathed on His apostles, which was unusual, I have never been in a room when someone has stood up and gone around breathing on people.

> John 20:22 And when he had said this, he breathed on them, and saith unto them, receive ye the Holy Ghost [Spirit].

These same apostles were not baptised in the Holy Spirit until later on in Acts 2:4, so this was something different. The Holy Spirit performs several functions and one of these, which is seen at work in the Old Testament and the New Testament, is spiritual enlightenment, causing believers to understand the spiritual things of God.[9] You have seen how before the crucifixion, Jesus kept on telling His disciples about His coming death and resurrection, yet no matter how many times He told them, they never understood, and in the end when everything happened just as He said it would, they were all completely surprised. From now until His departure for heaven in forty days, He had much to teach them which was important for them to understand, and so they are given spiritual enlightenment through the Holy Spirit, and from now on they will understand the things of the Spirit.

Jesus had met His chosen apostles and prepared them for their work, and we would think that they would now at last leave Jerusalem and go to Galilee, but no, they stayed right there in town. One of the apostles, Thomas was not there when Jesus visited the ten, and he still would not believe that Jesus was alive.

> John 24:24-25 [24] But Thomas, one of the twelve, called Didymus, was not with them when Jesus came.
>
> [25] The other disciples therefore said unto him, We have seen the Lord. But he said unto them, Except I shall see in his hands the print of the nails, and put my finger into the print of the nails, and thrust my hand into his side, I will not believe.

Thomas would only believe on the condition that he saw Jesus with his eyes and touched Him with his hands, and because of Thomas' unbelief they all stayed in Jerusalem.

[1] Acts 1:21-22

[2] Mark 16:14

[3] Luke 24:39

[4] Luke 24:40-41

[5] Luke 24:42-43

[6] Matthew 8:11

[7] Revelation 19:7-9

[8] John 18:36

[9] 1 Corinthians 2:1-16

THE SIXTH APPEARANCE OF JESUS WAS TO THE ELEVEN
John 20:26-31

Obviously, because this sixth appearance of Jesus was to the eleven, you know that this time Thomas was there, but look how much time had been wasted by the apostles in Jerusalem because of him.

John 20:26 And after eight days …

Over a week had past by and they were still in Jerusalem, so once again Jesus kindly came to them and told Thomas to look and see and feel His body and believe that He was truly alive.

John 20:27 Then saith he to Thomas, Reach hither [here] thy finger, and behold [look at] my hands; and reach hither [here] thy hand, and thrust it into my side: and be not faithless, but believing.

At last Thomas became a believer, and said something that shows the truth of Romans 1:4, which is that the resurrection proved that Jesus is the Son of God.

> John 20:28 And Thomas answered and said unto him, My Lord and my God.

Many Christians believe that the apostles were especially blessed to see the resurrected Lord, more than us who live many years later, but Jesus said that in fact we believers that have not yet seen Him are the ones that have been blessed.

> John 20:29 Jesus saith unto him, Thomas, because thou hast seen me, thou hast believed: blessed are they that have not seen, and yet have believed.

Those people that read the Bible and believe are especially blessed, because although they do not have the personal experiences the apostles had, they believe the Scriptures through the power of the Holy Spirit within them – what an honour. "Christ in you, the hope of glory."[1] John then tells us of the many signs performed by Jesus that are not in his gospel, and gives the reason why he wrote about the signs that are in it.

> John 20:39 But these things are written, that ye might believe that Jesus is the Christ, the Son of God; and that believing ye might have life through his name.

[1] Colossians 1:27

THE SEVENTH APPEARANCE OF JESUS WAS TO THE SEVEN
John 21:1-25

At last all eleven apostles arrived in Galilee, it had been a struggle but Jesus had finally got them there. Seven of them were fishermen, they had not worked seriously at their trade for three years, and when Peter decided to do some night fishing the other six joined him. They fished until it began to get light, and then headed back to the shore without catching a single fish. Jesus was waiting for them at the water's edge.

> John 21:4-6 ⁴ But when morning was now come, Jesus stood on the shore: but the disciples knew not that it was Jesus.

⁵ Then Jesus saith unto them, Children, have ye any meat? They answered him, No.

⁶ And he said unto them, cast the net on the right side of the ship, and ye shall find. They cast therefore, and now they were not able to draw it for the multitude [number] of fishes.

It was on the same Sea of Galilee, when Jesus had just called His disciples together for the first time, that a similar thing had happened. The men had been fishing all night and had caught nothing, but after Jesus told them to throw in their nets they caught so many fish that the nets began to break and two boats full of fish began to sink. Jesus performed that miracle before saying something that would be central in the lives of His disciples.

Luke 5:10 And Jesus said unto Simon, Fear not; from henceforth [now on] thou [you] shalt [will] catch men.

John remembered the event and understood why they had again netted a large catch of fish.

John 21:7 Therefore that disciple whom Jesus loved saith unto Peter, It is the Lord.

Peter also caught the significance of what was happening, jumped overboard and waded to the shore. The others brought in their boat towing the net full of fish. On the beach they found a fire with fish cooking and bread toasting. The lesson is that they will not have to go fishing any more. From now on they will be fishing for men and Jesus will provide all their needs.

Even though there were plenty of fish, cooked and ready for the disciples to eat, Jesus asked the disciples to haul in their nets, and it was found they had caught 153 fish. Preachers have attempted to make their talks more interesting by trying to find the number 153 somewhere and linking it to the fish. For example at one time there were 153 countries that were members of the United Nations. In the days of Jesus there were no synthetic fibres to make fishing nets, and so they had to be made of thread spun from animal or vegetable fibres, all of which rot when they are continually wet. Also they could not be made stronger and longer lasting by making them extra thick because the fish can see a thick net and swim away from it. In those days the nets that caught the most fish were made of thin thread which the fish could not clearly see, but because they were thin they were easily broken if too many fish were caught. Any fisherman from the Sea of Galilee would have told you, a net with 153 fish in it would have torn, but the apostles' net did not tear, that was a miracle, and is the point Jesus was making to His disciples, and the disciples were amazed by it.

> John 21:12-13 Jesus saith unto them, Come and dine. And none of the disciples durst [dared] ask him, Who art thou? Knowing it was the Lord.
>
> [13] Jesus then cometh [came], and taketh [took] bread, and giveth [gave] them, and fish likewise.

Although this was the seventh appearance of Jesus since His resurrection, it was only His third appearance to the apostles.

> John 21:14 This is now the third time that Jesus shewed [showed] himself to his disciples, after that he was risen from the dead.

Jesus next, three times asked if Peter loved Him, and three times Peter said he did. Three times during the trials of Jesus, Peter had said he did not even know who Jesus was, and to cancel that he now has to say that he loves Jesus three times. In the English language the one word, "love" is used in the Scripture, but the original Greek, accurately translates the Hebrew spoken by Jesus and Peter, using different words for "love," which if explained, make their conversation more interesting.

> John 21:15 So when they had dined, Jesus saith to Simon Peter, Simon, son of Jonas, lovest thou me more than these?

The word "lovest or love," here is from the Greek "agape," and is a decision, a matter of the will, you can decide to "agape" someone, even if you are not attracted to them, and you would show your love by being kind and helpful, even if you did not like them. It was this love that Peter was talking about when, at the last Passover, he said that he loved Jesus more than the other disciples. Peter had decided that he would "agape" love Jesus more than the others and he would show this by doing more for Him than them. Jesus then prophesied that Peter would deny Him three times before the cock crowed, and Peter had replied he would not, and even said that his decision, his will to love Jesus, was stronger than any other disciple.[1] That is why Jesus now asked him, "Lovest thou me more that these?" Was Peter's will to love Jesus stronger than the other six apostles he had been fishing with?

> John 21:15 He [Peter] saith unto him, Yea, Lord; thou knowest that I love thee.

Peter here used a different word for love, and he starts talking about the love close friends have for each other, the love of attraction, from the Greek word, "phileo." The reason Peter answered this way is because by denying Jesus three times he had not shown "agape" love, but he now says he "phileo" loves Jesus as his friend, he is strongly attracted to Him. Jesus then gave Peter the first of three assignments.

> John 21:15 Feed my lambs.

Lambs are young sheep, but Jesus is not talking about farming, He is telling Peter to make sure people who come to believe in Christ get good information, or food, so that they grow and develop a strong faith in Jesus. Today, Jesus' lambs can get a strong faith by reading the New Testament and living their lives as it says, but when Jesus said this, the New Testament had not been written. Lambs take different food from their mothers, they need milk, and Peter provided milk for new believers when he wrote to them in his first letter in the New Testament, as the following quotation shows.

> 1 Peter 2:2 As newborn babes, desire the sincere milk of the word, that ye may grow thereby.

Jesus asked if Peter *"agape"* loved Him a second time.

> John 21:16 He saith to him again the second time, Simon son of Jonas, lovest thou me?

The second time Jesus left off the words, "more then these," and just asked, "Do you love Me?" The question meant, "Peter, you could not say you *"agape"* loved Me more than the others, but do you *"agape"* love Me at all?"

> John 21:16 He [Peter] saith unto him, Yea, Lord; thou knowest that I love thee.

Peter again used the word *"phileo,"* because of how he had failed to show *"agape"* love by denying Jesus those three times. His answer in other words is, "I cannot say that I *"agape"* love you, but I do *"phileo"* love you, I am you friend." Jesus then gave Peter his second assignment.

> John 21:16 Feed [Shepherd] my sheep.

In this case the translation in the KJV Bible could be better, Jesus was telling Peter to be in charge of the believers. You will see him doing this as you read through the Book of Acts, in the New Testament.

Jesus asked if Peter loved Him for the third time, but because Peter could not say that he *"agape"* loved Jesus more than the others, or even at all, this time Jesus used the word *"phileo,"* "Are you my friend?"

> John 21:17 He saith unto him the third time, Simon, son of Jonas, lovest thou me?

Jesus meant, "Peter, you cannot say that you *"agape"* love Me at all, but can you even say, you are my friend?"

> John 21:17 Peter was grieved [hurt] because he said unto him the third time, Lovest thou me? And he said unto him, Lord, thou knowest all things; thou knowest that I love thee.

Peter really can promise Jesus that he loves Him like a true friend, and after that Jesus gives him a third assignment.

> John 21:17 Feed my sheep.

The sheep are believers in Jesus who have had lots of milk from the Word of God, have grown strong, and do not need any more baby food, they need good solid food to be able to recognise what is good and what is evil,[2] in people, churches, charities and all organisations. Peter presented them with solid food in the second of his letters found in the New Testament, where he speaks about false prophets, false teachers and the how before the second coming of Christ, many who claim to be Christian will in fact reject the ways of God as taught in the Bible, this is happening in most denominational churches today. The three denials of Peter have now been cancelled out, by his three honest answers to questions from Jesus, all declaring his love of his Lord.

Jesus next says that when he is an old man Peter will die as a martyr because of his belief that Jesus is the Messiah.[3] By dying for his faith Peter would prove his *"agape"* love for Jesus, at least as much as the others who were martyred. Peter therefore did have *"agape"* love as well as *"phileo"* love for Jesus. Out of all the apostles, only John, the writer of the Gospel of John, his three New Testament letters, and the Book of Revelation, died of old age. Peter knowing he would not die of old age, but would die a martyr, asked Jesus how John would die, and was told that was none of his business.[4] Jesus then said to Peter, "You follow me," meaning, "You must do what I tell you to do." We each have special assignments from Jesus which He has prepared for us, I have mine, and if you become a believer, you will have yours, Peter had his, and John had his, some are called to be martyrs, others are not.

> John 21:22 Jesus saith unto him [Peter], If I will that he [John] tarry till I come, what is that to thee? Follow thou me.

John ends his gospel by telling us that he has only told a very tiny bit of what he saw Jesus do and heard Him say, because to write it all down would have been impossible.

---

[1] Matthew 26:33-35

[2] Hebrews 5:13-14

[3] John 21:18-19

[4] John 21:20-22

THE EIGHTH APPEARANCE OF JESUS WAS TO OVER FIVE-HUNDRED BELIEVERS INCLUDING THE APOSTLES
Matthew 28:16-20, Mark 16:15-18, 1 Corinthians 15:6

Later when Paul wrote to the believers in the Greek city of Corinth, most of this large crowd of over five-hundred believers that had seen the risen Lord Jesus were still alive.

> 1 Corinthians 15:6 After that he [Jesus] was seen of above five hundred brethren at once; of whom the greater part remain unto this present, but some are fallen asleep.

In this section Jesus gives the second of the three final assignments He gave to the apostles, the first one was in John 20:21-23 during His fifth appearance. There are five parts to this second assignment. It should be noted that the words of Jesus here were not only for His disciples, but for others as well because He says, "I am with you always, even unto the end of the world," and that is still future, yet the disciples died long ago.[1]

The first part of this assignment says that Jesus is all powerful in heaven and on earth, and of this we have no doubt.[2] If therefore Jesus sends the apostles out they will have His authority and power to do whatever they are told to do.

The second part is also without doubt, and is, that they are to make disciples, something often missed by English readers of the Bible, so let's look at the whole verse.

> Matthew 28:19 Go ye therefore, and teach all nations, baptizing them in the name of the Father, and of the Son, and of the Holy Ghost:

As you can see in the KJV, there is nothing about making disciples, but since the Authorized Version was published in 1611, the translation has been looked at again, and later translations include the words, "make disciples." The reason is a matter of the grammar in the Greek manuscript, and what Matthew is saying is, "make disciples by going, baptizing and teaching," so we will look at these three ways of making disciples.

1. The first thing we have to do to make disciples is to go, and from Mark's gospel we are told where. "Go ye into all the world."[3] Many missionaries go and preach the gospel over seas and think they have done as Jesus instructed, but actually Jesus wants more, He wants disciples.
2. The second thing that has to be done for these disciples is to baptise them in the name of the Father, the Son and the Holy Spirit. Notice the Bible does not say, "in the names," but "in the name," there is only One God, but He is triune, Father, Son and Holy Spirit. If a missionary preaches the gospel and baptises he has not completed his assignment, often known as the great commission.
3. The third thing that must be done to make disciples is to teach the nations of the world, the Gentiles, what Jesus wants them to do, because it is important to obey Him. Jesus made a wonderful promise to the disciples in John 14:15-16, that if they followed His instructions, He would arrange for the Holy Spirit (Comforter) to come to them, and never ever leave. Obviously nothing will be impossible for a disciple working under the direction and power of the Holy Spirit.

We have already discussed in the previous chapter the command of Jesus to take bread and wine, the communion, in remembrance of Him. In Acts 2:46, we learn that after He had ascended into heaven, the disciples broke bread together in obedience to Him daily. What did Jesus promise if they obeyed Him? He promised the Holy Spirit, and the result was that the Church in Jerusalem grew bigger every day, and many miracles took place. The English lay preacher, Smith Wigglesworth 1859 – 1947, although a plumber by trade, went around the world healing the sick, casting out demons and even raising the dead by the power of God's Spirit. I do not believe it is just a coincidence that God performed so many signs using Smith Wigglesworth. Wigglesworth and his wife Polly used to take communion together daily, and if Polly was not available, then Smith would take the bread and wine by himself.

"Then said Jesus to those Jews which believed on him, If ye continue in my word, then are ye my disciples indeed. (John 8:31)."

The instruction to make disciples came from Jesus, speaking to over five-hundred believers including the apostles after His resurrection. He wants us to go to all nations baptising and teaching from the Bible, the Old Testament and the New Testament. In the New Testament the apostle Paul preaches several messages that certain churches today tend to ignore. In my estimation they are often what I consider dead or dying churches, without much spiritual life in them. He deals with homosexuality in Romans 1, immorality in 1 Corinthians 5 and 1 Corinthians 6, whether we should cover our heads or uncover them when we pray in 1 Corinthians 11, how women should behave in church meetings in 1 Corinthians 14, partnerships between believers and unbelievers in 2 Corinthians 6, and false teaching in Colossian 2. These instructions from Paul are there to help us get closer to God and to know the presence of His Spirit inside us.

> John 14:15-17 [15] (Jesus said) If ye love me, keep [follow] my commandments [instructions].
>
> [16] And I will pray the Father, and he shall give you another Comforter, that he may abide [stay] with you for ever [not only until you die];
>
> [17] Even the Spirit of truth; whom the world cannot receive, because it seeth [sees] him not, neither knoweth [knows] him: but ye know him: for he dwelleth [lives] with you, and shall be in you.

We next come to the third part of the second assignment.

> Mark 16:16 He that believeth and is baptised shall be saved; but he that believeth not shall be damned.

Some people use this verse to teach that you must be baptised in water to be saved, but it does not mean that. In the Book of Acts, new church members always believed first, and were baptised after believing, an example being the baptizing of the Ethiopian Eunuch.[4] Also one of the criminals crucified with Jesus was saved from Hell, and promised a new life, although he was not baptised.[5] The important thing is to believe in Jesus and His work of bringing men back to God through His death on the cross. Notice in Mark 16:16, it says, "he that believeth not shall be damned." It does not say, "he that believeth not and is not baptised shall be damned." The issue is believing, not being baptised.

In my own case God kindly let me know supernaturally that I had been baptised in the Holy Spirit, after I believed, probably because He knew I would wonder if I had been truly born again. Later, Lucy was born again and wanted to be baptised. We spoke to a mature believer about it, because I did not see the need for me to be baptised in water when I already had the Holy Spirit. He turned to me and said, "Do you object to being baptised?" I said, "No," and we got baptised. Jesus Himself was baptised in the River Jordan, by John the Baptist, "to fulfil all righteousness."[6]

The fourth part of the second assignment is in Mark 16:17-18, where Jesus gives five signs that will be seen among those people that have believed in Him.

1. They will speak with new tongues.
2. They will cast out demons.
3. They will heal the sick by laying their hands on them.
4. They will pick up snakes and not die.
5. They will drink poison and not die.

Some preachers teach that unless you perform all these signs, you are not a true believer. Well there are lots of believers in the New Testament who did not carry out all these things.[7] In Mark 16:16, it says, "he that believeth and is baptised shall be saved," talking about one individual person, because being born again is a personal thing, but in Mark 16:17, it says, "And these signs shall follow them that believe," speaking of a group of believers. Some of the signs are seen in various believers but not all the signs in all believers. In the Book of Acts the first four signs are seen at work in the early church, but not the fifth.

The fifth part of the second assignment is the promise that Jesus will stay with them until, "the end of the world [age]."[1]

---

[1] Matthew 28:20

[2] Matthew 28:18
[3] Mark 16:15
[4] Acts 8:26-38
[5] Luke 23:39-43
[6] Matthew 3:13-15
[7] 1 Corinthians 12:27-30

THE NINTH APPEARANCE OF JESUS WAS TO JAMES
1 Corinthians 15:7

> 1 Corinthians 15:6-7 ⁶ After that, he [the resurrected Jesus] was seen alive of above five hundred brethren at once; of whom the greater part remain unto this present, but some are fallen asleep.
>
> ⁷ After that, he [Jesus] was seen of James [the half brother of Jesus – not the apostle James]; then of all the apostles [including the apostle James].

Jesus had already been seen by James the apostle, four times, at His fifth, sixth, seventh and eighth appearances. The James He meets this time is His younger half brother, son of Mary and Joseph, who as a result of seeing Jesus alive becomes a believer, and in due course the leader of the Jerusalem church with the title of apostle.[1]

There were two kinds of apostles, and the first group of twelve which later included Matthias, had all been with Jesus from the time He was baptised by John, until He was taken up into heaven.[2] The second group had not seen Jesus baptised, but they had all seen Him after the resurrection, and included Barnabas, James and finally Paul, for whom our Lord returned especially from heaven to meet him on the road to Damascus, showing that Jesus wants us to know how extremely important the teaching of Paul and his New Testament letters are. Jesus had the following words to say regarding Paul, the man He returned from heaven to make an apostle, or in English, to send out.

Acts 9:15 He is a chosen vessel unto me, to bear my name before the Gentiles, and kings, and the children of Israel.

[1] Galatians 1:18-19, Galatians 2:9
[2] Acts 1:22-26

THE TENTH APPEARANCE OF JESUS WAS TO THE ELEVEN
Luke 24:44-49, Acts 1:1-8, 1 Corinthians 15:7

You will see that what happened at the tenth appearing of the risen Lord is only found in Luke and Acts, both of which were written by Doctor Luke. He tells us what Jesus had taught about in the forty days between His resurrection and His ascension into heaven. There were two main topics that He wanted the disciples to realise and to be informed of, the Bible prophecies about Himself, and the kingdom of God.

The prophecies concerning the Messiah are in all three divisions of the Old Testament, the Law, the Prophets and the Writings. The Writings begin with the Book of Psalms and are often called by that name, something you should know before reading the following verse.

Luke 24:44 And he [Jesus] said unto them, These are the words which I spake unto you, while I was yet with you, that all things must be fulfilled, which were written in the law of Moses, and in the prophets, and in the psalms, concerning me.

During the forty days after His resurrection, Jesus taught where the prophecies about Him are in all three sections of the Jewish Old Testament, and at last they really did understand.

Luke 24:25 Then opened he their understandings, that they might understand the scriptures.

His teaching about the kingdom of God was important because the Messianic Kingdom would not be established on earth yet. It would be postponed for the time being, because the Jewish nation had rejected its King, and the postponement would allow the gospel to be preached to non-Jews, giving them a chance to believe in Jesus and receive the gift of eternal life also.

> Acts 1:3 [The apostles] To whom also he [Jesus] shewed [showed] himself alive after his passion [suffering] by many infallible [reliable] proofs, being seen of them forty days, and speaking of the things pertaining to the kingdom of God.

Now, instead of the Messianic Kingdom, there would be the Mystery Kingdom for a while, which includes the true and false churches, and only after that would the Messianic Kingdom be set up. The teaching about the Mystery Kingdom caused the apostles to wonder about the promised Messianic Kingdom, they were expecting.

> Acts 1:6 Lord, wilt thou at this time restore the kingdom of Israel?

In other words, "Lord, is it now after you have been resurrected, you will be King of Israel?" Jesus refused to tell them when the Messianic Kingdom would be established on earth,[1] but He did have some work for them to do.

Jesus then came to the last of the three final assignments He gave to the apostles, an assignment with two very important parts. To begin with they were to wait, they had to stay there in Jerusalem, until the Holy Spirit came to them.[2] Three things resulted with the coming of the Holy Spirit.

1. After the Last Passover, one of the twenty-five promises made by Jesus to His apostles was that God the Father would send them the Holy Spirit, so that they would remember every single thing Jesus had said.[3] "And behold, I send the promise of my Father upon you" (Luke 24:49). The prophesy was fulfilled when the Holy Spirit came.

2. The Holy Spirit also gave the apostles the power to carry out the assignments given to them. "But you shall receive power, after the Holy Ghost is come upon you" (Acts 1:8).

3. Another result was Spirit baptism, something not mentioned before in the Bible. Although the Spirit was responsible for so much in the Old Testament, here we have for the first time,

baptism with the Holy Spirit. "Ye shall be baptised with the Holy Ghost not many days hence" (Acts 1:5). Baptism by the Holy Spirit shows membership of the true Church, the body of Christ. "For by one Spirit we are all baptised into one body, whether we be Jews or Gentiles, whether we be bond [slaves] or free; and have all been made to drink into one Spirit" (1 Corinthians 12:13). The Holy Spirit came and birthed the Church, it is spiritual, not earthly, it is not a Christian denomination controlled by men, men do not control the Holy Spirit, only Jesus is King.

The second part of the final assignment given to the apostles is found in, Acts 1:8, and was only to begin after they had been baptised with the Holy Spirit. They were to preach the gospel in four regions of the world, one after the other, not all together at the same time. The four regions were, Jerusalem, Judea, Samaria, "and unto the uttermost part of the earth," In Jerusalem and Judea they would be preaching to Jews, in Samaria to Samaritans, people of mixed Jewish and Gentile ancestors, and last of all to Gentiles. The meaning of the Jewish phrase, "the ends of the earth," is, the place where the Gentiles live, and by naming the regions Jesus was also telling the apostles who they were to preach to first of all, second, third, and last.

[1] Acts 1:7-8

[2] Acts 1:4-5

[3] John 14:26

JESUS ROSE INTO THE SKY
Luke 24:50-53, Acts 1:9-11

On the very top of Mount Olivet, is the Octagon Chapel of the Ascension, where in the middle of the floor is a rectangular slab of stone with a cavity in it. Visitors are told that the cavity is traditionally the foot print of Jesus, made as He blasted off into space. Pilgrims are encouraged to read parts of sermons while they are there, chant, and light candles. The trouble is that the chapel is one and half miles away from Bethany, the place where Jesus began to ascend into heaven while He was blessing the apostles.

> Luke 24:50-51 {superscript 50} And he lead them out as far as to Bethany, and he lifted up his hands, and blessed them.
>
> {superscript 51} And it came to pass, while he blessed them, he was parted from them, and carried up into heaven.

They watched as Jesus kept getting higher and higher before disappearing into a cloud,[1] and soon there they were all looking up at nothing except this cloud. Two angels appeared out of nowhere[2] and said to them, "Ye men of Galilee, why stand ye gazing up into heaven? This same Jesus, which is taken up from you into heaven, shall so come in like manner as ye have seen him go into heaven."[3]

> Mark 16:19 So then after the Lord had spoken unto them, he was received up into heaven, and sat at the right hand of God.[4]

The psalmist, King David had said this would happen more than a thousand years before.

> Psalm 110:1 The LORD said unto my Lord, Sit thou at my right hand, until I make thine enemies thy footstool.

The ascension also fulfilled the words Jesus said about Himself.

> John 16:28 I came forth from the Father, and am come into the world: again, I leave the world, and go to the Father.

The ascension of Jesus strengthens our faith by reminding us of several spiritual truths.

1. Jesus is in heaven preparing a place for us.[5] We know from other Bible verses that our own place there will be much better than anything we can think of or imagine.

2. Jesus has power and authority above all things.[6] We are without doubt on the winning side, and always will be.

3. Jesus is the Head of the Church.[7] He is in control of the spiritual Church, which He is growing bigger and bigger. Once His Church is fully grown, He will return to earth and destroy the enemies of His people Israel along with the enemies of His

Church, later on Satan and his friends will go into the everlasting flames, and Jesus will be Head of all that there is in heaven and on earth, King of Kings and Lord of Lords.

4. Jesus is the High Priest in heaven.[8] The High Priest is also our Brother, our Friend, and He is Almighty, we have nothing to fear.

5. It was only after the ascension that Jesus could send us the Holy Spirit.[9] From then on all believers are temples for the Holy Spirit, and the Spirit in us is our guarantee of eternal life.

6. Jesus is our forerunner into heaven, He went first so that we can follow.[10] He has chosen us to be with Him, not just 'til the cows come home, but for evermore.

7. Jesus, the Head of the Church, is now able to send spiritual gifts to believers.[11] I am amazed at His gift of teaching. The best teachers were a bunch of fishermen, a tax collector, a medical doctor, a youth, carpenter's sons and a tent maker, who were given the spiritual gift of teaching by Jesus, and many clever qualified men, from hundreds of universities, have not caught up with them yet, even after nearly two-thousand years, and never will, because the Church is first of all spiritual.

8. Lastly the ascension shows us how Jesus will return to earth from heaven.[12] He will come back bodily in the form of a man, not as a baby in a manger, and He has told us that when we see the signs that His coming is near, "Look up," because our rescue will then be about to happen.

[1] Acts 1:9

[2] Acts 1:10

[3] Acts 1:11

[4] Hebrews 1:3

[5] John 14:2

[6] Ephesians 1:20-22

[7] Ephesians 1:22-23, Colossians 1:18

[8] Hebrews 4:14-16

[9] John 16:7, Titus 3:4-6

[10] Hebrews 6:20

[11] Ephesians 4:7-11

[12] Acts 1:9-11

"And many other signs truly did Jesus in the presence of his disciples, which are not written in this book: but these are written, that ye might believe that Jesus is the Christ, the Son of God; and that believing ye might have life through his name" (John 20:30-31).

EPILOGUE IN THREE PARTS

Epilogue Part 1 - Advice

The Holy Spirit living in those that believe Jesus can overwhelm us with His presence. The joy of the Lord is something I will never forget and always crave.

One sunny summer day I walked down a grassy meadow towards the farmhouse, hands in the air, praising God. Suddenly the Spirit of God filled me with His love. He was too much for me. I prayed, "Heavenly Father, the joy in me is becoming more ecstatic than I can bear. Please reduce your presence just a little so that I am not crushed by the emotions of love, joy and peace." Immediately God answered me and I thanked Him. Walking on down the hill with my hands by my side I missed the strength of feeling I had just experienced and felt sorry for asking God to back off a little. At the same time I realised that my prayer had been necessary.

In the story of Mary and Martha, you will remember that Mary sat at Jesus feet while Martha worked hard getting the dinner ready. Jesus said that Mary had found the best part, meaning that it is better to be near Jesus than to serve Him. In my own experience this has proved to be true, but how are we to get near to the King of the Jews, the Lord of Heaven and Earth? In James 4:8, the brother of Jesus told us that if we move closer to God, God will get nearer to us. You may then wonder how we can draw near to this Holy, Almighty God. The answer is to spend time with Him.

One of the things I prayed for before we bought the farm was for a study room of my own where I could read the Bible and be alone with God. In fact I made it a condition, so that if we found a farm that was right in every way, but there was nowhere for my special room then we would not buy it. You, (my grandchildren), are either still at school or too young for school, but later on you will need to earn some money, and some employers may keep you busy and make you tired. Older readers will usually be able to find time to read God's word and pray to Him, but young people have many distractions and what I am going to say next is mainly for them.

It is important to spend time with God and read the Bible every single day. However, we do not have to spend hours in prayer. We can pray very effectively while walking down a grassy hill with our hands in the air, or a city pavement with our hands by our side. Now regarding the daily Bible reading, the Scriptures are our spiritual food, or if you like heavenly food, our bread from heaven that gives us strength, makes us grow and draws us closer to God. There is an example for us in Exodus of how God provided bread from heaven for the Jews in the wilderness after they left Egypt. It was called manna, which means a kind of bread. Every night when the Jews went to sleep while they were in the desert, they were surrounded by sand and bare rocks, with nothing to eat. During the night God sent them manna, bread form heaven, and the people collected it every morning except on the Sabbath. It was very nourishing indeed and kept them healthy and strong, just like our heavenly food, reading the Bible, keeps us spiritually healthy and strong. In the desert some people collected a lot of manna and some only a little but we know from reading Exodus 16:17-18, that no one had too much and everyone had enough. So read the Bible as much as you like. If you are very busy, you must still read it daily, but a little will be enough, just as a little manna every day was enough for the Jews while they were in the wilderness.

I pray and hope that reading this book often will cause you to understand the Bible clearly, and after you have asked the Messiah, into your life, to bring you very near to Him. In other words once your belief in the Son of God has been ignited, what you are reminded of by reading this book again, together with what you learn from the Bible will fan the flames of your faith, so that your excitement and joy overflows. Once that happens you will be able to help others find perfect peace, become close to Jesus and lead them to eternal life.

Epilogue Part 2 - Encouragement For Believers

New believers in Jesus should expect trouble to come into their lives. When this happens you can be sure that God really has chosen you for a special purpose. Don't try to overcome your difficulties in your own strength, because God does not want you to work through your difficulties by yourself. God wants you to turn to Him, so that you will experience Him helping you. In that way you will learn to trust Him more and more, until you trust Him so much that He can give you something important to do for Him, something so big that without His help, it would be impossible for someone like you. Another thing, the longer your trial the more you can expect to be used by God afterwards. Moses spent forty years looking after someone else's sheep before God asked him to lead the Israelites out of Egypt. Joseph was sold as a slave and spent years in an Egyptian prison, before God made him the second in command to Pharaoh. God often makes us go through difficulties before giving us something important to do.

> 1 Peter 4:12 Beloved, think it not strange concerning the fiery trial which is to try you, as though some strange thing happened unto you.

My fiery trial began three months after being born again. The company I had been working for, very successfully for 23 years, decided to get rid of me. After examining my work record and not finding any legal reason to dismiss me, they began to make my life so difficult that I would resign. My response was to turn to God. I was so comforted by my Comforter, (the Holy Spirit), after reading the Psalms, that my boss commented on my composure. At one meeting he said, "You look very calm, most people would have completely broken down by now!"

Whatever happens look to God, take courage and wait for Him to comfort you and show you the way out of your difficulties. The more the trouble and the longer it lasts, the greater will be God's blessing on you afterwards.

Isaiah 40:31 But they that wait upon the LORD shall renew their strength; they shall mount up with wings as eagles; they shall run, and not be weary; and they shall walk, and not faint.

One way God comforts His people when we are being tried was shown to me by three orphaned lambs of mine. Remember that Jesus is the Good Shepherd and we believers are His sheep. Likewise I was shepherd to the lambs. I had fed them with milk from a bottle, they knew my voice and trusted me.

One day the lambs were in a field and I was there also with my tractor. After work I began to drive the tractor back to the farm but the lambs decided to run in front of me. The way out of the field was through a narrow road with a gate at the end. Down the road ran the lambs until they came to the closed gate, and I followed them on the tractor. They were terrified. The tractor engine was very noisy and the lambs panicked, trying desperately to get through the gate, climb a stone wall on one side of the lane and push through a fence on the other side, but they were trapped and extremely frightened. Leaving the tractor engine running I got down to open the gate, and that made them even more scared, so I said, "Its all right boys!" As soon as they heard my voice they answered me and were completely at ease. The engine was still loud but they did not mind at all, their shepherd was with them and they feared nothing. They jumped up and stood on the front wheels, smelt the engine, got into the drivers cab and sniffed the gear levers, and generally got in the way, flocking around, underneath and in front of the tractor. What before had been a terrifying ordeal for them was now a non-event because they knew I was with them. We are the same when we know our Shepherd is with us.

Epilogue Part 3 - Prayer

Heavenly Father God, I know that my words, spoken or written, cannot convince anyone that you are real, that your Word is Truth, or that believing you leads to eternal life, all of which is your doing. Thank you for showing me the Truth, and for promising that I will come to you and be with you forever. Please cause all my grandchildren to believe you and give them everlasting life along with all the other readers of this book and the Holy Bible, who search them with the purpose of finding eternal life. I praise you Almighty God because you hear and answer all the prayers of your people which are according to your will. Jesus has shown us how to get to heaven. He believed You, His Heavenly Father and obeyed You. He died, was buried and then received from You, your kind of life. For this I love and enjoy praising and thanking you with all my heart, soul and might. In Jesus Name, Amen.

John Newcater

GLOSSARY

Abrahams's Bosom: Also known as Paradise, it was on the good side of Hades (Greek), or Sheol (Hebrew), but when Jesus rose from the dead it was emptied and the souls in it were taken to heaven to be with Jesus.

Aphikomen: The middle matza (unleavened bread) used in the Jewish Passover ceremony.

Abyss, The: A temporary prison holding fallen angels and demons situated in the bad side of Hades (Greek), or Sheol (Hebrew).

Bar Mitzva: The initiation ceremony for a Jewish boy aged thirteen years, after which he becomes responsible to keep the Jewish religious laws, and is recognised as an adult.

Born Again: The words used by Jesus to describe a believer's spiritual birth leading to everlasting life (see John 3:3-6).

Chanuka: The Feast of Chanuka is not in the Old Testament but God has approved it because Jesus went to the Temple and kept it. It was celebrated on the 25th of Kislev because on that day in 165 BC, a very small Jewish army defeated Antiochus, the great Hellenist-Syrian king, drove their enemies out of the Land of Israel, removed the idols from the Temple and rededicated it to the God of Israel. The menorah was lit, but there was only enough olive oil to last one day, however it miraculously lasted eight days while new oil was prepared.

Charoseth: A brown sticky preparation eaten at Passover to remind the Jews of the clay they had to make bricks with for Pharaoh while they were slaves in Egypt.

Christendom: The whole "Christian" community of the world, both good and bad, including people, churches and "Christian" countries.

Covenant: A promise, agreement, contract or pledge.

Cult: A system of religious worship. In this book the word refers to a system of religion that claims to be Christian, but does not worship according to the way the Bible teaches.

Denomination: A religious group under a hierarchy of leaders, that follow a declared set of doctrines, such as Baptists, Methodists, Anglican, etc.

Epistles: The word means, "letters," and refers to letters written to the early Church by their leaders, and which are now part of Scripture. They begin with the sixth book in the New Testament, the Epistle to the Romans, and continue until the twenty-first book, which was written by Jude, the half-brother of Jesus.

Essenes: A group that were a branch of the Pharisees from around 100 BC until AD 100, known for their strict observance of ceremonial purity.

Feast of Passover, Exodus 12:1-51: The feast celebrates the time the Angel of Death passed over all the Jewish homes that had the blood of a lamb painted on the outside of the doorposts and lintels of their doors. The next morning God rescued them from slavery and began to lead them to the land He had promised to give them (Genesis 35:12).

Feast of Pentecost, Leviticus 23:9-21: The feast comes 50 days after Passover. It is also known as, the Holiday of the Spring Harvest, as well as, the Holiday of the First Fruit Offering.

Feast of Tabernacles, Leviticus 23:33-44: During the feast the Jews build booths or temporary huts to entertain their guests in. The feast reminds them how they wandered 40 years in the desert living in tents (tabernacles) after they left Egypt, and how God protected them and supplied all their needs.

Great Commission (The): The great commission is the name given to the instructions Jesus gave for all believers, telling us to teach and make disciples in all nations right up until the end of the church age. "And Jesus came and spake [spoke] unto them, saying, All power is given unto me in heaven and in earth. Go ye therefore, and teach all nations, baptizing them in the name of the Father, and of the Son, and of the Holy Ghost: Teaching them to observe all things whatsoever I have commanded you: and, lo [look], I am with you alway, even unto the end of the world [church age]. Amen" (Matthew 28:18-20).

Gemara: The Jewish oral law written by the third school of scribes, and completed about AD 500.

Hanuka: See, Chanuka.

Jot: Corresponds to the Hebrew, "yod," the smallest letter in the Hebrew alphabet.

Jot and tittle: The smallest, least important part of the Jewish Law.

Karpas: The Green Vegetable Ceremony, in the Feast of Passover, which recalls the suffering of the Jews in captivity and their escape through the Red Sea.

Kindling of the Lampstands: At the Feast of Tabernacles lamp stands were set up throughout the whole Temple, and when lit they represented the Shekinar Glory of the presence of God.

King: As King, Jesus will have absolute authority over everyone and everything.

Law: The Laws given to the Jews by God, through Moses, in Genesis, Exodus, Leviticus, Numbers and Deuteronomy.

Matza: The unleavened bread eaten at Passover.

Menorah: Seven-branched lampstand used in Jewish worship.

Midrash: A book of ancient Jewish comments on parts of the Jewish Scriptures.

Mishnah: The Jewish oral law written by the scribes of the School of Sofer, and later the School of Teachers, which was completed about AD 200.

New Testament: Written by believers in Jesus after He had ascended into heaven.